Leading Issues in Competition, Regulation and Development

THE CRC SERIES ON COMPETITION, REGULATION AND DEVELOPMENT

Series Editors: Paul Cook, *Professor of Economics and Development Policy and* Martin Minogue, *Senior Research Fellow, Institute for Development Policy and Management, University of Manchester, UK*

Titles in the series include:

Leading Issues in Competition, Regulation and Development
Edited by Paul Cook, Colin Kirkpatrick, Martin Minogue and David Parker

Politics of Regulation
Institutions and Regulatory Reforms for the Age of Governance
Edited by Jacint Jordana and David Levi-Faur

Leading Issues in Competition, Regulation and Development

Edited by

Paul Cook
Professor of Economics and Development Policy, Institute of Development Policy and Management and Director, Centre on Regulation and Competition (CRC), University of Manchester, UK

Colin Kirkpatrick
Hallsworth Professor of Development Economics, Institute of Development Policy and Management and Co-Director of the Regulation Research Programme, Centre on Regulation and Competition (CRC), University of Manchester, UK

Martin Minogue
Senior Research Fellow, Institute of Development Policy and Management and Director of the Regulatory Governance Research Programme, Centre on Regulation and Competition (CRC), University of Manchester, UK

David Parker
Professor of Business Economics and Strategy, Cranfield University and Co-Director of the Regulation Research Programme, Centre on Regulation and Competition (CRC), University of Manchester, UK

THE CRC SERIES ON COMPETITION, REGULATION AND DEVELOPMENT

Edward Elgar
Cheltenham, UK • Northampton, MA, USA

Published by
Edward Elgar Publishing Limited
Glensanda House
Montpellier Parade
Cheltenham
Glos GL50 1UA
UK

Edward Elgar Publishing, Inc.
136 West Street
Suite 202
Northampton
Massachusetts 01060
USA

A catalogue record for this book
is available from the British Library

Library of Congress Cataloging in Publication Data

Leading issues in competition, regulation and development/edited by
Paul Cook, Colin Kirkpatrick, Martin Minogue, David Parker.
p. cm. — (The CRC series on competition, regulation and development)
Includes bibliographical references and index.
1. Industrial policy—Developing countries. 2. Trade regulation—Developing countries. 3. Competition—Developing countries. 4. Developing countries—Foreign economic relations. 5. Competition, International.
I. Cook, Paul, 1944– . II. Series.
HD3616.D452L43 2004
338.9'009172'4—dc22 2003065538

ISBN 1 84376 482 2 (cased)

Typeset by Cambrian Typesetters, Frimley, Surrey
Printed and bound in Great Britain by MPG Books Ltd, Bodmin, Cornwall

Contents

Figures

Tables and box

TABLES

BOX

Contributors

Rafaelita M. Aldaba is a researcher in the Department of Economics, University of the Philippines, a regional research partner with CRC, Manchester, UK

Thankom G. Arun is Lecturer in Development Economics in IDPM, University of Manchester, and a researcher in CRC, Manchester, UK

Ernest Aryeetey is Professor and Deputy Director of the Institute of Economic and Social Statistics at the University of Accra, Ghana, a regional research partner with CRC, Manchester, UK

Armando Barrientos is Senior Lecturer in Development Economics at IDPM, University of Manchester and a researcher in CRC, Manchester, UK

Ledivina V. Cariño is Professor in the National College of Public Administration and Governance, University of the Philippines, Manila, a regional research partner with CRC, Manchester, UK

Claude V. Chang is an independent consultant and former Secretary to the Treasury in Guyana, and a guest lecturer of the University of Guyana and Florida Atlantic University

Paul Cook is Professor of Economics and Development Policy in IDPM, University of Manchester, and Director in CRC, Manchester, UK

Richard Duncombe is Lecturer in Information Systems in IDPM, University of Manchester and a researcher in CRC, Manchester, UK

Derek Eldridge is a Lecturer in IDPM, University of Manchester, and Director of Capacity-Building in CRC, Manchester, UK

Raul V. Fabella is Professor and Dean of Economics in the University of the Philippines, Manila, a regional research partner with CRC, Manchester, UK

Richard Heeks is Senior Lecturer in IDPM, University of Manchester and a researcher in CRC, Manchester, UK

Graeme Hodge is Director of the Privatisation and Public Accountability Centre in the Law Faculty, University of Monash, Australia

Peter Holmes is Senior Lecturer in the Policy Science Unit, University of Sussex, UK

Colin Kirkpatrick is Professor of Development Economics at IDPM, University of Manchester and Co-director of the Regulation Research Programme in CRC, Manchester, UK

Malathy Knight-John is a Researcher in the Institute of Policy Studies in Sri Lanka, a regional research partner with CRC, Manchester, UK

Cassey Lee is Head of the Department of Economics in the University of Malaya, Malaysia, a regional research partner with CRC, Manchester, UK

J.S. Metcalfe is Stanley Jevons Professor of Economics and Director of the ESRC Centre on Research in Innovation and Competition (CRIC), University of Manchester, and a Research Fellow in CRC, Manchester, UK

Martin Minogue is Senior Research Fellow in IDPM, University of Manchester and Director of the Regulatory Governance Research Programme in CRC, Manchester, UK

Diana Mitlin is a Researcher in IDPM, University of Manchester, and in CRC, Manchester, UK

Kobus Müller is Professor of Environmental Studies, University of Stellenbosch, South Africa, a regional research partner with CRC, Manchester, UK

Anthony Ogus is Professor of Law, University of Manchester, and a Research Fellow in CRC, Manchester, UK

David Parker is Professor of Business Economics, University of Cranfield and Co-director of the Regulation Research Programme in CRC, Manchester, UK

R. Ramlogan is a Research Fellow in the Centre for Research in Innovation and Competition, University of Manchester, UK

Tan Wooi Syn is a Research Fellow in the School of Oriental and African Studies, University of London, UK

E. Uyarra is a Research Fellow in CRIC, University of Manchester, UK

Preface

Issues of regulation and competition have long been matters of both public policy discussion and academic research in developed economies, but until recently were relatively unexamined in relation to developing economies. The Centre on Regulation and Competition (CRC) was established in 2001, with funding from the UK Department for International Development, to conduct research into issues of competition, regulation and regulatory governance in developing countries. It works through a network of partnerships both in the UK, and overseas in Ghana, India, Malaysia, the Philippines, South Africa and Sri Lanka. This new series represents one of the many forms of dissemination of both conceptual studies and research findings, including conferences, workshops, journal publication and policy briefs. The editors will be glad to receive and consider book proposals for publication in the series.

The promotion of liberalised and deregulated markets by bilateral and multilateral aid donors, and by global institutions such as the World Trade Organisation, has led to significant attention to competition and regulation reforms in developing economies. This book draws together contributions from specialists ranging across different disciplines and types of economy, in order to examine both ideas and current practices in this field, including country and sector case studies. A particular focus is on the extent to which this reform process involves the transfer of policy models originating in developed economies, and the problems of applicability and adaptation that arise. The book presents a clear agenda for further empirical studies, and will make a valuable contribution to the literature on economic development.

Paul Cook
Martin Minogue
CRC, University of Manchester

PART 1

Competition and Regulation in Developing Countries: An Overview

1. Competition, regulation and regulatory governance: an overview

Paul Cook, Colin Kirkpatrick, Martin Minogue and David Parker

INTRODUCTION

Recent years have seen a movement away from state ownership towards more reliance on private markets to supply goods and services, including goods and services traditionally supplied by the state, such as telecommunications, water and electricity. These markets can be competitive, highly oligopolistic or even monopolistic. Where privatisation is associated with the creation of private monopoly then some form of continued state regulation is required to protect consumers from monopoly abuse. In cases where markets are oligopolistic or even competitive, state regulation may still be necessary to prevent the abuse of a dominant position, the creation of cartels, and in other ways to protect consumers through developing an effective 'competition policy'. Moreover, state regulation is also adopted internationally to protect society in the form of the regulation of working conditions, product quality, the environment, health and safety and the like. Indeed, in North America and the EU the regulation of markets has expanded at the same time as industries have been privatised (Blundell and Robinson, 2000). Therefore, contrary to the ambitions of leading advocates of 'privatisation', such as Milton Friedman in economics and Margaret Thatcher in politics, the 'frontiers of the state' have not been so much 'rolled back', but have been reshaped and redirected since the 1970s. This is evidenced, for example, in the shares of gross domestic product (GDP) controlled by the state in OECD countries, which have remained fairly stable.

The picture is much the same in many developing economies. Although 80 per cent of low-income countries are reported to have had some form of private participation in at least one infrastructure sector (Izaguirre and Rao, 2000), the scale of privatisation in many low-income economies has been very limited, especially outside of Latin America. In many countries privatisation seems to have been more talked about than carried out (e.g. Cook and Minogue, 1990; Parker, 2003). Only in the transition economies of Central and Eastern Europe and to a lesser degree China was there evidence of a substantial change in the extent of state involvement in the economy. But these countries are atypical, in the sense that before the late 1980s governments dominated the ownership of industry and commerce to a degree not found elsewhere. Also, in these countries (excluding China) privatisation and deregulation had an overriding political imperative; reform was driven by the desire to prevent the restoration of communism.

The shift in public policy over the last two decades away from state ownership and state responsibility for the provision of services, to private ownership and private provision with enhanced state regulation, is sometimes described as the rise of the 'regulatory state' (Majone, 1997). Alternatively, it has been referred to in terms of the 'invisible hand' of the market being supplemented by the 'visible hand' of regulators (Jackson and Price, 1994). In this regime the state ceases to be directly concerned with the provision of goods and services and instead concentrates on regulating private markets to promote economic and social welfare. This book is concerned with the regulatory state and in the context specifically of developing countries. Whereas there are now many publications on privatisation and regulation in developed economies and a growing number of studies of privatisation in lower income economies, for lower income countries the inter-related nature of competition, regulation and regulatory governance remains relatively under-explored. This book is intended to help fill this gap.

In this introductory chapter we set the scene by detailing the main research issues in competition, regulation and regulatory governance. We then provide a summary of the content of each of the following chapters, highlighting their contribution to addressing these research issues.

COMPETITION

The emphasis on the need to develop the private sector in developing economies has largely been predicated on the assumption, most often unstated, that privately owned enterprises operate under competitive market conditions. This could be seen in the lack of explicit attention being given to competition policy, in its antitrust form, to accompany the earlier shift towards private sector development in general. Further, if competitive conditions were absent then the presumption was that processes of privatisation and liberalisation would create the conditions in which competition between enterprises would flourish. And where privatisation was undertaken in some sectors such as utilities with no, or at best a marginal increase in competition, then some dedicated form of sector regulation would act as a surrogate for competition, even if temporarily. Competition policy is now rapidly being adopted in a whole range of developing economies with the encouragement of the international development institutions, and is an endorsement of the vital role that competition plays in the process of development.

Despite the centrality of the notion of competition in economic theory and its practice, its meaning and the ways in which it is perceived to work and contribute to development differ widely among theorists, policy-makers, bureaucrats and business people. Indeed, the history of economic thought provides some deeply contrasting views about the meaning of competition. These competing views of competition, in turn, have profound implications for the ways in which enterprises in the public and private sectors are perceived to contribute to development, and for the development of public policy approaches towards them.

For the classical economists writing in the nineteenth century, such as Adam Smith, competition was a process of rivalry between participants in the market who would compete by changing prices in response to market conditions, thereby eliminating excessive profits and unsatisfied demand. By the late nineteenth century the analytical development of the concept of competition had moved away from a behavioural approach to one that emphasised the importance of different market structures, and in which the organising concepts of the market relied on equilibrium and optimisation. This neoclassical approach generated the view that a market could be defined as competitive when there was a significantly large number of sellers of a homogeneous product, so that no sellers had enough of a market share to enable them to influence the product price by changing the quantity that they put onto the market. This idea was formally expressed in the notion of perfect competition, which has survived as the standard model for analysis and has ever since had a profound influence on policy-making concerned with the regulation of competition.

The classical and neoclassical concepts of competition differ, therefore, in their view of what competing means. The classical economists related the concept to business behaviour while the neoclassical view is more concerned with market structure. As Knight states 'perfect competition involves no presumption of psychological competition, emulation or rivalry' (Knight, 1946, p. 102).

The emphasis on market structure led to the development of the structure, conduct, performance approach to industrial organisation that has had such a significant influence on current-day thinking towards competition policy. In this approach it is argued that the performance of an industry, largely measured in terms of profitability, varies with market structure, which in turn influences enterprise behaviour. In this way, as with the process of 'getting prices right' under orthodox liberalisation programmes in order to maximise producer and consumer surpluses, 'getting the market structure right' by reducing levels of market concentration, will influence the behaviour of enterprises and prevent abuses from monopoly.

By contrast, the Chicago School of antitrust, as it has become known, drawing on the works of Alchian (1950), Peltzman (1976), Stigler (1971) and Posner (1974), and reflecting the influence of the Austrian School, challenges the notion that market behaviour performance is related strictly to market power. In their view, competition is a process that can lead to a variety of market structures providing efficient outcomes. They do not assume a constant state of market equilibrium, although competition can be expected to return the system to something resembling competitive equilibrium due to conditions of entry in the long run. Competition policy ought, therefore, to be directed predominantly towards removing regulatory barriers to entry. In contrast to static equilibrium theory and the market structure approach to competition policy, profits earned by successful entrepreneurs are not necessarily viewed as a sign of market inefficiency, but as a signal that entrepreneurs are responding to changing market conditions.

Apart from the convergence to a long run competitive equilibrium, this view of competition as a process is shared by the Evolutionary School of economics drawing on the works of Schumpeter. In particular, evolutionary theory is concerned with why the world changes endogenously, and with why technological competition is the driving force behind structural change and economic development (Metcalfe, 2000). Rather than the concern for profits, according to evolutionary economists the real cost of monopoly and collusive behaviour takes the form of stifling innovative effort and the long run competitive process by erecting barriers to challenging established market positions (Metcalfe et al., 2002).

Both the Chicago and the Evolutionary schools are sceptical about the performance, conduct, structure approach to competition policy. The Chicago School views the market structure approach, which emphasises the importance of market shares, as an inefficient policy that can lead to worsening market performance due to regulatory inefficiencies and regulatory capture (Stigler, 1971). In their view antitrust intervention is likely to be invoked by losers who allege unfair competition. The Evolutionary School believes there is an immense difference between competition policy as a negative discipline on enterprises, which sets out to break up market concentration and deviant behaviour as typified in conventional approaches to competition policy, compared with one that provides for positive incentives through the creation of better business opportunities. In the view of evolutionary economics, the search for an appropriate competition policy, particularly in economies where market institutions are underdeveloped, extends beyond measuring market power or excessive profits – it embraces the broader concerns of science and technology policy, and policy towards enterprise and innovation.

The discussion so far has directly and indirectly raised two key issues relating to the development of competition policy in developing economies. First, what might be included in competition policy and at what cost? Should it focus on rules and procedures to prevent enterprises from engaging in anti-competitive behaviour? Should it be primarily aimed at reducing the barriers to entry and exit and facilitating the conditions under which enterprises can compete? Will it be effective in meeting its objectives? How is general competition policy related to other government policies that have implications for competitiveness, and to the conduct of sector regulation in particular? Second, how will the framework that is developed for domestic competition policy be shaped and impacted upon by global rules for competition?

In relation to the first question, the debate has concerned the division between a behavioural and a market structure approach to competition, as well as the need to consider a wider range of factors other than those incorporated in an antitrust approach to competition policy. An argument for a market structure approach, which tends to be more rules oriented and more mechanistically applied, is that this suits the developing economy context in which market institutions and the capacity and skills to implement policy are poorly developed. This mitigates against a behavioural approach, which is more skill intensive and potentially more costly to implement. This need for simple, mechanistic rules is reinforced by arguments that the transactions costs of collusion are lower in developing economies, simply because monitoring technologies are less efficient, and enterprises have lower risk aversion and little to lose from colluding (Rey, 1997).

All of this should be viewed in the context of competition not being the automatic outcome of privatisation and deregulation in developing countries. This means that simply conditioning international development loans on the existence of privatisation and market liberalisation policies, or even on the creation of a competition law, will not ensure the creation of proper institutions for effective competition. This may require new institutions that are costly to establish. The budgetary constraints facing low-income economies may inhibit the speed with which complex regulation and new institutions can be introduced. Also, the danger in pursuing a rules-based market structure approach to competition policy, as opposed to a behavioural one, is that by overly relying on simplistic measures of market power there is a risk that enterprises are unjustifiably penalised if market shares do not adequately capture or measure anti-competitive behaviour (Cook, 2002).

The recommendations of the Chicago School that entry barriers be removed may also be problematic in developing economies where government-erected barriers have been most persistent. In such cases regulatory capture may not simply be a case of capture by powerful domestic private interests, who argue for the competition authorities to keep out new entrants by alleging unfair competition, but capture by government itself. The aims and pursuits of government may, therefore, conflict with competition policy. The conflict, however, may not necessarily be for the wrong reasons. Development policy may entail some degree of subsidy or protection to promote enterprises. The strategy of a sector regulator to expand a network activity (i.e. a developmental regulatory role) may on the surface appear as lax regulation, and one that conflicts with the introduction of more competition in terms of more market participants, but here, what is viewed as lax regulation may involve a legitimate trade-off between investment for the future and longer-term efficiency gains for the economy, and a current, static economic efficiency outcome.

The question of how international rules for competition are likely to affect domestic policy regimes is, of course, dependent on how far international rules are developed. There is mounting evidence that cross-border cartel activity has increased in recent years and is not being policed by international agencies (Evenett et al., 2001). One of the main arguments for international intervention is that anti-competitive practices in one area have spillover effects in others, as for example with import and export cartels and mergers involving foreign companies, and that domestic competition authorities are powerless to take action against them. Further, it seems that most host country competition authorities are unwilling to do so. Developing economy governments may have competition laws in place but be unable to gain evidence that anti-competitive practices are being undertaken. One result is the need for greater cooperation between competition authorities across countries. However, this policy outcome is constrained by the fact that at the present time the competition authorities in developed economies take into consideration the effects on their economies of anti-competitive actions worldwide, but do not specifically consider the effects of anti-competitive behaviour in their own countries on the developing world's economies (Holmes, 2003).

REGULATION

Regulation by the state can take many forms, from regulating employment terms, to health and safety legislation, to food safety, to regulating the environment, to regulating specific industries, and so on. In recent years with the privatisation of industries previously owned by the state in which competition is limited or absent, such as electricity, telecommunications, postal services, railways and water, regulation at industry level has increased. Sometimes this regulation has continued to be conducted from within government departments, but in other cases new, dedicated industry regulators have been created. Whatever the precise structure of the regulation adopted, however, all regulatory bodies face two fundamental challenges. The first of these relates to obtaining the necessary information to regulate effectively. Regulators need to have access to reasonably accurate information on the costs and revenues of the regulated firms, their capital investments, consumer demand and the costs of raising capital. In addition, they must anticipate changes in the market environment including macroeconomic events that might impact on the regulated firm, both adversely and positively. Inevitably, the information regulators receive will tend to be incomplete. Whereas the regulated firm presumably has insider knowledge of its operating environment, the regulator lacks this, leading to what is referred to in the economics of regulation literature as the problem of 'information asymmetry'.

The second challenge to effective state regulation relates to incentives. In principle, governments will have better information to regulate effectively and efficiently when they directly control or own the regulated business than when they are regulating private producers (Shapiro and Willig, 1990). This is a long-standing argument for state ownership and implies that state ownership is superior to private ownership with state regulation. But in practice state ownership is associated with major inefficiencies in the use of resources (Martin and Parker, 1997, Ch. 4). This inferiority of performance under state ownership relates to the relative incentives under private and state ownership for managers to manage their businesses efficiently and to the incentives that government as regulator faces in regulating effectively. Under state ownership the government is both the owner and the regulator of assets, leading to a potential conflict of interest. For example, government may have an incentive to overlook environmental damage caused by a state-owned water company because challenging the company to make improvements, by for instance introducing new water treatment processes, might lead to higher water charges or necessitate subsidies out of taxation. Either way costs will fall on consumers/taxpayers, for which government will get the blame. Also, some regulatory interventions may have an adverse impact on employment in the industry, leading to the wrath of the unions. The general result is an incentive for politicians and their officials to overlook regulatory infringements, especially those that are costly or politically controversial. In other words, state ownership is associated with disincentives to regulate effectively. More generally, politicians are accused of regulating for short-term political gain, leading to a reduction in the economic benefits from regulation and increasing the long-term economic costs.

Traditionally governments have regulated for a range of reasons. A number of these reasons are grouped together under the heading of 'market failure'. But as will be emphasised, state regulation may be used for other purposes that are more closely related to the workings of the political process, and in reality these may conflict with an analysis of market failure. These other reasons are usually summarised under the headings of 'regulatory capture' and 'political capture'.

Market failure exists when the market is unable to produce an outcome that maximises economic welfare. In competitive markets without such failings, consumers maximise their welfare or 'consumer surplus' given the competitive price. Consumers freely participate in the market and, under admittedly a very restrictive set of assumptions, the result can be shown to be Pareto optimal. A Pareto optimal outcome is one in which there is no possibility of making anyone else better off without making someone else worse off. Hence, no further resource reallocation would improve economic welfare. This condition and its assumptions are well drilled into economics students and the result is a situation where no regulatory intervention by the state could raise economic welfare. However, in practice the restrictive assumptions on intertemporal competitiveness required for a Pareto optimum are not met and markets can and do fail to maximise economic welfare. The following are the well-rehearsed reasons for market failure.

- There are information deficiencies or asymmetries in the market so that consumers and producers are unable to make decisions optimally in order to maximise their welfare. Information asymmetry is said to exist, for example, in the purchase of specialist health care, where the consumer is likely to be relatively poorly informed on the treatment necessary as compared with the health professional. The result may be that under private health care the consumer over-consumes medical treatment and medical costs become excessive.
- The market is a natural monopoly so that competition cannot flourish. A natural monopoly occurs where there are appreciable economies of scale or scope, such as in the network industries, where the duplication of gas and water pipelines, electricity transmission and distribution grids and fixed line telecommunication systems would be uneconomic (Sharkey, 1982). In developing countries natural monopoly may be pervasive because the market is insufficiently large to sustain a number of competing organisations operating at an efficient scale.
- There are pervasive externalities in the form of costs (or benefits) to agents who are not involved in the immediate transaction, such as when market production leads to significant pollution. Environmental impacts are a good example of externalities but externalities can exist wherever there is jointness in consumption.

Where there is market failure it is possible to demonstrate that state intervention, provided that it is optimally timed and executed, can lead to higher economic welfare than the unregulated private market. This conclusion is relevant when appraising the likely consequences of any privatisation measure. The benefits of privatisation are predicated on the existence of a competitive, well-functioning market process. But where this is absent, privatisation can lead to monopoly not competition. For instance, a study of privatisation in Brazil concluded that the result was the conversion of 'public monopolies into private monopolies with no beneficial impact' (Ayres, 1995; also see Saha and Parker, 2002). To make matters worse, the necessary regulatory reforms to address market failure had not been introduced to protect consumers from monopoly abuse.

Moreover, in the specific context of developing economies there may be additional market failures to those listed so far. These are related to the failure of private markets to produce the level and pattern of economic growth necessary to reduce poverty levels in lower-income economies. A Pareto optimal outcome is linked to one particular distribution of income. In developing economies there is usually a large gap between rich and poor, with many living in chronic poverty. A primary goal of state regulation, therefore, may be to ensure that markets contribute to poverty reduction. Markets can have both direct and indirect effects on poverty reduction: direct impacts may result from improving access for poor people to markets, as buyers or sellers; indirect impacts may occur through the 'trickle-down' effects of the overall rate and pattern of economic growth. But it is not self-evident that private markets will reduce poverty, indeed they may exacerbate it. Even where economic growth raises all incomes over time as private markets expand, the time period involved may be very lengthy indeed, and the distribution of the benefits may be very uneven. An important goal of state regulation of markets, therefore, may be poverty reduction. In this case, regulation is concerned with promoting economic development and raising income levels across the population and particularly among the poor, implying that the efficient private markets alone are unable to achieve this socially desirable outcome.

At the same time, however, state regulation may flourish for a set of altogether different reasons unrelated to market failure or development needs. This set of reasons for the regulatory state is associated not with the promotion of the public good but with private advantage. Because the state is powerful and probably omnipotent, it becomes a source of patronage and economic advantage. Political lobbying, including what in US political circles is known as 'pork barrel politics' under which politicians dispense political favours, leads to a very different perspective on the origins and nature of state regulation to that associated with market failure arguments. In this approach, regulation is either created at the outset to favour special interest groups or, even if its origins lie in a true concern with market failure, it is over time 'captured' by special interests intent on promoting their own economic rents (Stigler, 1971; Posner, 1974; Peltzman, 1976). In the regulatory state, governments wield considerable discretionary power to determine outputs and inputs and therefore income and wealth distribution. Not surprisingly, therefore, they become subject to continuous lobbying by interest groups to ensure that the regulatory outcomes are favourable to them.

Farming interests are a particularly good example of this in the EU, North America and Japan. Through lobbying, including street demonstrations and the occasional blockading of transport routes, they are able to win government financial support and restrict the import of cheap food from other parts of the world. The result is a higher income for domestic farmers but at a big economic cost in the form of higher prices to domestic consumers and lower incomes for farmers in other parts of the world. Such lobbying activities extend, however, well beyond agriculture to all areas of the economy where governments through their regulatory powers can successfully redistribute incomes. Lobbying groups are more likely to be monitored to reduce rather than increase competition. State regulation will then be associated with restricting market entry rather than the promotion of competition, even though the latter would lead to greater economic good (Djankov et al., 2002). The result is then a degree of 'state failure' that could even exceed the market failure that regulation is intended to address.

It can be simply demonstrated that provided the cost to an individual of participating in lobbying does not exceed the benefits that the individual anticipates from taking part in the lobbying, then lobbying of government will take place. Thus, for example, an industry threatened by closure in the absence of state subsidies or trade protection will quickly gather considerable support from its stakeholders. These stakeholders will include the workers, their trade unions, employer organisations, investors, suppliers and members of parliament in directly affected constituencies. Together they create a formidable lobbying force for protection from market forces. By contrast, taxpayers and consumers, although at risk of considerable welfare loss as a group from having to finance state subsidies or through having to pay higher prices, are unlikely to find it individually efficient to take part in lobbying activity. For this reason, state regulation tends to have an underlying momentum to expand continuously. Or, more correctly, to expand to such a point that the costs of regulation begin so obviously to outweigh any possible benefits that a public reaction takes place. Over time the consequence may be cycles of regulation and deregulation.

Allied to this tendency towards 'regulatory capture' is the notion of 'political capture'. Political capture involves the regulatory machinery being used primarily to further the political interests of members of the government, and the argument is related to a wider critique of government contained in 'public choice theory' or 'the economics of politics' literature (e.g. Niskanen, 1971; Tullock, 1976; Mitchell, 1988; Tullock et al., 2000). Under conditions of political capture regulation is shaped to further the interests of the political elite. For example, regulatory bodies may be staffed by members of this elite and regulatory measures may be shaped to enhance their economic welfare. The possibility of such capture is furthered by a lack of informed opinion outside government and the absence of an independent media and judiciary. In these conditions, which describe reality in many lower-income economies, capture may extend to cronyism in regulatory decision making and even outright corruption of officials (e.g. Theobald, 1990; Craig, 2000; Duckett, 2001; Tangri and Mwenda, 2001). Political capture is a form of regulatory capture under which regulation is designed and promoted to meet the needs of the political elite and to preserve its power. The regulatory state is then self-serving.

The market failure rationale for regulation contrasts dramatically, of course, with notions of regulation resulting from regulatory and political capture. In conditions of capture, state regulation is unlikely to gain widespread public sympathy or 'legitimacy'. Regulatory legitimacy exists when the regulatory institutions, while still subject to criticism because of particular decisions or behaviour, are generally accepted within society. Achieving this public acceptance occurs over time and as public confidence in the regulators is built. To achieve legitimacy, regulation is commonly linked to the following attributes of 'good' regulation (Haskins, 2000, p. 60), namely:

- transparency
- accountability
- targeting
- proportionality
- consistency.

Transparency refers to the regulatory process being open to public scrutiny. A transparent regulatory regime allows the public to appreciate the grounds for regulatory decisions and facilitates public consultation and challenge. An accountable regulatory regime is one in which regulation is answerable to the public or more usually to the public's representatives in parliament. A targeted regulatory system is one in which the regulations introduced to correct market failure are not so loosely drafted that they impact unintentionally on other parts of the economy. Proportionality is concerned with regulation introduced being proportional to the problem or market failure identified. The sledge hammer should not be used to crack the nut! Finally, consistency is a further important attribute of 'good' regulation. Consistency in regulatory decisions means that the regulator's actions become more predictable, leading to less disruption to the economy. Inconsistent regulation creates great uncertainty in the private sector and may well have a seriously damaging effect on investment.

In addition to this set of criteria for legitimacy, other important issues in the study of regulation relate to regulatory costs and regulatory risk.

Regulatory costs or the costs of regulation to an economy can be divided into the direct costs of administering the regulations, which will be reflected in the budgets of the regulatory departments, and the costs imposed on the remainder of the economy in terms of complying with the regulations. The latter are a form of 'compliance cost' (Parker, 2002). In principle, the administrative and compliance costs of regulation should be compared to the benefits accruing from the regulation, thereby promoting efficiency in the administration of regulation. However, it may be difficult to estimate the benefits, in which case the objective should be to minimise the costs of regulation to achieve a given (assumed) regulatory benefit. While governments can measure directly the administrative costs, compliance costs are usually hidden from view. But they can be appreciable; for instance in the USA they are said to be as much as $700 bn. This contrasts with a figure for direct regulatory costs borne by federal agencies of some $25 bn (Hopkins, 1996, cited in Blundell and Robinson, 2000).

In addition to the administration and compliance costs of regulation, the effects of regulation on the economy are related to the degree of 'regulatory risk' created. Whereas competitive, unregulated markets are associated with the normal commercial risks of trading, relating to changes in demand and supply and developments in the macro-economy such as interest rate changes, regulated markets suffer from an additional risk. Regulatory risk is an outcome of uncertainty and inconsistency in the regulatory regime, which leaves private agents including businesses fearful of current and future regulatory decisions. Where regulatory risk is appreciable, investors will seek compensation in the form of a larger expected return, so leading to a higher cost of capital. The higher the cost of capital, the lower will be the rate of investment (Guasch and Hahn, 1999; Hahn, 1998). Where regulatory risk becomes very high, private investment may even collapse. Lower-income economies with poorly developed institutional structures, including regulatory agencies, are likely to be associated with high regulatory risk (Levy and Spiller, 1996). This is an important reason for the study of regulation in the context of economic development, with the aim of improving regulatory decision making and processes in the developing world.

Regulatory impact assessment (RIA) is a term used to describe the process of systematically assessing the benefits and costs of a new regulation or an existing regulation, with the aim of improving the quality of regulatory policy. By assessing the positive and negative impacts of potential and existing regulatory measures, RIA can be used as a tool in the design and implementation of regulatory measures. By adopting the principles of transparency and accountability, RIA can also help in establishing the legitimacy of state regulation (Kirkpatrick and Parker, 2003).

Another set of issues in the study of regulation relates to the regulatory structures and regulatory instruments used. Regulatory structure is concerned with the form of administration that the regulation takes. Regulation may, for example, be conducted by government departments or it may be delegated to dedicated regulatory agencies, such as the Office of Telecommunications in the UK and the Federal Communications Commission in the USA. Such arm's length or 'independent' regulation – independent in the sense of being free from day-to-day political intervention though not of course free from public accountability – helps to reduce regulatory risk. The result should be 'better' regulation in terms of the above attributes of 'good' regulation and in particular consistent regulation. The result should be a lower cost of capital and therefore more investment in the regulated industries. This and related matters are pursued further in the discussion of regulatory governance in the next section of this chapter.

Regulatory instruments are the tools and techniques that the regulator uses in the pursuit of effective regulation. In particular, utility regulators will be concerned with the setting of prices and/or profits in the regulated business and with the quality of service. Although various differences exist in the precise instruments used, the approach to price and profit regulation tends to take one of three general forms; namely, cost of service regulation, price cap regulation or sliding scale regulation.

Rate of Return

- Cost of service regulation involves the regulator agreeing the level of operating costs (wages, fuel costs, etc.) and the capital costs (interest on debt financing and depreciation charges on the capital stock) for the regulatory period. To this is added a profit or agreed rate of return based on the firm's cost of capital. The product is the level of revenue needed to achieve the agreed rate of return given the anticipated costs of production. Once the volume of output is forecast then the necessary prices that need to be set are determined. This approach to regulation is sometimes referred to as 'rate of return regulation' and has been used widely in the USA and elsewhere for many years. Usually, if profits turn out to be higher than agreed, perhaps because costs turn out to be lower than forecast or the volume of sales expands more quickly than expected, then the firm is expected to cut its prices to restore the agreed level of profit. While seemingly simple in structure, cost of service regulation is associated with disincentives to reduce operating and capital costs because these can be passed through to consumers in higher prices, and incentives to over-invest, thereby expanding the asset base on which the allowed rate of return is calculated (Averch and Johnson, 1962; Kahn, 1995, pp. 49–59).
- A price cap is an alternative approach to regulating revenues in which profits are not determined by the regulator but are a residual. Under a

price cap the regulator agrees the forecast operating and capital costs with the regulated firm, as under cost of service regulation, but then applies an efficiency gain factor, 'X'. This X efficiency factor is normally based on some estimate of productivity growth in the industry compared with the economy in general. This estimate may result from benchmarking the firm's performance (or 'yardstick' comparisons) with other firms' efficiency growth across the industry or with similar industries or internationally. Whereas average productivity growth across the economy is reflected in price inflation or the Consumer Price Index (CPI), higher or lower than expected productivity growth in the regulated sector is reflected in the X factor price adjustment. The formula for the price cap is then, CPI+/–X. The result is an incentive for the firm to outperform in terms of reducing costs or attracting customers, leading to higher profits (Littlechild, 1983; Viehoff, 1995). The UK has championed price cap regulation because of its supposed incentive effects and price caps have now been adopted in many countries, including in some developing economies, to regulate their privatised telecommunications and electricity sectors.

- Sliding scale regulation involves some combination of the price cap and cost of service regime. Typically, with a sliding scale a price cap operates up to a given level of reported profit, but once the profit exceeds this level then prices are reduced to consumers pro rata to the level of the excess profit, thus sharing the efficiency gains more quickly between consumers and producers than with a pure price cap (Burns et al., 1995). This approach to regulation ensures that profits cannot be excessive for long periods and helps reduce political and social opposition to the regulatory regime that can exist when profits rise sharply, especially in what are perceived to be essential public services such as water and power (Parker, 1998). At the same time, however, when profits are clawed back the incentive for management to reduce costs is reduced. If profits are clawed back immediately, the regime can degenerate into a form of cost of service regulation.

These explanations of the three different approaches to price and profit regulation are by their nature very general and details do differ across the countries which use them. Also, and importantly, all these three methods of price and profit regulation are demanding in terms of information needs. With cost of service regulation, price caps and sliding scales the regulator must overcome the same information asymmetries so that costs, revenues, consumer demand, the asset base, and the true cost of capital can be computed reasonably accurately (Armstrong et al., 1994; Alexander and Irwin, 1996; Vass, 1997; Grout, 1997). In practice, this has proved to be no easy task even for regulators in OECD countries (Souter, 1994). The result can be lengthy appeals against regulators' decisions. For example, in the USA regulation is often appealed to the courts, leading to acrimonious arguments between the regulator and the regulated. Similarly, the UK mode of regulation based on price caps has produced animosity between industries and their regulatory offices, alongside consumer complaints about high profits and 'fat cat' management salaries (Parker, 1998, 1999).

Moreover, in developing countries these three different approaches to regulation are each likely to face difficulties because of a lack of regulatory capacity. Although the UK has exported price cap regulation in preference to the alternatives, it is not self-evident that all or even many developing countries have the regulatory capacity to operate a price cap effectively for long periods. Even in the UK the regime faces strains (Parker, 1998). Regulatory capacity is concerned with the resources available to government to regulate effectively. In developing countries regulatory offices are likely to have limited access to skilled regulatory staff. They may be unable to pay salary levels to attract skilled personnel because of depressed civil service pay scales, and may be subject to day-to-day political intervention even when the regulators are nominally independent. In the face of political capture, the regulatory process may lack legitimacy, so leading to deep suspicions on the part of investors as to the process and outcomes of the regulatory regime, especially if the head of the regulatory office is clearly a political appointment. All regulatory systems are prone to 'gaming' where the parties attempt to capitalise on information asymmetries to maximise their own rents (Bradbury and Ross, 1991; Veljanovski, 1991). But in developing countries, lacking a tradition of probity in government and perhaps an independent media and judiciary, and where the information asymmetries between the regulated and the regulator may be huge, such gaming can be expected to flourish.

This discussion suggests the following are important areas for research into regulation in developing countries:

- The nature of information asymmetries in the specific context of developing economies and how they might be best addressed.
- The role of incentives within different regulatory regimes and the lessons to be learned.
- The rationale for regulatory practice and the comparative roles of market failure and regulatory and political capture.
- The extent to which the attributes of 'good' regulation can be realistically achieved in a developing country context and the implications for regulatory reform.
- The optimal regulatory structures to adopt and particularly the relevance of 'independent' regulation and 'regulatory gaming' where there is a lack of regulatory capacity.

- The relative merits of cost of service regulation, price caps and sliding scales in economies very different to the developed countries where these methods primarily originated.
- The need for regulatory capacity building and the precise forms this should take.

REGULATORY GOVERNANCE

It is clear from the discussion thus far that the analysis of regulation (and indeed of competition policies and instruments) cannot be limited to the economic issues that until recently have been foremost in the literature on regulation in developed economies. Not only are ideological issues involved; that is, competing ideas on the best or most appropriate relationship of state and market, it is also the case that since it is governments that must take the initiative in designing and promoting these and related economic reforms, they become the subject of normal policy, political and bureaucratic processes. Both intentions and outcomes are therefore determined by a combination of economic, social, political and bureaucratic factors, and cannot be attributed to one set of factors alone. It is the acceptance that there is this broader framework to issues of competition and regulation that has produced the relatively recent focus on 'regulatory governance' in the literature relating to developed economies (for a survey of this literature see Minogue, 2001b, 2002b). This broader focus, and the involvement of other disciplines than economics (law and political science in particular) has also brought a degree of fuzziness in definitions of regulation. A simple broad definition is 'the use of public authority to set and apply rules and standards' (Hood et al., 1999). A distinction may then be made between the *regulation of business* (the controls exerted over private, non-state activities) and *regulation inside government* (the controls exerted within and between government agencies, and between levels of national government.) We might also add *international regulation* (regulation of national governments by supranational mechanisms); *self-regulation*, constituted by less formal alternatives than legislative or administrative rulemaking; and *metaregulation*, which implies an overarching system for reviewing regulatory mechanisms within government policy-making processes. Finally, the notion of *deregulation* falls within the field of analysis because of the essential relationship to regulation, while *competition* provides a significant framework of objectives for regulatory systems

When we turn to 'governance' we also find a lack of definitional clarity in the literature. Rhodes declares that 'governance has too many meanings to be useful, but the concept can be rescued by stipulating one meaning and showing how it contributes to the analysis of change' (Rhodes, 1997, pp. 52–3). The 'governance of regulation and competition' might be taken to cover:

- the whole range of government institutions involved in rule-making and implementation;
- the public policy processes which involve this set of institutions;
- the interactions of public organisations and actors with private organisations and actors;
- the significance of political factors: political will and leadership; the interactions of political and economic elites; political interventions in rule adjudication (especially in the actions of judicial or other regulatory actors); and the use of political relationships either to achieve regulatory capture *or* to build trust relationships which underpin effective informal regulation;
- the system of public values which provides the setting for regulation and competition.

A particular concern must be to establish which types of regulation are most effective in delivering benefits to ordinary citizens (and disadvantaged groups of citizens such as the poor) through improved and less costly services, whether provided by the public sector, the private sector, or jointly.

Another broad framework with some relevance is that provided by human rights issues. The practice of human rights necessarily operates within formal legal systems, but there is a more immediate realisation through mechanisms of economic regulation such as employment law and practice (child labour, equal opportunities). In the varied social and political cultures of developing economies the precise formulation of human rights gives rise to disputes about what regulatory claims can or should be made.

Literature reviews and initial 'mapping' surveys by the Centre on Regulation and Competition (CRC) at the University of Manchester and its network of research partners in both developed and developing economies have produced a number of tentative findings. In relation to *institutional structures and relationships*, these findings are:

- there are serious gaps in our knowledge and understanding of the regulatory process in developing economies;
- regulatory structures in developing countries appear to serve a range of objectives other than efficiency;
- due attention to governance and public policy processes (i.e. how things really work in practice) is essential to effective regulatory reform;
- direct regulation by the state machinery of government continues to be

widespread, so it is important to consider 'regulation inside government' as a likely province for regulatory reforms;

- nonetheless, there are certain obvious candidates for deregulation where bureaucratic controls (such as licensing) exert significant constraints on economic performance without conferring any discernible public interest benefit;
- transferred 'best practice' models demonstrate clear adaptive variations in different countries, and it is likely that the 'blind' importing of these models from developed economies will be counterproductive where no account is taken of differences in legal infrastructure, bureaucratic culture, market realities, and political values;
- self-regulation appears to be relatively unexplored as an alternative type of regulatory mechanism;
- regulatory agencies have done little to establish what are their own internal capacity-building needs; knowledge of dominant regulatory reform models is sketchy, and these are prone to local misinterpretation;
- a key task is to design regulatory structures so that opportunities for corruption are minimised.

In relation to *regulation, politics and poverty* the key findings are:

- political institutions and relationships constitute a primary operating context for economic reforms;
- but these political factors are frequently neglected or inadequately understood by external economic policy actors;
- regulatory agencies are as likely to be 'captured' at the policy design stage as at the implementation stage;
- well-organised and institutionally entrenched political interests will often succeed in controlling or subverting economic agencies;
- but authoritative and stable political interests can be a driver for economic reforms;
- market reforms of basic public services are likely to meet political and user resistance if they reduce access, affordability and quality;
- the impact of such reforms on the poor is under-researched and poorly understood.

THE POLITICS OF REGULATION AND COMPETITION

Earlier in this chapter a distinction was drawn between 'regulatory capture', largely construed to cover information asymmetries between regulatory agencies and regulated bodies, and 'political capture'. Politics might be treated in two senses here, both as ideology and as practice. At the level of ideas, different political philosophies involve different views about the appropriate relationship between the state and the market, and between the state and society. The debate between the more extreme paradigms of state–economy–society relations may well be dead, but the ship of state remains stubbornly afloat, if now pointing in a different direction. One commentator suggests that 'it is generally more appropriate to speak of shifting roles of government than of shrinking roles of government' (Kooiman, 1999).

This is doubtless because practical politics ensures that conflicting views over public–private boundaries are mediated through a process characterised by negotiation; that radical policies will be constrained by electoral cycles, or other mechanisms of appointment and replacement; and that substantial changes in rules (and especially in the structure of rule-making) operate over long rather than short time scales. Whether we call the process regulatory capture or political capture, what is at issue is effective control or domination of regulatory mechanisms by the interests who are the object of regulation. Both regulatory design and implementation may be seriously weakened by regulatory capture, and also by internal resistance where regulation inside government is involved. Political factors can be significant in their effects on regulation between levels of government; for example, where different political authorities control central and sub-central governments

A significant practical issue comes under the heading of 'policy transfer'. Since aid donors are likely to bring pressure to bear on developing country aid recipients to introduce competition and regulatory systems and methods which characterise the economic policy systems of developed economies, issues of appropriateness and adaptability arise. The problems of direct policy transfer across cultural boundaries are beginning to be well documented, but are still under-researched in relation to the wave of public management reforms of the past two decades. The literature on policy transfer as it relates to more general market-oriented governance reforms in developing economies is still fairly sparse, but what there is tends to the conclusion that reforms are largely rhetorical; blueprints are borrowed, but honoured in the breach more than the observance, with considerable local variation in reform trajectories, where such can be said to exist (Common, 1998, 1999; Parker, 2003). The blueprint itself has been subjected to critiques for being too 'top-down' (Wallis and Dollery, 2001) and for being inappropriate to the bureaucratic/managerial cultures characteristic in developing countries (Minogue, 2002a; Schick, 1998). Even in developed economies, the 'new public management' model has not been properly evaluated (Pollitt and Bouckaert, 2000), and, for example in the UK, has been substantially attacked for bringing more damage than benefit to the efficient provision of public services (Minogue, 2001a). The reforms associated with 'regulatory governance', privatisation and post-privatisation regulation are closely related in conceptual terms, but also in practice, to the general process of public management reform. The ways in which these reform ideas have been transferred and adapted to developing country economic and political systems needs to be examined in detail.

REGULATORY GOVERNANCE: THE RESEARCH AGENDA

Generally, regulatory systems both internal and external to government are weak in developing countries. The reasons for this weakness need to be established, and are hypothesised to lie partly in low levels of government legitimacy, partly in institutional underdevelopment, and partly in 'political capture'. While we are familiar with the existence of regulatory and political capture, we still do not have much research evidence on how this process operates in developing countries, where the political character of regulatory capture is more pronounced than in developed economies; and also where regulatory capture is often internalised within government itself. A related issue is the constraints on efficient and effective policy and administration that flow from the cultural characteristics of the government system; a good example here is the persistence and pervasiveness of corrupt behaviour (Minogue, 2002a). We need to understand better how these political and bureaucratic factors impede effective regulatory design and implementation. We also need a better understanding of the role and operation of legal institutions and actors in regulatory systems which are politically and behaviourally constrained. There is therefore a link between general public management reform and regulatory reform, in the sense that the effectiveness of any area of public policy, including regulation and competition policy, will be determined by whatever are the bureaucratic and political constraints and weaknesses inherent in the general system of governance. Political factors may be taken in principle to represent an opportunity for commitment to effective regulation (Moran, 2002; Braithwaite, 1999; Hood, 1998) but are more likely to be a potential source of inhibition.

This approach is strengthened by the recognition that, as noted earlier, regulatory governance embraces what has come to be called 'regulation inside government' (Hood et al., 1999). Regulation is frequently treated as something that is by definition external to and independent of government, but in principle government has always been heavily involved in regulation (hence the use of the term 'deregulation' to indicate the removal of government rules, restrictions, or even provision). In developed economies, despite the tendency of neoliberal reforms to take whole areas of economic activity outside government through privatisation, or to reduce government controls through deregulation, significant regulatory responsibilities remain with the state, and in some respects have been changed into new requirements for audit and oversight to fill the public interest accountability gaps left by privatisation and deregulation. In developing economies, where privatisation has pursued a rather erratic and patchy course, substantial regulatory responsibilities remain with both central and local public authorities. The tension between efficiency objectives and political imperatives is clearly marked, and is itself responsible for the relatively slow progress of institutional reforms. Public management reform may have a significant influence on economic reforms if the overriding need is to improve the quality of regulation inside government rather than to take regulation outside government.

A related area for investigation might be the interface between the public and private sectors created by new managerial initiatives through contracting and public–private partnerships. These initiatives have created new hybrid forms of action which are neither wholly public sector nor wholly private sector. They involve an attempt to separate public funding and accountability from operational delivery of services to the public; in some cases they also represent an attempt to draw in market investment to supplement scarce public resources; yet other variations draw in community resources to supplement both state and private provision. Research would seek to establish the regulatory patterns required by these new forms of public action in developed countries, and their applicability to developing economies.

Another related research possibility could focus on the concept of trust as an alternative to regulation. A main critique of contracting is that because it necessarily operates in a framework of directive formal rules, the relations of collaboration that underpin direct government provision are missing or damaged. An alternative approach is to concentrate on building relations of trust between public and private partners within a less formalised regulatory framework, as advocated for developed economies (Ayres and Braithwaite, 1992). The relative appropriateness of these alternatives (formalistic, or trust-based) for developing country regulatory systems needs to be explored.

A broader but related area for research is the possibility of 'regulation by values', focusing on regulatory mechanisms for the protection of economic and social rights, and on the creation of a public service ethics within governments. Both aspects deserve more attention in the light of the identifiably adverse consequences of economic liberalisation. Research of this kind would also draw in developing arrangements for the improvement of business ethics.

AN OUTLINE OF THE BOOK CONTENTS

The book consists of 21 chapters including this introduction. The chapters have been organised into three sections, with Part 1 providing an introductory overview. The chapters in Part 2 focus on *leading concepts and issues in competition, regulation and development*.

Chapter 2 by Paul Cook deals with the promotion of competition in developing countries. Despite differences, developing countries are generally characterised by lower degrees of market competition than their industrialised country counterparts. Until relatively recently, few developing countries had OECD-type competition policies. Cook demonstrates that the heightened interest in competition in developing countries has various explanations. He argues that in part it is undoubtedly linked to the wave of neoliberal economic reforms introduced since the 1980s, including privatisation. This view sees government control, and in particular regulation, as the main vehicle for enriching politicians and promoting corruption and, therefore, as a fundamental problem. As a consequence, deregulation and liberalisation are seen as inevitable solutions. Also, he contends that the increased emphasis on competition is linked to concerns in developing countries over weak systems of corporate governance, leading to greater enterprise inefficiency. Competition is often viewed as a substitute for corporate governance. But he also points out that the new interest in competition in developing countries has exposed how little is known of the effectiveness of competition policies and about the ways in which competitive processes work in developing countries. The purpose of the chapter is to select and examine a few critical areas that need to be considered when developing and evaluating competition policy in these countries. Different approaches to competition policy can then be characterised according to the relative emphasis that each places on the incentives for the acquisition of assets versus incentives for their use. The chapter draws on theory to consider issues relating to factors that inhibit competition and to discuss their implications for policy in developing countries.

Chapter 3 by J.S. Metcalfe, R. Ramlogan and E. Uyarra reviews some recent thinking on the connection between competition and development as a prelude to a study of wider concerns about innovation, income distribution, competition and development policy. The position taken by the authors is that the problems of competitiveness and economic development are isomorphic by virtue of being examples of the phenomenon of economic evolution. Economic evolution is a theory of how the world changes, or rather how it changes in such an uneven fashion. The authors review ideas on the history of the concept of competition and go on to develop an evolutionary approach to competition and competitive advantage, in particular examining issues relating to innovation and development. They conclude that competition is central to the development process, but that competition is a process not a state of affairs. Consequently competition policy is not reducible to a simple-minded concern with the exploitation of market power, rather in its fundamentals it is a matter of the creativity of an economic system.

Chapter 4 by David Parker and Colin Kirkpatrick identifies the main issues that need to be considered when examining economic regulation in developing countries. To provide a basis for this examination, Parker and Kirkpatrick draw on a range of theoretical propositions derived from the literature on the economics of regulation. Parker and Kirkpatrick examine six wide-ranging propositions that have implications for the success or failure of regulation. Principally these relate to the degree to which regulation is embedded in institutional arrangements; the extent of information asymmetries; the nature of regulatory contracts; the extent to which regulatory systems are prone to various types of capture; the trade-offs between effective and efficient regulation; and finally, the place for competition. Parker and Kirkpatrick then consider these propositions in relation to the needs of developing countries in order to establish a methodology for understanding how regulation works in these countries. They argue that both the theory and the experience of regulation in developed countries does have relevance for developing countries but the theory and its application cannot be naively transferred to them.

In Chapter 5, Peter Holmes discusses the issue of trade and competition policy that was put on the agenda of the WTO in 1996. In the chapter Holmes asks what justification there is for a multilateral agreement relating to competition and, critically, what it should include. He examines the legal position with respect to trade and law on competition policy and finds that current rules provide an unclear picture that could result in costly litigation to get clarification on what the rules mean. The final part of the chapter reviews the proposals for reform from a European Union perspective.

Graeme Hodge studies some critical issues in private sector development strategy in Chapter 6. The aim of this chapter is to reflect on the concept of a private sector development strategy (PSD strategy) and to articulate aspects of the PSD strategies of the Asian Development Bank and the World Bank, in order to identify both commonalities and differences. These strategies are reviewed as devices for corporate direction-setting and policy-making in the context of the privatisation of state-owned enterprises, economic regulation and competition. In particular, he considers issues arising when strategy is viewed as an evolutionary and learning phenomenon in organisations. The study argues that PSD strategy is essentially not strategy at all in the usual sense of corporate direction-setting and policy implementation, but is a mixture of affirmations, actions, goals, aspirations and belief. The consequence of this is that there are large gaps between the image of corporate direction-setting in development banks through definite initiatives for change and the actuality of generalised policy statements at senior levels, and both uncertainty and rhetorical conflict at officer level. The chapter also argues that, as a consequence, many of the traditional arguments, philosophical battles and failures to learn from empirical experience that have characterised decades of debate on privatisation, regulation and competition policy for development now continue beneath the surface of the PSD strategy paradigm. The chapter questions whether the development banks are capable of meeting the need for new models of regulation and competition. Meeting this challenge will require the banks themselves to redevelop PSD strategies that are more culturally relevant, to increase their internal capacity to learn from the breadth of experience to date and also to be more explicit about the inevitability of power sharing as part of successful reform. Thus far, the pattern seems to have been one of simply asserting private over public, markets over governments, and quick actions over more gradual, difficult but informed and effective reforms in privatisation, regulation and competition.

Chapter 7 by Anthony Ogus aims to identify and compare the key features of regulatory systems in industrialised countries. By way of essential background, the first section deals with the constitutional and cultural environment that underpins the systems, but it also includes a discussion of regulatory traditions and styles which, for example as between anglophone and continental European regimes, are significantly different. Institutional frameworks are discussed in the second section, covering, *inter alia*, the relationship between regulatory agencies and government, the breadth of remit of regulatory institutions and the degree of discretion conferred on them by legislation. The latter necessarily gives rise to issues concerning the forms and institutions of accountability. The chapter then considers regulatory procedures and management. Noteworthy here are, on the one hand, the systems of consultation and the extent to which public hearings are encouraged and, on the other, cost–benefit or regulatory impact analysis which, in some jurisdictions, is mandatory for regulatory policy-makers. The final section is concerned with legal instruments and concentrates on the growing distance between traditional 'command and control' methods and those relying on financial incentives and other economic instruments. A brief conclusion emphasises the pitfalls that attend an extension of the comparison to the different institutional contexts of developing countries.

The focus of Martin Minogue's chapter, Chapter 8, is on the conceptual and empirical problems that arise in the analysis of the administrative and political context of economic and social regulation in developing countries. After a discussion of the significance of dominant ideas in current debates on economic and social development policy, the chapter examines the main characteristics of regulatory governance in developed economies, since the privatisation and regulatory reforms recently introduced into developing economies are broadly modelled on developed country experience. It is argued that regulatory reforms need to be analysed in the broader context of the new public management (NPM) and governance reforms, which have been spreading across both developed and developing systems of government in the last two decades. One reason for close attention to systems of governance is that in developing countries, the state is likely to retain greater responsibilities for economic and social regulation than is now the case in developed economies. In this event, 'western' models of regulation will not be easily emulated or transferred because of the resistant political and administrative cultures that must receive them. The forms of this 'reality gap' are examined, and the implications for the reshaping of state–market relations in developing countries are considered, as well as the implications for pro-poor strategies.

A principal practical concern for regulatory agencies is to acquire and develop the internal institutional skills needed to secure effective regulatory performance. In Chapter 9, Derek Eldridge explores the utility of a specific diagnostic methodology linked to capacity-building issues and performance management. The chapter reviews the advantages and constraints associated with the application of this approach to regulatory organisations.

Chapter 10 by Richard Heeks and Richard Duncombe looks at how ethical trade – initiatives that seek to improve the social and environmental impacts of global supply chains – is growing because of perceived shortcomings in globalisation and in traditional forms of state regulation. This chapter analyses and categorises stakeholders, incentives and mechanisms of ethical trade. On the basis of current (limited) evidence, it summarises the impact of ethical trade via six performance measures: existence, extent, expedience, effectiveness, efficiency, and externalities. The mixed picture of impacts is analysed and understood from two perspectives: a design focus, and an institutional focus. The former sees impacts as guided by design–reality gaps in the planning and implementation of initiatives. The latter identifies key institutional elements affecting impacts: underlying stakeholder interests, regulatory incentives, asymmetries of power and information, and trust. The chapter concludes by looking at regulatory changes and challenges arising from globalisation; by critiquing current recommendations for ethical trade improvement; and by identifying ongoing research issues.

The chapters in Part 3 provide *case studies of policies and practice in developing countries*. Chapter 11 by Cassey Lee reviews the regulatory reforms that have been introduced as a consequence of privatisation in Malaysia since the mid-1980s. The author describes the sectoral approach to economic regulation that has been adopted in sectors where privatisation has taken place, and points out the limited attention given to competition regulation. Only the communications and multimedia sector has provisions for this. The author discusses the government's plans to introduce a national competition policy and analyses how the objectives of competition policy might conflict with other regulatory goals aimed at poverty eradication and wealth redistribution.

In Chapter 12, Kobus Müller examines the institutional and policy framework for competition and regulation in South Africa. Both the public and private sectors in South Africa are committed to changing the current situation of inequity, inequality and poverty. Competition and competitiveness are regarded as useful instruments to stimulate economic growth. South Africa has positioned itself as a country leaning towards the public interest model of government, and has adopted legislation providing for competition. International agreements in terms of competition have also been signed.

Major restructuring has taken place as regards institutional structures and regulatory responsibilities. Enterprises have been privatised, but are regulated by separate, state-funded bodies with judicial powers and accountability to taxpayers. There is potential conflict between regulatory and competition authorities about their roles.

Policies for social and economic regulation, designed to empower the disadvantaged, seem unable to promote growth and investment. According to the South African approach to privatisation the state remains the major stakeholder in partnerships. Self-regulation has increased, while regulatory measures have already had an impact on income statistics beyond ethnic lines.

The tripartite government alliance in the country is not in agreement on the regulation of the economy. Government, organised business and labour together with organised society formed the National Economic Development and Labour Council (Nedlac) to address issues of social and economic policy.

This chapter identifies gaps in the institutional and policy framework, which include representational, judicial, accountability, coordination, globalisation and ethical issues. The challenge is to find a balance between conflicting economic and social objectives, to enhance competition, reduce state debt and widen ownership in the economy.

In Chapter 13 Ledivina Cariño maps out the terrain of regulatory governance in the Philippines, describing the constitutional and legal frameworks of regulation and the economy. The examination of the institutional framework describes the role of the three branches of government, then the various means of organising the regulatory agencies, focusing primarily on how they tackle the joint pressures of involvement and independence. Emerging regulatory mechanisms in the private sector and civil society are also presented. This chapter argues that the contrasting pull of nationalism on the one hand, and globalisation and liberalisation on the other are the most significant forces shaping regulatory governance today.

The policy shift in the developing world over the last two decades, towards market mechanisms as instruments of economic growth and poverty reduction, has been paralleled by the emergence of a new role for the state from provider to facilitator/regulator. As Malathy Knight-John emphasises in Chapter 14, Sri Lanka has not been an exception in this regard. Although Sri Lanka moved from an import substituting and heavily state interventionist economy to a more liberalised one in 1977, competition legislation and legislation for regulating telecommunications, passenger bus transport, and the financial sector were only introduced later. Civil strife, pressures to finance the state's burgeoning fiscal deficit and the related move to opt for rapid privatisation contributed to placing competition and regulatory concerns on the backburner. Moreover, while the formal institutional and legal structures for competition and regulation now exist, distortionary intervention and bureaucratic micromanagement by the state are not uncommon. The study shows that regulatory practices have tended to stifle rather than enhance or promote competition in Sri Lanka. This raises important policy questions that Knight-John pursues.

Chapter 15 by Ernest Aryeetey discusses the development of the institutional and policy framework for regulation and competition in Ghana over the last ten years in response to the widespread liberalisation of the economy. Its objective is to highlight the different types of institutions and policies being employed to develop a level playing field for economic agents as they interact between themselves and also with consumers. In discussing the history of regulation over a longer period, it shows that while the professed goals have always been to provide equal opportunities for all economic agents, regulation has sometimes been also perceived as a tool for directing the involvement of distinct socioeconomic groups in the economy. The chapter also discusses the legal framework and major institutions for regulation and how they impact on the choice of regulatory approaches.

Chapter 16 by Diana Mitlin explores the impact of regulation and competition policy on the poor. There are a number of anticipated influences both in regard to the poor as consumers and as producers and/or suppliers of goods and services. Potential areas of influence include the impact of regulation and competition policies on the price of basic commodities and services; the quality of commodities and services; opportunities for access to markets for commodities and services; changes in market opportunities for employment and enterprise development (both positive and negative); and changes in externalities such as environmental degradation, and health and safety. Such areas have an evident impact on the well-being of the poor, their capacity to avoid poverty and their development options. The study focuses on a single sector – water services – and considers the impacts for the urban poor. Water was selected because it is a basic need in maintaining life and improving well-being in the short, medium and long term. For the poor, the objective is access to affordable and adequate supplies of water to meet a multitude of needs.

In Chapter 17 Armando Barrientos argues that there is an emerging consensus among multilateral institutions around the need for developing countries to develop and strengthen social protection policies and programmes, as an urgent response to economic crisis and rising vulnerability. The emerging social protection agenda gives regulation a very significant role in reducing social risk and vulnerability and encourages the reform and extension of existing regulation, and the development of new forms of regulation in developing countries. This includes the extension of labour standards as an important instrument in preventing and mitigating employment. The chapter begins with a characterisation of social protection as an emerging framework for social policy, and a brief discussion of the reasons for its prominence. The second section of the chapter shows, using the specific example of the introduction of individual insurance saving plans in Latin America and transitional economies, that the adoption of social protection has implications for the regulation of enterprises and markets. The third section examines empirically whether social protection regulation is linked to other regulatory domains, and especially the regulation of enterprises and markets. The indicators of labour regulation are shown to be positively correlated with indicators of contract enforcement, firm entry, and credit information regulation – suggesting linkages across regulatory domains.

The discussion in this chapter alerts us to the need to incorporate social protection within the study and evaluation of regulation in developing countries. Regulation constitutes an important component of social protection, especially in the context of the expansion of private and not-for-profit provision of social protection. Social protection regulation is also linked to other regulatory domains, and constitutes an important component of regulatory regimes. Further research is needed to determine these linkages, and to identify regulatory regimes with greater precision.

In Chapter 18, Tan Wooi Syn agrees that the state is central to the design and implementation of privatisation, as it must identify the industry or sector, select candidates, and regulate performance. State support is also necessary where the private sector is unable to bear all the risks in large projects such as infrastructure investment that involves externalities. However, such state intervention can undermine private incentives and reduce efficiency. The success of privatisation then depends on a country's institutional endowments, in particular its regulatory capacity. This chapter considers these issues in the case of Malaysia, where financial difficulties leading to state bailouts and renationalisations highlight the problems of patronage associated with its privatisation programme. Poor design and inappropriate choices of candidates weakened incentives to increase efficiency and investment, so emphasising the importance of institutional criteria in successful privatisation policies.

In Malaysia, political factors shaped privatisation policies and institutions; factional rivalries, centralised decision-making and increased patronage led to weakened institutions and poor service delivery. This case suggests that effective regulation is also likely to be circumscribed by the political context.

Chapter 19 by Raul Fabella and Rafaelita Aldaba examines the regulatory environment of the two most important energy sectors in the Philippines; namely, the power sector and the downstream oil industry sector. The authors show that significant deregulation in recent years could have profound implications for future industrial structures of these sectors. The chapter goes on to examine the legislation that underpins various reform initiatives and analyses the processes at work to both support and reverse the laws.

In Chapter 20, Thankom Arun provides a guide to the development strategies that have been pursued and to the evolution of regulatory laws and institutions in India. It examines the new legal basis for promoting competition in India, and uses the example of telecommunications to explore some of the economic and political issues relating to regulation of competition in this sector. It shows that regulatory issues need to be addressed in the early stages of reform and that the effectiveness of regulation will be enhanced by reducing the political element in regulatory decision-making.

Finally, in Chapter 21, Claude Chang discusses the development of telecommunications policy in Guyana. Guyana privatised its telecommunications system in 1990 but since the restructuring has been plagued by a series of problems and disputes with weaknesses in government regulation. In spite of some clear service improvements since privatisation, Chang highlights how changes in economic fundamentals and technology militate against maintaining practices and agreements over a long period of time, especially when they become no longer appropriate to the needs of the country. This chapter helps to bring together a number of the competition and regulation issues in earlier chapters through an interesting case study of both successes and failures in government policy. The case study underlines the need for a clear policy on competition and regulation and one which is constantly monitored and updated.

CONCLUSIONS

Developing countries are subject to privatisation, competition and regulatory reforms, often promoted by donor agencies such as the World Bank, IMF, OECD and Asian Development Bank. Recent research has confirmed the importance of sound institutions including regulatory regimes for economic development (North, 1990; Jalilian et al., 2003). This is reflected in the publications of the international agencies, including the World Bank, which have acknowledged the need for effective regulatory institutions if countries are to benefit fully from neoliberal reforms. For example, in 1997 the World Bank commented that 'although private sector expansion may relieve governments from certain tasks, it also imposes new responsibilities' (World Bank, 1997). More recently the World Bank has concluded that some developing countries 'have privatised badly, creating private monopolies still insulated from competition' and that 'the challenge of building effective regulatory agencies is enormous and will not automatically lead to better outcomes' (World Bank, 2003, pp. xv, 103).

This book provides a series of studies of competition, regulation and regulatory governance in an attempt to inter-relate these different aspects of the new regulatory state in the context of developing countries. In this sense the book bridges a gap between the literature on regulation and competition in developed economies and the market liberalisation agenda. The main purpose of the volume is to stimulate debate about the nature and form of competition, regulation and regulatory governance in the development process.

REFERENCES

Alchian, A. (1950), 'Uncertainty, evolution and economic theory', *Journal of Political Economy*, **58**, 211–22.

Alexander, I. and Irwin, T. (1996), 'Price caps, rate-of-return regulation and the cost of capital', *Private Sector* (September), 25–8.

Armstrong, M., Cowan, S. and Vickers, J. (1994), *Regulatory Reform: Economic Analysis and British Experience*, Cambridge, MA: MIT Press.

Averch, H. and Johnson, L.L. (1962), 'Behavior of the firm under regulatory constraint', *American Economic Review*, **52**, 1052–69.

Ayres, I. and Braithwaite, J. (1992), *Responsive Regulation: Transcending the Regulation Debate*, Oxford: Oxford University Press.

Ayres, R. (1995), 'Privatization and distributional equity: the case of Brazil', *International Journal of Social Economics*, **22** (12), 36–49.

Blundell, J. and Robinson, C. (2000), *Regulation without the State . . . The Debate Continues*, Readings 52, London: Institute of Economic Affairs.

Bradbury, R. and Ross, D.R. (1991), *Regulation and Deregulation in Industrial Countries: Some Lessons for LDCs*, Washington, DC: World Bank.

Braithwaite, J. (1999), 'Accountability and governance under the new regulatory state', *Australian Journal of Public Administration*, **58** (1), 90–7.

Burns, P., Turvey, R. and Weyman-Jones, T.G. (1995), 'General properties of sliding scale regulation', *Technical Paper 3*, London: Centre for the Study of Regulated Industries.

Common, R. (1998), 'Convergence and transfer: a review of the globalisation of New Public Management,' *International Journal of Public Sector Management*, **11** (6), 440–50.

Common, R. (1999), 'Accounting for administrative change in three Asia-Pacific states', *Public Management*, **1** (3), 429–38.

Cook, P. (2002), 'Competition policy, market power and collusion in developing countries', *Centre on Regulation and Competition Working Paper Series*, no. 33, University of Manchester.

Cook, P. and Minogue, M. (1990), 'Waiting for privatization in developing countries', *Public Administration and Development*, **10**, 389–403.

Craig, J. (2000), 'Evaluating privatisation in Zambia: a tale of two processes', *Review of African Political Economy*, **85**, 357–66.

Djankov, S., La Porta, R., Lopez-de-Silanes, F. and Shleifer, A. (2002), 'The regulation of entry', *Quarterly Journal of Economics*, **117** (1), 1–37.

Duckett, J. (2001), 'Bureaucrats in business, Chinese style: the lessons of market reform and state entrepreneurialism in the People's Republic of China', *World Development*, **29** (1), 23–37.

Evenett, S., Levenstein, M. and Suslow, V. (2001), 'International cartel enforcement: lessons from the 1990s', *The World Economy*, **24** (9), 1221–45.

Grout, P. (1997), 'The foundations of regulatory methodology: the cost of capital and asset values', paper presented at the CRI Conference, The Financial Methodology of 'Incentive'Regulation – Reconciling Accounting and Economics, London, 5 November.

Guasch, J.L. and Hahn, R.W. (1999), 'The costs and benefits of regulation: implications for developing countries', *World Bank Research Observer*, **14** (1), 137–58.

Hahn, R.W. (1998), 'Policy watch: analysis of the benefits and costs of regulation', *Journal of Economic Perspectives*, **12** (4), 201–10.

Haskins, C. (Lord) (2000), 'The challenge to state regulation', in J. Blundell and C. Robinson, *Regulation without the State . . . The Debate Continues*, Readings 52, London: Institute of Economic Affairs.

Holmes, P. (2004), 'Trade and competition policy at the WTO: issues for developing countries', in P. Cook, C. Kirkpatrick, M. Minogue and D. Parker (eds) *Leading Issues in Competition, Regulation and Development*, Cheltenham, UK and Northampton, MA, USA: Edward Elgar.

Hood, C. (1998), *The Art of the State: Culture, Rhetoric, and Public Management*, Oxford: Oxford University Press.

Hood, C., James, O., Jones, G. and Travers, T. (1999), *Regulation Inside Government: Waste-Watchers, Quality Police, and Sleaze-Busters*, Oxford: Oxford University Press.

Hopkins, T.D. (1996), *Regulatory Costs in Profile*, Policy Study no. 132, New York: Centre for the Study of American Business.

Izaguirre, A.K. and Rao, G. (2000), 'Private infrastructure: private activity fell by 30 percent in 1999', *Private Sector*, (September), 5—8.

Jackson, P.M. and Price, C. (eds) (1994), *Privatisation and Regulation – A Review of the Issues*, London: Longman.

Jalilian, K., Kirkpatrick, C. and Parker, D. (2003), 'The impact of regulation on economic performance in developing countries: a cross-country analysis', mimeo, Centre on Regulation and Competition, Institute of Development Policy and Management, University of Manchester.

Kahn, A.E. (1995), *The Economics of Regulation: Principles and Institutions*, vol. 2, Cambridge, MA: MIT Press.

Kirkpatrick, C. and Parker, D. (2003), 'Regulatory impact assessment and regulatory governance', mimeo, Centre on Regulation and Competition, Institute of Development Policy and Management, University of Manchester.

Knight, F. (1946), 'Immutable law in economics: its reality and limitations', *American Economic Review*, **XXXVI**, 93–111.

Kooiman, J. (1999), 'Social-political governance: overview, reflections, and design,' *Public Management,* **1** (1), 67–92.

Levy, B. and Spiller, P. (eds) (1996), *Regulations, Institutions and Commitment*, Cambridge: Cambridge University Press.

Littlechild, S.C. (1983), *Regulation of British Telecommunications' Profitability*, London: HMSO.

McCourt, W. and Minogue, M. (eds) (2001), *The Internationalisation of Public Management: Reinventing the Third World State*, Cheltenham: Edward Elgar.

Majone, G. (1997), 'From the positive to the regulatory state: causes and consequences of changes in the mode of governance', *Journal of Public Policy*, **17** (2), 139–67.

Martin, S. and Parker, D. (1997), *The Impact of Privatisation: Ownership and Corporate Performance in the UK*, London: Routledge.
Metcalfe, J.S. (2000), 'Competing concepts of competition and the evolution of competition policy in the UK', paper presented to Workshop on Regulation and Governance, 29–30 March, Manila, The Philippines: Centre for Research on Innovation and Competition, University of Manchester.
Metcalfe, J.S., Ramlogan, R. and Uyarra, E. (2002), 'Economic development and the competitive process', *Centre on Regulation and Competition Working Paper Series*, no. 36, University of Manchester.
Minogue, M. (2001a), 'Should flawed models of public management be exported?', in W. McCourt and M. Minogue (eds) *The Internationalisation of Public Management: Reinventing the Third World State*, Cheltenham, UK and Northampton, MA, USA: Edward Elgar, pp. 20–43.
Minogue, M. (2001b), *Governance-based Analysis of Regulation*, Working Paper no. 3, Centre on Regulation and Competition, University of Manchester, Manchester.
Minogue, M. (2002a), 'Public management and regulatory governance: problems of policy transfer to developing countries', Working Paper no. 32, Centre on Regulation and Competition, University of Manchester, Manchester.
Minogue, M. (2002b), 'Governance-based analysis of regulation', *Annals of Public and Cooperative Economics*, **73** (4), 649–66.
Mitchell, W.C. (1988), *Government As It Is*, Hobart Paper 109, London: Institute of Economic Affairs.
Moran, M. (2002), 'Understanding the regulatory state', *British Journal of Political Science*, **32**, 391–413.
Niskanen, W.A. Jr (1971), *Bureaucracy and Representative Government*, Chicago: Aldine.
North, D.C. (1990), *Institutions, Institutional Change and Economic Performance*, Cambridge: Cambridge University Press.
Parker, D. (1998), 'Price cap regulation, profitability and returns to investors in the UK regulated industries', *Utilities Policy*, **6** (4), 303–15.
Parker, D. (1999), 'Regulating public utilities: what other countries can learn from the UK experience', *Public Management*, **1** (1), 93–120.
Parker, D. (2002), 'Economic regulation: a review of issues', *Annals of Public and Cooperative Economics*, **73** (4), 493–519.
Parker, D. (2003), 'Inertia in the implementation of a privatisation programme: the case of a policy transfer in Taiwan', in W.M. De Jong, K.D. Lalenis and V. Mamadouh (eds) *The Theory and Practice of Institutional Transplantation: Experiences with the Transfer of Policy Institutions*, Dordrecht: Kluwer.
Peltzman, S. (1976), 'Toward a more general theory of regulation', *Journal of Law and Economics*, **14**, 109–48.
Pollitt, C. and Bouckaert, G. (2000), *Public Management Reform: A Comparative Analysis*, Oxford: Oxford University Press.
Posner, R.A. (1974), 'Theories of economic regulation', *Bell Journal of Economics and Management Science*, **5**, 335–58.
Rey, P. (1997), *Competition Policy and Development*, Toulouse, France: Institut d'Economie Industrielle, Universite des Sciences Sociales.
Rhodes, R. (1997), *Understanding Governance*, Buckingham: Open University Press.
Saha, S.K. and Parker, D. (2002), *Globalisation and Sustainable Development: Perspectives on the New Economic Order*, Cheltenham, UK and Northampton, MA, USA: Edward Elgar.

Schick, A. (1998), 'Why most developing countries should not try New Zealand's reforms', *World Bank Research Observer*, **13** (1),123–31.

Shapiro, C. and Willig, R.D. (1990), 'Economic rationales for the scope of privatization', in E.N. Suleiman and J. Waterbury, *The Political Economy of Public Sector Reform and Privatization*, Boulder, CO: Westview Press, reprinted in D. Parker (ed.) (2001) *Privatisation and Corporate Performance*, Cheltenham: Edward Elgar.

Sharkey, W. (1982), *The Theory of Natural Monopoly*, Cambridge: Cambridge University Press.

Souter, D. (1994), 'A stakeholder approach to regulation', in D. Corry, D. Souter and M. Waterson, *Regulating our Utilities*, London: Institute for Public Policy Research.

Stigler, G. (1971), 'The theory of economic regulation', *Bell Journal of Economics and Management*, **2**, 3–21.

Tangri, R. and Mwenda, A. (2001), 'Corruption and cronyism in Uganda's privatization in the 1990s', *African Affairs*, **100**, 117–33.

Theobald, R. (1990), *Corruption, Development and Under-development*, Basingstoke: Macmillan.

Tullock, G. (1976), *The Vote Motive*, Hobart Paper 9, London: Institute of Economic Affairs.

Tullock, G., Seldon, A. and Brady, G.L. (2000), *Government: Whose Obedient Servant?*, Readings 51, London: Institute of Economic Affairs.

Vass, P. (1997), 'The methodology for resetting X', in P. Vass (ed.) *Regulatory Review 1997*, London: CRI.

Veljanovski, C. (1991), 'The regulation game', in C. Veljanovski (ed.) *Regulators and the Market: An Assessment of the Growth of Regulation in the UK*, London: Institute of Economic Affairs.

Viehoff, I. (1995), 'Evaluating RPI-X', *Topics 17*, London: NERA.

Wallis, J. and Dollery, B. (2001), 'Government failure, social capital and the appropriateness of the New Zealand model for public sector reform in developing countries', *World Development*, **29** (2), 245–63.

World Bank (1997), 'The role of government and the private sector in fighting poverty', *World Bank Technical Paper no. 396*, Washington, DC: World Bank.

World Bank (2003), *Global Economic Prospects and the Developing Countries*, Washington, DC: IBRD/World Bank.

PART 2

Competition, Regulation and Development: Leading Concepts and Issues

2. Competition policy, market power and collusion in developing countries

Paul Cook

INTRODUCTION

Interest in promoting competition in developing countries has increased over the past decade. Despite differences, developing countries are generally characterised by lower degrees of market competition than their industrialised country counterparts. Until relatively recently, few developing countries had OECD-type competition policies. By the end of the 1980s only about a dozen developing countries had workable antitrust legislation and institutions (Gray and Davis, 1993). By the early 2000s the range of developing countries with competition policy had increased considerably, although to what effect is largely unknown.

The heightened interest in competition in developing countries has various explanations. In part, it is undoubtedly linked to the wave of neoliberal economic reforms introduced since the 1980s, and in particular to the issues raised as a result of privatisation. To many, privatisation was a response to the government failures encapsulated in the notion of the 'grabbing hand of government', a term coined by Shleifer and Vishny (1998). This, drawing on public choice theory, indicated that the key problem of state enterprises was government interference in their activities, which led them to pursue political rather than economic goals. Privatisation was viewed as a policy that would restrict the future influence of the state on enterprises previously publicly owned. This view sees government control, and in particular regulation, as the main vehicle for enriching politicians and promoting corruption and, therefore, as a fundamental problem. As a consequence, deregulation and liberalisation were viewed as inevitable solutions.

The issue of competition in relation to privatisation was important in at least two respects. First, the notion of privatisation was often associated directly with competition, moving from government-owned enterprises with monopolies and restricted entry to private ones operating under competitive market conditions. Second, and alternatively, privatisation was not always assumed to guarantee an improvement in competitive conditions because many public monopolies were transformed into private ones, and not all of these were so-called natural monopolies (Cook and Kirkpatrick, 1995; Shirley and Walsh, 2000). This raised new questions with respect to regulation and competition policy. How would natural monopolies operate in the private sector? Would sector regulation provide surrogate competition for them? Would competitive conditions eventually be encouraged and introduced? Would non-natural monopolies, created as a result of privatisation, be dealt with?

The interest in issues relating to competition has also been sparked off by recent developments in the global economy. These have included the recent spate of mega-mergers and the increased potential for cross-border anti-competitive practices (Evenett, 2002). In particular, concern has focused on the adequacy of developing country governments to deal with these, and to the role that global institutions can play in setting rules to ensure competitive markets flourish (Hoekman and Holmes, 1998; Evenett et al., 2001). While there are many bilateral and regional agreements on competition policy between countries, most multilateral principles for competition are currently voluntary.

The issue of competition has also received considerable attention in the aftermath of recent financial crises in various parts of the world. Among the causes that have been cited are those relating to over-investment resulting from a poor competitive environment, although the evidence supporting this explanation is weak (Glen et al., 1999). However, the increased emphasis on competition is linked to concerns in developing countries over weak systems of corporate governance, leading to greater enterprise inefficiency. Competition is often viewed as a substitute for corporate governance. This idea may be reinforced when it is considered how little is known about the way corporate governance works in developing countries outside the state-owned enterprise sector (Shleifer and Vishny, 1997).

In a broader sense the dramatic changes ushered in after the collapse of communism have contributed to the heightened interest in competition. The initial reaction in previously centrally planned economies was to leave the process of restructuring to unfettered markets; this was seen as a logical response to the rigidities of the former command system (Commander et al., 1999). The reality was that transitional economies developed weakly operating competitive markets and regulatory frameworks, although experience has varied, and some countries such as Poland and Hungary appear to have achieved better results as far as competitive pressures are concerned (Carlin and Landesmann, 1997).

The interest in domestic conditions for competition and attention to antitrust-type competition policy in developing countries has particularly resulted from the failures of economic reforms in the 1980s, that overly relied on trade liberalisation to promote domestic market competition. World Bank structural adjustments loans did not stipulate conditions for domestic competition policy (Gray and Davis, 1993). One general conclusion was that trade liberalisation did not do the whole job – it did not guarantee by itself a desirable level of competition in an economy, and correspondingly did not achieve all it was expected to in terms of increasing productive efficiency and competitiveness in international markets (Tybout, 1992). This raised questions over whether this was the right way to stimulate competition in developing countries. The idea that trade liberalisation would improve domestic competition has led to a reassessment that indicates that success in trade, and trade liberalisation, is itself dependent on establishing a competitive domestic market environment. This, in turn, is dependent on a view of competition policy that not only incorporates notions about the potential abuses of economic power by enterprises, but considers the broader aspects affecting the competitive infrastructure such as communications, financial and fiscal systems and regulatory constraints. The pessimism may have been reaffirmed by the experience of developed economies, which had become more open, and had long histories of competition policy, yet enterprises in these economies continued to engage in anti-competitive practices.

The new interest in competition in developing countries has, in turn, exposed how little is known of the effectiveness of competition policies and about the ways in which competitive processes work in developing countries. Up until 2000, there had been no systematic attempts to examine the ways in which competition policy influences competition in either developed or developing countries (Carlin and Seabright, 2001). Recent work by Dutz and Vagliasindi (2000), collecting information on competition law, implementation and its impact on competition in 20 transitional economies, concludes that effective competition policy implementation results in more intense competition.

The purpose of this chapter is not to provide a comprehensive review of all aspects of competition policy, but to select and examine a few critical areas that need to be considered when developing and evaluating competition policy in developing countries. A useful framework for considering competition policy is provided by Carlin and Seabright (2001). They suggest that competition can be viewed in terms of rivalry in relation to the acquisition of assets and rivalry in their use. Different approaches to competition policy can then be characterised according to the relative emphasis that each places on the incentives for the acquisition of assets versus incentives for their use. In particular, the Chicago School of antitrust economics emphasises the former, by considering policies that remove the constraints to the efficient acquisition of assets, while much of the traditional neoclassical approach to competition policy has been on ensuring that owners and managers of productive assets use them in the most efficient ways (Stigler, 1971; Peltzman, 1976; Bork, 1979; Singleton, 1986, 1997; Godek, 1998).

The rest of the chapter draws on theory to consider issues relating to factors that inhibit competition and to discuss their implications for policy. The aim of the remaining part of the chapter is to relate these to the development of competition policy in developing countries and draw conclusions.

THEORY OF COMPETITION POLICY

Competition analysis developed in the nineteenth century and the literature on it has grown ever since, with particular spurts in the 1930s, with the development of the theory of imperfect competition (Robinson, 1933; Chamberlin, 1933; von Stackelberg, 1934) and in the 1950s with the application of game theory (Nash, 1951). Useful reviews are contained in McNulty (1968), Vickers (1995), Neumann (2001) and Metcalfe and Uyarra (2002). Nevertheless, the theoretical literature concentrating on competition policy is still in the early stages of development compared with regulation theory (Rey, 2001). Much of the effort has focused on an analysis of the interaction of enterprises, involving collusion and mergers, with less attention paid to policy design and implementation. Furthermore, the theoretical literature comes almost exclusively from Europe and the US, and the models derived assume an institutional context developed in those countries. When issues relevant to developing countries are raised, there is often no attempt to adapt the theoretical framework to the particular conditions of developing countries comparable to attempts by those involved in the macroeconomics of development (Taylor, 1983; Agenor and Montiel, 1996). A useful start has been made by Rey (1997) in examining some of the implications of the theoretical literature on competition for developing countries.

This section examines three aspects of competition that affect the potential acquisition of assets and the use of existing productive assets. These relate to entry and exit conditions in markets, the potential for collusion between enterprises, and market concentration through merger activity.

Entry and Exit Conditions

Significant barriers to entry may exist in the form of government-induced barriers, structural barriers and entry-deterrent strategies of incumbent enterprises. Government-induced entry barriers include trade restrictions, regulations, price controls and procedures for the allocation of inputs. These arrangements have formed the basis for arguments that government-induced restrictions have opened the scope for rent-seeking activities by interest groups, particularly through attempts to seek preferential treatment (Frischtak, 1989). Structural barriers include legal and geographical barriers and the need for high sunk costs. Sometimes the high cost of the latter can be offset through fiscal mechanisms (Baumol et al., 1982). Strategic entry deterrence occurs through predatory pricing, product differentiation and advertising (Dixit, 1982).

Entry of efficient new enterprises increases competition and can stimulate innovation, and provide incentives for existing enterprises to improve their productivity. It can also cause poor performers to leave the market and release resources for others (Geroski, 1995). Entry of new enterprises can also serve as a vehicle for the introduction and diffusion of innovation which embodies new products or processes that in turn create new supply and demand conditions in markets (Geroski, 1991)

Contestable markets theory also indicates that under certain conditions the threat effect of potential new entry, as opposed to actual entry, can influence existing enterprises to change their behaviour (Baumol, 1982). The argument for the contestability of a market is based on potential entrants having access to the same technology as existing enterprises and there being no sunk costs, along with free entry and exit in markets.

The search for appropriate policies towards market entry and exit has been the subject of both theoretical and empirical research. Much of theory has examined the cost conditions in which different enterprises are likely either to be induced into an industry and gain from greater competition or to be deterred from entry as a result of increased competition (Tirole, 1988; Siefield and Evans, 1994; Aghion and Schankerman, 2000; Lipczynski and Wilson, 2001). Policies to improve the competitive environment have been directed to removing government-induced barriers through liberalisation and to promote the potential for productivity-enhancing entry. The latter has concerned policies that contribute to lowering overall costs of production by improving the broader infrastructure in which enterprises operate, and though privatisation, associated with enterprise break-ups, which reduce sunk cost requirements. Tackling strategic entry deterrence has proved more difficult.

Collusion

The literature on collusion has several strands. Considerable attention has been given to issues relating to formal cartels, which considers their optimal size, the potential gains from being inside and outside them, and their weaknesses (Stigler, 1966). These largely concern agreements to fix prices, with orthodox models typically predicting that outsiders will benefit from the formation of cartels (D'Aspremont et al., 1983). Also, cartel members gain when all members of the industry are included (Selten, 1973). Stigler (1964) examined the factors that facilitate effective collusion, and the central proposition states that successful collusion occurs when there exists an efficient method of policing the agreement. Cheats benefit unless they are detected and once detected they will cease to violate the terms of the agreement in fear that loyal members in the agreement will retaliate, even though the offender faces no obvious penalties. Williamson (1975) likened collusion to a problem of contracting – enterprises would devise their own means to enforce and punish deviant behaviour.

Of greater interest to competition agencies is the literature on the factors that determine implicit collusion, rather than explicit collusion found in cartels, referred to as tacit collusion. The problem facing competition agencies is how to detect collusion and what enforcement approach to use when it is discovered. Detection and proof of collusion involve significant information problems. Enterprises know whether they can collude or not, while competition agencies do not. Competition agencies can generally observe prices but not costs, and they can undertake investigations at a cost. Models incorporating asymmetric information can be found in reviews by Tirole (1992) and Laffont and Martimort (2000).

In practice, competition agencies can reduce the information problem by designing leniency programmes to allow favourable treatment if an enterprise informs: this is known as a 'revelation mechanism'. If a revelation can produce hard rather than soft information, then a competition agency can in principle encourage an enterprise to report collusion, rewarding the informant, and using the information against the remaining enterprises. Otherwise an investigation may take place and lead to financial penalties for all if evidence of collusion is found, although the probability of discovering such evidence may be quite low given the practical difficulties of detection.

The effectiveness of such revelation mechanisms appears to depend on the extent to which the industry can again collude once a revelation has been made. According to Rey (2001) if enterprises cannot collude at this stage, then the threat of financial penalties will work to deter collusion. If they can collude at this stage, revelation approaches will not work since non-selected enterprises would have an incentive to bribe the selected one and induce it not to report collusion. In this case financial constraints on competition agencies may prohibit the possibility of further iterative examinations.

The effectiveness of investigations may also be linked to the provision of leniency programmes and the seriousness of prosecutions of those found to collude. Motta and Polo (2000) model enforcement as a function of the resources available to a competition agency and point out that the offer of leniency can improve the performance of an investigation as long as there is a high commitment to prosecute the remaining offenders. This is needed to convince enterprises that it is in their interest to report.

Another strand of the literature on tacit collusion examines the role played by capacity constraints facing enterprises. Conventional analysis suggests that enterprises can maintain collusive prices if they believe that setting prices lower than their rivals would lead them into a price war which, given similar cost functions, would adversely affect their future profits. In this case a potential benefit from a deviation from a collusive agreement would be offset by longer run losses associated with a price war. Capacity constraints could affect these propositions in two principal ways. First, the existence of capacity constraints may reduce the incentive to deviate from an agreement, and second, they may affect the severity of a price war, in both cases then reinforcing the effect on collusion. These conclusions, however, are largely based on previous studies that have assumed that all enterprises have the same capacity.

The policy conclusions that result from this type of analysis are as follows. Any merger activity facilitates collusion because it reduces the number of competitors, making it easier to win support for a collusive agreement among fewer enterprises. Therefore, a policy of break-up or divestiture to other competitors will make collusion more difficult to sustain. This analysis and its policy implications may be all right if capacity constraints are not serious considerations. This policy position is also strongly reinforced by the application of conventional tests for concentration, derived from static analysis, because these typically associate symmetry in market shares with greater competition. The much referred to Herfindahl index to measure concentration predicts that, for a given number of enterprises, a more symmetric configuration of market shares is more likely to be competitive and the risk of collusion correspondingly lowered; that is, the index is at a minimum for a symmetric configuration.

Compte et al. (2000), following on from previous analyses by Mason et al. (1992) and Lambson (1994), examine the implications for collusion when asymmetric rather than symmetric capacity constraints are assumed. They also associate market shares that most facilitate collusion with those that are proportional to capacities (Rey, 1997). They show that a merger can make asymmetries in capacity worse when it involves the largest enterprise, and therefore can hurt the potential for tacit collusion. This is because the key issue for maintaining tacit collusion is to prevent the large enterprise from deviating. But a merger that increases asymmetry will result in smaller enterprises losing their ability to retaliate because capacity has been transferred to the larger enterprise. This, in turn, may increase the large enterprise's potential to gain from deviating from an agreement if it initially had a capacity constraint. If this is the case, then forcing the larger enterprise to divest part of its capacity to other competitors in order to reduce the dispersion in market shares may actually end up facilitating collusion rather than reducing it.

The analysis of concentration based on embodying asymmetric capacity constraints may therefore be more pro-competitive than a static analysis that assumes symmetry. The creation of greater concentration with asymmetric capacity constraints may hurt rather than increase the potential for collusion, while remedies that seek symmetry between competitors, while avoiding dominant positions, may facilitate tacit collusion.

Mergers and Acquisitions

Lipczynski and Wilson (2001) identify three main types of mergers. Horizontal mergers occur when enterprises producing similar products come together. Vertical mergers occur when enterprises combine their resources at different stages of production and hence involve enterprises that are both supplier and producer or producer and retailer. Conglomerate mergers occur when enterprises that are producing different goods and services combine their resources.

A horizontal merger means that the assets of rival enterprises come under the control of a single enterprise: this implies that their strategic behaviour can be coordinated. In the absence of cost savings resulting from the merger, conventional theory presumes that the merger, by reducing the intensity of competition, will be anti-competitive, by generating higher prices and lowering consumer welfare. This is more significant if entry barriers exist, since it is argued that existing firms will be under less pressure to reduce prices in response to new rivals. The merged enterprise will also have less incentive to increase output or capacity when a rival reduces output. Conventional analysis, as stated earlier, also indicates that mergers can be pro-competitive if a merger leads to more equal-sized enterprises, since these are likely to behave more competitively than unequal-sized enterprises (Gans, 2000).

In the analysis of mergers there then is a requirement to balance the potential gains in efficiency due to the merger against the potential welfare losses resulting from the increase in market power. Merger control, therefore, requires an assessment about future conduct, and is in contrast to the approach to price-fixing agreements between enterprises, which is essentially an ex post exercise. There is little consensus on how to handle the trade-off between the efficiency gains and welfare losses from mergers. The efficiency gains resulting from mergers are argued largely on the basis of economies of scale and scope and the sharing of know-how; the costs are modelled in terms of the market power effects of mergers on output and prices.

Rey (2001) points to two directions in which the theoretical literature has attempted to help develop merger policy. First, through models that have specifically attempted to model the trade-off between efficiency gains and economic power. Farrell and Shapiro (1990) show that in certain conditions mergers raise prices. They devise a simple test, based on market shares, to show the likely external impact of mergers on consumer surplus and outsider profits, and conclude that in limiting conditions a small reduction in output has a net positive effect on consumers and owners. If a merger is to be proposed when outsiders are highly concentrated, it is likely that the merger is motivated by a desire to reduce costs rather than by an attempt by the merging enterprises to increase their market power. This analysis has been criticised for overly relying on specific assumptions, for its practical application to merger policy and for requiring a significant amount of information on supply and demand conditions (Rey, 2001). Development along these lines would require incorporating the information problem into models.

The second approach consists of developing more practical guidelines for assessing the impact of a merger on market power. Dansby and Willig (1979) show that the average mark-up in an industry is related to measures of concentration, using the Herfindahl index, based on the sum of squares of enterprises' market shares. The Herfindahl index is, therefore, used as a screening device by some competition agencies.

Importantly, the application of quantitative criteria that are essentially derived from static models, has led to the accusation that attitudes towards merger control may become too rigid and ignore potential efficiency gains that would be derived from a more dynamic analysis and one that takes into account such factors as the risk of collusive or predatory behaviour.

COMPETITION POLICY AND DEVELOPING COUNTRIES

So far three critical areas that have significance for the application of competition policy have been examined; namely, market power relating to entry and exit conditions, collusion, and mergers. Each of these will be specifically examined in the context of problems confronting competition agencies in developing countries, pointing to gaps in knowledge and ways forward to improve the effectiveness of competition policy.

Entry and Exit

Dominant enterprises in developing countries may arise directly from government industrial policy in these countries, and from private rent-seeking behaviour (Khemani and Dutz, 1995). Undoubtedly, government-erected barriers, often embodied in industrial policy, continue to significantly affect entry conditions in developing countries. This was earlier recognised by the World Bank in its *World Development Report* in 1991, and has been reiterated more recently (World Bank, 2001). The 2001 *Report* states that in developing countries:

> the main institutional barriers to domestic competition are government regulations on exit and entry of firms. Even in the tradeable sector, international competition may not lend to domestic competition, partly because of institutional barriers to competition, such as government regulations in product and factor markets that deter firm entry, exit, and growth. Excessive and costly government regulations also facilitate corruption and lead to adverse distributional consequences by inducing workers and firms to escape into the informal sector. (World Bank, 2001, p. 135)

The extent to which these barriers have been reduced with respect to trade restrictions, regulatory entry and exit constraints and price controls remains unclear, and in some cases attempts to deregulate and introduce liberalisation measures may have resulted in new regulations replacing old ones, and achieving the same effect. Clearly, it is widely recognised that the implementation of reform programmes has been uneven (McGillivray and Morrissey, 1999). Explanations for the failure to reform have also varied. Governments in many developing countries have had very limited institutional capacities to implement reform (Addison, 2002). Political factors relating to the lack of commitment to reform and unrealistic expectations of donor agencies about how easy it is to introduce reforms have contributed to their slow implementation. Significant obstacles to reforming conditions for entry by enterprises into markets continue to be mounted by particular interest groups in the public sector, resisting competition for public enterprises, and by powerful private sector lobbies wishing to protect their markets (World Bank, 1995; Shirley and Walsh, 2000).

Governments in developing countries continue to have regulations that prevent enterprises from closing. Inadequate bankruptcy rules and policies to keep ailing public enterprises going for social and political purposes continue to be used. The current orthodoxy views these practices as wasteful, arguing that they are tying up resources that could potentially be used more productively elsewhere to stimulate employment and income growth, and that suitable social safety nets can better be provided through fiscal transfers and retraining and relocation schemes for displaced workers. While such arguments are attractive, they are dependent on well-functioning fiscal systems and institutions that can deliver appropriate training. These may also be inadequately supplied as evidenced in the cases of Ghana, Malawi and Bangladesh (Katalunya and Quartey, 2000; Khan, 2002).

Knowledge of the size distribution of enterprises in developing countries and what is happening over time to entry and exit patterns is at best patchy and clear conclusions are difficult to derive. Studies undertaken at various times for a limited number of countries are summarised in Tybout (1998). Studies cited have mainly used periodic industrial census data of varying quality, supplemented by information on micro enterprises, where it has been available. In summary, these studies suggest that small and micro enterprises are more predominant compared to the pattern exhibited in industrialised countries and medium-sized enterprises are relatively fewer. Various studies of rates of turnover appear to suggest that larger enterprises are challenged by newly formed enterprises more often than was earlier believed to be the case (Roberts and Tybout, 1996). And, contrary to earlier predictions, market shares are less secure among larger enterprises in developing countries as compared with those in OECD countries. There are, however, many unanswered questions concerning whether enterprises entering a market have lower productivity than those already in it, and whether inefficient enterprises are being replaced by more efficient ones. Even these studies have limited country coverage and reveal that most movement in and out of a market occurs among smaller-sized enterprises, leaving us to conclude as Tybout (1998) observes, that small producers never seriously challenge the larger entrenched incumbents.

Explanations for these patterns of size distribution and entry and exit are equally varied. First, at the broad level poor infrastructure, underdeveloped financial markets and overly complex administrative arrangements may provide formidable obstacles, not just to the entry prospects of new enterprises, but to the growth prospects for smaller existing enterprises. Second, Carlin and Seabright (2001) have argued that policies designed to favour small enterprises may have inadvertently contributed to the failure of small enterprises to grow into larger ones in developing countries, because these favourable measures have been abruptly removed once enterprises reach a certain size. The threshold for this is set fairly low in most developing countries. Recent survey results from Ghana and Malawi support the view that few small enterprises graduate to be large ones (Cook et al., 2002). Third, small enterprises surviving to graduate into medium-sized enterprises then tend to face a new set of regulations which may constrain their growth. Larger enterprises are more able to absorb the higher fixed costs associated with dealing with more extensive sets of regulations (Tybout, 1998).

Arguments such as these have led some policy analysts to argue that the primary focus for competition policy in developing countries ought to be a long run, entry-based one (Singleton, 1997). Whether or not this entails a concern for the competitive process or for the survival of small enterprises, as in the German model, is questionable, given the difficulties facing smaller enterprises not only for market entry but for growth, compared with larger enterprises. An entry-based approach to competition policy may, however, provide an opportunity to look more carefully at ruling out entry deterrence by dominant enterprises per se without a more critical examination of potential benefits that may be derived from intense rivalry between fewer competitors.

Collusion

Concentration levels are higher in developing countries than in industrialised countries. A few large enterprises dominate many sectors and account for the vast majority of output. In sectors where economies of scale are important, competition and market dominance may be spread across one or two large enterprises. Obstacles to entry and higher levels of concentration make it easier for enterprises to collude. An assessment of the potential for collusion ought then to form an integral part of competition policy in developing countries, whether it is merger that is being considered or the growth and expansion of existing enterprises.

High levels of concentration do not necessarily reduce competitive pressures; this all depends on how the intensity of competition is measured. What number of enterprises suffices to ensure enough competition is taking place is a controversial issue. Relatively few enterprises may exert enough competitive pressure when products are reasonably close substitutes. But if geographical and informational barriers exist, then competition may be quite low. In developing countries the poor condition of local infrastructure may call into question whether or not national markets exist, and fewer enterprises may supply local markets in collusion. This collusion may also extend to local officials who may gain from erecting and maintaining regulatory barriers that limit competition.

The risk of collusion may also vary between developing countries and developed ones. While the lack of a traditional focus on issues of collusion may be prevalent in developing countries, there may be important economic factors that are also relevant for considering the scope for collusion. First, the pattern of market shares in various sectors of developing countries may exhibit a more asymmetric pattern than in developed countries. Current research certainly indicates that market shares may be less stable in developing economies than in developed ones. According to Bernheim and Whinston (1990) enterprises with asymmetric market shares will find it more difficult to collude. Second, capacity constraints are quite significant in developing countries. Both are likely to be reinforced by the existence of foreign enterprises. Institutional barriers and weak capital markets increase the cost of investment and make it more difficult for enterprises to expand (Rey, 1997). When enterprises face similar capacity constraints they may be less inclined to defect from a collusive agreement, but when asymmetric capacity constraints are encountered the effect may be in the other direction. Smaller enterprises may then be unable to prevent the largest enterprise from exiting a collusive arrangement. A competition policy pursued by many developing countries that is based on a structural rather than a behavioural approach to concentration and dominance (i.e. using the Herfindahl index to measure concentration) may, therefore, actually increase the probability of collusive behaviour by creating an environment where market shares are more equal (i.e. symmetric). In this environment the incentives to deviate from a collusive agreement are reduced.

Third, what may be important in considering the risk of collusion in developing economies is not the concentration on market shares but the ability of competition agencies to detect and take action against collusive practices. The transactions costs of collusion may be significantly lower in developing countries. Laffont (1998) points out that this may be due to an implicit risk aversion by economic agents and to the perception that monitoring technologies used by competition agencies are fundamentally weak. Correcting this perception may be a key imperative.

The ability to deal with collusion in developing countries is complex. First, many developing countries do not have a history of combating collusion. Competition laws forbidding collusion have only just begun to be introduced. Second, the means to detect collusion may be fairly limited. The lack of civil society institutions, such as consumer lobbies and the absence of a relatively open media and an auditing tradition, may seriously undermine the disclosure of collusive practices. Third, Laffont (1998) has argued that the attempt to police collusion in developing countries may end up by replacing collusion between enterprises with a more complex process, involving collusion with the regulators. Fourth, the lack of financial resources available to competition agencies weakens their ability to investigate cases of collusion. This may reflect financial constraint, underestimation of the resources required for a serious competition policy, or lack of commitment. The introduction of leniency programmes may compensate for the lack of information and, although a potentially useful policy to pursue, they are conditional on sufficient financial resources to compensate informers and undertake investigations if required, and the ability and commitment to enforce penalties.

Mergers

Developing countries have witnessed an increase in merger activity in recent years. In domestic terms this may itself be a response to the removal of measures to protect enterprises from competition (Carlin and Seabright, 2001). When protection is removed, it may lead to inefficient enterprises exiting the market. Alternatively, it may encourage some form of rationalisation of an industry, principally through mergers. Mergers, acquisitions, joint ventures and international alliances have also been on the rise internationally. There have been large mergers in the telecommunications field, but also involved are other major infrastructure sectors, such as power, water and transport. A key feature of these mergers is the desire by the various participants to retain some ownership control. It has also permitted enterprises that were previously focused on a domestic market to expand and gain access to a partner market. Frequently, these have included a local partner in a developing country. Significantly, in the case of Latin America, mergers involve foreign investment and are critically linked to privatisation, particularly in the infrastructure and finance sectors (Amann et al., 2002). The increase in this type of activity is facilitated by the acceptance that the private sector should play a much more important role in the infrastructure sector than in the past, and a recognition that this may be the most efficient route to acquiring the latest technologies. Foreign investment may also view local partnerships as a means to acquire local knowledge about markets and regulation.

Whatever type of merger activity is going on, the competition agency's foremost problem is an information one. Enterprises have privileged information about their motivations for merger, in terms of efficiency gains, market power and the potential for collusion, which the competition agency wants. Getting this information is obviously difficult. The merging enterprises want to get their merger approved, while the competition agency wishes to ensure that the merger takes place without increasing the risk of abusive behaviour. With exceptions, the tradition of obtaining information about the prospects for a proposed merger from rivals and consumers is absent, not least because of the lack of an institutional presence with which consumers are able to exert their voice, other than in an ex-post sense through their purchasing decisions. The information constraint is also compounded by the relative lack of expertise in relation to competition policy and limited resources to improve the situation. In some countries qualified staffing levels are extremely low in competition agencies and budgets are generally small in relation to other regulatory functions.

The Farrell and Shapiro (1990) approach to merger analysis, despite its limitations, offered a way for competition agencies to trade off the anti-competitive and cost-reducing effects of a merger. Their tests are based on pre-merger market shares and demand elasticity that indicates whether or not a privately profitable merger is socially beneficial. As indicated, the tests require specific information on market conditions. Given the difficulty with the types of information required to assess merger cases and the implicit assumptions of such an approach, the use of 'undertakings' may prove a more promising avenue to take. They act as a signalling device and a kind of guarantee that the information is accurate (Fels et al., 2000). If a competition agency is concerned that a merger will result in a reduction in output, an undertaking by the merged enterprise not to reduce its output after the merger reveals information about its intentions. If in the post-merger situation, costs are reduced and output is increased then nothing is binding. A judgement is still required by the competition agency over what undertaking is to be established and to what extent a merging enterprise is willing to offer an undertaking rather than forgoing a merger. Effective undertakings may, therefore, help competition agencies evaluate mergers without having detailed knowledge of industry structure and the magnitude of potential cost reductions. Breaching an undertaking still requires a penalty, and the ability to enforce a penalty in part depends on how well the undertaking is specified. An undertaking may easily be manipulated by the merged enterprise if it is poorly specified and, therefore, becomes ineffective. There may be a concern that future entrants could be deterred from coming into an industry when there is an undertaking. A potential competitor may face an aggressive competitor as the merged enterprise will be forced to, for example, maintain output after the entry of the new enterprise. This may make entry less profitable. Where new entry leads to a substantial increase in output of other enterprises, then the undertaking on the merged enterprise could be lifted as the threat of reduced competition from the merger may have subsided. The use of undertakings, however, may be viewed as an entry point for regulatory capture if they are poorly specified and lack enforcement.

CONCLUSION

The discussion has focused on the rivalry for the acquisition of assets in terms of entry and exit constraints and on the rivalry in the use of assets by considering the factors that facilitate collusion. Recent developments in theory and in our knowledge of how competitive processes work in developing economies are beginning to provide guidance for the development of competition policy. The forms that effective policies take may differ from those employed in developed economies, although recent advances in theory may also be questioning these forms. The significance of how the wider competitive environment beyond antitrust considerations might critically affect these rivalries has also been recognised. Empirically, the scope for further research in developing economies is very wide.

Precisely how high barriers to entry are, and the forms that they take, in developing countries have not been systematically researched. Also, it has been argued that the scope for collusion may be higher in developing countries than in industrialised ones. How low might be the transaction costs of collusion in developing countries is another area that is relatively untouched by empirical or even theoretical research. Knowledge of the importance of asymmetric information and asymmetric capacity constraints and the ways in which they affect collusion is also empirically unexplained but explorable.

Given the newness of competition laws and the establishment of competition agencies in most developing countries, it can only be expected that research into their effectiveness is so far so limited. Attempts are beginning to be made to investigate more systematically what this competition policy terrain looks like in terms of laws, institutions and policies. Hopefully this will provide some insights into policy and practice. The next stage in examining the effectiveness of competition policy is to ask does it make a difference? This requires an assessment of the outcomes of policy decisions and the reasons why they were made – a much more complex step and one that has not been done that extensively even in industrialised countries. Such investigation will throw light on whether or not existing policies contribute to promoting or stifling the competitive process and hopefully will lead to the design of more effective competition policy.

REFERENCES

Addison, T. (2002), 'Structural adjustment', in C. Kirkpatrick, R. Clarke and C. Polidano (eds) *Handbook on Development Policy and Management*, Cheltenham: Edward Elgar.

Agenor, P. and Montiel, P. (1996), *Development Macroeconomics*, Princeton, NJ: Princeton University Press.

Aghion, P. and Schankerman, M. (2000), '*A* model of market-enhancing infrastructure', mimeo, University College London.

Amann, E., De Paula, G. and Ferraz, J. (2002), 'UK corporate acquisition in Latin America in the 1990s: lost opportunities in a new economic environment', CRC Working Paper, University of Manchester, August.

Baumol, W. (1982), 'Contestable markets: an uprising in the theory of industry structure', *American Economic Review*, **72**, 1–15.

Baumol, W., Panzer, J. and Willig, R. (1982), *Contestable Markets and the Theory of Industry Structure*, New York: Harcourt, Brace, Jovanovich.

Bernheim, B. and Whinston, M. (1990), 'Multimarket contact and collusive behaviour', *Rand Journal of Economics*, **21**, 1–26.

Bork, R. (1979), 'Antitrust and the theory of concentrated markets', *Industrial Concentration and the Market System*, American Bar Association Press, Washington, DC, 81–9.

Carlin, W. and Landesmann, M. (1997), 'From theory into practice? Restructuring and dynamism in transition economies', *Oxford Review of Economic Policy*, **13** (2), 77–105.

Carlin, W. and Seabright, P. (2001), 'The importance of competition in developing countries for productivity and innovation', background paper for *World Development Report*.

Chamberlin, E. (1933), *The Theory of Monopolistic Competition*, Cambridge, MA: Harvard University Press.

Commander, S., Dutz, M. and Stern, N. (1999), 'Restructuring in transition economies: ownership, competition and regulation', paper for annual World Bank Conference on Development Economics, Washington, DC, 28–30 April.

Compte, O., Jenny, F. and Rey, P. (2000), 'Capacity constraints, mergers and collusion', mimeo, Institut d'Economie Industrielle, Universite des Sciences Sociales, Toulouse, France.

Cook, P. and Kirkpatrick, C. (1995), *Privatisation Policy and Performance: International Perspectives*, Hemel Hempstead: Prentice Hall.

Cook, P., Katalunya, D., Nixson, F. and Quartey, P. (2002), 'Small enterprise development in developing countries', mimeo, University of Manchester.

D'Aspremont, C., Jacquemin, A., Gabszewicz, J. and Weymark, J. (1983), 'On the stability of collusive price leadership', *Canadian Journal of Economics*, **16**, 17–25.

Dansby, E. and Willig, R. (1979), 'Industry performance gradient indexes', *American Economic Review*, **69**, 249–60.

Dixit, A. (1982), 'Recent developments in oligopoly theory', *American Economic Review, Papers and Proceedings*, **72**, 12–17.

Dutz, M. and Vagliasindi, M. (2000), 'Competition policy implementation in transition economies: an empirical assessment', EBRD WP no. 47, London: European Bank for Reconstruction and Development.

Evenett, S. (2002) 'How much have merger review laws reduced cross border mergers and acquisitions', mimeo, World Trade Institute, Bern, February.

Evenett, S., Levenstein, M. and Suslow, V. (2001), 'International cartel enforcement: lessons from the 1990s', *The World Economy*, **24** (9), 1221–45.

Farrell, J. and Shapiro, C. (1990), 'Horizontal mergers: an equilibrium analysis', *American Economic Review*, **80** (1), 107–26.

Fels, T., Gans, J. and King P. (2000), 'The role of undertakings in regulatory decision-making', *The Australian Economic Review*, **33** (1), 3–16.

Frischtak, C. (1989), 'Competition as a tool of LDC industrial policy', *Finance and Development*, Washington, DC, International Monetary Fund, September.

Gans, J. (2000), 'The competitive balance argument for mergers', *The Australian Economic Review*, **33** (1), 83–93.

Geroski, P. (1991), *Market Dynamics and Entry*, Oxford: Blackwell.

Geroski, P. (1995), 'What do we know about entry?', *International Journal of Industrial Organisations*, **13**, 421–40.

Glen, J., Singh, A. and Matthias, R. (1999), 'How intensive is competition in the emerging market? An analysis of corporate rates of return from nine emerging markets', IMF Working Paper no. 32, Washington, DC, International Monetary Fund.

Godek, P. (1998), 'A Chicago-School approach to antitrust for developing economics', *Antitrust Bulletin* **43** (1), 261–74.

Gray, C. and Davis, A. (1993), 'Competition policy in developing countries pursuing structural adjustment', *The Antitrust Bulletin*, Summer, 425–67.

Hoekman, B. and Holmes, P. (1998), 'Competition policy, developing countries and the WTO', *The World Economy*, **21**, 875–93.

Katalunya, D. and Quartey, P. (2000), 'The policy environment for promoting small and medium sized enterprises in Ghana and Malawi', *Finance and Development*, May.

Khan, S. (2002), 'Financing small enterprise development in Bangladesh', PhD thesis, University of Manchester.

Khemani, S. and Dutz, M. (1995), 'The instruments of competition policy and their relevance for economic development', in C. Frischtak (ed.) *Regulatory Policies and Reform: A Comparative Perspective*, Washington, DC: World Bank, pp. 16–37.

Laffont, J. (1998), 'Competition, information and development', paper for the annual World Bank Conference on Development Economics, Washington, DC, The World Bank, 20–21 April.

Laffont, J. and Martimort, D. (2000), 'Mechanism design with collusion and correlation', *Econometrica*, **48**, 309–42.
Lambson, V. (1994), 'Some results on optimal penal codes in asymmetric Bertrand Supergames', *Journal of Economic Theory*, **62**, 444–68.
Lipczynski, J. and Wilson, J. (2001), *Industrial Organisation: An Analysis of Competitive Markets*, Hemel Hempstead: Prentice Hall.
McGillivray, M. and Morrissey, O. (1999), *Evaluating Economic Liberalisation*, Basingstoke: Macmillan.
McNulty, P. (1968), 'Economic theory and the meaning of competition', *Quarterly Journal of Economics*, **82** (4), 639–56.
Mason, C., Phillips, O. and Nowell, C. (1992), 'Duopoly behaviour in asymmetric markets: an experimental evaluation', *Review of Economics and Statistics*, **60**, 662–70.
Metcalfe, J. and Uyarra, E. (2002), 'Economic development and the competitive process', paper presented at the Centre on Regulation and Competition Workshop, September.
Motta, M. and Polo, M. (2000), 'Leniency programmes and cartel prosecution', mimeo.
Nash, J. (1951), 'Non-cooperative games', *Annals of Mathematics*, **54**, 286–95.
Neumann, M. (2001), *Competition Policy: History, Theory and Practice*, Cheltenham: Edward Elgar.
Peltzman, S. (1976), 'Towards a more general theory of regulation', *Journal of Law and Economics*, **19**, 211–40.
Rey, P. (1997), 'Competition policy and economic development', mimeo, Institut d'Economie Industrielle, Universite des Sciences Sociales, Toulouse, France.
Rey, P. (2001), 'Towards a theory of competition policy', mimeo, Institut d'Economie Industrielle, Universite des Sciences Sociales, Toulouse, France.
Roberts, M. and Tybout, J. (1996), *Industrial Evolution in Developing Countries: Micro Patterns of Turnover, Productivity and Market Structure*, New York: Oxford University Press.
Robinson, J. (1933), *The Economics of Imperfect Competition*, London: Macmillan.
Selten, R. (1973), 'A simple model of imperfect competition where four are few and six are many', *International Journal of Game Theory*, **2**, 141–201.
Shirley, M. and Walsh, P. (2000), 'Public versus private ownership: the current state of the debate', Mimeo, Washington, DC, World Bank.
Shleifer, A. and Vishny, R. (1997), 'A survey of corporate governance', *Journal of Finance*, **52** (2). 737–83.
Shleifer, A. and Vishny, R. (1998), '*The Grabbing Hand: Government Pathologies and their Cures*', Cambridge, MA: Harvard University Press.
Siefield, J. and Evans, L. (1994), 'Empirical studies of entry and exit: a survey of the evidence', *Review of Industrial Organisation*, **9**, 121–55.
Singleton, R. (1986), *Industrial Organisation and Antitrust: A Survey of Alternative Perspectives*, Columbus, OH: Publishing Horizons.
Singleton, R. (1997), 'Competition policy for developing countries: a long run, entry-based approach', *Contemporary Economic Policy* **15** (2), 1–10.
Stigler, G. (1964), 'A theory of oligopoly', *Journal of Political Economy*, **72**, 44–61.
Stigler, G. (1966), *The Theory of Price*, New York: Macmillan.
Stigler, G. (1971), 'Theory of economic regulation', *Bell Journal of Economics*, **2**, 3–21.
Taylor, L. (1983), *Structuralist Macroeconomics*, New York: Basic Books.

Tirole, J. (1988), *Theory of Industrial Organisation*, Cambridge: Cambridge University Press.

Tirole, J. (1992), 'Collusion and the theory of organisations' in J. Laffont (ed.) *Advances in Economic Theory*, vol. 2, Cambridge: Cambridge University Press, pp. 151–206.

Tybout, J. (1992), 'Linking trade and productivity: new research directions', *World Bank Economic Review*, **6** (2), 189–211.

Tybout, J. (1998), 'Manufactuing firms in developing countries: how well do they do and why?', Policy Research Working Paper 1965, Washington, DC, World Bank.

Vickers, J. (1995), 'Concepts of competition', *Oxford Economic Papers*, **47**, 1–23.

von Stackelberg, H. (1934), *Marketform und Gleichgewicht*, Wien and Berlin: Julius Springer.

Williamson, D. (1975), *Markets and Hierarchies: Analysis and Antitrust Implications*, Basingstoke: Macmillan.

World Bank (1991), *World Development Report*, Washington, DC: World Bank.

World Bank (1995), *Bureaucrats in Business: The Economics and Politics of Reform*, Washington, DC: World Bank, Oxford University Press.

World Bank (2001), *World Development Report*, Washington, DC: World Bank.

3. Competition, innovation and economic development: the instituted connection

J.S. Metcalfe, R. Ramlogan and E. Uyarra

INTRODUCTION

The concepts of competition and its correlates, competitiveness and competitive advantage, feature as highly in the current development agendas and policy debates of developing countries as they do in those of the developed world. As organising concepts aimed at informing policy, they are indispensable yet they are sufficiently opaque to make any discussion of their relation to economic development a matter that is negotiated with some difficulty. Economists write about competition, business scholars about competitive advantage, and the term 'competitiveness' is used by both camps but each uses these notions in very different ways. The common ground between these different approaches appears to be barren yet each perspective is indispensable for reaching an understanding that cuts to the heart of the problem of development; namely, the conditions for the growth and application of practical knowledge to better meet human needs.

How competition works in the context of a specific developing economy, for they are all different, naturally informs the policy issue of the regulation of competition and the deeper issue of the relation between competition and the elimination of poverty. Ultimately this link is made because competition is a social device for discovering better ways of meeting human needs and thus for improving the efficiency and effectiveness with which resources are defined and applied to economic activity. Competition is a device, therefore, for the augmentation of knowledge and capability. If an economy is to develop, it must be transformed from within, and to achieve this requires that its people be transformed – that they come to know things in relation to production, organisation and consumption that they currently do not know (Metcalfe, 2001). These are challenging issues and this chapter has no other purpose than to indicate how difficult it may be to answer the question of the relation between competition, development and the growth of knowledge.

Many problems of interpretation and misunderstanding arise precisely because competitive advantage is not a property of any individual firm, rather it reflects the interaction between firms in the market process. The identification of competitive advantage always involves comparison between firms or groups of firms and this comparison is contingent on the nature of the market environments in which the firms are operating, whether local or global. Thus while the contributions of business scholars often lack the wider systemic context, the contributions of economists are frequently lacking in any serious understanding of the competitive strategies and attributes of firms. Moreover, the endogeneity, the spontaneity of change that is competition is not an idea that fits easily into theories premised on the notion of equilibrium for which comparative statics and comparative dynamics are the normal tools of the trade.

In this chapter, we will review some recent thinking on the connection between competition and development, and, in the process, reflect wider concerns about innovation, income distribution, competition and development policy. Because there are contrasting views and approaches to competition, it is better to start with a clean sheet, as it were, and build up as coherent a position as we can in stages. This is our immediate purpose.

The position we take here is that the problem of competition and the problem of economic development are isomorphic by virtue of being examples of the phenomenon of economic evolution. Evolution is a theory of how the world changes, or rather how it changes in such an uneven fashion. The shifting balance of agricultural and manufacturing employment, the rise of modern manufacturing and the decline of handicraft industries, the changing distribution of economic activity between the town and countryside are well-documented examples of how development necessarily takes place in all economies. All economies are from our perspective developing, albeit in ways that are qualitatively different. Many of the great contributions to development theory recognise this important fact and place structural change and the discovery and use of new ways of deploying resources at the centre of what we mean by development (Bruton, 1985). Arthur Lewis is a prime example, with his emphasis on the redeployment of labour from unproductive and traditional backward sectors to more productive uses in the modern sector (Lewis, 1954). All economies are restless in the sense of the continual emergence of new, potential economic opportunities, the realisation of which requires structural change in the importance of different activities in the economy. Impediments to structural change are impediments to development, and among the more important of these are impediments to competition. Thus the fundamental development issues relate to the generation of new economic opportunities and the rate at which they can be realised, through investment in capacity and human capability and through the growth of markets. This is why a process of competition is so central to the process of development.

The restless capitalism theme will be an ever-present subtext in the following and we should add that by the adjective 'restless' we imply two properties.

Restless capitalism is uncomfortable capitalism; the opportunities for change always pose threats of change and how these inconsistencies are resolved can create major social and political issues. Past investments in material and human capital so frequently can be undermined by the process of differential development, and with these losses are carried the disappointment of hopes and expectations falsified. From this aspect, bygones are never bygones, rather they are the experiences around which alternative futures are imagined. However, there is a more positive side to restless capitalism – that of the ongoing search for economic improvement for better ways of adapting resources to meet human needs. At the core of this idea is the significance of the development of practical knowledge. This is Schumpeter's approach to development and competition with its emphasis on innovation, profits and the entrepreneur as the agent of improvement, together with the idea that it is the uneven development of knowledge that matters to processes of creative destruction. As he expressed the point (Schumpeter, 1928),

> what we unscientifically call economic progress means essentially putting productive resources to uses *hitherto untried in practice,* and withdrawing them from the uses they have served so far. (p. 378, emphasis in original)

The correspondence between evolution, competition and development is exact. Each is a theory of the growth of specified entities and populations of entities and since the focus is on differences in growth rates the natural implication is that development and competition entail structural change. The essential aspect of evolutionary theory is that it explains differential growth in terms of three related phenomena: economic variety and non-uniform behaviour, selection and sorting processes defined at various levels of an economic system, and processes to regenerate and replenish the economic variety on which the dynamics of evolution depend. In relation to the first, we emphasise the importance of differences between firms in their actual and intended competitive behaviour. In relation to the second, we see the importance of the competitive process and its link to structural change; and in relation to the third, we find the importance of innovation in the broad and indeed all those activities that enhance economic competence and create potentials for improvement within societies (Andersen, 1994; Nelson and Winter, 1984, 2002; Metcalfe, 1998; Dosi et al., 1988; Mazzacato, 2000).

What we mean by the development problem is, of course, the differential development over time of different economies and sub-economies. Forging ahead, catching up and falling behind are metaphors for differential growth (Abramovitz, 1986; Mytelka, 1999). When countries form a development strategy, they do so to catch up on their more advanced comparators and the vehicle for achieving this is a faster rate of growth of per capita income than the advanced countries. In turn, this requires faster growth of their productive activities and this is a reflection of a wider competitive process: activities that are more productive have to grow in importance relative to less productive alternatives. For traded goods, the relevant industries have to increase their share of world markets and establish a competitive advantage over foreign rivals. Competition is the development process in a microcosm. Thus competition and development are each processes premised on differential growth and, what is to be explained, is the origin of and constraints upon diversity in rates of growth. Differential growth defines development within industries and between industries and it maps onto competition within markets, between markets and for markets, although at each level the nature and dynamic of competition is different.

As a first step to unravelling different ideas about competition, we present next a brief history of the development of competing concepts of competition.

COMPETING CONCEPTS OF COMPETITION

It will be useful to begin with a review of some competing, well-established concepts of competition: for the meaning attached to this word is not easy to resolve, despite it being widely recognised as one of the core concepts of economic theory (Metcalfe, 1998; Dosi et al., 1988). Perhaps inevitably it has attracted multiple meanings and shades of emphasis, and it is surely odd that while competition is widely accepted as a legitimate economic concept, competitiveness is contested and surrounded in controversy (Stigler, 1965). Needless to add, the nature of a theory of competition will depend on the explanatory purpose in view. A theory that is designed to illuminate the allocation of given resources and methods to given ends, will be thoroughly different in character from one that is designed to explore the nature of economic development and the creation of resources and opportunities over time. If the first is perceived as the limiting outcome of the dynamic process implied by the second, the two could be seen as natural complements. Unfortunately, in this regard there are good grounds to be cautious; the limit of a competitive process is not normally the dispersal of economic influence but the very opposite, its concentration. Thus the continuation of competitive conditions comes to depend very much on matters of dispersed innovation and entry, a theme we explore at a later stage.

The required concept of competition should help with understanding why the economic world changes in the way it does and identify the sources of change, the processes of change, the consequences of change and the mutual interdependence between source, process and consequence. Moreover, the aim of competition policy should be to further development. It is inevitable that innovation, as a primary source of change, will loom large in this story but it is as well to recognise that innovations are not simply to be equated with changes of technology in a narrow sense.

Some History of the Idea of Competition

As far as the coordinating or order-imposing aspect of competition is concerned, the classical theory coalesced around two central propositions. First, that competition would tend to bring actual market prices into equality with natural prices. Second, those natural prices are also competitive prices: they correspond to a situation in which the allocation of investible funds across activities has established a uniform rate of profits on the capital invested (due allowance being made for risk), while the allocation of labour across activities has imposed a uniform wage for skill and effort of each given type (Kurz and Salvadori, 1995). The dynamics of competition consequently involve two steps. Competition *within* a sector drives market prices into equality with costs of production and competition *between* sectors establishes a pattern of costs consistent with a uniform rate of profits on the capital invested and uniform wages for work of the same kind. The resulting prices are called natural prices and are said to form centres of gravity to the price system in the presence of disturbances. The very meaning of natural prices implies the operation of competition – the two concepts are inseparable. The ultimate refinement of the classical method came with Marshall's attempt to deal with the time dimension of the competitive process in terms of temporal stages; so reducing a spectrum of market responses to a series of discrete categories – market period, short period, long period and secular period – each one reflecting the different velocities of economic adjustment. There can be little doubt that Marshall favoured a process view of competition and that he was always careful to emphasise that the data are never constant, so creating particular difficulties for any concept of an equilibrium, normal position. Indeed, it is worth noting that Marshall was reluctant to use the word 'competition', he much preferred the looser term 'freedom of industry and enterprise'.

Consider next the neoclassical perspective. The dominant themes of this alternative approach, ultimately connected with the work of Jevons, Edgeworth and Cournot, are competition expressed in terms of trading activity and competition as a state of equilibrium, as the limit to the process of rivalry. The equation of competition with trade and exchange was the natural outcome of the search for criteria to judge the efficacy of market institutions in coordinating the allocation of resources. The consequent emphases on the nature of market institutions, the distribution of information about rival offers and demands, and the matter of who, if anyone, sets prices, moved to the centre of the theoretical stage, and indeed moved economic theory away from questions of longer run development toward questions of the immediate allocation of given resources. This change in perspective on competition is tied in closely with the marginal revolution. Jevons (1871), for example, linked together his concepts of the market and competition in two requirements, that all traders have perfect knowledge of the conditions of supply and demand, and that there be complete freedom for anyone to trade with anyone else.

Important elements in our understanding followed, not least that the notion of a perfect market is quite distinct from the notion of perfect competition. As to who sets prices, and setting Walras's fictional auctioneer aside, there emerged a wealth of possibilities ranging from market makers, merchant-traders who release and absorb stocks and quote prices on organised anonymous exchanges, to individual firms who quote prices and sell to customer order on a personalised bilateral basis. In the latter case from whom one buys may be as significant as what one buys. Usefully, these categories of price setting were reduced by Hicks (1965) to a distinction between those market behaviours and institutions that promoted price flexibility and those that promoted price rigidity. Roughly speaking, a distinction between markets in which centralised, specialised merchant traders set prices and markets where individual firms set prices (Okun, 1981; Lachmann, 1986). There can be no question that this emphasis on the importance of the institutions of the market and the arrangements for diffusing information is of the first importance and an essential part of any study of the development of competition in an industry. However, this is not the aspect of the neoclassical revolution that has received most attention: much more pervasive has been the emphasis on competitive equilibrium as a state of rest relative to given data.

The crowning achievement of this strand of thinking is the theory of perfect competition, the central organising theme of the last century of economic theory and the theme against which all variants are judged. This brings together three independent ideas: that of a perfect market; that of atomistic behaviour; and that of freedom of entry and exit in the market. In the first and last respects it mirrors classical thinking. The crucial innovation is that of atomistic behaviour, the explicit hypothesis that no one trading in the market has a sufficient volume of sales or purchases to influence the market price (Knight, 1946). It is the foundation of the theory of general equilibrium and its offshoots in international trade theory, public finance and welfare economics, and it is the basis for judging the (in)efficiency of any market situations which depart from its axioms. Through the postulate of freedom of entry and exit, it encompasses the classical concern with resource mobility and the equalisation of suitably defined rates of return on investment. Through the conditions equating behaviour at the margin with market prices it gives a coherent set of standards for evaluating, at least in principle, whether given economic arrangements are efficient or otherwise, and it gives to market prices a deeper meaning as indexes of relative scarcity.

A wide range of economists have expressed their dissatisfaction with the neoclassical view. Thus Morgenstern (1972) claims that competition as a word employed by economists has lost touch with reality simply because it has replaced struggle and rivalry with equilibrium. Clark (1961) in his major contribution to this literature began by claiming that the shift from equilibrium to process was the most challenging question in the theory of competition. He suggested four broad elements necessary for effective competition, namely: competent customers able to appraise accurately the competing products on offer; freedom of individuals and organizations to engage in any trade or activity (remember Marshall!); access to all the necessary means of production; and, a climate of independence of attitude and strategy among firms in the industry. Given these elements, the actual conditions of competition would depend on the organisation of the market, together with the competitive behaviour of the rivals, and foremost among the competitive behaviours will be changes in the nature of what is supplied. In short, the elements of a theory of competition should not be chosen to characterise equilibria but to explain economic change. Particularly interesting in his appraisal of competition theory is Georgescu-Roegen (1967) who points to the fact that, as normally portrayed, competition is absent within the industry and only takes place between industries, 'the condition commonly labelled as a "perfectly competitive industry" actually involves no competition at all' (p. 32).

Thus we have a major paradox: competition only becomes active when we allow a monopoly element premised on the fact that firms are different, and scope for competition lies not in the number of firms but in the conditions creating diverse behaviour. Brenner (1987) is also a notable contributor to this literature, with the emphasis being placed on bets on new ideas and the insistence that 'Businessmen pursue strategies to discover a combination of customers and services with respect to which they have an advantage over those who they perceive as their competitors' (p. 49).

Among all the economists who have been critical of the equilibrium approach, none has been more devastating from a developmental perspective than Hayek (1948, 1978), with his view that an equilibrium concept of competition is a contradiction in terms. In a much-quoted passage, he suggests that

> if the state of affairs assumed by the theory of perfect competition ever existed, it would not only deprive of their scope all the activities which the verb 'to compete' describes but would make them virtually impossible. (p. 92)

Instead competition is a succession of events, a dynamic process, a voyage of exploration into the unknown in which successively superior products and production methods are introduced, and consumers discover who meets their particular needs and how. Neither producers nor consumers know in advance the outcome of the competitive process, for that is established only by trial and error; the market process is necessarily an experimental process. Again, we begin to see a link between the process view and the emphasis on differential behaviours of rival agents, and we should note Hayek's insistence that differentiation of this kind undermines any claim that agents can have complete knowledge of all the factors relevant to market behaviour. Knight too favoured an exploratory perspective on the economic process in which not only the capabilities of firms but also the preferences of individuals become the endogenous outcome of a trial and error economic process.

In many ways, this viewpoint has been most felicitously expressed by Fisher and colleagues in their compelling account of an ill-starred antitrust case against IBM:

> When new opportunities continually arise, one will see under competition a continuing process of change which carries with it continued opportunities for profit and growth. One cannot hope to understand the competitive nature of such a process by examining it in terms of static competitive equilibrium. (1983, p. 39)

The implications of such a position for the meaning and conduct of competition policy are, of course, profound. Here lies another clue to the contrast between different notions of competition: a competitive process creates patterns of change, something that Schumpeter understood well. Let us begin with the later Schumpeter, of *Capitalism, Socialism and Democracy*, for there he outlines the obvious fact that economic progress has continued unabated despite the absence of perfect competition as an organising principle in industry. Nonetheless, progress is linked closely with competition, which is 'intrinsic to the mechanism of capitalism which is by nature a form or method of economic change and not only never is but never can be stationary' (1944, p. 82).

The driving force in competition is not the adjustment of price but economic variation through innovation, the theory of which had occupied Schumpeter in two previous major works, *Business Cycles* (1939) and *The Theory of Economic Development* (1934). It is through innovation that firms command a decisive cost or quality advantage affecting not their marginal profits but their very existence. It is a matter of comparative indifference whether atomistic price competition in the ordinary sense operates more or less promptly. Capitalism is not to be judged in terms of its immediate efficiency in allocating given resources across given opportunities but in terms of its ability over time to create resources and opportunities and adapt to the potentials so created. Hence, the central idea of change driven from within, brilliantly captured in his phrase 'creative destruction'. Creative destruction, it should be emphasised, is not an optional extra to the capitalist process but is the capitalist process: equilibrium capitalism is for Schumpeter a contradiction in terms.

Let us take stock and summarise the specific charges brought against the equilibrium view of competition. We take them *seriatim*. Because the degree of competition is identified with the number of competitors, and not the behaviour of competitors, it ends up condemning attempts to create a competitive advantage as attempts to gain monopoly power. This was the complaint of Morgenstern and Hayek but it has been well put by Joan Robinson (1954) in the following terms: 'In the broad sense in which businessmen understand it, [competition] largely consists in destroying competition in the narrow economist's sense' (pp. 245–6).

Competitive behaviour is in part motivated by the search for monopoly positions. It is from this that an ambiguity in the interpretation of any firm's alleged monopoly profits follows naturally. Are these profits a consequence of the abuse of monopoly power or are they the consequence of superior productive behaviour? Of course, the number of competitors becomes a very imprecise concept as soon as we identify potential entrants currently outside the industry but willing to enter if prospects improve. It has been suggested that the threat of potential entry can be as strong a discipline as actual entry, a claim that is explored in depth in the literature on the contestability of markets (Baumol, 1982; Shepherd, 1984). Moreover, the identification of competition with the number of competitors, *simpliciter*, implies that those competitors are identical; otherwise they cannot be presented solely as a single number. This has several unfortunate consequences: it rules out behavioural heterogeneity, it equates competition with the opposite of monopoly (McNulty, 1967), and it ignores two other important implications of a greater number of competitors, as a barrier to collusion and in their role as multiple independent sources of variety in innovative behaviour. This is a point made by Clark (1961, p. 197) but it is perhaps most fully expressed in a famous passage in Marshall (1920):

> Every locality has incidents of its own which affect in various ways the methods of arrangement of every class of business that is carried on in it: and even in the same place and the same trade no two persons pursuing the same aims will adopt exactly the same routes. The tendency to variation is a chief cause of progress: and the abler are the undertakers in any trade the greater will this tendency be. (8th edn, p. 355)

Thus an industry is not competitive simply by virtue of the number of firms it contains but because increasing numbers implies increasing scope for differential behaviour (Loasby, 1982). The intensity of innovative competition is independent of the existing condition of the market, it depends on actions not structures and 'works even if the innovator is a monopolist' (Demsetz, 1995, p. 138). Consequently, there are as many dimensions of competitive intensity as there are possible competitive behaviours. As has long been recognised, output competition, the standard case, is only one of many possibilities.

Perhaps the most obvious and well-documented indicator of the lifeless nature of the equilibrium concept is its inability to encompass entrepreneurial behaviour. By definition, the rewards to entrepreneurship are transient and relate to the operation of markets in conditions of disequilibrium. Such rewards cannot be included in any definition of equilibrium, they are, in Schumpeter's words 'at the same time the child and the victim of development' (Schumpeter, 1934). Like Schumpeter, Baumol (1993) has emphasised the non-routine behaviour involved in entrepreneurship, encompassing such traits as imagination, boldness, ingenuity, leadership, persistence and determination in pursuit of wealth, power and position. These are not obviously amenable to Cartesian analysis. In equilibrium this group of attributes cannot be rewarded, all that can be rewarded is the routine behaviours that define the good stewardship of existing resources. We note in passing that entrepreneurial behaviour is necessarily differential behaviour, a theme to which we will return. Notice also that the transient incomes associated with innovation-related profits may provide the resources for further innovations and so create the possibility of a self-exciting economic system, which is permanently in transition.

Competition as Contests

In popular usage, the word 'competition' is reserved almost entirely for the concept of a contest, a race or game or sport, involving competitors playing according to agreed rules of the game. One of the first economists to elaborate on this connection was Frank Knight in his essay 'The Ethics of Competition' written in 1923. Here Knight makes the point that participation in business is stimulated not simply by the desire to satisfy wants but by the search for achievement and the satisfaction derived from participation, that is to say, by the desire for action. Here is a framework for interpreting competition that focuses on actions and behaviours and fits naturally with the evolutionary perspective. Any contest has a number of important characteristics. Chief among these is a clear set of accepted and enforceable rules of the game, the institutions of competition, including property rights and the rule of law, which determine the nature of the contest, the principles, by which contestants are rewarded, and the principles on which they can enter, or be eliminated from the contest. The rules of the game, an accepted code of conduct, serve to coordinate the behaviours of the rivals, define permissible behaviours and establish the set of prizes, and they are to be judged in terms of their neutrality or otherwise toward rival contestants; that is, by their fairness. The second element is the set of contestants and their particular attributes of skill, dexterity and effort. However, should these contestants be uniquely ranked in all circumstances we would hardly term the situation a contest, for its results would be perfectly predictable. Hence the contestants must show 'hidden' variation in their competitive attributes. From this follows the final element in any contest, the inherent unpredictability of outcomes. In part this may arise from uncertainty about the environment of the contest, since not all contingencies can be written into the rules, and in perhaps greater part from a lack of predictability about the behaviour of the contestants. Neither an outside observer nor the contestants can observe or anticipate the plans and strategies of the various rivals or predict the multiplicity of contingent circumstances that affect performance at a particular play. Luck is an essential part of all contests. The fall of the favourite, the emergence of the dark horse, are intrinsic to our idea of competition, and as this degree of unpredictability declines so often does the desire to call it a contest. In this regard, contests are discovery procedures to find the best behaviour out of a set of rival behaviours. Of course, what is best is entirely contingent on the rules of the game and entirely relative to the set of contestants. As Alchian (1951) so aptly remarked: 'As in a race, the award goes to the relatively fastest, even if *all* the competitors loaf. Even in a world of stupid men there would still be profits' (p. 213, emphasis added).

Hayek too would have found this idea of a contest fully compatible with his own insistence that the results of the competitive process are not foreseeable. In short, true contests have rivals competing according to established rules. The rivals apply skill and effort to different degrees to win prizes but the outcomes are neither entirely predictable nor entirely random. For, if they were entirely random there would be no incentive to apply effort to the conduct of the contest.

The process perspective on competition has a natural connection with the modern theory of evolution, and we now intend to explore this connection in more depth. The theme will be that contests are selection processes and the contestants are to be distinguished by their differential behaviours. A number of questions naturally arise at this point. What are the rules of the economic game, and to what extent do they depend on the institutions of the market place, the factors that condition trading as we outlined previously? What constitutes a good set of rules? What shapes the behaviours of the contestants, how different can they be and what processes result in those differences? What are the uncertainties that make economic contests unpredictable and indeed open-ended in their possible outcomes? Where does organisational and behavioural innovation fit into the competitive scheme of things?

AN EVOLUTIONARY FRAMEWORK FOR THE COMPETITIVE PROCESS AND DEVELOPMENT

It is clear from the preceding account that competition encompasses two broad sets of conflicting ideas, competition as a structure and competition as a process. In the first, competition is a statement about the organisation of the industry, not a statement of the characteristics of the individual firms, indeed the latter may as well be treated as if they are identical. In the second, it is the differential behaviour of firms that determines how much rivalry exists. How these differences are resolved into patterns of structural change and development depends on the coordinating role of the relevant markets. It is this developmental perspective that we now explore in more detail. What are the elements required for an evolutionary model of competition? We may list them as follows.

- There is a population of rival competing units, normally described as for profit firms or more accurately business units, producing a particular product range with the associated methods of production. Each firm is characterised by a set of operating procedures and strategic aims, a business plan that determines what is produced, and how the production and other processes, such as marketing, are organised.
- There is a set of markets, in which those business units jointly sell output and acquire inputs and which generate mappings from the bundle of competitive characteristics to a pattern of competitive advantage for the rival producers. This set of markets is not to be treated as invariant over time but to evolve as entrepreneurs succeed in creating new markets. Clearly the emergence of new markets implies innovation on the part of consumers as they adapt their preferences to the new exigencies.
- There is a set of rules of the game in relation to the requirements for entering a specific population together with the conditions for elimination from that population. There is also a set of rules of the game for the growth and decline of individual business units.
- Competitive advantages are a mapping from the competing characteristics of the set of rival firms into measures of firm performance over some time interval. These are measures of differential success and failure, and they fall into three broad categories: in relation to the profitability of a particular line of business; in relation to the ability to invest and grow that business; and in relation to the ability to innovate and transform that business.

The crucial step in this argument is that competitive performance follows from competitive advantage but unlike the competitive, firm characteristics, performance is not a property of any firm. Competitive performance is an emergent property of a competitive process and it arises from the interaction between rival firms in a market context, a struggle for custom, as any businessperson would understand. It makes no sense to talk of the competitive advantages of a firm outside of a particular competitive process and independently from a specification of the rival producers. A firm may be competitive relative to some rivals, uncompetitive relative to others. It is the differences in competitive characteristics across firms that matter, together with the manner in which the market environment evaluates those differences, that determines the distribution of competitive advantages at a point in time. Naturally, if the market rules change then so will the distribution of competitive advantages. There is a further important implication of this evolutionary view: the intensity of competition is measured by the changes that take place in the market in the relative positions of the rival producers over some time interval. A market in which shares are frozen is neutrally competitive, the actions of the rival firms cancelling out any competitive advantages. More normally, relative shares are changing and the rate at which structure changes provides a measure of the intensity of competition.

While the emphasis is rightly on the differences between firms, it is equally true that the evolutionary view also emphasises the role of markets in the competitive process. Firms set prices, as a general rule, but their freedom so to do is greatly constrained by the market environment. The more perfect the markets in which they buy and sell, the less the scope for firms to set prices, wages and cost of borrowing that reflect any superiority in their individual competitive characteristics. The better connected are the market participants, the more they share common information about rival offers to buy and sell and the less variability there will be in the prices and wages set by the rival firms. Thus the information structure and its support in market organisation matters greatly for the competitive process. Moreover, since market organization absorbs resources it is a legitimate question to ask who supplies those resources and what return they obtain for doing so.

In a world of uniform firms, there would be no basis for speaking of competitive advantage. Above normal profits could only be equated with the absence of competition or with transient economic states. As soon as we allow firms to be heterogeneous in their competitive characteristics, profits arise that are unrelated to market power and are premised entirely on the differential ability of the firms to attract custom and produce efficiently. Profits are the reward associated with superior competitive characteristics. Profits generated by different competitive characteristics have the attribute of quasi rents, and we normally expect quasi rents to be transient. This takes us to a second dimension of competitive advantage, which connects differential profitability with differential investment, and thus the differential growth in the productive capacities of the rival firms. Differences in profitability are the basis for enhancing or losing a market position and the simplest way to capture, short run fluctuations apart, is through the *changes* in market shares of the different competitors. Changes in market share reflect differences in rates of growth of capacity over the longer term and these changes are derived via the market environment from the causal and different competitive characteristics of the firms. On this view, a firm that is gaining market share over some interval *ipso facto* has a competitive advantage over any firm that is losing market share. Competition is a transfer process in which some firms gain in relative importance and others decline, it is a process of structural change and development. Notice carefully that this process is contingent on the market environment *and* the characteristics of the population of rival firms (Downie, 1958; Metcalfe, 1998). Moreover, this market environment includes the capital market, the labour market and the market relations in relation to the supply of produced means of production (Teubal, 1997). The competitive characteristics of a given firm may give it advantages in some circumstances and disadvantages in others. Hence we can see why benchmarking becomes relevant, to identify and copy 'good' sets of competitive characteristics: we can also see why it is a troublesome guide to good practice if either the market environment or what is 'best practice' is changing.

Finally, consider the third dimension of competitive advantage, the ability of firms to reposition themselves over time through changes in their bundles of competitive characteristics; that is, through innovation broadly conceived. To the extent that this ability is linked to the sums available to invest in innovation, it reflects the first dimension of advantage; to the extent that it reflects the scale of operation of the firm, it reflects the second. Over the longer term, it seems that this is the crucial dimension of competitive advantage, the ability to generate and follow through sequences of innovations more ably than rivals. Unfortunately for the firm, this appears the most difficult to sustain of all the foundations of competitive advantage, however, it is fortunate for the market process that this is so. If innovation depended only on resources invested, a firm that moves ahead would stay ahead, and concentration of output in a single producer would be the consequence. It is because innovation is unpredictable, that it depends on imagination and creativity and on luck, as well as on planned investments in R&D, that leaders become followers and conversely. Consequently, keeping competition active depends on the satisfaction of two conditions: the maintenance of open markets in which outsiders and insiders can freely challenge established positions, and continued commitments to innovation as the basic form of competitive rivalry.

It is a non-trivial task for a firm to attain and sustain relative superiority across all three competitive dimensions. Many are profitable but are unable or unwilling to expand with the general market and they decline in economic significance over time. Some small firms often make the strategic choice to remain small firms, even when their products and processes of production are very profitable. Growth is not preordained. Moreover, a relatively inefficient firm can increase its market share relative to a more efficient rival if it has superior abilities in relation to the investment process. Yet again, some can grow but only at the cost of a decline in efficiency. Some can be very profitable but are unable to sustain innovation beyond an initial success, so that rivals that are more creative erode their position. From this follows the joint importance of competition policy and innovation policy in a pro-development strategy, a matter we return to later.

Since development is about finding new uses for resources, it is also a creative, competitive process in which qualitative and quantitative change are intertwined. Innovation redefines the basis for generating profits and this reshapes the evolution of the economy. Innovation and development are also about enterprise. Entrepreneurship, the introduction of new productive combinations, is the driving force that continually creates new competitive advantages and opportunities for profit and growth. Furthermore, enterprise depends on the institutions of the market broadly defined. Open markets make possible and generate incentives to venture innovation-based challenges to established positions, efficient markets evaluate those challenges in the way that most favour growth in economic efficiency and effectiveness at meeting human needs over time. This is the basis for the idea of creative destruction and for the negative as well as the positive aspects of restless capitalism. It will be clear too that this is also a description of the development process in general. At root it is a matter of the development of human agency and thus of the development of knowledge.

This epistemic dimension, the connection between productive knowledge, competitive advantage and development, the issue of how firms acquire and develop their competitive characteristics, is of considerable importance. We cannot do justice to this rich literature here other than to draw attention to its emphasis on the acquisition of skills and capabilities, or rather the differential acquisition of skills and capabilities (Lall, 2001a). Building on the work of Penrose (1959), this literature places the evolution of a set of competitive characteristics under the control of managers – characteristics that include the use of technology, the specification of the products produced and the particular form of organization, distribution and marketing, brought together in a specific theory of the business opportunity addressed by the particular firm. In all these dimensions, firms are different and the basis for these differences resides in the knowledge and skills of all the employees and the way these are organised into distinctive capabilities. While these capabilities evolve, they must be sufficiently durable to give a firm relatively stable advantages and disadvantages in the market place in the short run. Moreover, in understanding the development of the firm, it is not sufficient to focus only on its internally generated capabilities. It is also necessary to take account of the ability to cooperate with external agencies in the acquisition of skills and knowledge. Firms frequently cooperate to develop competitive characteristics, and the availability of a rich ecology of potential collaborators is an important part of the development and competition connection. This is where the concept of innovation systems fits. In many sectors of industry the relative importance of 'distributed innovation systems' is increasing *vis-à-vis* the stylised model of a sovereign innovating firm (Coombs and Metcalfe, 2000, 2002; Coombs et al., 2003). The central point to grasp here is that market and other instituted processes provide the context in which new knowledge is generated and applied. Market experience shapes the problem sequences that emerge to guide the growth of knowledge and the course of innovation so that competition and innovation feed on one another. Each innovation opens up the possibility of further innovations, from which it follows that the growth of knowledge is embedded in, endogenous to, the competitive process. It is through this dynamic of knowledge accumulation in instituted contexts, market and non-market, that economies are self-transforming and development occurs from within. Without markets to test innovation experiments, to generate experience based on trial and error, to stimulate conjectures about different possible worlds, a major element in the framework for development is necessarily missing. Without the non-market institutions to support the innovative efforts of firms, the scope for combining the multiple sources of knowledge required for innovation is similarly absent.

Finally, it should be clear by now that a theory of development framed only in macroeconomic terms must necessarily miss the point, which is that the development process is a matter of micro inspired, self-transformation from within. Economies can grow only insofar as they also develop and this has always been so. While the idea of semi-stationary or proportional growth may have been helpful in the early stages of growth theory, as for example, in the Von Neumann growth model, it cannot help in the context of understanding development since it rules out, *ex hypothesi*, the most important of all the stylised facts, structural change. Economies never develop in a uniform fashion, for the imbalances that arise in the course of development are a natural consequence of the competitive processes through which the gradual and uneven growth of knowledge finds economic application (Hirschman, 1958; Streeten, 1959). None of this prevents one constructing and measuring macro indices of the rate of growth or the average level of productivity. However, these are not natural measures related to actual agency: as macro phenomena, they are necessarily constructed statistics and have no existence beyond their reflection in the underlying structure of the ensemble. While we can measure in macroeconomic terms we cannot comprehend in those terms, and this is a central tenet of the evolutionary approach. Consequently, there is no point approaching the study of development other than in terms of the internal properties of a particular economic system.

COMPETITION AND INNOVATION POLICY: RECENT VIEWS FROM A DEVELOPING COUNTRY PERSPECTIVE

We have argued that economic orthodoxy fails to address adequately the relationship between competition and development, concluding that, because of this failure, modern macro theories of economic growth fail to deliver a sound theoretical understanding of the development process. Moreover, it seems that the empirical evidence offers little support for such theories and consequently little guidance for the efficacy of any particular policy prescription (Kenny and Williams, 2001). In this section, we reflect on some of the issues related to competition, innovation and policy for development. We set out first a framework for competition policy that derives from an evolutionary understanding of the economy and of competition as a process dependent on innovation.

An evolutionary take on the competitive process carries over into new, or rather refocused, perspectives on competition policy. From an orthodox perspective the central issue in competition policy is the relation between market power, conduct and performance. Firms with market shares above some threshold are deemed to possess market power (the Lerner-Cournot rule) and are presumed to exploit that power, to price output higher than they would otherwise do. Large market shares are associated with above normal profits and these become the twin tests applied by competition authorities in many countries. Of course, any competition assessment has to establish the actions that firms take to distort the market and lever prices in their favour, for it is only in relation to such actions that remedies can be formulated.

From an evolutionary perspective, matters are seen differently, not in terms of market power but in terms of market capabilities. There is no presumption that 'excess profits' are the result of undue market power. They are more plausibly the result of superior performance created by superior innovative ability. As such we expect them to be transient but this depends on the abilities of rivals to compete away the rents. Similarly, the accumulation of a 'high' market share can be interpreted as evidence of the cumulative effects of superior competitive ability. Now, insofar as development is a matter of putting resources to more productive uses, it requires the 'better' firms to out-compete their inferior rivals in any line of activity. Competing means exactly this. Hence, the conventional tests for competition look quite different from an evolutionary viewpoint, as witnessed in the sharp controversy over the Microsoft antitrust case in recent years (Leibowitz and Margolis, 2001). Monopoly is not bad, *prima facie*. There is a natural affinity here with the

Chicago perspective on competition policy, in which unless there are strong reasons to believe the contrary, it is taken that the market process will always encourage the innovative entry that destroys an incumbent position (Roberts and Tybout, 1996).

However, these remarks do not justify a Panglossian view of the market process. Firms have an interest in distorting markets in pursuit of competitive advantage and governments an interest in discouraging and penalising such behaviour. Markets, whether for outputs or inputs that can be segmented or which contain artificial barriers to competition, will have the effect of distorting the competitive process and of slowing down the rate of economic evolution. Firms have a natural interest in preventing their customers from switching to rivals, in tying them in, as well as in erecting barriers to entry by innovating rivals, both of which are sufficient reason for a strong competition policy. The issue here is not simply the behaviours of the firms but rather the adequacy of the instituted rules of the market process. Policy to ensue a level playing field should be the aim so that rents are ability rents not distortion-based rents. Here we wish to emphasise how much this is a matter of the rules of the game that transcend competition policy in a narrow sense. The ease with which new business ventures can be created without administrative and regulatory burden is clearly crucial if competition is to be robust. Similarly, the continued survival of unprofitable firms through public or private subsidy also distorts and slows the competitive process. Rules for economic non-viability are of crucial importance to the competitive process. Equally important, in appraising market efficiency it is important that rival firms are evaluated on a 'level playing field' and that markets are open to the challenge of innovators whether from within or without the current set of rivals. Markets are important both for their efficiency and for their openness. Indeed it is a central feature of the market process in enterprise capitalism that no position is free from potential challenge. Markets provide the incentives to mount these challenges to the status quo and they actively facilitate them by keeping open access to customers and suppliers of inputs. However, markets are not given naturally, they are socially constructed and they are not costless to establish and operate. One striking implication of this is that the effectiveness of competition depends not only on the effectiveness of markets for specific goods but equally on the markets for labour and capital or inputs more generally. If more efficient and effective firms face barriers to the recruitment of labour or artificially limited access to free capital, the force of the competitive process is blunted and distorted. The second of our three dimensions of firm performance, the growth dimension, depends almost entirely on undistorted access to factor markets by the more profitable firms. Similarly, the market for corporate control can play a key role in promoting competition through innovation. The ability to efficiently add to or dispose from a set of business units is an important way in which companies build strong competitive position. While mergers and acquisitions should always be treated with caution, particularly between large firms, it remains the case that this route to competitive advantage is of considerable importance.

By far the most significant implication of the evolutionary view is the interdependence between competition policy, innovation policy and market regulation more generally. Since competition is driven by differential competitive characteristics, it follows that innovation policy has a role to play in stimulating enterprise and competition. New products and processes become the route to challenging established positions and to enhancing resource productivity. A low innovation economy is in all probability a low competition economy. Consequently, the dynamic case against monopoly or the concentration of economic power comes to depend on how this concentration influences the rate and direction of innovation in the economy. The real cost of monopoly and collusion more generally is that they stifle innovative effort and the long run competitive process, by erecting barriers to the challenge of established position. This is not usually a matter that concerns competition authorities but it should. By extension, science and technology policy and enterprise policy are complementary to competition policy. The essential point to grasp is that there is a great difference between competition policy as a negative discipline on firms, punishing deviant behaviour, and competition policy as a set of positive incentives to compete through the creation of better business opportunities.

All of this suggests that competition policy, especially in the context where market institutions are underdeveloped, requires attention to much more than the narrow search for market power or excess profits. In its essentials, it must be a pro-innovation policy. We turn now to explore how these ideas interact with some of the recent contributions to the recent economic development literature.

COMPETITION AND INNOVATIONS: POLICY DEBATES IN DEVELOPING COUNTRIES

Concerns about globalisation, technical change and the pace of liberalisation have given rise to numerous competitiveness studies, rankings and policy initiatives by governments, consultants and research institutions across many developed and developing countries. Part of this discourse relates to and interacts with the competition policy debate, although, for developing countries, explicit concern with this issue is a relatively recent phenomenon. Up to the 1990s, for example, formal competition policy appeared on the policy agendas of only 16 developing countries but this number has increased substantially in subsequent years with the encouragement and technical assistance of international institutions. More recently the new International Financial Architecture being constructed in the wake of the Asian crisis has brought renewed international pressures on developing countries to institute or reform their own competition policies if not to participate in some form of multilateral arrangement to ensure 'fair play' and 'level playing fields' between countries (Singh, 2002).

The issue is not a simple choice between whether developing countries should have a competition policy or not, it is rather the purpose and structure of that policy. For competition to favour development, we have argued that market processes must not distort the scope for better products and production processes to absorb an increasing share of the available economic resources. However, the types of policies adopted by developed countries need not necessarily be appropriate for developing countries. Moreover, the type of policy that may be appropriate for one developing country may not be adequately suited to another. The attention to allocative efficiency and lower prices that underlies competition policy in developed countries is too narrow and static from a development perspective. In practice, it may inhibit development if it is construed too narrowly. In order to focus competition policy on development, competition cannot be strictly perceived in the quantitative sense of more firms being better than fewer firms. Development may require in some instances that competition be restricted while in others be vigorously promoted. Thus Singh and Dhumale (1999) and Singh (2002) call for the emphasis to be on dynamic rather than static efficiency and the formulation of an optimal degree of competition (rather than maximum competition):

> that would entail sufficient rivalry to reduce inefficiency in the use of corporate resources at the micro economic level, but not so much competition that it would deter the propensity to invest. (Singh and Dhumale, 1999, p. 12)

Challenging the meaning of competition carries over into challenging the notion of competitiveness, a theme explored by Lall (2001b). He takes issue with the theoretical foundation of competitiveness measures (in particular the World Economic Forum (WEF) indices used for benchmarking countries) (WEF, 2000) that have become significant in the policy discussion in many developing countries. He starts his analysis by examining the logic of Krugman's objection (Krugman, 1994) to the use of a broad concept of competitiveness in which the focus is on structural factors such as productivity, innovation, capabilities and skills. Although he agrees with Krugman, that in the context of a general equilibrium framework, this concept of competitiveness is misplaced, he does not agree that competitiveness should be dismissed entirely as a non-economic issue. This is particularly so because market failure gives rise to valid issues relating to national competitive ability

(Arndt, 1988). Developing countries, in which market failure is particularly diverse and widespread, may require coordinated strategies to move their economies from low-skilled, low technology activities to higher valued activities. Lall suggests that a structuralist (selective intervention) rather than a market friendly approach may be more appropriate for developing countries in overcoming the impediments (diffuse information, coordination failures, cost of mastering tacit technology, existence of widespread externalities and linkages, pervasive weaknesses in factor markets and institutions) that constrain growth and development. He is clear in his understanding that strategies or policies for correcting market failure should in no sense be seen as 'remedying deviations from a perfectly competitive equilibrium' (p. 1505) as the goal for developing countries is not to attain some ideal static equilibrium but to create the conditions that will take them towards a non-equilibrium growth path. The point is to facilitate the self-transformation to a more productive economy.

In relation to the evolutionary theme, Lall's critique of the WEF 'model' and the derived competitiveness index is particularly incisive. He rightly perceives competitiveness as a 'multifaceted and complex' phenomenon perhaps too much so to 'permit easy measurement' (p. 1520). The WEF model/index suffers in several respects. First, it represents an oversimplification of the process of structural change in developing countries. The underlying assumption appears to be that markets are efficient in all countries and that the primary requirement for success is a competitive setting with full exposure to international markets. Second, the broad definition of competitiveness fails to distinguish between competing and non-competing activities, a particularly difficult exercise in practice. While it is acknowledged that a significant proportion of GDP may be accounted for by competing activities in small countries, Lall is concerned that such an approach dilutes the analysis of structural and dynamic factors affecting competitiveness. Overall, it is not immediately transparent what is being compared across countries in the competitiveness index and this raises questions whether such measures should form the basis of policy analysis and action. Lall admits that there is a strong case for constructing indices but cautions that such exercises should be more limited in coverage, use a smaller number of variables, and adopt a more modest approach.

The multi-faceted nature of the connection in evolutionary theories of competition between competitive characteristics and competitive performance is one reason why managerial notions of competition do not fit well with their economic counterparts. In the context of the debate that links new management concepts, such as inter-firm networking with Japanese-style organisational principles and competitiveness, Meyer-Stamer (1995) urges caution based on the evidence from developing countries, arguing that 'things are more complicated than they may first appear' (p. 143), that different paths to competitiveness exist and that no best practice is evident (p. 147). Meyer-Stamer's analysis is organised around three points. First, the discussion of new management concepts tends to be concentrated mainly on the production process, largely neglecting other functions of the firm such as marketing, logistics, R&D, and sourcing of capital, labour and produced inputs. Yet competitive advantage involves much more than a mastery of technical principles, it requires knowledge of human organisation and, crucially, knowledge of what consumers will buy. From a strategy point of view therefore, imitating the experience of other countries in one competitive dimension may fail because competitive characteristics necessarily form an interrelated bundle. Second, there may be multiple patterns of organization, through which firms can be competitive. In the case of China, for example, companies tend to be based on traditional internal organisational structures (small size, centralised, paternalist and cost-efficiency driven) but they are linked through dense networks of relationships, which allow them sustained close contacts, continuity in supplier relationships, regular exchange of information and low transaction costs (p. 146). Third, firms can be competitive without being organised around collective networks. Korean firms are also organised along traditional principles but their competitiveness rests on two pillars: efficient patterns of organisation at the firm level, and selective support of individual firms by associations and public sector institutions (p. 147). In the Korean context the state effectively substituted for the inter-company network by setting the institutional framework (technology, training, quality control, export marketing and so on) that supported the development of firm competitiveness. Competitiveness, concludes Meyer-Stamer, is created at firm level but it is partly derived from a systemic context that emerges from complex patterns of market and non-market interactions between government, enterprises and other actors, and will therefore exhibit different forms in each society.

The innovation dimension of the competition–development debate is explored in Mytelka (1999). Here the concern is with understanding the relationship between windows of opportunity in different industrial sectors for the entry of latecoming countries and their national policy initiatives. Drawing on empirical evidence from four developing countries, China, India, Korea and Brazil in the machine tools, telecommunications, petrochemicals and biotechnology sectors, Mytelka argues that that there are wide differences in the nature and pace of innovation and in the conditions of global competition during the period considered (1970–90). The traditional indicators of competitiveness (based on cost and price competition) have not applied to all industries at all times as new rules of competition were constantly being set. Thus different causal factors drive competitiveness in different industries and these can change over time (p. 211). The implication following from this is that no simple or clear policy guidelines are appropriate. This calls for:

> a better understanding of both the changing role of competition within industrial sectors and the attitudes, habits and practices of firms in these sectors notably with respect to competition and innovation would thus appear to be the essential first steps in the policy design phase. (Mytelka, 1999, p. 205)

One of her key insights is that competition policies (e.g. market opening policies) can have perverse effects if other conditions are not in place (p. 22). A distinction is to be drawn between different firm innovation strategies: *catching up*, *keeping up* and *getting ahead* and how these different strategies relate to firm capabilities, resources and competitive conditions. The general conclusion, which resonates strongly with Meyer-Stamer, is that 'the historical habits and practices of firms need to be considered when designing policies to stimulate innovation and competitiveness' (p. 22).

COMPETITION AND INNOVATION POLICY FRAMEWORKS

No evolutionary account of the link between development and competition can be complete without acknowledging the particular role of innovation in economic transformation. In a globalising world environment, a country's development is closely linked to its ability to be creative and innovative on its own account or through its use of technologies and organisational practices created elsewhere. An understanding of the competitive process needs to take account of how technology is generated, how it is absorbed and adapted and how market failures affect such processes. There is a growing literature on the policy implications of the innovation process, much of it produced by scholars working under a broad Schumpeterian if not evolutionary banner. Our purpose is not to review all its ramifications here but rather to draw attention to a few instances where it overlaps with the theme of competition and interacts with development (Metcalfe, 1995, 2001; Edquist et al., 2002). The central conclusion of this literature is not only that innovation processes are central to development but that competition policy and innovation policy need to be thought of together and be conducted in a complementary fashion in regard to each other and in regard to wider policies in relation to education, training and the supply of risk capital (Bartzoukas and Teubal, 2002).

Technological behaviour as Katz (2001) observes, originates from a co-evolutionary process. It is the outcome of the co-evolution of the micro- (learning strategies of individual firms), the meso- (the competitive and technological regime) and the macroeconomic forces (organisation, regulatory systems, institutions and public policies). Thus the way innovation (variety generation) occurs in relation to technology and organisation is not independent of market processes or their interaction with other non-market processes. Competitive pressures in open markets are sufficient incentive to stimulate innovation in search of competitive advantage, but the capabilities to innovate depend greatly on prior market experience, on trial and error experimentation, and on the support of non-market institutions and organisations. From such a perspective, the firm can be characterised as an experimental agency embedded in an institutional context that facilitates the growth of the practical knowledge of business opportunities. Competitiveness in this sense is the outcome of a continuous process of innovation that enables firms to catch up to, keep up with or move ahead of their rivals in the market processes. As we have intimated in the earlier discussion, a system that facilitates an open competitive process permits new firms to acquire customers and resources at the expense of established firms. Such systems are extremely competitive but not in the sense of notions of perfect competition. It is not a competitive economic structure that matters but rather a competitive economic process, embedded in product and factor markets, in which there is a high rate of business experimentation.

The traditional basis for innovation policy lies in the market-induced divergence between private and social rates of return to investment in knowledge and innovation (Arrow, 1962; Stoneman, 1988). Thus the role of the policy maker was simply to stimulate innovative activity by cleverly realigning the divergent incentives through suitable fiscal and other incentives. These policies are directed at the correction of market failures. Such corrective incentive policies, while especially relevant for developing economies, pale into insignificance besides the chasm in practical knowledge that exists between (and within) developing and developed countries. The innovation challenge is not simply a question of catching up with developed countries in established areas of world production; rather it is about developing an internal capacity for the independent development of technological and business knowledge. It is about learning to learn and that is demanding both of time and resources. Not only is the internal knowledge base for mastering technology in developing countries weak, the supporting networks (other enterprises, institutions and so on) are also underdeveloped. Hence, it is not market failures that are the policy problem but failures in innovation systems. The issue of how to overcome these formidable institutional gaps has been addressed by a number of scholars. Lall and Teuball (1998), for example, articulate a dynamic learning perspective to research and development activity. They place considerable emphasis on collective learning, externalities, spillovers, and the non-market exchanges of skill and information, that originate in networks of activities, and argue that one of the main aims of technology policy should be to tap, promote and extend collective learning by focusing on those activities that are externality-rich. This involves widening the policy intervention framework beyond a focus on selectivity (targeting sectors or industries) and functionality (improving factor markets) to incorporate a horizontal dimension geared at promoting selected activities across sectors for which markets are missing or are particularly difficult to create. Technological development thus involves a mix of functional, vertical and horizontal policies that are context dependent, both in terms of country and in terms of the capabilities of policy makers. This framework for a 'market stimulating technology policy' does not express *a priori* preferences for any policy mix but allows for policy learning and thus provides for a 'richer and more realistic framework for understanding policies'. The imperative for 'new innovation' policies specific to the needs of developing countries is made more urgent by the changing trends in the external and internal environments of developing countries, rapid technological change and deregulation. These lead Bartzoukas and Teubal (2002) to argue the case for more sophisticated policy frameworks. They propose a conceptual framework based on evolutionary and systems perspectives that goes beyond market failure analysis, together with a 'policy portfolio' and policy process framework based on a range of different types of programmes (both general and targeted), rather than a uniform, general policy promoting R&D. Moreover, this 'set' of policies should be subject to ongoing critical scrutiny, as no policy is valid indefinitely and applies to all circumstances (Teubal, 1997). The increased complexity and openness of systems of innovation imply new roles for policy in the areas of learning processes and coordination problems, institutions including the institution of policy itself, new patterns of knowledge flows, the complexity of capital markets and the allocation of resources in a global economy.

An interventionist view of technology policy for developing countries also finds favour with Chang and Cheema (2002) and Ahrens (1999). The latter argues that contrary to the Washington consensus, government activism is important for technology policy in developing countries. Indeed the East Asian experience implies that a neutral policy regime is neither a necessary nor a sufficient condition for successful development. Ahrens advocates the market enhancing view (Aoki et al., 1997) in which government acts not as a substitute for private sector coordination but as an institutional facilitator that supports private coordination and improves information exchanges between the private sector and itself. Chang and Cheema argue that the pro-market view of technology policy which focuses on efficient utilisation of given technologies does not seriously address issues of technological development and innovation. Market imperfections provide the rationale for a policy to foster learning and innovation rents in developing countries. For these authors, an activist technology policy is required to promote technological learning and this is to be achieved by socialising the risk involved in learning, and internalising the inter-temporal externalities associated with innovations. The success of such a policy depends partly on the underlying policy design but also on the underlying institutional and political conditions. Thus a state-promoting view starts from the premise that effective use of technology requires not only its adaptation to local conditions but in addition, a significant amount of investment in 'organisational and institutional adaptation'. The crucial condition for the successful use of learning rents is that the state is able and committed to monitoring relative firm performance and imposing penalties in the event of non-performance. This requires state autonomy, a capable state bureaucracy, intermediate institutions to manage information flows between the bureaucracy and the corporate sector (such as Japan's deliberation councils and Korea's export promotion meetings) and state-controlled institutions, such as the management of state-owned enterprises and the control over the financial sector.

These kinds of policy prescriptions draw partly from new theoretical directions and from the experience of the newly industrialising countries of East Asia and Latin America. Linsu Kim's early analysis (Kim, 1993) of Korea's national system of innovation provides many insights into the factors behind that country's rapid economic progress and technological development. Strong government, the promotion of technological learning in the private sector through *chaebols*, complemented by rapid formal education programmes and government-funded research institutes lie at the heart of Korean success. While not particularly relevant in the pre-1970 period, technology policy came into its own during the 1980s with the international economic slowdown and shift towards more protectionist trade policies in Europe and North America. Responding to the reluctance of foreign countries to transfer technologies, the Korean government set about a series of liberalising reforms and a major shift in science and technology policy. This was encouraged by various mechanisms such as tax incentives and preferential financing to set up research laboratories. The government-funded research institutes have been the backbone of national research and development since the 1980s (Kim, 2000). They played an important role in helping firms to acquire prior knowledge about technology and prospective technology suppliers in the early years of industrialisation, and joint research with these institutes enabled firms to assimilate and adapt technology rapidly. The skills and activities involved in reverse engineering allowed Korean firms to attain the capabilities necessary to approach the world technological frontier in several new industries. Moreover, strategies for reaching technology frontiers have followed a number of routes including setting up outposts in Silicon Valley to acquire state-of-the-art technology, the development of ties with multinationals, promoting industry ties with local public R&D institutes and heavy investment in in-house R&D activities. More recently, Westphal (2002) argues convincingly that entry into global markets, and the competitive challenge that created, enabled the South East Asian economies to acquire an increasingly sophisticated range of technological capabilities in which they have moved from assimilation of foreign technology to autonomous innovative capacity. Market engagement is crucial to their success but so is the contribution of active government that used trade policy to support technology policy. The outward orientation of these economies, as they accelerated their development, should not be confused with free trade; it has been the complementarities between learning firms, the competitive process and active government that made the difference. The role of government was to discipline firms and set performance standards as a condition of access to privileged resources. Interaction was a collective process of learning and revision of objectives and tactics whereby the South East Asian governments followed adaptive policies in which they learned from mistakes. They provide a sharp contrast with the experience of Latin America or Africa. As Bruton (1998) indicates, neither import substitution nor outward orientation will succeed unless they are linked to learning, knowledge accumulation, entrepreneurship and strong competitive processes.

Technology policy that favoured the strengthening of endogenous capability also featured highly in Latin American import substitution industrialisation strategies (Meyer-Stamer, 1997). In the case of Brazil, for example, Dahlman and Frischtak (1993) outline the impact of technological factors and the role of its innovation system in the development process. Sectoral technological initiatives closely aligned to the military government's interests started in the 1950s with the establishment of the National Research Council and the Technology Institute for Aeronautics. Towards the 1960s, however, the focus shifted towards strengthening technological competence in support of import substitution industrialisation, with various programmes for funding technical training, machinery and equipment acquisition in addition to a planning system for science and technology with strong emphasis on institutional development. This framework held such great promise that at the start of the 1970s there appeared to be little doubt that Brazil would close the gap with the OECD countries in much the same way that South Korea and Taiwan did in the 1980s (Meyer-Stamer, 1997, p. 33). Dahlman and Frischtak (1993), contend that apart from the agrotechnology and aerospace sectors, the government industrial R&D programme has been ineffective due to weak linkages with the productive sector. Moreover, public sector R&D, which accounts for 70 to 90 per cent of total R&D expenditure, remained low in comparison with other newly industrialising countries at a time when East Asian economies were increasing their R&D expenditure at a rapid pace. They further argue that in contrast to the Korean case, the education system was one of the main obstacles to technological upgrading. It is characterised by low primary and secondary education enrolment and the limited effectiveness of higher education in upgrading technological capabilities because of the poor quality of university education and the postgraduate system, and the small proportion of students in science, mathematics and engineering. This view is reinforced by more recent research which also identifies the failures to intensify R&D activity in the private sector in the context of rapid trade and market liberalisation, and the withdrawal of the state from productive activity in the 1990s (Amann and Baer, 2002).

Katz (2001) also notes the disarticulation between R&D and the productive sector in Latin America more generally but cautions about underestimating the achievements during the period of import substitution development. Public sector efforts in developing the scientific and technological infrastructure, training and large-scale production facilities, far from telling a story of failure, tell a story of success in accumulating domestic technological capabilities. While economic growth in Latin America was by no means as impressive as it had been in the East Asian countries, it was characterised by an increasing degree of technological sophistication. The consequent learning dynamics resulted in a rapid expansion of labour productivity and of manufacturing exports in Argentina, Brazil and Mexico in the 1970s (Katz, 2000). However, it proved impossible to sustain this progress in the international macroeconomic environment of the 1980s and 1990s when there was a rise of relatively low-technology, labour-intensive industries and a large shift of industrial specialisation towards raw material processing.

The essence of the problem for Latin America from Katz's vantage point (Katz, 2001) is that the national innovation systems that did develop were of a highly fragmented nature lacking in sense of purpose and depth. Their experience represents a failure of policy learning and policy adaptation. The key appears to lie with the bureaucratic culture that developed within and around the R&D institutes and the lack of linkages with the productive structure of the economy. Meyer-Stamer (1997) reinforces this perception, arguing that although there were elements of a system they were without systemic character (p. 85). While there were loosely linked activities in different sectors, there has been no continuous practice of a systematic, cross-sectoral technology policy. The concerns of the state appeared to weigh in favour of science – basic research – over activities dealing with applied research and technology development. Moreover, a nexus of technological cooperation between firms, universities and research institutions did not emerge. A balanced assessment of this experience would need to take account of some remarkable success stories including Brazil's world leadership in gene sequencing technologies and the basic science that underpins them (Harvey and McMeekin, 2003).

Clearly activist innovation policies have been employed with varying degrees of success in the recent past by East Asian and Latin American countries. Whether such an approach to policy is viable in view of the changing context of domestic and international contexts of technology policy is questionable. Chang and Cheema (2002) suggest that developing country deregulation and the emergence of a 'liberal' world order represented by the WTO are no longer conducive to such developments. Certainly the move towards liberalisation and deregulation in most developing countries is rendering a rent-creation mechanism more difficult to implement. Moreover, a move towards a more 'liberal' international regime marked by the establishment of the WTO constrains the freedom of individual countries in the use of trade, industrial and technology policies. Although not impossible, activist technology policy may require more careful policy design, focused on internal R&D effort rather than external acquisition of technology. Policy and policy makers may need to be more adaptive to changing circumstances. The Korean case is particularly instructive. While its innovation system was adequate for its development in the 1960s and 1970s, the formal and informal institutions were not sufficiently reformed to take account of the rapidly changing market and technology environment over recent years (Kim, 2000; Westphal, 2002). Thus, in an era when growth and development relies on collective knowledge and creativity, the continuation of that country's progress now appears to rest on wide-scale changes to its innovation system (Kim, 2000).

CONCLUDING THOUGHTS

Current thinking about development (and economic growth) has often failed to grasp the complex, causal nature of the social world and more often than not, presents an inappropriate and a-historical account of the economic process across countries (Kenny and Williams, 2001). It is no wonder then that Stiglitz (1998) notes that recent treatments of the development process have begun to re-emphasise the complex and interlinked nature of the economy reminiscent of writing in the 1950s and before. Our linking together of competition and development is offered in the same spirit, and it is a plea also to a return to earlier traditions of economic thinking (Nelson and Winter, 2002).

Our central conclusion is that competition, and by implication competition policy, involves complex and subtle issues that transcend the view of competition as a structural feature of specific markets arranged on a spectrum from monopoly to perfect competition. Instead, we have insisted that competition is a dynamic process not readily analysed in terms of states of equilibrium, and we have claimed that an evolutionary view of competition is isomorphic to an evolutionary view of development processes. Indeed, we conjecture that many of the great development economists could wear an evolutionary label with comfort. Did they not believe that development was a process of variation in which the institutions of society change from traditional to modern modes? We have argued that what connects competition and economic development, is their joint dependence on innovation and, thus, the neoclassical emphasis on equilibrium creates as many difficulties for the understanding of development as it does the understanding of competition. Both development and competition depend deeply on notions of coordination but coordination is not equilibrium it is order, and knowledge-based orders change from within. Developing economies are never in equilibrium because knowledge is never in equilibrium. The emphasis on order naturally places the operation of markets, the boundaries of markets and the regulation of markets at the forefront of the analysis. Indeed all markets are regulated as part of their instituted framework although much of this regulation can be informal, organised by the market participants and transcending matters of competition in the narrow sense.

Market processes play a key role in this view of development but not in the conventional way, if that means an emphasis on efficiency in the allocation of given resources to given ends. Rather the institutions of the market economy are to be judged in terms of the discovery of new uses for economic resources, as Schumpeter insisted. It is the role of open market processes in incentivising and facilitating creative change that matters. The socially and legally embedded rules of the game matter because they underpin this view of capitalism and competition as contest and enterprise. No economy attains high levels of development without building a rich ecology of market institutions to facilitate open competition. However, markets are the instruments and not the objective of economic progress; they are the necessary but not sufficient generators of development. It is innovation broadly conceived that is the root source of all economic progress and it is thus the link between innovation and competition that matters for competition policy, and any broad conception of innovation must recognise that there is much more to it than a command of science and technology. Thus competition policy turns out to be complementary to innovation policy with all that implies for the difficulty of assessing market power in relation to long run economic performance. Perhaps the best competition policy one can have is an innovation policy that stimulates multiple new business experiments.

In contrast to the general, direct and optimising perspective of market failure-based innovation policy, a structuralist and evolutionary perspective presents a multidimensional and multi-targeted focus, directed to a wide array of opportunities for business experiments, and employing multiple tools. Moreover, the selection of policy alternatives should not be a static process, as there is no policy adequate to the task of remaining relevant or effective over a prolonged period of time (Teubal, 1997; Bartzoukas and Teubal, 2002). It is an evolutionary perspective that justifies innovation policy in terms of system failures, deficiencies in the ecology of organisations and their interconnections (Edquist et al., 2002; Lipsey, 2002).

To conclude, competition is central to the development process, but competition is a process not a state of equilibrium. Consequently, competition policy is not reducible to a simple-minded concern with the exploitation of market power and the search for excess profits. It is in its fundamentals a matter of the creativity of an economic system; that is to say, the necessary and sufficient condition for competition is an open, experiment oriented, and innovative economy. This is one reason why pragmatism rules for competition authorities – they must be sensitive to inter-industry difference in relation to the main drivers of competitiveness in different industries: the role of innovation in competitiveness, the policies necessary to promote innovation, and the effect of competition on the innovation process.

REFERENCES

Abramovitz, M. (1986), 'Catching up, forging ahead and falling behind', *Journal of Economic History*, **46** (2) 385–406.

Ahrens, J. (1999), 'Governance and the implementation of technology policy in less developed countries', *Economics of Innovation and New Technology*, **11**, 441–76.

Alchian, A. (1951), 'Uncertainty, evolution and economic theory', *Journal of Political Economy*, **60**, 211–21.

Amann, E. and Baer, W. (2002), 'The development of Brazil's technological capabilities in the post war period: from dependence to self-reliance', *Latin American Business Review*, **3**, 1–29.

Andersen, E.S. (1994), *Evolutionary Economics: Post Schumpeterian Contributions*, London: Pinter.

Aoki, M., Murdock, K. and Okuno-Fujiwara, M. (1997), 'Beyond the East Asian miracle: introducing the market-enhancing view', in M. Aoki, H.-K. Kim, and M. Okuno-Fujiwara (eds), *The Role of Government in East Asian Economic Development. Comparative Institutional Analysis*, Oxford: Clarendon Press, pp. 1–37.

Arndt, H. (1988), 'Market failure and underdevelopment', *World Development*, **16**, 219–29.

Arrow, K. (1962), 'Economic welfare and the allocation of resources to invention' in R.R. Nelson (ed.), *The Rate and Direction of Inventive Activity*, New York: NBER.

Bartzoukas, A. and Teubal, M. (2002), 'A framework for policy oriented innovation studies in industrialising countries', *Economics of Innovation and New Technology*, **11**, 477–96.

Baumol, W.J. (1982), 'Contestable markets: an uprising in the theory of industry structure', *American Economic Review*, **12**, 1–15.

Baumol, W.J. (1993), *Entrepreneurship, Management and the Structure of Payoffs*, Cambridge, MA: MIT Press.

Brenner, R. (1987), *Rivalry: In Business, Science, Among Nations*, Cambridge: Cambridge University Press.

Bruton, H.J. (1985), 'The search for development economics', *World Development*, **13**, 1099–124.

Bruton, H.J. (1998), 'A reconsideration of import substitution', *Journal of Economic Literature*, **36**, 903–36.
Chang, H. and Cheema, A. (2002), 'Conditions for successful technology policies in developing countries – learning rents, state structures and institutions', *Economics of Innovation and New Technology*, **11**, 369–98.
Clark, J.M. (1961), *Competition as a Dynamic Process*, Washington: Brookings Institute.
Coombs, R., Harvey, M. and Tether, B. (2003), 'Analysing distributed innovation processes', CRIC Discussion Paper no 43, University of Manchester (forthcoming in *Industrial and Corporate Change*).
Coombs, R. and Metcalfe, J.S. (2000), 'Organising for innovation: coordinating for innovative distributed innovation capabilities' in N. Foss and V. Mahnke (eds), *Competence, Governance and Entrepreneurship: Advances in Economic Strategy Research*, Oxford: Oxford University Press.
Coombs, R. and Metcalfe, J.S. (2002), 'Innovation in pharmaceuticals: perspectives on the coordination, combination and creation of capabilities', *Technology Analysis & Strategic Management*, **14** (3), 261–71.
Dahlman, C. and Frischtak, C.R. (1993), 'National systems supporting technical advance in industry: the Brazilian experience', in R.R. Nelson (ed.), *National Innovation Systems: A Comparative Analysis*, Oxford: Oxford University Press.
Demsetz, H. (1995), 'The Intensity and Dimensionality of Competition', in *The Economics of the Business Firm*, Cambridge: Cambridge University Press.
Dosi, G., Freeman, C., Nelson, R., Silverberg, G. and Soete, L. (1988), *Technical Change and Economic Theory*, London: Pinter.
Downie, J. (1958), *The Competitive Process*, London: Duckworth.
Edquist, C., Malerba, F., Metcalfe, J.S. and Montobbio, F. (2002), 'New challenges for sectoral systems of innovation in Europe', paper presented to the Druid Summer Conference 2002, Copenhagen, Denmark.
Fisher, F.M., McGowan, J.J. and Greenwood, J.E. (1983), *Folded, Spindled and Mutilated*, Boston: MIT.
Georgescu-Roegen, N. (1967), 'Chamberlin's new economics and the production unit', in R. Kuenne (ed.), *Monopolistic Competition Theory. Studies on Impact*, New York: Wiley.
Harvey, M. and McMeekin, A. (2003), 'Brazilian genomics and bioinformatics: instituting innovation processes in a global context', mimeo, ESRC Centre for Research on Innovation and Competition, University of Manchester.
Hayek, F.A. (1948), 'The meaning of competition' in F.A. Hayek (ed.), *Individualism and Economic Order*, Chicago: University of Chicago Press.
Hayek, F.A. (1978), 'Competition as a discovery process' in F.A. Hayek (ed.), *New Studies in Philosophy, Politics, Economics and the History of Ideas*, London: Routledge and Kegan Paul.
Hicks, J. (1965), *Capital and Growth*, Oxford: Oxford University Press.
Hirschman, A. (1958), *The Strategy of Economic Development*, New Haven, CT: Yale University Press.
Jevons, W.S. (1871), *The Theory of Political Economy*, London: Macmillan.
Katz, J. (2000), 'The dynamics of technological learning during the import-substitution period and recent structural changes in the industrial sectors of Argentina, Brazil and Mexico', in R. Nelson, and L. Kim (eds), *Technology, Learning, and Innovation: Experiences of Newly Industrializing Countries*, Cambridge: Cambridge University Press.

Katz, J. (2001), 'Structural reforms and technological behaviour: the sources and nature of technological change in Latin America in the 1990s', '*Research Policy*', **30**, 1–19.

Kenny, C. and Williams, D. (2001), 'What do we know about economic growth? Or, why don't we know very much?', *World Development*, **29** (3), 1–22.

Kim, L. (1993), 'National system of industrial innovation: dynamics of capacity building in Korea', in R. Nelson (ed.), *National Innovation Systems: A Comparative Analysis*, Oxford: Oxford University Press.

Kim, L. (2000), 'Korea's national innovation systems in transition' in L. Kim and R.R. Nelson (eds), '*Technology, Learning, and Innovation: Experiences of Newly Industrialized Economies*', Cambridge: Cambridge University Press.

Knight, F. (1923), 'The ethics of competition', *Quarterly Journal of Economics*, **37**, 579–624.

Knight, F. (1946), 'Immutable law in economics: its reality and limitations', *American Economic Review*, **36** (May), 93–111.

Krugman, P. (1994), *Pop Internationalism*, Cambridge, MA: MIT Press.

Kurz, H. and Salvadori, N. (1995), *Theory of Production*, Cambridge: Cambridge University Press.

Lachmann, L. (1986), *The Market as an Economic Process*, Oxford: Basil Blackwell.

Lall, S. (2001a), '*Competitiveness, Technology and Skills*', Oxford: Oxford University Press.

Lall, S. (2001b), 'Competitiveness indices and developing countries: an evaluation of the Global Competitiveness Report', *World Development*, **29** (9), 1501–25.

Lall, S. and Teubal, M. (1998), 'Market stimulating technology policies in developing countries: a framework with examples from East Asia', *World Development*, **26**.

Leibowitz., S.J. and Margolis, S.E. (2001), '*Winners, Losers & Microsoft: Competition and Antitrust in High Technology*', Washington, DC: Independent Institute.

Lewis, W.A. (1954), 'Economic development with unlimited supplies of labour', *Manchester School*, **22**, 139–91.

Lipsey, R.G. (2002), 'Some implications of endogenous technological change for technology policies in developing countries', *Economics of Innovation and New Technology*, **11**, 321–52.

Loasby, B. (1982), 'The entrepreneur in economic theory', *Scottish Journal of Political Economy*, **29**, 235–45.

McNulty, P.J. (1967), 'A note on the history of perfect competition', *Journal of Political Economy*, **75**, 395–9.

Marshall, A. (1920), *Principles of Economics*, 8th edn, London: Macmillan.

Mazzacato, M. (2000), *Firm Size, Innovation and Market Structure: The Evolution of Market Concentration and Instability*, Lyme, US: Edward Elgar.

Metcalfe, J.S. (1995), 'The economic foundations of technology policy: equilibrium and evolutionary perspectives', in P. Stoneman (ed.), *Handbook of Economics of Innovation and Technology Change*, Oxford: Blackwell.

Metcalfe, J.S. (1998), '*Evolutionary Economics and Creative Destruction*', London: Routledge.

Metcalfe, J.S. (2001), 'Technology and economic development: a comparative perspective', background paper prepared for the World Industrial Development Report, UNIDO.

Meyer-Stamer, J. (1995), 'Micro-level innovations and competitiveness', *World Development*, **23**, 143–8.

Meyer-Stamer, J. (1997), *Technology, Competitiveness and Radical Policy Change: The Case of Brazil*, London: Frank Cass.

Morgenstern, O. (1972), 'Thirteen critical points in contemporary economic theory', *Journal of Economic Literature*, **10**, 1163–89.

Mytelka, L.K. (1999), *Competition, Innovation and Competitiveness in Developing Countries*, Development Centre, Paris: OECD.

Nelson, R. and Winter, S. (1984), '*An Evolutionary Theory of Economic Change*', Harvard: Belknap.

Nelson, R. and Winter, S. (2002), 'Evolutionary theorizing in economics', *Journal of Economic Perspectives*, **16**, 23–46.

Okun, A.M. (1981), *Prices and Quantities: A Macro Economic Analysis*, Oxford: Basil Blackwell.

Penrose, E.T. (1959), *A Theory of the Growth of the Firm*, Oxford: Basil Blackwell.

Roberts, M.J. and Tybout, J.R. (1996), *Industrial Evolution in Developing Countries*, Oxford: Oxford University Press.

Robinson, J.V. (1954), 'The impossibility of competition', in E.H. Chamberlin (ed.), *Monopoly and Competition and their Regulation*, London: Macmillan.

Schumpeter, J. (1928), 'The instability of capitalism', *Economic Journal*, **38**, 361–86.

Schumpeter, J. (1934), *The Theory of Economic Development*, Oxford: Oxford University Press.

Schumpeter, J. (1939), *Business Cycles*, New York: McGraw-Hill.

Schumpeter, J. (1944), *Capitalism, Socialism and Democracy*, London: George Allen and Unwin.

Shepherd, W.G. (1984), ' "Contestability" vs "Competition" ', *American Economic Review*, **74**, 572–86.

Singh, A. (2002), 'Competition and competition policy in emerging markets: international and development dimensions', http://ksghome.harvard.edu/~.drodrik.academic.ksg/ G24Singh.pdf

Singh, A. and Dhumale, R. (1999), 'Competition policy, development and developing countries', Trade Related Agenda Development and Equity (T.R.A.D.E) Working Paper No 7, South Centre.

Stigler, G.J. (1965), 'Perfect competition, historically contemplated', in G.J. Stigler, *Essays in the History of Economics*, Chicago: University of Chicago Press.

Stiglitz, J. (1998), 'Towards a new paradigm for development: strategies, policies and processes', the 1999 Prebish Lecture, Geneva: UNCTAD.

Stoneman, P. (1988), '*The Economic Analysis of Technology Policy*', Oxford: Oxford University Press.

Streeten, P. (1959), 'Unbalanced growth', *Oxford Economic Papers*, **11**, 167–90.

Teubal, M. (1997), 'Policies for promoting enterprise restructuring in national system of innovation: triggering cumulative learning and generating systems effects', in 'New Rationale and Approaches in Technology and Innovation Policy', *OECD STI Review*, **22** (Special Issue).

WEF (2000), Porter, M.E., Sachs, J.D., Warner, A.M., Cornelius, P.K., Levinson, M. and Schwab, K. (eds), *The Global Competitiveness Report 2000*, New York: Oxford University Press for the World Economic Forum.

Westphal, L.E. (2002), 'Technology strategies for development in a fast changing global economy', *Economics of Innovation and New Technology*, **11**, 275–320.

4. Economic regulation in developing countries: a framework for critical analysis

David Parker and Colin Kirkpatrick

INTRODUCTION

In the 1990s more than 120 developing countries introduced private investment in infrastructure schemes in the public utilities (Gray, 2001, p. 2). Traditionally the public utilities – electricity, gas, water services, telecommunications and transport – have been associated with economies of scale and scope in production that rule out competition in the market. For much of the last century state ownership of public utilities was the preferred option in most countries, including developing ones. Private-sector monopolies are not attractive given the possible threat of abuse of market power. More recently, however, in the face of evidence of 'state failure', the emphasis in public policy has switched from direct state ownership to private ownership but with state regulation.

State regulation is the means by which the state attempts to affect private sector behaviour. Economic regulation by government is associated with righting 'market failures', including ameliorating the perceived adverse consequences of private enterprise including its income and wealth distribution effects. An additional argument lies in the role of the state as a facilitator of economic growth. From the 1960s to the 1980s it was fashionable to promote industrialisation through import substitution, in which the state played a primary role as a regulator of both domestic and external trade and as a direct investor in industry and agriculture. However, following the apparent successes of privatisation and market liberalisation programmes in developed economies, including Europe and North America, and evidence of government failure in developing ones (World Bank, 1995), since the late 1980s international donor aid agencies have promoted market liberalisation and privatisation policies. This change is associated with a wider shift from the model of a positive or interventionist state to a regulatory one (Majone, 1994, 1997). The regulatory state model implies leaving production to the private sector where competitive markets work and using government regulation only where market failure exists (World Bank, 2001, p. 1).

Arguably, however, the performance of the new regulatory state remains under-researched, especially in the context of developing countries with their own peculiar economic and social problems. Where research has occurred it has exposed a number of regulatory failures (Noll, 1999). A NERA study in 1998, based on a questionnaire covering 12 infrastructure industries across six developing Asian economies, found much variation in practices and a considerable short-fall from regulatory best practice, as understood in the UK and the US (Stern and Holder, 1999). Cook (1999), based on case studies of utility sector reforms in developing countries, concludes that creating effective regulation and a competitive environment is at best a difficult and slow process. Brownbridge and Kirkpatrick (2000) identify difficulties in applying developed country models of regulation to developing economies in banking and finance. Campbell-White and Bhatia (1998, p. 5), in the context of Africa, conclude that: 'Regulation is being examined as part of individual sector initiatives, but these efforts are uncoordinated, and implementation is being left to follow privatization instead of being put in place concurrently.'

In recent recognition that not all is well, the World Bank (2001, p. v) stressed the importance of 'improving regulatory regimes and building institutions and capacity effectively to supervise the private sector' and the Asian Development Bank (2000, p. 18) emphasised the need for improved regulation. But this leaves open the question as to what precise forms of regulation are appropriate in the context of a developing country. It is not self-evident that the lessons of operating regulation in developed economies are directly transferable to the less developed world (World Bank, 2001, p. 54). Moreover, it is not at all clear that developing countries can be lumped together and analysed as a common unit, in particular, institutional capability can be expected to vary from one country to another.

In this chapter we explore a number of propositions from the literature on the economics of regulation. The objective is to identify the main issues that will have to be taken into account when studying regulatory issues in developing economies. The chapter is exploratory and largely conceptual, although illustrated with examples from developing countries. To make our task manageable we have chosen to concentrate mainly on economic regulation as it applies to the regulation of public utilities, sometimes referred to as the 'natural monopolies'. Our reasoning and conclusions are intended, however, to have wider applicability to other areas of state regulation. In the remainder of the chapter we review relevant aspects of the theory of economic regulation of natural monopoly, and then assess the theory in terms of the economic development needs and institutions of developing countries. The chapter then presents a framework for the study of economic regulation in developing countries, drawing on the earlier discussion. The final section provides the conclusions to the chapter.

PROPOSITIONS FROM THE THEORY OF ECONOMIC REGULATION

The theory of economic regulation developed from the nineteenth century and the literature is now vast (for recent reviews e.g. Laffont and Tirole, 1993, 2000; Levy and Spiller, 1994; Newbery, 1999). The case for economic regulation of public utility markets is premised on the existence of significant market failure resulting from economies of scale and scope in production, that lead to higher unit costs if more than one firm competes in the market. Another possible source of market failure is information asymmetries in market transacting. Markets are able to maximise social welfare where consumers and producers are perfectly (or at least well) informed when making choices in the market place. Where one party to a transaction has more information than the other about the quantity or quality of the outputs to be transacted, a condition known as 'asymmetric information', then this party could act 'opportunistically', exploiting its superior knowledge to gain utility at the expense of the other party.

Since the 1960s, however, the economics of regulation literature has also focused on circumstances where we might expect to find 'regulatory failure'; that is to say, circumstances where the regulation of markets might reduce rather than increase economic welfare. The seminal study in this literature is that by Averch and Johnson who, in 1962, presented a model of how regulation of a firm's rate of return could lead to incentives to over-invest. Following publication of Averch and Johnson's paper, studies highlighted other potential inefficiencies that could be introduced by rate of return regulation, notably distorted service quality and higher operating costs (e.g. Bailey, 1973).

Today the economics of regulation literature includes the following propositions (for further on these propositions see e.g. Kahn, 1988; Sidak and Spulber, 1998; Baldwin and Cave, 1999; Joskow, 2000; Viscusi et al., 2000).

- *The institutional context is critical to the process and outcomes of a regulatory regime*. As Granovetter (1985) recognised in his study of 'embeddedness', behaviour and institutions are constrained by social relations. This is true of any regulatory regime, which will be embodied in the specific institutional context of a country as reflected in its formal and informal rules of economic transacting and social behaviour. As Picciotto (1999, p. 3) comments: 'In all societies formal rules enacted by the state influence social behaviour only indirectly, filtered through layers of formal and informal social institutions, and normative patterns and practices.' In turn these institutional effects are credited with having important effects on the trajectory of economic development (Lal, 1999, Ch. 3). In consequence, the World Bank has been criticised for adopting an 'under-socialised approach' to policy reform (Torp and Rekve, 1998, p. 80).

Regulation in economies involves the setting of particular rules regarding market structure and business conduct and these rules both arise out of and influence the future shape of economic institutions. Levy and Spiller (1994) focus on regulatory arrangements to sustain private investment and how these vary with the institutional endowment in different countries. Also, 'new institutional economics' has had an impact on the economics of regulation especially through transaction cost theory. Transaction cost economics is concerned with the costs that enter into market transacting and that are associated with policing opportunistic behaviour in markets (Williamson, 1985; Allen, 1991). Economic development is seen not as simply a matter of amassing economic resources in the form of physical and human capital but a matter of 'institution building' so as to reduce information imperfections, maximise economic incentives and reduce transaction costs. Included in this institution building are the laws and political and social rules and conventions that are the basis for successful market production and exchange. Another important consideration is 'culture' or the way of doing things in society, which forms in North's analysis one of the 'informal' constraints on human interaction (North, 1990, 1991). Particularly relevant modes of conduct in the context of the regulatory state would seem to include probity in public administration, independence of the courts, low corruption and cronyism, and traditions of civic responsibility.

- *Regulation is associated with information asymmetries*. The regulator and the regulated can be expected to have different levels of information about such matters as costs, revenues and demand. The regulated company holds the information that the regulator needs to regulate optimally and the regulator must establish rules and incentive mechanisms to force and coax this information from the company. Given that it is highly unlikely that the regulator will receive all the information required to regulate optimally to maximise social welfare, the results of regulation, in terms of outputs and prices, remain 'second best' to those of a competitive market. Shapiro and Willig (1990) argue that state ownership provides more information to regulators than private ownership so contracting should be less problematic when the state both owns and regulates. However, state ownership is associated with inadequate incentives to gather and use this information to maximise welfare (Hayek, 1945). In other words, there tends to be a trade-off between state ownership reducing the information asymmetries and hence the transaction costs of regulation, and the relative incentives under state control and market transacting for agents to maximise social welfare (Grossman and Hart, 1986; Sappington and Stiglitz, 1987; Shapiro and Willig, 1990; Yarrow, 1999). This leads to 'credibility' and 'commitment' considerations: specifically, *credibility* on the part of investors that the regulatory rules will bring about the intended outcome; and *commitment* of government to the current regulatory rules, so that post-privatisation or post-concession award the regulator does not act opportunistically to reduce the prices and profits of the private regulated businesses. Regulatory credibility will be enhanced if the regulator faces high costs of deviating from a commitment.

- *Investment in a regulated environment is subject to a threat of hold up leading to under-investment*. Because the regulatory contract, whether formal or informal, is incomplete, it is vulnerable to post-contract opportunism. Public utilities are capital-intensive and therefore post-contract one or other party may have an incentive to adopt opportunistic behaviour to improve its own well-being. Utility networks involve sunk investments that are specific to the venture, so that once a network is created the balance of bargaining advantage at the time of a contract renegotiation may shift from the private-sector investor to the regulator (on behalf of the government) with implications for pricing and investment (Spiller, 1996; and for a recent review of the hold up literature, Schmitz, 2001). In principle prices could be reduced to short-term marginal costs. Where the investor fears this outcome, referred to as 'hold up', front-end loading of returns, take or pay contracts with governments and sovereign guarantees from the state or international agencies may be required by the private sector. In turn such guarantees reduce the net economic benefits of attracting private capital by reducing managerial incentives to control costs.

  The precise result of opportunistic behaviour depends crucially, however, on the relative bargaining power of the regulated and the regulator. Alternatively, the regulator and hence the government could be subject to 'hold up', where post-contract private investors demand a tariff or other contract adjustment in their favour and the regulator has no alternative supplier to turn to.
- *Regulatory regimes are prone to capture*. 'Regulatory capture' involves the regulatory process becoming biased in favour of particular interest groups and notably the regulated companies. Regulators can be assumed to care about the levels of both consumer and producer surplus because

both impact on social welfare – benefits to consumers are reflected in consumer surplus but producer surplus is necessary to stimulate innovation (Kirzner, 1997). A regulator that is neutral between consumer utility and profit would place an equal weighting on consumer and producer surplus. One that favours consumers would weight consumer surplus more highly. Regulatory capture is associated with a weighting favouring producer over consumer surplus. In the extreme case, the regulatory capture literature concludes that regulation *always* leads to socially suboptimal outcomes because of 'inefficient bargaining between interest groups over potential utility rents' (Laffont, 1999; Newbery, 1999, p. 134). In the Chicago tradition of regulatory capture (Stigler, 1971; Peltzman, 1976) regulators are presumed to favour producer interests because of the concentration of regulatory benefits and diffusion of regulatory costs, which enhances the power of lobbying groups as rent-seekers (Reagan, 1987). What is clear is that the capability of firms to influence public policy is an important source of comparative advantage (Shaffer, 1995).

Regulation is also subject to 'political capture'; indeed political capture may well be a much greater risk than capture by producer groups outside the political system. Where political capture occurs, the regulatory goals are distorted to pursue political ends. This is most likely to arise where the regulation is directly under the control of government ministers; hence the case for some kind of arm's length or 'independent' regulatory agency. Under political capture, regulation becomes a tool of self-interest within government or the ruling elite (Stiglitz, 1998).

Balanced against the risks of regulatory and political capture, however, is the possibility that regulators might develop a culture of arrogant independence, bordering on vexatious regulation. This creates some uncertainty about the desirable degree of regulatory independence. In principle three broad forms of regulation can be identified: (a) the regulatory authority is *integrated* into the normal government machinery, notably where it is a section of the ministry and controlled by the minister; (b) the *semi-independent agency*, which has some independence from the ministry but where decisions can still be over-ruled by a superior government authority; and (c) the *independent agency*, where there is no right of appeal to a superior government (political) authority, though there usually will be a right of appeal to the courts to ensure fairness and rationality in the decision-making process (in a number of jurisdictions known as an appeal on 'due process') (Smith, 1997; Von Der Fehr, 2000, p. 49). The independent agency is normally favoured by western advisers, who draw from the experience of regulation in the UK and US. However, regulatory independence and an impartial judicial review of due process may not be credible in some institutional structures: an issue we will develop further.

- *A regulatory system should be both effective and efficient*. Effective regulation achieves the social welfare goals set down by the government for the regulator at the time the regulatory office was established, and as subsequently amended after appropriate consultation. This can be achieved by regulation affecting (a) the structure of markets, and (b) conduct in markets through appropriate incentives and penalties. Efficient regulation achieves the social welfare goals at minimum economic cost.

  The economic costs of regulation take two broad forms: (1) the costs of directly administering the regulatory system, which are internalised within government and reflected in the budget appropriations of the regulatory body or bodies; and (2) the compliance costs of regulation, which are external to the regulatory agency and fall on consumers and producers in terms of the economic costs of conforming with the regulations and of avoiding and evading them. Both the administrative and compliance costs of regulation may rise over time, especially if economic regulation becomes an industry in its own right. It has been suggested that regulators could empire build: 'The self-interest of regulators will, in general, make them tend to exaggerate benefits, under-estimate costs and over-estimate the demand for action on their part' (Blundell and Robinson, 2000, p. 11).
- *Competition is superior to state regulation and should be preferred*. Economic regulation attempts to 'mimic' the social welfare results of competition, but it can do so only in a 'second best' way because competitive markets generate superior knowledge of consumer demands and producer supply costs (Sidak and Spulber, 1998, pp. 522–6). Indeed, government regulation can introduce important economic distortions into market economies: 'regulation . . . is far from being a full substitute for competition, it can create systematic distortions, it generally faces a trade-off between promoting one type of efficiency at the expense of another, and it is likely to generate significant costs, in terms of both direct implementation and exacerbation of inefficiency' (Hay and Morris, 1991, pp. 636–7). For such reasons, in the economics of regulation literature there is a strong preference for competition over state regulation and, where there is not a natural monopoly, for adopting regulation only until competition arrives.

This review of propositions from the economics of regulation literature incorporates observations on the importance of the institutional setting, regulatory rules and the regulatory process. While the search for practical solutions may lead countries to adopt regulatory policies that do not necessarily accord with the theory (Crew and Kleindorfer, 1996, p. 215), the theme of this chapter is that the theory is a useful starting point for analysing practice in developing economies. The propositions are now explored specifically within the context of developing countries.

ECONOMIC REGULATION IN DEVELOPING COUNTRIES: APPLYING THE THEORY

It should be noted at the outset that there is no separate economics of regulation literature designed for studying regulation in lower income economies. Hence, one obvious rationale for using the economics of regulation literature from the developed world is a lack of alternative theory or conceptual framework. However, as will be demonstrated, this is not a case of attempting to wear an ill-fitting shoe. The economics of regulation literature does have applicability in developing economies, if used with care. The approach adopted here is to analyse the needs of developing countries using the preceding propositions from the regulation literature, so as to build a methodology for studying regulation in these economies.

Institutional Context

Institutions act both as facilitators of economic development and as constraints, which can be divided into 'technical' and 'political'. Technical constraints include managerial deficiencies, lack of administrative and regulatory capacity, and weak capital markets. Political constraints include opposition from organised labour and the state apparatus, and fear of altering the balance of economic, ethnic and political power. Both sets of constraints may combine to provide an effective barrier to the speedy adoption and good performance of regulatory structures, even when the benefits for economic development are well understood (Parker, 1999a). As DFID (2000, pp. 23–5) comments:

> Effective governments are needed to build the legal, institutional and regulatory framework without which market reforms can go badly wrong, at great cost – particularly to the poor. Whilst excessive or cumbersome regulatory barriers stifle incentives and discourage investment, effective regulation remains essential – for instance to promote financial sector stability, to protect consumers, to safeguard the environment, and to protect human rights, including core labour standards.

Unfortunately, governmental effectiveness varies widely across the developing countries and excessive and cumbersome regulatory barriers are commonplace. While a number of countries have experimented for their public utilities with new forms of regulation based on examples from the UK and the USA, encouraged by western consultants, in a number of cases the results appear to have been disappointing, at least so far. For example, in Malawi the electricity industry regulator remains closely connected to the state electricity industry, compromising any notion of real regulatory independence and encouraging capture. Water sector reforms in a number of countries have been associated with second best outcomes and inefficiencies brought on by the institutional context within which reform has been attempted, especially a failure of the government machinery (Dinar, 2000). In India regulatory structures are associated with acute failures in institution building and with a bureaucratic approach that curtails enterprise and entrepreneurialism (Lanyi, 2000; *Financial Times*, 2001). South Africa's proliferation of regulatory bodies is associated with a lack of clarity about roles and responsibilities and with the adoption of policy-making roles independent of government (Schwella, 2002, p. 3). In contrast, under Malaysia's telecommunications regulatory regime the minister rather than the Malaysian Communications and Multimedia Commission continues to make all of the key regulatory decisions (Lee, 2002, p. 10). Meanwhile, experiences in the transitional economies are also educational. Studies have shown that there has been much variability in the independence of the new regulators established (Cave and Stern, 1998). For instance, in Hungary in 1996, the government found ways within the Electricity Law of reducing a tariff increase recommended by the regulator, the Hungarian Energy Office.

The substitution of state economic regulation for direct state ownership in developing economies is intended to remove the conflict of interest that exists where ownership, management and regulation of a firm are within one jurisdiction. But as Stelzer (1988, p. 78) recognises: 'Regulation is a business in which people make a difference.' The implementation of regulation is a human and not simply a technical function, so the quality of the regulators is important and regulatory expertise in developing countries is normally in scarce supply. The credibility of any kind of 'independent regulation', modelled on the UK or US regulatory structures, may be weak and even where it does exist, deciding on the appropriate degree of discretion to be given to regulators is likely to be particularly problematic in the absence of experience of delegating decision-making powers to quasi-governmental agencies.

Information Asymmetries

Information asymmetries and therefore the scope for 'opportunistic' behaviour by either the regulator or the regulated can be expected to be higher in developing than developed economies because of a lack of regulatory expertise and the need for regulatory capacity building. In particular, regulation is not the same thing as *management* of public utilities and this may not always be well understood. In any case the division can be obscure at the margin, leading to conflict between the regulator and the regulated; for example, pricing and investment are important management matters but they are also regulatory issues.

As an illustration, in Argentina there was a failure to determine the regulatory system ahead of a major restructuring of the telecommunications industry and the privatisation of the country's main operator, ENTel. The regulatory agency was created only after the sell-off. In the following months there was serious disagreement between the agency and company especially over the agency's powers to set new tariffs. Customer service complaints increased and investment was adversely affected by the general uncertainty created by the regulatory environment (UNCTAD, 1995, pp. 136–7; Cook, 1999). In Buenos Aires Metropolitan Region a 30-year water concession to a private-sector company led to a number of service improvements. But the industry regulator, ETOSS, complained about inadequate information supplied by the company, while the company, Aguas Argentinas, criticised the regulation for being too intrusive. In Guinea the private water operator, SEEG, earned more than twice the amount agreed with government from its water concession, but the state holding company and regulatory body, SONEG, failed to discover this until a World Bank audit (Bayliss, 2001, p. 14). This suggests ongoing regulatory weaknesses stemming from information asymmetry. In the Chilean electricity sector economic performance improvements were linked to regulatory improvements rather than privatisation per se (Cook, 1999). In 1995 Puerto Rico contracted the management of its water authority to the French multinational, Vivendi. An official report in 1999 condemned numerous failures, including deficiencies in supply, customer service and maintenance and repair, and noted that financial reports from the company to the regulator were either late or not submitted (Bayliss, 2002, p. 9).

Hold Up

Often concessions are used in developing countries for public utility investments and are prone to hold up. Typically the concession agreement will involve investment in long-life assets. The longer the concession period the less feasible it will be for any party at the outset to anticipate and build into the concession contract all future events that might impact on costs and revenues (Grossman and Hart, 1996). The risks include design/construction risk, operating cost risk, revenue risk, financing risks (including exchange rate movements e.g. when the debt is dollar denominated) and environmental risk (Kerf et al., 1998; Pongsiri, 2001).

The longer the time period the more likely it is that contract disagreements will arise between the concession holder and the regulator or government. In Jamaica a 25-year concession to operate the telecommunications sector, entered into with Cable and Wireless in 1988, provided for an agreed rate of return on equity. The concession is widely considered to have been disappointing with prices failing to fall and labour productivity growth remaining weak (Lodge and Stirton, 2002). It has now been replaced with a more liberalised telecommunications regime, but only after a difficult and lengthy process of renegotiation. In India the much publicised Dabhol Power Company dispute provides a pertinent lesson for international investors on the risks of hold up. The project, based in Maharashtra state, was initially considered to be a model for future independent power producers (IPPs) in India and elsewhere. Arranged in the late 1980s and refinanced at a cost of US$1.4bn in 1999, a new government in Maharashtra reviewed the contract and considered that it unfairly favoured the private investor over the people of Maharashtra. The result has been non-payment for power by the state electricity board and heated legal wrangling (*Project Finance International*, July 2000, p. 11). In South Africa the privatised water company at Dolphin Coast sought to renegotiate its contract after experiencing disappointing financial results. In April 2001 the company, Siza, refused to make a scheduled lease payment to the municipality. The municipality could have retaliated under the terms of the concession agreement by calling in a performance bond, but there was no obvious alternative supplier. Water prices were negotiated upwards by 15 per cent to restore Siza's profitability.

Expanding public services to populations previously un- or under-supplied can be expected to be a major objective of developing economies. However, to attract private investment requires a regulatory environment that minimises investor risk, while at the same time protecting local consumers and taxpayers from rent-seeking behaviour by private owners. This is not an easy balance and raises a number of issues relating to the relationship between economic regulation, social welfare and regulatory risk (Parker, 1999b). Gupta and Sravat (1998) provide an overview of the Dabhol and other private power projects in India and demonstrate that both opportunities and risks attach to private power projects. The lack of necessary regulatory reforms to introduce cost-based tariffs and to end non-payment for power, alongside incidents of contract reneging by the state, has led a number of international power companies to leave India, including EdF, Cogentrix and International Power. Also, the East Asian financial crisis of 1997 underlines that private investment is not a straightforward panacea for state failure to invest adequately. The use of IPPs in the Philippines during the 1990s led to a power glut with an estimated 59 per cent over-capacity in generation by 2001 (*Project Finance International*, October 2001, p. 53). In Indonesia, following unfavourable exchange rate movements, the government required the renegotiation of IPP contracts.

Regulatory and Political Capture

Public choice theory suggests that politicians and bureaucrats are self-seeking (Niskanen, 1971; Mitchell, 1988) and this has been a powerful argument for privatisation of state-owned utilities; but it is these very same politicians and civil servants who are expected to establish and maintain a credible regulatory structure after privatisation. By concentrating economic power in regulatory offices the risk of regulatory and political capture is likely to be increased, especially in societies with a culture of cronyism and clientelism (Guasch and Hahn, 1999, p. 137). Cronyism and clientelism, alongside patrimonialism and corruption, interweave creating a serious problem for public administration in developing countries (Theobold, 1990; also see the studies in Williams and Theobald, 2000) and therefore for regulatory credibility and commitment. In a developing country context, the risk of regulatory capture is reinforced by family loyalties, clan systems and other cultural norms favouring relationship contracting, such as the role of *guanxi* in transacting in Chinese societies (Duckett, 2001). Moreover, privatisation can concentrate power in a local political-business elite, compromising any chance of effective state regulation (see the papers in Saha and Parker, 2002). Rohdewohld (1993) details how Nigeria's privatisation programme from the mid-1980s was driven by the need to satisfy regional and ethnic interests. Patronage has been identified as a major problem in the privatisations that have taken place in many parts of Africa (Tangri, 1999; Tangri and Mwenda, 2001; Craig, 2000, 2001).

It is to be expected that in developing countries, as in developed ones (Brenner, 1980; Gale and Buchholz, 1987; Blau and Harris, 1992; Shaffer, 1995; Kerf and Smith, 1996), businesses and other interest groups will attempt to use public policy strategically so as to influence the content of regulation in their favour. In developing countries foreign companies may have considerable economic and political power to pursue rent-seeking goals, including negotiating exemptions from regulations by threatening to withhold investment. A study of the privatisation of the telecommunications and transport sectors in Latin America concluded that there was a real risk of regulatory capture because if multinational companies threatened withdrawal governments had no obvious alternative supplier. The study also identifies cases of political meddling in regulation and of incumbent private-sector firms actively lobbying government to prevent the development of competition (Ramamurti, 1996, pp. 30–3). Bitrán et al. (1999), reviewing the privatisation of Chile's public utilities, rate highly the likelihood of both regulatory and political capture.

Effectiveness and Efficiency

When assessing the efficiency and effectiveness of regulation in developing countries, allowance needs to be made for the role of state regulation as a facilitator of, as well as a possible obstacle to, economic development. Regulation can create a more certain environment for investment in developing countries and thereby produce more orderly economic development (World Bank, 2003). Regulatory agencies can be effective in controlling abuses of market power and thereby ensuring that markets remain contestable. In the utilities sector, where typically a small number of firms dominate the industry, recent research suggests that privatisation brings greater benefits in the presence of a regulatory authority (Wallsten, 2001; Parker et al., 2002).

Also, regulation in developing countries is likely to be not simply concerned with the pursuit of economic efficiency but with wider social welfare goals to promote economic sustainability and poverty reduction. This is significant because it suggests that regulation in developing economies may face a greater dichotomy than in developed countries between promoting economic and social goals. Until this is flushed out and properly articulated it is difficult to make proper sense of notions of regulatory effectiveness and regulatory efficiency in developing countries (Smith, 2000). What is deemed regulatory ineffectiveness in one context, for instance a failure to remove cross-subsidies that favour the poor, may not be in another context where poverty reduction is a primary goal of public policy. The impact of changing regulations that raise prices to industry for, say, power supplies, may have different consequences in a developing country dependent on foot-loose multinational companies than would be the case in those companies' home economies.

A meaningful assessment of the effectiveness and efficiency of economic regulation needs, therefore, to include the goals of poverty reduction and reducing social exclusion. For example, in South Africa policy is driven by the goal of empowering the black majority after decades of apartheid, leading to regulation to ensure universal and affordable access to essential services (Schwella, 2002, p. 18). Empowerment and participation along with poverty reduction are now on the agenda of donor institutions, but their link to regulation is not clearly made. For example, the continuing existence of service obligations and cross-subsidies alongside market liberalisation policies are issues that need to be addressed. There is argument in the literature as to whether privatisation necessarily improves economic efficiency (Martin and Parker, 1997, Ch. 4; Torp and Rekve, 1998, p. 78; Megginson and Netter, 2001; Cook and Uchida, 2001), but there can be little doubt that privatisation *alone* does not address the goals of macroeconomic stability and distributional improvements in developing economies (World Bank, 2001, p. 39). It is not necessarily the case that the poorest will lose out from privatisation (Estache et al., 2000; Birdsall and Nellis, 2002), but low-income consumers may not benefit unless their specific needs are addressed.

In particular, expanding services to the large numbers of the population who are currently inadequately supplied may be an important regulatory goal. In Kenya less than 2 per cent of the rural population are connected to mains electricity (World Bank, 2001, p. 11). In Rwanda there are merely 15 000 telephone lines for 8 million people. In developing countries some two billion people lack access to adequate sanitation and electricity, one billion lack access to clean water, and a half of the world's population has never used a telephone (Gray, 2001, p. 1). Therefore, arguably the effectiveness of economic regulation is, at least in part, appropriately assessed in developing countries by results in terms of an improvement in the scope and quality of services provided. This, in turn, implies the promotion of large-scale investment in system expansion. But, as Bayliss (2002, p. 11) concludes for developing economies: 'The usual pattern with electricity and water privatisation is a rapid expansion in the level of billing and installation of meters [to capture non-payers]. Increasing connections is a lesser priority and investing in the network infrastructure is at the bottom of the list.' In the province of Tucumen in Argentina a water concession necessitated sharp price increases that triggered a non-payment campaign by water users. Provincial elections and a financial crisis for the concessionaire led to difficult negotiations on a new tariff structure to help the poor and the case ended in international arbitration. In Zimbabwe, in 1999, the UK firm Biwater withdrew from a planned water project because it discovered that consumers would be too poor to pay the tariffs necessary to reach the company's profit target.

AN EVIDENCE-BASED APPROACH TO ANALYSING REGULATION IN DEVELOPING ECONOMIES

The discussion applying the economics of regulation literature to the specific example of developing countries does suggest that the main propositions from the literature can be usefully applied when researching regulation in developing economies. This section of the chapter builds on this discussion by detailing an analytical framework for studying regulation in developing countries.

Developing countries are heterogeneous and therefore any methodology needs to combine rigour with sufficient flexibility to incorporate the differing situations facing developing economies. The approach proposed here is rooted in a well-developed and respected theoretical literature, the economics of regulation, but uses the experiences of developing countries to refine and develop the theory, through an iterative process, so as to ensure that its detail is relevant and thorough. The methodology is intended to be valuable both for *ex ante* and *ex post* regulatory analyses; that is to say both when researching proposed regulations in developing countries and when reviewing existing regulatory regimes (it can therefore be linked to 'regulatory impact assessment' in policy-making), Kirkpatrick and Parker (2003). The aim is the gradual development of a rigorous analysis of regulation directly applicable to the challenges and circumstances of a low income economy which is meaningful in terms of lesson drawing (Rose, 1993).

The main propositions from the economics of regulation literature are incorporated into defined stages of a framework, in which particular attributes of each regulatory regime are assessed in terms of efficiency and effectiveness criteria (Figure 4.1). The research process goes through various stages involving an assessment of the regulatory goals, an assessment of the institutional context, an assessment of information asymmetries and their significance for regulatory procedures and processes, and an assessment of the scope for effective competition. This leads to conclusions on both regulatory capacity and policy.

In more detail, using this methodology would involve, first, an assessment of the regulatory goals and the weightings attaching to social goals as well as economic ones, leading to a relevant definition of regulatory effectiveness and efficiency for assessing the performance of regulation in a particular context. Second, an assessment of the institutional context within which the regulatory regime is embedded, including an assessment of (a) the political, economic and cultural values that either sustain or frustrate the intended regulation; (b) the scope for, or likelihood of, maintaining regulatory independence in the face of the forces for regulatory and political capture in a country; and (c) the extent of regulatory commitment, leading on to an assessment of regulatory credibility. Third, a review of the likelihood and extent of any information asymmetries, so as to develop an analysis of the consequences of asymmetry for the design of the most appropriate regulatory procedures and processes. Fourth, an assessment of the scope for competition, including the existence of a developed capital market and competition policy, so as to help define both the need for regulation and the relevant forms it should take. The fifth stage involves developing conclusions about the extent of regulatory capacity in a country and the policy implications, including the existing skills base and personnel and training needs. This stage would involve a consideration of mitigation and enhancing issues that could improve the outcomes. The result feeds back into the analysis with the aim of producing an improved outcome (in this sense this stage is similar to a 'regulatory impact assessment', see Lee, 2002).

Although, as drawn, Figure 4.1 may imply a linear process of analysis, albeit with feedbacks at each stage, it is not intended that the process should necessarily be linear. In the case of a particular country there may be grounds for altering the ranking of the stages to reflect research needs. However, what

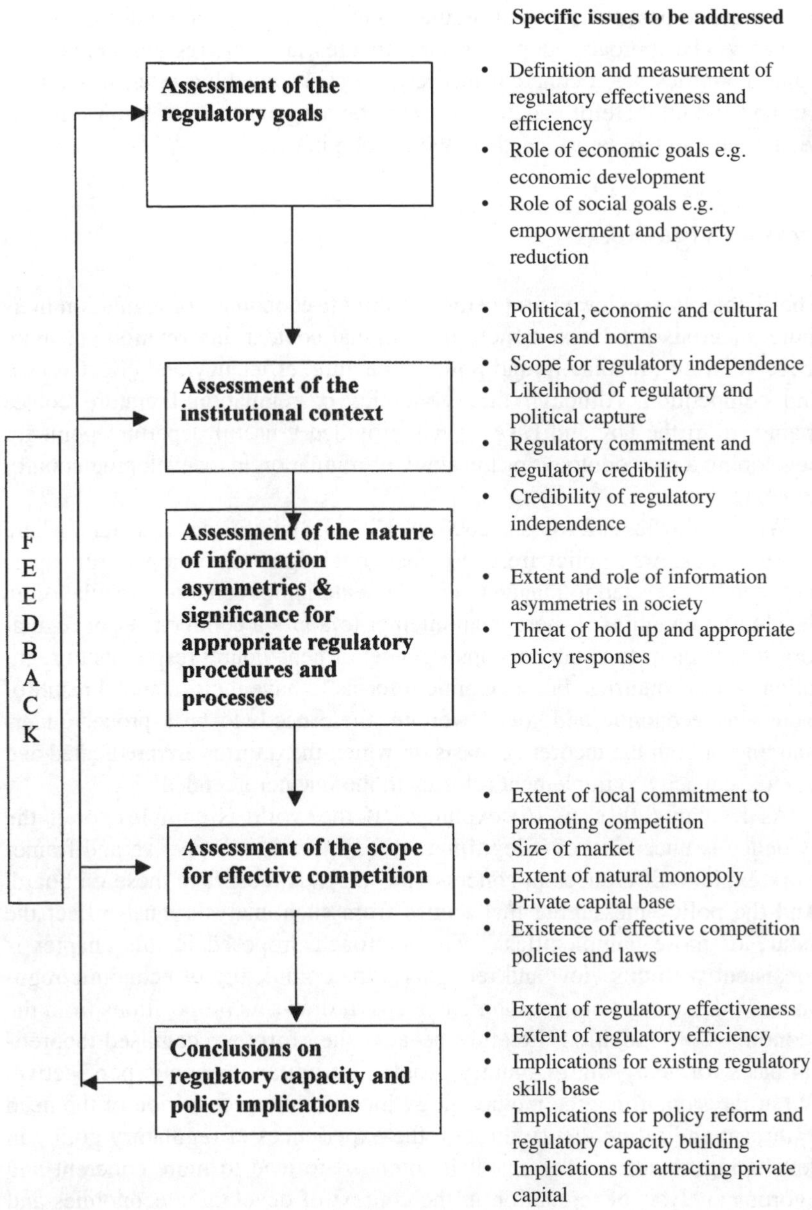

Figure 4.1 Framework for the study of regulation

the proposed research methodology is intended to do is to produce a systematic evidence-based analysis of regulation in developing economies grounded in theory. The approach adopted ensures that research into regulation in developing countries has a coherent theoretical base, something often missing so far, and should therefore contribute to the better generation of knowledge on regulation and regulatory needs in the developing world.

CONCLUSIONS

The chapter has reviewed propositions from the economics of regulation literature under six headings, namely institutional context, information asymmetries, 'hold up', regulatory and political capture, efficiency and effectiveness and competition. Although the economics of regulation literature comes mainly from the UK and USA, it has provided a useful departure point for developing a methodology for the study of regulation in a developing country context.

What Dolowitz and Marsh (2000, p. 17) call 'uninformed transfer', where a country borrows a policy from elsewhere but is ignorant of how it truly operates, can be expected to plague the implementation of economic regulation in developing countries if there is an attempt to apply a common set of regulatory standards or to assume a consistent set of behavioural responses to regulation across countries. For economic reforms to have their intended result of increasing economic and social welfare, there needs to be a proper understanding of both the theoretical basis on which the reforms are predicated and of local capacity to implement reforms in the manner intended.

As Kanbur (2001, p. 16) explains: 'If the world is complex, or if the evidence is uncertain, or if legitimate differences in perspective and framework explain differences in conclusions, analysis must take these on board. And the policy messaging that comes from such analysis must reflect the nature of those complexities.'[1] The approach proposed in this chapter is consistent with this view and recognises the complexity of economic regulation in the context of development needs. It draws on propositions from the economics of regulation literature because they form a recognised theoretical basis for analysing regulatory problems from an economic perspective. But at the same time, the methodology incorporates recognition of the need to inform and refine theory through the experiences of regulatory policy in developing countries. The result is intended to lead to more coherent and rigorous analysis of regulation in the context of developing economies and through this a symbiosis of theory and practice. In turn this should lead to improved regulatory capacity and ultimately, to enhanced regulatory policy outcomes.

NOTE

1. Kanbur was Director for the World Bank's Development Report on Poverty until he resigned in May 2000.

REFERENCES

Allen, D.W. (1991), 'What are transaction costs?', *Research in Law and Economics*, **14**, 1–18.

Asian Development Bank (2000), *Asian Development Report*, Manila: ADB.

Averch, H. and Johnson, L.L. (1962), 'Behavior of the firm under regulatory constraint', *American Economic Review*, **52**, 1052–69.

Bailey, E.E. (1973), *Economic Theory of Regulatory Constraint*, Lexington, DC: Heath.

Baldwin, R. and Cave, M. (1999), *Understanding Regulation: Theory, Strategy and Practice*, Oxford: Oxford University Press.

Bayliss, K. (2001), 'Does privatisation have a place in a poverty reduction strategy?', paper presented at the DSA Conference on Different Poverty, Different Policies, 10–12 September, University of Manchester.

Bayliss, K. (2002), 'Privatisation and poverty: the distributional impact of utility privatisation', Working Paper No.16, Manchester: Centre on Regulation and Competition, University of Manchester.

Birdsall, N. and Nellis, J. (2002), 'Winners and losers: assessing the distributional impact of privatization', Working Paper No. 6, Washington, DC: Center for Global Development.

Bitrán, E., Estache, A., Guasch, J.L. and Serra, P. (1999), 'Privatizing and regulating Chile's utilities, 1974–2000: successes, failures and outstanding challenges', in G. Perry and D.M. Leipziger (eds), *Chile – Relevant Policy Lessons and Emerging Challenges*, Washington, DC: World Bank Institute.

Blau, R.T. and Harris, R.G. (1992), 'Strategic uses of regulation: the case of line-of-business restrictions in the US communications industry', *Research in Corporate Social Performance and Policy*, **13**, 161–89.

Blundell, J. and Robinson, C. (2000), *Regulation without the State . . . The Debate Continues*, Readings 52, London: Institute of Economic Affairs.

Brenner, S.N. (1980), 'Corporate political activity: an exploratory study in a developing industry', *Research in Corporate Social Performance and Policy*, **2**, 197–236.

Brownbridge, M. and Kirkpatrick, C. (2000), 'Financial regulation in developing countries: survey article', *Journal of Development Studies*, **37** (1), 1–24.

Campbell-White, O. and Bhatia, A. (1998), *Directions in Development: Privatization in Africa*, Washington, DC: World Bank.

Cave, M. and Stern, J. (1998), 'Regulatory institutions and regulatory policy for economies in transition', in C. Robinson (ed.), *Regulating Utilities: Understanding the Issues*, London: Institute of Economic Affairs.

Cook, P. (1999), 'Privatization and utility regulation in developing countries: the lessons so far', *Annals of Public and Cooperative Economics*, **70** (4), 549–87.

Cook, P. and Uchida, Y. (2001), 'Privatisation and economic growth in developing countries', mimeo, Manchester: IDPM, University of Manchester.

Craig, J. (2000), 'Evaluating privatisation in Zambia: a tale of two processes', *Review of African Political Economy*, **85**, 375–86.
Craig, J. (2001), 'Privatisation and indigenous ownership: evidence from Africa', Working Paper No. 13, Manchester: Centre on Regulation and Competition, University of Manchester.
Crew, M.A. and Kleindorfer, P.R. (1996), 'Incentive regulation in the United Kingdom and the United States: some lessons', *Journal of Regulatory Economics*, **9**, 211–25.
DFID (2000), *Eliminating World Poverty: Making Globalisation Work for the Poor*, London: Department for International Development.
Dinar, A. (2000), 'Political economy of water pricing reforms', in A. Dinar (ed.), *The Political Economy of Water Pricing Reforms*, Oxford: World Bank and Oxford University Press.
Dolowitz, D.P. and Marsh, D. (2000), 'Learning from abroad: the role of policy transfer in contemporary policy making', *Governance: An International Journal of Public Administration*, **13** (1), 5–24.
Duckett, J. (2001), 'Bureaucrats in business, Chinese style: the lessons of market reform and state entrepreneurialism in the People's Republic of China', *World Development*, **29** (1), 23–37.
Estache, A., Gomez-Lobo, A. and Leipziger, D. (2000), 'Utility privatization and the needs of poor in Latin America: have we learned enough to get it right?', World Bank Policy Research Working Paper 2407, Washington, DC: World Bank.
Financial Times (2001), 'India urged to cut red tape to boost growth', 7 September, p. 10.
Gale, J. and Buchholz, R.A. (1987), 'The political pursuit of competitive advantage: what business can gain from government', in A. Marcus, A.M. Kaufman and D.R. Beam (eds), *Business Strategy and Public Policy: Perspectives from Industry and Academia*, New York: Quorum Books.
Granovetter, M. (1985), 'Economic action and social structure: the problem of embeddedness', *American Journal of Sociology*, **91** (3), 481–510.
Gray, P. (2001), 'Private participation in infrastructure: a review of the evidence', mimeo, Washington, DC: World Bank.
Grossman, S.J. and Hart, O.D. (1986), 'The costs and benefits of ownership: a theory of vertical and lateral integration', *Journal of Political Economy*, **94** (4), 691–719.
Guasch, J.L. and Hahn, R.W. (1999), 'The costs and benefits of regulation: implications for developing countries', *World Bank Research Observer*, **14** (1), 137–58.
Gupta, J.P. and Sravat, A.K. (1998), 'Development and project financing of private power projects in developing countries: a case study of India', *International Journal of Project Management*, **16** (2), 99–105.
Hay, D.A. and Morris, D.J. (1991), *Industrial Economics and Organization: Theory and Evidence*, Oxford: Oxford University Press.
Hayek, F.A. (1945), 'The use of knowledge in society', *American Economic Review*, **35**, 519–30.
Joskow, P.L. (ed.) (2000), *Economic Regulation*, Cheltenham: Edward Elgar.
Kahn, A.E. (1988), *The Economics of Regulation: Principles and Institutions*, Cambridge, MA: MIT Press.
Kanbur, R. (2001), 'Economic policy, distribution and poverty: the nature of disagreements', mimeo, Cornell University.
Kerf, M., Gray, R., Irwin, T., Levesque, C. and Taylor, R. (1998), 'Concessions for Infrastructure: A Guide to their Design and Award', Technical Paper No. 399, Washington, DC: World Bank.

Kerf, M. and Smith, W. (1996), 'Privatizing Africa's infrastructure: promise and challenge', World Bank Technical Paper No. 337, Africa Region Series, Washington, DC: World Bank.

Kirkpatrick, C. and Parker, D. (2003), 'Regulatory impact assessment: its potential for use in developing countries', mimeo, Centre for Regulation and Competition, IDPM, University of Manchester.

Kirzner, I.M. (1997), *How Markets Work: Disequilibrium, Entrepreneurship and Discovery*, Hobart Paper No. 133, London: Institute of Economic Affairs.

Laffont, J.-J. (1999), *Incentives and the Political Economy of Regulation*, Oxford: Oxford University Press.

Laffont, J.-J. and Tirole, J. (1993), *A Theory of Incentives in Procurement and Regulation*, Cambridge, MA: MIT Press.

Laffont, J.-J. and Tirole, J. (2000), *Competition in Telecommunications*, Cambridge, MA: MIT Press.

Lal, D. (1999), *Unfinished Business: India in the World Economy*, Oxford: Oxford University Press.

Lanyi, A. (2000), 'The institutional basis of economic reforms', in S. Kähkönen and A. Lanyi (eds), *Institutions, Incentives and Economic Reforms in India*, New Delhi and London: Sage Publications.

Lee, C. (2002), 'Telecommunications reform in Malaysia', Working Paper No. 20, Manchester: Centre on Regulation and Competition, University of Manchester.

Levy, B. and Spiller, P.T. (1994), 'The institutional foundations of regulatory commitment: a comparative analysis of telecommunications regulation', *Journal of Law, Economics and Organization*, **10** (2), 201–46.

Lodge, M. and Stirton, L. (2002), 'Globalisation and regulatory autonomy in small developing states: the case of Jamaican telecommunications reform', Working Paper No. 15, Manchester: Centre on Regulation and Competition, University of Manchester.

Majone, G. (1994), 'The emergence of the regulatory state in Europe', *West European Politics*, **17**, 77–101.

Majone, G. (1997), 'From the positive to the regulatory state', *Journal of Public Policy*, **17** (2), 139–67.

Martin, S. and Parker, D. (1997), *The Impact of Privatisation: Ownership and Corporate Performance in the UK*, London: Routledge.

Megginson, W.L. and Netter, J.M. (2001), 'From state to market: a survey of empirical studies on privatization', *Journal of Economic Literature*, **39** (2), 321–89.

Mitchell, W.C. (1988), *Government As It Is*, Hobart Paper 109, London: Institute of Economic Affairs.

Newbery, D. (1999), *Privatization, Restructuring and Regulation of Network Industries*, Cambridge, MA: MIT Press.

Niskanen, W.A. Jr (1971), *Bureaucracy and Representative Government*, Chicago: Aldine.

Noll, R. (1999), 'Telecommunications reform in developing countries', Working Paper 99–10, AEI-Brookings Joint Centre for Regulatory Studies.

North, D.C. (1990), *Institutions, Institutional Change and Economic Performance*, Cambridge: Cambridge University Press.

North, D.C. (1991), 'Institutions', *Journal of Economic Perspectives*, **5** (Winter), 97–112.

Parker, D. (1999a), 'Policy transfer and policy inertia: privatisation in Taiwan', *Asia Pacific Business Review*, **6** (2), 1–10.

Parker, D. (1999b), 'Regulating public utilities: lessons from the UK', *International Review of Administrative Sciences*, **65**, 117–31.

Parker, D., Kirkpatrick, C. and Zhang, Y-F. (2002), 'Electricity sector reform in developing countries: an econometric assessment of the effects of privatisation, competition and regulation', Centre on Regulation and Competition Working Paper No. 31, IDPM, University of Manchester.

Peltzman, S. (1976), 'Toward a more general theory of regulation', *Journal of Law and Economics*, **14** (August), 109–48.

Picciotto, S. (1999), 'Introduction: what rules for the world economy?', in S. Picciotto and R. Mayne (eds), *Regulating International Business: Beyond Liberalization*, London: Macmillan.

Pongsiri, N. (2001), 'Regulation and public private partnerships', Working Paper No. 12, Manchester: Centre on Regulation and Competition, University of Manchester.

Ramamurti, R. (1996), *Privatizing Monopolies: Lessons from the Telecommunications and Transport Sectors in Latin America*, Baltimore and London: John Hopkins Press University.

Reagan, M.D. (1987), *Regulation: The Politics of Policy*, Boston: Little Brown.

Rohdewohld, R. (1993), 'Deregulating the public sector: privatisation and commercialisation in Nigeria', *Annales de l'économie publique sociale et cooperative*, **64** (4), 501–30.

Rose, R. (1993), *Lesson-drawing in Public Policy*, Chatham, NJ: Chatham House.

Saha, S.K. and Parker, D. (eds) (2002), *Globalisation and Sustainable Development in Latin America: Perspectives on the New Economic Order*, Cheltenham: Edward Elgar.

Sappington, D.E. and Stiglitz, J.E. (1987), 'Privatization, information and incentives', *Journal of Policy Analysis & Management*, **6** (4), 567–82.

Schmitz, P.W. (2001), 'The hold-up problem and incomplete contracts: a survey of recent topics in contract theory', *Bulletin of Economic Research*, **53** (1), 1–17.

Schwella, E. (2002), 'Regulation and competition in South Africa', Working Paper No. 18, Manchester: Centre on Regulation and Competition, University of Manchester.

Shaffer, B. (1995), 'Firm level responses to government regulation: theoretical and research approaches', *Journal of Management*, **21** (3), 495–515.

Shapiro, C. and Willig, R.D. (1990), 'Economic rationales for the scope of privatization', in E.N. Suleiman and J. Waterbury, *The Political Economy of Public Sector Reform and Privatization*, Boulder, CO: Westview Press, reprinted in D. Parker (ed.) (2001) *Privatisation and Corporate Performance*, Cheltenham: Edward Elgar.

Sidak, J.G. and Spulber, D.F. (1998), *Deregulatory Takings and the Regulatory Contract: The Competitive Transformation of Network Industries in the United States*, Cambridge: Cambridge University Press.

Smith, W. (1997), *Utility Regulators: The Independence Debate*, Viewpoint 127, Washington, DC: World Bank.

Smith, W. (2000), *Regulating Infrastructure for the Poor: Perspectives on Regulatory Design*, mimeo, World Bank, Washington, DC.

Spiller, P. (1996), 'Institutions and commitment', *Industrial and Corporate Change*, **5** (2), 421–52.

Stelzer, I. (1988), 'Britain's newest import: America's regulatory experience', *Oxford Review of Economic Policy*, **4** (2), 68–79.

Stern, J. and Holder, S. (1999), 'Regulatory governance: criteria for assessing the performance of regulatory systems. An application to infrastructure industries in the developing countries of Asia', *Utilities Policy*, **8**, 33–50.

Stigler, G. (1971), 'The theory of economic regulation', *Bell Journal of Economics and Management*, **2** (Spring), 3–21.
Stiglitz, J. (1998), 'Private uses of public interests: incentives and institutions', *Journal of Economic Perspectives*, **12** (2), 3–22.
Tangri, R. (1999), *The Politics of Patronage in Africa*, Oxford: James Currey.
Tangri, R. and Mwenda, A. (2001), 'Corruption and cronyism in Uganda's privatization in the 1990s', *African Affairs*, **100**, 117–33.
Theobold, R. (1990), *Competition, Development and Under-development*, Basingstoke: Macmillan.
Torp, J.E. and Rekve, P. (1998), 'Privatisation in developing countries: lessons to be learnt from the Mozambican case', *Transformation*, **36**, 73–92.
UNCTAD (1995), *Comparative Experiences with Privatization: Policy Insights and Lessons Learned*, New York and Geneva: United Nations Conference on Trade and Development/United Nations.
Viscusi, W.K., Vernon, J.M. and Harrington, J.E. Jr (2000), *Economics of Regulation and Antitrust*, 3rd edn, Cambridge, MA: MIT Press.
Von Der Fehr, N.-H.M. (2000), 'Who should be responsible for competition policy in regulated industries', in E. Hope (ed.), *Competition Policy Analysis*, London: Routledge.
Wallsten, S. (2001), 'An econometric analysis of telecom competition, privatization and regulation in Africa and Latin America', *Journal of Industrial Economics*, **49** (1), 1–20.
Williams, R. and Theobald, R. (eds) (2000), *Corruption in the Developing World*, Cheltenham: Edward Elgar.
Williamson, O.E. (1985), *The Economic Institutions of Capitalism: Firms, Markets, and History*, Cambridge: Cambridge University Press.
World Bank (1995), *Bureaucrats in Business: The Economics and Politics of Government Ownership,* Washington, DC and Oxford: World Bank and Oxford University Press.
World Bank (2001), 'Private sector development strategy – directions for the World Bank group', mimeo, Washington, DC: World Bank.
World Bank (2003), *Global Economic Prospects and the Developing Countries*, Washington, DC: World Bank.
Yarrow, G. (1999), 'A theory of privatization, or why bureaucrats are still in business', *World Development*, **27** (1), 157–68.

5. Trade and competition policy at the WTO: issues for developing countries

Peter Holmes[1]

IS THERE A NEED FOR GLOBAL RULES?

Concerns about competition and trade have a long pedigree, back to Adam Smith who devoted a large fraction of the *Wealth of Nations* to the evil consequences of international trading monopolies such as the East India Company, which he said impoverished both Indian sellers and British consumers. The 1948 Havana Charter of the abortive International Trade Organization (ITO) included a requirement on members to police international restrictive business practices:

> Each Member shall take appropriate measures and shall co-operate with the Organization to prevent, on the part of private or public commercial enterprises, business practices affecting international trade which restrain competition, limit access to markets, or foster monopolistic control, whenever such practices have harmful effects on the expansion of production or trade and interfere with the achievement of any of the other objectives set forth in Article 1. (UNCTAD, 1948, Article 46, para. 1)

There was provision for the ITO secretariat to investigate cases and make recommendations to members. Of course the Havana Charter was not adopted as a whole, only the chapter on trade in goods which became the GATT. Discussions continued in other fora about the trade and competition interface, at the GATT, the OECD and UNCTAD. This work perhaps slightly obscured the fact that the heart of GATT did in fact touch on competition law. Article III of GATT requires non-discrimination (national treatment) in all domestic laws, regulations and taxes that may affect trade. This sweeping obligation was largely neglected by trade policy analysts before the WTO was created in 1994 because GATT obligations were not easily enforceable before the creation of the WTO dispute settlement mechanism.

As trade liberalisation advanced and the WTO was created, attention came to focus more on the 'non-border' barriers that might affect trade. The Uruguay Round brought regulatory barriers such as food safety and service rules into the WTO system, and more importantly armed the DS system to address other rules that might affect trade and which Article III could touch.

The topic 'trade and competition policy' was put on the WTO agenda by the Singapore Ministerial meeting in 1996. Along with a series of other 'new issues' the decision was taken to set up a working group to consider this interface.

DO WE NEED ANY FURTHER AGREEMENTS?

A fundamental requirement to justify a multilateral agreement on competition must be that, in some senses, anti-competitive practices originating in one jurisdiction may have spillover effects in the global economy as may national policies towards them. Examples include the following:

- worldwide market sharing arrangements;
- export cartels based in one country affecting consumers in another;
- import cartels operating to exclude foreign suppliers, or other private barriers to entry;
- mergers which may occur in competitive markets at home but where parties may have substantial market shares in other parts of the world;
- cross-border abuses of a dominant position in another country, including abuses of intellectual property rights.

Identification of a problem does not necessarily indicate a solution however.

It does not follow that the existence of spillovers automatically means that a WTO agreement could actually solve the problems created. To justify agreement at the WTO we need to show that a problem exists, that collective action could solve or mitigate it (at low cost) and that the WTO is the right forum. I suggest that we can make such a case but each step is separate.

The International Dimension of Antitrust vs Market Access

Two different issues arise in the debates about trade and competition. Restrictive business practices in one territory may exclude firms from another jurisdiction, giving rise to a *market access* problem, for example through control of distribution arrangements by local firms. This deprives consumers of choice but is likely to be felt most acutely by excluded producers. The other dimension of the problem is where the distortion in pattern of trade is the result of a deliberate strategic choice by exporting firms, whether in the form of a unilateral abuse or in agreement with firms in the importing market.

International antitrust concerns primarily relate to the effect on consumer welfare of agreements or acts by dominant firms or cartels. They may, for example, charge excessive prices for exports. A dominant firm or cartel may also use power in one market to leverage its position in another, such as by predatory behaviour.

The antitrust remedy is likely to be different from that for market access. Indeed, the dynamics are sometimes the opposite. In the case of market access, the problem is that the authority for the market in which the anti-competitive behaviour occurs (i.e. the exporting country) is unwilling to act, while the authority that wishes to act (the importer) has no jurisdiction. With antitrust the problem is that the authority of the economy experiencing the anti-competitive behaviour (i.e. the affected importer) has jurisdiction but is unable in practice to, while the competition authority in the exporting country has the means but is usually unwilling to do so!

Evidently, very different and complementary multilateral rules would be needed to deal with these two situations. And this dichotomy has direct relevance for policy because there is a tendency for developing countries to focus on one cause and the industrialised countries on the other. Developing countries are mainly concerned about abuses by northern exporters, while the EU and the USA worry about import cartels and the like.

The cross-border effect in the export cartel is failure by the home jurisdiction to act against the anti-competitive behaviour of 'its firms' in another market. Consider also the case of international mergers, which pose problems that were not foreseen when the GATT was created in 1947. A merger between two firms may be allowed by the competition authorities in the 'home' market because there remains plenty of domestic competition. But this may not be true of the markets in which their subsidiaries operate. There, the new combined entity may have a dominant position.

National competition authorities have as their objective only the welfare of their own jurisdiction. Thus, while the EU and the USA take into account in their decisions the effects on their economies of actions taken elsewhere, they do not consider the effect on foreign markets of actions by their firms; these are captured if at all only as a corollary of regulation of activities on the domestic market. Indeed, it is not unusual for competition laws specifically to exclude sectors of activity where foreigners may be the main victims of anti-competitive practice. Shipping conferences, for example, have traditionally been exempted, and many jurisdictions exempt export cartels either explicitly or implicitly. But many commentators have observed that even if there were no such exemptions the EU or the USA governments could not easily prosecute their own firms for harm done to consumers elsewhere without further legal changes.

If governments in the parent firm's home country cannot act, why cannot those in countries where the affiliates operate? The answer is they face a major practical problem. It is unlikely that governments in the affected country will be able to get the evidence needed to pursue infringers even if they have effective laws. The capacity of competition authorities to assess adequately all the factors in transnational mergers may well be limited even if there is willingness to act. The increasing number of international mergers and strategic alliances where the authorities are forced to rely on whatever information the parties supply clearly raises the question of the need for enhanced cooperation.

But if we accept that the problem is a real one, further questions arise before we can be confident that it is one that can be resolved by some sort of multilateral arrangement but cannot be resolved without one:

- what advantages does a multilateral agreement have over other forms of cross-border cooperation?
- if there is to be a multilateral agreement where should it be located?

Evidence on Anti-competitive Behaviour

There is indeed powerful evidence that cross-border cartels are active and are not being adequately policed. There is a long history of global cartels some of which have been investigated and some of which have not: we have seen the heavy electrical equipment cartel, the aluminium cartel, the vitamins cartel, the lysine cartel, and the international soda ash cartel.

In the 1990s the United States (US) Department of Justice became very active investigating and prosecuting cartels in industries such as vitamins, steel, and animal feeds. They uncovered evidence on a massive scale of global violations. The citric acid and lysine cartels involved global markets of around $2 billion in the late 1990s. These developments prompted the Department of Justice to set up an International Competition Policy Advisory Committee (ICPAC). Its report (ICPAC, 2000) found that cartels existed on a large scale.

Extensive work at the World Bank carried out and reviewed by Evenett et al. (2000) suggests that nearly 7 per cent of imports into developing countries were in sectors where firms had been found by the US authorities to be involved in cartels. Evenett and Clarke (forthcoming) show that the impact of the international vitamins cartel prosecuted by the US authorities appears to have been more serious in those developing countries that had no competition law.

Reasons for Intervening

As we have noted, it is very important to distinguish the two different reasons for attempting to curb anti-competitive activity because WTO members attribute different weight to them. They may involve market access, that is to say where private barriers to entry have been created by local firms against the will of certain foreign suppliers. Or they may involve pure international antitrust issues, where collusive or monopolistic behaviour by all firms is directed explicitly against consumers. In both cases consumers lose out, but a solution that 'shares' markets may satisfy exporters, although it does nothing for consumers. In neither case (although for different reasons) will uncoordinated action by domestic competition authorities solve the problem.

Market access

Anti-competitive collusion in a domestic market may be a very effective way to keep out imports, especially if distributors and wholesalers are involved. US policymakers and business circles expressed great frustration at US exporters' failed attempts to gain access to the Japanese market. From the mid-1980s onwards, the USA argued that the Japanese authorities had tolerated their own firms engaging in anti-competitive business practices, in particular through vertical integration between producers and distributors. A vast legal and economic literature emerged on whether Japan's markets were relatively more closed than other nations' markets, with little agreement emerging (Evenett et al., 2000 survey much of this debate).

In 1957 only Germany had a vigorous domestic competition policy. In the early years of the establishment of the European Common Market (EEC), the need to ensure market access led to the establishment of a supra-national competition policy with the goal of preventing private actions causing distortions to trade between member states. The Rome Treaty gave the European Commission powers to intervene directly and control anti-competitive behaviour by firms. This addressed the problem identified in the Havana Charter, but went further than the Charter in giving the executive the authority to act, not merely to report and recommend.

The jurisdiction of the European Commission was, and strictly speaking still is, limited to practices affecting cross-border trade. The EEC did not create a domestic competition regime for its members. At that time market access considerations led to a focus on the interests of exporters rather than consumers, but the effect has been positive for consumers as well as producers.

At the global level we have more of a problem. The governments of exporting states exercise no jurisdiction in the importer's market, and even though the 'effects doctrine' allows the importing country to claim jurisdiction over foreign firms whose actions affect it, they may have no ability to act. The EU has been able to attack alleged cartels by foreign firms in the 'Woodpulp' case and has also claimed jurisdiction over mergers of US based firms operating in the EU. But in practice, it is only the largest jurisdictions who have leverage to get the evidence and secure the compliance needed to really apply the effects doctrine. In the 1990s some suggestions were made, for example by Fikentscher and Ulrich (1995) for a multilateral agency to act directly in competition cases, but these were resoundingly rejected. Any international agreement would have to be between states and their competition authorities.

It is not surprising that when the view emerged that inadequate competition policy enforcement could undermine the expected market access gains from trade reforms, some began to argue that international disciplines on *national* competition policies were necessary to ensure market access. And it was natural to think of this taking place within the WTO: bargaining over market access concessions in multilateral trade negotiations has been the time honoured and highly effective means of lowering border barriers. But by 1996 the USA had come to the conclusion that it could use its own unilateral and bilateral instruments to achieve these ends. Consequently the demand that trade and competition should be on the post-Singapore WTO agenda came essentially from the European Union (EU).

WHAT IS THE CURRENT LEGAL POSITION?

Curiously enough a detailed examination of the current state of trade law leads us to the somewhat paradoxical case that one of the most powerful reasons for wishing to see an agreement at the WTO on competition policy is that competition rules are indeed covered already but in a haphazard and unclear way, and unless there is negotiation over what the obligations really mean, we risk a messy process where the dispute settlement body may be asked to define the rules in costly litigation, as in the notorious 'Kodak Fuji' case. We find in fact that there are two alternative motivations for addressing competition issues explicitly at the WTO. The minimalist agenda says: WTO obligations exist already but are imprecise and incoherent. Let us be more precise and consistent, and if necessary narrow down the meaning. The other is to say that WTO rules are currently too weak and we need a stronger and perhaps broader set of rules.

In fact, although the GATT 1947 made no explicit reference to private business conduct, its very general provisions almost certainly cover competition laws. As we noted, GATT Article III calls for 'national treatment' for all goods that have passed the frontier; it thus contains a general ban on any domestic rule or application of regulation in a manner that discriminates against imported products, for example tougher safety standards for foreign goods. The wording of Article III indicates that it was most obviously designed to deal with discriminatory taxation and basic quantitative restrictions, but the text refers to 'all laws, regulations and requirements affecting their internal sale, offering for sale, purchase, transportation, distribution or use'. The result is that if the way a country operates its competition policy discriminates against imports, then this becomes potentially actionable. The Appellate Body in its ruling on Japan – Taxes on Alcoholic Beverages (1996) stated firmly:

> The Article III national treatment obligation is a general prohibition on the use of internal taxes and other internal regulatory measures so as to afford protection to domestic production.

With the introduction of the system of binding dispute settlement since 1994, it now does matter exactly what the wording of the GATT and WTO agreements implies for competition issues. The OECD (1999) confirms that Article III could be used in this context. It must be remembered that Article III only covers discrimination by nationality of goods, not firms, and its equivalent in the GATT only refers to scheduled services. Significantly, the Appellate Body has ruled that the national treatment obligation currently applies to both *de jure* and *de facto* discrimination. This means that it is a violation of the GATT to have rules that are identical for home and foreign goods but which in practice are much harder for imports to meet.

Another element in the GATT is Article XXIII – the so-called 'non-violation article'. Article XXIII was for long an obscure and, until the 1990s, ignored article. It provided for dispute settlement in cases where it is alleged that a GATT signatory has introduced new laws or measures which, while not explicitly forbidden by the rules, nevertheless act so as to 'nullify or impair' elements of the trade liberalisation they agreed to in their GATT commitments: it is similar to Article III but is much harder to invoke. (It was used without success by the US to claim Japanese competition rules were unfair in the 'Kodak Fuji' case: but whereas under Article III any discrimination is a violation, under Article XXIII there has to be proof of 'injury'.)

Another interesting provision is the Uruguay Round agreement on safeguards (Article XIX) , the wording of which would explicitly outlaw industry to industry 'voluntary export restraint' agreements. The problem here is that such arrangements are in many cases already illegal under the national competition laws of importing countries, but the authorities often choose not to act, and there is room for a stronger obligation to do so.

GATT Article XVII authorises contracting parties to maintain state trading enterprises, even monopolies, so long as they do not discriminate between home and foreign goods in their purchases and sales. Article II requires that any trading monopolies authorised by the state must not restrict sales of imports in a manner inconsistent with tariff commitments. GATT obligations, dealing with *goods*, cannot require a state to open its trading sector, a service industry, to foreign competition, except where a specific offer to do so has been made under the General Agreement on Trade in Services (GATS).

Interestingly, the GATS does in fact incorporate a form of words recommended by a 1960s working group for adoption with respect to trade in goods. Articles 8 and 9 of the GATS lay down in very general terms an obligation that is not far removed from Article 46(1) of the Havana Charter. Article 8 requires that where a country has agreed to open up part of a service sector to trade, a supplier who retains a monopoly in a related market must not 'abuse its monopoly' when dealing in the unprotected market. Article 9 further says:

> Members recognise that certain business practices of goods suppliers may restrain competition and thereby restrict trade in services. Each member shall, at the request of any other member, enter into consultations with a view to eliminating such practices.

In the field of telecommunications the texts are more specific and do provide more detailed grounds for action in the event that a firm supplying a service, not subject to foreign competition under the GATS schedule of its government, leverages its market power into a supposedly open market segment. The GATS telecoms negotiations in fact continued after the end of the Uruguay Round as coverage of liberalisation was extended to basic voice telecommunications. In order to implement the commitments in the GATS to prevent foreclosure by dominant suppliers a 'reference paper' was agreed in 1997, which spelled out in more detail what these obligations entailed, including cost-based access of new operators to incumbents networks, although the focus is on the rights of competitors rather than users as would be the case in most national competition rules.

The other WTO agreement that makes specific reference to competition policy is the Trade-related Intellectual Property (TRIPs) agreement which requires all WTO members to adopt patent and copyright laws along the lines of developed countries, albeit with transition periods for less developed countries. Critics of the TRIPs agreement argue it gave considerable extra market power above all to pharmaceutical and agrochemical firms, without imposing restraints on potential abuses. However, the TRIPs agreement specifically referred to competition policy. It allows countries to take steps such as compulsory licensing when they can show that an anti-competitive abuse has occurred. It provides an incentive to have a competition law by making compulsory licensing easier when this route is used. It *allow*s the host countries of multinational corporations and importers to act in this way, but it does not *oblige* home countries to require their firms to behave in pro-competitive ways in foreign markets. No explicit mechanisms were established to deal with the information problems that might arise.

A key issue that has arisen is the treatment of parallel imports, vertical restraints and the international exhaustion of intellectual property rights

(IPRs). Some developed countries have argued that WTO rules should prevent countries from allowing unlimited parallel imports. The issue is basically whether a supplier of IPR protected goods, who lawfully sold them in one country, should be able to prevent those goods being sold on into another market. IPR holders frequently assign sole selling rights to their own subsidiaries or agencies, country by country, in a manner that permits international price discrimination, and do not license export sales. Competition law may invalidate such conditions. For example, any product sold in one part of the EU by a manufacturer to a wholesaler anywhere in the EU may be sold again anywhere else in the EU; on the other hand firms have the right to prevent the import into the EU of their branded or otherwise IPR protected goods that have previously been sold outside the EU. This issue is at the heart of the current dispute between South Africa and 39 drugs firms. The 1997 Medicines Act, challenged by pharmaceutical firms, would allow the South African authorities to import into South Africa products legally sold by the manufacturers at lower prices elsewhere, by-passing the official distribution channels. At first the US government backed the drugs firms but it has since acknowledged that the TRIPs agreement (Article 6) does allow member states to adopt their own policies on parallel imports (Maskus and Lahouel, 2000). This is a different issue from the import of products made or sold elsewhere without a licence (e.g. in India). The TRIPs agreement provides for the issuing of compulsory licences under a number of conditions, one of which is that a due-process competition investigation has found an abuse. TRIPs Article 31 (k) states:

> Members are not obliged to apply the conditions set forth in subparagraphs (b) and (f) where such use is permitted to remedy a practice determined after judicial or administrative process to be anti-competitive. The need to correct anti-competitive practices may be taken into account in determining the amount of remuneration in such cases. Competent authorities shall have the authority to refuse termination of authorization if and when the conditions which led to such authorization are likely to recur.

The subparagraphs 31 (b) and (f) mentioned here refer to the requirement, otherwise binding, that any compulsory licensing must be for home consumption, so, for example, ruling out Indian exports to Uganda.

Current WTO discussions are much preoccupied with how to allow compulsory licences for countries that do not have their own pharmaceutical industry. But it is clear that licensing could only work in a situation where prices were well above marginal cost (otherwise it would be cheaper to just buy from the patent holder), in a situation where competition rules come into play.

The weakness of the dispute settlement system of the GATT before the Uruguay Round may well have led policy-makers to underestimate the scope for litigation provisions. Before 1994 GATT contracting parties could refuse to accept a panel decision given against them, so contracting parties could operate their competition rules in whatever way they wished free of the fear that a GATT panel would declare their practice illegal. This assurance is no longer available. There are other provisions in the original GATT, which when combined with the teeth given to them by the WTO Dispute Settlement procedure, could be invoked in a competition case, as it has in Kodak Fuji[2] (where really there appeared to be no factual case to answer) and Mexican telecoms.[3]

WHAT SORT OF NEW AGREEMENT?

For a long time the EU and the US have included competition provisions in bilateral agreements with important partners. The EU has focused on ensuring that its close neighbours incorporate similar provisions to those of the EU on trade and competition into their laws. The US has signed a number of rather far reaching MLATS (Mutual Legal Assistance Treaties). The EU and the US have a rather weaker agreement including what is known as 'positive comity'.

In the late 1990s the EU was criticised (see for example Hoekman and Holmes, 1999) for putting forward an agenda derived from its bilateral trade agreements. The EU was apparently motivated by the wish to ensure that competition policy, or the lack of it, did not obstruct market access by EU firms into developing countries. Partly in the light of such criticisms the EU has since modified its position very substantially. Its papers to the WTO stress the need to have international competition rules that will be favourable to developing countries.

Marsden (2003) has in fact argued that market access is indeed still the underlying logic of the EU position, but EU representatives insist that while they recognise the usefulness of competition policy as a force for liberalisation, it is not the only objective of the EU (see Amarasinha and Garcia-Bercero, 2001).

The EU argues that bilateral arrangements need to be supplemented by multilateral agreements, and that few developing countries can profit from bilateral arrangements. Brazil is one of the few developing countries to have a bilateral arrangement with the US and there is some debate about how useful it has been.

The EU approach at the WTO is to seek an agreement to define core principles of competition policy as they apply to all WTO members. The EU argues that such an agreement would have to cover:

1. A commitment by WTO members to a set of core principles relating to the application of competition law and policy, including transparency,

non-discrimination, and procedural fairness in the application of competition law and/or policy.
2. A parallel commitment to the taking of measures against hardcore cartels.
3. The development of modalities for cooperation between member states on competition policy issues. These would be of a voluntary nature, and could encompass cooperation on national legislation, the exchange of national experience by competition authorities and aspects of enforcement.
4. A commitment to ongoing support for the introduction/strengthening of competition institutions in developing countries, in the framework of the WTO but in cooperation with other interested organisations and national governments.

Points 1 and 2 here would involve obligations, but what is rather interesting about the EU proposition is that, as we have seen, many of these points are already covered by WTO law. The EU position has been summarised thus:

> More specifically, we suggest that WTO negotiations should focus on three key issues:
>
> 1. core principles of domestic competition law and policy;
> 2. co-operation between competition authorities, including both specific cases and more general co-operation and exchange of information; and
> 3. technical assistance and capacity-building for the reinforcement of competition institutions in developing countries. (Mogens, 2001)

The EU is in fact proposing an agreement to define the existing competition provisions including national treatment more precisely; this proposal would probably narrow rather than widen existing obligations because the EU calls for the obligation of national treatment to be confined to their *de jure* wording of laws, not to their *de facto* application, and for derogations to be allowed. Thus the EU could reduce the 'depth' of obligations, but it would also extend the scope of coverage. It wants a comprehensive agreement that would extend such obligations from the their present scope – tradable goods and scheduled services – to all goods and services not covered by an exemption. At the same time the EU is proposing a general framework for voluntary cooperation, which would give some additional rights to those who accepted the redefined obligations. The EU is calling for:

> A competition agreement should include provisions to facilitate voluntary case-specific cooperation in relation to anti-competitive practices having an impact on international trade. Such provisions should apply to three main types of anti-competitive practices: practices that affect international trade (e.g. international cartels); practices that affect market access (e.g. import cartels, exclusionary abuses

> of a dominant position), and, practices with an impact on the trade flows to and from a different geographical market than that in which the practices have been conceived (e.g. export cartels, abuse of a dominant position by a foreign corporation). (WT/WGTCP/W/193, 1 July 2002)

Critics complain that the cooperation provisions are voluntary and that they make no provision for the exchange of confidential information. Case studies suggest however that non-confidential information can be of value: for example the EU has advised South Africa on how it defined the 'relevant market' in a number of cases, thus saving local resources and providing a solid legal footing for proposals for brand divestiture as a condition of merger approval.

Some critics are worried that the EU's proposals would undermine national development strategies by introducing a requirement of non-discrimination against foreign firms.[4] The EU argues that its proposals would apply very specifically to competition law, and most experts agree that it is hard to conceive of circumstances in which you would promote economic development by encouraging anti-competitive abuses by local firms.[5] Another possible concern is the South African commitment in competition law to 'black empowerment'. However, the South African Competition Commissioner and South African legal practitioners, when asked, have argued that the objective of helping their historically disadvantaged people can be achieved by firms of any ownership base.

The problem with the EU proposal is not so much that it imposes excessive burdens on developing countries, but rather that it imposes few if any additional obligations on developed countries.[6] Its requirements on developing countries are very flexible, but they are also very flexible with respect to international cooperation.

So far there are no comprehensive counter proposals. The US was deeply opposed to any negotiations at the WTO until July 2001, when a compromise agreement was made for the Doha agenda. The US now says they are prepared in principle to consider an international agreement but constantly picks holes in the EU proposals, mainly because they are too watered down. Latin American countries, with several years experience of competition regimes and using them to deal with international problems, tend to be more supportive, as is South Africa. Opposition comes mainly from Asia. India, Malaysia and Hong Kong have spoken vociferously against new WTO negotiations. Hong Kong argues its policy of free trade ensures an absence of monopolies and cartels: it argues that the worst anti-competitive practices are those sustained by EU and US anti-dumping rules. India has a long history of supporting calls for international action against international restrictive business practices and has spoken out in favour of the application of the UNCTAD (1980) 'Set of Multilaterally Agreed Equitable Principles and Rules for the Control of Restrictive Business Practices',[7] but it sees no benefit in what the EU is proposing. It already has a competition law and does not need an international agreement to get one, and it is suspicious of the EU's motives. India agrees that international competition issues are a proper matter for the WTO in principle, but argues that the time is not ripe. India's position on this almost wrecked the Doha agreement, but in early 2003 they took a slightly more constructive line. One of their main concerns is that no competition agreement should limit the existing scope for developmental industrial policy; advocates of the EU proposals argue there is no reason why it should do so. Malaysia is particularly suspicious of the risk that national development strategies could be undermined and its spokespersons argue that the EU is only interested in market access for its firms.

The summer of 2003 saw a number of countries modifying their position in the run up to Cancun. Scepticism about overload on developing countries has led to more calls for postponement or even abandonment of negotiations on trade and competition. The UK think tank, the Federal Trust, recently proposed (Federal Trust, 2003) that negotiations on competition policy be started after Cancun but on a separate long-term time horizon.

CONCLUSIONS

This chapter has looked at the debate over trade and competition at the WTO. It has deliberately avoided debates about the impact of competition and competition policy on economic development, but it takes as a premise that on the whole more rather than less competition in international markets would be favourable to developing countries, a viewpoint quite widely shared these days. The debate, therefore, becomes not so much whether this is a sensible aim, but whether a WTO agreement would be a good way to achieve this.

We argue that in principle there is a case for WTO negotiations, if only because there are extensive but unsystematic WTO rules at the moment, which need to be made more precise if we are not to run the risk of their being defined by the Dispute Settlement Body. The kind of obligations proposed by the EU would be very modest, and there is scope for derogations: the EU claims its main concern is these should be transparent and predictable. As we noted, the EU proposals would extend the scope of existing national treatment obligations from just tradable goods and scheduled services into non-traded goods and non-scheduled services. It would also extend the scope in this way of existing obligations on transparency and procedural fairness.

There are genuine fears that the extension of the national treatment obligation might restrict some aspects of development policy, but there has been little evidence that this is likely to be a real problem. The proposals on the table would allow countries to take exemptions from their existing obligations and would leave all other rules on subsidies, for example, unaffected. They would not require countries to open their markets to imports more than at present, except where imports were kept out by private barriers to entry.

The weakness in the EU proposal is rather that the proposals for voluntary cooperation are very weak. Could they deliver more? No competition authority in the world can guarantee that it will fully deal with all the complaints put to it by its own citizens, let alone offer an open-ended commitment to tackle complaints brought by foreign governments. Nevertheless, experience shows that competition agencies are more likely to respond to requests for assistance when there is a formal framework, even a voluntary one, and that the kinds of non-confidential information that can be so exchanged can be of great value. There is still room for debate about whether the WTO is the right forum for such a framework: ultimately the strongest argument for this is that WTO rules already cover competition and further elaboration is needed. And only in the WTO do the developing countries have at least a formal right of veto.

Ultimately however, the fate of any trade and competition deal will depend on bigger issues such as progress on agriculture. If the EU wants a trade and competition deal it will have to offer some further sweeteners within this area, but also it will have to show real flexibility on agriculture.

NOTES

1. This chapter draws heavily on earlier work with Rob Anderson of the WTO and Bernard Hoekman of the World Bank, who are responsible for many of the ideas but not for the remaining and newly introduced errors.
2. See WTO 'Japan – Measures Affecting Distribution Services', WT/DS45/1, 20 June 1996.
3. See WTO 'Mexico – Measures Affecting Telecommunications Services', WT/DS204/3, 18 February 2002.
4. See for example http://www.twnside.org.sg/title/twninfo42.htm.
5. See Evenett (2003) and Consumers International (2003).
6. For more detail on the issue of Special and Differential Treatment in this area see Holmes (2003).
7. http://r0.unctad.org/en/subsites/cpolicy/docs/CPSet/cpset.htm.

REFERENCES

Amarasinha, S. and Garcia-Bercero, I. (2001), 'Moving the trade and competition debate forward', *Journal of International Economic Law*, **4** (3), 481–506.

Consumers International (2003), 'Consumer policy and multilateral competition frameworks', Discussion Paper, March, available at http://www.consumersinternational.org/publications/ViewADocument.asp?regid=135&ID=352&CatID=141&langID=1.

Evenett, S. (2003), 'Competition policy, industrial policy, and a multilateral framework on competition', presentation to WTO Regional Workshop on Trade and Competition, Bangkok, 21–23 January, available at http://www.worldtradeinstitute.ch/index.html?research/publications.htm.

Evenett, S. and Clarke, J. (forthcoming), 'The deterrent effects of national anti-cartel laws: evidence from the international vitamins cartel', WTO Berne, available at http://www.worldtradeinstitute.ch/index.html?research/publications.htm.

Evenett, S and Suslow, V. (2000), 'Private international cartels and their effect on developing countries' (with Margaret Levinstein), background paper for *World Bank's World Development Report 2001*, December 2000.

Federal Trust (2003), 'Putting trade on track: a realistic negotiating agenda for the WTO', available at http://www.cix.co.uk/~fedtrust/wto.htm.

Fikentscher, W. and Ulrich, I. (eds) (1995), *Draft International Antitrust Code*, Baden-Baden: Nomos Verlag.

Hoekman, B. and Holmes, P. (1999), 'Competition policy, developing countries and the WTO', *The World Economy*, 875–93.

Holmes, P. (2003), 'The World Trade Organization and competition policy: implications for developing countries', *IDS Bulletin: Special and Differential Treatment in Terms of Trade*, **34** (2), April.

ICPAC (2000), 'International Competition Policy Advisory Committee to the Attorney General and Assistant Attorney General for Antitrust: final report', Washington, DC: International Competition Policy Advisory Committee, available at http://www.usdoj.gov/atr/icpac/finalreport.htm.

Marsden, P. (2003), *A Competition Policy for the World Trade Organization*, London: Cameron May.

Maskus, K. and Lahouel, M. (2000), 'Competition policy and intellectual property rights in developing countries', *World Economy*, 595–611.

Mogens, P.C. (2001), 'Towards basic rules on trade-related competition policy', speech by Director General, DG TRADE, Brussels, 2 March, available at http://europa.eu.int/comm/trade/speeches_articles/sp_mpc01.htm.

OECD (1999), *Competition Elements in International Trade Agreements*, available at http://www.olis.oecd.org/olis/1998doc.nsf/linkto/com-td-daffe-clp(98)26-final.

UNCTAD (1948), 'Final act of the United Nations Conference on Trade and Employment: Havana Charter for an International Trade Organization', Geneva: United Nations Conference on Trade and Employment, Havana Charter for an International Trade Organization, available at http://www.worldtradelaw.net/misc/havana.pdf.

UNCTAD (1980), *The Set Of Multilaterally Agreed Equitable Principles and Rules for the Control of Restrictive Business Practices*, available at http://r0.unctad.org/en/subsites/cpolicy/docs/CPSet/cpset.htm.

6. Private sector development strategy: some critical issues

Graeme Hodge

INTRODUCTION

The aim of this chapter is to reflect on the concept of a Private Sector Development Strategy (PSD Strategy) and to articulate aspects of the PSD Strategies of the Asian Development Bank and the World Bank, in order to identify both commonalities and differences. These strategies are reviewed as devices for corporate direction setting and policy making in the context of privatisation of state-owned enterprises, economic regulation and competition. In particular, we consider issues arising when strategy is viewed as an evolutionary and learning phenomenon in organisations. We will explore the degree to which PSD Strategy is implementable as a coherent set of actions, as well as analysing a range of perspectives of corporate strategy.

The argument will be put that PSD Strategy is essentially not strategy at all in the usual sense of corporate direction setting and policy implementation, but is a mixture of affirmations, actions, goals, aspirations and beliefs. The consequence of this is that there are large gaps between the image of corporate direction setting in Development Banks through definite initiatives for change and the actuality of generalised policy statements at senior levels, and both uncertainty and rhetorical conflict at officer level. It is also argued that, as a consequence, many of the traditional arguments, philosophical battles and failures to learn from empirical experience that have raged through decades of debate on privatisation, regulation and competition policy for development now continue beneath the surface of the PSD Strategy paradigm.

So what is PSD Strategy? How is it defined, what does it promise and how do commentators interpret it? These are the first questions to which we now turn.

THE ASIAN DEVELOPMENT BANK PSD STRATEGY

There is little doubt that the development of a strong and dynamic private sector is crucial to long-term economic growth. It is also a necessary condition for sustained poverty reduction. In the words of the ADB's PSD Strategy, 'differences in economic growth across the world's developing countries, as well as across countries [see Figure 6.1], largely explain the differences in poverty incidence' (Pernia and Quibria, 1999, cited in ADB, 2000, p. 5). Added to this we might also note the findings of the International Finance Corporation (IFC, 2000) that the single most important route out of poverty was finding a job. In locations such as Venezuela over 1997–98, for instance, some 80 per cent of people lifted out of poverty achieved this through getting a private sector job (IFC, 2000, p. 3).

In addition is the observation that state-owned utilities have effectively not delivered essential services to the most needy ahead of the middle class. Wallich (2001) for instance argues that despite the fact that 'access to reliable infrastructure matters hugely to poor people', 'public infrastructure monopolies have largely failed the poor'. She quotes the price of water being purchased from informal vendors as 20 times higher than the price of piped water, and argues that the poor pay ten times the cost of grid supplied power for paraffin in kerosene lamps. Wallich therefore advocates increased private sector involvement in the provision of infrastructure and essential services.

Of course none of this should be particularly surprising with institutions such as the IFC pursuing a corporate mission to '*promote private sector investment* in developing countries, which will reduce poverty and improve people's lives' (emphasis added). But sweeping statements concerning the role of privatisation, the need for better regulatory and competition policies as part of

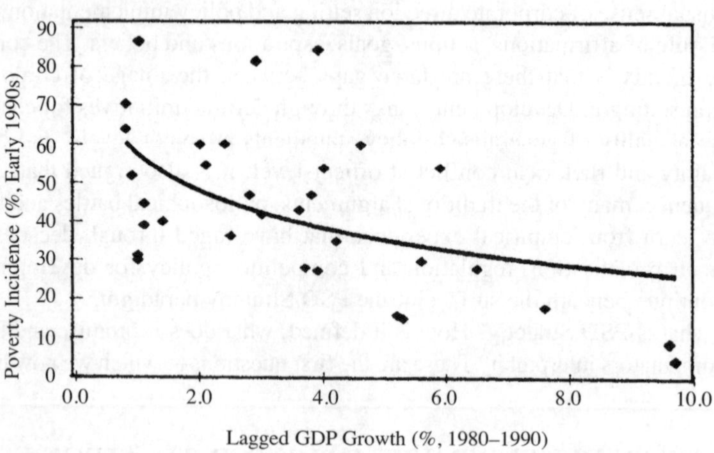

Source: Pernia and Quibria (1999).

Figure 6.1 Economic growth and poverty reduction

the 'enabling environment' did set the scene for what was to follow. The IFC (2000) report demonstrated an unqestioning acceptance of a business-centric model for solutions to development, indeed it went so far as to announce that 'Poverty is bad for Business'. The clear risk is that an unquestioning acceptance of PSD Strategy driven by these values without concomitantly greater accountability and regulatory strength could be accompanied by continued opportunism for private enrichment at the expense of the poor.

The private sector certainly plays an increasingly strong role in developing economies and probably is stronger than that of the development agencies. Wallich (2001) notes that donors gave about $50 billion to developing countries in the 1970s, about twice the level of private flows, which were only $25 billion. 'Now numbers are reversed: private flows are $300 billion, 6 times that of the donors' $50 billion' (Wallich, 2001, p. 3). This indicates a twelve-fold change in the importance of private capital flows over the past three decades. There have also been arguments mounted over the past few years that the use of private capital through partnerships can relieve pressure on public budgets as well as supporting urban development, generating jobs, and promoting entrepreneurship through, for example, the growth of SMEs and small vendors in China, Vietnam, Indonesia and Mongolia. The relative availability of such capital within the context of increasing populations and therefore increasing demand for basic infrastructure, health and education services presents a challenge to Development Banks to specify and implement PSD Strategy, and in particular, develop an 'enabling environment' for developing countries.

In formulating the Bank's PSD Strategy, a range of factors were reported as having been considered. Uppermost, according to ADB (2000, p. 9) was the Bank's overarching objective of poverty reduction and the development challenges facing the region. Also important were the private sector related activities of other multilateral agencies, the ADB's own institutional strengths (including understanding regional needs as well as multidisciplinary expertise) and lessons learned from existing PSD activities. Table 6.1 presents the three major 'strategic thrusts' of the Strategy:

1. Support of developing member country governments in creating enabling conditions for business;
2. To generate business opportunities in ADB financed public sector projects; and
3. To catalyse private investments through direct financing, credit enhancements, and risk mitigation instruments.

The first two thrusts are part of the Bank's public sector operations, while the third is part of its private sector operations. The three thrusts are argued as

Table 6.1 Three strategic thrusts of the Asian Development Bank's PSD Strategy: targeted outcomes and instruments

	Public sector operations		Private sector operations
Strategic thrusts	Creating enabling environments	Generating business opportunities	Catalysing private investments
Targeted outcomes	• Sound macroeconomic policy • Appropriate competition policy • Investment and trade liberalisation • Legal and judicial reform • Public administration reform • State enterprise reform • Tax reform • Product markets reform • Financial sector reform • Capital market reform • Pension and insurance reform • Labour and land markets reform • Sound environmental and social standards • Reform of infrastructure and other sectors • Good physical, social and technological infrastructure	• Private sector participation in Asian Development Bank (ADB)-financed public sector projects through contracts for – supply, – construction, – management, – concession, and – leasing • ADB-designed model build-operate-transfer and other types of projects will poverty reduction impacts reduction impacts • ADB-supported privatisation programmes	• Private sector projects with development impacts and/or demonstration effects • Priority to be given to – infrastructure facilities, – financial institutions, – investment funds, – specialised financial institutions for small and medium-sized enterprises and microenterprises, and pilot health and education projects
Instruments to use	• Policy dialogue • Economic and sector work • Programme loans • Sector development loans • Project loans • Technical assistance • Cofinancing • Partial credit guarantees	• Technical assistance • Program loans • Sector development loans • Project loans • Cofinancing • Partial credit guarantees	• Loans without government guarantees • Equity investments • Hybrid instruments • Co-financing • Partial risk guarantees • Partial credit guarantees

Source: ADB (2000, p. 11).

being 'mutually reinforcing when brought to bear on a development challenge' (ADB, 2000, p. 10).

In pursuing these three strategic thrusts, the Bank sees the focus as being on four areas of operations as follows:

1. governance in the public and private sectors;
2. financial intermediation;
3. public–private partnerships; and
4. regional and subregional cooperation.

These are outlined in Table 6.2. Ticks on this table indicate activities for which ADB strength exists 'based on its track record and for which the three strategic thrusts can achieve significant PSD outcomes' (ADB, 2000, p. 17). As well as outlining the need for the PSD Strategy and the broad thrusts making up the Strategy, the ADB's PSD Strategy document also outlines both the required internal changes for successful implementation of this Strategy, and a range of relevant implementation issues.

THE WORLD BANK PSD STRATEGY

The World Bank's Private Sector Development Strategy was released in April 2002. In its own words, it is 'about promoting growth, reducing poverty and helping people improve their quality of life' and is a 'way of doing things across sectors'. At its core, the Strategy is therefore formally 'about a good balance between the complementary functions of the state and the private sector' rather than about indiscriminate privatisation (World Bank, 2002a, p. i).

Broadly, the World Bank PSD Strategy aims first, to extend the reach of markets and enhance the investment climate, and second, to empower the poor by improving infrastructure, health and education. In support of these operational directions it proposes the measures summarised in Table 6.3.

The World Bank's PSD Strategy also documents a range of lessons learned from the past. It comments for instance that with regard to private participation in infrastructure, 'the introduction of private participation in infrastructure has been less easy to manage and presents more risks' compared with the privatisation of competitive sectors such as manufacturing or agriculture. The lesson here, according to the Bank (World Bank, 2002a, p. 42), centres around the importance of policy reform before introducing private participation. The Strategy also devotes attention to institutional and coordination issues in successfully implementing Strategy actions.

In going forward, the Strategy states that PSD 'is not a sector' itself, but is 'a means to do things better' (World Bank, 2002a, p. 44).

Table 6.2 Three strategic thrusts of the Asian Development Bank's PSD Strategy: applicability to the priority areas of operation

Strategic thrusts	Public sector operations		Private sector operations
Operational priorities	Creating enabling conditions	Generating business opportunities	Catalysing private investments
Governance			
Public sector governance	✓	✓	✓
Commercialization and privatization	✓	✓	✓
Private sector governance	✓	✓	✓
Financial Intermediation			
Financial institutions and markets			
Local currency financing	✓	✓	✓
Investment funds	✓	✓	✓
Small and medium-sized enterprises	✓	✓	✓
Public–private partnerships			
Physical infrastructure development	✓	✓	✓
Social infrastructure development	✓	✓	✓
Agriculture and rural sector development	✓	✓	✓
Regional and subregional cooperation	✓	✓	✓

Source: ADB (2000, p. 17).

Table 6.3 *World Bank Private Sector Development Strategy, 2002*

Strategic thrust	Extending the reach of markets	Access to basic services
Targeted measures	• Investment climate – Continued policy-based lending, consultation and reforms to build competition law, simplify business procedures – Reduce unjustified obstacles to private business investments – Legal and judicial reforms – Establish secure property rights regimes for poor people – Conduct systematic investment climate surveys and assessments to identify pro-poor investment climate features, track changes and compare countries – Institutional capacity building and improve corporate governance • Direct public support to firms – Continued support to entrepreneurs including rural credit and micro-credit finance – Improve performance of public financial and advisory support – Limit domestic taxpayers of poor countries by providing credit through IFC, not subsidies through WB – Target subsidies to capacity building/institution building activities and make transparent – Require minimum rate of return of lending and ensure subsidies are transparent	• Infrastructure supply – Support private participation in infrastructure – Improve regulatory regimes and build institutions to supervise the private sector – Develop principles for regulatory regimes reflecting emerging best practices of policy makers and regulators • Social Sectors – Continue investments in private health and education projects – Assess options for private provision based on infrastructure experience – Pilot 'output-based aid' projects that disburse public funds backed by donors for basic public services – Evaluate the effectiveness of pilots in the medium term and assess contracting and regulatory risks to – Capacity building of public and private institutions

Source: Developed from World Bank (2002a, pp. i–vi, and Annex 1).

OBSERVATIONS ON PSD STRATEGY

The content of the PSD Strategies for both the ADB and WB is interesting – first for what they say and, second, for what is not said.

In the first of these areas, the ADB's PSD Strategy has as its initial thrust the creation of 'the enabling environment'. This includes 'appropriate competition policy', 'legal reform' and 'public administration reform'. Its second thrust is to 'generate business opportunities' for 'private sector participation . . . in public sector projects'. At the operational level, it continues this same thrust, specifying priorities for governance (including 'public sector governance', 'commercialisation and privatisation' and 'private sector governance') and for public–private partnerships (covering 'infrastructure', 'social and agricultural and rural sector development').

Little further detail is available to indicate specific initiatives being undertaken in these areas. Under the general philosophy of creating the enabling environment, for instance, the ADB's PSD Strategy argues that reforms will need to enlarge the role of the private sector in the economy and that as this transition occurs, the government will need to concentrate more on facilitating and regulating private sector services to ensure markets work and to protect public interest as a neutral and objective regulator. It also notes under the operational priority area of public sector governance that 'improving public sector governance has been a major development objective of ADB since 1995', and that 'strengthening the rule of law', 'formulating sound and transparent sectoral regulations', and 'establishing efficient and competitive markets' will all be considered for assistance (ADB, 2000, p. 18). It adds that it will help ensure that benefits of economic growth will be maximised and fairly distributed.

The World Bank's PSD Strategy tells a similar story. It emphasises building an investment climate (including building competition law, simplifying business procedures, and reducing obstacles to business investments along with legal reforms). Operationally, it also aims to improve access to basic services through both better infrastructure supply and social services. In terms of supplying infrastructure, it covers private participation, better regulatory regimes/institutions to supervise the private sector, and development of regulatory principles reflecting best practices. In the case of social sector provision, investment in private sector health and education projects, piloting output-based aid project techniques, capacity building for public and private institutions, and assessing the effectiveness of pilot schemes in contracting private providers were emphasised.

Overall, then, we might observe first that the prescriptive actions were very general and that few specific strategic activities for regulatory and competition reform had been set. This observation is parallel to the comments of other observers such as Schulpen and Gibbon (2002, p. 6) who reviewed the case of OECD donors for PSD. They comment that 'only in a few cases do donor programs give clear intellectual precedence to specific levels or elements of PSD'. The few exceptions when reviewing the World Bank and ADB documents appeared to be the new emphasis and faith being placed in both output-based aid project delivery techniques, and public–private partnerships.

Perhaps this is not so surprising when we consider the degree to which PSD Strategy activities are inherent within much of the day-to-day work of both institutions. It has been argued for instance that 'typically, about two thirds of all World Bank operations include components that explicitly support private sector development' (ADB, 2000, p. 53). Yamamoto's review of the role of PSD in past strategy papers from the World Bank also revealed a large degree of longevity for central strategy ideas going back over a decade in the case of improving the business environment, privatisation of enterprises and support for entrepreneur development and policy work (Yamamoto, 2001). But to the extent that this is the case, then the expectations for the PSD Strategy as representing new directions and new activities far exceed the realities.

Second, we might also observe that very few 'poor-specific' PSD strategies seem to have been presented. Again this is echoed by the comments of Schulpen and Gibbon (2002, p. 6), who refer to the existence of 'policy incoherence' and a quote from van den Bosch (1998) who observed that 'the development of new PSD policy is in general disappointing [mainly because] activities in this field are seldom worked out and incorporated in a broader vision on poverty reduction and employment creation'.

We ought equally to comment about what does not appear to have been included in these PSD Strategies. One common element across both Strategies is the degree to which neither discussed explicitly nor addressed detailed actions for improving accountability. This is a surprising observation in the light of Woods' recent comment that institutions such as the World Bank (and by implication, the ADB) 'are now regularly accused of being secretive, unaccountable and ineffective' (Woods, 2001). She charges further that major reasons for this include unequal representations on executive boards, the practice of these boards not holding staff and management to account, and the fact that as these Banks have expanded their roles and impacts on stakeholders over the past two decades, this has not been accompanied by expansion in their accountability (Woods, 2001).

Another somewhat surprising omission from these two PSD Strategies is that neither pays particularly strong attention to the existence of specific winners and losers within general aid programmes or to the related issue of needing to offer specific protection for poor or otherwise vulnerable citizens during reforms. Likewise, little formal reference is made to reducing the effects of corruption, although there are considerable efforts being made to this end. In this respect, ways in which past lessons in protecting the interests of the poor can be operationalised in the current PSD Strategies are not clear in these documents.

In addition, the precise specification of research priorities for future PSD Strategy work has also been downplayed. This is perhaps understandable in an environment where the immediate needs of the poor are clear and applying resources in the field, rather than in research, is deemed a priority for action. But it is nonetheless a shortfall that has practical implications to the extent that research could lead to improved understandings of both the effectiveness of proposed PSD activities and their priority.

Lastly, reference should be made to the strategy process. The ADB document does not list either its stakeholders, or the ways in which they participated or contributed towards the development of the PSD Strategy – if indeed this occurred. In the absence of this information, it might be concluded that the ADB did not regard participation with its stakeholders as a priority in this exercise. To the extent that this observation is true, it is itself significant.

The way in which the World Bank's stakeholders contributed to its Strategy document was also not clear, but it was nonetheless obvious that the draft document (2001) was subject to considerable stakeholder feedback before it was released in its final version. Following earlier criticism of insufficient consultation with stakeholders and calls for increased accountability to those affected by its actions, and in the wake of an already demoralised staff after widespread criticisms of its policies from quarters such as the Meltzer Commission (2000), the inclusion of stakeholder feedback in the Strategy process was sensible and productive. Bayliss and Hall (2002) support this comment, seeing the revised PSD Strategy from the World Bank as having a 'somewhat more considered review of the issue [of privatisation]'. Their support, however, is conditional, given that the remainder of their comments present stinging criticism that the Bank's final Strategy had an unchanged strategy direction and implementation matrix compared to the earlier draft. To Bayliss and Hall, the precise objectives of the Strategy were not clear, and yet 'privatisation becomes the dominant goal', with 'silence on the subject of risk'. Although output-based aid was touted throughout the Strategy as an answer to public policy implementation problems, it was to Bayliss and Hall more a sales exercise than a set of actions that had resulted from serious self-examination (Bayliss and Hall, 2002, p. 5, p. 11).

This thrust was also reported by Globalisation Challenge Initiative (2002) who viewed strategies for increased private participation as resulting directly from a secretive strategy process, causing a weakened state capacity, and leading to what they termed 'in-service apartheid', whereby profitable and unprofitable services would be separated.

PSD STRATEGY AS CORPORATE STRATEGY

According to the Penguin English Dictionary (Garmonsway, 1980), strategy is a 'large scale plan or method for winning a war, battle of wits, contest, game'. In the business context, strategy has taken on a life of its own over the past four decades. Every business school throughout the world is now replete with suites of strategy courses covering its art and science. For a corporation, including a Development Bank, to be strategyless would be as suicidal as a political party being policyless.

In thinking about strategy from the corporate perspective, we might begin by noting that strategy can be defined in several ways; such as, a pattern of decisions defining how the firm will respond to the environment, how the firm chooses its position against competitors, the choice of services and products which make up its portfolio and in which it will invest and divest, and ways of achieving its goals and objectives. Most commentators in the public and not-for-profit sectors view strategy in terms of the last definition.

Arguably one of the most relevant lessons over the past two decades of corporate strategy is that successful strategy for public and not-for-profit organisations has usually required a greater sense of ownership from staff and from stakeholders than previously recognised. Whereas strategy was once seen to be top-down, fully formed thinking from knowledgeable corporate heads, more recent conceptions have seen successful strategy as equally a bottom-up, partially formed and evolutionary phenomenon. In this light, the apparent lack of attention to stakeholder involvement in strategy by the ADB is disappointing.

So how might we interpret PSD Strategy in the corporate context? Mintzberg and Lampel (1999) remind us of Mintzberg's ten 'schools of strategy formulation'; three prescriptive (or 'ought') schools of design, planning and positioning, along with seven descriptive (or 'is') schools including entrepreneurial, cognitive, learning, power, cultural, environmental and configuration. So far in this chapter we have commented that the PSD Strategy has been vague, with little detail and has suffered from insufficient stakeholder involvement. We will now draw briefly on the schools of learning, power and culture to comment further on the PSD Strategy.

The learning philosophy looks at strategy as an emergent process as the organisation grows in its understanding of its environment and of itself. Dating back to Lindblom's early ideas of incrementalism, strategies in this view 'are emergent, strategists can be found throughout the organisation, and so-called formulation and implementation intertwine' (Mintzberg and Lampel, 1999).

Strategy-making rooted in power sees powerful elites within the organisation developing strategy, or an organisation itself using its own power over other organisations and actors. This view is also both interesting and relevant.

Here the strategy process is about bargaining and persuading, and about the division of power among coalitions of actors and groups. Each seeks to gain influence and implement their ideas, and although they usually compete for such power, they may at times also cooperate in the pursuit of self-interest.

The cultural school of strategy-making sees strategy in terms of the reverse image of power – that is, culture. Strategy formulation is therefore rooted not in power and self-interest, but is seen more in terms of social processes around common interest and integration. Organisation culture and social culture are seen as central influences in strategy formulation, often discouraging change.

Each of these schools has something to say about our contention of PSD Strategy. First, we might observe that the PSD Strategies are overwhelmingly prescriptive. Perhaps this is not surprising. But to the extent that this view of strategy dominates, the organisation's ability to learn sensibly, its ability to understand that strategy will come from throughout the organisation, its willingness to make explicit discussions of strategy as power, and its ability to see strategy as a culturally centric process, may all suffer. This would seem to be true, to differing degrees, with both PSD Strategies.

Of course, PSD Strategy should be viewed as a public policy tool as well as the narrower version of corporate direction setting. Under this parallel perspective, broad policy frameworks, rhetorical visions and general promises are standard fare. Again, to the extent that these PSD Strategies are simply public policy statements, their usefulness in establishing the details of future corporate directions and setting the scene for definitive implementation actions to be delivered, and for which individuals and organisations might be held to account, is questionable. Given the power of development banks, this issue remains one of concern.

DISCUSSION

So, what can be learned here? Evidently, PSD Strategy is closer to the public policy framework and rhetorical statement of beliefs than it is to the notion of strategy as a designed set of actions setting corporate direction. PSD Strategy is more a complex mixture of affirmations, potential actions, fuzzy goals based on observations of developed economies, heartfelt aspirations and often strongly held beliefs. Although it is simultaneously held as a broad direction setting document as well as being hailed as a series of actionable challenges, it is difficult to see how it can successfully be both. It is certainly a rallying call for those who support its ethos as well as being a sign of the frustration of development banks in making progress towards poverty reduction through the idea of strengthening national economic engines.

Over the period October 2001 to April 2002, the ADB held a series of

'Awareness Sessions' for Bank staff, to increase awareness of the Bank's PSD Strategy, which had been adopted as a corporate priority in 2000.

From an educational perspective, the aims of the 2001–02 Awareness Sessions at the ADB were, in the formal sense, to increase the familiarity of Bank staff with the Bank's PSD Strategy, to share PSD Strategy experiences of staff in order to contribute to future Bank PSD Strategy work, and to reflect on some of the challenges faced. In retrospect, and adopting the power school perspective of strategy, the unofficial objectives of the PSD Strategy may well have had as much to do with a conspicuous show of force, with changing coalitions in the background, in order to be seen to triumph over factions resistant to the new strategic directions. Debates concerning the existence and veracity of evidence on both sides, or an explicit acknowledgement of ambiguities in the approach, were not a formal part of the Strategy. Intellectually, what evidence can be marshalled to support this view?

The first example concerns the debate around property rights, with Hernando de Soto proselytising the answer to the mystery of capitalism (de Soto, 2000), with obvious popularity within the World Bank, while Alan Gilbert (2002) takes the contrary view. To the World Bank's credit, the title of the discussion session of the 2002 PSD conference exploring this issue (World Bank, 2002b) was: 'Land Titles for the Poor: Panacea or Sham?' De Soto's thesis is that the failure of capitalism in the third world can be attributed largely to the lack of property titles. This notion has gained popular support from figures with global credentials such as Ronald Coase, Milton Friedman, Margaret Thatcher and Bill Clinton. Gilbert (2002), however, argues that this idea is 'dangerously flawed' because the argument is overplayed. To Gilbert's mind, de Soto is 'generating a myth about capitalism based on a populist dream'. Other debates are also absent, such as the effectiveness of loan conditionality on financial flows (Bird and Rowlands, 2001; Pender, 2001; Gilbert et al., 1999; Mosley et al., 1995) and the importance of domestic political economy factors in the success of aid programmes (Dollar and Svensson, 2000).

A second example concerns the arena of public–private partnerships (PPPs). In the midst of failed public provision, PPPs and output-based aid have both been hailed in these strategies as new thrusts to provide better essential services for the poor. While the potential for both private and other non-government organisations to better provide services does exist, it also needs to be acknowledged that worldwide controversies continue to dog the use of techniques such as PPPs in developed countries ranging from the United States and the United Kingdom, through to Australia and Denmark. Neither PSD Strategy appears to have seriously regarded the lessons learned to date from around the globe in the PPP arena (Hodge, 2002a; Osborne, 2001). Likewise, measuring the performance of public sector organisations along with public sector contractors through mechanisms such as contracting-out, outsourcing, partnerships, performance based contracting and a host of other contract techniques is hardly new. Much literature has been accumulated to provide lessons on which PSD could have drawn (Rhodes, 1994, 1998; Yates, 2000; Hodge, 2000). Such lessons, however, appear to have had limited, if any, impact on the Strategies. The same could also be said about the lack of explicit learnings from the privatisation of SOEs (Martin and Parker, 1997; Hodge, 2002b).

The third example might be found in the belief that developing countries ought to separate 'steering' from 'rowing' as put forward originally by Steve Savas in the United States and subsequently sold as part of 'reinventing government' package by Osborne and Gaebler (1993). This concept, though not referred to explicitly in the PSD Strategies, is nevertheless at the heart of much of the current discussion around the role of government. The proposition is that first, developing countries ought to aspire to contractualise government services and contract them out and, second, the real business of government is to 'regulate and facilitate rather than to do'. The inability of developed countries to look at the central place of government in their own historical development, and the cultural, political and sociological lessons from global experience to date, before recommending such techniques to poorer neighbours is disappointing. Also, we might comment that these concepts have been controversial in their application, have not received universal acclaim and, more importantly, are now recognised as requiring considerable new skills and capacities in government if they are to work effectively and cleanly (De Carvalho, 1998; Hodge, 2000).

We should also reflect that the possibility that encouraging governments to separate steering from rowing may tend to result in the belief that such separation is itself an answer to public policy questions facing the state. In other words, the wholesale inclusion of contracting-out and partnership techniques in PSD strategies may suggest that these are answers to public policy problems in economic development, rather than simply mechanisms for delivering some of the needed essential services. Separating steering from rowing has never been *the answer* to developing country problems – except of course in the post-modernist analysis, where words, symbols and signs are increasingly divorced from real world experience and where ideas for reinventing government are, according to Fox (1996), breathless in their salesmanship despite clear inconsistencies, and at times bizarre logic and linguistic manipulations.

CONCLUSIONS

What are the consequences of these observations, and what are our conclusions? The first point to make is that many of the traditional arguments, philosophical battles and failures to learn from empirical experience that have raged through decades of broader debates around privatisation, regulation, competition and development continue beneath the surface of the PSD Strategy paradigm. Also, experience within development banks shows that there are large gaps between the image of corporate direction setting in these institutions and the actuality of policy incoherence and fragmentation at officer level.

Perhaps the key consequence is that in the face of growing availability of private capital and the global power of private financial institutions, the breadth of the PSD Strategy policy platform and policy frameworks being espoused as 'strategy' means that a stronger emphasis needs to be placed by development banks on specific research directions attached to developing country reforms. It is even more imperative now that we research the effectiveness of modest initiatives and seek ways in which we might use the few reform successes to better advantage. Perhaps we need to lower our PSDS reform sights in order to undertake more realistic advances, and renew the emphasis on market transformation, market development and institution building research, with greater ownership of reforms by the developing countries themselves.

As Parker (2001) concluded, perhaps completely new models of regulation and competition are needed. This chapter not only comes to the same conclusion but goes further, and questions whether the development banks are capable of meeting this need. Meeting this challenge will require the banks themselves to redevelop PSD Strategies that are more culturally relevant, to increase their internal capacity to learn from the breadth of experience to date and also to be more explicit about the inevitability of power sharing as part of successful reform. This will be a challenge, given the observations made of PSD Strategy development to date. Thus far, the pattern seems to have been one of simply asserting private over public, markets over governments, and quick actions over more gradual, difficult but informed and effective reforms in privatisation, regulation and competition.

REFERENCES

Asian Development Bank (2000), *Private Sector Development Strategy*, March, Manila: Asian Development Bank.

Bayliss, K. and Hall, D. (2002), *Another PSIRU Critique of Another Version of the World Bank Private Sector Development Strategy*, available at http://www.psiru.org/reports/2002-01-U-WB-PSDrev.doc#_Toc60811.

Bird, G. and Rowlands, D. (2001), 'World Bank lending and other financial flows: is there a connection?', *The Journal of Development Studies*, **37** (5), 83–103.

De Carvalho, D. (1998), ' "The Captain is a Schizophrenic!" or Contradictions in the

Concept of the Steering State', *Australian Journal of Public Administration*, **57** (2), 107–14.

de Soto, H. (2000), *The Mystery of Capitalism: Why Capitalism Triumphs in the West and Fails Everywhere Else*, London: Bantam Press.

Dollar, D. and Svensson, J. (2000), 'What explains the success or failure of structural adjustment programmes?', *The Economic Journal*, **110**, October, 894–917.

Fox, C. (1996), 'Reinventing government as postmodern symbolic politics', *Public Administration Review*, **56** (3), 256–62.

Garmonsway, G. (1980), *Penguin English Dictionary*, 3rd edn, London: Penguin Reference Books.

Gilbert, A. (2002), 'On the mystery of capital and the myths of Hernando de Soto: what difference does legal title make?', presentation to The World Bank Group Private Sector Development Forum, 23–24 April, (also at http://rru.worldbalk.org/ and published in *International Development Planning Review*, Feb, 2002.

Gilbert, C., Powell, A. and Vines, D. (1999), 'Positioning the World Bank', *The Economic Journal*, **109**, November, 598–633.

Globalisation Challenge Initiative (2002), 'Growing dangers of service apartheid: how the World Bank Group's private sector (PSD) strategy threatens infrastructure and basic service provision', *News and Notices for IMF and World Bank Watchers*, **2** (5), (also at http://challengeglobalisation.org/).

Hodge, G.A. (2000), 'Privatisation: an international review of performance', in Paul A. Sabatier (ed.) *Theoretical Lenses on Public Policy Series*, Boulder, CO: Westview Press.

Hodge, G.A. (2002a), 'Who steers the state when governments sign public-private partnerships?', *Journal of Contemporary Issues in Business and Government*, **8** (1), 5–18.

Hodge, G.A. (2002b), 'Privatisation: lessons from the war', *Alternative Law Journal*, **27** (4), 177–83, Melbourne.

International Finance Corporation (2000), *Paths Out of Poverty: The Role of Private Enterprise in Developing Countries*, Washington DC: IFC.

Martin, S. and Parker, D. (1997), *The Impact of Privatisation: Ownership and Corporate Performance in the UK*, Series on Industrial Economic Strategies for Europe, London: Routledge.

Meltzer Commission (2000), *Report of the International Finance Institution Advisory Commission*, Washington, DC: US Congress.

Mintzberg, H. and Lampel, J. (1999), 'Reflecting on the strategy process', *Sloan Management Review*, Spring, 21–30.

Mosley, P., Harrigan, J. and Toye, J. (1995), *Aid and Power*, 2nd edn, London: Routledge.

Osborne, D. and Gaebler, T. (1993), *Reinventing Government: How the Entrepreneurial Spirit is Transforming the Public Sector*, Reading, MA: Addison-Wesley Publishing Co.

Osborne, S.P. (2001), 'Introduction: understanding public–private partnerships in international perspective: globally convergent or nationally divergent phenomena?', in Stephen P. Osborne (ed.) *Public–Private Partnerships: Theory and Practice in International Perspective*, London: Routledge Advances in Management and Business Studies, pp. 1–5.

Parker, D. (2001), 'Economic Regulation: A Preliminary Literature Review and Summary of Research Questions Arising', Working Paper No. 6, Oct, Centre on Regulation and Competition, University of Manchester.

Pender, J. (2001), 'From "structural adjustment" to "comprehensive development framework": conditionality reformed?', *Third World Quarterly*, **22** (3), 397–411.

Pernia, E.M. and Quibria, M.G. (1999), 'Poverty in developing countries', in Cheshire P. and E.S. Mills (eds) *Handbook of Regional and Urban Economics*, Amsterdam: North Holland.

Rhodes, R.A.W. (1994), 'The hollowing out of the state: the changing nature of the public service in Britain', *The Political Quarterly*, **65** (2), 138–51.

Rhodes, R.A.W. (1998), 'Different roads to unfamiliar places: UK experience in comparative perspective', *Australian Journal of Public Administration*, **57** (4), 19–31.

Schulpen, L. and Gibbon, P. (2002), 'Private sector development: policies, practices and problems', *World Development*, **30** (1), 1–15.

van den Bosch, F. (1998), *De ontwikkeleling van de particuliere sector-beleid, organisatie en programma's in de DAC donorlanden*. The Hague: DGIS.

Wallich, C. (2001), 'Infrastructure: commercialising public utilities and reaching the poor', paper presented at the Infrastructure and Poverty Reduction in Asia Conference organised by KFW and the Asian Development Bank, Berlin, 26 September.

Woods, N. (2001), 'Making the IMF and the World Bank more accountable', *International Affairs*, **77** (1), 83–100.

World Bank (2001), *Private Sector Development Strategy – Issues and Options, A Discussion Document*, 1 June, Washington, DC: World Bank.

World Bank (2002a), *Private Sector Development Strategy – Directions for the World Bank Group*, April 9, Washington, DC: World Bank.

World Bank (2002b), *Private Sector Development Forum*, 23–24 April, Washington, DC: World Bank.

Yamamoto, C. (2001), 'The role of private sector development in past strategy papers', 6 September, available at http://rru.worldbank.org/strategy/documents/.

Yates, A. (2000), *Government as an Informed Buyer: Recognising Technical Expertise as a Crucial Factor in the Success of Engineering Contracts*, Australia: The Institution of Engineers.

7. Comparing regulatory systems: institutions, processes and legal forms in industrialised countries

Anthony Ogus

INTRODUCTION

It might seem odd to include a chapter comparing regulatory systems in industrialised countries in a volume devoted to themes relevant to regulation and competition in developing countries. But if those from the (mainly) European and North American legal and regulatory traditions wish to venture into evaluative studies of equivalents in developing countries, they must have a firm basis from which to proceed – and an understanding of the conceptual framework used in their own and analogous jurisdictions would seem to serve very well for this purpose.

There are clearly many possible approaches to the comparison of regulatory systems. I focus on three characteristics: institutional structures; procedural and managerial systems; and legal forms. There is a generally accepted distinction (Ogus, 1994, pp. 4–5) between 'economic' regulation, which is the regulation of prices and quality of services supplied in a market characterised by monopoly or near-monopoly conditions, and 'social' regulation, which refers to those areas of state intervention, for example environmental and health and safety regulation, and consumer protection, generally justified by reference to externalities and information asymmetries. The determinants of the institutional framework are not always common to the two types of regulation. In this study, I cover both types, although in the main text there is a focus on economic regulation, with some reference to issues of social regulation.

Comparisons between national systems risk superficiality if no account is taken of the cultural and constitutional context in which the regime is to be found. This study begins, therefore, with an attempt to identify how regulation fits into that environment.

CONSTITUTIONAL AND CULTURAL ENVIRONMENT

Constitutional Framework

Regulation, in our conception, involves individuals and firms being induced to outcomes that, in the absence of the instrument, they would not have attained. It therefore necessarily involves the exercise of power by the state or an agency of the state. Constitutions control power and allocate it between different organs of the state, more specifically between legislature, executive and judiciary. Under most modern western constitutions, the power to regulate is acquired, if only implicitly, by the legislature. However democratic ideals must, to some extent, cede before other values and in consequence constitutional arrangements governing regulation are more complex. First, and most obviously, in practice much regulatory power is delegated by legislatures to the executive. Second, in some countries, notably France (Bell, 1992), the power of the executive to regulate, at least in some sectors, is derived directly from the constitution. This may reflect a political or ideological choice in favour of limiting democratic influences on decisions in such areas. A third exception is the residual power of the judiciary to regulate. In the common law world, judges have developed principles not only to constrain monopolistic behaviour, but also, under the doctrine of 'common callings' (Taggart, 1995, pp. 216–27), to guarantee services and to regulate prices.

In some countries the constitution itself may exert constraints on the power of the legislature to regulate; and this in turn will depend on the set of politico-economic values to which that document gives expression (Ogus, 1990). Thus we may have, as in the United States, a constitution which is interpreted as being based on a premise of freedom of economic activity. Then regulation has to find its constitutional legitimacy in the (admittedly broad) range of 'police powers' (e.g. protection of the health, safety and welfare of the community) the exercise of which can interfere with that freedom. This approach may be contrasted with another tradition which defines the role of the state as in some way directed towards social welfare ends which may diverge from unregulated market outcomes. The German Basic Law of 1949 has, at its base, the concept of *soziale Marktwirstchaft* (social market economy), implicitly legitimising more active regulatory interventions. But the language used to define such powers tends to be very vague, making constitutional challenges easy to resist. For example, Article 41 of the Italian Constitution provides that 'the law will set up appropriate schemes and controls in order that public and private economic activities may be directed and co-ordinated for the benefit of society'. This in turn should be distinguished from a third type of constitutional framework which assumes a planned economy and gives the legislature or government all the powers necessary to control it.

Administrative Law

There are major differences between countries regarding the character and effectiveness of administrative law and an obvious variable is the strength and independence of the judiciary who are primarily responsible for making and enforcing decisions against public institutions. However, significant variations also occur in countries which show equal respect for the separation of powers and ensure the independence of judges. There is, on the one hand, the continental European, civil law jurisdictions, which have a system of public law tribunals, separate from the main judicial system; and, on the other, the common law jurisdictions where administrative action is largely controlled by the ordinary courts, the state being regarded as simply *primus inter pares*.

And even within these two systems there are important variations. So, for example, the question of whether a court has the power to annul legislation on the ground that it is inconsistent with the constitution is not one that receives the same answer within each tradition (McWhinney, 1986). The German *Verfassungsgericht* has the power; but that of the French *Conseil Constitutionnel*, which in any event is not a court, is more limited. The United States Supreme Court has the power; the British House of Lords has not.

Then as between two of the leading common law jurisdictions, the USA and the UK, administrative law has clearly diverged (Schwartz and Wade, 1972). American judges take a harder look at the reasonableness of administrative actions (so-called 'substantive judicial review') whereas their English counterparts have rather concentrated on whether appropriate procedures have been observed. American administrative law has also gone further in terms of process values, requiring a greater degree of transparency of decision-making and encouraging participation by interested third parties.

Regulatory Traditions and Styles

Characterising and placing what we have come to call 'regulation' within legal systems are highly problematic tasks. The question is not unconnected with the politico-economic basis of the law. Thus we find that civil law systems which have rationalised the concept of the state, and particularly its role in the economy, have developed formal legal categories for this purpose, for example, the French *droit public économique* (Delvolvé, 1998) and the German *Wirtschaftsverwaltungsrecht* (Jarass, 1984). These terms have been used to bring under a single umbrella the law relating to public enterprise, public finance, state controls of private enterprise and competition law – and therefore without difficulty have incorporated the regulation of privatised entities. In contrast, in Anglophone jurisdictions with their common law emphasis on the control of government power, equivalent classifications do not exist. Of course, the same areas of law can be identified, but there has been nothing in legal doctrine to link them. Rather they have been seen as disparate aspects of administrative law, the main concern of which was to control executive discretion, rather than facilitate outcomes considered as economically desirable.

Paradoxically, the concepts of 'regulation' and 'regulatory law' that became so dominant in the 1980s and afterwards were predominantly Anglo-American in origin. They had as their base the economic notion of public law responses to instances of market failure and, as such, were rationalised by legal scholars from a law and economics background (Breyer, 1982; Ogus, 1994). Undoubtedly this literature had an impact on administrative lawyers who began to forsake their traditional preoccupation with discretion and judicial review. While public lawyers from the common law world were thus acquiring a vision which was closer to that of continental exponents of 'economic law', the latter were adjusting to the somewhat narrower notion of 'regulation' which became in French *réglementation* (Lévêque, 1998) and in German *Regulierung* (Reich, 1984).

Notwithstanding this convergence of the conception and rationalisation of regulation between the two principal legal cultures, the practical application retained important differences.

- The focus on the 'state' and the greater degree of state intervention in the continental tradition, leads to a culture of 'public interest' regulation which is somewhat broader than the Anglo-Saxon emphasis on 'market-failure' regulation (Dyson, 1992b).
- The style of the legislation used for regulatory purposes in common law systems tends to aim at a high level of precision, thus generating lengthy and very complex provisions; the continental approach adopts more general and abstract language, leaving more room for discretionary interpretation (Dale, 1988).
- Given their long tradition of state intervention and centralised bureaucracy, continental European systems have been less comfortable than common law jurisdictions with regulatory agencies which are, at least to some degree, independent of government (Majone, 1996, pp. 10–12).
- In common law systems, regulatory techniques and principles have tended to emerge piecemeal, with little attempt at coherence across different sectors. One consequence has been, in the USA, a tendency to use litigation rather than legislation as the engine of regulatory reform (Kagan, 2001). In contrast, in some European continental jurisdictions, particularly Germany, attempts have been made to develop general principles of regulatory administrative justice (Boujong, 2000).

INSTITUTIONAL FRAMEWORKS

Regulatory Agencies and Government

Regulatory systems must, of course, be enforced and therefore require some agency for this purpose. More than this, as we have seen, legislatures invariably delegate the task of detailed rule-making and this is often undertaken by the institutions responsible for enforcement. The first important issue which has to be addressed is the extent to which such institutions should be independent of government. There is here a spectrum of alternative arrangements ranging from complete government control to self-regulation. Although there are many possible variations, we can identify four main types.

- (I) An agency which is part of (central or local) government. External expert opinion may be consulted but the rules and decisions are made within the permanent bureaucracy, in relation to which a politician (the relevant minister) takes ultimate responsibility.
- (II) An agency which is semi-autonomous in the sense that while it is independent of, and not accountable to, government, the latter exerts some residual control through one or more of the following:
  - appointment of members;
  - some government representation;
  - an expectation, or requirement, that rules and decisions will be made in accordance with government policy or guidelines;
  - some form of ratification of decisions by ministers.
- (III) An agency which is independent of government in the sense that few, if any, of the controls in types (II) exist. It is a public institution, acting under powers conferred, and in accordance with principles enacted, by the legislature. Its member are experts drawn from non-government sources and without political affiliations.
- (IV) An agency which is predominantly self-regulatory as well as independent of government, in the sense that a significant proportion of the members are drawn from and directly represent the regulated sector. Some degree of public control may nevertheless be exercised through one or more of the following:
  - some members represent the public interest;
  - the principles and/or procedures to be followed are determined by the legislature;
  - rules and decisions can be challenged by reference to the courts or some superior public agency.

At the risk of over-simplification, a survey of practice, both historical and inter-jurisdictional, can lead us to some interesting generalisations. In the first place, in the last three decades or so, there has been a global tendency to shift along the spectrum away from central government control: this has been a major feature of what has been called the 'deregulation' movement (Ogus, 2000a). Nevertheless, second, the extent to which that phenomenon has occurred has varied between different countries and in accordance with different regulatory cultures.

Agency of type (III) is the classic form of American regulatory commission, developed at the end of the nineteenth century to govern utilities. Public ownership had been expressly rejected as a mode of governance and so the notion of a body of independent experts was wholly consistent (Landis, 1938). Other industrialised countries had typically adopted public ownership in this area, and when utilities were privatised and new forms of regulatory agency emerged, it was harder to sever the ties with governmental authority (Majone, 1996, pp. 14–15).

A third generalisation, and this applies to the USA as well as to Europe, is that agencies dealing with powers of social regulation, for example consumer protection and environmental protection, have more government involvement than those dealing with economic regulation, and indeed in many countries remain as type (I). Nevertheless, this should not be taken as necessarily implying exclusively centralist decision-making. In the important area of employment and particularly health and safety at work, a tradition has long been established of tripartite (state, employer representatives and employee representatives) governance structure (Baldwin and Daintith, 1992).

This last arrangement clearly involves some degree of self-regulation which, in any event, can assume a large variety of forms (Page, 1986, pp. 144–8). However, in its most blatant form, type (IV), self-regulation is used in most jurisdictions mainly in the area of professional regulation.

The theoretical arguments regarding these issues mainly relate to the costs of the information necessary for good decision-making and the ability to ensure that the agency's performance is consistent with the regulatory public interest goals – in other words the principal–agent problem (Macey, 1992). We can begin by recognising the advantages of delegating regulatory rule-making and enforcement to an agency which is largely independent of government (Mashaw, 1985). Expertise can be concentrated in ways not always possible within a permanent bureaucracy, and distance from government can reduce the degree of political interference – the history of public ownership has revealed too often that politicians are tempted to aim at short-term benefits, leading to, among other problems, uncertainty and instability (Zeckhauser and Horn, 1989). Nevertheless a role for government may be justified if aspects of regulation require essentially political judgements. This helps to explain the preference for type (I) in relation to social regulation and for type (II) as regards utilities regulation: while the primary questions of efficient price tariffs are for the independent agency, any social dimension, for example subsidisation and distributional preferences for certain customers, may more appropriately be determined by governments that are democratically accountable (Baldwin and Cave, 1999, pp. 289–91). Some residual government control or influence can also be justified on the basis that policy can thereby be coordinated with other relevant agencies and sectors.

One reason for the observed world-wide trend towards consensual, decentralised, regulatory rule-making is the growing recognition that governments cannot always be relied on to possess or properly to process the information necessary to meet the regulatory goals at low cost (Gunningham et al., 1998, p. 44). We can clearly see the advantage, for example, of large firms formulating their own rule-book which is then submitted to the regulatory agency to ensure compatibility with those goals (Ayres and Braithwaite, 1992). By themselves, however, these arguments do not justify adoption of the complete self-regulation model, type (IV), because here unconstrained agencies can exploit their regulatory power to advance private, rather than public, interests, in particular by creating barriers to entry (Faure et al., 1993).

Discretion and Accountability

We turn next to the power conferred on regulatory agencies, the nature of the discretion involved and the methods used to render them accountable. To enable regulators to apply the expertise that they are assumed to possess, a broad discretion must usually be conferred. However, the extent to which legislation directs, by specific rules or guidelines, how the discretion is to be exercised varies significantly between jurisdictions. To illustrate this, we can examine the provisions governing the control of electricity prices. Now we know that to achieve efficient pricing in monopoly conditions, regulators have tended to adopt either the long-standing American method of cost recovery based on a 'fair rate of return' or a price-capping technique, tied to inflation but incorporating productivity expectations, such as that devised by the Thatcher government for the privatised utilities in the 1980s (Ogus, 1994, pp. 305–13). But there is considerable diversity as to whether the legislation prescribes an appropriate method and, if so, with what degree of detail.

One finds that common law jurisdictions tend to use general language and thereby confer a very broad discretion on regulatory agencies. The legislation of continental European jurisdictions has tended to be more specific. The contrast may seem to be paradoxical in the light of what was said earlier about legislative styles, but it rather reflects differences of approach within administrative law, which themselves can be explained by reference to principal–agent theory. We may readily assume that everywhere the 'principal' is intended to be the public interest, justifying and therefore also constraining the regulatory system, but the extent to which the legislator is viewed as representing that interest is another matter.

The continental European tradition has always been to emphasise the link between legislatures and the public interest; particularising administrative functions within a strong, prescriptive statutory framework is therefore unsurprising. The American approach is somewhat sceptical of this link, recognising the key role that pressure groups and private interests play in the legislative process. Greater reliance is placed on ex post methods of constraint through the general principles of administrative law (Kagan, 2001). The expectation is that those enabled, by such principles, to participate in regulatory procedures or challenge regulatory decision-making in the courts will be more representative of the 'public interest' than the politicians (and bureaucrats) responsible for the legislation (Breyer and Stewart, 1985, pp. 26–32). For a period of over one hundred years, clarification of how regulators should control utility prices consistent with the notion of 'fair rate of return' emerged not from a legislative or executive source but rather from judges and the huge case law that emerged from judicial review of regulatory decision-making (Breyer, 1982, Ch. 2).

This discussion leads us into a more general consideration of accountability which can, of course, take a variety of forms, political and legal (Baldwin and Cave, 1999, Ch. 2). Inevitably, in jurisdictions where governments retain a major degree of control, independent agencies, if they exist, are accountable to them. But more typically, political accountability takes the form of submitting reports to the legislature which may have a special committee to scrutinise and debate its contents. In this connection, one may note that the British practice, not much imitated in other countries, to designate the regulator as a single person, rather than a committee or a commission, may strengthen political accountability, as the individual concerned has in consequence a much higher profile (Doern, 1998, pp. 40–41).

Legal accountability enables those aggrieved by a decision or an exercise of rule-making to issue a formal complaint or appeal. Where an agency's powers include that of issuing licences or conditions for individual firms, it may well have its own appeals panel for such purposes. Of greater significance is the right to bring claims to another institution. Here one observes a divergence between countries that establish specialist commissions or tribunals, such as the British Competition Commission, having powers to determine disputes only within that sector or a related sector, and those which rely exclusively on institutions having competence over general administrative matters. Examples of the latter include not only the system of administrative tribunals in civil law jurisdictions, but also the ordinary courts in common law jurisdictions, with their powers of judicial review. The main advantage of a specialist institution is that it can bring to bear expertise on the relevant regulatory issues, particularly where, as in the cited example, it includes economists as well as lawyers and administrators. But as we have already seen, the general jurisdiction of the American courts has not prevented them from developing a sophisticated approach to regulatory concerns (Foster, 1992, pp. 187–97); and in the civil law systems the high standing and profile of institutions such as the French *Conseil d'Etat* and the German *Bundesverwaltungsgericht* ensures effectiveness as well as legitimacy (Dyson, 1992a, pp. 12–13).

PROCEDURES AND MANAGEMENT

The Background: The Legal Character of Regulatory Systems

The choice of appropriate procedures and management systems is much dependent on the style and culture of regulatory systems and so, to explain their incidence, we must return to some of the fundamental aspects discussed earlier in this chapter. One is the distinction between social and economic regulation. Social regulation, such as that governing health and safety and environmental pollution, has a long history dating back to medieval times (Ogus, 1992) and is derived from the police powers of the state (Freund, 1932). As such, in its developed forms, it assumed the character of 'command and control', the machinery of government coercing desired behaviour from its citizens. Most of the procedures were therefore designed to ensure that the regulators did not exceed their legislative mandate, that the rules were reasonably required to meet the regulatory objectives and that the enforcement processes complied with the demands of natural justice and did not discriminate unfairly against firms or individuals – the 'bread and butter' of traditional administrative law (Baldwin and McCrudden, 1987, Ch. 3).

The origins of economic regulation are quite different. Although some form of inherent legal restraints on monopolies has existed in most jurisdictions, the control of prices and quality in natural monopolies has been a relatively recent phenomenon, simply because the most important instances of the latter have been associated with technological developments occurring after the industrial revolution. Also, the strategies of governments in dealing with the problem was at the outset, and at least in institutional terms, uncertain and incoherent (Arthurs, 1985). So in the nineteenth century, exploitative behaviour by private monopolists might be combated by ad hoc inquiries and adverse publicity, rather than by any systematic application of legal norms (Foster, 1992, pp. 227–35), while the ever-expanding public ownership of natural monopolies became subject mainly to internal procedural directives which did not always facilitate accountability to outsiders (Lapsley and Kilpatrick, 1997, Ch. 3).

The American distaste for public ownership led to the retention of private utilities, but with regulatory commissions controlling prices. These institutions acquired two related characteristics (MacAvoy, 1979, Ch. 2). With their principal function being to review price levels and structures proposed by the suppliers, they acted as adjudicators as much as rule-makers. Second, the facts that typically they were dealing with monopolists, with therefore a 'one-to-one' relationship, that some degree of cooperation from the regulated firms was required if they were to acquire the necessary information for good decision-making, and that some interchange of personnel was not unknown, all led to a concept of 'negotiated regulation', very different from that normally associated with command and control (see Peacock, 1984). Not surprisingly, there were allegations and evidence of 'regulatory capture' (Bernstein, 1955); and efforts were made to contain the phenomenon by (as we shall see) stringent procedural requirements.

The wave of privatisation in other countries in the 1980s and 1990s and the need to create regulatory agencies raised the question as to the extent to which the American model would be followed. Alternative strategies were to harness the new agencies to existing traditions of administrative proceduralism and management, and to imitate the institutions that already existed for social regulation. However, the same period also witnessed major changes to the latter, there being a significant move away from command and control towards systems involving economic incentives and more freedom for firms in meeting regulatory objectives (Ogus, 2000a).

Procedures

We may focus on three main categories of procedural rules designed to encourage transparency and third-party involvement in regulatory decision-making: notification, the one-way communication between the regulator and the public; consultation, the collecting of information relevant to the decision; and participation, the use of public hearings to allow oral representations and discussion.

The obligation to notify the public of proposed regulatory policies and rules is routinely applied in all jurisdictions. A requirement to publish reasons for decisions or rules is less commonly encountered. It obviously encourages good decision-making, but if regulators will in practice give reasons for their decisions, it may be counter-productive to make this the subject of formal requirements, since it may render the process unduly legalistic, causing additional costs and delay, and 'such procedures always work to the advantage of the regulated; they provide another route to regulatory capture' (Foster, 1992, p. 274).

This need to achieve the right balance between over-legalism and informality applies also to the other procedural issues. In the case of utility regulation, formal provision is typically made for consultation with a body representing consumers (Locke, 1998). But it is not clear that the lines of communication thus made open prove to be more effective than consultation that operates in a more ad hoc manner and appear to take place in most jurisdictions: 'consultation which focuses on only selected and well-organized interests may produce biased information which can skew regulatory decision-making' (OECD, 1994, p. 28).

Of course, there is little that can be done to control the weight that regulators attribute to various third-party communications, but procedural devices can at least be introduced to restrain attempts to influence decision-making by 'back-door lobbying': in the USA this is done by requiring that all communications between third-parties and regulators concerning proposals are placed on the official record (Breyer and Stewart, 1985, pp. 663–71).

Not surprisingly, given its adversarial culture, American administrative law has gone furthest towards a model of regulatory process involving public hearings (Breyer and Stewart, 1985, pp. 561–9). But such an approach would seem to be less appropriate in systems in which governments play a role in decision-making. Also it is arguable that oral debate can detrimentally oversimplify the complexities of some regulatory issues, including the determination of utility prices (Baldwin and Cave, 1999, pp. 318–19).

Managerial Systems

'Regulatory management' is a relative newcomer to the language of regulatory theory and policy. It has had its greatest impact in relation to social regulation as a reaction to the widespread perception in the 1970s and 1980s that many systems had to a greater or lesser extent failed to meet their targets (Sunstein, 1990, Ch. 3). This was a consequence of the facts that rules had become too numerous and too complex, that they imposed unnecessary burdens, especially administrative burdens, on firms and that they were too inflexible relative to changing technological and economic conditions (OECD, 1994, p. 17). The impact on regulatory policy has been significant (OECD, 1992). As we have already seen, there has been the deregulation movement involving more flexible regulatory instruments and a degree of self-regulation, but equally important has been the introduction of practices and procedures aimed at the better management of regulatory systems (Hill, 1999).

Among these reforms, we should highlight measures designed to coax bureaucracies towards better regulation. In a number of jurisdictions, so-called 'regulatory checklists' have been introduced, requiring officials involved in regulatory policy and the drafting of regulatory rules to reveal their awareness of characteristics that are considered desirable (OECD, 1993). In Norway the checklist includes questions such as: is government action necessary? If so, is it preferable at national or regional level? Have different regulatory techniques been considered to determine which is the most appropriate? Are the regulations drafted in a language and style that can be readily understood? Can they be effectively enforced? (Norway, 1994).

More ambitiously, in some countries, notably the USA, regulators must engage in some form of cost–benefit analysis of regulatory proposals, often known as regulatory impact analysis (Froud et al., 1998). This is somewhat controversial if it effectively requires officials to demonstrate that a measure is justified in cost–benefit terms, because the benefits of regulatory intervention are more difficult to quantify than the costs (McGarity, 1991). But typically the instrument is used more as an information device, enabling policy-makers to have a better understanding of the probable consequences of particular instruments.

In relation to areas such as environmental pollution and industrial health and safety, management systems of this kind have, it is claimed (e.g. Gunningham et al., 1998), promoted a better informed and a more sophisticated choice between regulatory instruments, and between regulatory and non-regulatory instruments. To what extent they have impacted on economic regulation is somewhat less clear. Of course, the latter embraces the quality as well as the price of monopolistic services, and good management systems can assist in the devising of effective controls, such as performance indicators (Ogus, 1994, pp. 286–7). But arguably they can also contribute meaningfully to what we have seen to be the crucial policy issues: the tension between price controls and competition policy; and, if there are price controls, the choice of an appropriate method for determining efficient prices (Better Regulation Task Force, 2001).

LEGAL INSTRUMENTS

Within the confines of this chapter it is clearly impossible to provide a comprehensive survey of the huge variety of legal instruments that are used to accomplish regulatory goals. Instead, we focus on a general theme concerning the style of the regulatory instrument: the extent to which the legal instrument should rely on coercion to achieve the desired outcome; and the extent to which it should rely on other types of incentive. In industrialised countries, there has been a significant trend away from the first, more traditional, method towards the second (OECD, 1994; Ogus, 2000a).

Command and Control

Traditional coercive, or command and control regulation is widely used across the social and economic fields. It comprises several features:

- it relies heavily on the imposition, or threatened imposition, of a sanction to achieve compliance;
- the burden of enforcement is assumed by a public agency, often that which is also responsible for detailed rule-making;
- the rules are predominantly 'activity-based', that is they control directly what individuals or firms do, rather than the outcomes of those activities.

Regulation of this kind gives rise to a number of problems, particularly in an era of rapidly developing technology (Sunstein, 1990, Ch. 3):

- activity-based intervention requires the agency to have adequate information resources both centrally, to formulate appropriate standards, and locally, to monitor their application;
- prescriptive regimes create little or no incentive for the regulated firms to develop cheaper means of meeting the regulatory goal;
- traditional 'rule-books' become very detailed and bulky;
- the more specific the prescription, the easier it is for regulatees to engage in behaviour which contradicts the spirit, but not the letter, of the law.

Innovations Within Command and Control

By the end of the twentieth century, many jurisdictions had significantly reformed their traditional regulatory techniques (OECD, 1994). The major catalyst for change was perhaps the perception that, as a consequence of the regulatory overload just described, 'traditional forms of command and control regulation . . . have reached the limit of their effectiveness' (Gunningham et al., 1998, pp. 46–7). But there was also the influence of increased globalisation of markets, and prescriptive and detailed national regulation often constituting barriers to trade (Esty and Geradin, 2001). There have been several modes of reform (Ogus, 2000a, pp. 89–93):

- controls shifted from activities to outcomes, thus enabling firms to devise their own methods of meeting regulatory goals;
- where prescriptive standards persist, they tend to operate as default rules, operative only if the firm fails to provide a reasonable alternative (Baldwin, 1995, pp. 80–121);
- standards agencies, such as the British Standards Institute and its European equivalents, provide rules that firms can adopt on a voluntary basis (Spindler, 1998);
- there has been a gradual broadening of powers of third parties to enforce regulatory law (Yeung, 1999).

Alternative Strategies and Instruments

There have been two main strategies or instruments developed as alternatives to command and control. The first comprises a number of variants on the idea of self-regulation; the second involves economic incentives rather than coercion.

If self-regulation is defined as a phenomenon where rule-making and enforcement are carried out exclusively by representatives of the regulated sector, it may well be declining. In industries where the regulated suppliers had traditionally wielded these powers, such as the professions and financial services, the powers have increasingly been transferred to public agencies (National Consumer Council, 2000).

If self-regulation is given a broader meaning, encompassing a spectrum of arrangements in which the regulated sector plays a lesser or greater role in the regulatory functions (Ogus, 2000b), then there has been increasing use of the phenomenon, based on the increasing realisation that those engaged in an activity are generally best informed as to what is the best and cheapest method of achieving a regulatory goal (Gunningham and Rees, 1997). What has thus emerged in the newer models of self-regulation is an attempt to devise institutional arrangements which retain the advantages of low-cost rule-formulation but involve some degree of public accountability. Some jurisdictions have adopted what has been referred to as 'co-regulation', in which self-regulatory agencies issue, and sometimes enforce, rules but with a degree of oversight from, or participation by, public agencies (Grabosky and Braithwaite, 1986). Of particular influence has been the model of 'enforced self-regulation' developed by Ayres and Braithwaite (1992). They envisage a public agency negotiating with individual firms regulations that are particularised to the latters' circumstances, with the threat of imposing less well tailored standards should the firm fail to cooperate. Another variant on the same theme is a regime in which the focus of public control is on the structure and appropriateness of the internal management system adopted by firms to address the regulatory goals, rather than on the activity itself (Gunningham et al., 1998, pp. 60–9).

Regulation by 'economic instruments' has attracted considerable attention as an alternative to command and control (Howse, 1993). The basic idea is to replace coercion by a system which harnesses regulatory goals to market incentives. It includes such devices as fiscal impositions, subsidies, trade in regulatory controls (e.g emissions trading) and conditions attached to public contracts. Advocates, many of them economists, claim that the instruments have several important advantages: they reduce information and administrative costs; their imposition is more certain; they are more adept at inducing marginal adjustments to behaviour; and they create incentives for technological development (Mitchell, 1988). In fact, when account is taken of practical aspects such as administrative costs, targeting and accountability, they are more problematic than the abstract models formulated by economists would tend to suggest (Ogus, 1998).

At the level of political rhetoric, economic instruments seem to attract much enthusiasm from governments but their actual use has been relatively modest. The trading of emission limits to atmospheric pollution appears to have been successfully established in the USA and Denmark (Cole, 2000). Although important proposals have been made by the European Commission for such a system to apply across the European Union, they remain controversial.

Financial charges have often been employed to induce behavioural change where legal compulsion is regarded as inappropriate. Taxes on alcohol, gambling and tobacco are the prime examples, but there is ambiguity and tension between the regulatory and revenue-raising functions: if the demand for the product or activity is highly inelastic, the imposition is a fruitful source of revenue, but relatively ineffective as a regulatory device (Ogus, 1999, pp. 254–58). Charges to combat road congestion have been much discussed (Button and Verhoef, 1998) and sometimes implemented, but efforts to apply the tax idea to other activities creating significant externalities, notably pollution, have been tentative. Although the taxation of water pollution has existed for some time (Andersen, 1994), the instrument has complemented, rather than replaced, conventional command and control regulation.

CONCLUSION: MODELS FOR DEVELOPING COUNTRIES?

This has not been an evaluative study, but rather a mapping exercise, attempting to identify the institutional structures of regulatory systems in different jurisdictions in terms of the choices available. To some extent, of course, those choices apply to developing countries and in consequence the study can be extended to evaluate models of regulation in those jurisdictions. However, equally obviously, there are other variables that come into play.

Take, first, the question of constitutional order. While important differences exist between the industrialised countries, the regulatory structures have been devised on the assumption of a limited role of the state in the economy and on the existence of checks and balances within political and governmental orders. The structures cannot easily be transplanted to countries where resource allocation through markets has been slow to emerge and where the tradition of an activist state is therefore much stronger; nor where power is unduly concentrated in a governing elite. Indeed, the central tenets of administrative law, from which regulatory institutional frameworks derive, require compliance with the law, and a degree of accountability to citizens, by governments and their officials no less than by those who are regulated. In short, western models of regulation will not function well without a consistent commitment to the 'rule of law' and its many connotations.

This does not mean that the regulatory models described in this chapter are irrelevant for countries without such a commitment. Rather, it points to the likelihood that some institutional frameworks will be more effective than others in meeting regulatory objectives. So, for example, with fewer constitutional checks and balances, centralised, command and control systems should be more successful.

Analogous considerations apply to corruption, another major hindrance to institutional reform. Now, it is obviously wrong to treat this phenomenon as a problem peculiar to developing, rather than developed, countries: many of the latter have a long history of public office being used for private gain. In any event, it is not always clear where the line is to be drawn between corruption and 'rent-seeking behaviour', the widespread, if generally lawful, practice of manipulating public institutions to serve private interests. Here we can draw on the prolific literature (surveyed in Tullock, 1993) to identify structural devices that can be used to constrain such behaviour. Some of these, for example the increased transparency of, and accountability for, public decision-making, imply a significant level of 'rule of law' commitment which may be absent in some developing countries. But others point to a strategy that may be more compatible with conditions prevailing in those countries: restricting the opportunities for corrupt and self-serving behaviour by, for example, limiting discretion and reducing the monopolistic power of regulatory officials.

REFERENCES

Andersen, M.S. (1994), *Governance by Green Taxes: Making Pollution Prevention Pay*, Manchester: Manchester University Press.

Arthurs, H.W. (1985), *Without the Law: Administrative Justice and Legal Pluralism in Nineteenth-century England*, Toronto: University of Toronto Press.

Ayres, I. and Braithwaite, J. (1992), *Responsive Regulation: Transcending the Deregulation Debate*, New York: Oxford University Press.

Baldwin, R. (1995), *Rules and Government: Non-Statutory Rules and Administrative Law*, Oxford: Oxford University Press.

Baldwin, R. and Cave, M. (1999), *Understanding Regulation: Theory, Strategy and Practice*, Oxford: Oxford University Press.

Baldwin, R. and Daintith, T. (eds) (1992), *Harmonization and Hazard: The Regulation of Workplace Safety in the European Community*, London: Graham and Trotman.

Baldwin R. and McCrudden C. (eds) (1987), *Regulation and Public Law*, London: Weidenfeld and Nicolson.

Bell, J. (1992), *French Constitutional Law*, Oxford: Clarendon Press.

Bernstein, M. (1955), *Regulating Business by Independent Commissions*, Princeton: Princeton University Press.

Better Regulation Task Force (2001), *Economic Regulation*, London: Cabinet Office.

Boujong, K. (ed.) (2000), *Karlsruher Kommentar zum Gesetz über Ordnungswidrigkeiten*, 2nd edn, Munich: Beck Verlag.

Breyer, S. (1982), *Regulation and its Reform*, Cambridge, MA: Harvard University Press.

Breyer, S. and Stewart, R. (1985), *Administrative Law and Regulatory Policy*, 2nd edn, Boston: Little Brown.

Button, K.J. and Verhoef, E.T. (eds) (1998), *Road Pricing, Traffic Congestion and the Environment: Issues of Efficiency and Social Feasibility*, Cheltenham: Edward Elgar.

Cole, D.H. (2000), 'New Forms of Private Property: Property Rights in Environmental Goods', in B. Bouckaert and G. De Geest (eds), *Encyclopedia of Law and Economics, Vol. III, Civil Law and Economics*, Cheltenham: Edward Elgar, pp. 274–314.

Dale, W. (1988), *British and French Statutory Drafting*, London: Institute of Advanced Legal Studies.

Delvolvé, P. (1998), *Droit Public de l'Economie*, Paris: Dalloz.

Doern, G.B. (1998), 'The interplay among regulators: mapping regulatory institutions in the United Kingdom, the United States and Canada', in G.B. Doern and S. Wilks (eds), *Changing Regulatory Institutions in Britain and North America*, Toronto: University of Toronto Press, Ch. 2.

Dyson, K. (1992a), 'Theories of regulation and the case of Germany: a model of regulatory change', in K. Dyson (ed.), *The Politics of German Regulation*, Aldershot: Dartmouth, Ch. 1.

Dyson, K. (1992b), 'Regulatory culture and regulatory change: some conclusions', in K. Dyson (ed.), *The Politics of German Regulation*, Aldershot: Dartmouth, Ch.11.

Esty, D.C. and Geradin, D. (eds) (2001), *Regulatory Competition and Economic Integration: Comparative Perspectives*, Oxford: Oxford University Press.

Faure, M., Finsinger, J., Siegers, J. and Van den Bergh, R. (eds) (1993), *Regulation of the Professions: A Law and Economics Approach to the Regulation of Attorneys and Physicians in the US, Belgium, the Netherlands, Germany and the UK*, Antwerp: Maklu.

Foster, C.D. (1992), *Privatization, Public Ownership and the Regulation of Natural Monopoly*, Oxford: Blackwell.

Freund, E. (1932), *Legislative Regulation*, New York: Commonwealth Fund.

Froud, J., Boden, R., Ogus, A. and Stubbs, P. (1998), *Controlling the Regulators*, Basingstoke: Macmillan.

Grabosky, P. and Braithwaite, J. (1986), *Of Manners Gentle: Enforcement Strategies of Australian Business Regulatory Agencies*, Oxford: Oxford University Press.

Gunningham, N. and Grabosky, P. with Sinclair, D. (1998), *Smart Regulation: Designing Environmental Policy*, Oxford: Clarendon Press.

Gunningham, N. and Rees, V. (1997), 'Industry self-regulation', *Law and Policy*, **17**, 363.

Hill, M.M. (1999), 'Managing the regulatory state: from "up," to "in and down," to "out and across" ', in G.B. Doern, M.M. Hill, M.J. Prince and R.J. Schultz (eds), *Changing the Rules: Canadian Regulatory Regimes and Institutions,* Toronto: University of Toronto Press, Ch. 11.

Howse, R. (1993), 'Retrenchment, reform or revolution? The shift to incentives and the future of the regulatory state', *Alberta Law Review*, **31**, 455–92.

Jarass, H.D. (1984), *Wirtschaftsverwaltungsrecht und Wirtschaftsverfassungsrecht*, 2nd edn, Frankfurt a.M: Alfred Metzner Verlag.

Kagan, R.A. (2001), *Adversarial Legalism: The American Way of Law*, Cambridge, MA: Harvard University Press.

Landis, J.M. (1938), *The Administrative Process*, New Haven: Yale University Press.

Lapsley, I. and Kilpatrick, K. (1997), *A Question of Trust: Regulators and the Regulatory Regime for Privatised Utilities*, Edinburgh: Institute of Chartered Accountants of Scotland.

Lévêque, F. (1998), *Economie de la réglementation*, Paris: La Découverte.

Locke, S. (1998), 'Modelling the consumer interest' in G.B. Doern and S. Wilks (eds), *Changing Regulatory Institutions in Britain and North America*, Toronto: University of Toronto Press, Ch. 7.

MacAvoy, P.W. (1979), *The Regulated Industries and the Economy*, New York: W.W. Norton.

Macey, J.R. (1992), 'Organisational design and political control of administrative agencies', *Journal of Law, Economics and Organization*, **8**, 93–110.

McGarity, T. (1991), *Reinventing Rationality: The Role of Regulatory Analysis in the Federal Bureaucracy*, Cambridge: Cambridge University Press.

McWhinney, E. (1986), *Supreme Courts and Judicial Law-making: Constitutional Tribunals and Constitutional Review*, Dordrecht: Nijhoff.

Majone, G. (1996), 'Regulation and its modes', in G. Majone (ed), *Regulating Europe*, London: Routledge, Ch. 1.

Mashaw, J. (1985), 'Prodelegation: why administrators should make political decisions', *Journal of Law, Economics and Organization*, **1**, 81–100.

Mitchell, C.N. (1988), 'Taxation, retribution and justice', *University of Toronto Law Journal*, **38**, 151–83.

National Consumer Council (2000), *Models of Self-Regulation: An Overview of Models in Business and the Professions*, London: NCC.

Norway (1994), *To Regulate – Or Not: Checklist for Use When Deciding on Instruments and New Regulation*, Oslo: Royal Ministry of Government Administration.

OECD (1992), *Regulatory Reform, Privatisation and Competition Policy*, Paris: OECD.

OECD (1993), *The Design and Use of Regulatory Checklists in OECD Countries*, Paris: OECD.

OECD (1994), *Improving the Quality of Law and Regulations: Economic, Legal and Managerial Techniques*, Paris: OECD.

Ogus, A. (1990), 'Property rights and freedom of economic activity', in L. Henkin and A.J. Rosenthal (eds), *Constitutionalism and Rights: The Influence of the United States Constitution Abroad*, New York: Columbia University Press, pp. 125–50.

Ogus, A. (1992) 'Regulatory law: some lessons from the past', Legal Studies, **12**, 1–19.

Ogus, A. (1994), *Regulation: Legal Form and Economic Theory*, Oxford: Clarendon Press.

Ogus, A. (1998), 'Corrective taxes and financial impositions as regulatory instruments', *Modern Law Review*, **61**, 767–88.

Ogus, A. (1999), 'Nudging and rectifying: the use of fiscal instruments for regulatory purposes', Legal Studies, **19**, 245–66.

Ogus, A. (2000a), 'New techniques for social regulation: decentralisation and diversity', in H. Collins, P. Davies and R. Rideout (eds), *Legal Regulation of the Employment Relation*, Dordrecht: Kluwer, pp. 83–98.

Ogus, A. (2000b), 'Self-regulation', in B. Bouckaert and G. De Geest, *Encyclopedia of Law and Economics, vol. 5, The Economics of Crime and Litigation*, Cheltenham: Edward Elgar, pp. 587–602.
Page, A.C. (1986), 'Self-regulation: the constitutional dimension', *Modern Law Review*, **49**, 141–67.
Peacock, A. (ed.) (1984), *The Regulation Game: How British and West German Companies Bargain with Government*, Oxford: Blackwell.
Reich, N. (1984), *Staatliche Regulierungzwischen Marktversagen und Politikversagen*, Heidelberg: Mueller Juristischer Verlag.
Schwartz, B. and Wade, H.W.R. (1972), *Legal Control of Government: Administrative Law in Britain and the United States*, Oxford: Clarendon Press.
Spindler, G. (1998), 'Market processes, standardisation and tort law', *European Law Review*, **4**, 311–36.
Sunstein, C.R. (1990), *After the Rights Revolution: Reconceiving the Regulatory State*, Cambridge, MA: Harvard University Press.
Taggart, M. (1995), 'Public utilities and public law', in P.A. Joseph (ed.), *Essays on the Constitution*, Wellington: Brooker's, pp. 214–64.
Tullock, G. (1993), *Rent Seeking*, Aldershot: Edward Elgar.
Yeung, K. (1999), 'Private enforcement of competition law', in C. McCrudden (ed.), *Regulation and Deregulation: Policy and Practice in the Utilities and Financial Services Industries*, Oxford: Clarendon Press, Ch. 3.
Zeckhauser, R, and Horn, M. (1989), 'The control and performance of state-owned enterprises', in P. MacAvoy et al. (eds), *Privatization and State-owned Enterprises: Lessons from the United States, Great Britain and Canada*, Boston: Kluwer.

8. Public management and regulatory governance: problems of policy transfer to developing countries

Martin Minogue

INTRODUCTION: THE DEBATE ON ECONOMIC DEVELOPMENT STRATEGIES

Analysis of regulatory governance in developing economies immediately encounters several difficulties. First, concepts of regulatory governance and the regulatory state are still relatively new in developed economies, and are generally the product of a post-privatisation phase of neoliberal economic reform. While recent surveys of privatisation on an international basis have been broadly favourable (Megginson and Netter, 2001; Shirley and Walsh, 2001) analysis of the application of privatisation and associated reforms in developing economies has been more critical, and it is clear that much more work is needed on their social effects. The picture is particularly blurred in respect of the reforms such as privatisation, contracting and regulation, which involve a new conception of state–market relations, and so add in the complexities of governance and political institutions in developing countries. Meanwhile, major players themselves appear now to be seriously divided about the appropriateness of current economic reforms and their relation to broader development strategies.

There can be no gainsaying the practical hold that neoliberal policies have exerted since the 1980s through their adoption and promotion by official aid agencies and bilateral donors. This has been characterised as the 'Washington consensus' – a broad set of ingredients in a recipe for successful economic growth and development originally spelled out by Williamson (1990, 1996) and regarded as agreed on by crucial Washington institutions, including the IMF, the World Bank, and the US Treasury. A key perception was that 'the role of the State was to "roll back" itself: liberalisation, deregulation, privatisation were the key watchwords' (Florio, 2002, p. 379). After more than a decade in which this policy consensus dominated official development policy agendas, it began to come under attack. This was in part because of the shocks administered by economic failures and crises in Russia, Asia and Latin America. If the proof of the pudding was in the eating, this particular pudding was causing severe indigestion. Some of the criticisms are highly relevant to discussion later in this chapter of the limits created by underdeveloped institutions. The clearest assault on the received thinking of the Washington institutions came from Joseph Stiglitz, a Nobel prize-winning economist. Stiglitz's now famous savaging of the IMF, while at the time Chief Economist at the World Bank, and his more recent attacks on the neoliberal orthodoxy subsequent to his effective dismissal, in truth do no more than follow the logic of his theoretical work, which draws attention to the limits to free markets of incomplete information, inadequate markets, and unworkable institutions. He is at pains now to point out that these limiting conditions are especially likely to be present in developing countries, and is particularly harsh on the shortcomings of premature privatisation, arguing that many developing and transitional economies do not have financial systems capable of handling such transactions, or regulatory systems capable of preventing harmful behaviours after privatisation; nor do they have systems of corporate governance capable of monitoring these restructured institutions (Stiglitz, 2002).

The point being stressed in this introductory section is that the big themes we deal with – states, markets, competition, regulation, poverty – are exceedingly complex, but are also characterised by contested understandings and conceptualisations. Effective development policy is not just a matter of getting the practice right, but of getting the ideas right. It is alarming to discover that influential aid donor policy initiatives often rest on ideas that are based on untested a priori assumptions, or are strongly disputed by other practitioners. This tension between theory and practice is marked in the case of public management and regulatory governance reforms.

PUBLIC MANAGEMENT AND REGULATORY GOVERNANCE: DEVELOPED COUNTRY MODELS

An earlier paper on regulatory governance made a number of basic linkages between regulation, 'new public management' (NPM) reforms, and broader concepts of governance (Minogue, 2001b).

1. The analysis of regulation goes beyond examination of the formal rules which govern relationships between the public and private sectors, to the broader framework of state–market relations.
2. Regulation is then seen as part of the whole range of neoliberal market reforms, which include privatisation and reshaped state–market mechanisms such as contracting and public–private partnerships.

3. Since much regulation is carried out inside government (Hood et al., 1999), it is appropriate to consider the effects on regulatory policy and practice of public management reforms that introduce into the state sector the entrepreneurial disciplines of the marketplace.
4. Since regulation can be categorised as a distinctive mode of policymaking (Majone, 1999) it is appropriate to examine its relation to the general public policy process.
5. Finally, the significant effects on regulatory systems and processes of political ideas, institutions and relationships of power require analysis of governance frameworks and an understanding of such concepts as 'the regulatory state', 'regulatory capture' and 'regulatory space'.

How should we tie in regulatory reforms to generic public management changes? First, we can do so by treating regulatory innovations as part and parcel of the generic reform movement labelled as New Public Management (NPM). The literature on NPM characterises it as a set of principles rooted in neoliberal thought, and involving a new conception of state–society, public–private relationships (best exemplified by influential hand-me-down derivatives of public choice theory such as Osborne and Gaebler, 1992). Conceptually, NPM is a response to perceived failures of the 'command and control' state, with its Keynsian philosophy of stabilisation and distribution, and strong internal values of public interest and public accountability. NPM rests on the following assumptions, which need to be critically examined for internal coherence as well as being tested against the results of reform practices.

1. The public interest state has led to extensive government failure and inefficiency, and should be replaced, as far as practicable, by superior market mechanisms.
2. A more efficient public sector requires the separation of policy from execution, which would be decentralised.
3. An entrepreneurial culture based on managerial incentives will produce better government performance than a public service culture based on public interest principles.
4. Accountability rooted in a direct relationship between 'manager' and 'customer' is preferable to legal and political forms of accountability.

In brief, the key idea is that the state has become too large, too interventionist, and too costly; that many of its activities could be transferred to a willing and capable private sector; and that the disciplines of the marketplace should be applied to any residual state bureaucracy.

It is clear that there are some highly debatable, not to say provocative, assumptions here. First, the notion that state failure is produced by an informal conspiracy by officials (both elected and appointed) to advance their own interests depends on the supposition that social behaviour is governed by individual self-interest. This argument rests on a highly simplified view of what constitutes and explains both government and market failure. Yet it is this same characteristic of self-interest that is held to make market-based forms superior, because the market resolution of self-interested transactions will produce optimal efficiency.

Second, the separation of politics from management is a major tenet, yet designing and implementing radical reforms of this type demand a substantial exertion of political will and leadership. Related to this, NPM requires the creation of managerial and institutional autonomy in a variety of decentralised forms, yet the effective implementation of such reforms must be driven by a centralised strategy, and strong central direction and resourcing. Because of these contradictions, commentators such as Hood (1994, 1995) suggest that NPM is conceptually incoherent, and mixes different types of reform strategy and managerial 'fashions'.

Whatever the view that might be taken of the concepts underlying NPM, there can be no dispute about the success of this model in dominating the public management reform agenda in developed economies in the past two decades (what follows summarises a more detailed account in Minogue, 1998). The explanation for this seems to lie in a combination of pressures on these governments to control rising levels of public expenditure while simultaneously holding down direct taxation, and to respond to political demands for improved levels of performance in the delivery of public services. With local variations, the design of the NPM model normally included a reduction of the size and scope of the public sector, particularly through privatisation (in social as well as economic spheres); restructuring and reduction of central bureaucracies; the introduction into state agencies of competitive disciplines through contracting of services and internal markets; and the use of performance management and auditing to increase operational efficiency. The aim of such reforms was to produce an entrepreneurial, results-oriented, performance driven public management culture inside an enabling rather than a direct provider state.

It is remarkably difficult to arrive at an informed judgement of whether this model has succeeded in practice. Given the emphasis of NPM on such elements as efficiency gains, performance measurement and auditing, and a commitment to results, it is surprising to find so little attention in the literature to evaluation. The implementation of the reform model has been extensive, particularly in the UK, New Zealand and Canada, and proponents (usually involved practitioners) claim real improvements in systems, processes, operations and cultures; but as Pollitt and Bouckaert (2000, pp. 97–133) show, there is an absence of persuasive empirical evidence with which to measure results on any of these dimensions. There is a genuinely changed discourse of reform, but little to link reforms of structures to processes and outcomes, whether in terms of better policymaking or better delivery of public services. Where the language of results-based management is employed this is often directed to the *introduction* of institutional changes, not to the *effects* of those changes as measured by outcomes. The UK provides a good illustration of the problems surrounding the evaluation of NPM reforms. While it is clear that a major structural transformation has taken place, with substantial privatisation across a whole range of public utilities and services, the restructuring and reduction of the central civil service, and the introduction of mixed public–private provision through mechanisms such as contracting out, public–private finance arrangements, and public–private partnerships, the results and impact of these changes are thoroughly contested. We might conclude at this point that as well as being a contested concept, NPM is also a contested practice in terms of judgement of its outcomes.

The relation of public management reforms to changing modes of regulation is also beset by potential contradictions. Lane (2001), for example, characterises public sector reforms as essentially a comprehensive shift from long-term contracting (primarily through government bureaucracies and public enterprises) to short-term contracting (primarily through contracting-out and tendering mechanisms). This move 'presupposes massive deregulation, opening up both the public sector and the regulated sector of the private economy to competition' (Lane, 2001, p. 43). On the other hand, this extensive reduction of bureaucratic-legal interventions, or what has been called the 'hollowing out' of the state (Rhodes, 1994) creates a new requirement for regulatory mechanisms to protect public interest concerns, to make good the loss or weakening of traditional forms of accountability, and to respond to what Moran terms the crisis of the collapse of self-regulation (Moran, 2002). Moran, summarising a 'complex political economy of regulation literature' (2002, p. 392) identifies a *pluralist* stream which emphasises that the nature of regulation is contingent on the distribution of power among different social groups, and will vary from case to case, and between different national political environments (the obvious contrast in developed country models being that between 'a litigious and adversarial regulatory culture in the United States and a British culture which stresses informal resolution of issues and a culture of consensus between regulators and regulated' (Moran, 2002, p. 392, drawing on Vogel, 1986). An alternative construct is a *rational actor* model in which the strategic pursuit of sectional interests produces benefits not to the public interest but to the powerful actors who dominate the process: politicians, business interests and bureaucrats. This latter approach is close to, and has roots in, the neoliberal paradigm which, as we saw earlier, contributed so significantly to generic ideas about the reform of the state–market relationship. In essence these two approaches represent familiar and competing explanatory frameworks for the origins and nature of regulation. Moran, examining the reasons for the growth of deregulation, identifies a loss of confidence in the regulatory state, partly because of persistent implementation failure, partly because of pessimism occasioned by regulatory capture. But his discussion reminds us that there is more than one version of the regulatory state. Sometimes the literature refers to all aspects of the 'command and control' state, and specifically to the expansion from traditional economic regulation to wider social regulation, particularly in respect of welfare, health and the environment: it has rightly been said that 'regulation . . . is as old as government itself' (Majone, 1996, p. 9). At other points the focus is much narrower, and refers to the creation of new regulatory institutions in the wake of privatisation and deregulation reforms, a phenomenon often termed 're-regulation'.

But if we create truly independent regulatory agencies, who will control them, or mediate any conflicts of interest between their actions and broader public interest concerns? This question might also be addressed to proponents of self-regulation as the only viable response to problems of regulatory overload (whether of the traditional or the post-privatisation kind). Here Moran turns to the formulation by Ayres and Braithwaite (1992) of 'responsive regulation' as a means of transcending the limits of legal formalism; regulation is essential to secure efficiency and to manage risk, but effective regulation 'in conditions of great complexity depends on fostering norms among the regulated such that they will voluntarily comply, and depends upon the creation of a constant dialogue between regulators and regulated' (Moran, 2002, p. 396). Elsewhere, Braithwaite (1999) argues that we have moved to 'a world where private powers pose many more threats to liberty than public power' and that accordingly we need to escape from traditional forms of political accountability, since these 'cause regulated actors to work defensively to avoid blame, instead of creatively to seize responsibility for achieving valued outcomes' (Braithwaite, 1999, p. 91). But this approach appears to beg two questions. First, who decides what the appropriate norms should be, or which values should inform what outcomes? If these norms and values are pre-determined, then they will have to be imposed, which will invite strategies of avoidance; if they depend on dialogue, they will represent a negotiated bargain, and opportunities for capture. As Moran admits, 'non-formal modes of regulation are themselves subject to the same sort of destructive influences as afflict formal modes' and both 'are undermined by the creativity of strategic actors searching for advantage' (Moran, 2002, p. 397).

What is missing from most accounts of regulation is understanding of the cultural elements that are essential to explanations of social behaviour, whether in general, in national systems, in organisations, or in particular groups; and of interactions and transactions between these various entities. This explanatory mode is well understood in social science, but is often neglected by the economists and lawyers who dominate the regulation literature. The commentators cited in this section (Moran, 2002; Inglis, 2000; Hood et al., 1999; Hood, 1998) all recommend a cultural analysis of the social relationships underlying regulation, and are attracted to the insights of anthropology in securing an adequate understanding both of why institutions work (or fail) as they do, and also of the ways in which trust can be built on shared values. According to Moran, 'the upshot is to paint a picture which subverts the efforts in the literature to develop some general theory of regulatory effectiveness' (Moran, 2002, p. 405); while Inglis, drawing his instances from the British education sector, mounts an excoriating attack on the pernicious ways in which neoliberal managerial reforms have subverted and damaged public service institutions built up on relations of mutuality and a commonality of public interest.

What then emerges as significant is the extent to which this debate must continue to include 'regulation inside government' (the title of Hood et al., 1999). The reshaping of the managerial state has brought into existence new regulatory institutions and practices, while at the same time leaving within the boundaries of the state some traditional regulatory responsibilities, in turn reconditioned by innovative regulatory practices (such as audit and performance management as already discussed briefly). We may add to this the regulatory responsibilities and relationships created by membership of the EU. Regulation therefore takes place inside government, outside government, across national government boundaries, and in institutions that cross the public–private divide. It is the wide-ranging nature of these arrangements that has brought into currency the idea of the 'regulatory state' but this too readily implies a replacement of other types of state, such as the 'traditional' state, or the 'welfare state', or the 'enabling state'. These are all crude labels, and in reality we are likely to find elements of each, and of the regulatory state, present in any particular national state we choose to examine. Perhaps this is why the notion of 'regulatory space' has been deployed. Drawn from the prior notion of 'policy space' in public policy studies, 'regulatory space' offers a canvas onto which we can paint a variety of occupants and their relational configuration; their provenance as state, non-state or hybrid actors matters less than their activities, transactions, motivations, and power or influence; this framework can also accommodate 'the variations introduced by differences in markets and issue arenas' (Hansher and Moran, 1989, p. 276). In sum, analysis of regulation involves analysis of ideas, institutions, processes, activities and actors, in all their myriad interrelationships in economic, social and political spheres. The conceptions of the regulatory state and regulatory space offer us the broadest possible analytical framework, in direct contradiction to the narrow formulations favoured in the standard literature on regulation.

POLICY TRANSFER ISSUES: PUBLIC MANAGEMENT IN DEVELOPING COUNTRIES

One justification for evaluating NPM reforms in developed economies is that the NPM model, or versions of it, has been widely imitated in developing countries, by the process we label 'policy transfer', principally through the mediating channels of the international and bilateral aid agencies (Common, 1998). Regulatory reforms are an integral part of the NPM model, specifically in being closely tied to market-oriented institutional changes such as privatisation and contracting. The preceding discussion sounds a number of cautionary notes. In the first place, it is not at all clear that the NPM reform model has been effective even in developed economies, and a critical literature places substantial costs as well as credits in the balance sheet. Consideration of the appropriateness for developing countries of developed country models of managerial and regulatory reform must incorporate a critical evaluation of the weaknesses in, and failures of, these models. Second, NPM entails a transformative conception of the state; while it is clear that the state in developing countries is much in need of renewal and reinvigoration, there is very little agreement on what kind of state this should be. Should we be trying to reduce the scope of that state, or should we be trying to build up its capabilities, powers and resources in order that it may achieve the developmental objectives required by its own citizens? Finally, the most obvious issue is that of cultural difference. Not only are developing economies distinctively different in economic, social and political terms from rich economies, but there is considerable variation between national cultures within these broad categories. Taylor (2001) has pointed to the problem that in transferring an NPM model to developing economies, we are making a double transfer, from developed to developing state, then across the public–private boundary. Both types of transfer are culturally problematic, and Taylor stresses the sociological naivety of those who promote NPM managerial practices that ignore or conflict with the social and political dynamics of public service organisations and systems in developing countries, an argument strongly expressed also by a leading practitioner of NPM in developed economies (Schick, 1998).

Once we begin to think about the crucial issue of the social and political dynamics likely to be encountered in the developing country state and its relations with both market and society, we must consider a further strand in the development agenda usually labelled as 'good governance'. This proposes that developing political systems must embrace what are regarded as universal principles of democratisation, political pluralism, human rights, the rule of law, and competent administration of public policy. 'Good governance' and 'new public management' are regarded as mutually supportive, with enhanced accountability and improved efficiency reinforcing each other. The main aid donors include in their good governance agenda the range of economic management reforms that encompass privatisation and regulation, and the interplay of public and private sectors (see e.g. UNDP, 1995; World Bank, 1994). This is logical enough, since the case for moving responsibilities out of the public sector rests largely on the presumption of government failure, institutional and administrative weaknesses in public management, and the distorting effects of political interventions and corruption. So we see that in the dominant development policy agenda espoused by the major aid donors, two transformative conceptions are brought together: a radical reshaping of the state and its relations with the market, and a particular model of state–society relations, incorporating 'universalist' political values. Moreover, this is an agenda that aid donors are intent on realising through both economic and political conditionalities attached to development assistance. Again, the ideas are strongly contested, and even on the most optimistic view, the application through practical reform programmes will encounter problems of adaptation to complex cultural systems. The specific issue of corruption (perhaps the defining limit of a range of governance pathologies) is used here to illustrate these difficulties, and to raise questions about the way that the standard literature on economic reforms treats the social and political contexts into which these reforms must be introduced (the following section draws heavily on Minogue, 2002).

CORRUPTION AND GOVERNANCE

If corruption is regarded only in moral terms, then it is unproblematic: it is bad, and should be eliminated. But this approach is neither adequate nor helpful, for it allows no room to treat corruption as a form of behaviour that has to be explained. The more persistent and widespread its occurrence, the more we need to understand it rather than indulge in high-minded condemnation. Corruption has in recent years received increasing attention as part of the good governance agenda being pursued by both multilateral and bilateral donors. Yet there is no hint in the plethora of publications that the analysis of corruption is another area of contested understandings. This is in no small part due to the dominance in this emerging literature of economistic treatments of corruption in terms of opportunistic, self-interested individuals who seize the opportunities to extract 'rents' provided by the bureaucratic pathologies of the 'third-world' state (Broadman and Recanatini, 2002; Rose-Ackerman, 1999; Gray and Kaufmann, 1998; Klitgaard, 1988). A telling example of the limitations of this approach is found in Huther and Shah (2001), who assert that 'corruption is a symptom of failed governance' and expound 'a framework based on the incentives for opportunistic behaviour by public officials'

(Huther and Shah, 2001, p. 2). The whole discussion is in terms of a calculation by individuals of their cost–benefit position set against a consciousness of expected gains and benefits. Policy, therefore, 'must change the cost–benefit calculations of public officials' (p. 3) and can do so by reducing the number of official transactions, and reducing the scope for gains. Their anti-corruption strategy envisages the de-monopolisation of public services, the promotion of competition in the private sector, and the injection of a new culture of contractualism in the public sector (we see here the whole thrust of neoliberal assumptions about state and market). In effect this analysis is merely a wish-list that makes no attempt to analyse wider social and political causation for the economic inefficiencies identified. The unrealistic nature of the analysis can be illustrated by one quotation: 'for a country in which few are held accountable for corrupt activities, anti-corruption efforts should focus on judicial independence resource' (p. 6). There is no recognition that, by definition, in such a country there would be no such thing as judicial independence. Again, they argue that 'widespread corruption is likely to be the result of multiple governance failures so successful anti-corruption campaigns are likely to be multipronged' (p. 6); but no attempt is made to analyse the reasons for multiple governance failures, or to acknowledge that whatever these reasons are would also defeat an anti-corruption campaign. Later, the authors judge that anticorruption policies work best where good governance systems are in place, but of course this is a tautology: if good governance systems are in place, by definition the incidence of corruption will already be low. Finally, they do the fashionable thing and discuss how levels of corruption might be quantified, but admit that such an approach is subject to 'large measurement errors' (p. 10).

A further example is provided by Lederman et al. (2001). This publication sets out to quantify the political determinants of corruption, with desirable political institutions being defined as those that increase political accountability or generate a competitive environment in the provision of public services, since it is assumed that these will reduce corruption. Their political analysis rests heavily on the modernisation model set out by Diamond et al. (1990), with no acknowledgement that this model is drawn from developed country political systems and bears little relation to the realities of political organisation and behaviour in developing countries. In relation to the structure of provision of public goods, the solutions recommended are either to decentralise government services, or introduce competition among government agencies. No practical examples are cited, and the evidence that liberalisation of public services can lead to increased corruption (Harriss-White and White, 1996) is ignored. It is difficult to avoid the conclusion that this whole discussion is as much about government failure and inefficiency as it is about corruption.

These examples have been cited to illustrate how the whole 'official' literature appears to assume that there is universal agreement on the definition of corruption, when there is not. Meanwhile, a range of non-economic treatments by anthropologists and political scientists is virtually ignored. An anthropological perspective immediately alerts us to the severe limitations of the economic orthodoxy. For example, Sissener (2001) counters the narrowness of the economic view of corruption, and its reliance on a 'public office' definition, with a contextual analysis which treats 'corrupt' behaviour as a 'social act . . . [whose] meaning must be understood with reference to the social relationships between people in historically specific social settings' (Sissener, 2001, p. 5). Using examples from India, China and Nepal, Sissener argues that 'a narrow definition of corruption makes it difficult to explain how behaviour that transcends Weberian borders of what is deemed acceptable for holders of public office is seen as legitimate and even laudable to those involved' (Sissener, 2001, p. 11). Ledevena (1998) analysing *blat* in Russia; and Yang (1994) on the pervasiveness of *guanxi* in China (both involving the use of personalistic networks to obtain goods, services or jobs in short supply, and both operating across public–private boundaries) are cited to support the contention that anti-corruption reforms are unlikely to have any effect in these conditions, where persistently rooted social behaviour is not seen as unacceptable by the practitioners. There is no mention of *blat* or *guanxi* in the lengthening list of World Bank publications on corruption.

Economists also frequently neglect the literature on the political dimensions of corruption. Yet Williams (1998) and Khan (1998, 2002) remind us of some well established certainties about political development; namely, that partisan organisation is at the heart of modern politics; that this requires 'spoils' to construct alliances and reward supporters; and that spoils are allocated (and have been in early modern British and American political history) on the basis that in political contests to control the state, there are always winners and losers. This process may be a necessary stage in the creation of modern political institutions and the political stability that is above all a precondition for effective economic progress and reform.

World Bank analysis of the political context of corruption is both condemnatory and superficial, striving to create a spurious rigour by establishing correlations between types of political institution, levels of corruption, and categories of economic performance. This approach makes indefensible or untested assumptions about causal relationships between democratic regime types and successful economic performance, and is rarely based on any empirical studies of actually existent corruption. The models produced by this type of exercise are so generalised and yet so narrowly conceived that they are almost worthless, and possibly mystifying, as tools of explanatory or causal analysis. Dominant neoliberal analysis assumes that neoliberal reforms, together with a contingent effect of economic growth, will bring economic efficiency and a corresponding reduction of corrupt practice and its deleterious economic effects. But there is evidence that these reforms have been associated with increased corruption, with both the privatisation of public monopolies, and the creation of new agencies of democratisation having increased, not reduced, what has been termed the 'new corruption' (Harriss-White and White, 1996; Duckett, 2001).

A more satisfactory approach is demonstrated by Khan (1996, 1998) who is concerned to distinguish between the 'allocative' effects and the 'corrosive' effects of corruption; that is, allocative because it gives access to resources otherwise not available to the recipient, and corrosive because this may be a wasteful and inefficient form of allocation. Khan draws attention to the absence in developing countries of a competent state that can protect property and other rights. Groups contending the existing allocation of rights strike bargains through a state-led patron–client model, sometimes described as 'patrimonial' (where a dominant state disperses resources to its supporters) or as 'clientelist' where powerful groups extract resources from the state. Since the detail and context of these political settlements vary, so do the associated effects of corruption so that, for example, 'while the South Korean state could impose performance criteria on its clients, the Pakistani state could not' (Khan, 1996, p. 15). He concludes that 'if the problem of inefficiency associated with corruption is due to the operation of corruption in a clientelist settlement, liberalisation may have little effect on corruption' (Khan, 1996, p. 20). Pointing to the possibility that the reduction of corruption in successful developers may have been the result rather than the precondition of such successful development, he calls for an explanatory framework that gives due weight to deeper structural causes (Khan, 1998). This approach is supported elsewhere, by Brinkerhoff (2000), who sees narrowly economistic treatments of corruption as 'unhelpful because they isolate corrupt practices from the political and institutional settings in which they occur' (Brinkerhoff, 2000, p. 241); and by Johnston (1997), a prolific writer on corruption, who points to the necessary limits of institutional reforms that neglect the social reality through which institutions must work, and suggests that in the long term, forms of social empowerment that transform 'the opportunities and alternatives that people have in life' is the more appropriate strategy (Johnston, 1997, p. 5). A similar problem arises with corruption.

GOVERNANCE REFORMS IN DEVELOPING COUNTRIES: THE REALITY GAP

The foregoing discussion indicates that analysts may be able to agree on what constitutes the practical economic reform agenda, while disagreeing on the appropriateness or likely effects of these reforms. Research may then have the valuable function of constituting a learning process in which both those who drive and fund the economic reform agenda (largely the aid donors), and those who receive and implement it (largely the maligned state bureaucracies) may co-operate in a necessary adaptation of preconceived blueprints to actual conditions. There is some evidence in relation to managerial reforms that this learning process is already developing (see e.g. Harrison, 2001).

The second, related problem arises directly from the condition of under-development itself. It is clear that the economic, social and political conditions for the range of neoliberal economic and political reforms favoured by the aid donors are rarely present in low and middle income countries. Development agencies are still inclined to proffer models based on conditions and practices in high income economies, then become frustrated when such models do not seem to work, or receive little more than diplomatic lip-service. Donor-led reforms are too often based on prior solutions, with little foundation in the complex social and political contexts into which reforms must be fitted. A good example is provided by Vietnam, where after a decade of donor-assisted economic and administrative reforms, there is almost no discussion in reform documentation of the Vietnamese Communist Party, dominant in the country's system of governance, and crucial to the effective implementation of state–market reforms. More empirical research is needed into specific country systems as the prerequisite for purpose-built reforms rooted in local social, economic and political realities, as an alternative to externally designed blueprints.

A central element in regulatory governance will be the analysis of accountability, since improved accountability and transparency are usually posited as the principal objectives of regulatory reform (assuming this to be defined as re-regulation rather than deregulation). The neoliberal version of accountability with which current regulatory reform is so closely implicated rests on evaluation of performance against pre-set standards or targets, and offers incentives to managers as well as some loosening of the traditional restraints. While financial and procedural accountabilities can be brought within such a framework (and improvements here would undeniably be a gain) it is a framework that sits uneasily with developing country governance (or substantive accountability: see Ogus, 2002). The degree of managerial and institutional autonomy involved, and reliance on a competitive model of public service delivery, assume the existence of market and civil society institutions that in many developing countries are more notable for their absence or deficiencies. Moreover, while the advantages of autonomous regulatory agencies standing at arm's length from state political control and intervention are obvious, there are serious disadvantages too, including the reduction of political accountability, and fragmentation at the heart of governments already suffering problems of institutional incoherence. In the political conditions of developing countries we cannot expect significant public agencies to operate as though politics did not exist, as the practice of privatisation has already demonstrated (Cook et al., 1998; World Bank, 1995). Moreover, giving to the managers of regulated services simultaneously more discretion and more financial responsibility appears to put in place precisely those conditions which may lead to increased corruption (Harriss-White and White, 1996); while giving more autonomy to regulators (by taking them outside government frameworks) is unlikely to reduce regulatory and political capture where constitutional, legal and public interest mechanisms of accountability offer no protection. As limited experiments with executive agencies in developing countries have shown, where there is a conflict between economic efficiency objectives and the internal dynamics of political governance, the imperatives of politics will usually prevail (Harrison, 2001; Therkildsen, 2000). One conclusion we might draw here is that accountability finally is underwritten less by formal institutions than by relations of trust – the argument that now makes the running in the regulatory literature in developed economies, as discussed earlier (Moran, 2002; Braithwaite, 1999). In this respect, rather than taking the negative, indeed contradictory attitudes adopted by the aid donors to the social and personalistic networks that characterise the governance institutions of many developing countries (contradictory because political networks are 'bad' while civil society networks are 'good'), we could regard these relations of trust as a foundation on which to build effective regulatory governance.

CONCLUSION

The principal thrust of this chapter has been to rehearse the problematic nature of policy transfer from developed to developing countries in the field of regulatory governance. In the first place, the dominant economic reform model is itself a contested conceptual model, and even in developed economies has produced a contested literature of evaluation and appropriateness. Despite these disputes, reflected in internal debates and power struggles in the major institutions promoting neoliberal reforms, it is this dominant model that is being 'transferred' to developing economies through aid programmes and by imitation. Problems of adaptation to different economic, social, political, legal and administrative cultures will inevitably arise, and must be the focus of a research agenda concerned to assess policy effectiveness in the context of the stubborn and complex realities of underdevelopment. This is a reminder, too, that the developmental state has an essential role; it will remain both the object and the subject of reform, and is likely to retain considerably greater direct regulatory responsibilities than is now customary in developed countries.

REFERENCES

Ayres, I. and J. Braithwaite (1992), *Responsive Regulation: Transcending the Regulation Debate*, Oxford: Oxford University Press.

Braithwaite, J. (1999), 'Accountability and governance under the new regulatory state', *Australian Journal of Public Administration*, **58** (1), 90–7.

Broadman, H. and F. Recanatini (2002), 'Corruption and policy: back to the roots', *Policy Reform* **5**, 37–49.

Brinkerhoff, D. (2000), 'Assessing political will for anti-corruption efforts: an analytical framework', *Public Administration and Development*, **20**, 239–52.

Common, R. (1998), 'The new public management and policy transfer: the role of international organisations', in M. Minogue, C. Polidano and D. Hulme (eds), *Beyond the New Public Management: Ideas and Practices in Governance*, Cheltenham, UK and Northampton, MA: Edward Elgar, pp. 59–75.

Cook, P., C. Kirkpatrick and F. Nixson (eds) (1998), *Privatisation, Enterprise Development and Economic Reform*, Cheltenham: Edward Elgar.

Diamond, L., J. Linz and S.M. Lipset (1990), *Politics in Developing Countries: Comparing Experiences with Democracies*, London: Lynne Rienner.

Duckett, J. (2001), 'Bureaucrats in business Chinese style: the lessons of market reform and state entrepreneurialism in the People's Republic of China', *World Development* **29** (1), 23–37.

Florio, M. (2002), 'Economists, privatisation in Russia and the waning of the Washington consensus', *Review of International Political Economy*, **9** (2), 374–415.

Gray, C. and D. Kaufmann (1998), 'Corruption and development', *Finance and Development*, March, 7–10.

Hansher, L. and M. Moran (1989), *Capitalism, Culture and Regulation*, Oxford: Oxford University Press.

Harrison, G. (2001), 'Post-conditionality politics and administrative reform: reflections on the case of Uganda and Tanzania', *Development and Change*, **32**, 657–79.

Harriss-White, B. and G. White (1996), 'Corruption, liberalisation and democracy', *IDS Bulletin*, **27** (2), 1–5.

Hood, C. (1994), *Explaining Economic Policy Reversals*, Buckingham: Open University Press.

Hood, C. (1995), 'Contemporary public management: a new global paradigm', *Public Policy and Administration*, **10**, 104–17.

Hood, C. (1998), *The Art of the State: Culture, Rhetoric, and Public Management*, Oxford: Oxford University Press.

Hood, C., O. James, G. Jones, and T. Travers (1999), *Regulation Inside Government: Waste-Watchers, Quality Police, and Sleaze-Busters*, Oxford: Oxford University Press.

Huther, J. and A. Shah (2001), 'Anti-Corruption Policies and Programs', unpublished paper.

Johnston, M. (1997), 'Fighting systemic corruption: social foundations for institutional reform', unpublished paper.

Inglis, F. (2000), 'A malediction upon management', *Journal of Education Policy*, **15** (4), 417–29.

Khan, M.(1996), 'A Typology of Corrupt Transactions in Developing Countries', *IDS Bulletin*, **27**, 12–21.

Khan, M. (1998), 'Patron–client networks and the economic effects of corruption in

Asia', in M. Robinson (ed.) *Corruption and Development: An Introduction*, London: Frank Cass, pp. 15–29.

Khan, M. (2002), 'State failure in developing countries and strategies of institutional reform', paper to World Bank Development Economics Conference, Oslo, June.

Klitgaard, R. (1998), *Controlling Corruption*, Berkeley, CA: University of California Press.

Lane, J.-E. (2001), 'From long-term to short-term contracting', *Public Administration*, **79** (1), 29–47.

Lederman, D., N. Loayza and R. Reis Soares (2001), *Accountability and Corruption: Political Institutions Matter*, November, Washington, DC: World Bank.

Ledevena, A.V. (1998), *Russias Economy of Favours:* Blat, *Networking, and Informal Exchanges*, Cambridge: Cambridge University Press.

Majone, G. (1999), 'The regulatory state and its legitimacy problems', *West European Politics*, **22** (1), 1–24.

Majone, G. (1996), *Regulating Europe*, London: Routledge.

McCourt, W. and M. Minogue (eds) (2001), *The Internationalisation of Public Management: Reinventing the Third World State*, Cheltenham: Edward Elgar.

Megginson, W. and J. Netter (2001), 'From state to market: a survey of empirical studies on privatisation', *Journal of Finance*, **49**, 403–52.

Minogue, M. (1998), 'Changing the state: concepts and practice in the reform of the public sector', in M. Minogue, C. Polidano and D. Hulme (eds) *Beyond the New Public Management: Ideas and Practices in Governance*, Cheltenham, UK and Northampton, MA: Edward Elgar, pp. 17–37.

Minogue, M. (2001a), 'The internationalisation of new public management', in W. McCourt and M. Minogue (eds) *The Internationalisation of Public Management: Reinventing the Third World State*, Cheltenham: Edward Elgar, pp. 1–19.

Minogue, M. (2001b), 'Governance-based analysis of regulation', Working Paper No. 3, Centre on Regulation and Competition, University of Manchester, Manchester.

Moran, M. (2002), 'Understanding the regulatory state', *British Journal of Political Science* **32**, 391–413.

Ogus, A. (2002), 'Comparing regulatory systems', in D. Parker and D. Saal (eds) *Privatisation Handbook*, Cheltenham: Edward Elgar, Ch. 23.

Osborne, D. and R. Gaebler (1992), *Reinventing Government*, Reading, MA: Addison Wesley.

Pollitt, C. and G. Bouckaert (2000), *Public Management Reform: A Comparative Analysis*, Oxford: Oxford University Press.

Rhodes, R. (1994), 'The hollowing out of the state', *Political Quarterly*, **65**, 138–51.

Rose-Ackerman, S. (1999), *Corruption in Government: Causes, Consequences and Reform*, Cambridge: Cambridge University Press.

Schick, A. (1998), 'Why most developing countries should not try New Zealand's Reforms', *World Bank Research Observer*, **13** (1), 123–31.

Shirley, M.M. and P. Walsh (2001), 'Public versus private ownership: the current state of the debate', Washington, DC: World Bank.

Sissener, T.K. (2001), 'Anthropological perspectives on corruption', *WP 2001:5*, Oslo: Chr. Michelsen Institute.

Stiglitz, J. (2002), *Globalisation and its Discontents*, New York: W.W. Norton.

Taylor, H. (2001), 'Human resource management and new public management: two sides of a coin that has a low value in developing countries?', in W. McCourt and M. Minogue (eds) *The Internationalisation of Public Management: Reinventing the Third World State*, Cheltenham: Edward Elgar, pp. 174–95.

Therkildsen, O. (2000), 'Public sector reform in a poor aid-dependent country: Tanzania', *Public Administration and Development*, **20**, 61–70.

UNDP (1995), *Public Sector Management, Governance, and Sustainable Human Development*, New York: United Nations Development Programme.

Vogel, D. (1986), *National Styles of Regulation: Environmental Policy in Great Britain and the United States*, Ithaca: Cornell University Press.

Williams, R. (1998), 'New concepts for old?', *Third World Quarterly*, **20** (3), 503–13.

Williamson, J. (ed.) (1990), *Latin American Adjustment: How Much Has Happened*, Washington: Institute for International Economics.

Williamson, J. (1996), 'The Washington Consensus Revisited', in L. Emmerij (ed.) *Economic and Social Development into the XXI Century*, Baltimore: Johns Hopkins.

World Bank (1994), *Governance: The World Bank Experience*, Washington, DC: World Bank.

World Bank (1995), *Bureaucrats in Business: The Economics and Politics of Government Ownership*, Oxford: Oxford University Press.

Yang, M. (1994), *Gifts, Favours and Bankrupts: The Art of Social Relationships in China*, London: Cornell University Press.

9. A diagnostic model for capacity building in regulatory agencies

Derek Eldridge

INTRODUCTION

Cook (2001, p. 161) refers to the effectiveness of regulation being judged according to a multiplicity of goals related to the needs of the various interested parties including owners, investors, consumers and government. Along with other researchers (Kirkpatrick and Parker, 2003; Vass, 2002; Majone, 1999) he describes the dividing line between success in regulation and lack of effectiveness, due to such phenomena as 'regulatory capture' and 'information asymmetries', an approach much in common with others concerned with the economic and legalistic interpretations of regulatory impact. On the other hand negligible research has been conducted on the manner in which internally located components in regulatory agencies contribute to externally experienced levels of effectiveness. This chapter addresses this deficit of knowledge by highlighting concerns faced by regulators, acting as chief executives, in securing adequate internal performance to enable regulatory policies to be put into effective practice. In line with the views of Minogue (2002), analysis of these institutional components can be undertaken within the language and concepts of the new public management and governance reforms currently being adopted by a range of developing countries. In other words the organisational and management theories discussed here will be familiar to the exponents, observers and critics of the new public management.

The chapter is based on a series of discussion held in the energy, multimedia and telecommunications sectors in three countries; namely, the Philippines, Malaysia and South Africa, in the period 2001–02. The objective of this research was to identify the critical internal components that are an inherent part of the translation of policies into effective regulatory outputs. Primarily, the research has enabled the construction of the diagnostic model shown in Figure 9.1, which places these parameters in a systemic framework that traces regulation from its policy origins to its delivery to recipient stakeholders. The advantage of this type of analysis is that it allows interactions between parameters within the system to be recognised and explored qualitatively as to their contribution to the regulatory process. This type of methodology as described by Pollitt and Bouckaert (2000, p. 21) provides a framework within which the main forces for and against management change can be identified, and within this chapter it is utilised, in particular, to investigate the interconnected roles of strategic planning, work system design and performance management. At a practical level the approach gives rise to the possibility that capacity building interventions initiated by regulators as chief executives are potentially not randomly chosen, but specifically focused and coordinated to strengthen the regulatory process (Asch and Bowman, 1989, p. 404). Is also enables the contribution of performance management to be discussed as a key component in building the human dimension to sustain the whole system, and in particular to support strategic planning and work system design processes. The chapter concludes by reviewing the issues arising in performance management that may potentially inhibit employee efforts and development in achieving effectiveness. The implication for regulators in this respect is how to initiate appropriate performance management as part of institution building and how to develop it in line with demonstrable needs, including the formalisation of the strategic planning and work system design process.

BASIC ASSUMPTIONS OF THE DIAGNOSTIC MODEL

The organisational system reflected in Figure 9.1 is explored from two interconnected perspectives: first, as a useful analytical means of unravelling the nature and scope of the management process within a regulatory agency and, second, as a specific tool for raising the agenda of institutional reform that regulators, as chief executives, may wish to promote. Both perspectives rest on the premise that such a system represents the ability of people to get the desired things done within an organisation, in other words the 'how' of institutional performance rather than the 'what', which refers specifically, in the regulation context, to the nature and scope of interventionist policies for promoting consumer well-being and enterprise viability. A management system adopted by a regulator of the type shown in Figure 9.1 is likely to be explained as the means by which the efforts of managers and staff alike can be harnessed towards the required regulatory results and through which progress towards them can be evaluated. Further, a regulator in setting up a new agency, or re-energising the work of an existing one, is likely also to give due weight to the importance of such a system as a prime means by which institutional capacity for delivery can be maximised.

The key organisation and management components of this system, namely strategic planning, work system design and performance management, are

Monitoring of External Impacts	Definition of Delivery Mechanisms	Specification of Organisational Capacity	Introducing Critical Enhancers for Capacity Building	Definition of Key Organisation and Management Components	Institutional Diagnosis	Policy Analysis
		Structural factors • *System* • *Outputs* • *Competences* • *Communication and information*	Adequate staff resourcing and development	Strategic planning	Identification of key transition factors for policy and practice	Policy formulation
Consumer well-being industry/sector viability	• Adequate regulatory practices • Enhancement of consumer awareness • Capable monitoring procedures		Individual, team and organisational learning capabilities	Work system design	Implication of key transition factors for organisation and management	Diagnosis of current organisational strengths and weaknesses
		Cultural factors • *Values* • *Sensitivity to various interests* • *Ways of working*	Owned accountability and transparency components	Performance management		

Figure 9.1 Conceptual framework for capacity building with a regulatory agency

further described in Table 9.1. They represent the basic building blocks by which regulators as chief executives can begin to discern institutional development needs, and by which diagnosis can be directly linked with management interventions for growth or change.

However, each of the key components of Table 9.1 is unlikely to be treated in an isolated fashion when looking at actions intended to raise institutional capability. Figure 9.1, drawing on ideas in Eldridge (2002), suggests the need for a congruency of thinking in terms of these three key components on the part of a regulator if the agency is to convert required policies into appropriate executive actions. They are central to institutional capacity building as interactive elements and all underpin the abilities of staff to understand the needs of the relevant external stakeholders, to design appropriate delivery systems to meet these needs, and to utilise the necessary management, technical, learning and accountability competencies. Their successful incorporation contributes towards overall systems viability for an organisation (Beer, 1985) and is at the heart of 'embeddedness of regulatory institutions' (Stirton and Lodge, 2002, Mehta, 2002).

Further, as suggested in Table 9.1, the strategic plan and the form of the work system for an agency are predominantly shaped by the types of regulatory policies to be enacted and the nature of the 'regulatory climate'. While the performance management system also is subject to these influences, its design and implementation strategy remain to some extent within the managerial remit of a regulator, as reflected in decisions about its objectives and form. There is a degree of independence for a regulator on the choices adopted for managerial style, the internal culture, the extent of team working to be encouraged and the degree to which staff members are to be empowered as individuals and in teams in securing effective organisational outcomes through performance management. While choices in these areas may reflect personal preferences on the part of a regulator, they are not exempt from the climate existing in similar organisations and the type of institutional ethos prevailing in regulation in the country concerned or the type of regulatory bodies favoured by governments.

At a strategic level, building on Cook (2001) the performance of a regulatory agency is likely to be judged under one or more of a number of the following headings:

- the degree of success achieved in regulation in relation to political and economic considerations as judged by government, the legislature or other influential stakeholders;
- the extent of implementation of any 'business plan' mandated by government/legislature for enhancing consumer interests and/or sector economic/financial viability;

Table 9.1 Key organisation and management components in a regulatory agency

Component	Likely source for information vital to component function (aims and content)
Strategic business plan	• The stated political aims of regulation • Legislation, including definition of the 'regulatory space' for intervention • Evaluation of previous regulatory practices in the sector concerned • Political climate for regulation including degree of emphasis on pro-poor provision • Views of key stakeholders including those of consumers • Financial/market performance of major private companies in sector • The type of relations expected between the regulatory agency and key stakeholders • Conditions under which 'regulatory capture' can be avoided
Work system development needs	• Nature and scope of the regulatory system implied by legislation and political objectives • Identification of supplier/client relationships in the regulatory system • Views of key stakeholders • Interpretation of key effectiveness criteria in regulation
Performance management system	• Definition of the above components – strategic business plan – system development needs (regulatory system) – Choice of management inputs – managerial style – culture – feedback mechanisms for increasing effectiveness • Knowledge of current skills and potential of the workforce • Views of staff and other stakeholders, such as human resource specialists

- the degree to which effective use has been made of any legislation underlying the work of the agency to address specific market issues;
- the extent to which a positive impact has been made in the markets in question from the perspective of consumers, consumer interest groups and the wider public;
- the extent to which views of the network of stakeholders within the industry/sector have been incorporated in the regulator's responses;
- the level at which monitoring procedures to gauge the effectiveness of regulation have been established.

While not all these criteria will be applicable at any one time in a specific agency, the combination of even two or three of them can give rise to quite complex strategic planning processes in terms of the range of stakeholders to be satisfied and the scope of the quantitative and qualitative information to be analysed and presented. Primary consideration has to be given in strategic planning, however, to the political decision making process which Bryson (1995, p. 11) sees as inductive and based on issues that, by definition, involve conflict, not consensus. Such conflict revolves around expressed opinions based on philosophy, ends, means, timing, location, political advantage and reasons for change, and is subject to efforts for resolution in the planning process. Out of this resolution can emerge policies and programmes that are politically acceptable to the involved or affected parties, but which are expressed as rationally applied intentions or plans. Guth and Macmillan (1989, p. 316) suggest that part of this process is the emergence of more general policies to capture, frame, shape, guide, or interpret the policies and programmes specifically geared to particular issues. A number of writers (Mintzberg, 1983; Pfeffer, 1992; Peters, 1995) also stress the importance of the interface between the political process and strategic planning as a prelude to the organisational rationale of writing vision, aims, objectives and targets and placing them within a consensually agreed statement. Consequently the strategic planning component of Figure 9.1 has at its heart strategic thinking which encompasses not only the interpretation of hard data on direction but also insights from key stakeholders, which broadens the consideration of issues and invokes a learning process (Mintzberg, 1994). Such plan formulation rests on intuition, creativity and building commitment – skills somewhat remote from the hard-nosed economic competences governing regulation, but ones which a regulator needs to have on board to ensure the adequate interpretation of political direction, to stimulate a dialogue to improve political decisions and understand what constitutes effective outcomes. This line of argument implies an institutional need to conceptualise strategic planning so that the political decision making model subsequently leads to consensual agreements on what policies and programmes will best resolve key issues through a rational planning model (Bryson,1995, p. 12). Furthermore the rational planning model potentially provides a feedback mechanism by which inconsistencies in the political outcome can be addressed (Katz and Kahn, 1978).

Coalescing with the political debate, stakeholder analysis is likely to be another key ingredient in the strategic planning process given the multiplicity of interests prevailing in a regulatory regime. Boschken (1994) refers to the inherent danger of not recognising the credentials of key stakeholders and not knowing the criteria of performance they would apply to an organisation. This lack of knowledge can contribute to inappropriate or ineffective standards of performance being accepted for the organisation. Bryson and Crosby (1992) picture a situation in which individuals and groups wrestle for control of the organisation's attention, resources and outputs – possibly an endemic feature of the regulatory process – and refer to the importance of stakeholder analysis in obtaining a more precise view of the contestants through surveys, interviews and group discussions. This is very much in line with the remit of the 'new public management' as exemplified in Osborne and Gaebler (1992), with its focus on customer needs and the generation of criteria of performance directly related to them. Bryson sees these criteria covering areas of organisation strength and weakness, overlaps, gaps, conflicts and contradictions in the quantity and quality of outputs. Most importantly he refers to a stakeholder analysis as being a process by which managers, in our case regulators, can place themselves in the shoes of others, especially outsiders, and make assessments of the organisation from these external perspectives. Not only does this form a basis for strengths/weaknesses/opportunities/threats (SWOT) analysis, strategic issue identification and strategic development, but it is an essential precursor for ethical action (Lewis, 1991). Additionally, stakeholder analysis may provide an understanding of what the organisation needs from each stakeholder group – an essential process in the delicate economic balances to be achieved in regulation. Mintzberg (1994, p. 111) reminds us that

> vision is unavailable to those who cannot 'see' with their own eyes. Real strategists get their hands dirty digging for ideas, and real strategies are built from the occasional nuggets they uncover.

WORK SYSTEM DESIGN

Regulators will only succeed if they are capable of harnessing internal efforts towards the required regulatory outcomes as specified in the strategic planning process. Systems of work have to be organised that enable agency staff to be coordinated in what they do and motivated to improve quality as the result of learning and group efforts. Job descriptions, as the usual organisational mechanism for ensuring that work proceeds in an effective manner, have to balance the 'upward demands' placed on job holders for accountability to senior staff with the 'lateral demands'; that is, participation in work systems that deliver results which may cut across departmental or functional lines of reporting. While the former mandate for job descriptions is a well practised discipline within public sector organisations, although still fraught with problems, the latter is an often neglected area much at the centre of the debate on public sector reform (Deming, 1994).

The art of dealing with this issue is for management to balance the needs of a job description, which by its very nature is individually centred, with those work system maintenance and development needs, which cannot be anything other than the responsibility of people acting in groups. Portraying jobs as part of work systems also encourages a sense of purpose that benefits clients, whether internal or external to the organisation. It also helps to avoid over-reliance by job holders on servicing the needs of the organisation's hierarchy, a 'disenfranchisement' particularly pertinent to public sector organisations, which may have too many layers of management. A sense of purpose can also inspire cooperation in work teams, and produce interdependence, and perhaps even interchangeability of individual roles, beyond the limits of formal job descriptions.

To understand the importance of work systems development in regulatory organisations one has only to look at the complex considerations that pervade regulation over and above the general demands of management in the public sector. A complete systemic understanding of the processes of furthering regulation from inception to delivery is important to avoid political and regulatory capture, to minimise information asymmetries and to maximise transparency of the criteria covering relationships with key stakeholders and the decisions affecting them. Limiting the randomness of approach among regulatory staff, ensuring the consistency of decisions and fulfilling accountability needs are also key aims that can only be met by an integrated and collaborative model of delivery. Such a model based on Tribus (undated) is envisaged in Figure 9.2 and represents a conceptualisation of the organisation well beyond what conventional job analysis can offer.

The demands of regulation as related to the continual need to improve its quality in meeting intentions, and to respond to underlying instabilities in the market being regulated, lead also, in the words of Ackoff (1999, p. 158) to the need for a systemic concept of the organisation that naturally inculcates a learning function. Such a possibility is demonstrated in the model of Figure 9.2 with its well developed system of feedback to improve performance. Latent within the system is the role of strategic planning, which gives rise to key questions in every box (node) of Figure 9.2, and these in turn potentially involve learning processes among those involved and provide vital feedback to the regulator. Note that Figure 9.2 represents a broad generic process and

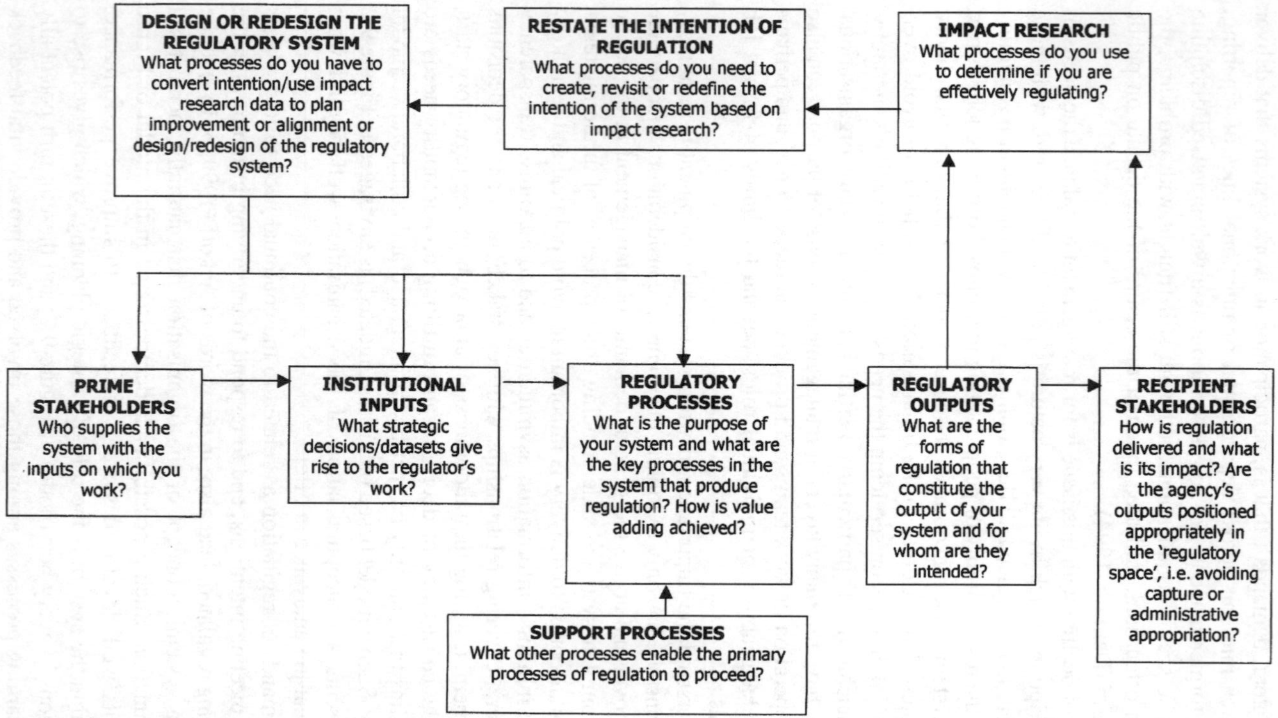

Note: This diagam has been developed specifically for this chapter based on a generic SIPOC model originally devised by Elane Torres and referenced in an article by Tribus (undated).

Figure 9.2 The supplier–input–process–output–customer (SIPOC) model as applied to the regulatory process

that in practice it would be necessary in a specific regulatory agency to map out processes in detail (using standard process mapping conventions), including the use of deployment charts to establish specific job roles.

Deming (1994, p. 61) refers to a system such as reproduced in Figure 9.2 as the 'real' organisation chart which, as the questions are answered, 'shows people what their jobs are, how they should interact with one another as part of a system'. He refers to a system (Deming 1994, p. 50) as a network of interdependent components that work together to try to accomplish the aim of the system, and in the case of Figure 9.2 it would give rise to an understanding of (British Deming Association, 1995):

- the various tasks contained with the process;
- how tasks are transformed into outputs;
- the decisions that need to be made at various stages;
- the essential interrelationships and interdependence between the process steps;
- where weak points are that may inhibit success of the total process.

This type of system exemplifies the situation in which work flows cut across departmental or functional boundaries which, through analysis, leads to an understanding of what constitutes client satisfaction. Burr (1990) refers to the most important outcomes of this approach being common knowledge among the employees involved on how each link in the chain fits together, and constitutes a learning process geared towards improvement. Deming (1994, pp. 54–60) suggests further that when change is proposed, flow diagrams allow the possibilities to be explored in terms of each component and the system as a whole, exposing for instance what constitutes value adding as against tasks conducted purely 'as norm'. Additionally, examination of process promotes a dialogue of:

- where things most easily go wrong;
- difficulties arising in staff relationships at 'transaction points';
- required criteria of performance to enable the system to function.

As a result, information is generated which is directly relevant to performance management.

PERFORMANCE MANAGEMENT

Performance management as portrayed in Table 9.1 is a derivative of the specifications of the strategic planning process and the work system development needs, but also represents the means by which these two components can be fully brought to fruition. To throw light on its scope within a regulatory agency and to provide the context for decisions that initiate an appropriate system, it is worth considering how this particular paradigm for management has evolved in recent years. Performance management has its origins not just in the broad range of behavioural theories relating to how people can be managed for improved contribution, but very specifically in the 'management by objectives' school of thinking that reached its height of influence in both public and private sector organisations in the 1970s and early 1980s (Humble, 1970; Reddin, 1970). It also represents a natural progression of performance appraisal, as this has moved from looking at contribution and its evaluation from the perspective of individual behaviours/traits, towards the measurement of job holder performance against objectives in a strategic framework (Locke et al., 1981). From the perspective of public sector reform, performance management also represents an attractive tool to create cultures more conducive to performance improvement (Cabinet Office, undated). In Table 9.2, Armstrong and Baron (1998) lay out their view of this progression of managerial ideas from MBO and through the experience of 'appraisal' that has resulted in today's understanding of the role of performance management.

The theory of performance management suggests that, when applied, role definitions for work units, teams and individuals emerge from the strategic planning process that reflect the preferred success criteria for an organisation. Also the feedback on which to judge the respective contributions is generated, which is then utilised in the improvement of performance and in recognising appropriate development needs. The form and arrangements for handling this feedback are open to a number of varying methodologies, but before these can be decided on regulators would need to make choices on the objectives, scope and major concepts for performance management, as discussed next. A major assumption underpinning the whole approach needless to say is that for professional staff, at the very least, knowledge of key success criteria for an agency would be essential and that any system would stimulate reflection on their contribution in meeting these criteria.

CHOICES IN INSTITUTIONAL FACTORS AND PERFORMANCE MANAGEMENT DESIGN

Obviously the design of a performance management system is challenging within the complexity of processes and the demands of regulatory interventions as indicated in Figure 9.1. Of fundamental importance in performance management is maximising meaningful feedback within the system to groups and individuals that indicates progress in achieving organisational goals, but

Table 9.2 Management by objectives, performance appraisal and performance management compared

Management by objectives	Performance appraisal	Performance management
Packaged system	Usually tailor made	Tailor made
Applied to managers	Applied to all staff	Applied to all staff
Emphasis on individual objectives	Individual objectives may be included	Emphasis on integrating corporate, team and individual objectives
Emphasis on quantified performance measures	Some qualitative performance indicators may also be included	Competence requirements often included as well as quantified measures
Annual appraisal	Annual appraisal	Continuous review with one or more formal reviews
Top-down system with ratings	Top-down system with ratings	Joint process, ratings less common
May not be a direct link to pay	Often linked to pay	May not be a direct link to pay
Monolithic system	Monolithic system	Flexible process
Complex paperwork	Complex paperwork	Documentation often minimised
Owned by line managers and personnel department	Owned by line managers and personnel department	Owned by management

Source: Armstrong and Baron (1998).

which is handled in a way acceptable to individuals and can be acted on by them for improvement. In achieving this positive institutional effect three important issues have to be resolved by regulators when initiating a performance management system. Note, in raising these issues reference is made to appraisal of performance, and while performance management has superseded more behaviourally based aspects of this, it remains a central methodology in any performance management system. The choices are also interdependent with the mandates established for the strategic planning process and for meeting work system design needs (see Table 9.1) but also reflect to a significant extent the type of management style the regulator wishes to adopt related to the contextual and individual options available.

Open versus Closed Assessment of Regulatory Staff in the Quest for Transparency

Open feedback in evaluating performance is likely to be seen as a potent tool to address performance issues (Anstey et al., 1976; Fletcher, 1993). However, the question arises whether prevailing organisational norms restricting openness and participation are intrinsic features of broader (national) cultures that the design of any assessment scheme must adapt to, or only express organisations' unfamiliarity with appraisal (and possibly with other systematic management practices). Evidence strongly suggests that open systems work less well in cultural settings that discourage open and frank discussions of (mutual) performance weaknesses by managers and staff; for example, in some South Asian organisations. Giving individuals feedback on performance in such organisations is often considered one sided and potentially damaging by the recipients, especially if conducted in an open manner. We may speculate in this particular debate how far openness in the appraisal of regulatory staff is to be encouraged in order to enhance transparency of operations, and whether it is possible that a closed system may be associated more directly with regulatory capture. In this respect Brigham and Fitzgerald (2001) refer to the need for 'visibility of reporting' to which performance management contributes, but also maintain that such a system constitutes a link between levels; that is, between organisational coordination and control. While admittedly referring to a regulated organisation rather than a regulator, their remarks remain pertinent on the value of performance management for the latter.

Formal versus Informal Performance Management Systems in Dealing with the Complexity of Regulation

McGregor (1957), one of the first critics of formal appraisal systems, notes that while organisations continue to require them in spite of their recognised weaknesses, many managers retain a belief that their day-to-day communication with staff, as part of an informal approach to performance management, is enough to give them all the information and influence they need. The response of Fletcher (1993, pp. 1–2), as a believer in officially designated systems, is that in the absence of formalisation, assessment does indeed take place as people work together but this is unstructured and perhaps highly subjective, leading to a potential for bias and unfairness. In a similar vein Walker (1980) notes that the clarification of job expectations, the reviewing of accomplishments, and the planning of future performance and development efforts, constituted as a formal system, are central to effective management; and also that objective performance evaluations are necessary as a legal defence to charges of discrimination on the basis of age, sex and race.

Looking at this debate from the perspective of a regulatory agency, it is difficult to envisage how an informal system would be adequate other than in situations in which staff numbers were quite small and operations relatively straightforward. In terms of Stirton and Lodge's (2002, p. 9) 'Presence of checks and balances against capture and administrative expropriation', transparency is recognised as fundamentally important, and it is hard to conceive of a situation in which staff accountability mechanisms on important matters are other than explicit, in recorded form and checked for consistency against the demands of regulatory practice. These aspects are integral to the achievement of transparency and a formally constituted performance management system is likely to have a major part to play in this.

However, a word of caution is raised against formally applied systems by Deming (1986), the originator of quality management, who argues that appraisal is one of the 'seven deadly sins' afflicting managers in North America. His view is that managers wrongly ascribe to individual employees responsibility for performance problems which really arise from the nature of the work system itself, thereby depressing the morale of staff while doing little to improve performance. Following Deming's lead, Bowman (1994) argues that formally constituted appraisal for individual employees is a mistake, as problems need to be tackled at the level of the organisation, not the lone staff member. Latham and Wexley (1993), however, suggest that Deming's scepticism about appraisal is not generally accepted. Even after systemic or organisational problems have been tackled, there remain psychological issues of performance that still have to be addressed at the level of the individual staff member through reviews involving feedback and discussion. However, Deming's views on reforming performance management objectives and practices are highly relevant and give rise to the need expressed in this chapter for congruency between work system design and performance management. Methods are required to assess the contribution of employees bound together in a work system for which they hold joint responsibility.

Performance Assessment versus Development versus Rewards for Employees

In reviewing work contributions, as in other areas of human resource management, the perspectives of the employee and of the organisation can be quite different. At one extreme, a performance management scheme designed exclusively for organisational benefit focuses on measuring past performance and setting performance targets for employees. From an opposite focus, a scheme designed wholly for the benefit of employees would focus exclusively on job satisfaction, and the training and development of staff.

In other words, the organisation's priority is more likely to be *assessment* for improvement, and the individual's to be personal and career *development*. These are different purposes: one points to comparing performance differences between individuals, the other to possible change in the performance of an individual now and in the future as a result of development. Can they be combined satisfactorily in a single review procedure? Randel et al. (1984, pp. 13–14) argue forcefully that they cannot and they make a distinction between interviews used for assessment (*performance reviews*), for development (*potential reviews*), and for determining pay and benefits (*reward reviews*). However, where it is already difficult to persuade managers to spend sufficient time on reviews of performance, it may be unrealistic to expect them to conduct several interviews with each appraisee. Yet the fact remains that an interview that combines assessment and development, and possibly reward, may result in the contamination of each by the others. Fletcher (1993, p. 10) concludes that it is best to see the function of appraisal as employee development and motivation because:

- this approach is acceptable and welcome to appraisees and most appraisers;
- it represents what is generally the highest priority for the organisation – a strategy for improving performance which relies on development and motivation;
- the effectiveness of appraisal for assessing individuals' performance relative to that of their peers is doubtful.

However, Fletcher's advocacy of *development* as the primary purpose of appraisal, runs counter to a central feature of performance management, as portrayed in reforming public sector organisations, which stresses an emphasis on target setting and review for improving work contributions as directly influenced by a strategic planning process. Additionally, much of public sector reform has focused on 'rightsizing', in some countries resulting in a reduction of posts in the public sector with a more than proportionate effect on those at a senior level. This affects promotion chances and impacts on assessment systems that have traditionally been used to identify staff for advancement. Regulatory agencies are certainly not going to be exempt from this type of dilemma in weighing up the pros and cons of the focus that assessment should take. In line with the trend seen generally in public sector organisations, and given their internal complexity of operations, it seems unlikely that they can avoid the primary focus primarily falling on the improvement of performance, but linked to a recognition of development needs.

Issues of rewards are also difficult to accommodate in the same interview as performance assessment and/or development. If appraisees believe that extra remuneration may result from an appraisal, this expectation may deflect them from a fully honest and open discussion of their performance or development needs, and this may be extremely problematic in regulation, when maximising 'undistorted' feedback is necessary.

CONCLUDING REMARKS

Consideration of the issues discussed here is fundamental in designing a performance management system that will prove resilient in the face of the complex demands made on the capabilities of regulators and which will enable strategic planning and work system design to be activated as precursors to the potential contributions of all staff. Resolution of the issues may be more taxing when the regulatory agency is part of the civil service sector or carries a residual of public sector culture from a previous existence. Such an agency may lack an ongoing and open dialogue on what constitutes effective performance and, further, may lack a mutual understanding of, and widely owned commitment to, performance improvement. Many studies suggest that any unilateral imposition of performance management by senior management in such circumstances may worsen rather than remedy matters (Deming Society, 1994). A paper based prescriptive approach for performance management, for instance, may focus discussion on the functional demands of the system, including definitions of annual output targets, rather than on establishing ongoing relationships between managers and others that provide continuous feedback for improving results. Such a weakness may be compounded by the possibility that targets set for a plan period become outdated, and underdeveloped manager/appraisee relationships may prevent adaptation to new conditions facing the agency. Further, there may be a failure to recognise the extent and type of change required, and to determine the necessary actions to bring it about through adaptations of the strategic plan or amendments of the work system.

On the other hand, an agency without a formalised performance management system, may already have working arrangements between managers and staff that are effective in achieving desired results or have the potential to do so. The issue in introducing performance management as an explicitly managed system then is whether it builds on those positive relationships, or disrupts them, leading to a fall in the quantity and quality of current outputs. Evidence from change management suggests that ignoring currently valued practice and experience when seeking improvement, runs the risk that new remedies imposed may not have the effect desired (Paton and McCalman, 2000). Further, it may deny current management capabilities and demonstrate an insensitivity to values that staff hold about themselves and their work. In other words, a new approach adopted from another context (which is typically how performance management has spread from one country to another), may be culturally inappropriate. This possibility becomes greater the more weight is given in strategic planning to budgetary requirements and output targets, at the expense of more qualitative aspects of service delivery, valued by clients, managers and staff alike.

The issue in introducing performance management into a regulatory agency is how to choose the appropriate set of concepts, bearing in mind the dilemmas portrayed in the previous section, while incorporating sound organisational practices which link it with the strategic planning process and the work system design requirements. Such an assessment enables a regulator to establish the framework for introducing performance management based on a consideration of the values held by staff in the organisation and of their affinity with the culture implied by any new system to be introduced. The time scale for this type of change puts in doubt the value of performance management systems imposed by outside consultants (or donors). What can look very attractive on paper as a performance management proposal towards a better delivery system so often fails to come to fruition because it is unacceptable to staff, and the time scales for its introduction are too short.

Complexity of performance management design and procedure can also cause problems. Again, on paper a new system might appear reasonably attractive to stakeholders. In practice, however, complications arise in relation to terminology, the ability to define work outcomes in a useful way, and purely technical issues of design. At its worst, paper outputs may expand to meet formal reporting requirements, but at the expense of a meaningful exchange of work experience and of ideas between managers and those being assessed. It may also inhibit adequate linkage with the strategic planning and work system design components.

Further, some areas of regulatory work may not fit easily into the methodology of performance management but this may not be necessarily recognised when systems are introduced. The danger is that all staff are required to follow the demands of the new system, regardless of how meaningful it is in specific job roles and in relation to perceptions held about the work outcomes expected. In addition, it is fruitless to set sophisticated standards of job performance in organisations that lack adequate information systems to produce the necessary control data.

One of the most criticised aspects of traditional ways of assessing people in the workplace flows from the work of Deming (1986), which suggests that individual target setting is nearly always destructive of customer-focused teamwork within or between work units. This is because it pressures individuals to demonstrate their own achievement in assessment, which they invariably perceive to be confined to the management reporting structure they find themselves in and which possibly represents 'pleasing the boss'. This pressure makes appraisees want to 'work around' the performance management system rather than improve it. 'Safe' targets may be negotiated at the start of a plan period, for instance, because they are perceived as easier to achieve, hence to gain approval from senior managers. Legitimate organisational targets seen as 'stretching', or just more difficult, may be left out or reduced in scope by appraisees. Deming's view is that, as a result of this effect, when objective setting passes down through the levels of a hierarchy, the inevitable result is sub-optimisation of what is possible. At its worst, it becomes a source of tactical games or defensive behaviour, thereby reinforcing obstacles to continuous improvement through team effort. Such a scenario would certainly jeopardise many of the qualities expected in a regulatory process of proportionality, accountability, consistency, transparency and targeting (Better Regulation Task Force, 2003).

As an alternative to the prescriptive performance standards and targets set by managers, Deming puts forward the idea of 'managing for results' as the main theme in performance management. This stresses how results are achieved rather than attributing results solely to the efforts and skills of individuals. It is process orientated, concentrating on the organisation of work and how teams can cooperate across traditional hierarchic boundaries to achieve the objectives of the organisation as a whole through commonly owned and developed work systems together with an understanding of strategic planning needs. Its key idea is building trust between stakeholders, which contributes to a reduction in confusion over planning and coordination, and minimises distorting behaviour induced by setting individual objectives.

The conclusion to be drawn from this line of argument is that an abiding feature for achieving institutional effectiveness in regulatory agencies is likely to be the instigation and management of quality processes that serve the needs of stakeholders within the framework of predetermined effectiveness criteria. Quality processes encouraged by regulators (the work system component) not only allow the intentions of regulation (the strategic planning component) to be appropriately enacted, but also promote the human effort in meeting the multifarious institutional demands by the choice of an appropriate performance management system.

REFERENCES

Ackoff, R.L. (1999), *Re-creating the Corporation*, New York: Oxford University Press.

Anstey, E., Fletcher, C. and Walker, J. (1976), *Staff Appraisal and Development*, London: Allen and Unwin.

Armstrong, M. and Baron, A. (1998), *Performance Management*, London: Institute of Personnel Development.

Asch, D. and Bowman, C. (eds) (1989), *Readings in Strategic Management*, Basingstoke: Macmillan.

Beer, S. (1985), *Diagnosing the System for Organisations*, Chichester: Wiley.

Better Regulation Task Force (2003), *Principles of Good Regulation*, London: Cabinet Office, Regulatory Impact Unit.

Boschken, H.L. (1994), 'Organisational performance and multiple constituencies', *Public Administration Review*, **54**, 308–12.

Bowman, J. (1994), 'At last an alternative to performance appraisal: total quality management', *Public Administration Review*, **54** (2), 129–36.

Brigham, B.H. and Fitzgerald, L. (2001), 'Controlling managers and organisations: the case of performance measurement in a regulated water company', Centre for Management Under Regulation Research Paper No. 01/1, Warwick.

British Deming Association (1995), *Flowcharting: How and Why?*, BDA Booklet A17, Salisbury: British Deming Association.

Bryson, J.M. (1995), *Strategic Planning for Public and Non-profit Organisations*, San Francisco: Jossey-Bass.

Bryson, J.M. and Crosby, B.C. (1992), *Leadership for the Common Good: Tackling Public Problems in a Shared Power World*, San Francisco: Jossey-Bass.

Burr, J.T. (1990), 'The tools of quality. Part 1: going with the flow(chart)', *Quality Progress*, **23** (6), 64–7.

Cabinet Office (undated), *Objective Setting in Personnel Review*, Main Report, London: Cabinet Office, Office of Public Service and Science.

Cook, P. (2001), 'Privatisation and regulation in developing countries', in W. McCourt and M. Minogue (eds), *The Internationalisation of Public Management, Reinventing the Third World State*, Cheltenham: Edward Elgar.

Deming, W.E. (1986), *Out of Crisis*, Cambridge, MA: MIT Institute for Advanced Engineering Study.

Deming, W.E. (1994), *The New Economics for Industry, Government, Education*, Cambridge, MA: MIT Press.

Deming Society (1994), *Performance Appraisal and All That*, London: Deming Society.

Eldridge, D. (2002), *Raising the Agenda for Capacity Building in the CRC*, Manchester: Centre on Regulation and Competition, Working Paper No. 19.

Fletcher, C.A. (1993), *Appraisal: Routes to Improved Performance*, London: IPM.

Guth, W.D. and Macmillan, I.C. (1989), 'Strategy implementation v. middle management self interest', in D. Asch and C. Bowman (eds), *Readings in Strategic Management*, Basingstoke: MacMillan.

Humble, J. (1970), *Management by Objectives in Action*, Maidenhead: McGraw Hill.

Kirkpatrick, C. and Parker, D. (2003), *Regulatory Impact Assessment: Developing its Potential for Use in Developing Countries*, Manchester: University of Manchester, Centre on Regulation and Competition.

Katz, D. and Kahn, R. (1978), *The Social Psychology of Organisations*, New York: Wiley.

Latham, G.P. and Wexley, K. (1993), *Increasing Productivity through Performance Appraisal*, Reading, MA: Addison-Wesley.

Lewis, C.W. (1991), *The Ethics Challenge in Public Service: A Problem Solving Guide*, San Francisco: Jossey-Bass.

Locke, E.A., Shaw, K.N., Saari, L.M. and Latham, G.P. (1981), 'Goal setting and task performance 1969–80', *Psychological Bulletin*, **90**, 125–52.

McGregor, D. (1957), 'An uneasy look at performance appraisal', *Harvard Business Review*, May–June, 89–94.

Majone, G. (1999), 'The regulatory state and its legitimacy problems', *West European Politics*, **22** (1), 1–24.

Mehta, P.S. (2002), 'Friends of competition', in *Capacity Building for an Effective Competition Regime in Developing Countries*, Jaipur: CUTS.

Minogue, M. (2002), *Public Management and Regulatory Governance: Problems of Policy Transfer to Developing Countries*, Manchester: Centre on Regulation and Competition, Working Paper No.32.

Mintzberg, H. (1983), *Power In and Around Organisations*, Englewood Cliffs, NJ: Prentice Hall.

Mintzberg, H. (1994), 'The fall and rise of strategic planning', *Harvard Business Review*, January–February, 107–14.

Osborne, D. and Gaebler, T. (1992), *Reinventing Government*, Reading, MA: Addison-Wesley.

Paton, R.A. and McCalman, J. (2000), *Change Management. A Guide to Effective Implementation*, London: Sage.

Peters, G. (1995), *The Politics of Bureaucracy*, New York: Longman.

Pfeffer, J. (1992), *Managing with Power: Politics and Influence in Organisations*, Boston, MA: Harvard Business School Press.

Pollitt, C. and Bouckaert, G. (2000), *Public Management Reform: A Comparative Analysis*, Oxford: Oxford University Press.

Randel, G., Packard, P. and Slate, J. (1984), *Staff Appraisal: A First Step to Effective Leadership*, London: Institute of Personnel Management.

Reddin, W. (1970), *Managerial Effectiveness*, Maidenhead: McGraw-Hill.

Stirton, L. and Lodge, M. (2002), *Embedding Regulatory Autonomy: the Reform of the Jamaican Telecommunications Regulation, 1988–2001*, London: London School of Economics, Centre for Analysis of Risk and Regulation.

Tribus, M. (undated), Quality in Education According to the Teachings of Deming and Feuerstein, Fremont, CA: Myron Tribus.

Vass, P. (2002), 'The Principles of "Better regulation" – separating roles and responsibility', Manchester, Centre on Regulation and Competition International Workshop, Manchester, September 2002.

Walker, J.W. (1980), *Human Resource Planning*, New York: McGraw-Hill.

10. Ethical trade: issues in the regulation of global supply chains

Richard Heeks and Richard Duncombe

INTRODUCTION

The growth of globalisation, including international trade, is typically regarded as a two-sided coin; bringing both benefits and problems. Implicit within many commentaries on problems is an assumption of market failure: that, left to their own devices, global production and international trade will fail to adequately reward and protect workers and their communities in the South. Put another way, the assumption is of failure to deliver public goods, such as good wages and working conditions; and of success in delivering 'public bads', such as pollution (Lee 1997).

Ethical trade can be defined as regulatory initiatives that seek to improve the social and environmental impacts of global supply chains. By definition, then, ethical trade can be seen as an attempted solution to a perceived problem of market failure, and it represents a growing form of regulation. Despite the name, trade per se is typically not the main preoccupation of such initiatives. The focus has been more on the conditions and impacts of production. For example, there has been a concern with International Labour Organisation core labour standards: freedom of association and right to collective bargaining, abolition of forced labour, elimination of child labour, and elimination of employment discrimination (ILO 1998). Code SA8000 includes all these, and adds health and safety, disciplinary procedures, remuneration, working hours, and management systems (SAI 2001). These issues of labour standards are the typical fare of ethical trade, but there has recently been recognition of the overlaps with, and value of integration with, environmental standards, which focus largely on limiting emission of pollutants (Blowfield 1999).

Given its social and environmental goals, the *impacts* of ethical trade are of significance to development. However, the *mechanisms* of ethical trade are also of significance, both practical and intellectual, because they place relatively little reliance on 'traditional' regulation; that is, on legal regulation by national governments. This chapter investigates both angles. It begins by analysing the mechanisms underlying ethical trade, seeking to order the rather chaotic proliferation of initiatives seen over recent years. It then runs through the (limited) evidence on impacts of ethical trade, and analyses ethical trade systems to understand factors underlying their success or failure. Finally, the chapter draws conclusions from ethical trade about regulation and about issues for further research.

ETHICAL TRADE AS REGULATION

Traditional state regulation has fallen out of favour as a way of addressing globalisation and its discontents. In its place has arisen a wide variety of methods which we will initially lump together as 'alternative regulatory mechanisms' (ARMs). These mechanisms themselves can be corralled under the 'ethical trade' label.

Traditional regulation is seen as dyadic: the regulating state and the regulated corporation are the key players. One characteristic of alternative regulatory mechanisms like ethical trade is that their design, ownership and implementation are spread across a much broader range of stakeholders (BRTF 2000). Step one in understanding ethical trade will consequently be to map out its stakeholders and their relations, as shown in Figure 10.1 (developed from Jenkins 2001).

Within these stakeholders, it is those involved in trade and production that have been the main focus for regulation. If that regulation is to work, then it must provide some lever, some incentive (reward or punishment) that affects those stakeholders. Otherwise, no action will be taken to address social or environmental impacts.

What are these incentives? In brief, they fall into six main categories: economic gain; avoidance of economic loss; social benefit; avoidance of social disadvantage; politio-legal benefit; and avoidance of politico-legal disadvantage. Specific examples include retention or loss of market share; ability or inability to charge a price premium; access to or loss of investment; acceptance or rejection from a peer group (e.g. trade association); and relief from or imposition of legal regulation.

There are various mechanisms that seek to apply these incentives. These can be *laws*, as found with traditional state regulation. However, other mechanisms are much more common in ethical trade.

- *Contracts* are used, for example between multinationals and their developing country suppliers; or by governments providing subsidies for particular firm activities.
- *Rules and codes* have had a high profile in ethical trade, typically being created either by individual multinationals, or by trade/sector associations.

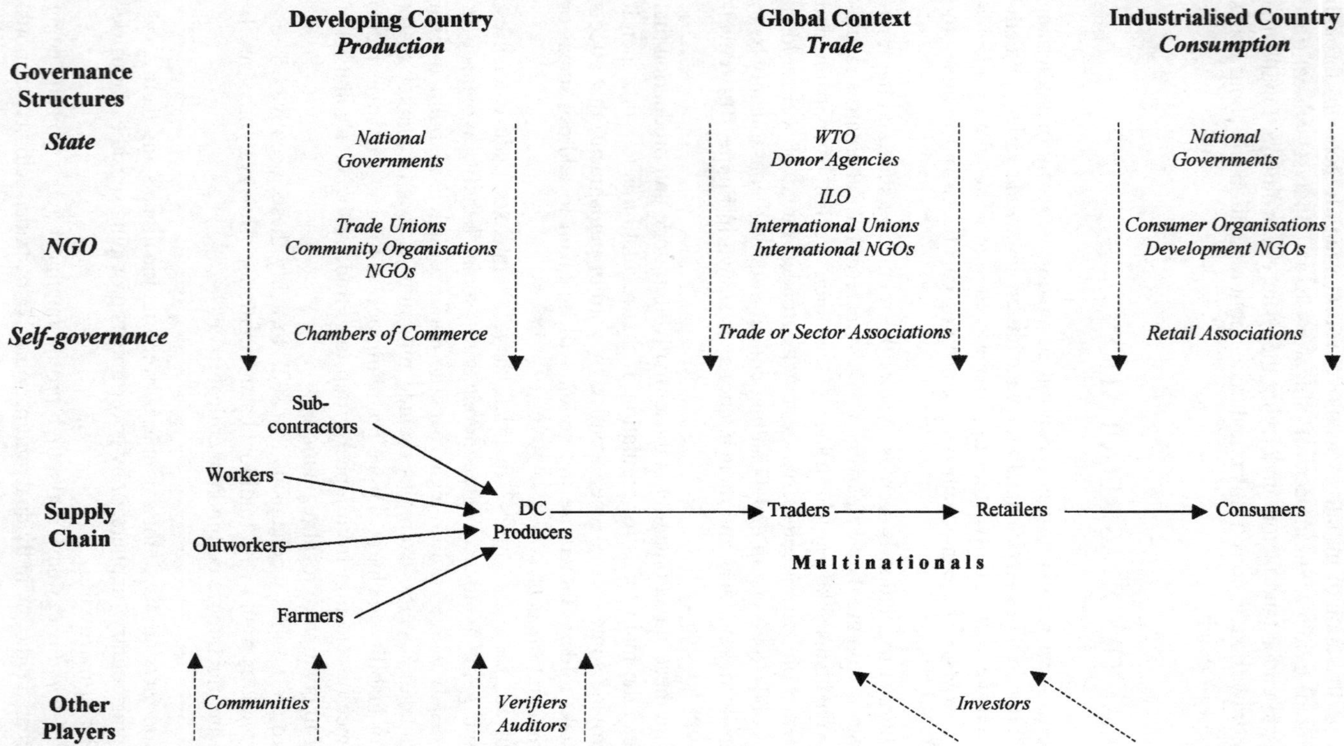

Figure 10.1 Stakeholder relations in ethical trade

In addition to hundreds of firm and sector codes of conduct, there are also core codes, intended to be widely applicable (such as SA8000 or the UK Ethical Trade Initiative's model code); and issue-specific codes, such as those dealing with child labour.

- *Informal agreements* are important, such as promises by government around future relief from, or shaping of, formal regulation.
- *Peer actions* can relate to permission to join or be excluded from particular associations. Competitors may also undertake 'market leadership' (Burns and Blowfield 1999). This occurs when a firm demonstrates that markets can be created from ethical behaviour. Fair trade can be seen as one example. Whereas most ethical trade seeks to improve the performance of existing global supply chains, fair trade creates new markets and new global supply chains based on alternative trading organisations that typically deal direct with small-scale producers and their communities (Tallontire 2000).
- *Supply flows* from capital and labour markets. This encompasses the actions of investors, especially major investors like pension funds, in deciding where to channel their investments. It also includes the actions of workers and the labour pool; actions that range from interest in recruitment to strikes.
- *Demand flows* from consumer markets. This is commonly seen as the driving force for ethical trade; the most potentially powerful alternative to state control. It covers loss of consumers for 'sub-standard' social/environmental performance, and retention/gain of market share, or the ability to charge higher prices, for 'good' performance.
- *Information flows* are wide-ranging. Every one of the mechanisms listed has an associated information flow, of which the *audit* flow is one of the most important. This gives feedback to producers and other stakeholders to help them know if decisions and actions have been appropriate, and what further action to take. Two examples are shown in Figure 10.2.

Information flows are also fundamental to *advocacy*; a widely used mechanism in ethical trade. This encompasses exhortations to producers to get them

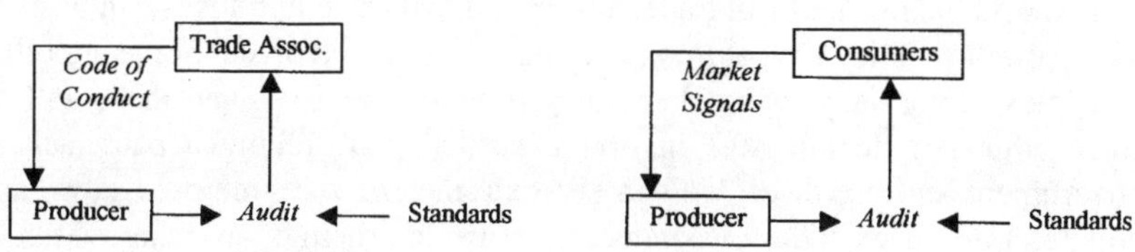

Figure 10.2 Audit-related information flows in ethical trade

to comply with social/environmental standards (e.g. trying to persuade them of the benefits of compliance); data for producers on best practice (e.g. on workplace health and safety); encouragement to governments to create new regulations (e.g. the ILO's attempt to get governments to ratify core child labour conventions); and data for consumers on production conditions. The most well-known form of the latter – forming the vertical flow to consumers in Figure 10.2 – is labelling schemes on products. Examples include Rugmark, that identifies child labour-free carpets, and the Forest Stewardship Council's label to identify products taken from sustainably managed forests (Zadek et al. 1998).

Some analyses categorise these mechanisms into mandatory and non-mandatory, with the laws of state regulation falling into the former, and all other mechanisms into the latter (Khanna 2001). The practical applicability of this categorisation must be questioned. There are government regulations that, while theoretically mandatory, have no impact because they are not implemented or because they are corrupted (Minogue 2004). Equally, there are supposedly voluntary mechanisms that firms feel they must react to. Consumer boycotts are one example, but codes of conduct can be another. Codes of conduct in the Kenyan flower industry, for instance, are non-binding but 'represent industry entry requirements' for new firms (Collinson 2001b, p. 2).

What actually matters is the contingent power of a particular incentive for a particular stakeholder in a particular situation; nonetheless, we can still categorise mechanisms as direct or indirect. To understand, we must see that the ultimate focus for almost all activity is the decisions and actions (behaviour) of developing country producers. It is they who have the immediate social and environmental impact. In this light, as summarised in Figure 10.3, virtually all mechanisms can be seen as indirect because, surprisingly at first sight, most regulatory activity is not focused on those stakeholders. Instead, it is focused on organisations that have some northern component, most of which are also multinationals: the retailers, or marketers, or traders who contract with developing country (DC) producers, or the multinational producers who own DC-based production subsidiaries. Even most self-regulation is self-regulation of organisations that themselves do not usually directly control social/environmental impacts of production in developing countries.

Figure 10.3 is complex enough, even though it presents only some of the main mechanisms of ethical trade. Yet real ethical trade initiatives can be even more complex. They are complex in terms of who is involved. Some are bilateral: pick almost any two stakeholders from Figure 10.3, and there will be some ethical trade initiative involving such a pair. Taking a pair such as government and producer, we can see extremes of state-imposed laws, and unilateral producer codes of conduct. In between, though, are many varieties of co-regulated rules and codes: from negotiated through approved and recognised to official (BRTF 2000). There are also complexities in the difference

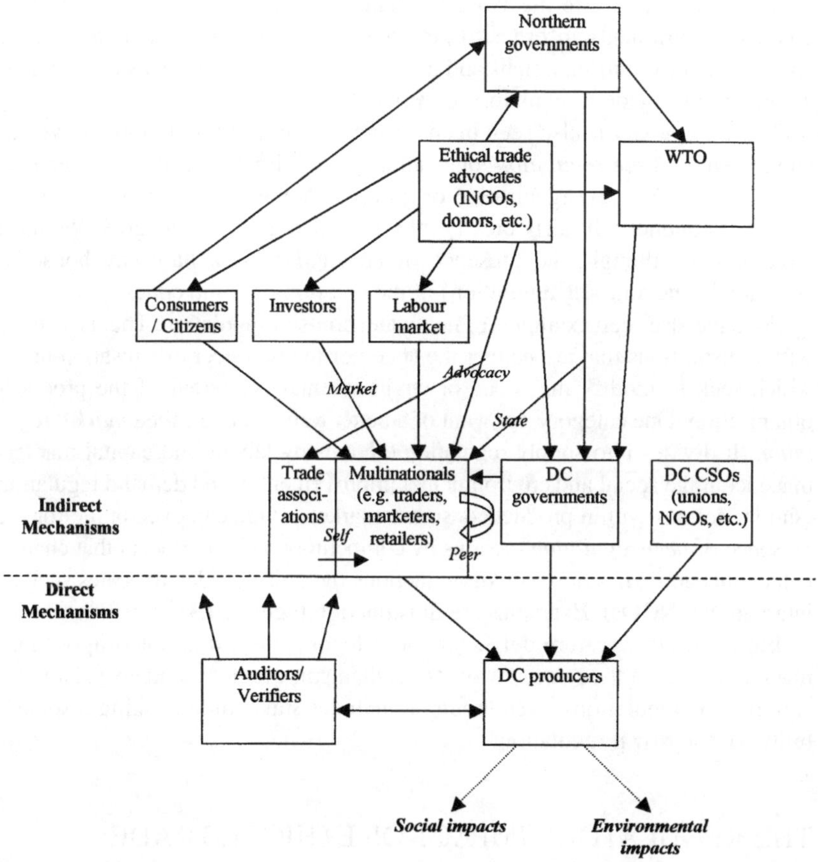

Figure 10.3 Indirect and direct regulatory mechanisms in ethical trade

between who *develops* the regulatory mechanism, and who *implements*, and who *is affected by* the mechanism. In addition, initiatives are increasingly not bilateral but multilateral (Barrientos and Blowfield 2001). Examples of multi-stakeholder initiatives (which typically bring together corporate, NGO and union stakeholders, often facilitated by government) include the UK's Ethical Trade Initiative, and the Dutch Clean Clothes Campaign.

Ethical trade initiatives are also complex in terms of what is involved. They often use multiple mechanisms. Sector-based initiatives, for example, can involve codes of conduct, audit of production impacts, labelling schemes, and broad-based advocacy. Other initiatives have many links: one element in a recent Christian Aid campaign aimed to get UK citizens to pressure the UK government to pressure the WTO to change the rules that affect developing country governments in order to get those governments to alter the trading environment for multinationals and local producers. Thus global supply chains are mirrored in global regulatory governance chains.

This complexity is also seen in analysing the form of regulation. As well as an element of *state regulation*, one can also see within ethical trade elements of *self-regulation*: an organisation or group of organisations regulating itself. Codes of conduct fall fairly clearly into the self-regulation category. We have already seen, though, the presence of *co-regulation* (a half-way house of combined state and self-regulation) in the creation of some codes.

We have also seen examples of non-state, non-self regulation. That is, actions within institutions that are neither the state nor the producer organisation itself, which seek to modify the social or environmental behaviour of the producer organisation. One category, for want of a better term, can be called *market regulation*. It divides into supply regulation (actions by labour and capital markets that encourage social and environmental improvements), and demand regulation (similar actions within product/consumer markets). One can even argue for the presence of *peer regulation* (actions by competitors and other peers that change behaviour) and *advocacy regulation* (actions by ethical trade advocates such as international NGOs). Examples are illustrated in Figure 10.3.

Ethical trade therefore defies simple categorisation. It is not simply 'non-mandatory', even though many of its mechanisms are not mandatory. Nor is it simply 'self-regulation', even though it includes stakeholders taking responsibility for their own regulation.

THE REGULATORY IMPACT OF ETHICAL TRADE

Having investigated the regulatory mechanisms of ethical trade, we now move on to look at the regulatory impacts. Is ethical trade producing the social and environmental improvements that are its goal?

This is not easily answered because of a dearth of impact assessment data, arguably due to the relative novelty of the topic. This has had a number of effects.

- Lack of research. New topics like ethical trade attract an inflow of researchers and research funds, but these take time to create a critical mass of work.
- Lack of impact research. Research tracks practice. A number of ethical trade initiatives only got underway in the late 1990s. Published research to date on these has tended to focus on their upstream elements (creation, design and content) and is only more slowly moving into the downstream elements of implementation and impact.

- Lack of good impact research. It is not easy to do regulatory impact research. There are relatively few guides, which self-reinforces with the lack of impact cases and data already noted. It is also difficult to tease out the specific impact of a given initiative when firms face multiple regulatory measures, and when one cannot readily identify control samples.

The result is a growing body of work that, in impact terms, remains dominated by hypotheticals rather than actuals. Nonetheless, we will review what data are available, classified according to six performance measures for ethical trade regulatory systems (developed from OCA 2000 and Barrientos and Blowfield 2001). Three of these are pre-implementation measures:

- Existence: is there a regulatory instrument?
- Extent: who and what is covered by the regulation?
- Expedience: are regulatory goals appropriate to social/environmental needs?

The other three are post-implementation measures:

- Effectiveness: does the regulation achieve the goals set?
- Efficiency: does it achieve its impact with minimum cost?
- Externalities: what other effects does the regulation have?

Each of these will now be discussed in turn.

Existence

There has been a sharp growth in the number of ethical trade initiatives in the past few years. At present, initiatives are strong in certain sectors but weak or absent in others (Jenkins 2001). Measures aimed at raising labour standards have been strong in areas with relatively low-cost branded consumer goods such as apparel, footwear, and toys. Measures aimed at environmental issues have concentrated in the primary sector (forestry, oil, mining) and resource-based manufacturing, such as the chemicals and wood product sectors. Within given sectors, measures tend to exist only for the traded segment and not for domestic market-focused producers.

Extent

Within a given global supply chain, the spotlight of ethical trade initiatives tends to fall on some areas and not others. Commentators analysing codes of conduct have tended to focus on what is not covered rather than vice versa, with concerns expressed about exclusion of home-workers and casual labourers (Barrientos 2000), and about exclusion of more peripheral production locations (Sharma et al. 2000).

Starting from the global level, ILO core standards or the broader set from SA8000 have been seen as something of a benchmark that certain initiatives fail to achieve; missing out on key standards (Curtis 2001). Starting from the local level, some initiatives fail to reflect the concerns of local workers and their communities; such as those expressed by women workers (Pearson and Seyfang 2001). In either case, the analysis has been that regulatory content reflects the interests of its creators, rather than the interests of its potential beneficiaries. This may also lie behind the fact that some initiatives are rather long on aspiration but correspondingly short on details of how exactly they are to be implemented (OECD 2001).

Expedience

The distancing between content and local beneficiaries just noted also rolls into a feeling that the goals of some ethical trade initiatives are too limited in what they seek to achieve. This has arisen particularly when commentators are comparing goals to those they feel state regulation would aim for or achieve. At the same time, ethical trade goals are at times judged unrealistic, with donors and NGOs setting social and environmental objectives that business cannot be induced to achieve (Lewis 2000). As with the points about existence and extent of measures, these matters can, in part, be put down to the ethical trade's relatively short history. If feedback and learning mechanisms are in place, then coverage and relevance should increase over time. This will only be true, though, if ethical trade regulatory mechanisms are seen to work and to work well. We now move on to consider the evidence on this.

Effectiveness

Despite the data limitations, there is evidence of ethical trade delivering on social/environmental goals. Examples include:

- Reductions in child labour in Central American garment manufacture (Sajhau 1998).
- Workers being reinstated and allowed to unionise in garment factories in Central America (Jeffcott and Yanz 2000).
- Reductions in the number of child labourers employed to make carpets in India (Sharma et al. 2000).
- Improvements in environmental management in electronics factories in Thailand (Foran 2001).

- Improvements in health and safety conditions in footwear factories in South-East Asia (Jenkins 2001).
- Reductions in water and air pollution emissions from factories in Asia and Central America (Khanna 2001).

In addition, pressures from socially responsible investment initiatives have been shown to affect multinationals' decision on product pricing for Africa, and on debt-forgiveness in South America (though these impacts lie outside the normal scope of ethical trade) (Slavin 2002, Bowers 2003).

Alongside this positive picture, there is rather more mixed evidence that highlights the limitations of alternative regulatory mechanisms. Relatively successful consumer campaigns – such as the growth of fair trade coffee – are overshadowed by the larger number that have little or no impact (Burns and Blowfield 1999). The successes achieved on child labour in India are put down to stricter enforcement of pre-existing state laws, with alternative mechanisms such as labelling having had only a 'limited impact' (Sharma et al. 2000, p. 74).

Voluntary mechanisms to encourage reporting on social and environmental issues by big firms have led only a small percentage of firms to comply (Doane 2002). Where self-regulated initiatives, such as codes of conduct, have been accepted by firms, they have come in for criticism as window-dressing: 'to date such [voluntary] initiatives have had a more visible effect on their [firms'] market image in the north than on the actual pay and conditions of workforces in the south' (Pearson and Seyfang 2001, p. 94). Labels have thus come in for criticism as being just a marketing tool to serve multinationals rather than a mechanism to deliver development benefits (Childs and Whiting 1998).

Efficiency

If there are few data on the effectiveness of ethical trade, there are even less on its efficiency, let alone the type of comparative cost/benefit analysis that could provide guidance on the optimum portfolio of regulatory instruments. Costs can be divided into administration costs (creating and implementing standards), compliance costs (fulfilling those standards), and social costs (the externalities discussed next) (Parker and Kirkpatrick 2002).

In terms of administration, theoretical work suggests, not surprisingly, that self-regulation costs more than no regulation (Collinson 2001a). It may attract lower administrative costs than state regulation because, with fewer stakeholders and use of 'insider knowledge', the information and transaction costs of formulating, interpreting, monitoring and enforcing standards should be lower (Ogus 2001). Even this quite simple conclusion is of uncertain value, though, because of the real-world imperfections in implementing state regulation, and because ethical trade is much more than just self-regulation: it often involves many stakeholders, raising the possibility of high information and transaction costs. All we can say for certain is that alternative regulatory mechanisms shift the balance of administrative costs between actors, with 'new' stakeholders, such as ethical trade advocates, facing new costs; and that costs will be affected by factors such as the number and asymmetry of stakeholders.

As regards compliance costs, the burden varies for producers depending on their 'starting position', for example how close they were to compliance before the regulation was introduced (Collinson 2001a). A comparative picture depends on what one compares this to. Some argue that ARMs present lower costs (and lower achievements) than state regulation but this assumes a feasibility, perfection and separation of state regulation that may well not exist in practice (Lazzarini and de Mello 2001).

Externalities

Before looking at the possible costs of externalities, we can first cite some of the benefits. In a very general sense, ethical trade has helped give a higher profile to social and environmental development, and helped citizens and firms in the North understand the consequences of their actions in the South. It is also catalysing an integration of debates on social, environmental and economic development; showing the indivisibility of issues that have been separated in the past (Pearson and Seyfang 2001).

Other benefits are equally intangible, and relate to the emergence of new institutional mechanisms for regulatory governance. Ethical trade often brings several stakeholders in the global supply chain together, creating informal institutional structures through which a dialogue can be established. This dialogue, and the mutual trust that it helps create, stands in contrast to the adversarial relationships that often existed previously (Blowfield and Jones 1999).

Breaking down these barriers can bring several benefits because regulatory systems based on trust and dialogue seem to outperform those based on confrontation (Minogue 2001). Flows of information and knowledge can be improved, thus reducing costs, because far more data are shared in situations of trust. Trust also enables the system to be more flexible. It can learn and adapt more readily than systems based on more formal organisational boundaries, and it can draw on resources wherever they reside within the system (Lewis 2000). This flexibility could lead as far as more formal, state-led regulation if stakeholders come to share goals and accept traditional mechanisms as the most effective means of achieving their goals. Something like this has happened in the European textile and clothing sector, where dialogue and institution-formation have produced an agreement with legal status and binding force that covers the four ILO core standards (EC 1999).

If the theme of positive externalities is institution-forming, then the theme of negative externalities is displacement. The analogy is that of squeezing the balloon: bearing down on a problem in one area will only cause it to emerge somewhere else. In some ways, this is a literal metaphor. Some of the children squeezed out of carpet-making in certain core locations in India re-emerged elsewhere, either in physical locations outside the core, or in other jobs such as beedi-making or weaving (Sharma et al. 2000). Southern jobs can also be lost, due to ethical trade, if producers centralise or automate or squeeze subcontractors in order to reduce their compliance costs (Collinson 2001a, Jenkins 2001). Whatever the deficiencies of employment in the export sector, they tend to be less than either employment in the domestic sector or unemployment. In other situations, it is production (rather than labour) that could move as contracts and capital flow to locations that are more loosely regulated (Burns and Blowfield 1999). This is the much-feared 'race to the bottom', used as an argument both by those opposed to regulation per se, and by those in favour of global regulation.

The final negative externality is institutional, with worries that ethical trade will undermine other regulations and institutions. In particular, it could weaken both unions and governments if it promotes the idea that regulation can take place perfectly well without those institutions. This parallels concerns (with some limited supporting evidence) that any window-dressing by multinationals is not just a marketing ploy to sell products, but also an effort to preempt formal regulation by the state (Curtis 2001).

In all, these externalities should not be overstated at present. They are more hypothetical than proven. Nonetheless, they form an important part of the overall picture of regulatory impacts of ethical trade.

ANALYSING THE REGULATORY IMPACTS OF ETHICAL TRADE

The overriding image of ethical trade impact to date is of the glass half-full . . . or half-empty. Multinationals and some ethical trade advocates have tended to take the former view, focusing on what ethical trade has covered and achieved. Many academic commentators have taken the latter view, with a tone that has tended more towards the critical than the supportive. Whether there is any overlap is hard to say, but there is also a sense that those coming from the right of the political spectrum have been more optimistic about ethical trade, whereas those from the left are more sceptical.

The division may relate to comparison with theory and with practice. It is quite easy to compare alternative regulatory mechanisms with some mythical situation in which a noble and independent government sets out ideal laws that are implemented by highly efficient, skilled and incorruptible civil servants. Such a comparison will cast ARMs in an unfavourable light. But it would be fairer to compare them with the reality of what state regulation has actually achieved and, indeed, of whether or not state regulation is even feasible (OCA 2000, Perry and Singh 2001). Seen this way, the limitations of current ethical trade may not appear quite so severe.

Whichever view one takes, it is hard to deny that ethical trade does currently have limitations and shortcomings. It would be useful to understand these as a step towards improvements. We can base such an understanding on two analytical approaches: design-focused and institution-focused.

Design-focused Analysis

Some analyses of ethical trade identify relatively practical issues behind shortfalls in the '6E' performance measures. We can frame these issues in terms of design–reality gaps: the notion that initiatives are more likely to fail when there is a significant gap between design assumptions/requirements and 'on-the-ground' realities (Heeks 2002). In some cases, this emerges as a general lack of implementation detail within initiatives, but there are also examples of specific design–reality gaps, including the following.

- Designs mismatched to the real availability of information channels, causing poor awareness of ethical trade initiatives among producers and workers in the South (ActionAid 2002).
- Designs mismatched to the real existence of other, overlapping initiatives, so that implementation costs rise as implementation effectiveness falls (Blowfield 2001).
- Designs mismatched to the real availability of funds, so that promised complementary supports to bans on child labour are not put in place (Sharma et al. 2000).
- Designs mismatched to the real availability of human capacities, so that audits can only rarely be undertaken, and those undertaken are done poorly (Prieto and Bendell 2002).
- Designs mismatched to the socio-economic realities of poor livelihoods, so that blunt-instrument bans on child labour cause more problems than they solve (Basu 1998).
- Designs mismatched to the socio-politics of the workplace, so that audits are seen by workers as a management initiative, causing them to paint a partial or falsely positive picture to auditors (Jenkins 2001).
- Designs mismatched to the complexity of supply chain realities, so that

only a small part of the supply chain is ever monitored (Sharma et al. 2000).

These design–reality mismatches undermine the crucial audit process by producing audit data that fall short on some of the key data criteria: completeness, accuracy, relevance, timeliness and appropriateness of presentation (Duncombe and Heeks 2002). More generally, design-reality mismatches explain the implementation gap between regulation on paper and regulation in practice.

We can attribute these design–reality shortcomings to problems with regulatory design or, going deeper, to problems with the *process* of design. This draws us back to a point made earlier, that ARM design reflects the interests of the designers. These designers are typically drawn from organisations in the North, since ethical trade has so far been largely a northern project (Blowfield 1999). In the case of self-regulatory mechanisms, they will be drawn from northern multinationals. It is thus predictable that design mismatches the realities, including needs and priorities, of workers and communities in the South.

Institution-focused Analysis

Design-focused analysis implicitly assumes that relatively straightforward improvements to the process and/or outcome of design can address the shortcomings of ethical trade. Institution-focused analysis provides a deeper critique that sees more inherent, and resilient, challenges to ethical trade.

This understands the '6E' shortfalls as a failure to close the gap between public and private interests, leading to negative public externalities of private actions and an inability of private firms to internalise the public benefits of socially and environmentally beneficial actions (Lazzarini and de Mello 2001). It models those interests as shown in Figure 10.4.

If we look at one of the key ethical trade stakeholders, the multinationals, then teasing out their underlying interests is not easy. However, surveys suggest that key interests include reducing costs, avoiding risks (including litigation and damage to reputation), and retaining/gaining market share (EC 1999, Khanna 2001). As enacted, those interests do not always match the public interest, as seen in the findings so far regarding limited impacts, 'window-dressing' and negative externalities. Why should this be? We can explain it in terms of the Figure 10.4 model, and issues that arise in the other elements of the model.

Incentives

If incentives are sufficiently strong, they modify multinational interests to

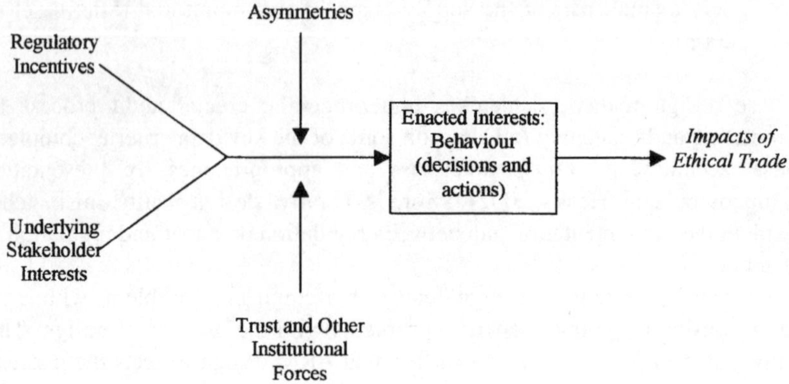

Figure 10.4 *An institutional model of ethical trade regulation*

cause behaviour in the public interest. Such incentives can be seen at work in the ethical trade effectiveness successes cited earlier. However, the incentives are often weak in many forms of ethical trade. The weaknesses of state regulation in some countries, and consequent failure to provide incentives for public interest behaviour, have already been noted. Only in countries with a credible state will state regulation, or desire to pre-empt state regulation, act as a viable motivator.

Other forms of ethical trade regulation include the following.

- Self-regulation: per se, self-regulation provides no clear incentives for behaviour change; a fact underlying some critiques of measures such as codes of conduct (Fitzgerald 2001). Any incentives tend to be comparative, and come from avoidance of other forms of regulation.
- Peer and advocacy regulation: having been studied relatively little, the incentive strength of these regulatory forms is unclear. Advocacy, though, may suffer from a lack of clear incentives: like self-regulation, any strength it derives tends to come indirectly from state or market incentives, such as the threat of consumer action.
- Supply market regulation: there is little evidence about strength of incentives from the labour market. Socially responsible investment can have an effect if well-focused, but there are few signs that firms which fail to adhere to social/environmental standards are affected by under-investment (Cowe 2002).
- Demand market regulation: if ethical investment has been undersold, ethical consumption may have been oversold as an incentive at least in terms of its practice, if not its potential. Perhaps more than anything,

> limits on change in consumer behaviour have limited the impacts of ethical trade to date. Doane (2002), for example compares the 89 per cent of UK consumers who say they are concerned about social/ethical issues, with the less than 5 per cent who make active choices on these factors in the majority of their purchasing decisions. Data on consumer willingness to pay a price premium for perceived ethical products are mixed, but at the pessimistic end lies work cited by Jenkins (2001) indicating that only 5 per cent of Canadian consumers would pay more for fair-traded products. The result, when motivation and willingness to pay are added to factors like brand loyalty, switching costs, lack of alternative products, and information asymmetries, is that consumers will generally not switch in large numbers from goods that rank poorly on ethical criteria to goods that rank well (Lazzarini and de Mello 2001). Only where consumers form a large demand bloc (such as major institutions) does the power of competition and the market start to work more effectively, providing the intended driving force for ethical trade.

If labour, capital and demand will not switch to reward good ethical performers and punish bad performers, this in practice creates disincentives. Good performers have to bear compliance costs that bad performers do not, with limited prospect of the market rewarding this behaviour (Doane 2002). The public benefits of compliance are spread unevenly throughout the supply chain, but concentrated at the production and pre-production end rather than with the multinationals. If the extra costs cannot be passed on to the consumer, they will either be avoided through bad performance or, perhaps, passed on to workers and producers in developing countries, potentially cancelling out any benefits, and creating some of the negative externalities noted earlier.

This is not to argue that public interest incentives are always deficient in ethical trade. We have seen cases where incentives work. However, we do argue that incentives are critical and yet often deficient in ethical trade. In such cases, companies are only likely to participate in an initiative where there is a small 'ethical gap' between their current interests/behaviour and the interests/behaviour required to comply with the initiative.

Asymmetries

Where incentives are weak in ethical trade regulatory systems, private interests will tend to dominate the behavioural motivation of stakeholders. However, the ability of particular stakeholder interests to dominate the outcomes of trade depends on the asymmetries that exist between stakeholders.

The fundamental asymmetry that exists in global supply chains is the asymmetry of power. Power relates to direct or indirect control over a basket of capital resources: financial capital, natural capital, physical capital (e.g. technology), human capital (e.g. skills), social capital (including relationships, brands and reputations), and knowledge capital (covering both knowledge and information). The greater the asymmetries of capital between stakeholders, the more the 'haves' can dominate the institutions of the global supply chain (markets, regulations, standards) and impose their interests.

Each supply chain will present a unique distribution of power and capital resources between stakeholders. However, a relatively common picture is one in which the multinational intermediaries are foremost, approaching oligopoly in some supply chains (Cawthorne 2002). In such situations, the exact form of regulation may not matter very much. Whatever the form, it is likely to be prone to outcomes of oligopoly that have also affected traditional state regulation (Lazzarini and de Mello 2001, Parker and Kirkpatrick 2002).

- Regulatory capture: the annexation of a whole regulatory mechanism or even initiative by a particular stakeholder group, skewing that mechanism/initiative to its interests.
- Regulatory hold-up: the use of oligopolistic power by one stakeholder in an otherwise neutral regulatory regime to force particular self-interested outcomes.

Both outcomes can be seen to lie behind the criticisms of poor performance of ethical trade regulatory systems, such as window-dressing.

Information asymmetries (highly unequal access to data between stakeholders) are both a cause and a consequence of oligopoly. This helps create a self-reinforcing cycle as dominant stakeholders seek to retain their power through non-disclosure of information, and as ethical trade systems create disincentives to disclosure. Exposing sub-standard social/environmental behaviour, for example, damages reputations even where the problem is being addressed (Nunez 2001). Concealment, and maintenance of information asymmetries, is the rational choice. The same point applies to audit where, because of power asymmetries, audited workers often prefer to say nothing rather than speak out, thus, again, preventing a reduction of information asymmetries (Barrientos and Blowfield 2001).

Information asymmetries damage the effectiveness of ethical trade. As well as enabling capture and hold-up, asymmetries between multinational intermediaries and state/NGO stakeholders also engender a lack of transparency and accountability, particularly for self-regulated mechanisms (Ogus 2001). Information asymmetries between multinationals and groups in the South limit the effective engagement of those groups in ethical trade, as do North–South disparities more generally (Blowfield 1999, Foran 2001).

Information inequalities between multinationals/producers and consumers lead to the problems of adverse selection (where consumers do not know enough about production conditions to differentiate between products from good and bad performers) and variants of moral hazard (where firms that initially perform well are tempted to abandon labour/environmental standards because consumers will not be able to detect this abandonment) (Khanna 2001). Both problems prevent good performers charging price premia or gaining market share. This, as noted before, helps undermine demand market regulation and prevents compliance costs being shared with consumers.

The informational component of many ethical trade initiatives has been described: attempts to redress the imbalances, particularly between multinationals and consumers. To date, though, the effectiveness of such work has been limited, partly because of data-gathering problems previously analysed.

Trust and Other Institutional Factors

The interaction of interest, incentives and asymmetries is both constrained and enabled by other institutional factors. In a general sense, societal values affect outcomes: for instance, market regulation by consumers works better in societies with greater awareness and valuation of social/environmental issues (Fitzgerald 2001).

More specifically, it is features of the institutions that seek to regulate (governments, markets, advocates, etc.) that matter (Parker and Kirkpatrick 2002). These features include their capacities, their autonomy, and their commitment to particular regulatory outcomes. Together this bundle establishes the credibility of the regulatory institution and, hence, the credibility of its related incentives. Credibility, in turn, establishes whether or not an institution is trusted by other stakeholders. As already described, trust between stakeholders is seen as crucial to the effective functioning of ethical trade, though this should not be taken too far. NGOs and unions that organise consumer boycotts or strikes may be seen as credible by producers without necessarily being trusted.

DISCUSSION AND CONCLUSIONS

Globalisation is fundamental to an understanding of ethical trade because it has changed the context for regulation (Barrientos 2000). On the one hand, globalisation has greatly increased the value and power – but also the vulnerability – of brands and of corporate reputations. These form an increasingly important part of the relationship between firms and markets as firms decreasingly come into direct contact with consumers, and as goods increasingly embody 'credence' components: elements like their social and environmental attributes that consumers cannot know but have to take on trust (Klein 2000, Nunez 2001). Coupled with a globalised media and global spread of information and communication technologies (ICTs), this has provided new levers for those seeking to regulate the social and environmental impacts of production.

On the other hand, globalisation, enabled by liberalisation and technological change, has been associated with a growing complexity and fragmentation of both supply chains and governance chains. This has generated many regulatory challenges.

- A growing divergence of interests as more, and more distant/different stakeholders are drawn into ethical trade. This divergence has grown since the promotion of poverty elimination goals for developing countries (Parker and Kirkpatrick 2002).
- A shift in power from producers to intermediaries as production becomes an outsourced commodity and as knowledge about design, brands, and markets becomes ever more important (Greig 2002, Ponte 2002). One developing country producer can become increasingly substitutable for another, while the oligopolistic power of multinational retailers, marketers and traders grows. Simultaneously, and despite the rhetoric, consumer power does not grow.
- A growth in information asymmetries as sites of production and sites of potential regulation (including supply and consumption markets) grow further apart, and as reputations are more strongly managed and protected. ICTs are a two-edged sword here. They can reconnect distant sites but, at the same time, they contribute to a data blizzard through which information on ethical trade penetrates with increasing difficulty (Duncombe and Heeks 2002).
- A growth in indirect rather than direct mechanisms of control. This has led to the 'denial of responsibility' defence (Greig 2002). Where a chain stretches from multinational retailer through developing country manufacturer and then sub-contractor to outworker, the multinationals may claim little control over, and little liability for, outworker conditions. It has also changed the nature of regulatory actions and incentives since these, too, are increasingly indirect (see Figure 10.3). Among other things, this makes it much harder to evaluate the impact of regulation.
- A decline in trust, partly due to greater distancing of stakeholders, partly due to the influx of new regulatory stakeholders with limited knowledge of each other and, in some cases, little track record of regulatory competence and/or some track record of confrontation.
- A growth in risk, uncertainty and change, all of which will encourage short-term, self-interested, opportunistic behaviour by stakeholders.

Ethical trade is still young in regulatory terms and there is much knowledge-building and learning to be done about the way in which its alternative regulatory mechanisms are facing up to the challenges of globalisation. Some see ARMs as particularly appropriate to globalised contexts given their flexibility and their capacity to tap into knowledge and expertise embedded in different organisations (BRTF 2000). However, the verdict to date on ethical trade is 'not proven', with evidence both for and against effectiveness and other performance measures. Ethical trade has achieved more than nothing, but less than hoped for and, to date, its institution-building and process benefits have been stronger than social/environmental impact gains.

The learning that has occurred thus far has produced a series of better practice recommendations. Some are relatively straightforward, and represent advice to close design–reality gaps; for example, by more appropriate design of audit procedures (Auret 2001).

Other recommendations are less clear, partly because there is an unavoidable tendency for writers to view the world through their own lens: activists recommend more activism (Klein 2000), researchers recommend more research (e.g. Foran 2001), union officials recommend more union recognition (e.g. Mansfield 2002), and so on. This might explain why some commentators make recommendations that are actually still one half of unresolved tensions. Examples include:

- Recommendations for more local flexibility and participation in order to match regulation to local needs. Others point out the value of uniform global approaches to avoid the race to the bottom that can ensue if countries have exploitable differences in regulatory standards (Fitzgerald 2001).
- Recommendations for multi-stakeholder initiatives to integrate a broad range of interests into regulation, to reduce opportunities for regulatory capture, and to increase the 'ethical space' (i.e. room for manoeuvre) for key actors (Blowfield and Jones 1999). Others point out the lower costs, greater flexibility and greater trust-building within bilateral initiatives (Mansfield 2002).
- Recommendations for greater focus within regulatory measures on outcomes. Others point out that process determines outcome, and that regulatory measures are thus often right to focus first on process (Blowfield 1999).

One tension that was much in evidence, though, now seems largely redundant: the opposition between state regulation vs. ethical trade. Ethical trade is often portrayed as something new: 'new means of facilitating the relationship between market and society' (Barrientos 2000, p. 564). Implicitly, it is categorised separately from the 'old': traditional regulation by nation states. We did the same here by describing its mechanisms as 'alternative' to state regulation. Of course, there are things here that appear new and different: making greater use of supply and demand markets for regulation; getting producers to regulate themselves; harnessing information for direct and indirect advocacy; drawing multiple stakeholders together.

The appearance of novelty does seem valid, even though concerns about global trade stretch back many years, and self-regulatory codes for multinationals emerged in the 1970s after bribery scandals (Jenkins 2001). The sense of separateness, however, is false (Perry and Singh 2001). Regarding level, ethical trade is global and local, but it also operates strongly at national level. It erodes the validity of mandatory vs. non-mandatory. And the state is a key actor among the many stakeholders involved. State regulation must be understood as one part of ethical trade; even where not directly involved, state regulation is frequently the threat, or promise, or benchmark, or ultimate goal behind many ethical trade mechanisms. Thus, state regulation is often the iron fist within the velvet glove of ethical trade.

Put another way, ethical trade stripped of any relationship to state regulation seems likely to deliver relatively limited social/environmental gains – more, perhaps, than no regulation; less, perhaps, than state regulation; and certainly less than a coordinated portfolio of state and non-state regulation. So ethical trade is not the 'white' that contrasts with the 'black' of state regulation. Instead, ethical trade represents many colours in a regulatory rainbow that includes traditional forms of regulation. 'Alternative regulatory mechanisms' could therefore be renamed 'supplementary regulatory mechanisms'.

Supplementary mechanisms grow outwards from, but always linked to, the state and its laws, typically seeking to encompass as broad a range of stakeholders and as broad a range of incentives and mechanisms as possible. They arise as those concerned with the market failures of trade seek out all possible means for achieving their goals. This might best occur in a relatively non-dogmatic manner; trying out a rich variety of regulatory avenues to see what will work and, hopefully, learning and improving along the way. This may include using supplementary mechanisms as a stepping-stone to return to improved state regulation.

In seeking ways forward, then, it seems inappropriate to ask 'improved state regulation *or* something else?', and better to ask 'what mix and what chronology of improved state regulation *and* something else?' The institutional analysis provided earlier demands a contingent answer to this question. What is feasible and what is desirable will differ from context to context depending on what fills in the particular institutional map (like that drawn in Figure 10.4).

Given this, we might argue that the nature of regulation is something of a red herring. Commentators can become somewhat obsessed by particular forms or mechanisms of regulation, getting drawn into specific design issues. Yet the shortcomings identified (inefficiency, ineffectiveness, capture, hold-up and, overall, the continuing divergence of public and private interests) arise with both state and non-state regulation. From a different perspective, we can see that the institutional factors in a context will 'infect' any form of regulation. Hence, arguably, we should be asking more questions about and paying more attention to the identified institutional factors: incentives, asymmetries, credibility and trust.

Using these analytical approaches, then, prescriptions for successful ethical trade would include:

- designs that have a relatively good match to the reality of the implementation context,
- incentives that give key actors a clear cost/benefit reason to act in the public interest,
- processes that enable development of trust between key players, and development of regulatory credibility,
- actions that reduce asymmetries, and
- mechanisms for learning and improvement.

Researching Ethical Trade

In this chapter, we have reviewed knowledge and issues to date on ethical trade. However, research on ethical trade is still in its relative infancy. Two particular knowledge gaps stand out.

First, we know far too little about the impact of ethical trade. Building knowledge on impacts will require development of regulatory impact assessment methodologies that are suitable to global supply and governance chains, and to the supplementary regulatory mechanisms that abound in ethical trade. We have some starting points on this (e.g. Mayoux 2001, Lee 2002), but much has still to be done.

Second, much of the work has been approached in a pragmatic manner with little recourse to conceptual models, let alone theories. There is a danger, putting the work on ethical trade together, that it represents a random scatter of pebbles rather than a growing cairn in which new studies stand on the shoulders of existing knowledge. Similar criticisms have been levelled at the study of regulation and development more generally (Parker and Kirkpatrick 2002).

We can use conceptual models to investigate specific angles on ethical trade. As already described, the notion of design–reality gaps can be used to understand the transfer of ethical trade models from North to South, and the relevance of regulatory systems to specific local contexts. We can also use information systems analysis to understand ethical trade because it is such an information-intensive activity and because ICTs are critical enablers of both global supply and global governance chains (see Duncombe and Heeks 2002).

But ethical trade must also be viewed holistically and, from this perspective, it is institutional models that offer the best theoretical basis. Figure 10.4 has offered just a simple model, but a deeper grounding probably lies in the body of work on 'network/chain analysis' since this integrates a number of economic, political and contextual components (e.g. Gereffi 1999, Kaplinsky 2000, Raikes et al. 2000, Henderson 2002). Using such institutional analysis, we can start to build knowledge on ethical trade with both theoretical and practical value.

REFERENCES

ActionAid (2002), *The Kimberley Process Scheme to End Trade in Conflict Diamonds*, ActionAid, London.

Auret, D. (2001), 'Code compliance?', *Insights*, **36** (March), 3–4.

Barrientos, S. (2000), 'Globalization and ethical trade: assessing the implications for development', *Journal of International Development*, **12**, 559–70.

Barrientos, S. and Blowfield, M. (2001), 'Richer or poorer? Achievements and challenges of ethical trade', *Insights*, **36** (March), 1–2.

Basu, K. (1998), *Child Labour: Cause, Consequence and Cure*, Policy Research Working Paper, World Bank, Washington, DC.

Blowfield, M. (1999), 'Ethical trade: a review of developments and issues', *Third World Quarterly*, **20** (4), 753–70.

Blowfield, M. (2001), 'Death by a thousand codes', *Insights*, **36** (March), 5.

Blowfield, M. & Jones, K. (1999), *Ethical Trade and Agricultural Standards: Getting People to Talk*, Natural Resources Institute, Chatham Maritime, UK, available at http://www.nri.org/NRET/IFASpapr.htm.

Bowers, S. (2003), 'BFG drops Guyana claim', *The Guardian*, 18 March.

BRTF (2000), *Alternatives to State Regulation*, Better Regulation Task Force, London.

Burns, M. and Blowfield, M. (1999), *Approaches to Ethical Trade: Impact and Lessons Learned*, Natural Resources Institute, Chatham Maritime.

Cawthorne, P. (2002), 'The proliferation of ethical business codes in the UK and Europe', paper presented at 'Home and Away' workshop, 16–17 July, University of Sydney.

Childs, C. and Whiting, S. (1998), *Eco-labelling and the Green Consumer*, Department of Environmental Science, University of Bradford.

Collinson, C. (2001a), *The Business Costs of Ethical Supply Chain Management: South African Wine Industry Case Study*, NRI Report No. 2606, Natural Resource Institute, Greenwich.

Collinson, C. (2001b), *The Business Costs of Ethical Supply Chain Management: Kenyan Flower Industry Case Study*, NRI Report No. 2607, Natural Resource Institute, Greenwich.

Cowe, R. (2002), 'Wanted: shareholders with a global conscience', *The Observer*, Business Supplement, 24 Nov., p. 6.

Curtis, M. (2001), *Trade for Life: Making Trade Work for Poor People*, Christian Aid, London.

Doane, D. (2002), *Market Failure: The Case for Mandatory Social and Environmental Reporting*, New Economics Foundation, London.

Duncombe, R. and Heeks, R.B. (2002), 'Information, ICTs and ethical trade', Centre on Regulation and Competition working paper no. 41, IDPM, University of Manchester, Manchester, http://idpm.man.ac.uk/crc.

EC (1999), 'Codes of conduct and social labels', *European Social Dialogue*, special edition, May.

Fitzgerald, E.V.K. (2001), *Regulating Large International Firms*, Technology, Business and Society Programme Paper No. 5, United Nations Research Institute for Social Development, Geneva.

Foran, T. (2001), *Corporate Social Responsibility at Nine Multinational Electronics Firms in Thailand: A Preliminary Analysis*, Nautilus Institute, Berkeley, CA.

Gereffi, G. (1999), 'Commodity Chains Framework for Analyzing Global Industries', mimeo, Dept. of Sociology, Duke University, Durham, NC.

Greig, A. (2002), 'The struggle for outwork reform in the Australian clothing industry', *Journal of Australian Political Economy*, **49**, June, http://www.jape.org/.

Heeks, R.B. (2002), 'Information systems and developing countries: failure, success and local improvisations', *The Information Society*, **18** (2), 101–12.

Henderson, J. (2002), *Globalisation on the Ground*, Centre on Regulation and Competition working paper no. 38, IDPM, University of Manchester, Manchester, http://idpm.man.ac.uk/crc.

ILO (1998), *ILO Declaration on Fundamental Principles and Rights at Work*, ILO, Geneva.

Jeffcott, B. and Yanz, L. (2000), *Codes of Conduct, Government Regulation and Worker Organizing*, ETAG Discussion Paper no. 1, Maquila Solidarity Network, Toronto.

Jenkins, R. (2001), *Corporate Codes of Conduct: Self-regulation in a Global Economy*, Technology, Business and Society Programme Paper no. 2, United Nations Research Institute for Social Development, Geneva.

Kaplinsky, R. (2000), *Spreading the Gains from Globalisation: What can be Learned from Value Chain Analysis?*, IDS Working Paper no. 110, IDS, University of Sussex.

Khanna, M. (2001), 'Non-mandatory approaches to environmental protection', *Journal of Economic Surveys*, **15** (3), 291–324.

Klein, N. (2000), *No Logo*, Flamingo, London.

Lazzarini, S.G. and de Mello, P.C. (2001), 'Governmental versus self-regulation of derivative markets', *Journal of Economics and Business*, **53**, 185–207.

Lee, E. (1997), 'Globalization and labour standards: a review of issues', *International Labour Review*, **136** (2), 173–89.

Lee, N. (2002), *Developing and Applying Regulatory Impact Assessment Methodologies in Low and Middle Income Countries*, Centre on Regulation and Competition working paper no. 30, IDPM, University of Manchester, Manchester, http://idpm.man.ac.uk/crc.

Lewis, D. (2000), *Promoting Socially Responsible Business, Ethical Trade and Acceptable Labour Standards*, Social Development Department, DFID, London.

Mansfield, B. (2002), 'Union experiences with standards and codes', paper presented at 'Home and Away' workshop, 16–17 July, University of Sydney.

Mayoux, L. (2001), *Impact Assessment of Fair Trade and Ethical Enterprise*

Development, EDIAIS Information Resource, IDPM, University of Manchester, Manchester, http://www.enterprise-impact.org.uk/informationresources.

Minogue, M. (2001), *Governance-based Analysis of Regulation*, Centre on Regulation and Competition working paper no. 3, IDPM, University of Manchester, Manchester, http://idpm.man.ac.uk/crc.

Minogue, M. (2004), 'Public management and regulatory governance', in P. Cook, C. Kirkpatrick, M. Minogue and D. Parker (eds), *Leading Issues in Competition, Regulation and Development,* Edward Elgar, Cheltenham.

Nunez, J. (2001), 'A model of self-regulation', *Economics Letters*, **74**, 91–7.

OCA (2000), *An Evaluative Framework for Voluntary Codes*, Office of Consumer Affairs, Industry Canada, Ottawa.

OECD (2001), *Codes of Corporate Conduct*, OECD, Paris.

Ogus, A. (2001), *Regulatory Institutions and Structures*, Centre on Regulation and Competition working paper no. 4, IDPM, University of Manchester, Manchester, http://idpm.man.ac.uk/crc.

Parker, D. and Kirkpatrick, C. (2002), *Researching Economic Regulation in Developing Countries: Developing a Methodology for Critical Analysis*, Centre on Regulation and Competition working paper no. 34, IDPM, University of Manchester, http://idpm.man.ac.uk/crc.

Pearson, R. and Seyfang, G. (2001), 'New hope or false dawn? Voluntary codes of conduct, labour regulation and social policy in a globalizing world', *Global Social Policy*, **1** (1), 77–106.

Perry, M. and Singh, S. (2001), *Corporate Environmental Responsibility in Singapore and Malaysia*, Technology, Business and Society Programme Paper no. 3, United Nations Research Institute for Social Development, Geneva.

Ponte, S. (2002), 'The "latte revolution"? Regulation, markets and consumption in the global coffee chain', *World Development*, **30** (7), 1099–122.

Prieto, M. and Bendell, J. (2002), *If You Want to Help Us Then Start Listening to Us!*, New Academy of Business, Bath.

Raikes, P., Jensen, M.F. and Ponte, S. (2000), 'Global commodity chain analysis and the French *filiere* approach', *Economy and Society*, **29** (3), 390–417.

SAI (2001), *Social Accountability 8000*, Social Accountability International, New York.

Sajhau, J.P. (1998), *Business Ethics in the Textile, Clothing and Footwear Industries: Codes of Conduct*, SAP 2.60/WP.110, ILO, Geneva.

Sharma, A., Sharma, R. and Raj, N. (2000), *The Impact of Social Labelling on Child Labour in India's Carpet Industry*, International Programme on the Elimination of Child Labour working paper, ILO, Geneva.

Slavin, T. (2002), 'New rules of engagement', *The Observer*, Business Supplement, 1 Sept, p. 11.

Tallontire, A. (2000), 'Partnerships in fair trade: reflections from a case study of Cafedirect', *Development in Practice*, **10** (2), 166–77.

Zadek, S., Lingayah, S. and Forstater, M. (1998), *Social Labels: Tools for Ethical Trade*, European Commission, Brussels.

PART 3

Competition and Regulation in Developing Countries: Policies and Practice

11. Regulating competition in Malaysia

Cassey Lee

INTRODUCTION

Competition regulation became important in Malaysia following the regulatory reforms that accompanied the government's ambitious privatization programme. Sectoral regulation in the pre-privatization period involved mostly economic regulation and this was purely a matter of 'self-regulation' by the government. With privatization, new regulatory institutions and mechanisms have been established to regulate privatized entities. In the absence of a national competition policy or law, a sectoral approach to competition regulation was adopted. This approach to competition regulation has thus far been limited and ineffective. The Ministry of Domestic Trade and Consumer Affairs is currently formulating a national competition policy that, if implemented, will eventually lead to a national competition policy. The future transformation from a sectoral approach to a national approach in competition regulation will not be easy. This chapter discusses the existing state and future directions of competition regulation in Malaysia. The next section begins with a brief discussion of development policies in Malaysia since 1970. This is followed by a discussion of the sectoral competition regulation in the country, then a focus on the ongoing efforts to implement a national competition policy. The fifth section concludes.

DEVELOPMENT AND REGULATORY CONTEXT SINCE 1970

An important event in the post-independence era in Malaysia was the racial riots in May 1969. The government responded to the event with an extensive interventionist development policy called the *New Economic Policy* (NEP). The NEP was implemented to eradicate poverty as well as to redress the economic imbalance between the major races in the country. In the latter case, specific targets were set for ownership in the commercial and industrial sectors. This was achieved through many means from outright purchase of equity by trustee companies (representing the Bumiputra (i.e.

indigenous) community's interests) to licensing, quotas and government procurements. An example is the *1975 Industrial Coordination Act* (ICA) which required manufacturing firms exceeding a given size threshold (e.g. 25 or more employees or paid-up capital exceeding RM250 000) to apply for licences to operate. The use of the ICA to control entry into an industry was to ensure compliance with the NEP (in terms of ownership and employment).

By the early 1980s, the government embarked on another phase of interventionist policies by promoting heavy industries such as the national car project (Proton) and the steel plant (Perwaja). The objective was economic diversification to enhance industrial linkages in the economy. Investments in these projects were accompanied by increases in import duties on both automobiles and steel. Not long after these policies were implemented, the severe recession in the mid-1980s brought about another major shift in government policy, this time in the form of economic liberalization. The government's privatization policy, which had already begun by then, gained further momentum after the mid-1980s. Despite the extensive privatization that has taken place, regulatory reforms have lagged behind. The redistributive emphasis of the NEP remained an important element in the implementation of privatization. For example, the *Privatization Guidelines* state that at least 30 per cent of equity in privatized projects should be allocated to the Bumiputra community. However, since the financial crisis of 1997/98, several projects that were privatized in the 1980s (but subsequently experienced substantial losses) have been re-nationalized. These include two LRT systems in Kuala Lumpur (STAR and PUTRA), the national sewage system (IWK) and the national airline (MAS). Industry consolidation, involving the reduction of operators and firms through mergers, has also been an important feature of the economy since 1997. This has mostly taken place in the financial sector (commercial banking, finance companies, brokerage houses, insurance companies) and the communications and multimedia sectors.

Over the past 30 years, the most important types of economic regulation were those used to support redistributive objectives. These were mainly in the form of control over entry conditions such as licensing (especially in non-tradable sectors such as infrastructure) and government procurement. In contrast, competition regulation has been virtually non-existent. The impact of some of the government's policies on competition has not been addressed. These include liberalization in the haulage sector (which led to the entry of too many firms) and the consolidation of the commercial banking sector (which reduced the number of commercial banks to ten).

SECTORAL COMPETITION REGULATION

Since independence, economic sectors in Malaysia have been regulated primarily at the sectoral level, mainly in the form of economic regulation in which the government exerted control over entry conditions, and in some cases prices. In the regulatory reforms that took place following privatization, new regulatory agencies were established, and economic regulation continues to be the main focus of regulation in these sectors (see Table 11.1). However, new legislation in two sectors has expanded the scope of regulation to include competition regulation. Both the *Communications and Multimedia Act 1998* (CMA 1998) and the *Energy Commission Act 2001* (ECA 2001) contain statements that make competition regulation a function of the regulator. The statement on the competition regulation function of the Energy Commission in the ECA 2001 is fairly general:

> to promote and safeguard competition and fair and efficient market conduct, or in the absence of a competitive market, to prevent the misuse of monopoly power or market power in respect of the generation, production, transmission, distribution and supply of electricity and the supply of gas through pipelines. (ECA 2001, p. 14)

The CMA 1998 identifies more specific anti-competitive conducts that it considers illegal such as collusion, rate fixing, market sharing, boycotting of competitors and tying. The mechanism for competition regulation in the communications and multimedia sector is slightly more advanced than in the energy sector. The Communications and Multimedia Commission has published three documents that serve as guidelines on competition regulation in the sector, namely:

- *Guideline on Substantial Lessening of Competition* (CMC 2000a). This document clarifies the various notions (e.g. market, potential rivalry), anti-competitive conducts (e.g. predatory pricing, foreclosure, etc.) and conditions (e.g. intentionality) in which such a conduct is deemed illegal under the CMA 1998. The document also provides an analytical framework for analysing cases where substantial reduction in competition is thought to have occurred.
- *Guideline on Dominant Position in a Communications Market* (CMC 2000b). This document clarifies the concept of dominance and the various structural characteristics (market shares, vertical integration, barriers to entry) and anti-competitive practices (pricing and supply behaviour) that might be associated with the presence of a dominant firm. The guideline also makes provision for an analytical framework for determining dominant position in a market.

Table 11.1 Sectoral regulatory institutions and mechanisms in Malaysia

Sector	Regulatory agency	Legislation	Type of regulation
Distributive trade	Ministry of Domestic Trade and Consumer Affairs (MDTCA)	Consumer Protection Act 1999, Price Control Act 1946 and the Supply Control Act 1961	Prices of essential goods are regulated. No provision for competition regulation
Roads	Public roads are regulated by the Road Transport Department (Ministry of Transport)	Road Transport Act, 1987	Price regulation (toll rates) by Ministry of Works
	Privatized roads are regulated by the Malaysian Highway Authority under the Ministry of Works		Commercial vehicle licensing (entry) by Commercial Vehicle Licensing Board, Ministry of Entrepreneurial Development
Railways	KTMB was corporatized but continues to be regulated by the Railways Department (Ministry of Transport)	Railways Act 1991 and Railways (Successor Company) Act 1991	Price regulation (fare rates) by Ministry of Transport
Ports	Corporatized ports are regulated by the respective Ports Commission (e.g. Johor Port Authority, Bintulu Port Authority, Klang Port Authority etc.)	Ports Authorities Act 1963, Ports Act (Privatization), 1990, and the various port commission acts for each port	Price regulation by port commission
	Federal ports are regulated by the Ministry of Transport		
Airports	Civil Aviation Department, Ministry of Transport	Civil Aviation Act, 1969; Landing, Parking and Housing, Passenger Services and Air Navigation Facility Charges (and) Regulations 1992	Price regulation by Ministry of Transport

Table 11.1 continued

Sector	Regulatory agency	Legislation	Type of regulation
Communications and multimedia	Communications and Multimedia Commission	Communications and Multimedia Act 1998	Price regulation and Competition regulation – CMC advises the Ministry of Energy, Communications and Multimedia
			Entry is regulated via licensing
Electricity supply	Energy Commission	Energy Commission Act 2001, Electricity Supply Act 1990, Electricity Supply (Successor Company) Act 1990	Regulation of wholesale prices via agreements between IPPs and Tenaga Nasional (incumbent distributor company)
			Retail tariffs regulated by Ministry of Energy, Communications and Multimedia
Water supply	Water Supply Department, Water Board, PWD	Water Supply Act, and state legislation	For privatized supplier prices are regulated concession agreements

- *Process for Assessing Allegations of Anti-competitive Conduct: An Information Paper* (CMC 2000c). This paper sets out in greater detail the sequence of actions to be taken by the CMC when it investigates incidents and firms involving the substantial reduction in competition and presence of dominant market position.

Several clauses in these guidelines are worth highlighting. They exemplify some of the difficulties that are encountered in regulating competition sectorally in the communications and multimedia sector.

First, there is a specific statement that provides for the protection of smaller operators in the absence of a general competitive policy or trade practices regulatory regime (Section 4.3, CMC 2000a). This statement suggests that sectoral-level competition policy ought to compensate for the absence of national competition policy.

Second, conduct that might be anti-competitive (i.e. breaching the Act) may be tolerated provided it can be shown that the 'national interest' requires it. However, 'national interest' is not defined in the Act or in any of the guidelines published thus far (Section 5.4, CMC 2000a). Such exemptions are probably too ill-defined to be of any use, and may instead generate regulatory uncertainty.

Third, it is also re-emphasized in the guidelines that judgement as to whether conduct is anti-competitive or not is divided between the Minister and the CMC (Section 5.7, CMC 2000a). Under Section 144 of the CMA, the Minister is invested with the power to take decisions to prevent or mitigate anti-competitive conduct involving agreements between licensees and a foreign network facilities provider and/or network service providers. Other types of anti-competitive conducts are within the jurisdiction of the CMC. It is not clear whether this division of regulatory responsibilities is optimal or is sufficiently well-defined, since the Ministry's influence on CMC is substantial.

TOWARDS A NATIONAL COMPETITION LAW: THE FAIR TRADE ACT

At present, Malaysia does not have a national competition policy or law – the Malaysian government has thus far adopted a very cautious approach to the implementation of such legislation. Work on a competition law began as early as 1991 under the aegis of the Ministry of Domestic Trade and Consumer Affairs (MDTCA), which is responsible for regulating the distributive sector. Previous efforts to implement a competition policy were unsuccessful, partly due to political and bureaucratic resistance. Despite these past failures, the

MDTCA remains committed to implementing a competition law in the country. For example, the *Eighth Malaysia Plan 2001–2005*, the country's most recent five-year plan, contains a specific reference to the implementation of a national competition policy and law:

> During the Plan period (2001–2005), efforts will be made to foster fair trade practices that will contribute towards greater efficiency and competitiveness of the economy. In this context, a fair trade policy and law will be formulated to prevent anti-competitive behaviour such as collusion, cartel price fixing, market allocation and the abuse of market power. The fair trade policy will, among others, prevent firms from protecting or expanding their market shares by means other than greater efficiency in producing what consumers want. In addition, a national policy and master plan on distributive trade will be formulated to facilitate an orderly and healthy development of the sector.

This formal commitment is not the only force driving the implementation of a competition policy and law in Malaysia. The spectre of WTO-sponsored negotiations on multilateral agreements on competition has provided further impetus to implement a competition policy and law in the country. Even though this is far from inevitable, government officials consider this implementation to be crucial before any multilateral negotiations.

The MDTCA considers competition policy and law as supplements to the existing laws that protect consumers in the country, such as the Trade Descriptions Act 1972, the Hire Purchase Act 1967, the Weights and Measures Act 1972, the Direct Sales Act 1993, the Money Lenders Act 1951, and the Consumer Protection Act 1999. These statutes provide protection to consumers via laws that set out not only the rights of consumers but also the various actions (on the part of the seller) deemed unethical and illegal. Many of these statutes are meant to be applied to specific sectors such as the distributive sector (Trade Descriptions Act, Weights and Measures Act, Direct Sales Act) and financial sector (Hire Purchase Act, Money Lenders Act). However, these laws do not deal with competition issues such as the impact of market power and collusion.

The Secretary General of the MDTCA has indicated in a recent speech that a competition law may be enacted before the end of 2003. To ensure that the law is successfully implemented, the MDTCA has been actively engaging other ministries via a series of dialogues with the purpose of addressing their concerns as well as for consensus building. These efforts would probably be followed by an initiative to seek an endorsement for a competition policy (tentatively entitled the *Fair Trade Policy*) at cabinet-level in 2003. Once the cabinet gives its approval, a competition law (i.e. *Fair Trade Act*) will be drafted and eventually enacted. The *Fair Trade Act* will be aimed at preventing and uprooting anti-competitive conduct in the various economic sectors.

Several challenges lie ahead in implementing a national competition law in Malaysia. First, the government will have to reverse the sectoral devolution of competition regulation. Sectoral regulators are likely to resist efforts to centralize competition regulation at national level. Furthermore, existing national-level regulators (such as the Securities Commission which currently regulates mergers and acquisition of companies listed on the KLSE) will also need to be convinced that competition-related issues ought to be regulated by a new agency (e.g. a Fair Trade Commission).

Second, the competition law and policy may come into conflict with some of the industrial and socio-economic policies that are adopted in Malaysia. These include selective import substitution policies (such as the national car project), bank consolidation (to strengthen domestic banks), and wealth-redistribution policies. To accommodate these policies that have a different set of objectives, exemptions and authorizations are likely to be important elements in the proposed competition policy and law in Malaysia. In this regard, the Malaysian government will need to be careful as too many exemptions may weaken competition regulation and make it vulnerable to regulatory capture.

CONCLUSION

Competition regulation in Malaysia is at a very nascent stage – it exists formally in only two economic sectors: namely, the communications and multimedia sector and the energy sector. The Ministry of Domestic Trade and Consumer Affairs is currently in the process of formulating a national competition policy and law. If implemented, this is likely to accommodate existing socio-economic policies with other objectives such as industrial development, poverty eradication and wealth redistribution. The real challenge in implementing the competition law will be to accommodate these other objectives without rendering the competition law ineffective.

REFERENCES

Communications and Multimedia Commission (2000a), 'Guideline on substantial lessening of competition', Discussion Paper No. RG/SLC/1/00(1).

Communication and Multimedia Commission (2000b), 'Guideline on dominant position in a communications market', Discussion Paper No. RG/DP/1/00(1).

Communication and Multimedia Commission (2000c), 'Process for assessing allegations of anti-competitive conduct: an information paper', Information Paper No. IP/Competition/1/00(1).

Malaysia (2000), *Eighth Malaysia Plan 2001–2005*, Kuala Lumpur: Government's Printer.

12. The institutional and policy framework for regulation and competition in South Africa

Kobus Müller[1]

INTRODUCTION

South Africa is a country characterised by inequity, inequality and poverty. The public and private sectors have shown a commitment to the need for change and have also implemented policies and services to address these burning issues in the country. There is a need to balance the desire to ensure centralised control, to ensure an even-handed approach to policy implementation and service delivery to all sectors of the population, focusing on the areas of greatest need. At the same time, this centralised approach must be balanced with the need for growth in the economy through a focus on competition and competitiveness. This chapter attempts to map the institutional and policy framework and the context from which it has emerged since the demise of the apartheid state.

THE LEGAL FRAMEWORK FOR COMPETITION AND REGULATION IN SOUTH AFRICA

The transition to democracy in South Africa in 1994 brought fundamental changes to the form and function of the state and the accompanying institutional and policy framework. Before the introduction of the new dispensation, parliament was considered to be sovereign. This changed in 1994 when South Africa became a constitutional democracy after incisive debate among a wide-ranging group of role-players in the socio-political-economic discourse and concluded in the constitutional negotiation process.

The new Constitution of the Republic of South Africa (Act 108 of 1996) 'is the supreme law of the Republic. Law or conduct inconsistent with it is invalid, and the obligations imposed by it must be fulfilled' (The Constitution, 1996: section 2). The cornerstone of democracy in South Africa is the Bill of

Rights (The Constitution Ch. 2: section 7–39) which 'applies to all law, and binds the legislature, the executive, the judiciary, all organs of state' and 'binds a natural or juristic person'. The Bill of Rights applies to, and sets out the rights of all people in the country in some detail. Such rights relate to Equality (section 9), Freedom and Security of the Person (section 12), Freedom of Religion, Belief and Opinion (section 15), Freedom of Association (section 18) and Labour Relations (section 23). It is also at this level of the legislative framework in South Africa that the first examples of regulatory authorities emerge in the form of various commissions and authorities established to evaluate and monitor certain of the issues and themes arising from the Bill of Rights.

It is important to refer briefly to specific legislation, enacted in terms of the Constitution, and relating to access to information and administrative justice. The legislation promoting access to information (Act 2 of 2000) was enacted 'to give effect to the constitutional right of access to *any* information held by the State and any information that is held by another person and that is required for the exercise or protection of any rights'. Coupled with this, is legislation promoting administrative justice (Act 3 of 2000) that deals with the right of a person 'to administrative action that is lawful, reasonable and procedurally fair and to the right to written reasons for administrative action'. The preambles of each of these laws refer to transparency, accountability and (in the case of the latter legislation) openness. It is clear that these two laws can, and will have a fundamental effect on the manner in which proceedings relating to regulation and competition will be conducted.

The reform of competition law in South Africa came to the fore in 1998 in response to the publication of a policy document the year before (Proposed Guidelines for Competition Policy, 1997). The preamble to the new legislation (Competition Act, Act 89 of 1998) states (in part) that 'credible competition law, and effective structures to administer that law, are necessary for an effective functioning economy' that will 'create greater capability and an environment for South Africans to compete effectively on the international markets'. This will lead to the regulation of the 'transfer of economic ownership in keeping with the public interest' and the monitoring of 'economic competition', and provides for the establishment of regulatory bodies. It is apposite to refer to the case law and precedent that has already begun to emerge in South Africa, especially following the promulgation of the Competition Act. A number of well-known international companies and organisations have utilised legal processes to ensure fair and equitable competition in the corporate environment in South Africa. Many of the industries that have been the subject of adjudication in the Competition Commission, the Competition Tribunal and the Competition Appeal Board are located in arenas that are highly regulated by the state and that are subject to a high degree of state control and organisation such as the petrochemical, pharmaceutical and banking industries.

It is important to remember that South Africa, as a member of the international economic and financial community, is also subject to international conventions and agreements that set a particular framework for regulation and competition. South Africa is a signee or member of a wide variety of organisations and institutions that, in many if not most cases, imply regulation and/or competition rights elements and responsibilities with which the country must comply. Provision is also made in the Constitution that international agreements, customary international law and international law are binding on the Republic of South Africa, unless inconsistent with the Constitution or an Act of Parliament (The Constitution, 1996, Ch. 14: section 231–2). It is important for South Africa to appreciate the multilateral trade implications of competition law and policy, because the interpretation, application and enforcement of South Africa's competition law are bound to have international implications. At present, there are no legally binding multilateral disciplines on competition policy within the World Trade Organisation (WTO) framework. There are, however, many provisions in various WTO agreements that have a direct impact on competition policy and of which any national competition law and authority must take account.

REGULATION AND COMPETITION IN SOUTH AFRICA: THE INSTITUTIONAL FRAMEWORK

The fundamental changes to the form and function of the state in 1994 had a dramatic impact on the contours of the institutional landscape. The establishment of constitutional democracy in South Africa in 1994 has brought with it a restructuring of intergovernmental relations and a redefinition of the social and economic regulatory responsibilities of the different spheres of government as delineated in the Constitution of 1996. All government action is governed by the Constitution that establishes the regulatory competence of the different spheres of government. The regulatory map is made up of institutions in the national, provincial and local government spheres. These distinctive, interdependent and interrelated institutions each have their own legislative and executive capacities and accompanying regulatory functions.

At national level, Parliament (consisting of two houses, the *National Assembly* and the *National Council of Provinces*) is the principal legislative body with regulatory and control functions relating to the President and the Cabinet. It controls the regulatory performance of all administrative institutions. In turn, the *Constitutional Court*, as the highest court in the country dealing with constitutional matters, exercises control over (among other aspects) the constitutionality of the actions of Parliament. Constitutional democracy is strengthened and supported by a number of institutions. For example, the *Human Rights Commission*, the *Commission for Gender Equality* and the *Independent Electoral Commission* were all established in terms of the Constitution.

A diverse population of organisational forms covering the full spectrum from 30 national government departments (e.g. *Department of Labour* in the occupational health and safety sector) on the one hand, to miscellaneous statutory control bodies and regulatory councils (e.g. the *National Gaming Board*, the *Independent Communications Authority of South Africa* and the *Competition Commission*) on the other are responsible for social and economic regulatory functions in the national sphere. As far as regulation within government is concerned, the South African institutional landscape is not unique and follows the pattern found elsewhere, with institutions such as public audit bodies, professional inspectorates, ombudsman agencies and central agency regulators (e.g. the Auditor-General, the Independent Complaints Authority, the Public Protector and the Public Service Commission).

This pattern is more or less replicated in the provincial sphere of government within the nine provincial administrations, and in the local sphere within the 284 municipalities. The new local government dispensation that also provides for municipal service enterprises and local public–private partnerships will probably lead to the creation of even more regulatory authorities at local level, adding to the existing myriad. The complexity of the regulatory landscape in terms of both the number of institutions involved and the diversity of organisational type is probably higher at this time in the national sphere than in the other two spheres of government. With the increasing number, extent and complexity of regulatory activities, some institutions such as state departments and other public institutions with executive functions have been given authority to extend the provisions of acts by proclamation, regulation and other binding instructions. This has led to the establishment of numerous administrative tribunals with judicial powers within the frameworks of the relevant acts.

As far as the economic regulation of business is concerned, the *Competition Commission* plays a crucial role in investigating anti-competitive conduct, the assessment of the impact of mergers and acquisitions on competition and the monitoring of competition levels and market transparency in the economy. The Competition Commission is an independent body. Its decisions may be appealed to the *Competition Tribunal* and the *Competition Appeal Court*.

The initial steps towards privatisation taken by the previous government had lost some momentum by the beginning of the 1990s and were eventually put on hold during the period of constitutional negotiations in the period immediately prior to the advent of the new dispensation in 1994. The African National Congress (ANC), suspicious of the then government's approach to privatisation and the possible hidden agenda of selling the family silver before a new government could come to power, effectively put a halt to these initiatives.

With the new constitutional framework firmly in place, the new government has proceeded very cautiously with privatisation in pursuit of what is now euphemistically referred to as the 'restructuring of state assets'. The existence of powerful state-owned enterprises (SOEs) raises numerous issues in respect of competition regulation in South Africa, as it does elsewhere. South Africa has a number of very large SOEs in the transport, telecommunications and broadcasting, energy and armaments sectors. Although these SOEs were previously nominally responsible to a government department, they were for the most part, in practice, laws unto themselves. Many have now been privatised, partly privatised, or are in the process of being privatised, or are undergoing major restructuring. Newly privatised SOEs have been granted specified periods of exclusivity in exchange for a contractual commitment to meet specified public service mandates.

The establishment of a regulatory regime prior to the restructuring of a public monopoly has become standard practice in South Africa and many regulators are the result. A selected group of regulatory authorities in one sector provides a first order view of the way in which regulatory agencies are created and institutionalized in this country. The *Independent Broadcasting Authority* (IBA) had been established in terms of the Constitution to take over broadcasting regulatory tasks previously performed by the Ministry of Home Affairs and the Postmaster-General. At the same time the *South African Telecommunications Regulatory Authority* (SATRA) regulated the telecommunication industry. In 2000 the IBA and SATRA were merged to establish the *Independent Communications Authority of South Africa* (ICASA) that now regulates telecommunications and broadcasting in South Africa, combining the functions of SATRA and the IBA. This example illustrates the rapidly changing regulatory landscape in just one industry.

The rapid evolution and proliferation of the more 'independent' type of regulatory bodies in the relatively short period since 1994 have raised questions about the types of autonomy conferred on these bodies and on their officials, and the forms of control exercised over them. These various regulators, established in terms of acts of Parliament, are financed mostly with money appropriated by Parliament (though additional income could be raised by way of fees or licences), are subject to audit by the Auditor-General, and must submit an annual report to the relevant minister (for example, the Competition Commission or ICASA). But apart from these provisions they are independent and the controls over them are limited to the abovementioned measures. The fact that ministers have expressed concern that certain regulators have adopted a policy-making role independent of government serves as an indication of their level of independence.

The debate in South Africa concerning inter-agency relationships, and the division of responsibilities between different agencies and levels in the system has just begun. The issue of the relationships and potential jurisdictional conflicts between competition and regulatory authorities has received attention in a recent policy document (Radebe, 2000). Both the rapid increase in the number of regulators and the lack of clarity about roles and responsibilities are seen to contribute to market uncertainty that could eventually undermine the achievement of restructuring objectives. The arguments and debates that have reached the High Court[2] turn on the question of whether the jurisdiction for competition matters should rest with sector regulators, with competition authorities, or both. The jurisdictional conflict over which authority should regulate which area, leads to expensive litigation over purely procedural matters. In order to ensure the consistent application of the legislation guarding competition matters across sectors, the Competition Commission may negotiate agreements with other regulatory authorities, participate in their proceedings and advise or receive advice from any regulatory authority. However, the sector regulators regard themselves as better guardians of the public interest than the competition authorities. The distinction between technical regulation and competition regulation is often blurred. As an example, technical decisions regarding spectrum use in the telecommunications sector and accompanying decisions about licensing may profoundly impact on the intensity of competition in the sector.

Administrative and managerial issues linked to accountability and autonomy arise from the financing and staffing of those authorities that are mostly financed from public funds, and thus should be publicly accountable. However, to function properly they need a fair amount of managerial autonomy and separation from the constraints normally imposed on government departments. This may create a need for less control and accountability and more independence. The issue is one of balancing the tension that seemingly exists here. A practical manifestation of this issue relates to the procurement and retention of expert staff. As a result of their higher levels of managerial autonomy, these classes of institutions with the use of public funding often compete successfully with ordinary state sector employers for expert staff by offering much more attractive benefits packages than can be offered by government departments.

On the question of the existence of codes, guidelines or other constraints which induce regulatory officials to respond to public interest considerations, it should be noted that government institutions in every sphere of government, so-called organs of the state (which include the independent regulatory bodies) as well as public enterprises are subject to the basic values and principles governing public administration defined in the Constitution. These include *inter alia* values and principles relating to professional ethics, the effective and efficient use of resources, and the requirement that services must be provided impartially and fairly. Furthermore the right to just administrative action is enshrined in the Bill of Rights and given effect in national legislation (Promotion of Administration of Justice Act, 2000, Act 3 of 2000). It would therefore seem that judicial review can act as an important constraint on regulatory administrative action, at least as far as procedural accountability is concerned.

A further, related political/administrative issue involves the control and accountability of independent regulatory authorities. In the relatively short period of its existence before it was merged with SATRA to form ICASA, serious accountability problems were raised during the late 1990s concerning the abuse and misappropriation of funds to benefit IBA councillors and staff. Authorities have thus drawn public criticism for actions based on a lack of public control and accountability. This is a manifestation of the classic question, 'who guards the guardians?' or, for present purposes, 'who regulates the regulators?' There have been different approaches to the structuring and functioning of these control and accountability relationships, ranging from the requirements for reporting to ministers and/or departments to direct accountability to Parliament. The ideal is probably direct accountability to Parliament or to any other democratic legislative authority, but given the time, resource and technical constraints of these bodies, this ideal is likely to be over-ambitious. This leaves open the issues of properly legislating for, and structuring, a functional system of public accountability for these bodies.

The influence and participation of customers or users in regulatory authorities is normally promoted in prescriptions regarding the composition and appointment of the governing boards, commissions or councils. The prescriptions in this regard vary from the very specific (for example in the case of the *Judicial Service Commission* where the representation of the professions and other roleplayers is prescribed in detail) to the fairly vague where it is left to the responsible minister or the President (sometimes on the recommendation of the National Assembly) to appoint 'suitable' persons (for example in the case of the *Competition Commission*). The process sometimes prescribes participation by the public in the nomination process, requiring transparency and openness and the publication of a shortlist of candidates (for example in the case of ICASA).

CURRENT POLICY SETTING FOR REGULATION AND COMPETITION

South Africans are apparently quite protective of their perceptions of their uniqueness. This applies to their ideas, their models of regulation and competition as well as their policies. To gain some insight into the government's philosophy of state–market relations it is necessary to refer to two important post-1994 macro policy statements – namely the Reconstruction and Development Programme (RDP) and the Growth, Employment and Redistribution Plan (GEAR).

The RDP was basically the first policy statement of the ANC Alliance after coming to power in 1994 and was modelled on its 'Ready to Govern' election platform. The RDP is important from the perspective of social regulation as it focuses mainly on the provision of housing and food, land tenure reform and infrastructure provision, all generally provided for or controlled by the state. The RDP has aimed to combat unemployment and poverty in the first instance by pursuing the goal of improving production and household income through job creation, increased productivity and economic efficiency, improved conditions of employment and the creation of opportunities for all to sustain themselves through productive activity; second, by improving living conditions through better access to basic services, health care, education and training; and third, by establishing a social security system and other safety nets to protect the poor, disabled, elderly and other vulnerable groups.

The RDP was criticised for its emphasis on development and redistribution rather than on investment and growth. The RDP objectives were restated during 1996 and the second major policy statement in the form of a macro-economic plan, the Growth, Employment and Redistribution Plan (GEAR), was announced in May 1996. GEAR in turn focused on the importance of creating macro-economic conditions that would facilitate economic growth and development within the context of structural change under way in both the South African, and the global economies. Thus a line was drawn in the regulatory arena that differentiates between issues of social and economic regulation. These two major policy statements highlighted a potential fault line between the social and economic regulatory dimensions that runs through the subsequent policy debate and policy strategies adopted by government. This tension exists within government between the Alliance partners (the ANC, the South African communist Party (SACP) and Congress of South African Trade Unions (COSATU)) as well as between actors in society at large; that is, labour, business and government.

This tension is evident in the government's competition and privatisation policies. It is the government perception that there is an excessive concentration of economic power in the South African market, which necessitates the 'transfer of economic ownership in the public interest'. The Competition Act follows mainstream European Union, and to an extent United States competition law by prohibiting practices in restraint of trade whether vertical (between firms, supplier, or customer) or horizontal (between firms and abuses of dominance by dominant firms). It has an underlying social and economic objective. The social objective is to promote 'the ability of small businesses owned by historically disadvantaged persons to become competitive'.

In addition, government argues in its policy statement (DTI, 1997) that because of the challenges that flow from the legacy of economic distortions, a uniquely South African approach to competition policy is required. There is the need to fuse the two policy imperatives, on the one hand to pursue competitiveness and efficiency in the economy, and on the other hand to ensure that this process will ensure access on the part of many more people previously denied an equal opportunity to participate in the economy.

The importance of Black Economic Empowerment (BEE) is illustrated by the fact that in 2000 and 2001 respectively, 11 and 13 black economic empowerment deals were approved. As a result, historically disadvantaged persons are now increasingly securing business opportunities and participating at board and management levels to influence strategy. BEE mergers have been seen as useful vehicles for implementing accelerated employment equity programmes to achieve corporate affirmative action goals, and to develop market access and penetration strategies.

The South African policy approach to privatisation is well summarised in the 2000 policy document (Roux, 2000, p. 2). According to this document the South African approach to restructuring and privatisation is unique, with its general thrust being to shy away from Thatcherite, former Eastern Bloc and Latin American approaches to regulation and competition. South Africa, for example, puts more emphasis on the restructuring of the state sector than on privatisation. South Africa's approach seems in some respects reminiscent of the French example where the state remains a majority shareholder when state assets are privatised. However, where the French prefer domestic private investors as venture partners, the South African approach has been to involve foreign investors, but then only as minority partners. Restructuring is also driven by means of strategic alliances leading to long-term collaborative partnerships. Examples include acquisitions, mergers, equity relationships, joint ventures, public–private partnerships (PPPs) and marketing and purchasing agreements.

On the matter of self-regulation in South Africa there has long been a tradition that the rights of practice and the rules of conduct for professional occupations are determined by bodies drawn exclusively or predominantly from members of the professions concerned. These forms of self-regulation are exercised through councils or institutes normally, but not always, with statutory backing (e.g. the *Health Professions Council of South Africa* or *South African Institute of Chartered Accountants*). Such groups regulate their own affairs under powers given to appropriate institutions (control bodies). Practitioners in the relevant professions, elected or nominated members and members of the public service are normally represented on these control bodies. The appointment of an industry Ombudsman (e.g. the *Banking Ombudsman* or the *Life Insurance Ombudsman*) as a form of voluntary regulation has also gained popularity in the last 10 years. The agricultural sector is an interesting case in point of self-regulation as many of these control boards were transformed into producer or shareholder controlled marketing associations, some of which perform a form of self-regulating function (e.g. *Agri-inspec* which oversees the importation of agricultural products). The levies paid by the producers are not compulsory, which may cause some problems for these associations to function properly – for example to undertake the relevant research.

Concern over the incidence of white-collar crime and corrupt and improper practice in South Africa has thrown into sharp relief cogent issues of ethics and not least has raised questions as to the efficacy of current self-regulatory arrangements, practices and mechanisms. These self-regulatory arrangements have evolved in an ad hoc manner over time and are provided for in diverse pieces of subordinate legislation administered by individual departments of government. No comprehensive picture exists of the nature and extent of the self-regulatory regime in South Africa that has evolved from these various arrangements.

As stated earlier, the most fundamental policy issues emanating from the context of regulation and competition in South Africa derive from an approach that simultaneously provides for growth and development as well as for the alleviation of poverty and inequality (DTI, 1997). In excess of 20 million South Africans subsisted in a state of poverty in 1996 according to census estimates (Statistics SA, 1996). The number of poor households typically has risen faster than the number of lower and middle-income households. At the same time the share of national income of black middle-income households is rising and that of their white counterparts declining. Income distribution remains an emotive issue in the poverty debate. These statistics suggest the emergence in South Africa of a new order in which inequality is less a matter of race than of increasing relative affluence of higher income groups across the racial divide.

Rising income inequalities within population groups are largely a function of changing patterns in the demand for skills in South Africa. While the total number of black people employed has declined, implying increased unemployment within this group, substantial increases have occurred in the relative number of black people employed in highly skilled occupations and in their earnings. Changing labour market demand, particularly for unskilled labour, is adduced demonstrably to have been a function of the regulatory environment, applying particularly to the labour market in South Africa. Rising poverty can thus not be dissociated from the issue of regulation. Politically the stand-off on the issue of regulation of the economy turns to a large degree around the issue of regulation of the labour market. With the Congress of South African Trade Unions (COSATU) commanding a membership that in effect equates to a minority percentage of the South African labour force, the question is legitimately asked as to whether current regulatory regimes that in effect accord COSATU, as an alliance partner in government with the ANC and the SACP and a strong proponent of labour market regulation, a disproportionate voice, do in fact in any meaningful sense represent an equitable arrangement. On the basis of current trends income inequality will increase, with declining employment in the unskilled and semi-skilled categories and increased demand for highly skilled and productive workers remunerated at commensurately higher rates. This is consistent with the present industrially driven economic growth path of South Africa and has clear implications for the prospects of the generally lower-skilled poor.

To win support for competition goals and competition systems, the authorities should be seen to be grappling with employment problems and other major social issues. Ordinary citizens must be convinced by seeing the relationship between effective competition policy – and systems, one may add – and the realisation of their social goals (Lewis, 2000, p. 3).

META-POLICY REFORM IN SOUTH AFRICA

The meta-polity of competition and regulation in South Africa has both international and domestic dimensions. With the advent of the new political dispensation, South Africa has once again been admitted to the international community of nations. Where in the previous dispensation the country was isolated, it now finds itself readmitted to the international mainstream. This has of course had significant implications for policy, adding a new dimension to the meta-polity of competition and regulation in South Africa.

The current phase of globalisation and liberalisation that has paralleled South Africa's readmission into the international community in particular, and the advent of the World Trade Organisation (WTO), have added new and complex dimensions to competition issues within the context of South Africa's emerging multilateral trade relations. The WTO, the World Bank and the International Monetary Fund (IMF) are increasingly setting the parameters of member governments' economic policies, with significant domestic policy implications. Specifically the activities of the WTO Working Group on the Interaction between Trade and Competition Policy are significant in the context of competition and regulation. South Africa since 1994 has therefore at once been confronted with the challenge of re-establishing its competitive position in world markets after isolation, while at the same time accommodating the dynamics of a rapidly evolving international trade environment. South Africa has significant obligations with implications particularly for the regulatory regime in terms of agreements concluded in the WTO as well as within the United Nations framework. Of significance also are those arrangements concluded within the UN Conference on Trade and Development (UNCTAD) and other forums such as the Non-aligned Movement (NAM), the Organisation for Economic Co-operation and Development (OECD), the African Union (AU – formerly the Organisation for African Unity (OAU)) and the World Customs Organisation (WCO). South Africa's interest specifically in UNCTAD derives from that organisation's role in researching interrelated issues of trade, technology, investment, services, competition and sustainable development in developing countries; in capacity building; and as a forum for intergovernmental dialogue and consensus-building between the hemispheres on these issues.

With South Africa's re-emergence on the international scene after 1994 the country has been the focus of a number of capacity-building and advocacy initiatives on the part of international agencies. Certain of these initiatives have specifically addressed issues of competition and regulation.[3] In addition domestic research and advocacy capacity with a bearing on competition and regulatory issues has resided in academic research institutions at universities and technicons within South Africa. However, both the international and domestic dimensions of the meta-polity specifically of regulation and competition in South Africa have until comparatively recently been relatively amorphous. The establishment of the Trade and Industry Policy Secretariat (TIPS) in 2001 as an initiative of the Department of Trade and Industry (DTI) promises to provide focus on a wide range of policy issues, not least issues of competition and regulation. The establishment of TIPS has coincided with the establishment by the Southern African Development Community (SADC) of the Southern Africa Trade Research Network (SATRN) which is managed by TIPS.

In the past SADC countries have lacked sufficiently strong incentives to participate in the General Agreement on Tariffs and Trade (GATT), now the WTO. SADC however recognises that the nature of multilateral negotiations has changed, with issues such as competition policy, trade in services, and labour standards gradually superseding in importance the traditional issues of tariff levels, trade preferences and differential treatment. Trade and competition policy has been identified as a specific field of interest for SATRN, with special emphasis on legislation and other measures such as sectoral regulations and privatisation policies aimed at promoting competition in the national economies of the region.

POLITICAL, SOCIAL AND EXTERNAL INFLUENCES

The evolution of participation by the organs of civil society in the regulation and competition system in South Africa cannot be divorced from the evolution of the broader political and democratic landscape within the country. The challenge of reconciling the complex and often contradictory roles of a variety of players in a society in transformation inevitably also impacts on the regulatory and competitive regime. There is frequently an inherent tension in alliances established to facilitate democratic transition that are manifesting divisions in its aftermath. As stated this has also been evident in South Africa within the Tripartite Alliance with significant divergences of view emerging on key economic issues between the ANC, the SACP and COSATU, not least on the regulation of the economy, and most particularly the regulation of the labour market and the privatisation of state assets.

The ongoing debate between the ANC and its alliance partners in government, the SACP and COSATU, still strongly reflects an emphasis on the centrality of the state in the economy. While the need to involve and engage civil societal elements in the processes of governance is conceded, the focus of participation does not necessarily reflect recognition that civil society may play a progressive role independently of, or even in opposition to, government. Clearly the evolving role of civil society will be determined by the extent to which this tension can be resolved and to which an inclusive view is espoused that accommodates both these dimensions.

The Reconstruction and Development Programme (RDP), the ANC's policy platform in the election of 1994, itself had its origins largely in civil society, specifically in COSATU policy documentation of the early 1990s. The RDP recognised civil society organisations as crucial actors in the development process. Its decline since 1994 from strategic policy prominence and its replacement at centre stage by the essentially macro-economic preoccupations of GEAR was accompanied for a period by an eclipse in the role in governance of civil society at large which was largely relegated to the margins as merely another vehicle for sectarian interest. Recognition of the centrality of macro-economic issues to the transition process led in 1992 to the launching of the National Economic Forum (NEF) as a trilateral institution composed of government, organised business, and labour. The labour movement ended its boycott of the state-aligned National Manpower Commission that merged with the NEF after 1994 to form by act of Parliament (NEDLAC Act, 1994) the National Economic Development and Labour Council (NEDLAC). NEDLAC constitutes the nexus of the formal relationship between government, organised business, organised labour and organised community in pursuit of consensus on issues of social and economic policy. It therefore stands at the commanding heights of a wide range of regulation and competition policy issues in South Africa.

Debate on the efficacy of NEDLAC has largely revolved around the allegation that it has in effect marginalised a large component of the grassroots community from the economic policy process in which it is engaged. At the flood tide of popular demand for inclusive participatory democracy, so the argument goes, it in effect represents a consociation of organised elites, while lack of capacity and of a platform for participation has modulated the voices of a number of legitimate grassroots organisations relative to those of organised business and labour in South Africa.

Nevertheless, the advent of open democracy in South Africa has served as the genesis for a variety of emergent civil society structures with watchdog roles, not least in the monitoring of legislation and of consumer affairs. Indeed many civil societal structures have begun to adopt new roles as participants in the policy-making process as receptiveness, albeit grudgingly at the outset on the part of government, to their engagement on a broader front in an essentially consultative role in governance issues has grown since 1994. This has implied on the part of such organisations a shift in orientation, mode of interaction, structure and skill. In particular it has seen the shifting of focus of organs of civil society away from spontaneous reaction to the issues of the day toward more cogent response to substantive longer-term issues.

At the level of the legislative process, NGOs are particularly prominent in the dissemination and monitoring of legislation at the committee stages in the Parliamentary process.[4] Through their monitoring, lobbying and capacity-building programmes, they strive to ensure that policy and legislative processes are transparent, accessible and accountable. These organisations enjoy no official status with Parliament but play an important role in disseminating information on a subscription basis and in encouraging debate around legislative and regulatory issues. Human rights organisations locally and internationally play a role in sustaining such activities in the promotion of open democracy.[5] In only one of the nine provinces in South Africa (Kwazulu-Natal) is a similar function performed in respect of the provincial legislative process.[6]

At the national level, the Free Market Foundation of South Africa (FMF), a member of the Global Economic Freedom Network, plays a relatively unusual role in promoting competitive economic practice in South Africa for its own sake, rather than on behalf of vested commercial interests. This NGO monitors legislative processes and has long been actively engaged in lobbying in the cause of the promotion of economic freedom. As with other similar bodies the FMF is partly supported by its subscription base and partly by donations and project funding.

South Africa does not have a particularly developed record of consumerism. At the time of the transition in 1994 the then South African Consumer Council merged with a number of other consumer bodies to form the National Consumer Forum (NCF), a new umbrella body representing consumer affairs in South Africa. The NCF is a non-governmental organisation with affiliated member consumer bodies throughout the country. It is affiliated to Consumers International. Parallel to the NCF is the SA National Consumer Union, also a national NGO that has been in existence for 40 years and that is affiliated to the NCF. Neither the NCF nor the Consumer Union enjoy special recognition by government whose own National Consumer Affairs Office (NACAO) within the Department of Trade and Industry, supported by 24 provincial consumer offices, develops policy, legislation and regulations in the areas of consumer credit services, industry regulation and product standards. The institutions of civil society per se therefore do not play a formalised role. This is generally reflective of the current approach in South Africa according to which the formal role of institutions of civil society in the regulatory regime is essentially confined to the area of self-regulation.

The efficacy of regulation is a function essentially of two elements; namely, respect for the law and for the authority of the regulator on the one hand, and the capacity to implement regulatory measures and to bring transgressors to book on the other. On both these scores South Africa currently encounters problems. In the first place respect for governing authority has historically been eroded not least by a culture of civil disobedience against the then apartheid regime that accompanied the freedom struggle. The efforts required, for example, of the South African Revenue Services (SARS) in bringing to book large numbers of serial tax evaders, and of the South African Broadcasting Corporation (SABC) in at once encouraging and enforcing positive compliance with the requirement for television licensing bears testimony to the resource, and other implications of enforcement in prevailing circumstances. Elements of this psyche of non-compliance persist, complicating the regulatory environment and occasioning the recent pronouncements by President Mbeki on the need for moral regeneration in the country and the launch of the Moral Regeneration Movement at a Summit held in April 2002 (Moral Regeneration Summit, 2002).

CONCLUSION

In this chapter an attempt has been made to draw the contours of an unfolding preliminary map describing the institutional and policy framework of regulation and competition in South Africa. Transformation in South Africa since 1994 has not been an event but a process – as yet not concluded – that in its conjuncture and its essential features constitutes part of a global movement towards democratisation, dismantling of authoritarian control and the refocusing of relationships between society, economy, nation state and the international environment.

Issues that have emerged in the present mapping exercise and which could serve as pointers to the identification of gaps in the institutional and policy framework and to direct future research are:

1. concerns that some regulators have adopted a policy-making role (accountability issues);
2. a proliferation of regulators with no coordination of policies and rules (coordination issues);
3. the allocation of jurisdiction between competition and sector regulators, administrative tribunals and courts of law (judicial and procedural issues);
4. lack of objective criteria for the appointment to some regulatory bodies (representational issues);
5. lack of guidelines in cases with conflicting objectives (e.g. evaluation of mergers on competitive grounds versus the advancement of black ownership or black employment);
6. the effects of regional integration and inequitable competitive conditions internationally (globalisation issues);
7. the effectiveness of current approaches to self-regulation;
8. the achievement of maximal voluntary compliance with regulation in South Africa (issues of compliance and ethics).

It would seem that the regulatory challenge in South Africa is to find the optimal balance between potentially conflicting economic and social objectives – between enhancing competition, reducing state debt, increasing foreign direct investment flows, and facilitating economic growth and improved industrial competitiveness on the one hand; and widening ownership in the economy and engagement at its commanding heights by historically disadvantaged South Africans according to the ideo-political agenda on the other. The paradox to be resolved is that greater social delivery and development itself is constrained by slow economic growth.

NOTES

1. Kobus Müller is co-ordinator of the CRC project team for Working Paper 47 on which this chapter is based. The contributors are (in alphabetical order) J. Ackron, A. Burger, E. Schwella, F.M. Uys and K. van der Molen.
2. The question of whether the Competition Commission or the Financial Service Board should regulate in the case of the hostile bid by Nedcor to take over Standard Bank in 2000.
3. CUTS Centre for International Trade, Economics & Environment (CUTS/CITEE) Comparative Study of Competition Regimes in Select Developing Countries of the Commonwealth) – a study funded in 2000 to 2002 by DFID.
4. The Institute for Democracy in South Africa (IDASA); the Parliamentary Monitoring Group (PMG); the Contact Trust.
5. *Inter alia* the European Union Foundation for Human Rights in South Africa.

6. The Provincial Policy Programme (PPP) is a project of four organisations: Lawyers for Human Rights (LHR), the Institute for Multi-Party Democracy (IMPD), Black Sash and the Institute for Democracy in South Africa (IDASA).

BIBLIOGRAPHY

Cloete, J.J.N. (1994), *Public Administration and Management – New Constitutional Dispensation*. J.L. van Schaik Academic.

Community Agency for Social Enquiry (CASE) (2002), *Civil Society and the State in South Africa: Past Legacies, Present Realities, and Future Prospects.*

Competition Act, 1998 (Act 89 of 1998), *Government Gazette*, 30 October 1998, 400 (9412). Cape Town: Government Printers.

Department of Finance (1996), *Growth, employment and Redistribution: A Macro Economic Strategy*. The Republic of South Africa, Pretoria.

Department of Local Government (2001), *IDP Guide Pack, Guide II: Preparation.* Formset Printers Cape (Pty) Limited, Cape Town, http://www.salga.gov.za/IDP/idp index.htm.

Department of Trade and Industry (1997), *Proposed Guidelines for Competition Policy: A Framework for Competition, Competitiveness and Development*, 27 Nov. 1997, South African Government information, 27 Oct. 2000, http://www.polity.org.za/govdocs/policy/competition.html.

Estate Agency Affairs Act, 1996 (Act 112 of 1996) as amended.

Goodin, R. (1999), *The Theory of Institutional Design*, Cambridge: Cambridge University Press.

Hahlo, H.R. and Khan, E. (1968), *The South African Legal System and its Background*, Cape Town: Juta & Co.

Housing Consumers' Protection Measures Act, 1998 (Act 95 of 1998) as amended. Government Gazette, 2 November 1998, 4001 (19418), Cape Town: Government Printers.

Joyce, P. (1989), *The South African Encyclopedia*, Cape Town: Struik Publishers.

Lewis, D. (2000), 'Competition regulation: the South African experience', paper presented to ISCCO Conference 2000, Taipei, Competition tribunal, 20 August 2000, http://www.comptrib.co.za/TeipeiConferenceSpeech.htm.

Moss Kanter, R. (2001), 'The end of the end of big business: maybe we went a bit too far with that "reinventing government" stuff', *Business 2.0*, Dec 2001 (Magazine, selected articles online). Retrieved 8 April 2002 from http://www.business2.com/articles/mag/0,1640,35199,FF.html.

Promotion of Access to Information Act, 2000 (Act 2 of 2000), *Government Gazette*, 3 February 2000, 416 (20853), Cape Town: Government Printers.

Promotion of Administrative Justice Act, 2000 (Act 3 of 2000), *Government Gazette*, 3 February 2000, 416 (20853), Cape Town: Government Printers.

Proposed Guidelines for Competition Policy: A Framework for Competition, Competitiveness and Development (1997) Department of Trade & Industry.

Public Finance Management Act, 1999 (Act 1 of 1999) *Government Gazette*, 2 March 1999, 405 (19814), Cape Town: Government Printers.

Radebe, J. (2000), *Policy Framework for an Accelerated Agenda towards the Restructuring of State-owned Enterprises*, Department of Public Enterprises, 26 Oct.

Roux, A. (ed.) (2000), *Business Futures*, Institute for Future Research, University of Stellenbosch.

Schwella, E. (2002), *Regulation and Competition in South Africa*, Working paper series no. 18, Centre on Regulation and Competition.
Standards Act, 1993 (Act 29 of 1993) as amended.
Statistics SA (1996), 'The people of South Africa, population census 1996', 10 April 2002, http://www.statssa.gov.za/default1.asp.
Statistics South Africa (2000), *Measuring Poverty in South Africa,* Pretoria.
South African Civil Aviation Authorities Act, 1998 (Act 40 of 1998), *Government Gazette*, 4 September 1998, 399 (19212), Cape Town: Government Printers.
Telecommunications Act, 1996 (Act 103 of 1996), *Government Gazette* (Government documents online). Retrieved 15 April 2002 from http://www.gov.za/gazette/acts/1996/a103-96.htm.
The Constitution of the Republic of South Africa, 1996 (Act 108 of 1996) as adopted on 8 May 1996 and amended on 11 October 1996 by the Constitutional Assembly: annotated version / (Christina Murray, Friedrich Soltau).
The Republic of South Africa (1994), *The Reconstruction and Development Programme: A Policy Framework*, http://www.polity.org.za/govdocs/rdp/rdp.html.
The NEDLAC Act (1994), *National Economic Development and Labour Council Act*. Act 35 of 1994.
Van Heerden, H.J.O. (1991), *Grondslae van die Mededingingsreg*. Cape Town: HAUM.
Whiteford, A. and van Seventer D.E. (1999) *Winners & Losers: South Africa's Changing Income Distribution in the 1990s*, Johannesburg: WEFA Southern Africa.

Relevant website links

African National Congress (ANC): http://www.anc.org.za
African Union: http://www.africa-union.org
Banking Ombudsman: http://www.oba.org.za
Commission for Gender Equality: http://www.cge.org.za
Competition Commission: http://www.compcom.co.za
Competition Tribunal: http://www.comptrip.co.za
Congress of South African Trade Unions (COSATU): http://www.cosatu.org.za
Constitutional Court: http://www.concourt.gov.za
Department of Labour: http://www.labour.gov.za
Department of Trade and Industry (DTI): http://www.dti.gov.za
Free Market Foundation of South Africa (FMF): http://www.freemarketfoundation.com
General Agreement on Tariffs and Trade (GATT): http://www.ciesin.org/TG/PI/TRADE/gatt.html
Growth, Employment and Redistribution Plan (GEAR): http://www.gov.za/reports/1996/macroeco.htm
Health Professions Council of South Africa: http://www.hpcsa.co.za
Human Rights Commission: http://www.sahrc.org.za
Independent Broadcasting Authority (IBA): http://www.iba.org.za
Independent Communications Authority of South Africa: http://www.icasa.org.za
Independent Electoral Commission: http://www.ellections.org.za
Institute for Democracy in South Africa (IDASA): http://www.idasa.org.za
The Institute for Multi-Party Democracy (IMPD): http://www.idpm.org.za
Lawyers for Human Rights (LHR): http://www.lhr.org.za
Moral Regeneration Movement: http://www.gov.za/issues/mrm

National Assembly: http://www.parliament.gov.za/na/index.asp
National Consumer Affairs Office (NACAO): http://www.dti.gov.za/review.asp?ISDiv=69&iEVENT_ID=110
National Consumer Forum (NCF): http://www.ncf.org.za
National Council of Provinces: http://www.parliament.gov.za/ncop
National Economic Development and Labour Council (NEDLAC): http://www.nedlag.org.za
National Economic Forum (NEF): http://www.nedlac.org.za/about/nef.htlm
National Gaming Board: http://www.ngb.org.za
Non-aligned Movement (NAM): http://www.nam.gov.za
Organisation for Economic Co-operation and Development (OECD): http://www.oecd.org
Parliamentary Monitoring Group (PMG): http://www.pmg.org.za
Provincial Policy Programme (PPP): http://www.ppp.org.za
Reconstruction and Development Programme (RDP): http://www.gov.za/gazette/whitepapers/1994/16085.pdf
South African Broadcasting Corporation (SABC): http://www.sabc.co.za
South African Communist Party (SACP): http://www.sacp.org.za
South African Institute of Chartered Accountants: http://www.saica.co.za
South African Revenue Services (SARS): http://www.sars.gov.za
South African Telecommunications Regulatory Authority (SATRA): http://www.icasa.org.za/satra/default.htm
Southern Africa Trade Research Network (SATRN): http://www.tips.org.za/satrn
Trade and Industry Policy Secretariat (TIPS): http://www.tips.org.za
World Customs Organisation (WCO): http://www.wcoomd.org

13. Regulatory governance in the Philippines: a profile

Ledivina V. Cariño[1]

INTRODUCTION

This chapter maps out the terrain of regulatory governance in the Philippines. The first section introduces the country. The second describes the constitutional and legal framework of regulation. The third discusses the institutions involved in regulatory governance, and the fourth presents lessons learned and remaining challenges.

THE PHILIPPINES

The Philippines, the world's second largest archipelago, is located in Southeast Asia. The total population as of 2000 was about 76.5 million growing yearly at 2.36 per cent. The country's experience as a colony, first under Spanish and much later American occupation, has left distinctive marks in its economy. On the eve of Philippine independence in 1946 and practically as a condition for it, the United States offered to help rehabilitate the country in exchange for the grant of parity rights to Americans. Parity rights meant that rights that the 1935 Constitution reserved for Filipino citizens – to exploit and develop natural resources, and to operate public utilities – were given also to Americans. The parity clause caused the amendment of the 1935 Constitution and remained in effect until 4 July 1974.

President Carlos P. Garcia in 1958 enunciated the 'Filipino First Policy' geared toward achieving national economic independence. Basically, he opposed the economy's return to free enterprise as he believed this would only facilitate the continued domination of foreigners. The economy then was controlled by American Chinese, and to a certain extent, Spanish, more than by Filipino interests. Later, multinational corporations would enlarge their share but Filipinos would remain on the bottom rung of the economy. This explains why nationalism pervades the economic provisions of all Philippine constitutions.

President Arroyo now presides over an economy that the World Bank classifies as middle-income. Independent risk assessments show an economy poised to recover economically. It is still beset by a high proportion of people living in poverty, high unemployment, high wealth concentration, and a secessionist movement and terrorism in Mindanao, the country's second largest island.

THE CONSTITUTIONAL AND LEGAL FRAMEWORK

The Constitution of 1987 and Philippine WTO membership have set the tone for economic reforms in concept and practice. These reforms have been conceived not only for economic growth but also for the country's integrity as a sovereign state and as a democracy; they do not only contemplate changing the face of the market but seek also the participation of the citizenry in its fruits. In a country marked by inequality, this means putting these reforms into the service of social justice. It thus requires appraising the system of regulatory governance against a wide range of values collectively called the 'public interest'.

The Nationalistic Constitutional Framework

The goals of regulatory governance are set forth in the 1987 Constitution (Article II, Section 9):

> The State shall promote a just and dynamic social order that will ensure the prosperity and independence of the nation and free the people from poverty through policies that provide adequate social services, promote full employment, a rising standard of living, and an improved quality of life for all.[2]

Article II, Section 19 further provides that 'The State shall develop a *self-reliant and independent national economy effectively controlled by Filipinos*' (emphasis added). Article XII (National Economy and Patrimony) gives the state the duty to:

- Protect Filipino enterprises against unfair *foreign* competition and trade practices (Sec.1);
- Enact measures that will *encourage the formation and operation* of enterprises whose capital is *wholly owned by Filipinos* (Par. 1, Sec. 10);
- Give *preference to qualified Filipinos* in the granting of rights, privileges, and concessions covering national economy and patrimony (Par. 2, Sec. 10);

- *Regulate and exercise authority over foreign investments* in accordance with its national goals and priorities (Par. 3, Sec. 10); and
- *Promote the preferential use* of Filipino labor, domestic materials and locally-produced goods, and adopt measures that help make them competitive (Sec. 12). (emphasis added)

Moreover, only Filipino citizens or corporations with majority Filipino ownership may be franchised to operate public utilities (Art. XII, Sec. 11). The practice of professions is also limited to Filipino citizens, 'except in cases prescribed by law' (Sec. 14, Art. XII).

The 1987 Constitution follows the philosophy articulated by earlier Constitutions. After reviewing the 1935, 1971 and 1987 Constitutions and a long list of Supreme Court decisions, Sereno came to the following conclusions (2002, p. 8):

- All the Constitutions soundly rejected *laissez faire*.
- The Supreme Court defined the economic philosophy of the Constitution in terms of (its) 'social justice' clauses, which in their view have a strong preference for redistributive and affirmative action legislation and programmes.
- This social justice orientation . . . empowers an interventionist government, and . . . interventionism is the primary way by which the problem of mass poverty can be addressed.
- The Constitution has been invariably interpreted to be nationalist, as to opportunities, licences, and rights in the economic sphere.
- Since the Constitution is strongly nationalist, in the cases decided by the Court, in effect, 'nationality-indifferent' and 'market-oriented' economic policies appear to bear the burden of having to be proven as not contravening the Constitution.
- (But) there are 'seeds' of thought in more recent jurisprudence which are open to a more market-oriented economic system.

Constitutional Provisions in Support of Free Enterprise

Support for 'a more market-oriented economic system' is explicitly provided by Article II, Section 20: 'The State recognises the indispensable role of the private sector, encourages private enterprise, and provides incentives to needed investments.' The embrace is limited by the following duties of the State:

- To ensure the right to own, establish, and operate economic enterprises, subject to the duty of the State to promote distributive justice and to intervene when the common good so demands (Sec. 6); and

- To regulate or prohibit monopolies when the public interest so requires, and prohibit combinations in restraint of trade or unfair competition (Sec. 19). (emphasis added)

Nevertheless, these provisions do allow for Philippine entry into international economic organisations and its efforts to give the leading role to the private sector. Perhaps the clearest statement in support of globalisation and liberalisation is found in the current Medium-term Philippine Development Plan (MTPDP, 2001–04). MTPDP reiterates that 'the philosophy of free enterprise shall continue to underpin government policies in stimulating business activities and promoting competition'. However, it manifests the continuing tension between the society's embrace of free enterprise and its political and social commitments as it enjoins government to ensure that 'the benefits from globalisation shall be balanced with stronger regulatory capability, more transparency and effective implementation of safety nets'.

MAJOR LAWS REGULATING THE ECONOMY

The regulatory regime is shown in three types of laws: laws regulating the whole economy or specific portions of it; laws restricting entry and competition; and laws promoting agriculture, industry and social services. The last set 'necessarily intertwines' with the conduct of trade and commerce (Medalla, 2000), but as they could encompass all existing Philippine law, they cannot be covered here.

Regulation of the conduct of business

The first law regulating trade and investment was the extension of Spain's *Codigo de Comercio* to its colony (Royal Decree of 6 August 1888). Its provisions relating to commercial contracts, joint accounts, and the conduct of maritime commerce are still in force (Catindig, 2001). Others have been superseded by the Corporation Law, Act No. 1459 (1906) or by the Corporation Code of the Philippines, *Batas Pambansa Blg*. 68 (1980). These laws govern the conduct of trade and commerce, covering all industries and even non-stock corporations. Stock corporations are further regulated by the Securities Regulation Code (SRC), Republic Act No. 8799 (2000). Lilia Bautista, the new head of the Securities and Exchange Commission (SEC) describes the SRC as 'incorporat(ing) international best practice standards' (September 2000).

The Corporation Code is complemented by the law creating the Department of Trade and Industry, Executive Order[3] Nos. 133 and 242 (1987), the law for the protection of consumers (RA 4109, 1964 and the Tariff and Customs Code (RA 1937, 1987).

Other laws seek to liberalise and reform specific industries and institutions. Banking and finance laws[4] have effected decontrolling interest rates, domestic licensing of some foreign banks, lifting of the moratorium on new commercial banks and relaxing regulations on setting up bank branches. In the insurance industry, 100 per cent foreign-owned insurance companies are now allowed to operate in the country (RA 8179, 1996). RA 7925 (1995) deregulated telecommunications and abolished the effective monopoly of several decades of the Philippine Long Distance Telephone Company. Both the maritime industry and civil aviation have also been opened up (EO 185, 1994, EO 213, 1994, EO 125, 1987, EO 219, 1995). The energy industry reforms are embodied in the Electric Power Industry Reform Act of 2001 (RA 9136) and the Downstream Oil Industry Deregulation Act of 1998 (RA 8479). The Metropolitan Waterworks and Sewerage System (MWSS) was the object of the largest privatisation effort in the world (RA 8041, 1995).

Significant reforms in the investments sector[5] include the Foreign Investments Act of 1991 (RA 7042) that allows 100 per cent foreign equity participation except in specified sectors. In 1996, the Act was amended to allow greater foreign participation in some of the previously prohibited sectors. Now only two areas have remaining restrictions: those sectors reserved to Filipinos by the Constitution and other laws (Negative List A); and sectors related to matters of security, health and morals, and protection of local industries (Negative List B). The reforms have resulted in an increase in the value of the country's foreign direct investment, although it still lags behind other Southeast Asian countries in attracting foreign capital (Austria, 2001).

Catindig (2001) has classified these foreign investment laws, along with the Build-Operate-and-Transfer Law,[6] the deregulation acts on telecommunications, oil and electric power, the Special Economic Zone Act of 1995 (RA 7916) and the Retail Trade Liberalisation Act of 2000 (RA 8762), as 'the new laws to maintain the country's competitive edge'.

Reflective of the new mood of the country, RA 8762 deserves special treatment. The law reverses almost half a century of prohibiting non-Filipinos from engaging in the retail business. The Retail Trade Nationalisation Law (RA 1180, 1954) was born out of fear of alien domination during the 1950s. It aimed not to create a public enterprise (as 'nationalisation' connotes in the United Kingdom) but to protect the thousands of small Filipino *sari-sari* ('Mom-and-Pop') stores from the incursion of Chinese retailers all across the country. RA 1180 was repealed by RA 8762, with the country 'finally succumbing to the strong winds of trade liberalisation' (Catindig, 2001, pp. 2–3). The repeal follows the Tariff Reform Programme and the Liberalisation Programme aimed to reverse the country's long history of protectionism and import substitution (Austria, 2001). Trade liberalisation has increased the competitiveness of the manufacturing industry (particularly export industries) based on the decrease in the ratio of domestic resource cost to the shadow exchange rate from 1.5 in 1988 to 1.2 in 1994. The more efficient establishments have also increased their share in the total value of production, indicating better allocation of scarce resources. Liberalisation, however, has yet to result in growth in the manufacturing sector.

Other laws are direct results of government's commitments to international organisations. These include: the Intellectual Property Code of the Philippines, RA 8293 (1997), the Electronic Commerce Act, RA 8792 (2000), the Safeguard Measures Act, RA 8800 (2000) and the Anti-money Laundering Law (RA 9160, 2001).

The country's response to globalisation demands is dramatically illustrated in the last law, which, in a sense, was passed with the country under the gun. The criminalisation of money laundering is part of the Philippines' global commitments.[7] The Financial Action Task Force (FATF) established by the G-7 Paris summit in 1989 had recommended that its member countries apply countermeasures to the Philippines if it failed to pass such a law by 30 September 2001. The government met the deadline, but barely, with President Arroyo promising amendments even as she signed the bill into law. Such an amended law closer to more FATF demands was passed in March 2003 (RA 9194).

The Philippines has further commitments due to its membership of multilateral and regional trade organisations. In the WTO, the country has committed to, among other things, convert quotas on agricultural imports into tariffs; bind tariff rates at 10 percentage points above the 1995 applied rate for 63 per cent of the total tariff lines; bind all current restrictions on market access in financial, communications, transport and tourism sectors; and impose zero tariff rates on certain IT product lines. The ASEAN Free Trade Area (AFTA), of which the Philippines is an original signatory in 1992, imposes a Common Effective Preferential Tariff (CEPT) scheme that aims to reduce intra-regional tariffs within the 15-year period beginning 1993. Other measures under AFTA include harmonisation of standards, reciprocal recognition of tests, certification of products, removal of barriers to foreign investment, and so on. Of major concern is the country's commitment to eliminate tariffs on 60 per cent of its product lines by 2003, given that as of 1999 it was still at the 1.4 per cent level (Austria, 2001).

The country is also a member of the Asia-Pacific Economic Co-operation (APEC). APEC's goal is to achieve free and open trade and investment in the Asia-Pacific region by 2010 for developed member economies, and 2020 for developing member countries (Austria, 2001). The Philippines is targeting a gradual decrease to a uniform tariff rate of 5 per cent in all areas excluding sensitive agricultural products by 2004. Based on the 1999 Philippine Individual Action Plan, the country has already complied with seven of the twelve APEC Non-binding Investment Principles (Austria, 2001).

Despite these efforts, economic analysts see the need for further reforms to improve the Philippines' competitive position and receive more benefits from liberalisation. Austria (2001) suggests expansion and deeper participation in regional trading arrangements and a fully articulated competition policy. Intal and Basilio (1998), meanwhile, seek the creation of a more facilitative macroeconomic environment.

Restrictions to entry and competition

Restrictions may be classified into limitations for nationalistic reasons, and all other restrictions. The Constitutional economic preference for Filipinos has already been discussed; RA 8800 (2000) seeks to protect local industries from increased imports that cause or threaten to cause serious injury to them, and RA 8751 (1999), amending the Tariff and Customs Code of the Philippines likewise seeks 'to protect domestic industries from unfair trade competition'. Under this measure, countervailing duties will be imposed on imported subsidised products that have caused or threaten to cause material injury and retardation of growth or prevent the establishment of domestic industry.

Non-nationalistic restrictions to entry and competition include public utility franchises,[8] monopoly rights given to public enterprises, licensing, and rules to remove barriers to competition. The last may involve licensing regimes and other similar arrangements that limit the number of producers and/or the volume of production. Entry into a particular market may also be limited by the imposition of minimum standards, industry-specific regulatory regimes, and restrictions ranging from price control to generally accepted ethical practices for consumer protection and increased competition (Cabalu et. al., 1999). While the Philippines has no overall legislative scheme for licensing of business, it does license certain industries and activities. For instance, the Insurance Code provides for the regulation of entry into the insurance business and the General Banking Act requires banks to comply with prudential requirements. The Department of Trade and Industry (DTI) undertakes licensing and standard-setting activities.

Another form of regulation aims to remove restrictions on competition set up by the firms themselves. Such activities are aimed toward maximising profits at the expense of the other players in the market and are generally associated with cartel-like arrangements. Arrangements include price fixing, geographic market division, limiting or boycotting dealings with a customer or class of customers, tie-in arrangements and resale price maintenance. Since blanket prohibitions may be counter-productive, a *competition test* may be used to determine the practical and beneficial effects of these practices in order to determine the level of regulation necessary in a particular case (Cabalu et. al., 1999).

Devolution of regulation

Some central functions were transferred to local government units (LGUs) by the Local Government Code, RA 7160 (1991). Their explicit regulatory powers include the 'power to reclassify agricultural lands, enforce environmental laws and the Building Code, process and approve subdivision plans, inspect food products and regulate the operation of tricycles' (Legaspi, 2001). Local governments may also regulate the provision of health, agriculture, social welfare and other devolved services. LGUs also have the power to tax property and businesses and give business licences and permits. The area of local regulation can grow larger since LGUs have been given broad powers under a general welfare clause (RA 7160, Chapter 5, Sec. 16).

INSTITUTIONAL FRAMEWORK

Economic policy-making is the shared responsibility of the three branches of government. This section discusses how regulatory governance takes place within this framework. The work of regulatory mechanisms outside government will also be explored.

Legislative and Judicial Involvement in Regulation

This section will deal with how the legislative and judicial branches get involved in regulation. It ends with an illustration of the system of checks and balances involved in an economically relevant law.

The legislature

Congress is composed of the Senate and House of Representatives. The Senate has 24 members elected at large nation-wide, while the House has around 250 members elected by districts.[9] Congress has powers not only to make laws, but also to conduct investigations, in aid of legislation, into any aspect of the economy and society. Constitutional provisions explicitly state the Congressional power to set trade and taxation policies that are the bases of the Executive's regulatory practice.

The judiciary

By constitutional mandate, the judiciary may review any decision of any agency, including regulatory institutions. Judicial interpretation becomes particularly important in defining what constitutes unlawful practices like monopolies and oligopolies, combinations in restraint of trade, and unfair competition practices. A case in point concerns the Oil Deregulation Law (RA 8180), which the Supreme Court declared unconstitutional in November 1997.

The Court found that RA 8180's 'provisions on tariff differential, stocking of inventories, and predatory pricing inhibit fair competition, encourage monopolistic power, and interfere with the free interaction of market forces' (Garcia vs. Corona et. al., 17 Dec. 1999, 321 SCRA 218). This decision was basically anchored on the constitutional prohibition against restraint of trade. Congress then enacted RA 8479, a deregulation law without the questioned provisions of the earlier one. A test of the constitutionality of the new law, filed in 2000, is pending as of the end of 2002 in the Supreme Court.

Checks and balances in practice

The system of checks and balances among the three branches occasionally results in inter-branch conflicts and policy gridlock. Such a case occurred in relation to the Expanded Value Added Tax (E-VAT) law (R.A. 7716, 1994). One of the measures towards liberalisation, the bill was certified by the Executive and survived deliberations in both Houses, mainly due to the domination of the ruling party. Members of Congress opposed to the bill then filed a case with the Supreme Court questioning its constitutionality. Ultimately, the Court cleared the law, but not before substantial delay (de Dios, 1999).

In analysing this and similar cases, de Dios found that small-group interests are able to influence economic policy-making particularly through the legislature. Interest groups have multiple channels of lobbying efforts through the different members of Congress. If one is unreceptive, other more accommodating members may be willing to question and distort the objectives of policies advanced by the executive that seem disadvantageous to certain interests. However, contrary to popular sentiment that the legislature wields excessive power that enables it to intervene and adversely affect executive initiatives, de Dios argues that the legislature's obstructive behaviour is mainly due to its subordination to the executive. The legislature may find it in its best interest to play the nuisance role in order to preserve the system of checks and balances, advance local interests and even partake of the 'benefits' of interest-group competition. De Dios therefore suggests that the executive power needs to be weakened, preferably through devolution of powers and the development of a stronger bureaucracy to enable the legislature to internalise all contending interests, both local and national, and ultimately disregard particularistic interests.

The Executive Branch and Regulation

As of 2002, there are 18 government agencies engaged primarily in economic regulation, as practically every law touching on an industry or process creates a corresponding regulatory agency. Regulating banking and finance are the *Bangko Sentral ng Pilipinas* (BSP, the new Central Bank), Securities and Exchange Commission (SEC), Philippine Deposit Insurance Corporation

(PDIC), and the Office of the Insurance Commissioner (OIC). Trade and commerce are regulated by the Department of Trade and Industry (DTI), the Tariff Commission and the Board of Investments (BOI). The Department of Energy (DOE) and the Department of Transportation and Communication (DOTC) and their attached agencies regulate public utilities. Virtually all have been either recently created or transformed to align them with the current liberalisation thrust. Table 13.1 shows the agencies found in each sector whose functions are primarily regulatory in nature.

The organisational characteristics of this system of regulatory governance are discussed in the next section.

Organisational status

In general, the extent of autonomy given to a regulatory agency may be determined by where it is placed in the Executive branch. The Bangko Sentral enjoys the highest status, having been established as 'an independent central monetary authority' with substantial administrative and financial autonomy (RA 7653, 1993). The chair of the Monetary Board, its governing authority, is its own governor. The vice chair is a cabinet official designated by the President; at present, that is the Secretary of Trade and Industry.

Regulatory bodies 'attached to a department' occupy the second level. 'Attachment' in Philippine legal parlance is the lateral relationship between a department and an agency for policy and programme coordination. The department has a representative in the regulatory board who ensures alignment with department policies. However, the representative may not interfere with internal operations (Tendero, 2000, p. 67). Attached boards have regulatory and adjudicatory powers outside the control of the department to which they are attached.

At the next level are regulatory agencies that are under the administrative supervision of a department. This pertains largely to the alignment of their personnel and financial resources and policies with the department and does not extend to control over their regulatory and adjudicatory powers, just like the attached agencies. This is the relationship of the Board of Investments with the Department of Trade and Industry, and the National Water Resources Board with the Department of Public Works and Highways.

Finally, a department may exercise control and supervision over a regulatory agency (Tendero, 2000, p. 66). This type of jurisdiction can be observed in the DTI's exercise of control over its bureaux and by the DOTC's over the Land Transportation Franchise and Regulatory Board.

Governing structure

Commissions or boards, acting collegially, generally govern regulatory institutions. The governing boards of NWRB and MARINA are completely

Table 13.1 The regulatory agencies

Sector/Agency	Mandate
Finance	
Securities and Exchange Commission (SEC)	Absolute jurisdiction, supervision, and control over all corporations, partnerships and associations in the Philippines
Insurance Commission	Regulation and supervision of the insurance industry
Bangko Sentral ng Pilipinas (BSP)	Central monetary authority
Philippine Deposit Insurance Corporation (PDIC)	Regulation of banks under receivership
Trade & commerce	
Tariff Commission	Investigatory, adjudicatory, and advisory agency on trade in goods and in tariff and trade remedy laws
Department of Trade and Industry (DTI0	The primary coordinative, promotive, facilitative and regulatory agency for trade, industry and investment activities
Bureau of Trade Regulation and Consumer Protection (BTRCP)	Safeguard interest of consumers and the public and formulation and monitoring of programmes for effective enforcement of trade laws
Bureau of Product Standards (BPS)	Development, implementation and promotion of standards
Board of Investments (BOI)	Encouragement and facilitation of investments
Water	
Metropolitan Waterworks and Sewerage System Regulatory Office (MWSS-RO)	Responsibility for ensuring that all provisions and performance targets specified in the Concession Agreement are met
National Water Resources Board (NWRB)	Coordination and regulation of all activities related to water resources management including water utilities operations
Energy	
Department of Energy (DOE)	Overall supervision and control of energy exploration, development, utilisation, distribution and conservation
Energy Regulatory Commission (ERC)	Promotion of competition, market development, and customer choice, and penalising of abuse of market power in the restructured electricity industry
Transport & communications	
Civil Aeronautics Board (CAB)	Regulation of the economic aspects of air transportation, and general supervision and regulation of and jurisdiction and control over air carriers
Maritime Industry Authority (MARINA)	General jurisdiction and control over the maritime industry
Land Transportation Franchising and Regulatory Board (LTFRB)	Rationalisation, regulation and supervision of all motorised land-based public transportation services
Air Transportation Office (ATO)	Implementation of rules and regulations in civil aviation to assure safe, economic and efficient air travel
National Telecommunications Commission (NTC)	Promulgation of rules and regulations to encourage more effective use of communications & broadcasting facilities and to maintain effective competition among private entities.

composed of ex officio government officials, while those of the BSP, PDIC, and CAB have ex-officio members as chair.[10] This arrangement promotes close linkage between government policies and those of the respective boards. Since officials who are not ex officio presumably come from outside government, the fact that two – BSP and PDIC – explicitly require members to be from the private sector seems to imply an expectation of greater independence from them.

Only four boards – BSP, SEC, PDIC and BOI – have terms fixed by law. These agencies are then relatively insulated from external pressure since the concerned authority cannot threaten a member of that body with removal from office. They may also span presidential terms. Most other board members are appointed by the President to a fixed term. However, since that is not set by law, the appointee has less security of tenure and may be more easily persuaded to vacate the office in case of policy disagreements with the President, especially after the incumbency of the original appointing power. The stated qualifications of members generally relate to 'recognised competence' in an academic field or profession. Membership of the bar is required in four boards, and lawyers are appointed to boards even though that qualification is not required by law. This may be traced to the society's legalistic orientation, the preponderance of lawyers among lawmakers, and the mistaken assumption that quasi-judicial proceedings require competence in law. However, broader qualifications, such as in 'economic and social disciplines' (in two laws) or a combination of disciplines (in three), are appearing in new laws. Civil engineering has made its first appearance (in LTFRB). This suggests a new recognition that issues of regulation have wider societal underpinnings than just knowledge of legal matters. Other important qualifications are manifested in two laws. Only the BSP has an explicit provision regarding conflict of interest, and only the BOI gives a direct role to civil society since the President can only choose members from a list of nominees of business and other organisations. However, explicit mention is made only of the Chamber of Commerce rather than organisations of labour, consumers and the poorer sectors.

Regulatory agencies generally have collegial decision-making bodies, with important exceptions being departments and offices that are also regulatory agencies. A department, the primary sectoral subdivision of the Executive branch, usually performs service provision functions. It is not independent of the President since the department secretary is considered his or her alter ego. The Air Transportation Office and the Office of the Insurance Commissioner are the only other regulatory agencies headed by a single executive. Both are treated like line bureaux of their respective departments.

Fiscal autonomy

Most regulatory agencies generate income from operating fees, fines and charges. The BSP and the PDIC are the only ones independent of outside control concerning the management of their financial resources.

Appeal against decisions

The independence of an agency is also determined by where appeals against its decisions may be lodged. For some agencies, the petition for review or appeal is to the next higher authority in the Executive Branch, while for the others, the appeal can only be made to the proper judicial courts. Generally, all decisions promulgated as part of quasi-judicial or adjudicatory functions are appealable to the Court of Appeals. Decisions of three agencies (SEC, CAB and NTC) may be brought for appeal only before the Supreme Court. Although only having the status of attached agencies, their respective department secretaries cannot thus intervene in their decision-making or interfere with the performance of their quasi-judicial functions. Meanwhile, some agencies have to follow the principle of exhausting administrative remedies before resort to the judiciary. The decisions of such agencies are appealable to the next higher authority. In some cases, to avoid bribery and corruption, the Secretary may review the decisions of a board *motu propio,* for instance in the case of the Secretary of Transportation and Communications regarding decisions of the Land Transportation Franchise and Regulatory Board.

Accountability

Aside from performing their designated functions, regulatory institutions are accountable to the public. Financial accounting systems, reporting to next-in-rank authorities, and performance reviews are mechanisms for such accountabilities. Every agency of the government has a resident auditor from the Commission on Audit (COA) to ensure that its financial and other resources are managed and expended well. It must also submit public accomplishment reports. Some agencies such as the DTI and NTC have service centres that accept complaints and comments from the public. The DTI has established consumer welfare desks and facilitates the formation and strengthening of consumer groups such as Women's Consumer Groups.

In addition, all agencies are guided by RA 6713 (1989), the Code of Conduct and Ethical Standards for Public Officials and Employees, and the Anti-graft and Corrupt Practices Act (RA 3019, 1960) with their strict conflict of interest and corruption prohibitions. In addition, the Securities Regulation Code has provisions on the proper conduct of its officials and employees.

Overlapping jurisdictions: the case of the cement industry

The multiplicity of agencies raises questions of jurisdiction and the lack of a holistic approach to regulation. This problem surfaced in an issue involving the cement industry in 2002. The Philippine Cement Manufacturing

Corporation (Philcemcor) petitioned the Secretary of Trade and Industry to issue a provisional tariff as a safeguard measure against foreign-manufactured cement. (The provisional tariff was to be paid in the form of cash bonds to be collected by the Bureau of Customs, under the Department of Finance.) The DTI Secretary, after preliminary investigation, granted the petition and then asked the Tariff Commission (which is under NEDA) for a formal investigation. The Tariff Commission found that no safeguard measure was necessary and sent its recommendation back to the DTI for promulgation. The DTI refused and sought the opinion of the Secretary of Justice as to the legality of the Commission's action. The Secretary of Justice opined that without the intervention of the President, the TC's recommendation should prevail. The DTI Secretary then brought the matter to the President, through the Committee on Tariff and Business Matters that he himself chairs. In the meantime, the Court of Appeals issued a temporary restraining order preventing the DTI Secretary from implementing the TC recommendation. This was what he wanted in the first place. However, the proper venue for appeals for tariff is supposed to be the Court of Tax Appeals, not the Court of Appeals.

Beyond the issue of jurisdiction, this case shows how the public interest may be defined from different perspectives. The DTI Secretary sought to issue a provisional tariff to protect the economy from dumping and unfair foreign competition and to safeguard jobs. The Tariff Commission did not see any injury to the local cement industry or to employment. The Citizens Alliance for Consumer Protection (CACP), a civil society group, sided with the Commission, as it declared local cement as substandard and high-priced, thus against the interests of consumers. Other groups denounced the local manufacturers as a price-fixing cartel. From this viewpoint, nationalism and globalisation seemed to be on the same side, while DTI and Philcemcor saw differently.

It remains unclear which decision truly supports the public interest and it is possible that the national interest does not depend on *who* is already in the country. If the contentions of the TC and citizen groups are true, then the interests of domestic consumers and foreign distributors may coincide. Even domestic construction labour would not be served by the substandard quality of cement. Moreover, the domestic industry is not necessarily a Filipino industry to be protected by nationalism. On the other hand, if dumping is indeed taking place, the citizenship of the domestic producers does not matter, since they are the object of unfair competition that even a liberalising world does not condone.

Non-state Regulatory Mechanisms

In addition to boards created by law for every aspect of the economy, the state has also sought to give the private sector some powers of regulation. This has introduced two relatively new regulatory forms, the self-regulatory organisation, and an organisation created out of privatisation. Their nature, and the problems they raise, are discussed next.

Self-regulating organisation

In a country where poverty and inequality reign, the state will tend to see itself as the guardian of the people's interest unless the private sector is able to show that it can regulate itself. Fraud, insider trading and other anomalies have made imperative the explicit declaration of the status of the Philippine Stock Exchange (PSE) as a self-regulating organisation (SRO).

Two requirements of an SRO were written into the new Securities Regulation Code. First, the Board President and a majority of the remaining members, should not be 'associated with any broker or dealer or member of the Exchange for a period of two (2) years prior to his/her appointment' (Sec. 33.2(g)). Second, the exchange must be de-mutualised. This transforms the PSE from a non-stock to a stock corporation, wherein a broker or a dealer does not automatically become a member of the exchange, and a person need not be a stock broker or dealer to be a member. The self-regulatory nature of the PSE got into the news in 2002 on two occasions. First was the election of officers of the exchange, in which all eight non-brokers in the Board voted for the same (and winning) candidate, taking control of the exchange away from brokers.

The second issue concerned a problem about a seeming stock manipulation. SEC Chair Bautista warned that the SEC would step in and remove the PSE's self-regulatory status if it did not clean up its own house. The SEC had in fact suspended the SRO status of the PSE on 7 March 2000 after the PSE's Compliance and Surveillance Group resigned in protest at the alleged white-washing by the PSE Board of its investigative report. SRO status was restored only on 8 September 2000, after passage of the Securities Regulation Code and compliance by the PSE with SEC terms and conditions (SEC, 2001).

It is clear that an organisation can enjoy self-regulation only if it follows principles of the market accepted by the state. In Bautista's terms (August 2000), the market should be FELT (fair, efficient, liquid and transparent).

Regulation by the private sector

Another mechanism is a regulatory office set up by the private sector such as the Regulatory Office of the Metropolitan Water and Sewerage System (MWSS). The MWSS was privatised in 1998 and its functions of providing water to Metropolitan Manila divided between two concessionaires: Maynilad for the western sector, and Manila Water Company for the east. The MWSS retained ownership of the water system and other assets, including the land

and building where the two concessionaires hold office. The terms of the concession were set forth in a concession agreement signed by MWSS, Maynilad and Manila Water. The agreement created the MWSS Regulatory Office (MWSS-RO) so that the government could continue to maintain some form of control over water, a basic and vital public good. The Regulatory Office is organisationally placed under the Board of Trustees. This gives rise to the first problem. In theory, the Board should not have any clout over the Regulatory Office because it is a party to the agreement that the RO is supposed to enforce. In reality, however, the Board of Trustees can practically dictate what actions and decisions RO should make.

First, as mentioned earlier, the Office was only created by a contract between the government and private companies. As such it does not have legal personality, and may not enter into official agreements and/or contracts. Due to this impediment, the Regulatory Office has to rely on the MWSS Board when entering into contracts, thereby limiting its independence from the latter. Moreover, all RO decisions are subject to Board approval. The Regulatory Office may validate or review petitions for water rate hikes but approval is at the Board's discretion.

The second problem is the RO's relation to the concessionaires. Under the agreement, the private operators equally finance the RO's annual operating budget through concession fees, making the Office totally financially reliant on them. A recent controversy elucidates the RO's problems. On 11 October 2001, the MWSS Board terminated the services of two deputy regulators purportedly after they lost the Board's 'trust and confidence'. The presidents of the private operators also signed the termination letter. Coincidentally or not, the two fired regulators were opposed to Maynilad's petition for water rate hikes. The regulators' dismissal is still in question, since one of them wants to take up the issue in court, invoking the provision in the agreement that appointed regulators may only be removed through action by an Appeals Panel with representation from an international arbitration body. However, the fact that the Board can coerce members of the Regulatory Office to resign from their posts clearly shows its control and influence over the RO. This unwritten and unofficial power of the Board circumvents provisions in the agreement that are in place to ensure the regulators' independence.

Another problem involves the RO's powers and functions. In specifying its initial and transitional powers, the concession agreement uses passive terms such as 'monitoring' and 'review', never the power to 'regulate'. While it can be argued that these terms may be used interchangeably, 'regulation' connotes a more pro-active course of action than the terms used in the contract. The agreement recognises that the RO's functions 'will change over time as the regulatory regime is established and developed', although it is unclear how and when these functions can be amended and/or modified.

There is already an attempt to improve the existing regulatory environment in the form of a bill to create a Water Regulatory Commission, an independent central regulatory body for the entire water sector in the country. However, even if such an agency is created, it may not be able to exercise authority over the MWSS service area as the provisions in the agreement, including the regulatory aspects, are supposed to be valid and binding until the end of the concession period, in 2022. Any changes in the agreement can only be introduced with the concurrence of all parties concerned. It is unlikely that the concessionaires will agree to measures strengthening the regulatory framework, thereby compromising their present advantageous position.

LESSONS LEARNED

This chapter on competition and regulation in the Philippines shows that many challenges remain to be confronted. Some directions for further research and policy development are summarised next.

Philosophical and Ethical Underpinnings

As a colonial society and even as an independent state, the Philippines has suffered from the domination of alien interests in its economy, politics and society. It is thus understandable that all Philippine Constitutions have a strong nationalistic tone, reserving for its nationals vital sectors of the economy and seeking to protect them not just from unfair competition, but from unfair *foreign* competition. The strength of Filipino enterprises in their own land would be a strong source of national pride, even as it provides jobs and quality goods to the people. On the other hand, if nationalism were only to shield inefficient firms, then Filipinos would not be served by keeping out aliens. The country has shifted back and forth between these extremes, hewing close to liberalisation as global pressures increase, and moving back to nationalism in protecting national heritage and social justice. International commitments may force more concessions, as the process of passing the money laundering law has shown. The problem may lie not so much in embracing one or the other philosophy, as in taking a holistic view of the economy instead of seeing it cut up into separate pieces as the parcelling out of regulatory governance to several uncoordinated agencies is wont to do. A strategy that reconciles the two philosophies in pursuit of the public interest thus seems to be required.

This introductory study has pointed out the need to look into at least two other ethical issues. The first is how the benefits and losses not only from globalisation or nationalism but from the processes of regulation themselves are distributed and affect the lives of the poor. The second is to understand how regulation may provide opportunities for rent-seeking, regulatory capture, and other manifestations of corruption and unequal treatment.

Modes of Regulatory Governance

Bearing in mind that the end-goal of all regulation is the safeguarding and attainment of the public interest, the Philippines has created many organisations so that no stone is left unturned in meeting significant national needs. It thus has a wide array of mechanisms varying in organisational status, governing structure, fiscal autonomy, appeal from decisions, and accountability. This chapter has indicated where autonomy and independence may be achieved in each of these areas. However, their proper combinations within agencies and the expected inter-relationships of agencies to each other need to be analysed. Moreover, since the chapter has looked primarily at the laws and at a few cases of implementation, the strength of any arrangement cannot yet be determined. The same may be said of the different forms of regulatory agencies which were discussed briefly, but need to be more intensively examined. Further analysis should also include not only central state mechanisms but also those of local governments as well as those provided by civil society and the private sector.

NOTES

1. Ledivina V. Cariño is coordinator of a CRC research team including Jose P. Tabbada, Ma. Fe V. Mendoza, Erwin Gaspar Alampay, Eva Minerva Baylon, Rene M. Lopos, Rommel Rabanal, and Mark Anthony Gamboa.
2. This is followed by Section 10, which speaks of the duty of the State to promote 'social justice in all phases of national development' and Sections 14 to 18, which further underscore the duty of the government to ensure the fundamental equality before the law of men and women; protect and promote the right to health of the people; protect and advance the right of the people to a balanced and healthful ecology; give priority to education, science and technology, arts, culture and sports to foster patriotism and nationalism, accelerate social progress, and promote total human liberation and development; and protect the rights of workers and promote their welfare.
3. These executive orders have the force of law since President Corazon Aquino made them in her capacity as sole legislator during the one-year revolutionary government following the ousting of Marcos (1986–87). In all other years, an EO is an implementation of an Act or law.
4. The New Central Bank Act, RA 7653 (1993), the Philippine Deposit Insurance Corporation Act, RA 7400 (1992), Financing Company Act of 1998 (RA 8556), the General Banking Law of 2000 (RA 8791), and the Foreign Banks Law (RA 7721, 1994).
5. Republic Act 5186 creating the Board of Investments (1967), the Omnibus Investments Code of 1987 (EO 226) as amended by RA 8756 (1999), the Foreign Investments Act of 1991 (RA 7042), as amended by RA 8179 (1996) and the Investors' Lease Act (RA 7652, 1993).
6. RA 6957 (1990), as amended by RA 7718 (1994).
7. This includes its ratification of the UN Convention against Illicit Traffic in Narcotic Drugs

and Psychotropic Substances, and its participation in the Asia-Pacific Group on Money Laundering (Catindig, 2001).

8. But note that by Constitutional directive, all franchises for public utilities can be given only to Filipinos or to firms 60 per cent owned by them.
9. Twenty per cent of the members of the House should be 'party-list representatives', that is, members representing organisations chosen at large by the voters, following a constitutional formula.
10. Note, however, that the ex officio chair of the Bangko Sentral (BSP, the Central Bank) is not an outsider but the governor of the Central Bank himself.

REFERENCES

Austria M.S. (2001), 'Liberalisation and regional integration: the Philippines' strategy to global competitiveness', Philippine Institute for Development Studies (PIDS) Discussion Paper Series No. 2001–09.

Bautista, Lilia (August 2000), 'The Securities Regulation Code 2000: is it a new beginning or is it the end?', speech delivered to the Association of Securities Analysts of the Philippines, Makati Sports Club.

Bautista, Lilia (September 2000), 'Implementing guidelines for the Securities Regulation Code', speech delivered to the FINEX Seminar on the Securities Regulation Code, Makati: Manila Peninsula Hotel.

Cabalu, H., Doss, N., Firns, I., Jefferson, T., Kenyon, P., Koshy, P., Lim, L.K., and Brown, P. (1999), 'A framework for competition policy in the Philippines', Curtin University.

Catindig, Tristan A. (2001), 'The Major Laws of the Philippines relating to Trade and Investment', paper presented at the ASEAN Legal Systems and Regional Integration International Law Conference, Kuala Lumpur, Malaysia: ASEAN Secretariat and the Asia-Europe Institute and Faculty of Law of the University of Malaya.

de Dios, E.S. (1999), 'Interest-group competition, legislative obstruction, and executive power', in Dante B. Canlas and Shigeaki Fujisaki (eds) *Studies on Governance and Regulation: The Philippines*, Tokyo: Institute for Developing Economies.

Intal, Ponciano Jr and Basilio, Leilani Q. (1998), 'The international economic environment and the Philippine economy', Philippine Institute for Development Studies (PIDS) Discussion Paper Series No. 98–25.

Legaspi, Perla E. (2001), 'The changing role of the local governments under a decentralised state: some cases in Philippine local governance', Dilemma, Queen City: National College of Public Administration and Governance, University of the Philippines.

Medalla, E.M. (2000), 'Government policies and regulations: interrelationships with competition policy objectives', online copy obtained from Philippines-APEC Study Center Network website: http://pascn.pids.gov.ph.

Securities and Exchange Commission (2001), 'Country Report of the Philippines', paper submitted to the OECD 3rd Round Table on Capital Market Reform in Asia.

Sereno, M.L.A. (2002), 'The power of judicial review and economic policies achieving constitutional objectives', paper read at the Forum on the Role of the Judiciary in Philippine Economic Development, Manila: PHILJA-AGILE-USAID Project on Law and Economics.

Tendero, A.P. (2000), 'Theory and practice of public administration in the Philippines', revised edn, Mandaluyong: Fiscal Administration Foundation, Inc.

Philippine Government Documents

Act no. 1459: The Corporation Law (1906).

Royal Decree of 6 August 1888.

1980 Batas Pambansa Blg. 68: Corporation Code of the Philippines.

1936 Commonwealth Act no. 83: Securities Act.

1935, 1973 and 1987 Constitution of the Philippines.

1979 Executive Order No. 546: Creating a Ministry of Public Works and a Ministry of Transportation and Communications.

1982 Executive Order No. 797: Reorganising the Ministry of Labour and Employment, Creating the Philippine Overseas Employment Administration, and for other Purposes.

1987 Executive Order No. 125: Reorganising the Ministry of Transportation and Communications Defining Its Powers and Functions and for other Purposes.

1987 Executive Order No. 133: Reorganising the Department of Trade and Industry, Its Attached Agencies, and for other Purposes.

1987 Executive Order No. 202: Creating the Land Transportation Franchising and Regulatory Board.

1987 Executive Order No. 226: The Omnibus Investments Code of 1987.

1987 Executive Order No. 242: Amending Executive Order No. 133, Series of 1987 Entitled 'Reorganising the Department of Trade and Industry, Its Attached Agencies, and for other Purposes'.

1987 Executive Order No. 247: Reorganising the Philippine Overseas Employment Administration and for other Purposes.

1987 Executive Order No. 307: Establishing an Occupational Safety and Health Centre in the Employees' Compensation Commission

1994 Executive Order No. 185: Opening the Domestic Water Transport Industry to New Operators and Investors.

1994 Executive Order No. 213: Deregulating Domestic Shipping Rates.

1995 Executive Order No. 219: Establishing the Domestic and International Civil Aviation Liberalisation Policy.

1999 Garcia vs. Corona et. al., 321 SCRA 218.

House of Representatives. Media Affairs Office.

2001 http:\\www.congress.gov.ph.

National Economic and Development Authority.

1999 Philippine Medium Term Development Plan, 2001–2004.

1974 Presidential Decree no. 474: Maritime Industry Decree.

1974 Presidential Decree no. 612: The Insurance Code.

1975 Presidential Decree no. 1067: The Water Code of the Philippines.

1948 RA 265: The Central Bank Act.

1952 RA 776: The Civil Aeronautics Act of the Philippines.

1953 RA 911: An Act Creating a Tariff Commission, Defining its Powers and for other Purposes.

1954 RA 1180: Retail Trade Nationalisation Law.

1957 RA 1937: Revising the Tariff and Customs Law.

1960 RA 3019: Anti-Graft and Corrupt Practices Act.

1963 RA 3591: An Act Establishing the Philippine Deposit Insurance Corporation, Defining its Powers and Functions and for other Purposes.

1964 RA 4109: An Act to Convert the Division of Standards under the Bureau of Commerce into a Bureau of Standards, to Provide for the Standardisation and/or Inspection of Products and Imports of the Philippines and for other Purposes.

1967 RA 5186: Investment Incentives Act.

1989 RA 6713: Code of Conduct and Ethical Standards for Public Officials and Employees.

1990 RA 6957: An Act Authorising the Financing, Construction, Operation, and Maintenance of Infrastructure Projects by the Private Sector, and for other Purposes.

1991 RA 7042: Foreign Investments Act of 1991.

1991 RA 7160: The Local Government Code.

1992 RA 7400: The Philippine Deposit Insurance Corporation Act.

1993 RA 7652: Investors' Lease Act.

1993 RA 7653: The New Central Bank Act.

1994 RA 7716: An Act Restructuring the Value Added Tax (VAT) Law System, Widening Its Tax Base and Enhancing Its Administration, and for these Purposes Amending and Repealing the Relevant Provisions of the National Internal Revenue Code, as Amended, and for other Purposes.

1994 RA 7718: An Act Amending Certain Sections of Republic Act No. 6957, entitled 'An Act Authorising the Financing, Construction, Operation, and Maintenance of Infrastructure Projects by the Private Sector, and for other Purposes.'

1994 RA 7721: Foreign Banks Law.

1995 RA 7916: Special Economic Zone Act.

1995 RA 7925: An Act to Promote and Govern the Development of Philippine Telecommunications and the Delivery of Public Telecommunications Services.

1995 RA 8041: The National Water Crisis Act.

1996 RA 8179: An Act to Further Liberalise Foreign Investment, Amending for the Purpose Republic Act No. 7042, and for other Purposes.

1996 RA 8180: The Oil Deregulation Law.

1997 RA 8293: The Intellectual Property Code of the Philippines.

1998 RA 8479: The Downstream Oil Industry Deregulation Act.

1999 RA 8751: An Act Strengthening the Mechanisms for the Imposition of Countervailing Duties on Imported Subsidised Products, Commodities or Articles of Commerce in order to Protect Domestic Industries from Unfair Trade Competition, Amending for the Purpose Section 302, Part 2, Title II, Book I of Presidential Decree No. 1464, Otherwise Known as the Tariff and Customs Code of the Philippines, as Amended.

1999 RA 8756: An Act Providing for the Terms, Conditions and Licensing Requirements of Regional or Area Headquarters, Regional Operating Headquarters and Regional Warehouses of Multinational Companies Amending for the Purpose Certain Provisions of Executive Order No. 220, Otherwise Known as the Omnibus Investments Code of 1987.

2000 RA 8762: Retail Trade Liberalisation Act.

2000 RA 8791: The General Banking Law.

2000 RA 8792: The Electronic Commerce Act.

2000 RA 8799: The Securities Regulation Code.

2000 RA 8800: Safeguard Measures Act.

2001 RA 9136: The Electric Power Industry Reform Act.

2001 RA 9160: The Anti-Money Laundering Act.

2003 RA 9194, An Act Amending Rep. Act No. 9160, otherwise known as the 'Anti-Money Laundering Act of 2001'.

14. Competition, regulation and regulatory governance in Sri Lanka

Malathy Knight-John

INTRODUCTION

The policy shift in the developing world over the last two decades, towards market mechanisms as instruments of economic growth and poverty reduction, has been paralleled by the emergence of a new role for the state from provider to facilitator/regulator. Liberalization and privatization have been accompanied by competition policy and rules-based regulatory systems in an effort to address distributional concerns. The integration of the regulatory process into the policy framework and its effectiveness in addressing its stated objectives, however, has depended to a large extent on the political economy priorities and governance standards of the state.

Sri Lanka has not been an exception in this regard, as the ensuing discussion in this chapter illustrates. Although Sri Lanka moved from an import substituting and heavily state-interventionist economy to a more liberalized one in 1977, competition legislation was enacted only a decade later, with legislation for regulating telecommunications, passenger bus transport, and the financial sector also being introduced later. The civil strife that has engulfed the nation for over two decades, pressures to finance the burgeoning fiscal deficit and the related move to opt for rapid privatization contributed to placing competition and regulatory concerns on the backburner.

Moreover, while the formal institutional and legal structures for competition and regulation do exist, distortionary intervention and bureaucratic micromanagement by the state are not uncommon. Regulatory practices have tended to stifle rather than enhance or promote competition. This raises important questions such as, are competition and regulation weak because the institutional and legal framework is flawed? Or, more insidiously, are the real political economy objectives of the state different from the stated goals of equitable growth and poverty reduction championed by successive political regimes since liberalization?

This chapter is essentially a mapping exercise laying out the profile of competition, regulation, and regulatory governance in Sri Lanka. It is also an attempt to evaluate the effectiveness of competition and regulatory reform and to get a flavour of the political economy realities that shape this public policy process. The chapter is structured as follows. The next section describes and analyses the policy setting, subsequent sections look at the legal and institutional structures, respectively, for competition and regulation and identify the political, social and external influences impinging on regulation and competition policies. The chapter ends with a summary of the main conclusions.

THE POLICY SETTING

Public policy in Sri Lanka is the joint responsibility of the executive and the legislative branches of government with the directive principles of state policy being specified in the constitution. In practice, however, these fundamental principles of good governance are seldom adhered to, with the checks and balances mechanism built into the executive-legislative structures being undermined by short-term partisan politics. The permeation of disruptive politics into the policy-making process has intensified more recently with the chief executive (the president) and the legislature coming from different political parties.[1] Moreover, even when the executive and the legislative bodies have been from the same political party, the electoral cycle has prompted ad hoc policies reflecting the incentive to maximize narrow, short-term political interests.

The political dynamics that have shaped the policy-making process in general have also influenced state policy with respect to competition and regulatory reform. Although successive governments since 1977 have made explicit policy statements defining state–market relations, with the state as facilitator-cum-regulator and the private sector as the engine of growth, the state still has an 'inefficiently excessive' presence in the economy. State enterprises continue to be used as avenues for political patronage and employment creation. Even with the privatization programme that has resulted in the divestiture of 86 entities from 1989 to date, the Central Bank (2001) reports that there were over 70 state-owned enterprises (SOEs) operating in the economy, with cumulative losses from these entities amounting to around 2 per cent of GDP in 2000.

More recently, however, an unsustainable and ever-expanding budget deficit (9.9 per cent of GDP in 2000 and 10.9 per cent in 2001) and the signing of a stand-by arrangement with the IMF, with attached conditionality on structural reforms, in April 2001, appear to have contributed to a more concerted policy effort to embrace public–private partnerships. Policymakers see these partnerships as a means of developing vital infrastructure services such as public transportation, highways, electricity/energy, water and telecommunications and as a way to finance the state deficit and retire debt through the sale of shares in SOEs.

Some of the more prominent examples of public–private partnerships are in the telecommunications sector, where the government sold 35 per cent of its shareholding in Sri Lanka Telecom Ltd. (SLT), the incumbent fixed telephony operator, to Nippon Telegraph and Telephone (NTT) of Japan; in the airline sector, where 40 per cent of government shares in the national carrier were sold to Emirates Airlines; and in the energy sector, where 51 per cent of state shareholding in the Colombo Gas Company was sold to the Dutch company, Shell Overseas International BV/Royal Dutch (Shell).

The decision to intensify the public–private partnership approach in the reform process also highlights the importance of the regulatory regime, particularly in the utilities sector, where balancing producer and consumer interests to ensure sufficient incentives for private investment and to address price and access issues is crucial. However, as pointed out in Jayasuriya and Knight-John (2002) and as will be discussed later in this chapter, policy-makers have paid insufficient attention to the need for effective competition policy and regulatory structures to support the reform process.

As mentioned earlier, competition legislation was introduced only in 1987 with the liberal trade regime being used as a proxy for competition policy during the early years of liberalization. The articulation of a clear and comprehensive competition policy is still pending and competition policy concerns are handled in an arbitrary and piecemeal fashion in response to a particular sector need or as dictated by political economy priorities at a given time.

As of now, the new 'competition' authority has no power to investigate monopolies and mergers and while reports of a separate Monopolies and Mergers Commission abound in the press, there has been no specific policy statement to this effect or concrete measures to institutionalize such an entity. Although it is conceivable that the government may want to avoid the perception of a restrictive regulatory regime to attract investment, this lacuna in the competition policy framework is a recipe for disaster.

The privatization process has also been at odds with competition, with the maximization of fiscal benefits through the granting of monopoly power taking precedence over long-term sector efficiency and consumer welfare. As detailed in Knight-John (forthcoming a) the ill-effect of this process is apparent particularly in the telecommunications sector, where there has been abuse of a dominant position with negative impacts on competitors and consumers.

Regulatory principles are laid out in the specific legislation pertaining to a particular sector, while sector policy, which currently exists in a structured format only in the telecommunications sector, is developed by the government in response to sector needs. This sectoral approach to regulation is a function both of sector-defined line ministries and of the sector-defined loans provided by donor agencies for the reform process.

However, with the change of government in December 2001 the centralization of policy development functions under the prime minister led to a policy initiative, supported by the World Bank and the Public–Private Infrastructure Advisory Facility (PPIAF), to move away from the sectoral approach to regulation to a multi-sector model for utilities. The rationale for the multi-sector approach is the degree of commonality in the object of regulation (e.g. rights of way), the degree of commonality in the form of regulation (e.g. price caps), economies of regulation relating to the assumption that public hearings, cost studies, etc. are substitutable across sectors and the belief that a multi-sector body will be less vulnerable to political and regulatory capture. The multi-sector agency – the Public Utilities Commission (PUC) – will initially include the water and electricity sectors with sufficient flexibility to add other utilities to its brief as the reform process progresses.

As at the time of writing, telecommunications regulation continues to be handled by the Telecommunications Regulatory Commission (TRC) because the emphasis of regulation in the planned convergence model for telecom, internet, broadcasting and cable – access, interconnection, and the allocation of spectrum resources – differs from the emphasis on controlling monopoly revenues in the electricity and water sectors. The bus transport sector is also excluded from the PUC as policy-makers are of the view that a constitutional controversy, stemming from the fact that transport is a devolved subject, and relating to the division of powers between the National Transport Commission (NTC) representing the centre and the provincial councils representing the regions, would hinder the multi-sector reform process.

These concerns do have practical and technical validity. However, the failure to include the broader energy industry – including the Liquefied Petroleum Gas (LPG) sector – in the PUC, on the grounds that this sector is characterized by competition, is worrying given the anti-competition issues that have arisen in this sector since the Shell privatization[2] and given the fact that there is currently no regulator in this sector.

Regulators are bound, even where sector policies contradict regulatory principles, to recognize government policy (and priorities), therefore exposing regulators to the vagaries of the political process. An example of regulatory failure that results from such contradictions is the policy requirement that the TRC 'maintains' the international monopoly conferred on the incumbent telecom operator after privatization, contrary to its regulatory mandate to facilitate and promote competition in the sector. This particularly ominous concession afforded to SLT/NTT contributed to several instances of abuse of a dominant position (such as the refusal to implement the closed numbering plan drawn up by TRC and the blocking of calls originating from competitors), anti-competitive behaviour with respect to interconnection, and legal disputes over the use of enhanced voice services by other operators for international calls (Jayasuriya and Knight-John, 2002).

This example also calls into question the real rationale for regulation. Although the government's stated objective of regulation is, purportedly, to enhance competition and consumer welfare, regulatory practice has focused on shielding the incumbent operator from competition. Was this simply an extension of the international monopoly granted to SLT/NTT so as to maximize the fiscal benefits of privatization? As argued in Jayasuriya and Knight-John (2002), the answer lies in the changed rent-seeking opportunities for politicians and favoured bureaucrats, who viewed anti-competitive regulation as a complement to the one-off rent extraction opportunity at the time of privatization, and therefore as a means to ensure continued rent extraction.

These regulatory deficiencies are compounded over time with no review or impact assessment mechanisms in place to evaluate regulatory strategies objectively, locate areas of weakness and rectify past mistakes. Given the manner in which policy is formulated and implemented in Sri Lanka – to maximize rent-seeking opportunities or to cater to narrow political interests – donor pressure or conditionality may, ironically, be the only solution.

THE LEGAL FRAMEWORK

According to the constitution, governing power in Sri Lanka is divided between the executive, the legislature and the judiciary. As already mentioned, the president is afforded utmost power, with his or her decisions granted immunity from any judicial challenge. Unique to the Sri Lankan judiciary branch is its comparatively narrow power of review – any prospective Bill can be challenged in the Supreme Court on constitutional grounds only within seven days from the date it is presented to parliament. After this time, the courts have no authority to review an Act and it can only be amended by parliament.

The constitution makes no specific reference to matters regarding regulation or competition. As a result, there is no constitutionally defined role for the courts in cases involving competition and regulatory issues, excepting instances that involve a question of fundamental rights (e.g. prejudicial dismissal/hiring policies etc.). The principal legal forms governing regulation and competition are the Acts of Parliament, used to establish competition and regulatory agencies. The general procedure for an Act to be passed involves the following sequence: Line Ministry – Cabinet approval – Line Ministry – Legal Draftsman – Attorney General (to check constitutionality) – Line Ministry – Parliament.

The rest of this section will focus on specific pieces of legislation in an effort to map out the existing legal mechanisms for implementation, arbitration and enforcement of competition and regulation in Sri Lanka. It is important to note, however, that legislation only sets out general and broad principles, leaving the task of developing detailed rules to specialized competition and regulatory agencies.

Competition Law

Competition law in Sri Lanka was introduced with the enactment of the Fair Trading Commission Act No. 1 of 1987 (FTCA). This provided for the establishment of the Fair Trading Commission (FTC) to control monopolies, mergers and anti-competitive practices and to formulate and implement a national price policy. Consumer protection legislation that provided for the setting up of the Department of Internal Trade (DIT) to regulate internal trade and to establish fair trading practices had been introduced in 1979. In principle, the DIT was to deal with day-to-day consumer complaints and the FTC was to provide industry oversight with emphasis on anti-competitive behaviour and price manipulation. In practice, however, there was considerable overlap in the functions of these two institutions, pointing to potential cost savings from their amalgamation. Attempts to address this problem resulted in the drafting of new legislation in the 2001 to 2002 period. The first piece of legislation – the Consumer Protection Authority Bill of 2001 – provided for the establishment of a Consumer Protection Authority and Consumer Protection Council, with investigative and adjudicative powers, respectively, to replace the FTC and the DIT. This proposal was drastically changed after more than a year of uncertainty regarding its status.

The new version – The Consumer Affairs Authority Bill of 2002 – has been stripped of provisions to investigate monopolies and mergers and is perhaps indicative of a shift in the management of competition issues under the current political regime, with increased emphasis on creating an investor-friendly climate free of undue regulatory hassle. Whether this route is the most optimal with respect to fostering investor perceptions of credibility and of predictability and of securing the type of investment conducive to the medium to long-term development and welfare of the country, however, is left to be seen.

The Consumer Affairs Authority (CAA) and the Consumer Affairs Council (CAC) are to function under the Ministry of Commerce and Consumer Affairs and their Chairs and members are to be appointed by the Minister, as was the case with their predecessors. Among the qualifications required for these positions are law, economics, commerce, administration, accountancy, and science. A significant improvement in the new legislation is the provision that the Minister can only terminate the appointment of the Chair or other members for misconduct or for physical or mental incapacity. The FTCA allowed the Minister to remove the Chair or any member without reason.

The objectives and functions of the CAA, as stated in the Bill, focus almost entirely on protecting consumers from unfair trade practices and anti-competitive practices, with the power to investigate monopolies and mergers being removed from its ambit. Some positive additions to its list of functions include the mandate to undertake public and private sector efficiency studies and to assist in the establishment of consumer organisations.

Moreover, the powers of the new entity have been broadened to include areas such as, *inter alia*, finance, shipping, entertainment, utility services, transportation, and professional services (legal, medical, engineering, etc.). The inclusion of utility services and the provision of concurrent jurisdiction *vis à vis* the sector regulators and the PUC is a noteworthy development in the public policy process. The FTCA had failed to address the relationship between the sector regulators and the competition authority and turf battles initially surrounded the establishment of the CAA and PUC.

A perturbing aspect in the new legislation, however, is the apparent reversal of the move away from price control since 1990. Whereas the FTC could only fix or vary the maximum retail price of pharmaceuticals, the new Bill prohibits price increases of 'specified' goods and services, with the Minister in consultation with the CAA having the power to declare any good or service considered 'essential to the life of the community' as 'specified'.

The new Bill, like the FTCA, defines anti-competitive practices very generally, as those that restrict, distort or prevent competition in connection with the production, supply or acquisition of goods or the supply or securing of services. The problem with this broad definition of anti-competitive practices was illustrated in the case of Ceylon Oxygen vs. FTC. Here the courts held that the Commission did not have the power to investigate predatory pricing, discriminatory rebates and exclusive dealings and could only look into practices such as monopolies, mergers and anti-competitive practices, as specified in Section 11 of the FTCA. Evidently, the court did not consider predatory pricing, discriminatory rebates and exclusive dealings to be instances of anticompetitive practice.

In line with the behavioural (as opposed to structural) approach to antitrust in Sri Lanka's competition legislation, anti-competitive practices are considered illegal only if it is proved that they are contrary to the public interest. Public interest considerations to be taken into account are outlined in the Bill – for instance, concepts such as effective competition, price, quality and variety of goods and services, cost reduction, facilitating new entry, and so on are specifically mentioned in the legislation. The Consumer Affairs Council – a new entity in the competition regime – is to hear and determine all applications made to it by the CAA or any other person or association of traders, based on public interest considerations.

Similar to the FTCA, the new Bill specifies that any person who fails to comply with a provision of the law is guilty of an offence and will, on conviction in the Magistrate's Court, be liable to fines, imprisonment, or both. However, while the level of penalties was general and applied across the board to corporate and non-corporate bodies in the FTCA, the new Bill differentiates between these two groups. In the case of the FTC, the penalties set out in the Act failed to have a deterrent effect, perhaps because the Commission itself lacked legitimacy as an entity that would actively pursue cases contravening the law. The institutional factors that prompted this image of the FTC will be discussed in the fourth section of this chapter.

Utility Regulation

Currently, a legal framework for utility regulation exists in the telecommunications and bus transport sectors and for the establishment of the PUC, in the form of the Public Utilities Commission Bill of 2002. Legislation for water is at a draft stage and legislation for electricity sector regulation has been prepared and steps are being taken to synchronize these statutes with the PUC Bill. Specifically, policy-makers have decided to include the constitution, funding and powers of the multi-sector authority in the 'umbrella' PUC legislation and to contain the industry-specific bits of regulation in a set of separate industry statutes.

An interesting precedent being established in the PUC is the involvement of the Constitutional Council (CC) in the appointment of Commissioners. This is an attempt to move away from partisan politics and to add objectivity and independence to the regulatory process. The CC is a recent legal development introduced in October 2001 under the 17th Amendment to the Constitution with the mandate to appoint independent commissions for the elections office, public services, judicial service, police department, and so on. It comprises the prime minister, parliament speaker, opposition leader (all as ex officio members), one person appointed by the president, five persons appointed by the president on the nomination of the prime minister and opposition leader, and one person appointed by the president and nominated by a majority of the members of parliament from political parties other than those to which the prime minister and the opposition leader belong.

The Commissioners to be appointed to the PUC are to be qualified in the fields of engineering, law and business management. Moreover, they are to be appointed on staggered terms and they cannot be removed without parliamentary approval and for a specified reason. They are also subject to conflict of interest rules.

The Bill includes two substantive sections on competition and consumer protection and the mandate of the PUC includes the investigation of monopolies, mergers and anti-competitive practices in relation to the public utilities that it regulates, while also providing for concurrent jurisdiction with the competition authority. The PUC Bill specifies the activities that might be viewed as anti-competitive, such as abuse of a dominant position.

Another notable feature in the PUC legislation, absent in any other competition or regulation legislation in Sri Lanka, is the provision to ensure cooperation and facilitate the exchange of information between the Commission and other bodies, such as the Central Environmental Authority, the Urban Development Authority and the TRC, by way of a written memorandum.

Although it is clearly too soon to make any conclusive remarks on the PUC, inbuilt legal safeguards such as the inclusion of the CC, of Parliament, of concurrent legislation, and so on are indicative of a shift towards a more progressive genre of regulation. The institutional features of the PUC that complement its legal framework will be discussed in the next section of this chapter.

The telecommunications industry is governed by an Act passed in 1991 and amended in 1996. The 1991 legislation led to the trifurcation of the industry, with operational functions assigned to the SLT, regulation to a single member regulatory body and telecommunications policy to the line ministry. The legislative amendments of 1996 saw the creation of the TRC as a five member Commission with three appointed and two ex officio members. While the replacement of a single member regulatory entity, with a diversified group of Commissioners appointed by the line Minister from the fields of law, finance and management, was a progressive measure, the independence of the TRC was compromised by the appointment of the Secretary to the Ministry as its ex officio Chairman.

Under the existing legislation, the line Minister can issue 'general or specific' directions with which the Commission must comply. Moreover, while the TRC can *recommend* the issuing of telecom licences to the Minister, he or she can reject these recommendations, with reasons, and give out licences at his or her discretion. In the area of tariff control, however, the TRC has more discretion – it has a mandate to determine tariffs *in consultation* with the Minister.

Public interest considerations outlined in the Act include protecting the interests of consumers with regard to telecom service charges, quality and variety, maintaining effective competition between operators, and promoting the rapid development of domestic and international telecom services. The Act only indicates the general public interest rationale for both price regulation and universal service obligations (USOs). Detailed methods of price regulation – price cap regulation– and the particulars of USOs are specified in network licences.

At the time of writing, SLT's licence specifies an RPI-X formula, where X is 2 per cent. There was a provision to suspend price cap regulation for a five-year tariff-rebalancing period between 1998 and 2002. The two fixed access wireless loop operators (WLLs) were also exempted from tariff regulation for a five-year period (until 2000), to give them time to develop their markets. All other operators in the industry are covered by price cap regulation, as per their licence agreements.

The WLLs have USO commitments built into their licences; each operator was required to have at least ten working telephones in each secondary switching area by the end of 2000, with an annual penalty of US$80,000 for failure to meet these targets. SLT, on the other hand, was exempt from formal service rollout obligations.

The TRC also has the power to *approve* interconnection charges when operators reach an agreement on the charges, and to *determine* such charges when operators are unable to reach an agreement. Attempts by the Commission in 1996 and in 1998 to assist the three fixed access operators to develop an interconnection regime, given their inability to reach a negotiated settlement, were not successful. The 1996 determination disadvantaged the WLLs, compelling the Commission to make a second determination in 1998. Although none of the three operators was satisfied with the 1998 arrangement, the WLLs complied with the regulatory directive, while SLT continued with the pre-1998 arrangement and challenged the TRC decision in court. Currently, there is an informal interconnection agreement between the three operators, which the Commission is attempting to build into the formal regulatory framework.

Although the Commission entertains complaints from the public and has the power to investigate and make determinations in disputes between customers and operators, it encourages the public first to attempt to resolve the problem with the operator. The TRC's role in disputes between operators rests on its powers to set and enforce licence conditions rather than on explicit powers to resolve disputes. TRC decisions can be directed to the Court of Appeal within 30 days of the decision being made public.

The liberalization of Sri Lanka's bus transport sector in 1977 and the entry of private sector operators into an industry that had been a stronghold of the state for decades, demonstrated the need for external regulation. A Department of Private Omnibus was set up for this purpose in 1983. This was later dissolved with the establishment of the NTC in 1991, following advice from the World Bank.

The mandate of the NTC, as set out in the legislation that governs it, includes regulating the quality and quantity of service, the provision of adequate services on socially necessary but unremunerative routes, ensuring healthy competition between operators, determining route permit fees and regulating subsidized transport (for instance school services). In practice, however, the NTC has functioned mainly as a route-permit-issuing entity and has been extremely ineffective in achieving its other objectives.

The potential for excessive ministerial interference is also rife, given that the line Minister appoints five members of the Commission, with the three ex officio members coming from the line Ministry, the Ministry of Policy Planning and the Ministry of Finance. Moreover, as was the case in the FTC, the Minister can remove any Commissioner without reason and with no provision for the removal to be challenged in court. The Minister also has the power to give 'general directions' to the NTC, as in the case of the TRC. Although the Commission has the power to cancel permits, licensees can appeal to the Minister.

Financial Sector Regulation

This section provides a brief overview of the legislation currently governing the securities market, the banking and insurance sectors and auditing and accounting standards in Sri Lanka. It should be noted, however, that plans are underway to establish a single financial regulator for the securities market, the insurance industry and accounting and auditing standards.

The Securities and Exchange Commission of Sri Lanka (SEC) was established under an Act of Parliament in 1987 to regulate the securities market and to provide licences to stock exchanges, stockbrokers and stock dealers. An amendment to the Act in 1991 also gave the SEC the power to license unit trusts, while a recent amendment in 2003 broadened the Commission's mandate to regulate market intermediaries such as underwriters, fund managers, and so on as well. Under the Company Take-Overs and Mergers Code of 1995, the SEC can also look into takeovers and mergers.

The Commission is made up of six members with experience in the fields of law, finance, business and administration appointed by the Minister of Finance, a Deputy Governor of the Central Bank nominated by the Governor of the Bank, and three ex officio members – the Deputy Secretary to the Treasury, the Registrar of Companies, and the President of the Institute of Chartered Accountants. This diversified structure of the Commission limits the powers of the Minister.

The Chairman and Director General (DG) of the SEC are appointed by the Minister of Finance from among the Commission members, and on the recommendation of the Commission, respectively. The DG heads a Secretariat that functions under the general direction of the Commission and is answerable to, and can be removed by, the Minister. While the Minister can only remove the DG on the recommendation of the Commission, Commissioners can be removed by the Minister.

The legal framework for Sri Lanka's banking sector is set out in an Act of

Parliament passed in 1988. This sets guidelines for the regulation of the banking sector and gives broad supervisory powers to the Monetary Board of the Central Bank of Sri Lanka. This Board is made up of the Governor of the Central Bank, the Secretary to the Ministry of Finance and Planning and a member appointed by the Minister of Finance and Planning. It is widely respected for its independence – in contrast to some of the other Commissions discussed earlier in this chapter. This perception of the Board is particularly relevant in the current context in Sri Lanka, where several attempts have been made by investors to purchase banking stocks to obtain a dominant position in the banking industry. As per the current legislation, an individual is not permitted to hold more than 10 per cent of the shares of a bank, while the corresponding maximum share for a company is 15 per cent.[3]

The Insurance Board of Sri Lanka (IBSL), established by way of legislation passed in 2000, regulates Sri Lanka's insurance sector. As in the case of the SEC, the diversified composition of the Board provides for a degree of independence from political intervention.

The Sri Lanka Accounting and Auditing Standards Monitoring Board (SLAASMB) was established under an Act of Parliament in 1995, to look into the accounting and auditing practices of 'specified business enterprises' (such as companies with a turnover in excess of Rs 500 million or with a staff in excess of 1000 employees). One of the principal differences between the SEC and the SLAASMB is that the former's jurisdiction is limited to quoted companies, while the latter has a broader ambit.

Institutional Structure

This section of the chapter completes the triad of policy, law and institutions that provides the foundation for competition, regulation and regulatory governance in Sri Lanka. Its principal focus is the issue of establishing institutions that promote and sustain effective competition, provide for investment to flow into the economy, and ensure that consumer interests are accommodated in the regulatory process.

What is required to build such institutions? Samarajiva (2002) argues that the most critical factor for competition and regulatory agencies to be effective is that they are independent of operators and of the government. Where government ownership is a factor to contend with, however, absolute independence is not possible. Moreover, independence should not be viewed as an exemption from accountability. As such, the issue is really one of achieving *workable independence*.

This section looks at formal methods of securing workable independence, such as procedures for appointment, removal and reporting (and the extent of direct political involvement in these processes) and the financial autonomy of competition and regulatory agencies. It also considers what Samarajiva (2002) characterizes as informal modes of independence – winning legitimacy through communicative processes with stakeholders – by looking at variables such as user participation and influence and commitment to the public interest.

Several aspects of the formal mechanisms for independence, such as the appointment, dismissal and reporting procedures in competition and regulatory agencies, were discussed in the preceding section of this chapter. Direct ministerial influence, provided for by the law, is a prominent feature in most of those agencies, although less so perhaps in the PUC and in the financial sector regulators. A pertinent question is the degree of independence that these agencies and their officials have from government (and from special interest groups) after appointment. Some useful indicators in this regard are the nature of the service contract for Commissioners (e.g. part time/full time appointees and the specified term of the contract), mechanisms for accountability (e.g. review by legislature, judicial review, regulatory impact assessment and consultative processes before reaching a decision) and financial autonomy.

As set out in the competition legislation, the CAA is to consist of a Chair and not less than ten other members, all appointed by the Minister, with the Chair and three of the members selected by the Minister to serve as full-time members for a period of three years. As mentioned above, the Minister has the power to intervene in the decision-making procedures of the FTC, particularly with regard to price control issues.

As is the case in other public institutions, the Commission is subject to financial scrutiny by public audit bodies, under Article 154 of the Constitution. It is also, similar to most other public agencies, subject to judicial review and to legislative review, though the latter is not a very effective process given the political dynamics of policy-making outlined earlier in this chapter. The judicial process does allow for more independence and autonomy, but the long delays in Sri Lanka's courts and the fact that most judges lack the expertise required to tackle regulatory issues, undermines its usefulness as an instrument for accountability.

As mentioned earlier, the FTC, the competition authority that preceded the CAA, was not considered to be a very effective entity and lacked legitimacy in the eyes of its stakeholders. Perhaps one of the most significant contributing factors was a severe resource constraint. The Commission required Treasury approval for all expenses as funds were allocated by Parliament. The authority was one of the most poorly funded public bodies with an average annual budget of around 0.00363 per cent of the total government budget, and with staff salaries less than those paid by other public sector institutions. As a result, there was an acute shortage of skilled persons in the FTA, with only around 13 of the 27 positions being filled over the last few years. Although the

FTC had the powers of a District Court to investigate monopolies, mergers and anticompetitive practices *sui moto,* there were very few investigations initiated given the capacity constraints. A positive development in the new legislation is the attempt to expand the fund of the new authority by securing independent sources of finance through the sale of forfeited goods, retention of a third of every fine collected, and grants and donations.

Under the current structure of the TRC the Director General is the only full-time member. As mentioned earlier, the power of the Minister to intervene in the workings of the Commission continues even after the appointment of members. This is so because the Chair is the Secretary to the Ministry and the Minister can issue 'general or specific' directions at any time.

The TRC however, has a relatively better record than the FTC in terms of consultative procedures in decision-making, particularly in the 1998/1999 period under the leadership of a proactive Director General. The TRC also has greater financial autonomy when compared to the FTC, given that it does not receive any government monies. Its financing comes mostly from licence fees. In addition, salary scales are also higher than those in the public sector, enabling the TRC to recruit qualified and skilled staff.

Turning to the institutional structure of the SEC, this allows for considerably more autonomy than exists for both the FTC and the TRC, given the appointment procedure. Also, specific measures of accountability are built into reporting, with the Director responsible to both the Commission and the Minister, the Minister monitoring Commission members, and the Commission monitoring the staff. Like the TRC, the SEC is not dependent on state monies and finances itself through a tax collected from brokering costs and from market transactions. Also, it pays salaries that are close to private sector levels. As a result, it has been able to maintain a staff of about 50 employees in six divisions.

The PUC Bill also contains significant improvements with regard to independence, such as the involvement of the CC in appointments, staggered terms and conflict of interest rules. In addition, all members of the PUC are to serve on a part-time basis.

While the formal modes of ensuring independence in the regulatory process outlined here are important, particularly when bad governance is ubiquitous, winning and sustaining legitimacy in the eyes of stakeholders is vital for the survival of competition and regulation agencies. How successful have these agencies been in this regard in the Sri Lankan context? Clearly, the FTC was not able to build an image for itself as a credible entity free from political capture with the ability to take on a proactive role in regulating competition – it was often referred to as a watchdog with 'teeth that cannot bite'. The TRC, by contrast, went through a short period – 1998/1999 – when it was considered to be an example of regulatory best practice by several countries in the region. This was also the period when user participation was actively encouraged through public hearings and consumer consultations, and public interest considerations were manifested in the decisions of the Commission – a case in point being the decision to introduce special tariff schemes partially to shield low and medium users from tariff increases in the first two years of rate rebalancing. Since then, however, most stakeholders have not considered the TRC a legitimate entity. The appointment of an ex-employee of the incumbent operator as Director General contributed to this loss of credibility, underlining that leadership – somewhat of an 'intangible' commodity – plays a key role in regulatory agencies in winning legitimacy.

Political, Social and External Influences

In general, consumer and user groups have had very little influence on the competition and regulatory process in Sri Lanka. They have had a minimal opportunity to participate in and contribute towards the development of policies, laws and institutions that, in the final instance, have a tremendous impact on their welfare. Perhaps the most significant factor explaining the lack of consumer involvement in the process is that there are no active consumer organizations in the country. Given the absence of a bottom-up consumer/user network, the involvement of such groups in the competition and regulatory process has largely been at the initiative of the regulatory agencies.

The absence of active consumer groups to counter other interest groups, particularly those representing the chambers of commerce, which are a very powerful lobby group in Sri Lanka, was felt very strongly when the new competition Bill was being drafted. Provisions including the rights of consumers were rejected and the chambers of commerce were successful in opposing the payment of a registration fee from companies to secure non-government funds to finance the competition authority. The strong role of business interests in the regulatory process is also reflected in the TRC's inclination in its regulatory decisions to support the incumbent operator, SLT.

Trade unions have had more of an impact on reforms such as the privatization process than on regulatory reforms. Not surprisingly, labour groups have not been very supportive of privatization, given the job security in state-owned enterprises and the perception, cultivated over the years of government intervention in the economy, of a benefactor state. The presence of vociferous trade unions with strong bargaining power and the ability to create industrial unrest has prompted the government to introduce several measures, such as Employee Share Ownership Plans (ESOPs) and retrenchment packages, to placate workers, very often at high financial cost to the state.

International organizations and external agencies have had an impact on the competition and regulation process primarily through technical and financial assistance channels. For instance, the World Bank is currently helping the Sri Lankan government to develop a consolidated strategy for infrastructure regulation and the SEC was created with the assistance of the US Agency for International Development (USAID). However, contrary to the claims of groups opposed to the involvement of these external agencies in domestic affairs, the influence of international donor agencies has not been exceptional and has certainly not exceeded that of domestic political interest groups. It might even be the case that Sri Lanka requires more external pressure to counter the negative influence of these political interest groups and to achieve a more effective competition and regulatory policy regime.

CONCLUSION

The main conclusions that emerge from this analysis of competition, regulation and regulatory governance in Sri Lanka are that regulatory failure, stemming from systemic weaknesses in policy formulation and implementation and in the institutional and legal structures governing competition and regulation, is rampant, and opportunities for political capture are abundant. In essence, the underlying message is that government in Sri Lanka does not work well.

This raises the conundrum of how to build effective competition and regulatory structures and to create the conditions for good regulatory governance in a milieu where bad governance is omnipresent. Given the apparently extensive government failures in the system, should the competition and regulation reform process rely on more of a 'market approach' to the delivery of public interest? For instance, would light-handed regulation, fewer and simpler regulatory rules, and so on have a more beneficial impact on consumer and producer welfare? Can such an approach actually guarantee insulation from political influence, given that vested interests with political connections are not confined to the state sector alone? What impact will such an approach have on equitable growth and poverty alleviation? Clearly, there are no simple answers to these questions. Addressing gaps in our understanding of the dynamics of competition and the regulatory process in Sri Lanka should be the principal focus of future research.

NOTES

1. While such a situation may have a beneficial impact on policy-making in countries with good governance practices, it tends to have the opposite effect in Sri Lanka.
2. The privatization contract specified that Shell would be given a five-year monopoly in the LPG business.

3. The Monetary Board has the authority, in exceptional situations, to authorize holdings in excess of these limits on grounds of national interest.

BIBLIOGRAPHY

Central Bank of Sri Lanka (various years), *Annual Report*, Colombo, Central Bank of Sri Lanka.

Cook, P. (2002), 'Competition and its regulation: key issues', Working Paper No. 2, Manchester: Centre on Regulation and Competition.

Consumer Unity & Trust Society (2002), *Towards a New Competition Law in Sri Lanka*, Jaipur: CUTS.

Fair Trading Commission (various years), *Annual Report*, Colombo: Fair Trading Commission.

Jayasuriya, S. and Knight-John, M. (2002), 'Sri Lanka's telecommunications industry: from privatization to anti-competition?', Working Paper No. 14, Manchester: Centre on Regulation and Competition.

Kelegama, S. and Cassie Chetty, Y. (1993), *Consumer Protection and Fair Trading in Sri Lanka*, Colombo: Law & Society Trust.

Kirkpatrick, C. (2001), 'Regulatory impact assessment in developing countries: research issues', Working Paper No. 5, Manchester: Centre on Regulation and Competition.

Knight-John, M. (forthcoming a), 'Distributional impact of privatization: the Sri Lankan experience', in J. Nellis and N. Birdsall (eds) *Distributional Impact of Privatization*, Washington, DC: Centre for Global Development.

Knight-John, M. (forthcoming b), *A Preliminary Impact Assessment of the Glaxo Wellcome-SmithKline Beecham International Merger on the Respiratory Segment of Sri Lanka's Pharmaceutical Market*, Colombo: Institute of Policy Studies and Law & Society Trust.

Minogue, M. (2001), 'Governance-based analysis of regulation', Working Paper No. 3, Manchester: Centre on Regulation and Competition.

Ogus, A. (2001), 'Regulatory institutions and structures', Working Paper No. 4, Manchester: Centre on Regulation and Competition.

Parker, D. (2001), 'Economic regulation: a preliminary literature review and summary of research questions arising', Working Paper No. 6, Manchester: Centre on Regulation and Competition.

Samarajiva, R. (2002), 'Utility regulation and competition policy in Sri Lanka: prospects for change', in M. Knight-John (ed.) *Competition Policy and Utility Regulation: The Sri Lankan Experience*, Colombo: Law & Society Trust.

Sri Lanka (1987), *Fair Trading Commission Act No. 1 of 1987*, Colombo, Government Publications Bureau.

Sri Lanka (1987), *Securities Council Act No. 36 of 1987*, Colombo: Government Publications Bureau.

Sri Lanka (1988), *Banking Act No. 30 of 1988*, Colombo: Government Publications Bureau.

Sri Lanka (1991), *National Transport Commission Act No. 37 of 1991*, Colombo: Government Publications Bureau.

Sri Lanka (1991), *Sri Lanka Telecommunications Act No. 25 of 1991 as amended by Sri Lanka Telecommunications (Amendment) Act No. 27 of 1996*, Colombo: Government Publicity Bureau.

Sri Lanka (2002), *Consumer Affairs Authority: A Bill*, Colombo: Government Publications Bureau.

Sri Lanka (2002), *Public Utilities Commission of Sri Lanka: A Bill*, Colombo: Government Publications Bureau.

Wanasinghe, S. (2001), 'The implications of the changing role of governance in Sri Lanka', *Research Studies: Governance Series No. 7*, Colombo: Institute of Policy Studies.

Wickramaratne Rupesinghe, P. (2002), 'Competition law in Sri Lanka' in M. Knight-John (ed.) *Competition Policy and Utility Regulation: The Sri Lankan Experience*, Colombo: Law & Society Trust.

World Bank (2002), *World Development Report 2002: Building Institutions for Markets*, Washington, DC: World Bank.

15. The institutional and policy framework for regulation and competition in Ghana

Ernest Aryeetey

INTRODUCTION

The reforms that Ghana has undertaken in the last two decades are basically for the development of a stronger market economy. These have not only changed the nature of government economic policies, but have incorporated into them the design of regulation and institutional strengthening at all stages. The introduction of more effective regulation is premised on the idea that as the public sector withdraws from the direct production of goods and services, the revitalized private sector will require some regulation to ensure that it functions in the interest of the wider public. There are new regulatory arrangements in many of the major areas where new economic agents have taken over activities previously carried out by the public sector. But beyond that, areas that were hitherto unregulated have also come in for some regulation. This is, first, a consequence of government being required to do so under the new governance arrangements, particularly the constitution, and second, a consequence of greater demand by donors, as increasing use is made of aid for those activities.

Some of the prominent new areas for regulation following restructuring are the water, electricity and telecommunications sectors. Similarly, new regulatory arrangements have been instituted for the financial sector following major reforms. In the area of production, government has pulled back extensively from direct involvement in the manufacturing and agricultural sectors and has sought to encourage more extensive private sector participation, at both the small-scale and large-scale ends of the market. The expanded role of the private sector in the management of forest resources has led to an expansion of the capacity of the regulatory infrastructure for the forests, taking into account the environmental considerations that need to be made at the same time as rapid economic growth is expected. The form that regulation for enterprise development takes is far less clear-cut and its objectives appear to be less appreciated. But, besides the utilities, this is where considerable interest for many consumers and producers lies.

THE LEGAL FRAMEWORK FOR REGULATION IN GHANA

The new interest in the freedoms of economic agents has influenced considerably choices made in fashioning the current system of governance. The need for institutions to be created with oversight responsibilities for the actions of economic agents, and independent of the central arms of government has been a major facet of the new legal framework. The evolution of the current constitutional system and how it is used to ensure accountability in the markets, is discussed next.

The Evolution of the Constitutional System and Economic Reforms

Ironically, Ghana began its economic reforms in 1983 under an authoritarian regime that had been put in place by the military. In that regime, the issues of distribution were considered more important than production and growth. The leaders believed that the poor economic situation was a simple outcome of corruption that was related to incompetence; once the issues of equity were resolved through the institution of sanctions for wrong-doing the situation could be resolved.

As the control regime failed to work, the need for economic reform became even more urgent. Working together with the World Bank and the IMF led to the liberal policies that have characterized the economy since. The increased flow of resources in the mid-1980s that accompanied the new policies led to an expansion of the economy. With the increased level of economic activity and associated economic independence for various agents, the sense of empowerment that evolved was one that appeared incompatible with the authoritarian political structures. Economic liberalization and diversification were perceived to be increasingly incompatible with autocratic rule. As private investment continued to elude Ghana's quest for development, various explanations continued to attach importance to the uncertainty involved in dealing with a government that could not guarantee individual freedoms (Aryeetey 1994). There were many that questioned the legitimacy of the reform process in the absence of political legitimacy (Ninsin 1991). There were other pressures on government to search for a more inclusive arrangement for development, particularly as it had committed itself earlier to a decentralized form of government. Coupled with this was the pressure that came in the wake of the collapse of the Soviet Union and the eastern bloc for political reforms that would lead to democratic governance (Afari-Gyan 1995).

The current constitution of Ghana is often described as a mixture of the American and French constitutions, with a smattering of principles enshrined in the British style of government. It provides for a unitary state in which the executive, the unicameral legislature and the judiciary share the powers of government. The constitution sets up several institutions and offices and guarantees their independence from central government. They are made distinct from government departments that are associated with particular organs of government under the control of the executive. An example is the Electoral Commission. Indeed, the development of a system of checks and balances underlies the principles of the constitution.

The constitution seeks to guide the government of Ghana on how it should govern. This is what drives the inclusion of 'directive principles of state policy' to guide governments. These principles basically indicate what the state's development obligations towards the people are, within the resource constraints of the country. They provide for political objectives, including the promotion of democracy and the avoidance of abuse of power and corruption; economic objectives that suggest a need for equity in the use of national resources; social objectives that seek to guarantee freedom, justice, probity and accountability; educational objectives that seek to guarantee all Ghanaians free education at all levels; and cultural objectives that seek to promote customary and cultural values that are judged useful for a developing society. The directive principles serve only as a guide and are therefore not legally enforceable.

Legal Forms for Governing Regulation

One area the constitution is particular about is the issue of equal access to natural resources. It requires the creation of regulatory bodies that would focus on judicious use and equity. An example is the requirement for a Lands Commission and a Minerals Commission, and their empowerment to deal with the relevant sectoral issues. The constitution provides for parliament to make laws by passing bills that seek to direct general courses of action in a manner not adequately dealt with by existing law.

The laws for creating regulatory agencies are quite similar in structure, with a little variation in content to suit the relevant sector. The law that set up the Public Utilities Regulatory Commission (PURC), Act 538, is presented in five parts. The first part deals with the establishment and functions of a Public Utilities Regulatory Commission. The second is devoted to 'provision of service and rates' for public utilities. Complaints and enforcement of the decisions of the commission are provided for in part three. Part four makes administration and financial provisions for the commission, while the final part (five) defines what constitute offences and the penalties for them under that Act, as well as other miscellaneous provisions. The Act setting up the Energy Commission is structured only a little differently.

Act 490 (1994), which set up the Environmental Protection Agency, makes provision for the establishment of the institution, enforcement and control, the national environment fund and finally for the administration and financial matters of the agency. Similarly the Bank of Ghana Act provides for its role as a regulator of the banking industry, as indeed does the law on the setting up of the Ghana Investment Promotion Centre that requires the Centre to help develop a sound investment climate for Ghana.

But by far the most significant attempt to protect consumers of goods and services with a law is planned under the draft 'Protection Against Unfair Competition Act, 2000' (Act 589) to be administered by the Minister for Justice. The draft law seeks to stop the 'causing of confusion with respect to another's enterprise or its activities', among other things. It also has clauses dealing with:

- damaging another person's goodwill or reputation;
- misleading the public;
- discrediting another person's enterprise or its activities;
- unfair competition in respect of secret information; and
- unfair competition in respect of national and international obligations.

The Minister of Justice is authorized to cause the issue of legislative instruments for the purpose of developing regulations aimed at protecting the public, as consumers and also as producers of goods and services, from unfair competition.

The main approach to developing instruments for regulation is the enactment of legislative instruments. For example, Act 568 gives the PURC the power to make regulations that are necessary for the implementation of its mandate. Two such regulations are the Public Utilities (Termination of Service) Regulations 1999, LI 1651, that set out the circumstances in which utility service to consumers may be terminated, and the Public Utilities (Complaints Procedure) Regulations 1999, LI 1665, specifying the procedures by which any person (utility or consumer) may lodge a complaint with the Commission.

Legal Mechanisms of Implementation, Arbitration and Enforcement

The various acts for regulation provide for specific means to be applied in implementing the regulations. The regulation on public utilities is probably the most illustrative of how the legal mechanisms work. Typically, the act enjoins the utility provider to:

- Maintain its equipment and property used in the provision of the service in such condition as to enable it to effectively provide the service;
- Make such reasonable effort as may be necessary to provide to the public service that is safe, adequate, efficient, reasonable and non-discriminatory; and
- Make such repairs, changes, extensions and improvements in or to the service as may be necessary or proper for the efficient delivery of the service to the consumer.

After requiring providers to achieve the above outcomes, the PURC is then empowered as follows:

> Where the Commission discovers on its own or upon a complaint that the service provided by a public utility is not in accordance [with the above requirement], the Commission shall in writing direct the provision of the adequate or reasonable service that should be provided by the public utility and may include such other directions as to secure compliance with [the requirements above].

The act on public utilities empowers the regulatory body to seek compensation for a consumer if necessary, pressure the utility to employ technology that improves service delivery and/or reduces cost for the consumer over a reasonable time period. The PURC is required to monitor standards of performance by public utilities. The act further requires that whenever a public utility enters into an agreement with any body corporate the agreement be complied with as entered into. There are also provisions on refusal to provide service which do not permit any public utility to refuse to serve any body except with the permission of the Commission, guidelines for fixing rates and demanding payments with the approval only of the Commission, cost of production, and so on. Public utilities are required to publish all rates charged. The regulatory body is required to put in place a procedure for the lodging of complaints by the public and also to investigate all of these except where it is of the opinion that the complaint 'is trivial, frivolous, vexatious or not made in good faith'.

Enforcement of decisions of the regulatory bodies may be done through the courts. Considering the over-burdened nature of the judicial system, however, the time dimension for the legal enforcement of such decisions is crucial.

A number of complaints have come before the PURC since it began work in 1997, most of which are related to billing, tariff increases and quality of service in that order. The Commission received 184 complaints in 1999 and 186 in 2000. It was able to resolve 180 of these in both years. The remaining cases are still pending and have not yet been sent to the courts for determination.

An explanation for the absence of a 'hard-nosed' approach to regulation of public utilities is the fact that the regulatory body considers itself to be still developing the standards that have to be applied by the utilities in their dealings with consumers. With the standards not fully in place, the strategy is to reduce arbitrariness in enforcement. The same applies to the Energy Commission and the Environmental Protection Agency.

Significant Legal Cases or Determinations

One interesting case in which the legal system is used by a consumer to assert his rights and enforce a contract to deliver a service has been the case of *Hasnem Enterprises Ltd* (Plaintiff) *vs. Electricity Corporation of Ghana* (Defendant). The case started before a regulatory body was put in place for the utilities. In the original case, the plaintiff sued the defendant for negligence resulting in damage to equipment used at the premises of the plaintiff for business in 1981. This was after a break in an underground cable belonging to the defendant and delivering electricity to the premises of the plaintiff caused damage to the plaintiff's equipment. The break occurred outside the premises of the plaintiff. The High Court threw out the case. The judge found that the plaintiff had not established a case of negligence against the defendant despite the application of the notion that negligence did not have to be proven so long as it could be reasonably established that the absence of action on its part on property belonging to the defendant was the cause of the damage to the plaintiff's equipment. On appeal at a higher court in 1996, the decision of the lower court was upheld. The plaintiff continued with a further appeal to the Supreme Court, which decided in his favour in January 1998, overturning the decisions of the two lower courts.

The most interesting aspect of the Supreme Court decision is the way it has been perceived to open the way for holding utility companies and other service organizations liable for negligence leading to loss of income. The Court ruled that the defendant knew from evidence available that there were technical problems with the power supply in the area that the plaintiff operated from, but failed to take corrective action. The defendant also knew what the possible consequences of such problems could be for users and yet took no action. It therefore found the defendant liable for damages and ordered payment.

From a different perspective, another interesting case, supposedly for the protection of the consumer, arises from the legal suit between Accra Brewery Ltd and Guinness Ghana Ltd. This was an application brought by the plaintiff (Accra Brewery Ltd) seeking an order of interim injunction to restrain the defendant (Guinness Ghana Ltd) from entering into or in any other way enforcing an agreement entitled 'Guinness means profit' with outlet owners of the plaintiff.[1] In the supporting affidavit, the plaintiff claimed that it produced products which competed with the product of the defendant. The plaintiff contended that the defendant had entered into an agreement with a number of their common retailers through a monetary inducement, which obliged them to stock only the defendant's products and to put up only advertisements from the defendant. They argued that, as a result of the agreement, the retailers refused to stock the plaintiff's products and had refused to sell these products. The plaintiff further argued that the defendant's actions were unlawful by inducing their mutual customers to break their contracts with the plaintiff. It was further argued by the plaintiff that

> the conduct of defendant [was] preventing the Ghanaian public from exercising its freedom to choose any alcoholic or non-alcoholic beverages in drinking bars or other authorized places where plaintiff's and defendant's products [were] sold.

A further argument by the plaintiff was that

> the defendant's act of inducement contravene[d] the tenets of social and economic liberty and prosperity, particularly the liberty of the individual to trade with whom he pleases and the prosperity of the nation by the expansion of the total volume of trade.

The plaintiff contended that he had lost substantial income as a consequence of the activity of the defendant.

In this case the judge ruled against the plaintiff, arguing that there was no indication of the defendant seeking to create a monopoly. He said there was no evidence that the defendant by his action was seeking to prevent customers from buying a similar product more cheaply from elsewhere. This was so since the products had the same sale price, which was determined by agreement between the producers, and that consumers were free to choose which outlets they would buy from. He also contended that there was no evidence that the defendant's market share had risen as a consequence of the agreement. With respect to the public interest issues, the judged ruled that there was no evidence that the public interest was likely to suffer as a result of the agreement between the defendant and selected retailers since consumers still had a choice.

This second case came up shortly before the law on 'protection against unfair competition' (Act 589) was drafted, and it was obviously influenced by the case. While the draft law on unfair competition is quite specific on the grounds under which such unfair competition may occur, it also has the umbrella clause that 'any act or practice in the course of industrial or commercial activities that is contrary to honest practices constitutes an act of unfair competition'. It is certainly not clear how a judge would determine what constitutes or does not constitute honest practice in this instance.

It is remarkable that despite the new constitutional and democratic arrangements strengthening the hand of consumers and other economic agents enormously, the number of suits or legal cases brought up in relation to consumer rights and unfair competition remains insignificant.[2] This may be attributed to a number of factors including a general apathy in relation to legal matters. Another possible explanation is the fact that the financial costs of litigation tend to be beyond the means of most economic agents, who tend to seek informal solutions to their grievances.

Methods for Price Regulation

Issues of regulation and competition for many of the new regulatory bodies tend to focus much less on profits and prices than on other aspects of public interest. The Public Utilities Regulatory Commission (PURC) and the National Communications Authority (NCA) are however, directly involved in setting prices. The PURC is required to file a proposal at least 60 days prior to the commencement of a new service or the effective date of new tariffs. These proposals have to be published widely in the media. The Commission is enjoined to take reactions to these proposals in written form or from representations made at public hearings for tariff review considerations. After the Commission arrives at decisions following consultations with providers and consumers in this manner, these are published in the *Gazette*. The law requires that in negotiating tariffs, the PURC take into account:

- consumer interest;
- investor interest;
- the cost of production of the service;
- assurance of the financial integrity of the public utility;
- economic development of the country;
- best use of natural resources;
- uniformity of prices throughout the country;
- competition among utility companies.

These are fairly standard requirements in utility pricing worldwide. In particular the Commission must determine whether costs provided by public utility providers are justified. In pursuit of this, the PURC prepared guidelines for setting electricity tariffs in 1998 and in 2002, applying a price cap regulation approach. The PURC has determined that the following considerations are important in arriving at rates:

1. Fair apportionment of total cost of supply to various classes of consumers and provision of a certain minimum level of service at an 'affordable' price to residential customers who may not be able to pay the full cost;
2. Appropriate rate of return on investments to satisfy the interests of investors in the national interconnected system;
3. Setting of a bulk supply tariff to ensure that distribution facilities procure at least cost from wholesale power suppliers, electricity for distribution and retail to regulated customers;
4. Setting of transmission service charge to ensure economically efficient, reliable and secure operation of the transmission system by the electricity transmission utility;
5. Setting of distribution service charge to ensure economically efficient, reliable and secure operation of the distribution system by distribution utilities;
6. Provision of adequate revenue to ensure financial viability of the power utilities;
7. Allowance for 'special rates' for priority consumers whose activities may enhance economic development.

The PURC has also worked out charges for the utility buying power wholesale from the Volta River Authority (VRA), and distribution service charges to be paid by consumers. For the purpose of computing the bulk generation charge, it is indicated that a two-component tariff shall represent the price of capacity and energy that distribution utilities purchase from the spot market as follows.

1. A capacity charge that shall be set at a value equal to the investment annuity plus the fixed operating and maintenance costs for developing a single cycle gas turbine for peaking capacity required in the national interconnected system; and
2. An energy charge derived from the expected short-run marginal costs of supplying energy in the national interconnected system, based on a 12-month forward simulation economic merit order dispatch of all generation facilities in the national interconnected system.

Each year VRA shall compute for the PURC a levelized energy charge that shall apply to electricity purchases from the spot market. The levelized energy charge will be adjusted in June and December each year, taking into account annual hydrology of the reservoir for VRA's hydroelectricity facility at Akosombo. To this is added the transmission charges and the distribution charges. The distribution service charge consists of standard distribution losses of power and energy, standard investment, maintenance and operation costs, and costs associated with the user, independent from his or her demand for power and energy. The annual average inflation (CPI), a productivity factor (G) set by PURC, a quality of service penalty/reward (QSP) set by PURC and a cost of capital adjustment factor (CCAF) set by PURC are also factored in. Thus the distribution service charge (DSC) is derived as

$$\text{DSC} = \frac{\text{Annuity} * (1 + \text{CCAF}) + \text{O\&M}*(1 + \text{CPI} - \text{G}) + \text{QSP}}{\text{Distribution System Max Demand}}$$

The total expenses of a utility company are distributed between different user categories on the basis of the actual costs incurred by the distribution company in providing the service, and the distribution service expenses are allocated to each class of customers as energy or demand related costs on the basis of their contribution to coincident peak demand.

In the case of water, the PURC uses a modified approach but with the same principles. In this case, the tariff will be structured taking into account projections of sales volumes, the number of customers in each tariff class, and PURC expectations of the overall efficiency of water delivered to water supplied. PURC will also take into account the Government of Ghana water sector policy in balancing tariffs between different classes of customers.

Due to difficulties in determining acceptable and practical operating standards in prevailing institutional and environmental circumstances, rates are set largely as an outcome of an iterative process that takes into account material on costs provided by the utilities with very limited independent assessment of these by the PURC.

Other Legal Requirements Relating to Quality of Service

The law requires various regulatory bodies to make clear what the environment for producing and delivering the output should be. For example, Act 541 requires the Energy Commission to work together with the PURC to develop standards of performance for the supply, distribution and sale of electricity or natural gas to customers by licensed public utilities. The standards include voltage stability, maximum number of scheduled and unscheduled outages, number and duration of load shedding periods, and metering. The law provides for the payment of compensation where the utility fails to satisfy standards set by the regulatory body.

However, as earlier indicated, the regulatory bodies may find it difficult to specify the maximum number of power outages when it is obvious that the capital required by the electricity utility for improving its service has not been made available as the sector undergoes restructuring in the hope of privatization.

INSTITUTIONAL FRAMEWORK

It may be argued that regulation is intended to provide equal opportunities for businesses as they engage in their lawful economic activities, producing goods and services for the public. But there is also the perception that regulation has sometimes been used as an instrument for ensuring that specific powerful groups are able to protect themselves and their economic interests. There are certainly elements of both in the way regulation institutions have grown with time.

The Evolution of Regulation and Competition Institutions in Ghana

The earliest cases of regulation may be linked to the colonial government's early attempts to regulate the influx of mining capital in what was then the Gold Coast. Bentsi-Enchill (1986) has documented extensively the rapid growth of mining activity involving both indigenous miners and foreign mining concerns in the latter part of the nineteenth century. As the mining companies entered into contractual agreements with local chiefs for land concessions, this often alienated local interest in terms of usage rights. The initial opposition of the colonial government to the rapid growth of concessions to mining companies soon gave way to active support for it. The terms of concessions were such that they literally gave away the land for very little to the concessionaires. Soon Ghanaian small miners began to enter the concessions granted by chiefs to the foreign companies, usually in areas not yet mined by the mining companies. Sometimes this was with the approval of the mining company for a fee or for a share of the produce. At other times this was considered an interference with legal contracts. The growing confusion surrounding how such concessions were issued and managed by chiefs finally led the colonial government to issue the 1900 Concessions Ordinance. This Ordinance made it clear that no byelaws made under the Native Jurisdiction Ordinance could interfere with the terms of a validated concession. What many analysts see was an attempt to bring some discipline into the mining and land industry by the colonial government, but more an attempt to protect foreign capital that was using its influence to alienate local people from their natural resources. Indeed, the different mining regulations that have come into being since the colonial days have largely been perceived as an attempt to protect large foreign interests against small indigenous interests and not necessarily for fostering competition (Bentsi-Enchill 1986).

In post-colonial Ghana, the regulation of the financial market by the central bank was institutionalized early with its creation in 1958. But here, regulation was used as an instrument to protect local interests against perceived foreign exploitation through the segmentation of the market and the reservation of different parts for different user groups (Aryeetey et al. 1992). This is what led to the creation of different development banks for different sectors by the government.

But regulation in other markets has been far less clear and often only implied in the functions of institutions that supervise other public sector organizations. Thus, for example, while there have been different departments that have been responsible for the production and delivery of water to consumers since 1928, there was never an institution assigned the specific role of regulating the water sector until 1997.

Institutional System Governing Regulation and Competition Issues

Aside from the statutory bodies created recently, the constitution also makes provision for a decentralized local government system, which requires that all public departments operating in any administrative district report to the representative District Assembly. Thus each of the decentralized public service departments is responsible to both a national ministry and the local government structure. The essence of decentralization is basically to allow for representatives of users of the services to have an input into how such publicly provided services are derived. The District Assembly system has thus become the main rallying point for consumer input into public service delivery, particularly in rural communities (see Figure 15.1).

There are public services that are not necessarily provided by any single department, but which have become community issues. One such is the provision of rural water and sanitation. There is a Community Water and Sanitation Agency responsible for assisting and coordinating the provision of water and sanitation services in rural communities using community management approaches. So while district assemblies assume part of the financial responsibility for the provision of water in towns and villages, with the communities also sharing in that responsibility, the agency provides technical support for the development and installation of rural water systems. The agency reports to the Ministry of Works and Housing and liaises with the local government bodies.

Autonomy of Regulatory Bodies

Most of the independent regulatory commissions set up in the last decade have a responsibility to 'advise the Minister [responsible for the sector] on policy formulation and development strategies for the [sector or industry]'. They are usually required to take from a minister 'such directions of a general character as appear to him to be required in the public interest relating to the discharge of the functions of the [regulatory body]'. It is not obvious what 'directions of a general character' may mean in some instances and this could

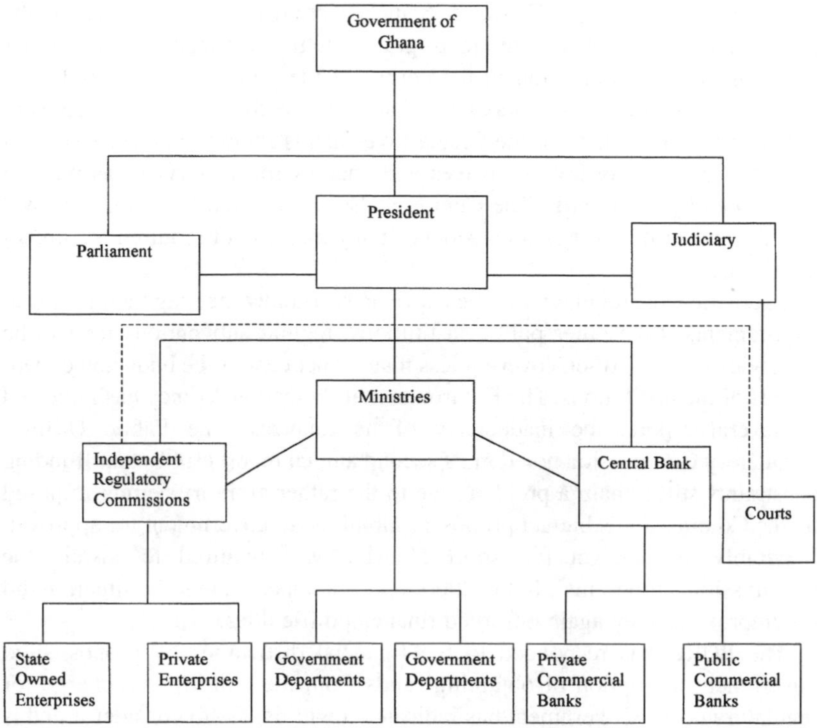

Figure 15.1 Institutional arrangements for regulation

therefore be subject to abuse, but the commissions have access to parliament and can seek protection from such abuse through other guarantees embedded in the constitution.

For the Public Utilities Regulatory Commission, however, the law states that, 'subject to the provisions of this Act, the Commission shall not be subject to the direction or control of any person or authority in the performance of its functions'. The reasoning behind this provision is to protect the consumer from utilities that are still largely owned by the state in the fixing of price caps and the setting of standards. The most important checks on the authority of this commission are the appointment of its board and management by the President and its financing from funds approved by Parliament.

Financing and Staffing of Regulatory Bodies

Regulatory bodies are generally funded through annual government budgetary allocations. For the PURC, Act 538 makes provision for it to add to the government subvention through loans granted to the Commission, any monies accruing to the Commission in the course of the performance of its lawful functions, and grants. The legal provisions made for funding indeed vary considerably as the law for the Ghana Investments Promotion Centre suggest that the Centre 'may levy such fees and charges for its services as may be determined by the Board'. The Centre is also empowered 'with the approval of the Board (to) invest as it considers fit any monies not required for immediate use'.

In practice, the regulatory bodies have had difficulty meeting their financial requirements. Like other public institutions, regular subventions tend to be largely inadequate, often covering less than 70 per cent of the budgeted expenditures of the institutions. The Environmental Protection Agency has indicated in several reports the inadequacy of its finances. The Public Utilities Regulatory Commission noted in its second annual report (1999) that 'funding constraints still remain a problem due to the rather arbitrary ceiling imposed on the Commission's budget proposals submitted to government for approval. Inevitably, the budget fell short of what was required to sustain the Commission's programs'. In the 2000 report, it appeared that the situation did not improve as they again observed financial difficulties.

The PURC has responded to the financial difficulties by proposing to government the option of obtaining funds from the utilities as a charge for regulatory costs. Government has indicated a willingness to consider it and is currently discussing the proposal with the utility companies who appear to have no difficulty with it. The idea of having a fee for regulation is seen by PURC as a major step in securing its financial independence.

The governing bodies of the regulatory organizations are free to hire and fire personnel of the institutions with the exception of the chief executives who are appointed by the President. For many of them, the financial difficulties that they face imply that their ability to hire staff for their various functions is constrained.

Codes, Guidelines on Public Interest

The main tool for giving effect to the regulatory functions of agencies is the power of the agencies to cause legislative instruments to be drawn up, either through a ministry or on their own authority. The main source of inducement to officials of the regulatory bodies to respond to public interest considerations comes, however, from the growing public awareness of the obligations of public institutions and other service deliverers. In the liberal environment, Ghanaians have once again found 'their voices' and have begun to articulate quite loudly their views and expectations of all manner of public institutions.

With the growth of mass media, duly reflected in the number of private newspapers and radio stations, public views on most issues of interest to consumers are loudly expressed. There is indeed hardly a day when no one calls a radio station to express dissatisfaction with water services, power services, telecommunications, roads, health, education, and so on in specific areas, often urban.

Forms of Accountability

All regulatory bodies are accountable to parliament, which may summon any regulatory body to explain any regulation and its enforcement at any time. This has been increasingly so in the cases of water, electricity and telecommunications. The authority of parliament is amply reflected by the procedure for issuing regulations. The PURC, for example, goes through the following steps to issue new regulations. It first prepares an initial draft of the regulation and sends it to the Attorney General's office for legal drafting. On consideration of the draft by the Commission, this is presented to parliament's select committee of subsidiary legislation. Unless parliament rejects the draft within 21 days, the regulation becomes effective.

POLICY SETTING

Policies for regulation have evolved over the years as a consequence of specific interest groups championing change in the way business is conducted; but these are not necessarily consumers. Early regulation policies were intended to strengthen the state's position in the economy, while later policies are largely intended to ensure that in the aftermath of the withdrawal of the state no one group dominates the scene. But it is not at all clear how far the state can retreat into a smaller area in specific sectors.

Regulation and Competition Strategies

A feature of the reforms of the last two decades has been the attempt to promote the 'private sector as the engine of growth'. Since the last elections, the slogan has been changed to achieving the 'golden age of business'. Essentially, emphasis has been placed on developing an appropriate enabling environment to foster the expansion of the private sector. Decentralization and privatization have been key strategies to foster competition and the efficient use of public resources.

The issue of public–private partnerships in the delivery of goods and services has been given attention in official pronouncements. It was stated in the second medium-term policy document of the last government that public–private partnerships will underscore most of their development initiatives. There have been a number of developments that already make this an essential and still-growing part of institutional processes in Ghana.

Despite these laudable goals, the privatization experience of Ghana in the 1990s shows how the strategy of involving both the state and the private sector in the economy has worked with difficulty to date.[3] An interesting example is the divestiture attempts with water, electricity and telecommunications. The government first tried several rehabilitation exercises with each of these as full-fledged SOEs in the early 1980s. These included institutional improvements through capacity-building initiatives and decentralization, financial restructuring with the withdrawal of significant subsidies, and finally operational improvements, expansion and rehabilitation of infrastructure. In the water sector, for example, tariffs were increased 14 times up to 1986 with 25 per cent annual rises. Institutional improvements included the adoption of performance contracts for all three sectors in 1989–90. The World Bank has judged that these performance contracts had little effect on the performance of the respective SOEs and it attributed this to low targets that had little reflection on the potential productivity of the enterprises. Having failed with these performance contracts, the government is today contemplating a wider scope for privatization. Today, in the water sector, there is a re-assessment of the role of the government, a desire to move it away from being an active and exclusive operator to either a partner in the provision of water, or a purchaser of water services, or an enabler and regulator. The ambition is to attract substantial capital investments in infrastructure through private equity and to contain borrowing for the sector through efficient operation and cost recovery measures.

Institutions, Processes and Actors for Implementing Regulation and Competition Policies

There is a general tendency in the 'new' laws on institutions for regulation to grant the regulatory bodies the authority to enforce or implement their policies/decisions, either on their own or with the assistance of other public agencies. The National Communications Authority (NCA), for example, has been given the authority to develop regulations for the sector and implement them through a number of steps. The main function of issuing and withdrawing licences to communications operators is the most significant tool for ensuring compliance with regulations. This is different from the electricity sector where the licence to operate is issued by the Energy Commission, but the regulation with respect to standards and tariffs is done jointly with the Public Utilities Regulatory Commission, and the latter does not issue any licences to operators.

Act 524 provides for the NCA to grant exemptions from licences, the treatment of applications for licence, conditions of licence, non-transferability of licence, renewal of licence, power to modify licence, designation of standard and approval of equipment, monitoring of performance of equipment and compensation for damage, access rights of licensed operators, suspension or cancellation of licence, appeals, standards of performance, and information levels of performance. It also provides for the assignment of frequencies for communications systems. The law requires all operators to establish a procedure for dealing with complaints by customers or potential customers, and such procedures must be approved by the NCA and widely publicized. The NCA has subsequently issued 'arrangements of regulation' in which it basically provides details of policies on regulation. The NCA is the body that must settle all disputes between operators after they have applied for such a settlement, and after this an appeal can be made to the minister in charge of communications if dissatisfied with the determination by the Board of the authority working through a hearing panel.

Under fair competition the regulations provide that an operator who controls a network or facility may not limit access to his/her network for competitors. Similarly, a dominant operator in a geographic market specified in a licence 'shall not resort to conduct or practices that unfairly disadvantage rival operators or that are calculated to keep out competition'. Thus limiting access to a network or interconnection is not allowed; neither is the provision of sub-standard access. Despite these provisions, most mobile phone service operators complain that their difficulties in providing satisfactory services to customers arise because they have sub-standard access to the network of the large partly privatized public telephone company. This is probably one area in which, despite the growth in the number of service providers, there is considerable public concern about the low level of competition, reflected in the perceived high prices for the service. Indeed, the issue of mobile phone services and access to the largest phone operator's network remains one of the biggest challenges facing the regulatory body and is seen as a test of how effective the new regulatory environment is for fostering competition.

Self-regulation

By far the best-known forms of self-regulation are associated with the operations of various professionals in the private sector. By statute (The Professional Bodies Registration Decree NRCD 143 of 1973), any person who seeks to practise a profession for which there is a recognized association or professional body must be a member of such an association in order to be so recognized or permitted to practise. There are 16 such professional bodies recognized by law, and they regulate their members.

Each recognized professional body publishes its conditions for membership eligibility, which include largely acceptable and relevant minimum academic qualifications for the profession, adequate experience and acceptance of the institutions' codes of ethics and conduct. The institutions are intended to promote the profession through continuing education while securing the members against 'unfair competition' from non-members. By regulating the practices of their members they seek to ensure that those members remain 'in good standing' in the eyes of the public and do not bring the profession into disrepute. Some professional bodies are widely acknowledged to have successfully regulated their professions, ensuring that most practitioners have been duly licensed/approved by them, and work using standards that are generally accepted as high.

Rationale for Regulatory Instruments and Competition Rules

The main regulatory instruments identified from the new statutes are the application of negotiated price caps for the public utilities (power and water) and licensing for many other economic activities. Licensing and binding settlement of disputes between operators and between customers and operators are the main instruments available to many of the regulators, including those for telecommunications. The competition rules tend to emphasize 'free entry' into the regulated sectors by different operators, as seen with the telecommunications and the power sectors.

The rationale for obliging unhindered entry into the networks of various service providers by other operators is very much in line with the liberal economic policies, which seek to minimize the number of both state and private monopolies. The logic behind free entry for operators assumes that the entry costs are not prohibitive and that an increasing number would lead to a reduction in prices. As indicated earlier, this was expected to happen most readily in telecommunications where, indeed, the number of mobile operators has increased steadily but prices have also risen relatively fast. The very large demand for telephone services in an environment where the infrastructure for telephony is still inadequate ensures that there is ample room for the operators to derive monopoly profits in the segmented markets. The rural and urban markets are quite distinct in structure, further deepening the segmentation that is not addressed under the current conditions for regulation. In essence the inability of the huge state monopoly in the provision of fixed-line telephones to expand its infrastructure reduces the incentive for mobile operators to invest in further expansion of their services beyond their urban segments of the market. Even worse is the poor access for other firms competing for fixed-line telephone service provision, as exhibited by the exacerbating conflict between Ghana Telecom and Westel Communications. There is a growing perception that the regulator has little effective control over the partly state-owned Ghana Telecom.

Implementation Deficiencies

An obvious defect in the implementation of regulation policies is the inadequate attention paid to the enormous information requirements for sound regulation. The notion of regulation suggests that the consumer and the operator of a service have certain basic information about the processes associated with the production of that service, and the costs that go with the production and distribution. In view of the possible information asymmetry, a regulator is required to fill the gap between the position of the consumer and the operator. Thus, in effect, the regulator is expected to broker information exchange at the negotiation table for the benefit of both the operator and the consumer. But, in many developing countries, the ability of the regulator to acquire such information is severely limited by the fact that there are very few credible sources. There are several examples in Ghana of the poorly resourced Ghana Water Company Limited being the only source of not-so credible information on costs for water production (World Bank 1995). And the scope of information required is even larger in these poor environments. In effect, the information gap between the consumer and the operator is often too large for the regulator to adequately fill. The current difficulty in preparing guidelines for setting water tariffs is testimony to the difficulty in obtaining useful information on the costs of production and distribution of water.

An illustration of the implementation deficiencies is provided by the public outrage over the revision of rates for the utilities in Ghana. At the beginning of 2002, the Volta River Authority and the Electricity Company requested an increase of about 105 per cent in the end-user tariff for electricity. In July, the PURC decided on a 60 per cent increase with effect from August 2002 and another average 12 per cent increase to take effect in March 2003, taking into account the fact there had been no increase for three years in a high-inflation environment. Similarly for water, the PURC approved a two-step increase of 40 per cent effective from August 2002 and a 12 per cent increase to take effect in March 2003, compared with a request for a 77 per cent increase requested by Ghana Water Company Ltd. In the PURC's view, the fact that the increases were done in stages was a reflection of its efforts to protect consumers from the increases that had to take place in order to cover costs in an efficient manner.

The public uproar that was generated by the steep increases led the government to issue statements that suggested that the regulatory body had acted improperly in making the decision to announce increases. While the public questioned the basis for such a steep increase, regarding it to be far higher than was required to keep the utility companies running efficiently, and obviously beyond the means of many households, the utility companies argued that the increases were far less than they required to provide an efficient service. In effect, none of the parties to the negotiation of tariffs was happy with the outcome, even when it was not obvious what would have been a more satisfactory outcome for the two parties besides their initial positions. The starting positions for the two parties were too far apart for the PURC to effectively bring them closer. But this is the nature of the problem that regulatory bodies face in an environment riddled with poverty, high-risk investment and poor information quality and quantity.

The government obviously did not help the situation by suggesting that the decision of the PURC was problematic for it. The government's comments could only damage the long-term credibility of the regulatory processes. This experience shows clearly the difficult socio-political context within which regulation takes place.

The poverty of a large number of people makes regulation even more difficult. Poverty limits the choices open to users of various public services. They are obliged to search only for those services that are not expensive. This means that the technology in use must be one that provides services as cheaply as possible. But service providers in many developing countries have much less control over the technologies to be utilized than is often assumed. Globalization simply means that they often have to rely on internationally available technology, which may be out of the reach of poor households. The fixed costs associated with these are often enormous and can only be covered with significant state intervention. The dilemma that regulators face is 'how much state intervention is warranted to make regulation meaningful for the poor?'

Evaluation, Review and Impact Assessment Mechanisms

The issues of evaluation, review and impact assessment of regulation policies has not featured prominently in the operations of the new regulatory bodies, even though the need to do that is often implied under the statutes. For example, the Energy Commission is required 'to prepare, review and update periodically indicative national plans to ensure that all reasonable demands for energy are met'. The Commission is also required to develop a comprehensive database for national decision-making on the extent of development and utilization of energy resources available. Similarly, the PURC is required 'to conduct studies relating to economy and efficiency of public utilities', while the Ghana Investments Promotion Centre is enjoined to 'evaluate the impact of the Centre on investments in the country and recommend appropriate changes where necessary'.

The various regulatory bodies have indicated that they are in the process of setting up and equipping appropriate research departments that will undertake these functions, either by themselves or through consultants. The PURC currently carries out research through its Bureau of Technical Operations and Rate Economics, which has the function of monitoring the performance of the utilities. While the unit is acknowledged to suffer obvious capacity problems, it has nevertheless carried out some review activities that have been applied in the revision of rates for the utilities. Its annual reports have included sections that deal with the financial impact of tariffs on utility companies as well as the impact of tariffs on energy-intensive industries.

POLITICAL, SOCIAL AND EXTERNAL INFLUENCES

It is important to point out that with a growing civil society, the number of initiatives from outside government to introduce regulation has increased. The last decade has seen the organization of many workshops, conferences and seminars intended to bring together different actors in the provision of social and other public services. Such gatherings have become major tools for promoting the adoption of new regulations. An example of such initiative is seen with the environment where a number of NGOs have led sustained campaigns for changes.

Organized Interests

The political climate in Ghana has become much more conducive to the organization of pressure groups. The situation improved steadily after 1992 when the fourth republic was introduced. The number of opposition parliamentarians who raise questions on the floor of parliament in search of probity and accountability has risen steadily. While such questioning does not necessarily lead to action, they are generally acknowledged to put public institutions on their toes. The standing committees of parliament have been used increasingly for discussions with regulatory agencies, even if these are not necessarily public.

The last decade has also seen the emergence of the National Association of Consumers. Despite its existence for a decade, it is not a widely known body. It recently came into prominence when it voiced its rejection of the new tariffs decided by the PURC for electricity and water. It had earlier made submissions to the PURC regarding the proposals it received from the two utility companies and campaigned steadily for a much lower rise in the tariffs than was decided by the PURC. The National Association of Consumers does not have any formal roles within the regulatory system.

Another interesting development of the more liberal economic and political environment is the emergence of independent think tanks that exert some pressure on government and other public institutions. These include the Centre for Policy Analysis (CEPA), the Institute for Economic Affairs (IEA), and the Centre for Democracy and Development. The growing interest of civil society organizations in regulatory and competition issues has perhaps been most forcefully highlighted by the emergence of the non-profit organization called the Centre for Public Interest Law (CEPIL). While the centre has not yet made any significant impact on the development of regulations, its existence is beginning to generate considerable interest in the role of civil society. CEPIL has started a project on mining and timber intended to offset the negative outcomes of expanding mining and timber activities following investment incentives offered to foreign firms. It is also attempting to build a legal support network that will assist communities and individuals whose rights are violated by powerful actors. It has indicated that it will put pressure on regulatory agencies to ensure that they operate more effectively in the public interest.

There are a number of economic groups that show interest in the regulatory environment. These include the Association of Ghanaian Industries, Federation of Associations of Ghanaian Exporters, Ghana Association of Women Entrepreneurs, Ghana Employers Association, Ghana Chamber of Commerce, Ghana Chamber of Mines, Trades Union Congress and many others. In the last few years, these interest groups have become quite active in lobbying government for particular policy changes, particularly those relating to corporate and personal income taxation. While their role in the regulatory systems is not fully formalized, considerable attention is paid to these bodies as their members are appointed to serve on the boards or commissions that provide regulatory services. Thus, for example, the Trades Union Congress and the Association of Ghanaian Industries are both represented on the Public Utilities Regulatory Commission. Indeed, private sector as well as consumer representation on the regulatory commissions has become very much the norm. What is not clear is the qualification of chosen representatives for the task. In general, government does not provide any explanation for the appointment of particular persons to the boards of the various regulatory bodies, and in a number of cases there have been obvious questions about the suitability of board members.

It is interesting that despite the active participation of the consumer interest groups in the setting of rates by the PURC, these groups have been strongly critical of the recent tariffs for water and electricity. While it is obvious that they reflect the genuine concerns of the majority of members, it is not equally obvious that the groups are adequately organized to discuss the issues of regulation and how these affect their membership. In effect the contributions of those who represent consumers at the regulatory agencies tend to reflect more the individual preferences or positions rather than those of organized groups. The Ghana Chamber of Mines has emphasized the cost difficulties that the latest tariffs will impose on mining. While this is certainly the case, it does not however reflect the concerns of small-scale or informal miners whose operations are largely illegal on account of the nature of the regulations on mining activity and who do not have access to the Chamber of Mines.

Alongside the growing organized interest in regulatory matters, it is important to acknowledge the similar rapid growth in the less organized parts of civil society. The increase in access to communications facilities has come with a surge in the numbers of people expressing public concern about the performance of various institutions. As mentioned earlier, there are always several calls to radio stations to complain about water services, electricity services and telecommunications services in particular areas on each day, but there is no formalized structure for getting the utility companies to respond to these complaints, besides that provided by the PURC.

Role of External Agencies

The role that donors have played in shaping the economy of Ghana in the last two decades cannot be over-emphasized. Several contributors to the volume edited by Aryeetey et al. (2000) argued that most of the significant growth that Ghana has seen since economic reforms began can be linked to policy reforms that have taken place. But those policy reforms would not have been easy or even possible without aid, which came with significant conditionality. A major reform requirement was the privatization of state-owned enterprises, and the creation of the necessary regulatory arrangements. The role that donors have played in this regard has had two dimensions, first ensuring the development of a new management practice of regulating economic agents, and, second, imposing regulatory approaches that are not necessarily intended to solve the structural problems facing the economic agents as they operate in a poorly developed economic and political environment.

With regard to the first dimension of helping to entrench a new form of regulation, it is important to underscore the fact that not only did donors require that regulation of private economic agents accompany the greater involvement of the private sector, they also partly financed the creation of many of the regulatory bodies. In the reforms of the financial sector, focus on regulation and supervision of banks saw the World Bank and other bilateral donors provide Ghana with significant technical advice. The Banking Law was amended to require that each bank be examined at least once a year. Regulation was extended to semi-formal financial institutions through the Rules and Regulations and Control Measures for the Establishment and Supervision of Savings and Loan Companies issued by the Bank of Ghana in 1990.

For the public utilities, the major rehabilitation and restructuring exercises pursued since the mid-1980s have all been carried out with support from the World Bank. The Bank initially assisted the government in the 1980s to enter into performance contracts with Ghana Water Company Ltd, Electricity Company Ltd and Ghana Telecom. By its own reckoning the contracts with public managers were fraught with several problems which made outcomes not always satisfactory.

Currently, with the establishment of the PURC, donors continue to play a major role in its operations. The World Bank, USAID and DFID have been the major sponsors of its institutional development as well as the development of its programmes.

SUMMARY AND CONCLUSIONS

New independent institutions have been created that draw their mandate directly from the constitution, using standard regulatory approaches. The institutions may or may not be subject to limited controls from government ministers. While authorized to carry out regulatory functions in order to protect the public interest and promote fair competition in the use of resources, they do suffer enormous logistical difficulties as a result of the limited funding that they receive. The limited financial support makes it difficult for them to attract and hire key technical personnel for the development of enforceable standards.

But by far the most significant structural constraint of the new regulatory agencies remains the wide information gap existing between providers of services and the users of those services. The information gap is engendered by the poverty of the users of services and the 'inappropriateness' of the technology used by the service providers, and the absence of any common ground for determining the most suitable approach to production and delivery. When service providers use technology that is well beyond the means of the majority of the users of the service, the regulator's task of setting tariffs becomes extremely difficult to carry out meaningfully.

The growth of civil society has been supportive of the development of a new culture for regulation. Their initiatives seek to move government away from what is perceived as a regulation culture that only entrenches powerful groups against less powerful groups, particularly in the exploitation of national resources. Public interest issues are now being pushed forward much more forcefully in relation to regulation. While consumer groups are not very visible in this cause, organized non-profit organizations are seen to be actively influencing new legislations for regulation, particularly those relating to environmental causes.

In sum, the regulation institutions of Ghana are still in the early phase of their development and have become part of a new culture in Ghana that supports private participation that could be competitive. As their logistical problems are dealt with over time, and as greater attention is paid to narrowing the information gap between service providers and consumers, regulation is bound to have greater positive impact on achieving effective competition.

NOTES

1. Guinness Ghana Ltd entered into an agreement with 183 retailers of alcoholic beverages out of an estimated 7000 outlets in 1999.
2. Personal communication with Mr. Kojo Bentsi-Enchill, a highly respected attorney.
3. Eboe Hutchful (2002) has a very comprehensive discussion of the reform of the public sector in the 1980s and 1990s, and its links with the private sector through divestiture of SOEs.

REFERENCES

Afari-Gyan, K. (1995), *The Ghanaian Constitution: An Introduction*, Friedrich Ebert Foundation, Accra.

Aryeetey, E. (1994), 'Private investment under uncertainty in Ghana', *World Development*, **22** (8), Oxford.

Aryeetey, E., J. Harrigan and M. Nissanke (eds) (2000)), *Economic Reforms in Ghana: The Miracle and The Mirage*, James Currey, Oxford and Woeli Publishers, Accra.

Aryeetey, E., Y. Asante and A.Y. Kyei (1992), 'Mobilizing domestic savings for African development and diversification: a Ghanaian case', mimeo, International Development Centre, Queen Elizabeth House, University of Oxford.

Bentsi-Enchill, K. (1986), 'Colonial land policy in Ghana, 1874–1962', mimeo, Department of Land Economy, Cambridge University, Cambridge.

Hutchful, E. (2002), *Ghana's Adjustment Experience: The Paradox of Reform*, UNRISD and James Currey, Heinemann and Woeli Publishers, Oxford, Portsmouth and Accra.

Ninsin, K. (1991), 'The PNDC and the problem of legitimacy', in D. Rothchild (ed.) *The Political Economy of Recovery*, SAIS African Studies Library, Lynne Rienner, Boulder and London.

World Bank (1995), *Bureaucrats in Business, The Economics and Politics of Government Ownership*, A World Bank Policy Research Report, Oxford University Press, Oxford.

16. Competition, regulation and the urban poor: a case study of water

Diana Mitlin

INTRODUCTION

This chapter explores the impact of regulation and competition policy on the poor. There are a number of anticipated influences both in regard to the poor as consumers and as producers and/or suppliers of goods and services. Potential areas of influence include the impact of regulation and competition policies on the price of basic commodities and services; the quality of commodities and services; opportunities for access to markets for commodities and services; changes in market opportunities for employment and enterprise development (both positive and negative); and changes in externalities such as environmental degradation, and health and safety. Such areas have an evident impact on the well-being of the poor, their capacity to avoid poverty and their development options. The study focuses on a single sector, water services, and considers the impacts for the urban poor. Water was selected because it is a basic need in maintaining life and improving well-being in the short, medium and long term. For the poor, the objective is access to affordable and adequate supplies of water to meet a multitude of needs.

The significance of politics and policy in influencing outcomes such as access and affordability is emphasised by Spiller and Savedoff (1999, pp. 1–2):

> why is it so difficult to properly manage and operate water systems in the region, and more generally in the developing world? The problem is not related to project finance or lack of technical or manpower capabilities, but rather to the political economy of the sector.

In southern cities, water markets are complex: typically, there are one or more of three major types of suppliers. Each may operate individually or may co-exist with other suppliers (of the same or different types). Large-scale suppliers (public or private) that are part of the formal enterprise sector have some level of monopoly power granted by the state. This monopoly may be universal (for example, sole supplier in a city) or it may have spatial restrictions (supplier to part of the city), or it may be shared. Smaller-scale private vendors may be formal or informal. They generally do not operate piped networks, although there are exceptions. They vary in size from companies large enough to own tanker fleets to household enterprises selling water to their neighbours. Community-managed water services are a third option, offering some residents opportunities for non-profit sources of supply.

Water, whether provided by the private or public sectors, is very much located within the area of public policy. Industries that are dominated by monopoly providers, as is the case for piped water services, require regulation. A number of further features of water services in the South add to regulatory challenges.

- Many urban poor live in settlements without a piped supply of water and hence small-scale informal suppliers may be the only source of water.
- Smaller, sometimes informal, suppliers may or may not be formally regulated as a part of the water supply sector.
- The significance of water for well-being raises environmental health issues regardless of the type of supply.
- Policy issues outside the water sector may influence access to supplies. In particular, land use policies and regulations regarding squatter settlements may be important.
- Local community management of water supplies extends the consideration of regulation and regulatory issues beyond government agencies into civil society.
- Competition and regulatory issues are currently being reconsidered in the context of growing private sector participation.

The chapter considers the significance of water for the poor, analyses issues of private sector involvement in large-scale networks, considers the role of regulators, examines smaller-scale, sometimes informal, water providers and community-managed systems, and looks at collaboration between providers.

WATER AND POVERTY

Water is critical to human well-being. The significance of water for health has long been recognised. Increasingly, there is a greater awareness of the importance of water for other uses including in informal enterprise activities (Moriarty 2002; Nicol 2000).

The relationship between water availability and the incidence of disease has long been acknowledged (see Hardoy et al. 2001, pp. 39–43; Thompson et al. 2000, p. 43; Stephens 1996, p. 15). It is recognised that many low-income areas lack adequate basic services and infrastructure resulting in significant health problems. Etherington et al. (2002, p. 22) report that 16 per cent of all deaths in one Kathmandu hospital between 1992 and 1998 were due to waterborne diseases. Alcazar et al. (2000, p. 6) note that 'waterborne and water related diseases are a major cause of morbidity and mortality especially in the poorer neighbourhoods of Lima. The medical costs and lost wages from such diseases were a high part of household income for the poor, 27 per cent by one estimate.'

The importance of water extends beyond health issues to consumption, production and amenities. Johnstone and Wood (2001, p. 5) argue that a lack of access to adequate and affordable water has several important consequences for livelihoods such as increased costs, time and physical effort to obtain water, reduced consumption, an increased health burden and lost productivity. A study of the contribution of water to household livelihoods in nine East African towns noted its importance for drinking, cooking, bathing, cleaning, washing, gardening and beer brewing (Thompson et al. 2000, p. 43).

The burden of lacking adequate supplies of water does not fall equally within households. Women suffer particularly from the lack of adequate supplies of water. In many contexts, women are responsible for reproductive households needs and associated tasks (including drinking, bathing and washing). Many women combine these household tasks with working from home in a range of formal and informal occupations. Some jobs such as the preparation of street foods further increase their need for water. In addition to direct expenditure on water, other factors such as the time taken to secure water (such as distance travelled and/or queues at standpipes) and the health burden of carrying heavy loads result in considerable indirect costs.

WHO-UNICEF (quoted in OECD 2003, p. 19) estimates that 1.1 billion do not have access to safe water supplies. Many of these have only limited or no access to piped supplies. The estimated proportions of households living in selected low-income urban settlements without adequate provision are, respectively for Africa, Asia and Latin America, 35–50 per cent, 35–50 per cent and 20–30 per cent (United Nations Human Settlement Programme 2003).

LARGE-SCALE PIPED NETWORKS AND THE PRIVATISATION OF SUPPLY

Many urban dwellers receive their water through public piped networks, either directly from the manager of the network or indirectly through water vendors who buy and on-sell water. Such piped supplies may be direct to the residence (as is common in the North) or to a public standpoint (when supplementary vending services may occur).

Private sector involvement in the water sector has been increasing in the last decade. However, it is not clear how widespread it is. Johnstone and Wood (2001, p. 1) quote Silva et al. (1998) to suggest that, in relation to private sector participation in the water supply industry, by 1997 'a total of 97 projects had been implemented in 35 developing countries'. Although this suggests that private sector involvement has grown, it should be noted that, by implication, there are many cities, regions and countries in the South in which major suppliers remain public.

The traditional model of service provision with public ownership and subsidised prices has been associated with poor service quality and limited coverage. Prices have been low but the benefits have not been shared equally (Walker et al. 2000, p. 1). Menard et al. (2001, p. 5) provide an insightful summary of the general problems with public supply in their study of the water supply sector in Guinea: few people were connected to the public network (less than 40 per cent of residents in the capital city), few of those connected were billed (less than 12 per cent in 1982) and few of those billed paid their bills (only 12.5 per cent). As a result, public subsidies were directed at higher-income families, and the network could not be extended to low-income households.

Even for those with access to piped networks, there is some evidence to suggest that the quality of provision has fallen in recent years. Thompson et al. (2000, pp. 43–4) exemplify such problems in a longitudinal study of water supply in nine East African towns.

The poor outcomes of public ownership and management are explained by political intervention in decision-making due to industry characteristics and consumption needs (Spiller and Savedoff 1999, p. 2; Nickson 1997, p. 165); and by monopoly conditions enabling agencies to pursue their own interests or those of their staff (Rees 1998, p. 95). Spiller and Savedoff (1999, p. 29) argue 'the sector is prone to government opportunism, triggering a downward spiral of low prices, low investment, low quality, low coverage and high levels of corruption'. Nickson (1997, pp. 167–8) argues in favour of private sector involvement to address public sector failures and due to the intrinsic nature of the good. Water, he suggests, has neither of the two characteristics of public goods: non-excludability (supply to one means supply to all) nor non-rivalry (consumption by one person does not reduce the amount available to others). However, this analysis takes no account of the problem of illegal tapping of water lines. Ferguson and Maurer (1996) (quoted in Hardoy et al. 2001, p. 61) suggest that up to 70 per cent of the water entering the supply system may be illegally tapped in some cities.

Private sector involvement is also associated with a number of factors. The linking of political demand for services with payments is increasingly popular (Manor 1999, pp. 28–9). Financial constraints on central government have increased their incentive to pass on their responsibilities (for an example, see Chisari et al. (1999, p. 357)). Donors (particularly the World Bank) have been active in supporting privatisation (Bayliss 2001a, pp. 3–4). An alternative explanation of the trend towards private sector involvement in basic services argues that it reflects the investment needs of a wealthy elite. (See Loftus and McDonald (2001, pp. 180–81) for a discussion of this issue in Argentina.) Collignon and Vezina (2000, p. 10) also argue that business interests (rather than public interests) have tended to influence private sector involvement in water services.

Finally, it should be noted that there is no single model for private sector involvement. Nickson (1997, p. 176), Rees (1998, pp. 98–9), Budds (2000, pp. 9–10) and Johnstone and Wood (2001, pp. 10–12) summarise the multiple possibilities of private sector involvement in the water sector. These include: service contracts for specific tasks, management contracts, operating leases, Build Own Operate and Transfer contracts, concessions, shared ownership, and full divestiture.

The Winners and Losers from Privatisation

Who are the winners and losers from private sector involvement in water services? Studies in Mexico City (Haggarty et al. 2000, p. 21), Argentina (Chisari et al. 1999, p. 375 and Van den Berg 2000) and more general assessments (OECD 2000, pp. 7–10) inform our understanding. Broadly speaking, the winners are the private companies, and residents who gain connections and/or whose services improve (when these are valued more than the costs of price rises). There may be benefits from the improved quality of water services. The state may also be considered to be a winner if water services improve, although state agencies will have to pay more for their water as prices rise.

Losers are customers who have to pay more, employees and heads who might be laid off and lose status and benefits. There are particular concerns that the poorest residents may suffer from rising prices. For example, in an assessment of a private concession in Parana, Argentina, the first design resulted in an estimated consumer loss of US$25 million over 30 years (Van den Berg 2000). The redesigned concession predicted net consumer benefits of US$3 million; however, the urban poor were estimated to lose by US$3 million, with anticipated benefits of US$6 million for better-off consumers.

The situation for employees is mixed. Reductions in the labour force following privatisation appear to be relatively common. In Cartagena (Colombia), the number of employees fell from 494 to 262 following the introduction of private sector participation (Nickson 2001a, p. 17). In Manila, over 3000 employees lost their jobs (Hall et al. 2001, p. 7). In Buenos Aires, the privatisation of water and sewerage works resulted in the workforce falling from 7600 to 4000 employees (Loftus and McDonald 2001, pp. 195–6).

However, in Lima, where privatisation was rejected in favour of public sector reform, the workforce also fell from 3769 to 1359 due to measures to improve efficiency (Alcazar et al. 2000, p. 13).

The International Market in Privatised Water Supply Services

Of further relevance in understanding how the nature of competition influences outcomes is the high level of global concentration in water services. Johnstone et al. (2001, p. 35) suggest that five firms now account for over 50 per cent of all projects involving private sector participation.

Choice may be further restricted if companies are only interested in business in the larger cities (Budd 2000, p. 11). Etherington et al. (2002, pp. 11–12) discuss the process of setting up a management lease contract in Nepal. The government of Nepal requires such companies to have experience in two operations of a size similar to Kathmandu (1.1 million urban residents, 70 per cent of whom are connected to the water network), one of which must be in a southern country. Only seven companies globally are thought to qualify. By 2002, two companies were serious about continuing their participation in the bidding process (Etherington et al. 2002, pp. 11–12).

Such a high level of concentration in the international market raises questions about how freely countries and cities can set conditions and regulators can operate. Johnstone et al. (2001, p. 35) note that this high level of concentration may favour the companies who know a lot more about regulatory options and their potential consequences than the regulators themselves.

Privatisation, Water and the Poor: Summary

It is evident that competition and regulatory outcomes depend on many things, including both the policies themselves and the broader context within which they are located. Outcomes also depend in part on the enforcement capacity of state agencies. At the same time, the urban poor themselves are not a single group. Different groups of the urban poor face different needs and have different opportunities to secure water services. Private sector involvement has assisted some of the poor to secure access to piped supplies but others have not benefited and it is likely that some are worse off. The high level of concentration among international providers favours the companies rather than the public interest.

THE ROLE OF REGULATORS

Alongside greater private sector involvement in water services, there is broad agreement that the nature of the market for water requires continuing state regulatory intervention (Komives and Brook-Cowen 1999; Nickson 1997; Spiller and Savedoff 1999). The natural monopoly in the supply of water, positive and negative externalities associated with consumption and the fact that water is a merit good (with the implication that consumers may underpurchase being unaware of the full benefits) are all reasons for public sector intervention (Johnstone et al. 2001, p. 27).

Regulation of water services is complex. Rees (1998, p. 100) lists the following regulatory tasks: price control, promotion of operating efficiency, service standards, control of externalities, maintenance of public good functions, ensuring that assets can be serviced over time, ensure development of essential infrastructure, control over land speculation, control over unfair trading practices, safety net regulations, promotion of efficient use and ensuring responsiveness to consumer needs. Rivera (1996, p. 62) suggests that a model for successful regulation needs to include regulatory objectives together with the design of instruments and incentives, development of expertise, enforcement strategies, and strategies to maintain the independence of the regulator plus legitimacy and transparency of the process. The complexity of water services and particularly the involvement of environmental and economic interests mean that multiple agencies may be involved. For example, Mazzucchelli et al. (2001, p. 63) identify five agencies with regulatory responsibilities for the Buenos Aires concession.

Recent experience has resulted in concern about the capacity of regulators: they have been accused of being corrupt (Loftus and McDonald 2001, pp. 187 and 194); ineffectual (Loftus and McDonald 2001, 193; Alcazar et al. 2000, p. 11); insufficiently free of political interference (Alcazar et al. 2000, p. 11); unable to offer a sufficient profit to stop firms leaving the sector (Bayliss 2001b, p. 14); insufficiently strong institutional capacity (Nickson 1997, p. 184; Rivera 1996, pp. 61–2); and prone to regulatory capture (Johnstone et al. 2001, p. 34). Capacity issues may be particularly difficult where municipalities are the primary public agency responsible for the contract (Nickson 2001b, p. 5; Castro and Cruz 2002, p. 10).

Experience with privatisation is now raising questions about whether or not the shift to a 'private provider – public regulator' model avoids the dangers of politicisation. Esguerra (2002, p. 2) discusses the pressure put on the regulators and the state by the two water companies that won the concession in Manila. The two companies (formed by partnerships between two of the wealthiest families in the Philippines and international companies) have sought to amend their contracts with the regulatory agency. When outcomes were not sufficiently favourable, they pursued legal and political channels. Rees (1998, p. 96) points out that regulation has to be

> seen not just as a negative set of rules, monitoring and policing arrangements but as a bargaining process which has to strike a balance between providing private companies with the incentives to invest and operate efficiently and protecting the interests of other social and economic actors.

Private sector investment in water services has not avoided political involvement in decision-making but merely made negotiations more complex, with the addition of a further major interest group.

Further Challenges for Regulation

In addition to the complexities of managing large corporations and the different imperatives of private profitability and public interest, there are further challenges for regulation in the water sector in the South. First, there is the issue of water quality and standards. Second, lack of affordability has resulted in problems for regulators seeking to enforce requirements for the extension of piped networks. Third, as discussed in the penultimate section, there may be particular regulatory challenges to arrangements that bring together different kinds of providers.

In regard to standards, Johnstone and Horan (1994, p. 451) argue that increasing environmental standards related to water quality is associated with economic development and increasing aspirations, and note that in the US, the number of regulated water quality parameters increased from 9 to 110 between 1925 and 1988. In the South, the trade-off between the cost of improved supplies and affordability can raise difficult choices. These problems are exemplified by the issue of arsenic in the groundwater in some regions of Bangladesh that was first found in the 1980s, where the Bangladeshi government has adopted the prevailing European and American standard of 50 ppb (parts per billion) for arsenic rather than the WHO guideline of 10 ppb. Standards in Europe are becoming stricter and by 31 December 2004 it will fall to 10 ppb with the USA following shortly afterwards. WaterAid (a UK NGO) use the standard of the Bangladeshi government, and note that using European and USA standards would result in 50–70 fewer deaths from arsenic related cancers each year. However, UNICEF estimate that 260 000 children under the age of five die each year from diarrhoeal disease, with some 26 per cent of these deaths likely to be caused by drinking poor quality water. The closure of tubewells that would result if high arsenic related standards were imposed would result in more people using bacteriologically less safe alternative water sources, and hence more deaths and ill-health. This example illustrates the dilemmas in determining what standards are appropriate, given the cost of securing those standards and the alternative uses to which such money might be put.

A second regulatory challenge is emerging from recent experience with privatisation. Contracts commonly require companies to extend services. However, an emerging difficulty for regulators is that the poor are unable to pay enough to cover consumption and amortisation costs, and ensure a reasonable return on capital. In Guinea and Buenos Aires, coverage rates appear to be limited because of the high cost of water, and hence the inability of the poor to afford supplies (Bayliss 2001b, p. 7; Menard et al. 2001, p. 12; Loftus and McDonald 2001, p. 188; Chisari et al. 2001, p. 2). There is a growing awareness on the part of both public and private agencies of the need for subsidies to secure adequate water supplies for the poor – it is difficult to see how regulators alone can easily respond to such issues.

Requirements about flexibility of payment schedules may also be important. Solo (1999, p. 126) and Collignon and Vezina (2000, p. 21) argue that the advantages of the small-scale private operators include flexible payment systems including daily payments. Meters can also be linked to systems of pre-payment as well as the regular distribution of a fixed free or subsidised amount of water. Marvin et al. (2001, p. 213) suggest that pre-payment meters may help affordability. However, they are concerned about some of the consequences and argue that 'marginal users [should] have a voice in shaping new innovations in metering systems'.

The Role of Regulators: Summary

Regulatory capacity remains a significant issue for those concerned with reform of water services. It is now evident that privatisation has not removed politics from decision-making. Local regulatory capacity appears to be weak. Regulatory agencies have significant challenges even without the additional task of managing political involvement and private influence. Difficult decisions need to be made about appropriate standards. Contracts may require the extension of networks but problems of affordability are emerging. The poor may not be able to afford piped water without subsidies.

COMPETITION AND SMALL-SCALE VENDORS

Large numbers of the urban poor lack access to the public network. As a consequence, many of them use a range of services provided by small-scale informal water vendors. The significance of small-scale private providers is not disputed (although it was ignored for a considerable time). Collignon and Vezina (2000, p. 5) argue that, in ten towns across West and East Africa, between 17 and 78 per cent of household water needs are met through the formal distribution network with the remainder serviced by informal providers (or direct groundwater sources). In Bamako, for example, 18 000 households are served by the city water agency and 92 000 by independent providers. Their importance appears to have grown. Thompson et al. (2000, p. 45) note that, in 1967, small-scale vendors were not a significant supplier in nine East African towns, but by 1997, they were supplying 24 per cent of the water needs of those households without piped water.

There is a growing recognition of the diversity within this sector of the water supply industry. Albu and Njiru (2002, p. 15) make a useful distinction between wholesale vendors (who may buy a tanker or even have a small network), distributing vendors who sell directly to consumers via door-to-door sales, and direct vendors who sell to consumers who come to them. Competition between vendors appears to vary. Collignon and Vezina (2000, p. 40) note that, in general, they found little strongly competitive behaviour between the informal suppliers in ten East and West African towns. However, Crane (1994) quotes Shugart (1991) to suggest that vendor competition in Jakarta is limited by family or ethnic links.

In some cases, small-scale informal water providers are included within the regulatory systems that apply to larger companies, and hence prices may be controlled. But even where the informal sector has been brought within the regulatory system, formal controls may be weak. Collignon and Vezina (2000, p. 11) found formal contracts with private operators to manage publicly funded standpipes in nine of ten cities in an East and West African study. However, written terms had little relationship with actual practice; retail prices may be twice as high as that specified in the contract and bribes may be paid by the private operators to agents of the public company (ibid.).

Unit prices of water purchased from small-scale vendors are generally higher than the unit price of piped water. Johnstone et al. (2001, p. 27) summarise six city studies and suggest that the ratio of unit costs between vendors and piped connections is between 5.5:1 and 300:1. Hardoy et al. (2001, p. 48) draw on studies in 14 cities to suggest a narrow differential of 4:1 to 83:1. Collignon and Vezina (2000, p. 21) report that in ten selected East and West African towns, water delivered to the door costs four times as much as water from a public standpipe and six times as much as water from a home tap. However, they argue that:

> Independent providers are sometimes criticised . . . for reaping high profits . . . But the surveys carried out for this study found no evidence to support this view. On the contrary, the survey results indicate rather that the market for water and sanitation services is extremely competitive and profit margins low. Most operators surveyed earn just enough to maintain and replace equipment and pay themselves a modest wage. (Collignon and Vezina 2000, p. 42)

Small-scale Vendors: Summary

Small-scale vendors are significant providers of water services for some urban poor groups. In some places, competition and regulatory authorities ignore small-scale vendors. A major issue for authorities that wish to integrate small-scale vendors into the formal system is how this might be done. In respect of competitive practice, water markets appear to be strongly influenced by their local context and outcomes differ considerably in different locations. Interventions may be counterproductive if they do not take account of contextual factors.

THE THIRD WAY: COMMUNITY-MANAGED SERVICES

Alongside public networks (with or without private sector involvement) and small-scale private providers, there are also community-managed services. Gross et al. (2001, p. 26) suggest that such models have become popular in the last ten years. However, it should also be recognised that community models build on much longer traditions of self-managed assets (Lammerink et al. 2001, p. 25). The growth of community-managed water supply systems appears to reflect a broadly based interest in participatory development.

Community management offers users a voice and choice in aspects such as technology, level of service, service provider, financing arrangements and management systems in exchange for making contributions (in cash or in kind) (Gross et al. 2001, p. 26). Such models often seek to engage community members from the beginning of the service delivery process in order to build community ownership and strengthen local capacity to manage services. They are driven by the understanding that many communities are willing and able to develop their own water supply systems rather than wait for government provision, often because their household expenditure is likely to fall if they work together to improve on existing provision.

There is no single model for community-managed supplies. They may be supported by an external agency, most probably an NGO. The attitude to subsidy varies considerably, as does the actual division of responsibilities within the project. One of the best known examples of community managed sanitation is the Orangi Pilot Project in Karachi which has assisted more than 100 000 households to manage lane-based sanitation schemes that have over the last 16 years developed connections to the main sewerage network. With the support of the Orangi Pilot Project, communities in Faisalabad have developed similar methodologies to provide themselves with water. Box 16.1 describes their work – and also demonstrates the continuing significance of political forces in the provision of water supply.

BOX 16.1 COMMUNITY-MANAGED WATER PROVISION: THE POLITICS AND THE PIPES

In Faisalabad, the Anjuman Samaji Bahbood (a welfare organization run by local residents) sought to improve water provision in low-income settlements. One settlement called Hasanpura was chosen as a pilot area because there was no potable water in the settlement although (saline) underground water from boreholes was available for washing clothes and some other activities. The 1,000 households in the settlement were spending a daily average of Rs 5 on water. High levels of disease imposed further costs on residents. The project sought to connect the settlement to mains water located 1,100 feet away, with individual lanes then laying pipes to connect households to mains water. Each household's share of the costs of the mains water pipe was Rs 1,300. The cost of connection was an average of Rs 600 and the charge to connect to the public network was Rs 1,175.

Initially local authorities showed little interest. One official demanded a bribe when the household needed a licence to bring a water pipe across a road. The community decided to do this portion of their work at night, confident that once it was completed they would be able to keep the pipe and pay a fine. When the community completed the connection to the mains water supply, their successes were judged by some to be more of a threat than an achievement. One local politician sought to undermine their activities by promising households free connections if they stopped participating in the programme. The politician started to lay his own line but the work was sub-standard and the community lost interest.

In addition to a sceptical local authority, ASB faced local households who were unwilling and unable to invest a large amount in water and sanitation. A grant from an NGO enabled the organization to construct secondary pipes, thereby establishing the beginnings of a network that families could connect to. Families were asked to pay the connection costs for their house to the lane sewer and their share of the cost of the secondary pipe, enabling further expansion of the network. Families were willing to do this. External donor finance and local visionaries were successful in catalysing a change in attitudes.

When the local authority saw that families were willing to pay the cost of piped water, they became interested. The leader of the organization was invited to participate in a number of government activities. Within a few months, state funds were available to extend activities to other settlements. At the same time, interaction increased between local staff of the water authority and ASB activists. ASB offered their own area plans to assist in state financed improvements and were asked to assist in monitoring private contractors on a state programme.

Source: Alimuddin, S., Hasan, A. and Sadiq, A. (2001) 'Community driven water and sanitation: The work of the Anjuman Samaji Behbood and the Larger Faisalabad context', Poverty Reduction in Urban Areas Series, Working Paper 7, London: International Institute for Environment and Development.

Community-managed water supplies are often contentious, in part because they overlap with the political interests of formal sector supplies and threaten the entrepreneurial activities of the informal sector. Matin (1999, p. 11) further develops this point when discussing interventions by an NGO in Dhaka to improve the water supply. 'Access to scarce resources is a recurring source of conflict in a slum and often provides a power base for a distinct social leadership, which dictates the terms and conditions under which residents in a particular neighbourhood have to live.' In this case, the first community-managed initiative was sabotaged by the local leader who stole water to sell. As a result, the NGO created and strengthened community teams that were able to manage finance and staff.

Community-managed services may fail because the tasks place further burdens on communities that are already struggling to address their multiple needs. Etemadi (2001, p. 96) studies Communal Water Associations (CWA) in Cebu City (the Philippines). These associations are provided with faucets by the city council in order to improve water provision in a city in which only 41 per cent of residents have access to piped water. She concludes:

> Many CWAs are beset with management problems . . . such as lack of active participation by members, undemocratic if not oppressive management style, irregular or no annual election resulting in monopoly of leadership, and a lack of financial transparency and accountability. It is not uncommon to hear that a CWA official has disappeared with the association money to the dismay and consternation of the members.

Community-managed systems may raise difficult issues for regulators and competition authorities. Communities may be responsible for enforcing regulations but they may have a limited capacity and be vulnerable to coercion. Regulations to promote community management may be unrealistic. Models to promote large-scale community management may be lacking and hence community-management options may not be able to compete with formal piped provision or small-scale vending of water. Community-managed systems may be self-governing but this does not mean they always work in the best interests of all the community. It is not clear how the interests of the more vulnerable might be protected.

Community-managed Services: Summary

Communities have been interested in providing themselves with water services because of the absence of acceptable alternatives. Such services raise new and interesting challenges for regulators. However, the extent to which community-managed services can provide a real alternative source of water services for the urban poor is not clear. They are likely to require additional capacity within the community to be successful.

COLLABORATION BETWEEN PROVIDERS

There appears to be a growing recognition of the potential synergy between different types of suppliers within the water sector. Nickson (1997, p. 166) argues that there is a 'new consensus on managing UWS [urban water systems]'. He suggests that this consensus is based around two principles: first, the recognition that water companies (however owned and managed) should be treated as commercial enterprises and, second, that water management should be based on a participatory approach involving users, planners and policy-makers (Nickson 1997, p. 166). Johnstone and Wood (2001, p. 15) also suggest that NGOs and CBOs may become more important with increased private sector participation.

Despite this interest, Mazzucchelli et al. (2001, p. 99) argue that within the Buenos Aires concession, collaboration has not been well developed. Aguas Argentinas, the company with the concession, introduced a new programme to work with low-income communities to reduce installation costs and improve billing and collection (Hardoy and Schusterman 2000, p. 65). Such models pass over management responsibilities to low-income communities who develop their own systems for installation and management. Over time, four specific strategies have emerged in Buenos Aires although each is small-scale with initiatives in one or two places (Mazzucchelli et al. 2001, p. 99):

- 'community-led' with an agreement between the community and the company;

- 'NGO-led' with the NGO coordinating relationships between the company and community;
- 'municipal-led' with the municipality subsidising connection charges; and
- 'job-creation' with the state financing community involvement as part of a job-creation programme.

In other cities, private companies are also being encouraged to explore collaboration with low-income groups to reduce supply costs (Mazzucchelli et al. 2001; Nickson 2001b, p. 17). Experiences are mixed and it has not been possible to identify a successful large-scale example. In Cordoba (Argentina) management responsibilities have been passed on to representative local organizations (Nickson 2001a, pp. 17–19). However, Nickson (2001a, p. 25) notes: 'there is a danger that community leaders will become viewed by residents as "tax collectors" on behalf of AGUACAR and thereby lose their legitimacy'.

In the case of small-scale vendors, Collignon (1999, p. 4) is generally pessimistic about the possibilities of collaboration with piped providers; he notes that only Mauritania has developed a system in which small operators have concessions from the water distribution network. Collignon and Vezina (2000, p. 10) find that in ten West and East African cities, the response of municipalities is generally to fine activities, restrict the informal laying of water pipes and limit the number of standpipes. Collignon and Vezina (2000, p. 31) note that resale is also allowed in Abidjan where SODECI (the city-wide agency) has formally licensed about 700 households for the resale of domestic water to neighbours. There are further examples of collaboration in Dhaka (Bangladesh) and Cartagena (Colombia) (Solo 1999, p. 119 and Nickson 2001a, p. 26 respectively). However, in Cordoba (Argentina), the assumption is that small private water companies that supply through their own networks will gradually be absorbed into the concessionaire (Nickson 2001b, p. 22), and, in some cases, this has been achieved by court action (Nickson 2001b, p. 22).

One reason for the lack of experience may be Johnstone and Wood's (2001, p. 52) suggestion that there is no easy route to combine formal and informal systems. Solutions by community groups or private vendors 'are usually a short-term response to the crisis resulting from inadequate access' Johnstone and Wood (2001, p. 52). They go on to suggest: 'perhaps the most difficult task facing the regulator is to ensure that positive aspects of the small-scale operators are preserved, while ensuring that services are provided efficiently and do not generate externalities elsewhere' (Johnstone and Wood 2001, p. 52).

Collaboration: Summary

It appears that, except for pilot programmes, there has been relatively little experience of collaborative systems to date, either between large companies and community-managed models or between large companies and small-scale vendors. Cooperation between providers is likely to be a difficult area for regulatory policy. While there are recognised benefits, as outlined, there is little experience of bringing together formal and informal providers.

CONCLUSION

As evident from this discussion, water services remain inadequate for many of the world's urban poor but the market for water appears to be highly contested. A major reason for this is that water is a critically important basic need. There are interventions by both politicians and government officials who are under pressure (for a multitude of reasons) to change the distributional impacts of policies and practices. At the same time, deficiencies in public supply combined with the scale of need mean that there are many opportunities for private entrepreneurship and such enterprises may seek to control their markets to increase their profits. The significance of water for the livelihoods of the poor has resulted in a number of other social initiatives to address water need through community management. However, as shown, these have to struggle for space among political and private interests.

The debate about the impact of privatisation on improving conditions of poverty is particularly contentious. Bayliss (2001b, p. 1) argues that there are two opposing views on poverty reduction: on the one hand, the World Bank suggests that privatisation is essential to promote the growth needed for poverty reduction; on the other, she argues that the privatisation of basic services is associated with unemployment, rising prices and contractions in service. As argued, there are winners and losers associated with private sector involvement. While those who have gained access to piped services are likely to have benefited, others have lost out or have not seen improvements.

This chapter has shown that the challenge for competition and regulatory authorities extends beyond the regulation of private sector involvement in piped water supplies. Authorities need to recognise the significant role of small-scale vendors as well as the actual and potential contribution of community-managed services. Working in this context offers a considerable challenge to such authorities and their relevance to poverty reduction. It calls for a much more holistic understanding of the ways in which basic services are secured by the poor and a willingness to adapt theory and practice to addressing their needs.

REFERENCES

Albu, Mike and Cyrus Njiru (2002), 'The role of small-scale providers in urban areas', *Waterlines* **20** (3): 14–16.

Alcazar, Lorena, Lixin Colin Xu and Ana Maria Zuluaga (2000), 'Institutions, politics and contracts: the attempt to privatise the water and sanitation utility of Lima, Peru', World Bank Policy Research Working Paper, WPS 2478, Washington, DC.

Bayliss, Kate (2001a), *Water Privatisation in Africa: Lessons from Three Case Studies*, Public Services International Research Unit, University of Greenwich.

Bayliss, Kate (2001b), *Does Privatisation Have a Place in a Poverty Reduction Strategy*?, Preliminary draft.

Budds, Jessica (2000), *PPP and the Poor in Water and Sanitation*, An interim review of documents, Water, Engineering and Development Centre, University of Loughborough.

Castro, Luis and Saul Cruz (2002), *A Mexican Probe on the Effects of PSP in Water and Sanitation on the Poor: A Comparative Field Study*, London Water Aid – Tear Fund.

Chisari, Omar, Antonia Estache and Carlos Romero (1999), 'Winners and losers from the privatisation and regulation of utilities: lessons from a general equilibrium model of Argentina', *World Bank Economic Review*, **13** (2): 357–78.

Chisari, Omar, Antonio Estache and Catherine Waddams Price (2001), 'Access by the poor in Latin America's utility reform', WIDER Discussion Paper No. 2001/75, World Institute for Development Economics Research, United Nations University, Helsinki.

Collignon, B. (1999), *The Potential and the Limits of Private Water Providers: Independent Sellers in Francophone Africa*, UNDP, Washington, DC.

Collignon B. and M. Vezina (2000), *Independent Water and Sanitation Providers in African Cities*, UNDP-World Bank Water and Sanitation Program, Washington, DC.

Crane, Randall (1994), 'Water markets, water reform and the urban poor: results from Jakarta, Indonesia', *World Development*, **22** (1): 71–83.

Esguerra, Jude (2002), *The Corporate Muddle of Manila's Water Concessions: How the World's Biggest and Most Successful Privatisation Turned into a Failure*, WaterAid, London.

Etemadi, Feliz (2001), 'Towards inclusive governance in Cebu', Urban Governance, Partnerships and Poverty Research Working Paper No. 25, Stage 2 Case Study, University of Birmingham.

Etherington, Alan, James Wicken and Dinesh Bajracharya (2002), *Preparing for Private Sector Management of Kathmandu Urban Water Supply*, WaterAid, Nepal.

Ferguson, B. and C. Maurer (1996), 'Urban management for environmental quality in South America', *Third World Planning Review*: 117–54.

Gross, Bruce, Christine van Wijk and Nilanjana Mukherjee (2001), *Linking Sustainability with Demand, Gender and Poverty*, Water and Sanitation Programme, World Bank, Washington, DC.

Haggarty, Luke, Penelope Brook and Ana Maria Zuluaga (2000), 'Thirst for reform? Private sector participation in Mexico City's water sector', Policy Research Working Paper WPS 2311, World Bank, Washington, DC.

Hall, David, Kate Bayliss and E. Lobina (2001), 'Still fixated with privatisation: a critical review of World Bank Water Resource Sector Strategy', paper prepared for the International Conference on Freshwater, Germany.

Hardoy, Jorge, Diana Mitlin and David Satterthwaite (2001), *Environmental Problems in Third World Cities*, Earthscan Publications Ltd, London.

Hardoy, Ana and Ricardo Schusterman (2000), 'New models for the privatisation of water and sanitation for the urban poor', *Environment and Urbanization*, **12** (2): 63–75.
Johnstone, D.W.M. and N.J. Horan (1994), 'Standards, costs and benefits: an international perspective', JIWEM **8**: 450–8.
Johnstone, Nick and Libby Wood (2001), 'Introduction', in Nick Johnstone and Libby Wood (eds) *Private Firms and Public Water: Realising Social and Environmental Objectives in Developing Countries*, pp. 1–20, Edward Elgar Publishing, Cheltenham.
Johnstone, Nick and Libby Wood (2001), 'Water and sanitation in low income neighbourhoods: the scope for service differentiation and decentralised management', in Nick Johnstone and Libby Wood (eds) *Private Firms and Public Water: Realising Social and Environmental Objectives in Developing Countries*, pp. 45–54, Edward Elgar Publishing, Cheltenham.
Komives, K. and P.J. Brook Cowen (1999), 'Expanding water and sanitation services to low-income households: the case of La Paz–El Alto concession', *World Bank Public Policy for the Private Sector*, Note No 178.
Lammerink, Marc P., Eveline Bolt, Dick de Jong and Tom Schouten (2001), 'Strengthening community water management', *PLA Notes: Community Water Management*, **35**: 21–8.
Loftus, Alexander J. and David A. McDonald (2001), 'Of liquid dreams: a political ecology of water privatisation in Buenos Aires', *Environment and Urbanization*, **13** (2): 179–99.
Manor, James (1999), *The Political Economics of Democratic Decentralization*, World Bank, Washington, DC.
Marvin, Simon, Nina Laurie and Mark Napier (2001), 'Prepayment: emerging pathways to water services', *Third World Planning Review*, **23** (2): 213–22.
Matin, Nilufar (1999), *Social Inter-mediation: Towards Gaining Access to Water for Squatter Communities in Dhaka*, Water and Sanitation Program – South Asia/Swiss Agency for Development and Cooperation/WaterAid/Dushtha Shasthya Kendra, Dhaka.
Mazzucchelli, Sergio A., Martín Rodriguez Pardinas and Margarita González Tossi (2001), 'Private sector participation in water supply and sanitation: realising social and environmental objectives in Buenos Aires', in Nick Johnstone and Libby Wood (eds) *Private Firms and Public Water: Realising Social and Environmental Objectives in Developing Countries*, pp. 55–116, Edward Elgar Publishing, Cheltenham.
Menard, Claude, George Clarke and Ana Maria Zuluaga (2001), *The Welfare Effects of Private Sector Participation in Urban Water Supply in Ghana*, Development Research Group, World Bank, Washington, DC.
Moriarty, P. (2002), 'Sustainable livelihoods approaches: an explanation', *Waterlines*, **20** (3): 46.
Nickson, Andrew (1997), 'The Public Private Mix in Urban Water Supply', *International Review of Administrative Sciences*, **63** (2): 165–86.
Nickson, Andrew (2001a), 'Establishing and implementing a joint venture: water and sanitation services in Cartagena, Colombia', Building Municipality Capacity for Private Sector Participation Series – Working Paper 442 03, GHK International, London.
Nickson, Andrew (2001b), 'The Cordoba water concession in Argentina', Building Municipality Capacity for Private Sector Participation Series – Working Paper 442 05, GHK International, London.

Nicol, A. (2000), 'Adopting a Sustainable Livelihoods Approach to Water Projects: Implication for Policy and Practice', Working Paper 133, Overseas Development Institute, London.

OECD (2000), 'Joint Working Party on Trade and Environment, Environmental Services: the "win-win" role of trade liberalization in promoting environmental protection and economic development', Organization for Economic Cooperation and Development, Paris.

OECD (2003), *Improving Water Management: Recent OECD Experience*, Organization for Economic Cooperation and Development, Paris.

Rees, Judith A. (1998), 'Regulation and private participation in the water and sanitation sector', *Natural Resources Forum*, **22** (2): 95–105.

Rivera, D. (1996), *Private Sector Participation in the Water Supply and Wastewater Sector: Lessons from Six Developing Countries,* World Bank, Directions in Development, Washington, DC.

Shugart, C. (1991), *An Exploratory Study of the Water and Pipe-Vendor System in Jakarta*, Harvard Institute for International Development, Cambridge, MA.

Silva, G., N. Tynan and Y. Yilmaz (1998), 'Private participation in the water and sewerage sector – recent trends', *Public Policy for the Private Sector*, World Bank Note No. 147, Washington, DC: World Bank.

Solo, Tova Maria (1999), Small scale entrepreneurs in the urban water and sanitation market', *Environment and Urbanization*, **11** (1): 117–31.

Spiller, Pablo T. and William D. Savedoff (1999), 'Government opportunism and the provision of water', in W.D. Savedoff and P.T. Spiller (eds) *Spilled Water: An Institutional Commitment to the Provision of Water Services*, pp. 1–34, InterAmerican Development Bank, Washington, DC.

Stephens, Carolyn (1996), 'Healthy cities or unhealthy islands? The health and social implications of urban inequality', *Environment and Urbanization*, **8** (2): 9–30.

Thompson, John, Ina T. Porras, Elisabeth Wood, James K. Tumwine, Mark R. Mujwahuzi, Munguti Katui-Katua and Nick Johnstone (2000), 'Waiting at the tap: changes in urban water use in East Africa over three decades', *Environment and Urbanization*, **12** (2): 37–52.

United Nations Human Settlement Programme (2003), *Water and Sanitation in the World's Cities: Local Action for Global Goals*, Earthscan/UN-Habitat, London.

Van den Berg, Caroline (2000), 'Water concessions: who wins, who loses and what to do about it', *Public Policy for the Private Sector*, Note No. 217. World Bank, Finance, Private Sector and Infrastructure Network, Washington, DC.

Walker, Ian, Fidel Ordonez, Pedro Serrano and Jonathon Halpern (2000), 'Pricing, subsidies and the poor: demand for improved water services in Central America', *Policy Research Working Paper WPS 2468*, World Bank, Washington, DC.

17. Regulation and social protection

Armando Barrientos[1]

There is an emerging consensus among multilateral institutions around the need for developing countries to establish and strengthen social protection policies and programmes as an urgent response to economic crisis and rising vulnerability (IADB 2000; ADB 2001; ILO 2001; World Bank 2001).[2] The interest in social protection is a consequence of globalisation trends which increase risk and vulnerability and therefore the demand for social protection, but also restrict the capacity of governments to respond to this demand (Rodrik 1997; Alesina 1999; Tanzi 2000). As an emerging paradigm of social policy in developing countries, social protection covers a wider range of programmes, stakeholders, and instruments than alternatives such as 'social security', 'social insurance', or 'safety nets'. This chapter explores the implications arising from the adoption of social protection for the regulation of enterprises and markets.

The emergence of social protection has important implications for the regulation of enterprises and markets. Regulation is here understood as rules, norms, and institutions, aimed at achieving stated public policy goals. The emerging social protection agenda gives regulation a very significant role in reducing social risk and vulnerability. It encourages the reform and extension of existing regulation, and the development of new forms of regulation in developing countries (World Bank 2001). This includes the extension of labour standards as an important instrument in preventing and mitigating employment related income risk. It also includes mandated employee insurance covering health expenditures, work related injuries and disability, and old age and dependant pensions (ILO 2001). The extension of insurance plans and the participation of private providers necessitate access and prudential regulations applying to financial institutions and other private social protection providers (Barrientos 1999). Self-regulation in the form of codes of conduct or sectoral agreements binding participating firms to risk-sensitive behaviour, provides another important instrument of social protection (Barrientos and Ware Barrientos 2002). It also includes the development of environmental and health and safety regulations as a means of preventing health risks, the materialisation of which may adversely affect consumers and employees. As is apparent from this list, the regulation of enterprises and markets constitutes an important component of the social protection agenda, and the adoption of social protection will involve a significant extension and development of regulation in developing countries.

It is an interesting question whether the predicted changes in regulation encouraged by social protection will have any effect on the regulatory environment in developing countries. Regulation arising from social protection policies is perhaps a small subset of the overall regulation, but a handful of studies focusing on linkages between different regulatory domains suggest social protection can have important implications for the regulation of enterprises and markets. A study on the relationship existing between product market regulation and employment protection for OECD countries finds that countries having tight product market regulation also have strong employment protection policies (Nicoletti et al. 2000). Studies on advanced economies have shown a relationship existing between the openness of an economy and the development of social insurance, redistribution, and wage compression norms (Atkinson 1997, 1999; Agell 1999, 2000). These studies show the presence of linkages between regulatory domains, including those arising from social protection, which could be fruitfully explored in a developing country setting. Furthermore, to the extent that regulatory regimes, understood as distinct articulations of regulatory domains, can be identified in developing countries, social protection may have implications for these as well.

These are the issues addressed in this chapter. The aim is to explore the interactions existing between social protection and regulation with a view to identifying key issues and trends, and a methodology for analysing them. The chapter is organised as follows. The first section discusses the main features of social protection and briefly reviews the main factors behind its emergence as a social policy framework. The next section discusses the implications of social protection for regulation. Given the breadth of social protection, the discussion focuses on the regulatory implications of increased reliance on government mandated insurance plans. The third section explores the potential implications of social protection for other regulatory domains, and argues for the need to identify and evaluate regulatory regimes. A final section summarises the main conclusions.

WHAT IS SOCIAL PROTECTION?

In the 1990s, the concept of social protection underwent an important transformation.[3] Within the context of economic crises, structural adjustment and globalisation, social protection has been increasingly adopted as an appropriate framework for social policy in developing countries. Social protection is now defined as consisting of 'public actions taken in response to levels of vulnerability, risk, and deprivation which are deemed socially unacceptable within a given polity or society' (Conway et al. 2000). Social protection is generally taken to be broader than social security, which is normally associated with compensatory, comprehensive, welfare state programmes existing in advanced economies.[4] Social protection is also broader than social insurance, normally restricted to contributory programmes covering a specific range of contingencies, and it is broader than social safety nets, which are mainly short-term interventions in response to food or income crises. There is an emerging consensus around the view that social protection can provide a more appropriate framework for addressing rising poverty and vulnerability in the context of current conditions in developing countries.

A number of factors explain the rise of social protection as a dominant agenda for social policy, but the impact of globalisation in the context of trade, finance and labour market reforms is the most important. The greater openness of developing economies implies a greater exposure to changes in global markets, and a greater concentration of social risks on the less powerful participants. Within developing countries, social risks concentrate on the more vulnerable sectors; globalisation therefore raises the demand for social protection (Rodrik 1997). At the same time, globalisation reduces the tax base of national governments, for example through the migration of high skilled workers, the restrictions on taxes brought about by the need to remain competitive in international markets, and the growth in internet commerce (Tanzi 2000). In reducing the tax base, globalisation undermines the capacity of governments, especially in developing countries, to meet the greater demand for social protection. An important implication is that effective social protection cannot rely solely on public programmes and on direct public provision. While governments retain a central role in the production of social protection, a wider set of providers, instruments and programmes is needed to meet the increased demand for social protection, and this is an important driving force behind the emerging social protection paradigm.

Social protection has a number of distinctive strands:

- Social protection focuses on poverty reduction and on providing support to the poorest (de Haan, 2000). This is different to the income redistribution focus of social security in developed countries, and the largely income-contingent focus of social insurance.
- Social protection seeks to address the causes of poverty, and not simply its symptoms (World Bank 2001), which has far reaching implications. It is postulated that the causes of poverty are to be found in the multiple social risks faced by the poor, in their vulnerability to the realisation of these risks, and in adverse effects of their behavioural response to risks. The realisation of social risks affects the welfare of the poor directly but,

in addition, their greater vulnerability to risks leads to risk averse behaviour with long-term detrimental implications for their welfare. Social protection aims to reduce the exposure of the vulnerable to risks, ameliorate the effects of the realisation of risks, and enable welfare improving behavioural responses to risks. It can also be argued that by focusing on social risks, social protection addresses the dynamic nature of poverty (de Haan 2000).

- The focus on risk and vulnerability as the main cause of poverty also implies that social protection is 'forward looking' in underlining the need to develop ex ante interventions to reduce risk and vulnerability. Public interventions are evaluated as investments rather than costs (World Bank 2001), and seek to develop the capacity of the poor to reduce, ameliorate, or cope with social risk. Social protection draws particular attention to human capital investment, and more generally to productive investment as the key to poverty reduction.
- Social protection acknowledges the variety and heterogeneity of risks affecting individuals, households and communities, and therefore acknowledges the multidimensional nature of poverty (Lund and Srinivas 2000). Employment and labour market risks are taken to be highly significant, and interrelated with other sources of risk and vulnerability. Labour market social protection instruments are therefore given a key role.
- Social protection draws attention to a wide range of stakeholders, programmes and institutions, and instruments, involved in the provision of social protection in developing countries, from formal social insurance programmes to the universal provision of health and education, to informal social networks, micro-insurance, and intra-household support (Esping-Andersen 1999, 2002). It draws attention to the need to 'crowd in' and articulate existing forms of social protection (Murdoch 1998).
- Social protection addresses the impact of globalisation on the demand and supply of social protection. While acknowledging the important role of public provision of social protection, and the key role of governments in supporting and strengthening other forms of provision, the articulation of a broader set of providers and instruments, including private, not-for-profit, and household provision, is taken to constitute a necessary response to globalisation.
- Social protection acknowledges the relevance and importance of a gender dimension to the distribution of risk and vulnerability, and therefore to poverty reduction strategies (ILO 2001, p. 39; World Bank 2001, pp. 27ff).
- Social protection highlights issues of governance and participation in the design, financing, and provision of social protection instruments and programmes (World Bank 2001).

Taken together, these strands of social protection amount to a very comprehensive and timely statement on the social policy agenda and priorities for developing countries. They also reflect a significant shift in perspective, and an emerging consensus, among the multilateral agencies in the field.

There are important nuances in the social protection perspective adopted by different multilateral institutions reflecting their specific outlook. The Social Protection Strategy Paper from the World Bank, for example, moves beyond 'traditional' social protection in defining a 'social risk management' framework adding macroeconomic stability and financial market development to typical social protection programmes. Social risk management (SRM) consists of public interventions 'to assist individuals, households and communities in better managing income risks' (Holzmann and Jorgensen 1999, p. 1008). The emphasis on agency and income protection is in line with the Bank's broader approach to development. The ILO, on the other hand, sees social protection as arising from basic rights.[5] It is defined by 'entitlement to benefits that society provides to individuals and households – through public and collective measures – to protect against low or declining living standards arising out of a number of basic risks and needs' (van Ginneken 2000). The emphasis on rights is also in line with the ILO's basic approach.

In sum, in the context of economic crises, structural adjustment and globalisation, social protection is being increasingly adopted as the appropriate framework for social policy in developing countries. There is emerging consensus around the view that social protection can best address rising poverty and vulnerability in developing countries.

THE IMPLICATIONS OF SOCIAL PROTECTION FOR THE REGULATION OF ENTERPRISES AND MARKETS

The emerging social protection paradigm gives regulation a key role in preventing and mitigating social risk and vulnerability, by encouraging the reform and extension of existing regulation, and by encouraging new forms of regulation. This section focuses on insurance mandates, a new form of regulation arising directly from social protection. Social protection will have wider effects on regulation, but insurance mandates provide a distinctive case study. In Latin America and transitional economies, a number of countries have replaced direct public or quasi-public provision of old age, disability and health insurance with government regulated (mandated) employee insurance. This involves a change in the role of government from provider to regulator, and an expansion of private provision of social protection. This section explores the implications of introducing insurance saving mandates for enterprises and markets, and their regulation.

Economic crises and restructuring have placed strong pressure on government finances, both through restrictions on the tax base and through pressure to reduce fiscal deficits. Where governments are responsible for social security programmes, such as those covering old age, disability, or health insurance, these pressures have translated into a deterioration of benefit coverage and levels, and growing pressure for reform. In the context of Latin America and transitional economies, governments have sought to reform these programmes by transferring responsibility for insurance to the workers themselves and, to a lesser extent, to their employers. In place of direct provision, governments now mandate participation by workers in retirement income or health expenditure insurance saving plans, and have actively encouraged the establishment and development of private insurance providers (Barrientos 1998a, 1999; Barrientos and Lloyd-Sherlock 2000).[6] Mandating insurance saving plans is increasingly replacing direct or indirect public provision, and has become a key instrument in the provision of social protection in Latin America and transitional economies (Barrientos forthcoming).

There is an extensive literature on government mandates as an instrument of social protection, but it is not possible to provide a full review here. Summers argues that government mandates have advantages over alternative forms of organising provision: direct public provision has implications for public finance, while leaving insurance provision to be freely bargained by employees and employers often results in sub-optimal insurance cover (Summers 1989).[7] There is also a growing literature on individual insurance saving plans as an instrument of social protection (World Bank 1994; Barrientos 1998a; James 1998; Folster 1999; Barrientos and Lloyd-Sherlock 2000).

The Implications of Mandated Insurance Saving Plans for Enterprises and Markets

The introduction of government insurance saving mandates will have implications for firm size and sectoral choice (formal–informal). A simple model of the impact of government mandates on the profit function of firms can illustrate this point (Squire and Suthiwart-Narueput 1997). In Latin America and transitional economies, the involvement of employers in mandated insurance saving plans is normally restricted to ensuring their employees comply with the mandate, collecting their contributions, and depositing these with the provider of choice. The costs associated with compliance may differ by firm size, and the extent of managerial specialisation within firms. Assuming the employer profit function is:

$$\pi(r, w) = \max_{K,L} F(K,L) - wL - rK \qquad (17.1)$$

where π is profits, K and L are capital and labour, respectively, and w and r are wages and rate of return to capital, respectively. The introduction of a mandated pension and health insurance generates for the firm costs ξ per worker. These costs are most likely decreasing in firm size, so that $\xi(L)$, $\xi(L)'$ > 0, and $\xi(\mathrm{L})'' < 0$. The range of possible responses by the firm includes compliance, evasion and avoidance. Avoidance assumes that the mandated coverage is such that it is possible for the firm to reorganise employee input so as to avoid compliance, but at a transaction cost η per worker, with $\eta > 0$. The firm can alternatively choose to evade the mandate, but risks a penalty P with probability of inspection λ, with $1 < \lambda > 0$. The impact of the different responses on the firm's profit function π^M is:

$$\pi^M (r, w) \left| \begin{array}{ll} \pi^m (r, w) - \xi(L) & \text{if comply} \\ 1 - \lambda\, \pi^M (r, w) + \lambda\, \pi^M (r, w) - P - \xi(L) & \text{if evade} \\ \pi^M (r, w) - \eta L & \text{if avoid} \end{array} \right. \tag{17.2}$$

The firm will avoid rather than comply if

$$\eta L < \xi(L) \tag{17.3}$$

and the firm will evade rather than comply or avoid if

$$\lambda \,/\, 1 - \lambda\, [P + \xi(L)] < \eta L < \xi(L) \tag{17.4}$$

Assuming that avoidance transaction costs per workers are constant, and that fines are independent of firm size, there will be a size of firm for which avoidance will be preferable to evasion. Furthermore, with compliance costs decreasing in relation to firm size, there will be a larger size of firm where compliance will dominate avoidance. The firm's strategy in response to the mandated benefit collection and administration costs can be summarised in

$$\gamma = \min \{\lambda \,/\, 1 - \lambda[P + \xi(L)],\, \eta L\ ,\, \xi(L)\} \tag{17.5}$$

This simple model demonstrates that regulation associated with the introduction of insurance plan mandates could have implications for enterprises and markets. Research into the determinants of insurance plan coverage in countries which have introduced such mandates found a strong positive correlation of employee affiliation and establishment size, consistent with the implications arising from this model (Barrientos 1996, 1998b).

The Implications of Mandated Insurance Saving Plans for the Regulation of Private Providers of Social Protection

The introduction of individual insurance saving plans as an instrument of social protection creates the conditions for the development of new financial and insurance providers specialising in social protection: pension fund managers, health and unemployment insurance providers, and so on. In addition, existing financial intermediaries are encouraged to expand the range of financial instruments associated with these developments, such as annuity provision. Regulation of social protection providers is important in facilitating the bedding down and success of the reforms (Shah 1997; James et al. 1998; Queisser 1998; Vittas 1998; Barrientos 1999; Yermo 2000; Barrientos and Boussofiane 2001). Providing that regulation is well designed and implemented, the new providers could play a very significant role in opening up financial and insurance markets, thus improving households' access to credit and insurance and therefore their ability to self-protect against social risks.[8]

Extensive regulation of private providers of social protection is needed because of information asymmetries affecting insurance provision. In the absence of product and price regulation, private providers of insurance have an incentive to select low-risk, high-income groups, and repel high-risk, low-income groups. They also have an incentive to exploit superior information by absorbing the returns to investment in the form of high costs and profits. In the absence of regulation, private insurance providers also have an incentive to take excessive risk with the investment funds in their charge, a case of moral hazard arising from the role of governments as guarantors of last resort. Regulation is also needed because of the relative underdevelopment of financial and insurance markets in developing countries, which sometimes requires a significant injection of competition, and at other times calls for the creation of new markets. In setting out the regulation of these providers, the challenge is to make insurance markets work for the benefit of the more vulnerable groups in the population.

In conclusion, the adoption of social protection will, in all likelihood, have significant implications for the regulation of enterprises and markets as a result of governments playing an increasing role as regulators of social protection, and in the extension of regulation needed to accommodate a stronger role for private providers of social protection.

SOCIAL PROTECTION, LINKS BETWEEN REGULATORY DOMAINS, AND REGULATORY REGIMES

This section considers whether social protection is likely to have implications for other regulatory domains, and for the overall regulatory regime.

There are few studies exploring the linkages existing between social protection regulation and other domains. For advanced economies, Agell puts forward the hypothesis that 'increased openness may lead to increased institutional involvement in the labour market' as a means of reducing vulnerability to global markets (Agell 1999, p. F160). This is also discussed by others (Rodrik 1996; Atkinson 1997), but there is little consensus on the links between increased openness, economic risk and volatility, and the demand for and supply of social protection (McCulloch et al. 2001). A study by Nicoletti et al. (2000) focuses on the linkages between social protection and product market regulation in OECD countries.[9] They find that product market and employment protection regulation, defined by a broad array of indicators, are correlated. As they put it, 'restrictive product market regulations are matched by analogous employment protection legislation restrictions to generate a tight overall regulatory environment for firms in their product market as well as in the allocation of labour inputs' (Nicoletti et al. 2000, p. 51). One possible interpretation of these findings is that firms that are relatively sheltered from competition in the product market may feel less urgency in pressing for employment protection liberalisation.

The presence of linkages across regulatory domains often figures in policy discussions. For developing countries, this issue arises, for example, in the context of discussions of the political economy of structural reforms. To the extent that regulatory domains are interconnected, reform in one domain will need to take account of regulatory reforms in other domains. Indeed, the substance, timing and sequencing of reforms may well be dictated by interconnected regulatory domains. Vittas, for example, discusses in some detail the sequencing of regulatory changes needed to facilitate social security reform in developing countries, which include a host of regulatory changes in public financial arrangements as well as in corporate regulations, regulation of the finance and banking sectors, and employment regulation (Vittas 1995). In his view, social security reforms introduced without regulatory changes in these other related areas have little chance of success.

The concept of a regime goes a step further – it poses the question of whether regulations in different domains of an economy exhibit a measure of interconnectedness such that specific types of regulation can be recognised across regulatory domains. A regulatory regime describes a distinctive articulation of regulatory domains; that is, a distinct institutional framework for regulation. The identification of regulatory regimes is a challenging task because of the detailed and complex nature of regulation. It is also made difficult by the fact that regulation usually develops in a piecemeal fashion, with each regulatory intervention addressing very specific public policy objectives. Cross-country comparisons add further complexity, and regulation tends to be differentiated across countries.

However, these difficulties underline the potential advantages of such an approach. Identifying common or connected features in regulation across domains, and similarities across countries, can considerably facilitate discussion of regulatory structures and of their impact on development. The complex nature of regulation suggests that mono-causal explanations will be deficient in the context of regulatory regimes. The notion of regulatory regimes helps unveil regulatory constraints and path dependence, which are usually obscured where single regulatory interventions are considered. Investigating whether countries cluster around a handful of regulatory regimes can help analyse the effects of regulation on the development process.[10] An advantage of this approach is that the grouping of countries around a regulatory regime is not done at the expense of ignoring country specificity, or path dependence, and without the presumption of regulatory convergence.[11]

The discussion in the remainder of this section will attempt to explore these issues empirically, asking whether there is a measure of interconnectedness existing between social protection regulation and other regulatory domains, and whether countries cluster around identifiable regulatory regimes. The data used come mainly from the DoingBusiness dataset (World Bank 2002a) constructed by the World Bank, supplemented with economic indicators from the 2002 *World Development Indicators* (World Bank 2002b) and other indicators from the ILO's *World Labour Report 2000* (ILO 2000).

To investigate the extent to which regulatory domains are interconnected, Figures 17.1 to 17.3 show a scatterplot of an index of labour regulations and three separate measures of product market regulation: an index of formalism in contract enforcement, the number of procedures required by firm entry regulations, and the extent of credit information provided on firms measured as a percentage of 21 information characteristics. The values for the different measures are all increasing in regulation. An advantage of the DoingBusiness dataset is that the data have been carefully standardised and cover a large group of countries. Except where indicated, the datapoints are for 2000–02. The figures show the association between variables by region, as preliminary work showed strong differences by region.

Figure 17.1 shows the association existing between an index of labour regulation and an index of formalism in contract enforcement. The index of labour regulation is the sum of an index of employment laws, covering alternative employment contracts, conditions of employment, and employment protection; and an industrial relations index covering regulations on trade unions, workers participation and collective bargaining. The labour regulations index therefore captures a wide range of social protection indicators. The index of formalism in contract enforcement, on the other hand, summarises a number of indicators of procedural interventions in the enforcement of commercial contracts, with a higher value for the index indicating increasing formalisation of the contract enforcement process. As can be seen in Figure 17.1, there is a strong association across regions in these two indicators of regulation. With the exception of Sub-Saharan Africa, which shows little association between these variables, and the Middle East and North Africa region, which shows a negative association, all other regions show a positive association between these two indexes representing different regulatory domains.

Figure 17.2 shows the association existing between the labour regulation index and a measure of the regulation applying to firm entry: the number of procedures required for firm entry. The latter measure was constructed by recording all interactions needed by a new company to obtain all the necessary

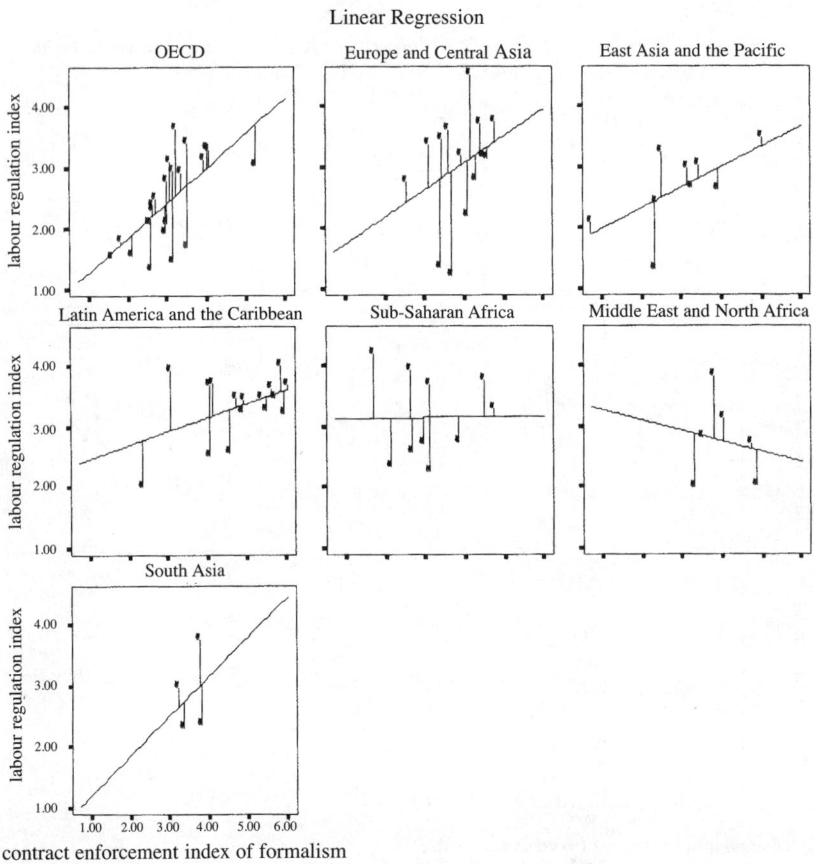

Figure 17.1 Scatterplot of labour regulation index and an index of formalism in the enforcement of commercial contracts

permits and licences, and the 'inscriptions, verifications, and notification to enable the company to start operation' (World Bank 2002a). Figure 17.2 shows that a positive association between these variables can be observed for most regions, except for Latin America where there is little association between the measures, and Europe and Central Asia where the association is strong and negative. In the main, regions that have more regulated labour markets also have stronger firm entry regulations.

Finally, Figure 17.3 shows the association existing between the labour regulation index and a measure of the extent of regulation on credit information provided by a public credit registry agency. The measure was constructed

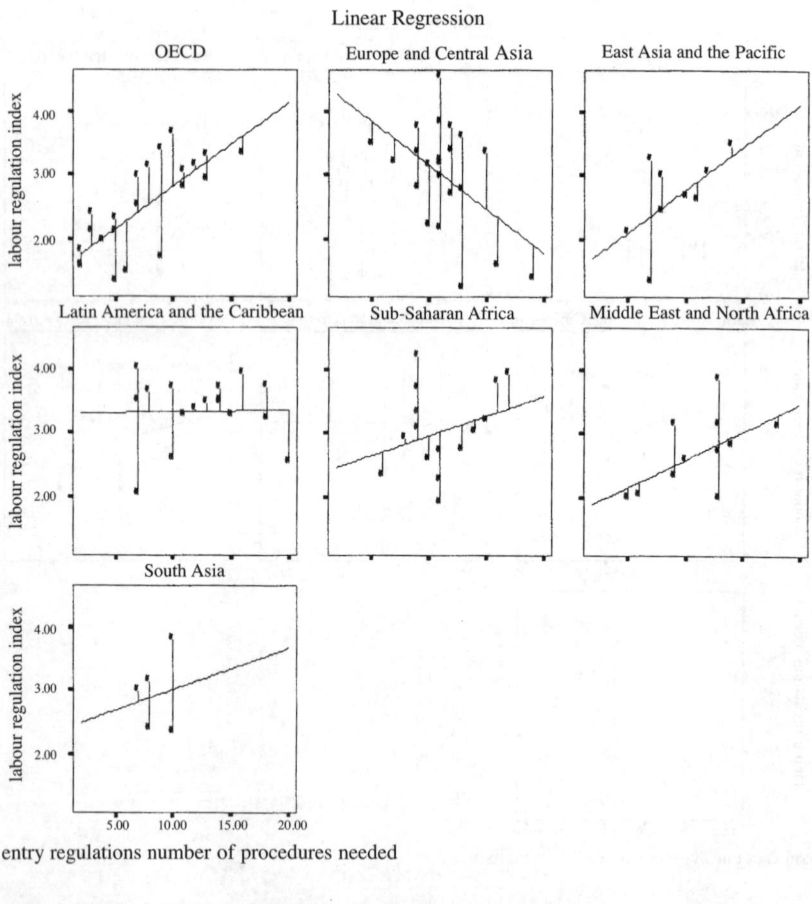

Figure 17.2 Scatterplot of labour regulation index and the number of procedures required by firm entry regulations

by setting out a list of potential information items provided on firms (e.g. name of owner, assets and liabilities, bankruptcies, etc.) and checking for each country the proportion of information items released. The measure captures the extent of credit information regulation provided, and therefore the extent of regulation in credit markets. The indicator is available for a reduced number of countries. Figure 17.3 shows a weak positive association for most regions, except South Asia where the association is negative. On the whole, there is weaker evidence that labour regulations are positively related to credit information regulation.

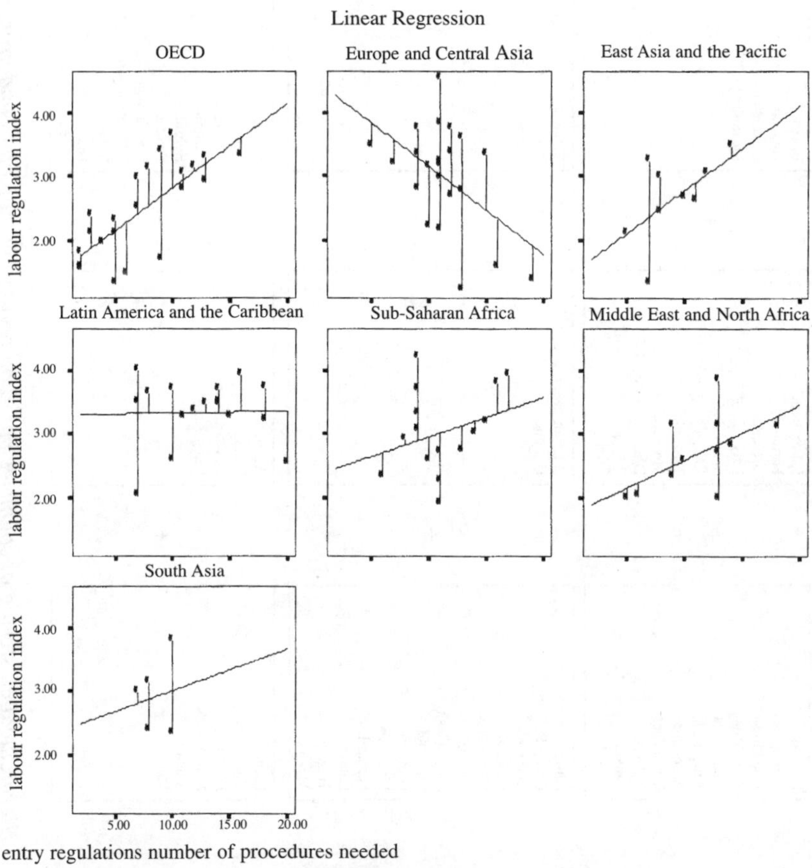

Figure 17.3 *Scatterplot of labour regulation index and the scope of credit information on firms provided by a public credit registry agency*

	Sub-cluster One		Sub-cluster Two		Sub-cluster Three		Sub-cluster Four
Cluster One	Ecuador Philippines Honduras Kazakhstan Guatemala Venezuela Argentina Costa Rica Bolivia Panama Peru	+	Korea Rep. Portugal Greece Italy Spain Jordan Tanzania Morocco Dominican Republic	+	Brazil Uganda Colombia Mozambique	+	Romania Uruguay Pakistan Nigeria Croatia Egypt Poland South Africa
Cluster Two	Chile Czech Republic Indonesia Sri Lanka Slovenia Lebanon Bangladesh Thailand Hungary Lithuania Senegal Latvia Tunisia Mexico	+	Russian Federation Ukraine	+	Jamaica Zambia Malaysia	+	India Kenya Malawi Vietnam Ghana China Georgia Turkey
Cluster Three	France Germany Finland Netherlands Singapore Japan	+	Australia Canada New Zealand Hong Kong	+	Denmark Norway Switzerland Austria Belgium Sweden United States United Kingdom Ireland Israel Taiwan	+	

Figure 17.4 Hierarchical clustering of countries based on regulation indicators and gross national income per capita

The next step is to seek to identify whether there is enough commonality in these regulatory domains across countries to identify regulatory regimes. Figure 17.4 shows the results from a basic clustering exercise, taking the four indicators of regulation used in Figures 17.1–17.3 plus a measure of gross national income per capita. The intention here is to investigate possible groupings of countries along the regulatory domains examined. A hierarchical clustering routine was used, which basically groups countries with similar scores until they are all in one group.[12] Identifying the number of distinct clusters relies on a stopping rule based on measuring the distance of sub-clusters to be joined, with a large jump in this distance indicating further clustering to be unhelpful. Figure 17.4 shows the progressive clustering of countries, and the exercise suggests there are three distinct clusters: one dominated by Latin American and Southern Mediterranean countries, a second cluster containing several transitional and Commonwealth countries, and a third cluster containing mainly OECD countries. Some of the sub-clusters are recognisable in terms of shared characteristics, and particularly in terms of broad legal frameworks. The clustering of countries on the basis of regulation indicators suggests the feasibility of identifying regulatory regimes, and the role of social protection regulation within them. Further research is needed to extend the analysis to include indicators from other regulatory regimes, and to relate the clusters to explanatory variables and outcome measures of development.

Although more research is needed before reaching stronger conclusions, the exercise suggests the usefulness of examining linkages between regulation domains, and of including social protection and product market regulation. There are important linkages across regulatory domains, suggesting that social protection is likely to have an impact on other regulatory domains. The identification of regulatory regimes can provide useful information, although more work is needed to refine the empirical investigation and link its explanatory patterns.

CONCLUSIONS

This chapter discussed the implications of the growing consensus around the need to establish and strengthen social protection in developing countries. It began with a characterisation of social protection as an emerging framework for social policy, and a brief discussion of the reasons for its prominence. Social protection involves an extension of the range of instruments, stakeholders and programmes in the production of social protection. Regulation is an important component of social protection, and in the second section the chapter showed, with the specific example of the introduction of individual insurance saving plans in Latin America and transitional economies, that the adoption of social protection has implications for the regulation of enterprises and markets. The third section examined empirically whether social protection regulation is linked to other regulatory domains, and especially the regulation of enterprises and markets. This showed that indicators of labour regulation are positively correlated with indicators of contract enforcement, firm entry, and credit information regulation, suggesting linkages across regulatory domains. The correlation between regulatory domains differs across regions, in both strength and quality. Finally, an attempt was made to identify regulatory regimes on the basis of the different indicators using cluster analysis. The exercise showed that it is feasible to cluster countries around regulatory regimes.

The discussion in this chapter should alert us to the need to incorporate social protection within the study and evaluation of regulation in developing countries. The emergence of social protection as the framework for social policy in the developing world will have important implications for regulation. Regulation constitutes an important component of social protection, especially in the context of the expansion of private and not-for profit provision of social protection. Social protection regulation is linked to other regulatory domains, and constitutes an important component of regulatory regimes. Further research is needed to determine other linkages, and to identify regulatory regimes with greater precision, but the chapter has indicated the advantages of doing so.

NOTES

1. I am grateful to Colin Kirkpatrick and participants at the Centre for Regulation and Competition Conference at the University of Manchester held in September 2002 for helpful comments. The errors that remain are mine alone.
2. The World Bank's Social Protection Sector Strategy paper argues there are important similarities between social protection and the sustainable livelihoods approach of the UNDP and DFID (World Bank 2001).
3. For a discussion of the transformation of social protection within the World Bank, see World Bank (2001), and for a restatement of social protection within the ILO see ILO (2001).
4. In the ILO's perspective, for example, social security is restricted to 'statutory schemes'.
5. In the more recent *Social Security. A New Consensus*, a painstaking effort is made to broaden the organisation's emphasis on social security in the direction of social protection by drawing a parallel between the latter and the 'decent work for all' strategy. As noted in this document, one 'of the essential features of the decent work approach is that everybody is entitled to basic social protection' (ILO 2001, p. 39). This is taken to be an extension of the 1948 Universal Declaration of Human Rights article 22 stating that 'everyone, as a member of society, has the right to social security', via the 1966 International Covenant on Economic, Social and Cultural Rights article 9 stating 'the right of everyone to social security, including social insurance' (ILO 2001).
6. In Latin America, individual retirement insurance plans have been introduced in Chile, Argentina, Peru, Colombia, Uruguay, Bolivia, Mexico, El Salvador, Nicaragua and Costa Rica. Individual health insurance saving plans have been introduced in Chile, Argentina, Colombia and Mexico. Individual unemployment insurance plans have been introduced in Chile and Colombia. Chile and Colombia are also experimenting with demand subsidies for the financing of education, which could easily be complemented by saving plans.

7. See also Mitchell 1990; Ippolito 1997.
8. In the case of Chile, the introduction of mandated insurance plans has extended access to financial and credit markets to groups otherwise unattractive to the banking and insurance sectors, for example by developing low cost voluntary saving plans in parallel with retirement plans. Regulation can also extend this access to workers in informal and vulnerable employment. The introduction of low cost severance plans for domestic workers is an example of this. Employers are required to contribute 4.11 per cent of domestic workers' pay into a severance plan with one of the pension fund managers. The balance of the plan is invested in the same assets as retirement insurance plans, and is available to domestic workers in the event of the termination of employment.
9. Their study generates a number of interesting and relevant findings. With regard to links between outward and inward oriented regulation, they find no close correlation between these two for the OECD countries studied. It appears that 'high standards of openness to trade and international finance' are not carried over to domestic regulation (Nicoletti et al. 2000, p. 36).
10. In the domains of social security and labour market regulation, the use of welfare regimes as an organising concept has proved to be very useful (Esping-Andersen 1999; Gough 1999; Barrientos forthcoming).
11. Discussing labour market regulation, for example, Freeman finds that there is significant variety in regulatory structures across advanced countries and also across developing countries, and little sign of convergence towards a single model (Freeman 1993, 1998, 2000). He also finds significant variation in outcomes (countries with similar regulations showing different outcomes, and countries with different regulations showing similar outcomes, on the relevant variables) and strong path dependence.
12. The clustering was done using z-scores for the different indicators to ensure the different variables used have equal weighting.

REFERENCES

ADB (2001), *Social Protection Strategy*, Manila: Asian Development Bank.

Agell, J. (1999), 'On the benefits from rigid labour markets: norms, market failures, and social insurance', *Economic Journal*, **109** (453), F143–164.

Agell, J. (2000), 'On the determinants of labour market institutions: rent-sharing vs. social insurance', mimeo, Uppsala: Department of Economics, Uppsala University.

Alesina, A. (1999), 'Too large and too small governments', in V. Tanzi, K.-y. Chu and S. Gupta (eds), *Economic Policy and Equity*, Washington, DC: International Monetary Fund, pp. 216–34.

Atkinson, A.B. (1997), 'Bringing income distribution back from the cold', Economic Journal, **107** (441), 297–321.

Atkinson, A.B. (1999), *The Economic Consequences of Rolling Back the Welfare State*, Cambridge, MA: MIT Press.

Barrientos, A. (1996), 'Pension reform and pension coverage in Chile: lessons for other countries', *Bulletin of Latin American Research*, **15** (3), 309–22.

Barrientos, A. (1998a), *Pension Reform in Latin America*, Aldershot: Ashgate.

Barrientos, A. (1998b), 'Pension reform, personal pensions and gender differences in pension coverage', *World Development*, **26** (1), 125–37.

Barrientos, A. (1999), 'The emerging pension fund management market in Latin America', *Journal of Pensions Management*, **5** (1), 60–8.

Barrientos, A. (forthcoming), 'Latin America: towards a liberal-informal welfare regime', in I. Gough and G. Wood (eds), *Insecurity and Welfare Regimes in Asia, Africa and Latin America*, Cambridge: Cambridge University Press.

Barrientos, A. and A. Boussofiane (2001), 'The efficiency of pension fund managers in Latin America', CRC Working Paper 11, Manchester: IDPM, University of Manchester.

Barrientos, A. and P. Lloyd-Sherlock (2000), 'Reforming health insurance in Argentina and Chile', *Health Policy and Planning*, **15** (4), 417–23.

Barrientos, A. and S. Ware Barrientos (2002), 'Social protection for workers in the informal economy: case study on horticulture', Social Protection Discussion Paper 0216, Washington, DC: World Bank.

Conway, T., A. de Haan and A. Norton (eds) (2000), *Social Protection: New Directions of Donor Agencies*, London: Department for International Development.

de Haan, A. (2000), 'Introduction: the role of social protection in poverty reduction', in T. Conway, A. de Haan and A. Norton (eds), *Social Protection: New Directions of Donor Agencies*, London: Department for International Development, pp. 5–20.

Esping-Andersen, G. (1999), *Social Foundations of Postindustrial Economies*, Oxford: Oxford University Press.

Esping-Andersen, G. (2002), 'The sustainability of welfare states: reshaping social protection', in B. Harris-White (ed.), *Globalization and Insecurity. Political, Economic and Physical Challenges*, London: Palgrave, pp. 218–32.

Folster, S. (1999), 'Social insurance based on personal savings', *The Economic Record*, **75** (228), 5–18.

Freeman, R.B. (1993), 'Labor market institutions and policies: help or hindrance to economic development', *World Bank Economic Review*, **7** (3), 117–44.

Freeman, R.B. (1998), 'War of the models: which labour market institutions for the 21st Century?' *Labour Economics*, **5**, 1–24.

Freeman, R.B. (2000), 'Single peaked vs. diversified capitalism: the relation between economic institutions and outcomes', Working Paper 7556, Cambridge, MA: National Bureau of Economic Research.

Gough, I. (1999), 'Welfare regimes: on adapting the framework to developing countries', Working Paper, Bath: Institute for International Policy Analysis.

Holzmann, R. and S. Jorgensen (1999), 'Social protection as social risk management: conceptual underpinnings for the social protection strategy paper', *Journal of International Development*, **11**, 1005–27.

IADB (2000), *Social Protection for Equity and Growth*, Washington, DC: Inter-American Development Bank.

ILO (2000), *World Labour Report 2000*, Geneva: International Labour Office.

ILO (2001), *Social Security. A New Consensus*, Geneva: International Labour Office.

Ippolito, R.A. (1997), *Pension Plans and Employee Performance. Evidence, Analysis and Policy*, Chicago and London: University of Chicago Press.

James, E. (1998), 'New models for old-age security: experiments, evidence and unanswered questions', *The World Bank Research Observer*, **13** (2), 271–301.

James, E., G. Ferrier, J. Smalhout and D. Vittas (1998), 'Mutual Funds and Institutional Investments. What is the most effective way to set up individual accounts in a social security system?', mimeo, Washington, DC: The World Bank.

Lund, F. and S. Srinivas (2000), *Learning from Experience: A Gendered Approach to Social Protection for Workers in the Informal Economy*, Geneva: International Labour Organization.

McCulloch, N., L.A. Winters and X. Cirera (2001), *Trade Liberalization and Poverty: A Handbook*, London: Centre for Economic Policy Research.

Mitchell, O.S. (1990), 'The effects of mandating benefits packages', in R. Erhenberg (ed.), *Research in Labor Economics*, Greenwich, CT: Jai Press, pp. 297–320.

Murdoch, J. (1998), 'Between the state and the market: can informal insurance patch the safety net?', *The World Bank Research Observer*, **14** (2), 187–207.
Nicoletti, G., S. Scarpeta and O. Boylaud (2000), 'Summary indicators of product market regulation with an extension to employment protection legislation', Economics Department Working Paper 226, Paris: OECD Economics Department.
Queisser, M. (1998), 'Regulation and supervision of pension funds: principles and practices', *International Social Security Review*, **51** (2/98), 39–55.
Rodrik, D. (1996), 'Understanding economic policy reform', *Journal of Economic Literature*, **34** (March), 9–41.
Rodrik, D. (1997), Has Globalization Gone Too Far?, Washington, DC: Institute for International Economics.
Shah, H. (1997), 'Towards better regulation of private pension funds', Working Paper 1791, Washington, DC: The World Bank.
Squire, L. and S. Suthiwart-Narueput (1997), 'The impact of labour market regulations', *The World Bank Economic Review*, **11** (1), 119–43.
Summers, L.H. (1989), 'Some simple economics of mandated benefits', *American Economic Review*, **79** (2), 177–83.
Tanzi, V. (2000), 'Globalization and the future of social protection', IMF Working Paper WP/00/12, Washington, DC: IMF.
van Ginneken, W. (2000), 'The extension of social protection: ILO's aim for the years to come', in T. Conway, A. de Haan and A. Norton (eds), *Social Protection: New Directions of Donor Agencies*, London: Department for International Development, pp. 33–48.
Vittas, D. (1995), 'Sequencing social security, pension, and insurance reform', Policy Research Working Paper 1551, Washington, DC: The World Bank.
Vittas, D. (1998), 'Regulatory controversies of private pension funds', mimeo, Washington, DC: The World Bank.
World Bank (1994), *Averting the Old Age Crisis*, London: Oxford University Press.
World Bank (2001), 'Social protection sector strategy: from safety net to springboard', Sector Strategy Paper, Washington, DC: The World Bank.
World Bank (2002a), 'DoingBusiness Dataset', World Bank, 2003, http://rru.worldbank.org/DoingBusiness/default.aspx.
World Bank (2002b), *World Development Indicators 2002*, Report, Washington, DC: The World Bank.
Yermo, J. (2002), 'Institutional investors in Latin America: recent trends and regulatory challenges', in OECD (ed.), *Institutional Investors in Latin America*, Paris: OECD, pp. 23–120.

18. The political economy of privatization in Malaysia

Tan Wooi Syn

INTRODUCTION

The state is central to the design and implementation of privatization as it must identify the industry or sector, select candidates, and regulate performance, particularly if monopolies are involved. State support is also necessary where the private sector is unable to bear all the risks in large projects such as infrastructure development that involve externalities. However, such state intervention can undermine private incentives and reduce efficiency. The success of privatization then depends on a country's institutional endowments, in particular its regulatory capacity, and the quality of information available.

This chapter considers these issues in the case of Malaysia, where financial difficulties leading to state bailouts and renationalizations highlight the problems of patronage closely associated with its privatization programme. Poor privatization design, selection and regulation arguably led to inappropriate choices of privatizations and candidates, and weakened incentives to increase efficiency and investment. This in turn emphasizes institutional criteria for the success of privatization policies.

Why the government proceeded despite these problems, and why poor institutions were allowed to persist, demands examination of the political factors that shaped privatization policies and institutions. Privatization was part of a redistributive process that sought to develop entrepreneurial capacity by promoting capital accumulation. But this process also undermined 'learning', compromising the quality of candidates, and increasing patronage. Growing factional rivalries within the ruling Malay party led to centralized decision making and weakened institutions, resulting in poor choices.

Despite its authority, the government was unable to ensure service delivery. This suggests that while successful regulation will depend on the ability to determine appropriate prices/subsidies and monitor performance, it must also be able to enforce credible sanctions for non-delivery. But the ability to do so may be circumscribed by the political context, specifically the available entrepreneurial capacity, social cost of bankruptcy, and national importance of the enterprises.

PRIVATIZATION THEORY AND PRACTICE

Privatization is said to improve efficiency by changing the objectives of the firm's ultimate owners, possibilities for government intervention and ways of monitoring managerial performance (Vickers and Yarrow 1991). According to property rights theory, the principal (government) is unable to provide the appropriate incentives to the agent (state-owned enterprises or SOEs) and to monitor performance due to information problems. Private ownership is seen as the most efficient way to monitor performance in the absence of complete contracts and where 'the nonseparability of products . . . raises the cost of assessing the marginal productivities' of employees (Alchian and Demsetz 1972: 794). The clear designation of property rights – through the combination of residual control (ownership) and residual return (profit) – is said to provide incentives to improve efficiency by introducing the profit motive.

This is rarely the case in privatization, particularly of monopolies or public goods, where the owner 'cannot capture the whole social and economic benefits generated' (Fayard 1999: 12–13) because government regulation is required to address issues of efficiency and equity. The need for price 'caps' or subsidies means that the owner does not necessarily have all the rights to the residual and, as such, does not enjoy all the gains of any improvements. It is also now known that both public and private provision of goods and services involve significant delegation of authority and hence share similar problems relating to incentives and monitoring. The clear designation of property rights does not guarantee economic efficiency because managers in public or private firms remain largely rewarded by salary (Mansfield and Poole 1991, cited in Martin and Parker 1997: 403), hence 'neither has the incentive to design good incentive structures' (Stiglitz 1996: 174) leading to managerial discretion. Information impactedness and 'friction', along with shareholders' bounded rationality, further limit the disciplinary mechanism of capital markets on managerial discretion.

Private ownership is also said to offer a more credible promise for the state not to intervene, thus providing beneficial incentive effects. The starting point of most privatization theories is that 'public enterprises are inefficient because they address the objectives of politicians rather than maximize efficiency' (Boycko et al. 1996: 309). According to public choice theory, SOEs are constrained by the behaviour of politicians and bureaucrats who pursue their own utility rather than the public interest, as political motives usually outweigh efficiency considerations (Vickers and Yarrow 1991). SOEs are inefficient as they lead to excessive political intervention, and any economic intervention by the state is viewed as a potentially counter-productive policy response and an invitation to rent-seeking behaviour; the greater the regulation, the more private resources are absorbed by rent-seeking activities (Buchanan 1980).

Because SOEs, through the allocation of rents, are seen as a vehicle to redistribute wealth or promote politically motivated redistributive arrangements (Jones and Mason 1982), privatization is desirable as it 'effectively drives a wedge between politicians and managers' by depoliticizing firms and making it too costly for politicians to subsidize them (Boycko et al. 1996). By placing some distance between the government and the producer, and substantially increasing the transaction costs of such interventions, privatization is said to make more credible the promise not to use public funds to subsidize losses (Sappington and Stiglitz 1995).

In reality, privatization involves state economic intervention rather than its negation. The existence of monopolies, public goods, and high capital costs has required the state to play a central role through regulation and by sharing risks. Subsidies and grants play an increasingly significant part in infrastructure investment because of the very high capital costs and the need to subsidize public goods or to compensate for positive externalities.[1] Government guarantees may be needed to secure long-term loans, and tax breaks to reduce the tax burden at the beginning of the loan period (Fayard 1999), and the state needs to regulate firm behaviour because large fixed and sunk costs preclude duplication and limit the scope for effective competition in infrastructure privatizations (Vickers and Yarrow 1995). A certain degree of state intervention is now generally acknowledged as necessary (Fayard 1999), and a feature of privatization has been the increase in public–private partnerships to ensure project viability, and which involve a high degree of government financial assistance.[2]

While privatization is meant to provide new funding sources for capital intensive projects such as infrastructure, the private sector in fact faces difficulty financing such high cost projects without government guarantees (Windsor 1996), and many infrastructure projects that offer positive economic and social benefits cannot break even (Poole 1996; Fayard 1999), or cost more when externalities are included (Rosenau 2000a). Private sector financing also costs more due to project-specific risks and limited liability (Daniels and Trebilcock 2000), while the market for private financing of transit services appears to be highly fragmented and disorganized compared with similar investment alternatives (Windsor and Atherton 1984, cited in Windsor 1996: 72). The state can also keep costs down by providing long-term loans, as long maturity is more important than low interest rates (see Fayard 1999: 5–6).

If the private sector is to have incentives to improve efficiency, it must either be able to control revenue and/or bear risks. In reality, these incentives are diluted because full divestitures have been limited and risks have largely been borne by the public sector (Fayard 1999). In the case of large-scale projects such as infrastructure, the state must reduce either the private sector's share of the cost, or its risk, to ensure the project is viable for private sector participation, but the sharing of risks leads to risk-incentive trade-offs (Daniels and Trebilcock 2000; Heilman and Johnson 1992). As the private owner no longer owns the residual return (profit), privatization does not solve the problems of incentives and monitoring. The institutional structure, in particular the regulatory framework, is of great importance in addressing these issues. Careful regulation is needed to determine appropriate prices/subsidies to provide some insurance to the private sector while not dampening incentives; to monitor performance to ensure service delivery; and to enforce credible sanctions in the event of non-delivery.

INSTITUTIONAL REQUIREMENTS FOR PRIVATIZATION

The success of privatization can be said to depend on the country's institutional endowment, and it is crucial that the chosen method of privatization is consistent with the problems to be resolved, information available, and the existing institutional framework. Where the aim is to improve operational efficiency and raise capital, a concession can be ideal (Stottmann 2000). By transferring all commercial risk and responsibility for capital investment to the operator for the duration of the contract, a concession theoretically passes full responsibility for operations and investment to the operator and so brings to bear incentives for efficiency in all aspects of management and operation.

In the case of utilities, the choice of privatization will depend crucially on the quality of information available about the enterprise's present condition and performance. This includes information on (or identifying as unavailable) the present and projected service area; current characteristics of the service; a basic inventory of the assets and their condition and serviceability; human resources; financial performance and tariffs (level and structure, subsidy arrangements, collection performance, disconnection policy); and consumer preferences, affordability and willingness to pay (Stottmann 2000).

This information should be made available to bidders so that bids are realistic and viable. The selection process should be competitive, and the contract awarded to the bidder proposing the lowest future tariff levels (indicating the highest efficiency).[3] Poor quality information results in renegotiations, but contract renegotiation is also inevitable due to future uncertainties that cannot be covered. Careful provision must therefore be made to deal with unexpected events over the life of the contract, including conditions under which adjustment can be made; guidelines determining when and under what conditions contract renegotiation must occur rather than price or service adjustment by agreement or by regulatory discretion; the process by which renegotiation must be initiated and conducted; and a definition of clear arbitration provisions (Stottmann 2000).

Regulation is important as large-scale privatized projects usually require some form of state financial assistance (due to the high capital costs, especially in the construction stage) and subsidies (as tariffs usually cannot cover costs). As the long duration of such concessions creates opportunities for rents, the state will also seek to keep profits consistent with market conditions to achieve economic efficiency through a price 'capping' mechanism. This is achieved by directing the private sector to implement the socially optimal plan based on the common information about industry conditions and the firm's behaviour. In practice, the presence of asymmetric information means that managers are much better informed about industry conditions, and their behaviour can be monitored only imperfectly (Vickers and Yarrow 1995).

It is therefore difficult to determine how much profit the operator actually makes and hence the appropriate amount of subsidies or level of price cap. This has disincentive effects by encouraging the operator to artificially inflate costs. Incentive regulation seeks to induce firms to improve efficiency by granting some, but not complete, discretion to the firm. It is most appropriate where competition alone is insufficient to compel industry participants to pursue social goals, where the regulated firm has better information than the regulator about its environment and/or its actions, and where the goals of the firm and society are not entirely congruent (Sappington and Weissman 1996).

As the level of regulation and monitoring will also depend on the mode of privatization (e.g. a concession requires far more regulation and capacity than a management contract), regulatory capacity can determine which privatization option is most appropriate. Regulatory capacity will depend on the information available, technical competence, and the country's institutional endowments. The quality of information is crucial to determine the appropriate rate of return, benchmark or price cap, while sophisticated regulatory training and technical ability are needed to calculate realistic benchmarks. Simpler regulation such as RPI-X, on the other hand, requires credible restraints on arbitrary changes, credible conflict-resolution mechanisms, and checks and balances that must be built on long-standing constitutional arrangements and informal norms (Levy and Spiller 1994).

The choice of privatization thus needs to be compatible with the legal framework and human resource capacity, and the success of a regulatory system depends on how well it fits into a country's institutional setting (Levy and Spiller 1994). Decisions about the privatization option, industrial structure, and regulatory framework are therefore closely linked; a concession would be difficult to implement where regulatory capacity is weak, political commitment is low, the regulatory environment uncertain, and information poor (Stottmann 2000).

THE MALAYSIAN CASE

The privatization of Malaysia's national sewerage system, airline, car project, and light rail transit (LRT) system was part of the government's attempts to improve efficiency and increase investment through owner-managed enterprises. All these sectors required some form of subsidy given the high capital costs, low margins (at least in the medium term), and large externalities. State support was also required because the owners could not charge tariffs or fares to cover their operating costs and, in the case of Proton, the national car project, learning rents in the form of protection were needed.

An adequate regulatory framework was therefore necessary to ensure that incentives were in place to induce the owners to improve efficiency and invest. But regulation was weak, with the government intervening on an ad hoc basis through various ministries. The evidence of efficiency gains was mixed at best, long-term investment targets were not met (most notably in the case of the sewerage system and one LRT operator), and all four projects were eventually renationalized following ongoing losses and mounting debt. These failures can be blamed on institutional failure that led to incorrect privatization choices, poor screening and selection, and weak regulation.

The privatization of the sewerage system proceeded without sufficient information on the performance, assets and condition, and customer base of the existing system, or an adequate legal framework. This led to the operator having to take over and maintain more assets than originally agreed, three tariff revisions following consumer opposition, and bill collection problems, which raised operating costs and reduced revenue and cash flow. The privatization of public transit systems is not feasible without some form of state support, given the cost of infrastructure and general inability of such systems to cover operating costs.[4] While most countries underwrite the cost of construction and subsidize operations, the Malaysian government chose to leave the financing of the LRT system largely to the private sector.[5] The government's failure to ensure project viability was compounded by grossly overestimated passenger forecasts (resulting in the operators running at less than one third of their forecast demand) and cost over-runs (Halcrow Consultants 1999; FinanceAsia.com 26 July 2000).[6]

In the case of Malaysian Airlines (MAS), the poor purchase structure and industry problems would have made it difficult for private ownership to address the airline's long-term capital investment requirements. The purchase was financed entirely through loans, but low profit margins, large externalities, and regular bankruptcies inherent to the industry meant that revenues could not be guaranteed to generate sufficient profits to repay the loan, let alone increase investment. Proton, on the other hand, was arguably not viable to begin with. An ambitious project to spearhead Malaysia's industrialization process, it was closely modelled on the Korean car industry's success but failed to take into account the different global market conditions, necessary scale economies (which were beyond the domestic market), high capital costs, and excess global capacity due to intense competition. It was therefore unlikely that privatization would have made a difference.

The absence of open bidding in all four cases can be said to have compromised the quality of candidates. With the exception of one LRT operator[7] and Proton's owner, none of the candidates had the necessary experience. Berjaya Group, the company which headed Indah Water Konsortium (IWK – the consortium awarded the sewerage treatment concession), was seen to lack relative experience in public works (aside from small road-building projects) (Gomez and Jomo 1997); the owner of MAS had an interest in airlines but had never run an airline; and the remaining two LRT operators[8] did not have experience building or operating public transport systems. Proton's owner was an automotive engineer with relevant experience, but even then the government bypassed a far more experienced local car assembly industry. The poor choice of candidates was reflected not only in the financial difficulties of these companies (with the exception of Proton which remained protected and profitable), but also in the performance of the owners' other businesses, all of which were debt-ridden. This reduced the ability of the owners to continue financing the privatized projects, and the government was forced to renationalize these when the owners ran out of money.[9]

Regulatory failure was best exemplified by the government's 'arbitrary administrative action' when it revised tariffs not once but three times in the case of IWK. The government also effectively failed to regulate the LRT system by not accounting for the large externalities that necessitated some form of state support. The unlikelihood of repaying the capital costs meant that the operators had lost incentives to be efficient (Halcrow Consultants 1999).

The Privatization Master Plan (Malaysia 1991) highlighted these institutional weaknesses: namely, the lack of clear guidelines on activities to be privatized and the proper role of the state; lack of assessment of optimum modes of privatization; inadequate criteria for selection of candidates; absence of criteria to screen SOEs to determine the suitability for privatization; and lack of transparency in decision making. Privatization thus failed because of weak institutions and problems arising from reduced incentives and poor regulation. It was incompatible with the country's institutional endowments, and undertaken despite the lack of adequate information, legal framework or regulatory capacity. Although the government may have lacked the necessary information or technical skills to devise a detailed regulatory framework or to determine tariffs and the desired level of efficiency, there appeared to be little attempt at regulation, with the government intervening in an ad hoc manner.

As a result, privatization was characterized by arbitrary administrative action that undermined incentives to improve efficiency or to undertake investment.

PRIVATIZATION AND PATRONAGE

Meeting the necessary institutional conditions for privatization, however, will often be difficult, especially in developing countries as 'what is privatized and how represents the state's continuing intervention within the economy, favouring certain capitals at the expense of others' (Fine 1997: 376). Decisions to 'establish, retain or divest a public enterprise are not made in a political vacuum' and 'ownership and control of economic units are instruments for advancing certain interests and frustrating others' in the struggle for power among various interest groups (Jones and Mason 1982: 16). As it is essentially a redistributive process, privatization is highly politicized and often potentially conflictual. The state may also seek to ensure its interest is protected, and this will determine how (to whom) privatization is allocated. Political criteria thus usually take precedence over institutional requirements, and Malaysia's privatization programme has been closely associated with patronage and cronyism, where the focus has been on securing profits from shorter-term rents, usually in construction, rather than from longer-term investment.

Privatization increased rent-seeking and money politics to secure positions in UMNO, the ruling Malay party, which in turn facilitated access to rents (Gomez 1991). The allocation of major privatizations tended to favour a relatively small group of Malays that the government argued was selected on the basis of their ability to manage large projects. The emergence of this group of Malay businessmen who benefited disproportionately from privatization led to allegations of cronyism and a lack of transparency, where the 'granting of projects to Bumiputra [Malays] and to interests close to the ruling coalition (in particular UMNO) has become a common feature of the implementation of privatization in Malaysia' (Barraclough 2000: 355; Ho 1988; Jomo 1990).

Private interests were seen to be working hand in hand with the politically powerful to dominate the financially profitable but more rentier-based activities in what has been described as 'cronyistic privatization' (Rasiah 1998, 2001). Patterns in bidding for contracts in the early 1990s suggested the existence of formal and informal collusion (e.g. cartel-like agreements) among bidders, with some companies enjoying special influence and privileged information to consistently bid successfully (Jomo 1994). This was compounded by the absence of an open tender system as a result of a 'first come, first served' policy which allowed the government to select beneficiaries on the basis of political and personal connections, while consistent share underpricing with the increasing allocation of new privatized shares since early 1991 further encouraged the belief that privatization was primarily a means of rent capture to aggrandize its politically influential beneficiaries under government auspices and patronage (Jomo 1994).

The awarding of contracts to those with political connections led to patronage, rent-seeking and corruption. Productive efficiency was sacrificed as the beneficiaries of privatization were not competent enough to manage the enterprise or project because their selections were not based on strict economic criteria. Cronyism insulated many ventures from market competition and there was little evidence that privatization strengthened domestic capital accumulation in export-oriented manufacturing, technological upgrading or other needed structural changes (Jomo 1994; Gomez and Jomo 1997) and rapid growth allowed crony ventures to flourish after 1986 without immediate debilitating consequences (Rasiah 2001). There was also official acknowledgement that most of the economic rents through privatization were not efficiently deployed through productive investments to significantly accelerate industrialization or to consolidate genuine Malay entrepreneurship (Jomo 1994; Rasiah 2001).

Instead, 'changing forms of crony rentierism' and a conglomerate style of growth meant that when rents associated with tariffs fell following deregulation in the 1990s, captured rents were reinvested in the protected domestic economy (e.g. unproductive property and real estate sectors, construction, finance and other investments with a short-term horizon) (Jomo 1994; Rasiah 2001; Rasiah and Ishak 2001). The speculative and unproductive nature of this form of diversification can be gauged from the increase of bank lending in the property sector and share purchases, instead of manufacturing, agriculture and mining[10] (Chin and Jomo 2000; Jomo and Gomez 2000).

As a result, the Malay bourgeoisie was largely limited to finance, property and construction, and generally dependent on state patronage. Given that several such ventures enjoyed state guarantees of domestic market control, a significant section of the newly created managerial class arguably hardly showed elements of entrepreneurship in the absence of risk-bearing (Rasiah 1998). This was acknowledged by the prime minister, Mahathir Mohamad, who emphasized the need to 'improve the resilience of the Bumiputra to enable them to sustain their corporate equity holdings and not succumb to divestment for short-term profits or when the country is faced with an economic crisis' (Malaysia 2001: point 44).

The poor choice of candidates due to patronage is thus a strong theme in explanations of failed privatization. The owners of IWK, MAS, Proton and the LRT system were all closely linked to UMNO, in particular its leadership, and patronage can be said to have led to the poor choice of candidates, so weakening incentives to increase efficiency and investment. But patronage does not satisfactorily explain why the government made these choices in the first placc. To understand why patronage and poor selection featured strongly requires locating privatization within Malaysia's ongoing redistributive programme, initiated under the New Economic Policy (NEP) in 1970, and which not only pre-determined the choice of candidates, but arguably compromised their quality due to learning failure.

PRIVATIZATION AND CAPITAL ACCUMULATION

Malaysia's privatization programme was implemented within the context of the NEP to develop Malay entrepreneurial capacity by promoting capital accumulation. Privatized public sector assets were to provide the basis for further corporate growth of the Malay private sector and ownership conditions were to reduce ownership imbalances between Malay and other interests (Malaysia 1985; Galal et al. 1994). The policy emphasis on growth and redistribution thus necessitated a trade-off between economic efficiency and political stability, and necessarily shaped the character of the privatization programme and related institutions.

State intervention is crucial in promoting the process of capital accumulation through transfers that include the creation of new property rights and the provision of rents. The creation of rents can increase capital formation by redistributing income from consumption to investment activities (Choi 1993) and rents are also important for learning. As privatization basically confers on recipients additional income above what they would have otherwise received, it has the character of a rent.

The privatization of the sewerage and LRT systems, despite their lack of feasibility, can be seen to facilitate the process of capital accumulation through the allocation of short-term (construction) and long-term (concession) rents. The concessionaire can thus earn profits at the end or at the beginning, by overstating construction costs.[11] The 60-year concession period for the LRT privatization can be seen in terms of providing long-term monopoly rents, while the decision to privatize infrastructure construction, instead of underwriting capital costs and privatizing operations, as is the case in most cities, offered further rents. This was also consistent with the types of investment in the country that were increasingly related to construction. Similarly, by creating a monopoly from an essentially decentralized sewerage system run by 144 local authorities, the potential efficiency gains from privatizing to several different operators[12] were arguably ignored to ensure monopoly rents. Hence, where regulation is normally needed to prevent monopoly rents, this may not be the case where the state seeks to promote such rents as part of a capital accumulation process.

Due to the problem of excess demand in developing countries, resources are usually allocated in personalized and partisan ways, and through patron–client networks, rather than through a transparent process, invariably leading to rent-seeking and corruption (Khan 1998, 2000). Moreover, if the dominant intention of a government is to remain in power, then the transfer of economic resources through privatization will be closely aligned to its interests. In Malaysia's case, the choice of candidates was necessarily tempered by ethnic and political criteria, and it was important that those selected were loyal to the government and trustworthy. Such a selection process cannot be transparent.[13]

Nonetheless, the choice of candidates remained important given the national significance of many of these projects, and the government was aware of the risks and the need for careful assessment of track records, credit ratings, and intent: 'They must not be the kind of people who would sell their shares for quick gains' (Mahathir 1998a: 29). The government believed it had made the correct choice, and the prime minister consistently defended this by arguing that successful candidates 'had already proven their ability to run big operations' (*New Straits Times*, 27 November 1995) and were already rich, successful businessmen (Mahathir 1998b). The emergence of leading Malay businessmen running conglomerates comparable to large non-Malay corporations was said to be an indication of their ability to improve the performance of companies to be privatized (Mahathir 1998a).

Part of the decision to privatize was based on the belief that there was a sufficient pool of candidates following a decade of NEP entrepreneurial training programmes and opportunities. However, the continued dependence of Malay capitalists on subsidies and bail-outs after privatization suggests that the quality of candidates was compromised by policies under the NEP which promoted capital accumulation through preferential access in business, employment and education, and through the quick transfer of wealth to the Malay community, all of which created perverse incentives and discouraged learning.

Under the NEP, Malay businessmen were supported with easy credit, reserved (and discounted) corporate shares, business licences, government contracts and other forms of preferential treatment.[14] These measures were designed to minimize risk, and in the purchase of shares, provide windfall gains (Jesudason 1989), but also meant that the very essences of entrepreneurial risk-taking were ignored. Insulation of politically linked businesses and SOEs from market competition and easy access to finance undermined market discipline, while the speed of asset acquisition undermined their 'learning by doing' (Gomez and Jomo 1997). The rapid ascent of the Malay bourgeoisie was due to access to enormous funds from the banking system, especially state-controlled and state-owned banks, and to cheap shares using borrowed money, as a key to capital accumulation (Jesudason 1989).

Economic opportunities and state protection did not necessarily translate into increased business acumen (Bowie 1991), but instead created a 'soft environment', perpetuated Malay dependence on the state and promoted rentier activity. The NEP fostered a 'dole', 'subsidy' or 'get rich quick' mentality among Malays with a 'permanent middle class' dependent on the government (Khoo 1995), and an inefficient and fragile Malay bourgeoisie (Jesudason 1989). Many Malay businessmen were highly geared to loans and dependent on preferential 'Bumiputra share allotments' acquired under the NEP (Khoo 1995). Malay productivity was low (Bruton 1992) and Malay business contribution to employment generation and diversification was minimal, since much of its expansion came from buying companies at good prices, and selling its shares when prices were right (Jesudason 1989).

Privatization accelerated the transfer of corporate assets to Malay businessmen, many of whom were groomed as managers in state agencies under the NEP, again bypassing the learning process as they were handed entire companies rather than having to build these up. These large transfers concealed inefficiencies and long-term opportunity costs (which included the large-scale exchange of assets rather than productive investment) (Jesudason 1989) and encouraged a conglomerate style of growth, where the rentier constantly moves in order to capture available opportunity, regardless of previous experience or expertise (Gomez and Jomo 1997). Instead of 'Malay self-reliance and competitiveness [privatization] merely sculpted one gigantic "crutch" ' (Mahathir, cited in Khoo 1995: 129), and the poor quality of candidates reduced the chances of successful privatization. But why did poor selection and bad policy persist?

POLITICAL CONFLICT AND WEAK INSTITUTIONS

A large part of institutional failure – the poor choice of industries and candidates – was due to the highly centralized decision-making process which followed Mahathir's consolidation of power. This was in turn in response to the growing factionalization in the Malay ruling party that resulted from the changing political dynamics within the Malay middle class.

The expansion of the Malay middle class was a direct result of the NEP. Between 1970 and 1990, the proportion of the Malay workforce working in middle-class occupations grew from 12.9 per cent to 27 per cent (Crouch 1993). Malay representation increased in eight prized professions[15] (from 5 per cent in 1970 to 25 per cent in 1988) (Jomo 1990), managerial posts[16] (especially in the commercial and industrial sector), and among university graduates (who moved into business following the exhaustion of employment opportunities in the public sector) (Jomo 1990).

Corporate restructuring increased the Malay proportion of share capital from 1.5 per cent in 1969 to 19.4 percent in 1988, and individual shares[17] in the Malay stake increased to 67 per cent[18] (Jomo 1990). State efforts to control the 'commanding heights of the economy' (e.g. plantations and tin mines), driven by concerns with finding the quickest way to accumulate assets and control well-managed, profitable companies (and fuelled by the rising influence of Malay nationalists), also created a new corps of state managers who were central and powerful in Malaysian corporate life (Jesudason 1989). By the late 1980s, professional and trustee Malay executive directors represented an important new element in the strengthening of a Bumiputra commercial and industrial community (Searle 1999).

Despite its continued dependence on the state, the Malay business class grew in organization and influence, and its views were often shared by the political leaders themselves (Jesudason 1989). By the 1980s, the growing number of Malay businessmen fostered by the NEP had become an increasingly important element in the Malay political elite, the composition of which gradually changed from politicians and 'administocrats' to a combination of politicians and businessmen (Leigh 1992). As a result of the NEP there were significantly more Malay politicians active as businessmen (on their own and on UMNO's behalf) and Malay businessmen active in politics (Ho 1988).

This shift in power was also accompanied by changes in the occupational background and outlook of the elite (symbolized by Mahathir's assumption of leadership) and mirrored by the changing occupational background and disposition of UMNO leaders and grassroots members, where schoolteachers and other local leaders were replaced by businessmen and university-educated professionals produced by the NEP (Crouch 1992; Searle 1999). 'Middle class elements' were able to take over UMNO completely by the early 1980s (Jomo 1999), and by the time privatization was introduced, there was already a large Malay middle class, including a younger, more professionally trained managerial cadre whose support was important, and who had to be accommodated (see e.g. Milne and Mauzy 1999: 45).

The changing composition of the Malay middle class also led to increasing factionalization and conflict, centred around the nature of redistributive policies. While the NEP was seen to have promoted economic growth and stability, it also created divisions within the Malay community by the very nature of the process of capital accumulation that widened intra-ethnic inequality.[19] The NEP had increased the scope of patronage tremendously and contributed to the rapid growth of Malay businessmen in the late 1970s and 1980s who became an important force in the internal politics of UMNO through the party's extensive patronage network (Khoo 1992; Crouch 1992).

The NEP also changed the nature of the patron–client relationship. Elected members of parliament who were previously political patrons (providing political support in return for economic benefits) greatly increased their control of the district development machinery that allowed them to distribute development benefits and thus purchase continued support (Shamsul 1986). This reshaped internal politics within UMNO local branches, increasing bitter factional struggles for nomination and leading to the rise in outbreaks of violence at UMNO branch and division meetings after 1984.[20] Growing factional rivalries culminated in an open party split in 1987 (Khoo 1992; Crouch 1992). Mahathir's victory in intra-party struggles owed much to the successful creation under the NEP of a 'Malay rentier-business cadre' who stood to benefit (disproportionately) from greater business opportunities following privatization, and whose support was crucial (Jomo 1993; Felker 1993).

Increasing authoritarianism since 1987 was seen as a response to the fragmentation following the arrival of the Malay middle class (Kahn and Loh 1992a). With his re-election as party president, Mahathir consolidated his authority both within UMNO, where he amended the constitution to increase his power (Milne and Mauzy 1999), and in government, with the concentration of power in a few key regulatory agencies directly under the Prime Minister's Department (Searle 1999). UMNO's control of key economic and technocratic agencies of government, specifically the Ministry of Finance, Ministry of Trade and Industry, and Economic Planning Unit (EPU) (located in the Prime Minister's Department) meant that decision making became increasingly centralized, allowing Mahathir to bypass key bureaucratic interests (Felker 1999), and impose his own views on economic policies,[21] with even the EPU having to defer to the prime minister on his choice of key projects.

This narrowing and concentration of the decision-making process, combined with Mahathir's particular personal preferences (including an obsession with 'mega' projects) his nationalist bent, and the country's abundant natural resources,[22] arguably reduced the government's ability to learn and increased the likelihood of poor choices and repeated mistakes. The failure of Proton, for example, can be attributed directly to Mahathir who initiated and pushed through the project despite objections and concerns within his administration.[23] The prime minister's personal interest in the car project also undermined the viability of the LRT system by promoting the ongoing construction of privatized highways that only served to limit the use of public transport. The government failed to subsidize operations, or regulate private vehicle traffic to create the necessary passenger volume (*The Edge*, 26 August 1996). The LRT system was poorly integrated physically, operationally, or as part of a cohesive public transportation system.

Poor design and regulatory failure arguably reduced incentives. For example, the owner of MAS and both operating LRT companies would have had little incentive to improve efficiency, given their debt burdens that made the prospect of breaking even unlikely. In the case of MAS, this was in part due to the poor purchase structure and externalities inherent in the airline industry. In addition, previous management decisions on fleet expansion added to the new owner's debt burden and the government continued to make crucial decisions on domestic airfares and international routes that impinged on the airline's revenue stream.

The picture that emerges then is that entrepreneurial failure, compounded by the poor choice of industries and weak regulation, led to renationalization in all four cases. Persistent policy failure was partly due to a combination of a highly centralized (and insulated) political executive, and the country's rich natural resource endowment (e.g. see Bowie 1988; Jesudason 1989) that diluted imperatives for economic efficiency. But why did the government not intervene earlier to ensure service delivery given the national importance of these privatized enterprises?

LACK OF CREDIBLE SANCTIONS

Mistakes by the government do not explain why it failed to act against non-performing companies, particularly given the prime minister's authority. Faced with financial difficulties, the owners of Proton, MAS, and the LRT system were apparently unwilling to carry out further capital investment or to repay loans for investments already undertaken, so forcing the state to take over the enterprises at great cost.

MAS had incurred huge debts following several fleet expansions and the 1997 currency crisis. The owner also faced a large personal debt from the purchase of the airline, and his other publicly listed (telecommunications) company also faced debt problems. After successive losses and mounting debts between 1998 and 2000, he claimed he could no longer finance MAS (*Business Times*, 28 November 2000), and sold his share back to the government for RM1.79 billion[24] or RM8 per share on 20 December 2000.

Similarly, Proton's parent company DRB-HICOM[25] had an estimated RM5 billion in debts (*The Edge*, 6 March 2000; *Malaysian Business*, 1 April 2000) following an aggressive conglomerate-style expansion (*The Edge*, 12 April 1998). Although Proton remained profitable,[26] DRB-HICOM needed to sell Proton to survive (*The Edge*, 9 November 1998; *The Edge*, 6 March 2000; *Malaysian Business*, 1 April 2000) and was unable or unwilling to sustain Proton given an impending lifting of tariffs and an estimated RM1 billion needed in capital injection for R&D. The parent company of PUTRA, the least efficient LRT operator, was the country's largest corporate debtor with over RM25 billion in debts (*Far Eastern Economic Review*, 21 December 2000) and needed to be bailed out by the government, while the third LRT operator, KL Monorail (also the owner of IWK), failed to complete its LRT project due to financial difficulties.

While the ability to monitor informs the principal whether the agent is performing, it does not in itself guarantee that the agent will actually deliver, and the principal must be able to enforce discipline to ensure delivery. Regulatory failure will thus also occur when the government is unable to threaten punishment for non-delivery. In the western context, the state simply gives the contract or transfers the company to someone else, and the private operator who failed to deliver is allowed to go bankrupt. In developing countries, the scarcity of capital and high social costs of bankruptcy mean that there is a lack of credible sanctions.

In the case of Malaysia, there was a lack of entrepreneurial capacity and an unwillingness to let key enterprises fail. Given the size of the enterprises, it was unlikely there would have been many, if any, suitable candidates to begin with. In addition, the fact that all four projects were of national importance, and that the prime minister had a personal interest in Proton, meant that the owners would have been aware that the government could not afford to allow the projects to fail. But why then did the government not just save the projects and discipline the owners?

Instead, the owners were rewarded for non-delivery when the government bought back the companies. The government paid RM8 per share for MAS when MAS shares were trading at RM3.80. The price was justified on the basis of a premium for a controlling stake, although the government already owned 49 per cent of the airline on 12 December 2000 through various state agencies.[27] In the case of the LRT system, the operators continued managing operations after renationalization. Even though the government replaced some of these owner-entrepreneurs with professional managers who could be sacked for not performing (see *Asiaweek*, 7 September 2001), this remained a minor threat in comparison with the potential loss of ownership.

This suggests that aside from incentives to induce efficiency and investment, a regulatory framework must be backed by credible sanctions if it is to work. But its effectiveness will be circumscribed by the political context, including the available entrepreneurial capacity, social cost of bankruptcy, and national importance of the enterprise. It also complicates the transfer of effective regulatory frameworks from developed to developing countries.

CONCLUSION

The failure of privatization policies has been blamed on institutional failure; namely, the poor choice of industry/enterprise and mode of privatization, selection of candidates, and inadequate regulatory framework. This was clearly the case in Malaysia, where privatization has been closely associated with patronage and cronyism, and the shift of investment into short-term and unproductive activities. The wrong choice of candidates arguably led to poor performance and eventual failure.

However, privatization was part of a process of capital accumulation that sought to develop (Malay) entrepreneurial capacity through the provision of short-term and long-term rents. The choice of candidates, as a result, was politically and ethnically motivated, with patronage becoming a key feature. The nature of this redistributive process resulted in learning failure, which further compromised the quality of candidates. Nonetheless, given the lack of entrepreneurial capacity, and the political and economic nature of the privatizations (which involved huge capital costs and externalities), it is unclear whether the state could have found the best candidates. In any case, failure was compounded by the poor choice of privatizations, some that were not viable to begin with, and others that were not feasible to privatize. It is unlikely that the right choice of candidate would have made a difference in these circumstances.

This highlights the importance of identifying the right *sectors* to privatize. The government's poor choice was largely due to weak institutions, in this case a highly centralized and autocratic decision-making process which was in reaction to increased factional rivalries within the ruling Malay party. It is therefore necessary to locate institutional failure within the wider political context, as the solution then becomes more complex than simply strengthening institutions.

The government failed to design an effective regulatory framework to determine tariffs and subsidies, set efficiency targets, or monitor performance. Although regulatory design was further complicated by multiple (often social) objectives, there did not appear to have been any attempt at regulation, which was at best ad hoc, consisting of ministerial interventions. This may have been due to the centralization of power in government (i.e. the prime minister may have felt regulation was unnecessary). Given that the government was cognizant of non-delivery problems, the question then is why it failed to intervene earlier. Were the subsequent bailouts and renationalizations simply due to regulatory failure?

An effective regulatory framework must not only be able to determine appropriate tariffs and subsidies, and monitor service delivery. Without the threat of credible sanctions, the government will be unable to guarantee service delivery. Rather than 'ex post government opportunism', regulatory failure was due to the inability or unwillingness of the private sector to continue financing projects. While this was due to a combination of entrepreneurial failure, poor project viability and externalities, the owners were able to opt out because the government lacked credible sanctions. It could not threaten to pass the project to someone else (due to the scarcity of capital), or let the projects fail (due to the high social costs of bankruptcy and their national importance).

NOTES

1. For example, a study of water resource management in Europe revealed that government grants contributed 42.5 per cent of capital investment in wastewater treatment in Germany, 40 per cent in France, a 'high proportion' in the Netherlands, and 'significantly' in Portugal (Correia 1998).
2. The 'fiscal illusion' of moving government expenditure off budget also makes public–private partnerships politically appealing.
3. However, this may not be the case in the context of asymmetric information. The producer bidding the most, and promising to conform most closely with government objectives, may neither carry out those commitments nor be the one for whom the asset is most valuable due to limited liability and imperfect enforceability of commitments. A willingness to bid higher may simply reflect a higher probability of defaulting on promises (Stiglitz 1996: 194).
4. For example, fares only covered 30 per cent to 40 per cent of operating costs in the US and 55 per cent in the UK (Hakim et al. 1996a). In the case of the two operational LRT systems, this figure was 44 per cent (STAR) and 22 per cent (PUTRA) in 1999 (Halcrow Consultants 1999).
5. According to the former head of the government's Corporate Debt Restructuring Committee (CDRC), infrastructure projects required state funding as only the state, and not banks, could provide long-term funds given the long gestation period (FinanceAsia.com, 26 July 2000). The government provided long-term, low interest loans directly (in the form of government and infrastructural support loans) and through state institutions (e.g. the Employees Provident Fund and Development and Infrastructure Bank).
6. According to the former head of the CDRC, many infrastructure projects did not meet the forecasts, and many were unbankable, with a wide gap between funding and cash flows (FinanceAsia.com, 27 July 2000). A former government minister was also quoted as saying: 'From Day One we knew it wasn't going to be a profitable project' (*International Herald Tribune*, 27 December 2000).
7. STAR was a consortium formed and headed by Taylor Woodrow (a UK housing, property development, construction and engineering company) and Adtranz (a train manufacturer owned by DaimlerChrysler, which was later sold to Canada's Bombardier Transportation in 2000). Although Taylor Woodrow and Adtranz had a majority 30 per cent share in the consortium, state institutions had a combined share ownership of 50 per cent.
8. PUTRA and KL Monorail (formerly People Rapid Transit).
9. According to the new head of the CDRC in 2001, the subsequent replacement of these owners with professional managers was to separate the powers between chairman and chief executive officer in order to 'alleviate the problems of owner-managers who have their own debt problems' (*Far Eastern Economic Review*, 18 October 2001).
10. Loans for construction, housing and real estate increased from 21.6 per cent in 1977 to 35.9 per cent in 1988, while loans to the manufacturing, agriculture and mining sectors comprised barely a quarter of commercial bank loans (Chin and Jomo 2000). Loans could be obtained without proper procedures and were often given for speculative get-rich-quick schemes rather than productive investment (Chin and Jomo 2001; Gomez 1994, cited in Chin and Jomo 2001).
11. See interview with Chellappah Rajandram, the former head of the CDRC (FinanceAsia.com, 26 July 2000).
12. For example, the government could have privatized sewage treatment to more than one

operator along the lines of the 19 urban centres outlined in the national sewerage development programme (see Pillay 1994). According to Ridzuan Halim, associate professor at the Faculty of Business, University of Malaya, there is 'no advantage organizing sewerage works on a national basis since there is little sense centralizing or collecting sewerage on a national basis' (*The Edge*, 1 June 1998).

13. The selection process reflected the government's strategy of handpicking candidates, many of whom were closely linked to then Finance Minister Daim Zainuddin (see *Far Eastern Economic Review*, 19 July 2001, 23 August 2001).
14. See, for example, Khoo (1995); Gale (1981); Crouch (1996); Jesudason (1989); Bowie (1991); and Gomez and Jomo (1997).
15. Doctors, lawyers, engineers, veterinary surgeons, dentists, accountants, surveyors, and architects.
16. From 7400 in 1971 to over 61000 (1985) or an annual average of 16.6 per cent (Ismail and Osman 1991: 39).
17. As opposed to Malay ownership held in trust by state agencies.
18. These figures have been argued to be grossly underestimated (Jomo 1990), ostensibly to justify continued affirmative action policies under the NEP.
19. Inter-racial income inequality was replaced by intra-ethnic inequality, particularly among the Malays, with mass poverty at the bottom and the concentration of wealth and control of corporations in the hands of a very small number of Malay individuals (Tan 1982: 182; Schlosstein 1991). Only 1.3 per cent of eligible Malay investors in the National Unit Trust Scheme (ASN) owned 75 per cent of shares in the late 1980s (Jomo 1990), with less than 2 per cent managing to acquire shares above RM5000 in 1990 (Ismail and Osman 1991).
20. Although factions were arguably already present in all levels of UMNO (Ahmad 1985), the rise of money politics was closely related to, if not a direct result of, the NEP (Shamsul 1986).
21. Besides a close circle of advisers – only a few of whom were in the Cabinet – Mahathir was seen to have kept his own counsel (Jesudason 1989; also see Milne and Mauzy 1999).
22. See Bowie (1988). Petronas, the state oil company, was used to renationalize Proton and had previously 'bailed out' several other companies.
23. The national car project was implemented before a largely negative report on project feasibility was released (Bowie 1988). Despite the government postponing the lowering of tariffs (as part of the Common Effective Preferential Tariff programme under the ASEAN Free Trade Agreement) from 2003 to 2005 (*The Sun*, 21 June 2000), Proton's alternative (Japanese) director stated that Proton may not even be competitive by 2005 (*The Sun*, 25 July 2000).
24. In 1998 the government pegged the Malaysian ringgit to the US dollar at RM1 to US$0.263.
25. The death of Yahya Ahmad, DRB-HICOM's original owner in 1997, was widely perceived to have had an adverse effect on the company.
26. Pre-tax profit for 2000 was RM141.3 million, compared to RM1.03 billion in 1997, when Proton was the fifth most profitable company on the main board of the Kuala Lumpur Stock Exchange (*The Edge*, 22 December 1997).
27. Following KWAP (the state pension fund) increasing its stake in MAS to 20.04 per cent through the purchase of an additional 9 per cent (72.12 million) MAS shares from the Brunei Investment Agency (*Business Times*, 12 December 2000; *The Edge*, 11 December 2000) at RM4 each for RM280 million (*Business Times*, 4 December 2000). The RM8 price was reportedly decided by then Finance Minister Daim Zainuddin who subsequently resigned in 2001 after the political fall-out following the renationalization (*Far Eastern Economic Review*, 23 August 2001, 27 June 2002).

BIBLIOGRAPHY

Ahmad, Atory Hussain (1985), *Pembentukan Dasar Awam Malaysia* [*Malaysia's Public Policy Formation*], Kuala Lumpur: Utusan Publications.

Alchian, A. and Demsetz, H. (1972), 'Production, information costs, and economic organisation', *American Economic Review*, **62**, 777–95.

Anderson, T. and Hill, P. (eds) (1996), *The Privatization Process*, London: Rowman and Littlefield Publishers.

Applebaum, R. and Henderson, J. (eds) (1992), *States and Development in the Asian Pacific Rim*, London: Sage Publications.

Bailey, E. and Pack, J. (eds) (1995), *The Political Economy of Privatization and Deregulation*, Aldershot: Edward Elgar Reference Collection.

Barraclough, S. (2000), 'The politics of privatisation in Malaysia', *Contemporary Southeast Asia*, **22** (2), 344–57.

Bowie, A. (1988), 'Redistribution with growth? The dilemmas of state-sponsored economic development in Malaysia', *Journal of Developing Societies*, **4**, 52–69.

Bowie, A. (1991), *Crossing the industrial Divide*, New York: Columbia University Press.

Boycko, M., Shleifer, A. and Vishny, R. (1996), 'A theory of privatization', *The Economic Journal*, **106** (435), 309–19.

Bruton, H. (1992), *The Political Economy of Poverty, Equity and Growth: Sri Lanka and Malaysia*, Washington: Oxford University Press.

Buchanan, J. (1980), 'Rent seeking and profit seeking', in J. Buchanan, R. Tollison and G. Tullock (eds) *Toward a Theory of Rent Seeking Society*, Austin: Texas University Press.

Buchanan, J., Tollison, R. and Tullock, G. (eds) (1980), *Toward a Theory of Rent Seeking Society*, Austin: Texas University Press.

Chin, K.F. and Jomo, K.S. (2000), 'Financial sector rents in Malaysia' in M.H. Khan and K.S. Jomo (eds) *Rents, Rent-Seeking and Economic Development*, Cambridge: Cambridge University Press.

Chin, K.F. and Jomo, K.S. (2001), 'Financial liberalisation and system vulnerability', in K.S. Jomo (ed.) *Malaysian Eclipse: Economic Crisis and Recovery*, London: Zed Books.

Choi, B.S. (1993), 'Financial policy and big business in Korea: the perils of financial regulation', in S. Haggard, C.H. Lee and S. Maxfield (eds) *The Politics of Finance in Developing Countries*, London: Cornell University Press.

Cook, P. and Kirkpatrick, C. (2000a), *Privatization in Developing Countries*, Volume I, Cheltenham: Edward Elgar Publishing.

Cook, P. and Kirkpatrick, C. (2000b), *Privatization in Developing Countries*, Volume II, Cheltenham: Edward Elgar Publishing.

Correia, F. (ed.) (1998), *Institutions for Water Resources Management in Europe*, Volume 1, Rotterdam: AA Balkema.

Crouch, H. (1992), 'Authoritarian trends, the UMNO split and limits to state power', in J. Kahn and F. Loh (eds) *Fragmented Vision: Culture and Politics in Contemporary Malaysia*, Sydney: Allen & Unwin.

Crouch, H. (1993), 'Malaysia: neither authoritarian nor democratic', in K. Hewison, R. Robison and G. Rodan (eds) *Southeast Asia in the 1990s: Authoritarianism, Democracy and Capitalism*, Sydney: Allen & Unwin.

Crouch, H. (1996), *Government and Society in Malaysia*, New York: Cornell University Press.

Daniels, R. and Trebilcock, M. (2000), 'An organisational analysis of the public–private privatization', in P. Rosenau (ed.) *Public–Private Policy Partnerships*, London: The MIT Press.

Fayard, A. (1999), 'Overview of the scope and limitations of public–private partnerships', Paris: Seminar on Public–Private Partnerships (PPPs) in Transport Infrastructure Financing, European Conference of Ministers of Transport.

Felker, G. (1993), 'Political economy and Malaysian technology policy', in K.S. Jomo and C. Edwards (eds) *Malaysian Industrialisation: Performance, Problems, Prospects*, London: Routledge.

Felker, G. (1999), 'Malaysia's innovations system: actors, interests and governance', in K.S. Jomo and G. Felker (eds) *Technology, Competitiveness and the State*, London: Routledge.

Fine, B. (1997), 'Privatization: theory and lessons from the UK and South Africa, *Seoul Journal of Economics*, **10** (4), 373–414.

Galal, A., Jones, L., Tandon, P. and Vogelsang, I. (1994), *Welfare Consequences of Selling Public Enterprises*, Washington: Oxford University Press.

Gale, B. (1981), *Politics and Public Enterprise in Malaysia*, Singapore: Eastern Universities Press.

Gomez, E.T. (1991), *Money Politics in the Barisan Nasional*, Kuala Lumpur: Forum.

Gomez, E.T. (1994), *Political Business: Corporate Involvement of Malaysian Political Parties*, Townsville: James Cook University.

Gomez, E.T. and Jomo, K.S. (1997), *The Political Economy of Malaysia*, Cambridge: Cambridge University Press.

Haggard, C., Lee, C.H. and Maxfield, S. (eds) (1993), *The Politics of Finance in Developing Countries*, London: Cornell University Press.

Hakim, S., Seidenstat, P. and Bowman, G. (1996a), 'Review and analysis of privatization efforts in transportation', in S. Hakim, P. Seidenstat and G. Bowman (eds) *Privatized Transportation Systems*, London: Praeger.

Hakim, S., Seidenstat, P. and Bowman, G. (eds) (1996b), *Privatized Transportation Systems*, London: Praeger.

Halcrow Consultants (1999), 'Kuala Lumpur public transport restructuring final report', Kuala Lumpur: Corporate Debt Restructuring Committee.

Heilman, J. and Johnson, G. (1992), *The Politics and Economics of Privatization*, London: University of Alabama Press.

Hewison, K., Robison, R. and Rodan, G. (eds) (1993), *Southeast Asia in the 1990s: Authoritarianism, Democracy and Capitalism*, Sydney: Allen & Unwin.

Ho, K.L. (1988), 'Indigenizing the state: the NEP and the Bumiputera state in Peninsular Malaysia', PhD dissertation, Ohio State University.

Ismail, Salleh and Osman, Rani (1991), *The Growth of the Public Sector in Malaysia*, Kuala Lumpur: ISIS.

Jesudason, J. (1989), *Ethnicity and the Economy: The State, Chinese Business, and Multinationals in Malaysia*, Singapore: Oxford University Press.

Jomo, K.S. (1990), 'Whither Malaysia's new economic policy?', *Pacific Affairs*, **63** (4), 469–99.

Jomo, K.S. (1993), 'The way forward?: The political economy of development policy reform in Malaysia', Faculty of Economics and Administration, Kuala Lumpur: University of Malaya.

Jomo, K.S. (1994), *U-Turn? Malaysian Economic Development Policy after 1990*, Queensland: James Cook University.

Jomo, K.S. (1999), 'A Malaysian middle class?: Some preliminary analytical considerations', in K.S. Jomo (ed.) *Rethinking Malaysia*, Hong Kong: Asia 2000.

Jomo K.S. (ed.) (2001), *Malaysian Eclipse: Economic Crisis and Recovery*, London: Zed Books.

Jomo, K.S. and Gomez, E.T. (2000), 'The Malaysian development dilemma', in M.H.

Khan and K.S. Jomo (cds) *Rents, Rent-seeking and Economic Development*, Cambridge: Cambridge University Press.

Jones, L. and Mason, E. (1982), 'Role of economic factors in determining the size and structure of the public enterprise sector in less-developed countries with mixed economies', in P. Cook and C. Kirkpatrick (2000a) *Privatization in Developing Countries*, Volume I, Cheltenham: Edward Elgar Publishing.

Kahn, J. and Loh, F. (1992a), 'Introduction: fragmented vision', in J. Kahn and F. Loh (eds) *Fragmented Vision: Culture and Politics in Contemporary Malaysia*, Sydney: Allen & Unwin.

Kahn, J. and Loh, F. (eds) (1992b), *Fragmented Vision: Culture and Politics in Contemporary Malaysia*, Sydney: Allen & Unwin.

Khan, M.H. (1998), 'Patron–client networks and the economic effects of corruption in Asia', *European Journal of Development Research*, **10** (1), 15–39.

Khan, M.H. (2000), 'Analysing corruption as process: competing paradigms in economics and political economy', forthcoming.

Khan, M.H. and Jomo, K.S. (eds) (2000), *Rents, Rent-seeking and Economic Development*, Cambridge: Cambridge University Press.

Khoo, B.T. (1995), *Paradoxes of Mahathirism*, Kuala Lumpur: Oxford University Press.

Khoo, K.J. (1992), 'The grand vision: Mahathir and modernisation' in J. Kahn and F. Loh (eds) *Fragmented Vision: Culture and Politics in Contemporary Malaysia*, Sydney: Allen & Unwin.

Leigh, M. (1992), 'Politics, bureaucracy, and business in Malaysia: realigning the eternal triangle', in A. McIntyre and J. Kanishka (eds) *The Dynamics of Economic Policy Reform in Southeast Asia and South West Pacific*, Singapore: Oxford University Press.

Levy, B. and Spiller, P. (1994), 'Regulation, institutions, and commitment in telecommunications', in P. Cook and C. Kirkpatrick (2000b) *Privatization in Developing Countries*, Volume II, Cheltenham: Edward Elgar Publishing.

Lubeck, P.M. (1992), 'Malaysian industrialisation, ethnic division and the NIC model: the limits of replication', in R. Applebaum and J. Henderson (eds) *States and Development in the Asian Pacific Rim*, London: Sage Publications.

Mahathir, Mohamad (1998a), *The Way Forward*, London: Weidenfeld & Nicolson.

Mahathir, Mohamad (1998b), *The Challenges of Turmoil*, Subang Jaya: Pelanduk Publications.

Malaysia (1985), *Guidelines on Privatisation*, Kuala Lumpur: Government Printers.

Malaysia (1991), *Privatisation Master Plan*, Kuala Lumpur: Government Printers.

Malaysia (2001), *Tabling The Eighth Malaysia Plan, 2001–2005*, Kuala Lumpur: Government Printers, available at <http://216.239.53.100/search?q=cache:kInMuRjN52oC:jtr.gov.my/bi/rm8speech.htm+rancangan+malaysia+kelapan&hl=en&lr=lang_en&ie=UTF-8>.

Mansfield, R. and Poole, N. (1991), 'Advancing the horizons: central role of the manager', paper presented to the British Academy of Management Conference, University of Bath.

Martin, S. and Parker, D. (1997), 'Privatisation: the conceptual framework', in P. Cook and C. Kirkpatrick (2000a) *Privatization in Developing Countries*, Volume I, Cheltenham: Edward Elgar Publishing.

Milne, R. and Mauzy, D. (1999), *Malaysian Politics under Mahathir*, London: Routledge.

Pillay, M.S. (1994), 'Privatization of sewerage services in Malaysia', paper presented at the 20th Water, Engineering and Development Centre (WEDC) Conference, Columbo, Sri Lanka, available at <http://www.lboro.ac.uk/departments/cv/wedc/papers/20/plenary/pillay. pdf>.

Plane, P. (1997), 'Privatisation and economic growth: an empirical investigation from a sample of developing market economies', in P. Cook and C. Kirkpatrick (2000b) *Privatization in Developing Countries*, Volume II, Cheltenham: Edward Elgar Publishing.

Poole, R. (1996), 'Privatisation for economic development', in T. Anderson and P. Hill (eds) *The Privatization Process*, London: Rowman and Littlefield Publishers.

Rasiah, Rajah (1998), 'Capital expansion, cronyism and contraction', *Journal of the Asia Pacific Economy*, **3** (3), 358–78.

Rasiah, Rajah (2001), 'Pre-crisis economic weaknesses and vulnerabilities', in K.S. Jomo (ed.) *Malaysian Eclipse: Economic Crisis and Recovery*, London: Zed Books.

Rasiah, Rajah and Ishak, Shari (2001), 'Market, government and Malaysia's new economic policy', *Cambridge Journal of Economics*, **25**, 57–78.

Rosenau, P. (2000a), 'The strengths and weaknesses of public–private partnerships', in P. Rosenau (ed.) *Public–Private Policy Partnerships*, London: The MIT Press.

Rosenau, P. (ed.) (2000b), *Public–Private Policy Partnerships*, London: The MIT Press.

Sappington, D. and Stiglitz, J.E. (1995), 'Privatisation, information and incentives', in E. Bailey and J. Pack (eds) *The Political Economy of Privatization and Deregulation*, Aldershot: Edward Elgar Reference Collection.

Sappington, D. and Weissman, D. (1996), *Designing Incentive Regulation for the Telecommunications Industry*, London: The MIT Press.

Schlosstein, S. (1991), *Asia's New Little Dragons*, Chicago: Contemporary Books.

Searle, P. (1999), T*he Riddle of Malaysian Capitalism*, Honolulu: Allen & Unwin and University of Hawaii Press.

Shamsul, A.B. (1986), *From British to Bumiputera Rule*, Singapore: ISEAS.

Stiglitz, J. (1996), *Whither Socialism?* Cambridge, MA: The MIT Press.

Stottmann, W. (2000), 'The role of the private sector in the provision of water and wastewater services in urban areas', in J. Uito and A. Biswas (eds) *Water for Urban Areas: Challenges and Perspectives*, New York: United Nations University Press.

Tan, T.W. (1982), *Income Distribution and Determination in West Malaysia*, Kuala Lumpur: Oxford University Press.

Uito, J. and Biswas, A. (eds) (2000), *Water for Urban Areas: Challenges and Perspectives*, New York: United Nations University Press.

Vickers, J. and Yarrow, G. (1991), 'Economic perspectives on privatisation', *Journal of Economic Perspectives*, **5** (2), 111–32.

Vickers, J. and Yarrow, G. (1995), *Privatisation: An Economic Analysis*, London: The MIT Press.

Windsor, D. (1996), 'Creative financing options for urban transport privatization', in S. Hakim, P. Seidenstat and G. Bowman (eds) *Privatized Transportation Systems*, London: Praeger.

Windsor, D. and Atherton, W.C. (1984), *Administrative Impacts of Private Financing Technologies for Urban Transportation*, Washington, DC: US Department of Transportation.

Newspapers and Magazines

Asiaweek
Business Times
Far Eastern Economic Review
International Herald Tribune
Malaysian Business
New Straits Times
The Edge
The Sun

19. The regulatory environment of the energy industry in the Philippines

Raul V. Fabella and Rafaelita M. Aldaba

INTRODUCTION

This chapter surveys the two important energy industries and the regulatory environment in which they operate in the Philippines. These two industries are the electricity or power industry and the downstream oil industry. The chapter first gives a brief historical account of the evaluation of these industries' respective regulatory environments before landmark reform and restructuring laws were passed. The various regulatory and competition policy dimensions of these new laws are singled out and examined. The corresponding regulatory watchdogs, their functions and the scope of their mandates are brought into focus. Where early outcomes are already available, these are discussed including the reversive challenges that are currently being mounted. Whether these laws are allowed enough time to take root and deliver the promised favourable outcomes remains to be seen. While the rules of the game as set down in the acts and the implementing rules and regulations appear clear, the actual application of these rules to particular cases still depends on the people appointed to critical positions, especially in the regulatory watchdogs, and the attitude and actions of politicians. The next section focuses on electricity and this is followed by a review of the downstream oil industry. The final section contains the conclusions.

AN OVERVIEW OF ELECTRICITY

The State as Regulator 1930–70

Before the 1930s, the electric power industry was completely private and autonomous, apart from the grant by the Commonwealth government of a 50-year franchise to Manila Electric Rail and Light Company (MERALCO) for the building and operation of an electric railway and light heat power system in Manila in 1905.

State involvement of the power sector commenced with the Commonwealth Act 120 in 1936, which created the state-owned National Power Corporation (NPC) to develop domestic power generation. The idea was to develop, own and manage generating facilities. In the same year, the Commonwealth Act 146 created the first regulatory watchdog in Philippine history, the Public Service Commission (PSC), which would oversee and regulate power and other public services. These developments reflected neatly the dominant thinking on state–industry relations in the USA of which, at that time, the Philippines was a territory.

State Ownership and Control 1970–86

This state of affairs remained largely intact until 1971, when Republic Act 6137 was passed in response to the increase in gasoline prices as a result of devaluation of the peso. The Act created the Oil Industry Commission (OIC) which took over responsibility for the regulation of the oil industry from PSC, and was further mandated to ensure the supply of oil-based products. Regulation was slowly becoming fragmented and specialized.

The PSC next lost the power to regulate water and electricity to the Board of Power and Waterworks (BPW) and was eventually abolished in 1972 by Presidential Decree 40. The year 1972 was significant because martial law was declared and the era of Presidential Decrees (PD) under President Marcos started. The same nationalized MERALCO decree declared NPC the sole operator in the generation and transmission of power. Another Presidential Decree, PD 269 in 1973, created the National Electrification Administration (NEA) to support electric cooperatives. The nationalization of MERALCO had less to do with efficiency than with the fact that the Lopez family, an influential political opponent, owned it. Politics was becoming a more intrusive influence in the power sector.

Energy became a cabinet level concern with the creation of the Department of Energy (DOE) by PD 1206. The OIC was replaced in the same decree by the Board of Energy (BOE), which was responsible for regulating energy products (electricity and oil products). In 1979, NPC raised its share of generated power from 30 per cent to 90 per cent when it acquired the thermal power generation facilities of MERALCO. The PD era ended in 1986 with the overthrow of President Marcos. MERALCO was returned by the new dispensation to its previous owners at this time.

The problems facing the largely state-run power industry began to glare in the early 1980s. The average production of electricity per 1000 people went from 0.35 kWh in 1977–80 to 0.39 kWh in 1985–88. The contrast with the growth in other developing countries was stark. At the same time, the number of new households that were electrified fell from the peak of 330 000 in 1982 to 100 000 in 1986 and to 30 000 in 1988 (World Bank, 1993). The Philippine government wrestled throughout the 1980s with a devastating debt crisis which decimated maintenance investment and resulted in the drying up of external finance for new power projects. In 1986, the Bataan Nuclear Power Plant, that was programmed to come on-stream in the mid-1980s, was mothballed for safety and political reasons. The decision was undoubtedly influenced by the Chernobyl disaster. Low maintenance and underinvestment resulted in the crippling power crisis in the early 1990s. Table 19.1 shows the number of days with brownouts, energy sales and megawatts per day lost. Apart from this, the average tariff was relatively high for the ASEAN region. In 1991 MERALCO's tariff was $0.03 higher than PLN in Indonesia and TNB in Malaysia, and $0.04 higher than EGAT in Thailand (World Bank, 1993).

Note as well that the MERALCO rate was about $0.03–$0.04 above the NPC rate, representing up to 80 per cent margin. By contrast, the margin was only $0.02 in Malaysia. While NPC was therefore accumulating losses, MERALCO was not. It was apparent that the pricing structure, especially of NPC, was increasingly politicized and involved mounting state subsidies.

First Deregulation Era 1987–2000

In 1987, Executive Order (EO) 215 abolished the monopoly of NPC in power generation and allowed the entry of private firms, but the uptake by private players was next to nil. The state, strapped for cash, unable to borrow and

Table 19.1 Average production of electricity (in million kilowatt hours per 1000 people)

Country	1977–80	1981–84	1985–88
Philippines	0.35	0.39	0.39
Brazil	1.01	1.23	1.44
Chile	0.99	1.07	1.23
India	0.17	0.20	0.27
Indonesia	0.06	0.12	0.20
South Korea	0.93	1.30	1.77
Malaysia	0.64	0.83	1.50
Mexico	0.86	1.08	1.25
Thailand	0.30	0.38	0.54
Turkey	0.51	0.57	0.79

Source: *UN Yearbook of Energy Statistics* as cited in *The World Bank Country Report*, April 1993.

determined to honour foreign debt obligations, could not alter the generation capacity. Likewise, the rules for participation of the private sector were unclear. The incentives on offer were paltry, given the overall state of macroeconomic and political uncertainty. More had to be done.

This came in the form of the Build-Operate-Transfer (BOT) Law (Republic Act (RA) 6957) of 1990. With the rules on entry and government intervention set in clearer terms, the uptake improved but the delivery lag allowed the power crisis to reach crippling proportions. In 1992, RA 7638 re-created the Department of Energy (which was abolished by the Aquino administration) to plan and manage the development of the energy sector. The years 1993 and 1994 were banner years for private sector participation in the power sector. The Emergency Power Crisis Act (RA 7648) gave President Ramos the authority to speedily approve power procurement contracts with private suppliers, also known as independent power producers (IPP). In 1994, the BOT law was amended to accommodate the growing variants of build-operate-transfer schemes. The generous incentives embodied in the power purchase contracts (PPA), together with the emerging attraction of East Asia as a destination for direct foreign investment, created a surge of entrants. In a typical power purchase contract, the Philippine government shouldered risks associated with market demand, exchange rate, fuel cost, retail tariff and sovereign risks. In effect, IPPs were market risk-less investments.

While the increase in PPA-mediated power generation capacity effectively ended the power crisis by 1995, the contingent liabilities embodied in these contracts became a fiscal minefield in the next five years. The PPA stipulated that NPC purchase power from IPPs regardless of the level of dispatch (the 'take-or-pay' feature), so NPC must pay for between 25 and 80 per cent of the agreed-on generated power even if it took up none of this. This resulted in power costing up to 25 per cent more than the power NPC generated in its own facilities (Tuaño, 2001; Reside, 2001). When excess power capacity came on stream, this became a fiscal nightmare; NPC's loss was ₱5.9 billion in 1999 and ₱9.9 billion in 2000. When NPC attempted to recoup the cost by raising the NPC tariff, it stoked a political firestorm (more later).

PRE-REFORM STRUCTURE OF THE ELECTRICITY SECTOR

The Industry Profile

The structure of the sector in the period 1987–2000 is reflected in Figure 19.1. The regulatory and policy framework consisted of the Energy Regulatory Board (ERB), the DOE, and the NEA. The ERB regulated MERALCO and other private utilities, the Electric Cooperatives and the state-owned NPC. The DOE formulated development projects and policies for the whole industry; the NEA either owned or supervised the Electric Cooperatives (which were partly government-owned). The *generation sector* consisted of the IPPs and NPC-owned generation facilities. The IPPs either sold power directly to MERALCO, to the distribution utilities (DUs) or to the NPC which, in turn, re-sold it to distribution utilities. NPC completely owned the transmission grid and auxiliary facilities. The distribution utilities, MERALCO and the electric cooperatives, owned subtransmission assets that conveyed electricity from high voltage transmission to consumers at tariffs approved by the ERB.

The pre-reform rules did not allow pure suppliers or aggregators who, while not owning subtransmission assets, nevertheless also supplied electricity to end-users using the subtransmission assets of existing distribution utilities as fees. This required the unbundling of the distribution business into *wire* – involving subtransmission assets – and *non-wire* – involving pure electricity trading and the supply business. This industry structure was dictated by the special features of electricity (Guasch and Spiller, 1998).

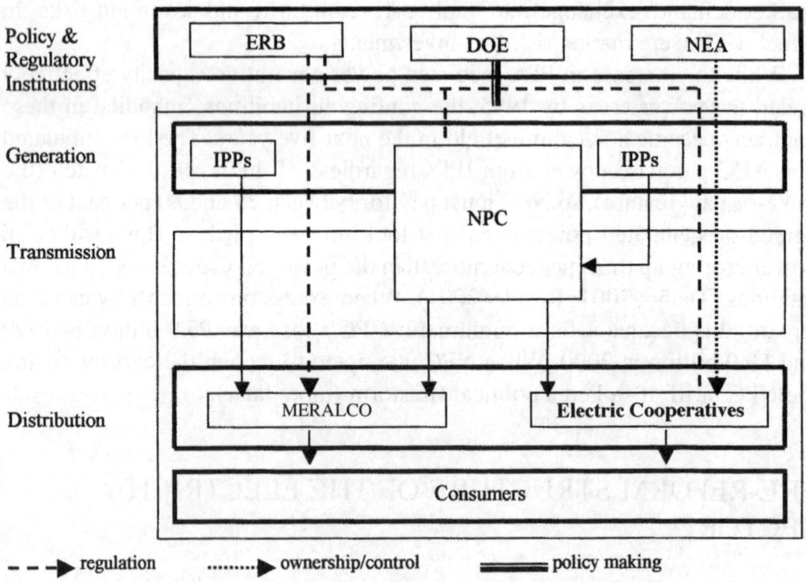

Sources: Philippine Department of Energy and World Bank (2000).

Figure 19.1 Structure of the Philippine electricity industry after first deregulation attempt

In the Philippines, power generation consists largely of coal- or diesel-fired generation, hydroelectric generation and geothermal generation. In the pre-reform set-up, the Energy Regulatory Board licensed generation companies or gencos, and the same body regulated their rates. In the previous arrangement, electric power transmission facilities were owned and operated by the NPC. These consisted primarily of the Luzon Grid at 230 kV and beyond, the Visayas Grid with 69 kV and above, and the Mindanao Grid at 138 kV and above. NPC also owned subtransmission assets.

The price regulation approach used by the ERB and its predecessors was the rate of return on rate base (RORB). A reasonable rate of return on asset investment was pegged at 12 per cent. Utilities were allowed tariff adjustments to recover NPC rates plus operating costs, including system losses. The incentive drawback of this strategy was evident with utilities happily incurring inefficiency costs and passing them on.

The State Involvement and Regulation

As already observed, the state was the main player in the power industry's generation and transmission sector. The National Power Corporation (NPC), a government-owned and operated corporation, owned the majority of the power generation capacity that included diesel-, coal-, geothermal- and hydro-powered generation. The private sector owned some gencos (IPPs), which sold directly to the NPC. The NPC wholly owned and operated the transmission systems, and also enjoyed some tax and tariff-free importation of petroleum products. The regulatory functions were vested in the state regulatory board that approved all tariffs of DUs, ECs, NPC and gencos. The Department of Energy created in 1996 (RA 7638) was charged with the responsibility of planning for the future; that is, forecasting power needs and developing and implementing projects to meet such needs.

State intervention occurred at many points in the industry. It stepped in on the financing side, either by guaranteeing NPC debentures or by granting generous guarantees to BOT investors; it gave tariff-free import privileges; it regulated tariffs at various nodes; and it mandated missionary electrification in areas that could not be served by power grids and imposed lifeline rates for poor households. The state also imposed a structure of subsidies: inter-class (specifically, commercial and industrial users paid more than household users), and inter-grid and within-grid subsidies (some regions paying higher rates so that other regions may pay less).

ELECTRIC POWER INDUSTRY REFORM ACT (RA 9136) OF 2001

A tectonic shift in the regulatory environment came with the Electric Power Industry Reform (RA 9136) of 2001. The fiscal deficit trap had become intolerable and further financing through state borrowing was much harder to access.

RA 9136, in effect repealed, among others, the following: RA 7638 or the 'Department of Energy Act of 1992', RA 6396, the NPC Charter, EO 172 creating the Energy Regulatory Board (ERB), and PD 269, also known as the National Electrification Administration (NEA) Act.

The 'Electric Power Industry Act of 2001' (RA 9136) provides a radical and ambitious blueprint for the electric power industry of the Philippines. Of the declared goals in Section 2, the following are most relevant and indicative:

> To ensure transparent and reasonable prices of electricity in a regime of free and fair competition and full accountability;
> To provide for an orderly and transparent privatization of the assets and liabilities of the National Power Corporation (NPC);
> To establish a strong and purely independent regulatory body and system . . . and enhance the competitive operation of the electricity market.

These goals reflect the main thrusts of the Act, which are state disengagement in ownership and financing and greater market determination of outcomes under a fair and transparent regulatory framework.

Market Safeguards and Transparency

Market safeguards were mandated first via the prohibition on cross-ownership of the Transmission Company (Transco). Specifically it stated: 'No generation company, distribution utility or stockholder or official thereof shall be allowed to hold ownership in the Transmission Company or its concessionaire and vice versa' (Rule 11, Section 3 (a), (b)). Likewise, limits on the concentration of ownership of generation capacity were established. To quote RA 9136: 'No company . . . can own or control more than thirty percent (30%) of the installed generating capacity of a Grid and/or twenty five percent (25%) of the national installed generating capacity' (Rule 11, Section 4 (a)). Limits on bilateral supply contracts by DUs were also set: 'No Distribution Utility shall be allowed to source from bilateral power supply contracts more than fifty percent (50%) of its total demand from its affiliate engaged in generation.'

These rules meant that cross-ownership between generation and distribution was allowed although transactions between affiliates were limited. This provision was reached after intense lobbying by entrenched players. Transmission, however, was wholly insulated from cross-ownership. The ownership and affiliate contract limitations were meant to inhibit market power abuse, discriminatory access, transfer pricing and cross-subsidization.

By Section 36 of RA 9136, every participant in the electric power industry was to structurally unbundle its activities; that is, separate different activities according to generation, transmission, distribution and supply, through the creation of separate divisions within the same company or even different juridical entities with clear accounting and auditing separation, especially as between regulated and non-regulated activities (Rule 10, Sec 1, IRR). This was to serve the interest of transparency. Rule 15 provided for the unbundling of rates. Section 3 stipulated that:

> An electric power industry participant shall identify, separate and unbundle its rates, charges and costs.

and

> In determining the eligible costs of service to be charged to the end-users, the ERC shall establish the minimum efficiency standards . . . including systems losses, and interruption frequency rates parameters among others.

The ERC prescribed the rate unbundling methodology for transmission and distribution wheeling rates and the retail rates of the distribution utility (Rule 10, Section 4, 5): 'These rates must be such as to allow the recovery of just and reasonable costs and a reasonable RORB to enable the entity to operate viably.'

Privatization

Chapter V, Section 47 of the Act mandated that 'All assets of NPC shall be sold in an open and transparent manner through public bidding, and the same shall apply to the disposition of IPP contracts' (Section 47 (d)). The privatization of the assets of NPC was to be implemented by the Act-enacted and the government-owned asset management corporation, the Power Sector Assets and Liabilities Management Corporation (PSALM Corp.), which inherited all the assets and liabilities of NPC, including the transmission assets.

Of the assets inherited by the PSALM Corporation, the transmission assets, the Small Power Utilities Group (SPUG) and the Agus and Polangui complexes in Mindanao were excluded from privatization. The transmission assets were to be managed and operated by the Transmission Corporation (TRANSCO), a corporation wholly owned by the PSALM Corp., Agus and Polangui, as well as SPUG.

Sectoral Regulatory Classification

Generation is ruled out of the regulatory process. Section 6, Chapter II of the Act declares that, 'Generation of electric power shall be competitive and open.' Thus, (a) it shall not be a public utility operation requiring a local or national franchise; (b) the prices charged by a generation company for supply of electricity shall not be subject to regulation by the ERC.

Section 29 Chapter II stipulates that the supply sector when serving the contestable market 'shall not be considered a public utility operation . . . The prices to be charged by suppliers for the supply of electricity to the contestable market shall not be subject to regulation by ERC.' The 'contestable market' is defined as the segment of 'electricity end-users who have a choice of a supplier of electricity as may be determined by ERC in accordance with this Act'. Thus it has a different meaning to that found in economics textbooks – it is a bureaucratic definition rather than an economic one. For example, all end-users with 'a monthly average peak demand of at least one megawatt for the preceding twelve (12) months' constituted the initial contestable market. This was to be lowered to 250 kW after two years and so on down (Section 4, Rule 12, IRR).

Suppliers to contestable markets under the Act were further required to: (a) secure from ERC a licence to operate; (b) not own any interest in TRANSCO or its concessionaire; (c) unbundle its supplier charge into its components; (d) comply with Competition Rules and the Wholesale Electricity Spot Market (WESM).

Transmission, however, remained within the regulatory ambit. Section 7, Chapter 11 states that, 'The transmission of electric power shall be a regulated common electricity carrier business, subject to the ratemaking powers of the ERC.' The transmission system is wholly owned by TRANSCO which, in turn, is wholly owned by the government-owned and operated PSALM Corporation.

Distribution also falls under regulatory scrutiny. Chapter II, Section 22 mandates that the 'distribution of electricity to end-users shall be a regulated common carrier business requiring a franchise'. Franchises can be granted only by the Congress of the Philippines (Section 27, Chapter II) and the ERC has to approve the retail rates of distribution utilities (Section 24, Chapter II). These rates must be unbundled into components: wires, generation and supply. Where businesses related to distribution are undertaken, Section 26 further mandates that separate accounts are to be maintained for each business undertaking to ensure that the distribution business does not subsidize it. This is an explicit preventive measure to transfer pricing and other obfuscative activities. Inter-connection is provided for when it states that 'a distribution utility shall provide open and non-discriminatory access to its distribution system to all end-users, including suppliers and aggregators' (Rule 7 (c); Chapter II, Section 23 and 31, RA 9136).

On the issue of DUs, Chapter II mandates that in every generation and in every distribution utility, 'the holdings of persons, natural or juridical . . . shall not exceed twenty-five percent (25%) of the voting shares of stocks' unless the company is listed in the Philippine Stock Exchange.

Removal of Cross-subsidies

Section 24, Chapter VIII mandates that 'Cross subsidies within a grid, between grids and/or classes of customers shall be phased out as a period not exceeding three (3) years from the establishment by the ERC of a universal charge.'

REGULATION AND PROMOTION

The Electricity Watchdog: ERC

The regulatory watchdog of the electricity industry is the Energy Regulatory Commission (ERC), which inherits the mantle from the Energy Regulatory Board (ERB) created under EO 172. The Commission has four members and a Chair who has to be a lawyer.

Section 44, Chapter IV of the Act states that 'The ERC shall promote competition, encourage market development, ensure customer choice and discourage/penalize abuse of market power in the restructured electricity industry.' It has to: (i) formulate and enforce the Grid and Distribution Code, Competition Rules and limits to recovery of system losses; (ii) establish performance standards for TRANSCO and concessionaires, DUs and suppliers; (iii) approve and enforce rules of the WESM; (iv) formulate the methodology for determining and fixing wheeling and retail rates to captive markets and after public hearings approve or disapprove such charges as petitioned by 'an affirmative vote of three (3) members' the ERC has exclusive jurisdiction over rates and fees; (v) determine the universal charge to be imposed on all end-users; (vi) implement abolition of all subsidies; (vii) set lifeline rates for the poor; (viii) monitor and penalize abuse of market power, cartelization, discriminatory behaviour and rules on ownership. In this, the ERC exercises quasi-judicial power. It can then amend or revoke the licence to operate of any participant; and (ix) implement the rules on functional and rate unbundling.

Not only does the ERC act as chief regulator of the transmission, distribution and supply sectors of the electric power industry through its approval of wheeling and retail rates, it also acts as the competition watchdog.

The Department of Energy and the Wholesale Electricity Spot Market (WESM)

The Department of Energy is the state agency charged with the development and upgrade of the electric power industry. It formulates and updates the 'Philippine Energy Plan' that encompasses exploration utilization, distribution, conservation and the pursuit of non-conventional and renewable energy sources.

Section 30 of the Act mandates that the DOE establishes the 'Wholesale Electricity Spot Market' (WESM). The WESM is run by the 'Independent Market Operator (IMO)', under the DOE. The DOE, jointly with electric power participants, formulates the WESM Rules that cover the methodology for determining the price of power not covered by bilateral contracts, which is approved by ERC, the dispatch instructions, the conditions for entry to and termination from the market, and procedures for billing and settlement.

Rate Determination Methodology

As observed, the ERC's principal responsibility is fixing the wheeling and retail rates for captive end-users. 'The rates must be such as to allow the recovery of just and reasonable costs and a reasonable RORB to enable the entity to operate viably.' (Section 43 (f)) states that 'the ERC may adapt alternative forms of internationally accepted rate-setting methodology' (Rule 15, Section 5 (a)). Although the latter gives the ERC methodological leeway, if RORB is adopted, the following must be observed: (i) asset revaluation allowed once every three years; (ii) interest expense (except in construction) cannot be deducted from permissible rate base; (iii) RORB cannot include management inefficiencies such as cost of project delays; (iv) procurement by petitioners must be transparent and satisfy industry standards; and (v) rate filing petition should be unbundled.

Table 19.2 lists the major components of price recognized and allowed by the ERC and highlights the role of the PPA and CERA for MERALCO and the FCA for the NPC. The mid-2002 furore over electricity price increases is associated with these items.

Transitory Oversight

Section 62 of the Act also mandates the creation of the Joint Congressional Power Commission (Power Commission) to monitor and ensure that the Act is properly implemented. The 14 members of this Commission come from both the lower and the upper houses of Congress. Among its tasks that are

Table 19.2 Current price regulation by the ERC

The effective selling price consists of two components:

- basic rate covering the operating and maintenance expenses, cost of purchased power and the cost of fuel used in operating the electric power plants. It remains the same until the utility files for a change subject to ERC approval
- cost adjustment mechanism is a method to allow utilities to automatically recover additional cost resulting from factors that are beyond the control of the utility such as imported fuel prices, currency depreciation, and cost of electric power bought from independent power producers

For MERALCO, the cost adjustment mechanism is made up of the following:

- purchased power adjustment (PPA) recovers changes in cost of power purchased from the NPC and its own IPP not covered by basic rate and the cost of distribution system losses
- currency exchange rate adjustment (CERA) recovers changes in foreign–denominated operating costs and principal debt repayment due to exchange rate movements

For NPC, it is composed of the following:

- purchased power cost adjustment (PPCA) recovers changes in power purchased from IPPs
- fuel cost adjustment (FCA) recovers changes in operating costs due to changes in fuel prices
- foreign exchange adjustment (FOREX) recovers changes in foreign disbursement due to changes in foreign exchange rates

Source: Philippine Energy Regulatory Commission.

relevant to the regulatory environment are: 'Endorse the privatization plan prepared by PSALM for approval of the President of the Philippines' as well as 'Determine weaknesses in the law and recommend necessary remedial legislation'.

INDUSTRY STRUCTURE IN RA 9136

The new industry structure envisioned in RA 9136 is summarized in Figure 19.2. As shown, the ERC regulates the distribution utilities and Transco, the state-owned (i.e., PSALM-owned) transmission company. The ERC exercises oversight over gencos and aggregators, and coordinates its activities with the DOE and PSALM. The state-owned PSALM owned Transco and other assets of Genco NOPC prior to privatization. The DOE formulates policy for the whole industry and supervises the NPC and the NEA. The NPC in turn owns SPUG, while the NEA supervises cooperatives, and the DOE supervises the independent market operator, which runs WESM.

The Power Commission can compel, under threat of punishment, any industry participant to submit any data and information pertinent to the performance of the industry. The Power Commission will exist for ten years after the effectivity of the Act 'but may be extended by a joint concurrent resolution'. The Power Commission adds another layer of oversight and being of a legislative nature could pose a threat to the stability of the Act and its provisions. Function (g) is especially pertinent because of reversal possibilities.

THE FIRST TEST

The debate accompanying RA 9136 was strident and, at times, highly contentious. The passage necessitated carrots such as the ₱200 billion subsidy by the government to bear part of the estimated ₱800 billion stranded cost;

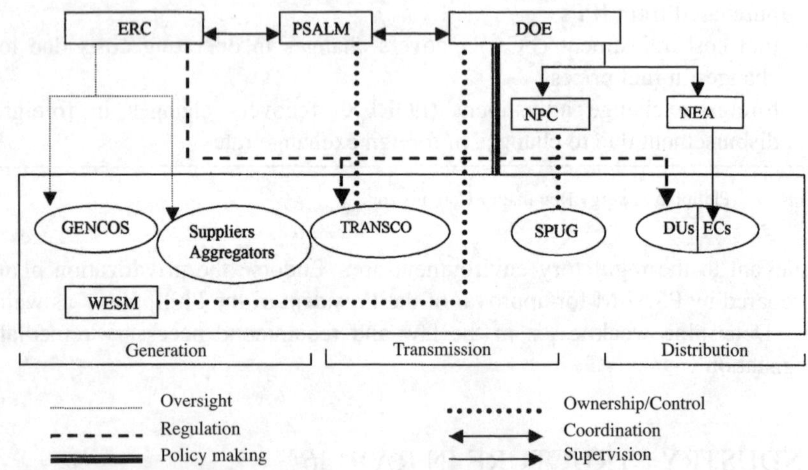

GENCOS generation companies
WESM wholesale electricity spot market
SPUG small power utilities group
DUs distribution utilities
ECs electric cooperatives

Source: Philippine Department of Energy.

Figure 19.2 Power industry structure after RA 9136

mandated, if time-bound, by reduction in tariffs, lifeline rates, and Mindanao facilities exemptions.

In 2002 the NPC got a ₱1.25 per kWh increment as a *purchased power adjustment* (PPA). This coincided with MERALCO's petition for ₱1.12 per kWh as its own PPA. The steep rise in end-user tariff caused a public outcry that prompted the President of the Republic to order NPC to postpone the increment, which was to pay for NPC's own debt and the liabilities incurred as guarantees (then only contingent liabilities) to IPPs during the BOT heyday. The suspension of the PPA adjustment meant that the government had to go to NPC's rescue to the tune of ₱15 billion at a time when the fiscal deficit was a big headache. As expected, the members of Congress rushed to exploit the row. A three-year relief from PPA is being proposed for consumers and one year for industries and a cap on MERALCO's PPA is also being proposed. In addition, even more drastic measures are contemplated. For all the glowing verbiage of RA 9136, the reality of its implementation threatens to completely undermine the law. Only time will tell if RA 9136 was worth the exercise after the political gauntlet has taken its toll. Politics and the imperatives of elections may, in the end, determine its outcome.

AN OVERVIEW OF OIL

Prior to 1971, the downstream oil industry, whose various parts are shown in Figure 19.3, operated without government intervention, with outcomes determined by market competition among six oil refiners: Shell, Caltex, Esso, Filoil, Mobil and Getty. Only one, Filoil, had substantial equity controlled by Filipino capital. These directly imported their petroleum requirements for refining. Foreign ownership also substantially affected the debate and policies in the sector.

The balance of payments crisis in 1969–70 precipitated the devaluation of the peso which, in turn, led to hefty increases in the price of gasoline. The public and jingoistic rhetoric of the time blamed the 'oil industry cartel' and foreign oil companies for the price increases and called for state regulation of oil prices. In response, RA 6173 created the *Oil Industry Commission* (OIC). State intervention thus began on a brew of anti-foreign and anti-cartel sentiment.

This sentiment was to push state involvement beyond regulation. PD 334 created the state-owned Philippine National Oil Company (PNOC). PNOC was designed to be a market player, owning and operating refining, storage and distribution assets. PNOC struck a joint venture with Mobil Oil and promptly acquired Esso and Filoil. The OIC, created in 1971, was restructured into the Board of Energy (BOE) in 1977, and was charged with the responsibility of setting prices for petroleum products, oil pipeline rates and

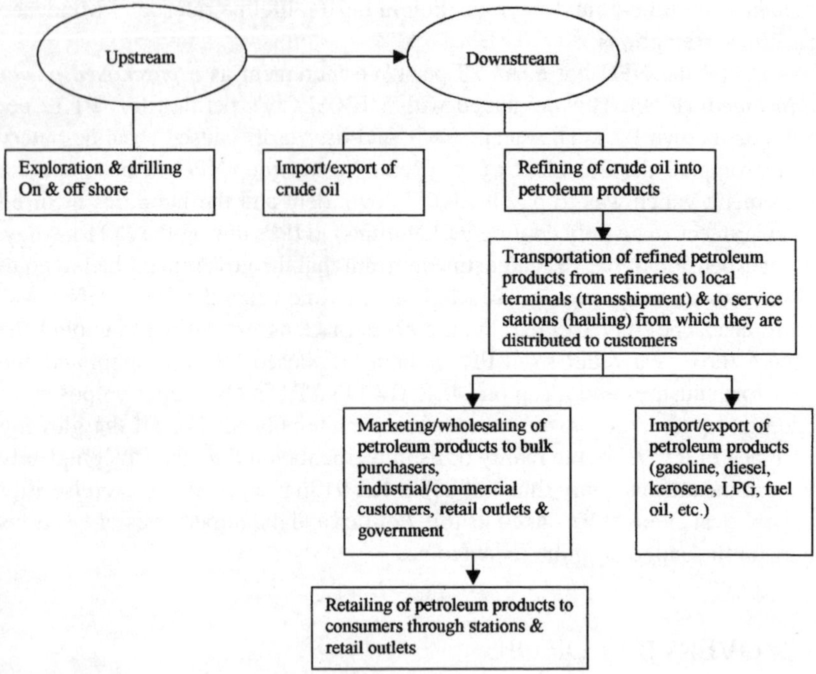

Source: PDCP Bank 'Oil Deregulation', *Industry Digest*, 1997.

Figure 19.3 Oil industry segments

electricity. A Department of Energy was created to formulate energy policies and programmes.

To maintain a stable pump price of gasoline, the Oil Price Stabilization Fund (OPSF) was created. The idea was to use orthodox price stabilization: achieving smooth retail price fluctuation by setting the price at a long-term average petroleum price so that a premium is collected by the Fund when the actual petroleum price is lower than the average, and disbursed when this is higher than the average. If properly set, the OPSF would be sustainable, but it also required that a rise (fall) in the intercept was to be accompanied by a raised (reduced) price, and this never became part of the political rhetoric. Downward shifts in the world petroleum price were reflected in pump prices but upward shifts were strongly resisted. The spectre of foreign predatory behaviour was permanently raised, with the result that the OPSF became a fiscal quagmire that helped weigh down long-term economic performance. In 1990, the government infused an additional ₱5 billion into the OPSF, which was used up within two years.

By the middle of the 1980s, the industry had only three refinery operators: Caltex, which bought Mobil, Shell which bought Getty, and the state-owned PNOC, which swallowed Filoil and Esso with a combined share of 90 per cent of oil industry output. As observed earlier, EO 172 transformed the BOE into the Energy Regulatory Board, which fixed petroleum product prices, gas and electricity prices. The DOE regulated the importation of crude oil, the refineries and other facilities, and product quality. The mechanism used for determining petroleum prices was a recovery approach based on a mark-up over the landed cost of crude oil over the previous two months. This guaranteed a baseline profit for firms. Differential taxes were imposed on the products based on affluence of consumers. By the 1990s, it was becoming clear that the whole set-up was unworkable, threatening the fiscal health of the economy. Few investments were being undertaken in view of the heavy hand of the state and its unpredictability.

THE DOWNSTREAM OIL INDUSTRY DEREGULATION ACT OF 1998

The 'downstream oil industry sector' refers to 'the business of importing, exporting, re-exporting, shipping, transporting, processing, refining, storing, distributing, marketing and/or selling crude oil, gasoline, diesel, liquefied petroleum gas (LPG), kerosene and other petroleum products' (Section 4 (h)). 'Downstream' then embraces everything that pertains to the oil business except oil exploration and extraction, which constitute the 'upstream' activities.

The basic law regulating the downstream oil industry sector in the Philippines is RA 8479, otherwise known as the 'Downstream Oil Industry Deregulation Act of 1998'. In its wake are repealed a cumulation of many laws: RA 6173 as amended, EO 172 as amended, LOI 1431 (October 1984), LOI 1441 (November 1984), LOI 1460 (May 1985), PD 1889, EO 137. Thus RA 8479 brings under one roof the whole regulatory framework of the oil industry sector.

Chapter II of the law sets down the principal reformation thrust of RA 8429. Section 5 entitled 'Liberalization of the Industry' states that 'any person or entity may import or purchase any quantity of crude oil and petroleum products from a foreign or domestic source, lease and/or operate refineries and other downstream oil facilities and market such crude oil and petroleum products'. This, in effect, (a) abolishes the crude oil import monopoly of the government, (b) extends the importation to 'other petroleum products' such as gasoline, (c) grants the import privilege to 'any person or entity' who satisfies the four provisions/conditions set down in Section 5, and (d) opens up the domestic market to new players who may not be refinery operators but who meet the conditions that only domestic refiners dependent on oil purchasing can service the domestic market.

Section 6 specifies a single and uniform tariff duty on imports of crude oil and refined petroleum products of 3 per cent. Thus the implicit protection to domestic refinery operators in the form of a tariff cascade (i.e. a 4 per cent differential between the tariffs of refined petroleum products and crude oil) is eliminated. The original version of RA 8479, RA 8180, provided precisely for such a protection for refinery operators. This provision, among others, was challenged before the Supreme Court, which declared RA 8180 unconstitutional. The Legislature passed RA 8479, which dropped the constitutionally invalid provisions (more on this later).

Section 7 spells out the market competition policy, requisite safeguards and the regulatory responsibility pertinent thereto: 'The Department of Trade and Industry and DOE shall take all measures to promote fair trade and prevent cartelization, monopolies, combinations in restraint of trade and any unfair competition in the Industry'. Thus anti-market behaviour will be punished. It also delineates the three other basic functions of the DOE: (1) to monitor the industry players and industry outcomes, such as the domestic and world prices of oil, product quality and refining processes; (2) to conciliate dispute over contractual obligations among industry players; (3) to market-make, which includes: encouraging entry of new players to increase competition, including a package of incentives such as but not limited to tax incentives, and especially promoting retail competition to embrace training of potential retailers and loan financing.

THE REGULATORY STRUCTURE

The DOE, as observed, is the central regulatory agency charged with the responsibility of implementing oil safeguards and other provisions of RA 8479. In this section, the tasks assigned to the DOE, are outlined.

Implementation of Anti-trust Safeguards: DOE–DOJ Task Force

The law prohibits anti-market behaviour in the form of cartelization monopolies and predatory pricing. To enforce this safeguard, the law created the *Joint (DOE–DOJ) Task Force* (Chapter IV, Section 14 (d)). This task force receives and reports complaints and investigates cases of anti-market behaviour related to any 'unreasonable' rise in prices, and prepares a report of its findings. When a violation is in evidence, the task force refers the case to local prosecutors who pursue it with the regional trial courts. If a private entity is a victim, the entity is entitled to sue for relief or damages with the regional trial court. Thus the joint task force is only an investigative body and is bereft of any quasi-judicial powers.

Monitoring and Standards

The DOE monitors and publishes such industry pertinent outcomes as an oil inventory, world and domestic prices (via Price Display Boards) and product quality. The monitoring of the latter is set against standards set by the Bureau of Product Standards (BPS) of the DTI in cooperation with DENR, DOE, DOST, and representatives of suppliers and consumers. Where such standards are violated, the DOE may recommend revocation of the permit to operate, recommend readjustments of the business or stop operations (Chapter IV, Section 14 (a), (b), (c), (e)).

Within the DOE, the pertinent agency in charge of gathering information and receiving and processing reported submissions and notice filing is the Energy Industry Administration Bureau (EIAB) (IRR of RA 8479, Rule II, Section 5).

The EIAB requires (i) every industry player to file a notice of operation providing details of its business and legal personality, including name, address, facilities and pertinent permits such as SEC registration; (ii) a notice of importation prior to loading which includes type, quantity, FOB price, port of destination and entry, bill of lading and invoices; (iii) a notice of exportation to include details such as bill of lading, name and address of exporter, type of cargo, ports and dates; (iv) all refinery operators, importers and marketers to produce a monthly report of actual and future imports, exports and local purchase.

Dispute resolution also falls under the DOE's mandate. Thus 'The DOE shall conciliate and arbitrate any dispute that may arise with respect to the contractual relationship involving the dealer's mark-up, the freight rate in transporting petroleum products and the margins of LPG distributors' (Rule III, Section 10 (b) of IRR). The DOE Secretary acts as the arbitrator over these disputes, and as such exercises quasi-judicial powers. The arbitration proceeding is specified whether oral or written. Any decision is appealable to the judicial courts.

The DOE is tasked with the duty to make the market more competitive (Section 8, RA 8479). The IRR in undertaking this task joins the DOE to: (i) grant the same incentives to new oil industry investment as are granted to BOI-registered enterprises in preferred areas of investment by the Omnibus Investment Code of 1987. These include tax breaks among others; (ii) attract new players; and (iii) promote retail competition through the training of potential retailers and provide loans.

REARGUARD ACTION

The public debate over the deregulation of the oil industry was strident and acrimonious in the mid-1990s. While there has been outright opposition (the anti-transnational cartel rhetoric), other views are more tempered and hold out for provisions that would, in effect, limit the extent of the deregulation and preserve the franchise value of old players. The compromise bill, RA 8180, which was passed in March 1996, removed price controls, the pump price stabilization mechanism, the Oil Price Stabilization Fund (OPSF), the exchange rate guarantee and liberalized entry. While radical, RA 8180 carried provisions that discriminated against potential new entrants and would have emasculated the market orientation of the law. In the bill predatory pricing was defined so that new players could not use lower prices to gain market share, in effect, ensuring that new players would be scarce. Also new entrants would be penalized because they were required to carry a 60-day inventory which added to their costs.

These new provisions were challenged before the Supreme Court, and in a landmark decision in October 1996, the Supreme Court declared RA 8180 unconstitutional on account of these anti-market provisions. The challenge was all the more interesting because it was an attempt to derail the deregulation altogether and, in part, it succeeded since the Supreme Court turned down the whole bill rather than just the offending provisions. But the ploy backfired when a revised bill, RA 8479, was passed. In this bill predatory pricing was referred to as pricing below average variable cost and a 3 per cent uniform tariff on all imported petroleum products and the elimination of the inventory requirement was proposed.

Increases in the pump price of gasoline, due to increases in the world petroleum price and the drastic exchange rate adjustment in the wake of the Asian Crisis, gave opponents of deregulation a field day. The 'still' heavily concentrated structure of refinery operators, and so-called excessive cartel profits, were blamed for price increases. The calls for re-intervention coalesced in the proposal for a 'National Oil Exchange', which would consolidate the economy's oil demand needed from world suppliers. In effect, the state monopoly over imports of crude oil would be reinstated. However, interest in the National Oil Exchange proposal waned when the world price of oil softened, but the forces against deregulation have not rested.

EARLY OUTCOMES

Since the passage of RA 8479 in February 1998, new players have appeared in retail marketing, bulk marketing and terminaling. The number of domestic refinery operators has remained constant. It is in retail business that the visibility of new players is most pronounced. As of February 2000, the number of petrol stations selling new players' gasoline reached 145 nationwide, with most of these being in Luzon where their oil depots are located. This occurred despite new players not being allowed to own their own stations, in contrast to old refinery operators who own gas stations.

SUMMARY

The Philippines has witnessed three phases of governance in the energy sector over the last century. From 1930–70, the electricity and the downstream oil industry operated with the state acting as the regulator and the private sector as the owner and producer. The 1970s with its oil crisis, the availability of petrodollars, the success in Europe of the 'commanding heights' viewpoint, and the exigencies of local politics, led to the deep politicisation of decisions to the state as the owner and producer. This experiment foundered in the 1980s.

Deregulation in the Philippine electricity industry started in 1989 with the demonopolization of power generation. In 1990, the BOT Law clarified the rules and incentives which facilitated private sector entry in power generation. Government guarantees in the mid-90s created the heyday of private participation. The Electric Power Industry Reform Act of 2001 envisaged a radically transformed electricity industry, with the state privatizing its generation and transmission assets and opening distribution to competition. It also provided for a spot market for wholesale electricity. In this case the state became purely a regulator in transmission and distribution of the RORB.

The 'Downstream Oil Industry Deregulation Act of 1998' abolished the monopoly over oil imports and opened up the domestic market to new players. Price stabilization in the form of the 'Oil Price Stabilization Fund', was also abolished and prices became market determined. Thus the state's role has evolved from being a regulator before 1971, a regulator and an owner and monopoly petroleum importer up to 1997, to being a competition watchdog after that. How much will be achieved from these initiatives remains uncertain.

BIBLIOGRAPHY

Achacoso, L. and G. Domingo (2000), 'Fuel for growth: a look at the Philippine petroleum industry', W. Sycip Policy Center, Asian Institute of Management, Makati, Philippines, September.

Aldaba, Rafaelita (2002), 'Regulatory policies and reforms in the power and downstream oil industries', June, unpublished monograph.

Churchill, Anthony (1995), 'Regulating the power sector', in Claudio R. Frischtak (ed.) *Regulatory Policies and Reform: A Comparative Perspective* (Chapter 15), Private Sector Development Department, Washington, DC: The World Bank.

Galang, Roberto and Chani Marie Solleza (2001), 'Deregulation under fire: an assessment of the downstream oil industry', W. Sycip Policy Center, Asian Institute of Management, Makati, Philippines.

Newbery, David (1995), 'Regulatory policies and reform in the electricity supply industry', in Claudio R. Frischtak (ed.) *Regulatory Policies and Reform: A Comparative Perspective* (Chapter 14), Private Sector Development Department, Washington, DC: The World Bank.

RA No. 8479 (1998), 'An Act Deregulating the Downstream Oil Industry, and for Other Purposes'.

RA No. 9136 (2002), 'An Act Ordaining Reforms in the Electric Power Industry, Amending for the Purpose Certain Laws and for Other Purposes'.

Reside, Renato Jr (2001), 'The future of the Philippine power sector: reason to be cautious (lessons from California and the United Kingdom)', in Canlas and Yasuhiro Nimura (eds) *Socio-economic Reform Program in the Philippines – Impacts and New Directions*, Institute of Developing Economies, Japan External Trade Organization.

'Rules and Regulations to Implement Republic Act No. 9136 entitled Electric Power Industry Reform Act of 2001'.

Spiller, Pablo and J. Luis Guasch (1998), 'Managing the regulatory process: design, concepts, issues, and the Latin America and Caribbean story', mimeo, Washington, DC: The World Bank.

Tuaño, Philip Arnold (2001), 'Privatization of a state enterprise: the NAPOCOR case', in *Economic Reforms and Governance in the Philippines – Eight Case Studies*, Ateneo School of Government and Ateneo Center for Social Policy and Public Affairs.

World Bank (1993), *World Bank Country Report*, Washington, DC: The World Bank.

World Bank (2000), *Philippines Country Framework Report for Private Participation in Infrastructure*, Washington, DC: The World Bank.

20. Regulation and competition: emerging issues from an Indian perspective

Thankom G. Arun

INTRODUCTION

The processes of globalisation and liberalisation have brought a considerable awareness towards improving the competitive process in developing economies such as India. Until recently most of the developing countries have operated without a structured competition policy, and have justified the interventions by the state over economic activities. The task of creating and maintaining an active competitive environment and developing a competition policy seems to be challenging in developing countries, particularly in the presence of many other competing alternatives, such as sectoral regulators, in ensuring a competitive environment. To what extent the new competition policies are helpful in enhancing investment and technological capabilities of firms and sectors is also an issue of concern. India is an interesting case study for looking at these issues in detail. India has experienced two periods of development with different policy regimes and institutional frameworks. Since independence, the transformation and development of the Indian economy has taken place within a planned, rigidly regulated and relatively closed economic framework. This changed in 1991 and since then, the country has embraced more liberalised policies.

This chapter is organised as follows. It begins by providing a brief outline of the basic governance structure of the country. It then explores the nature of the development strategy and regulatory legislation that were implemented during the import substitution regime. This is followed by an overview of the interrelationships between issues such as reforms, regulation and competition in developing countries in general, and India in particular. This section also discusses the new legal basis for a competitive regime in India. The final part of this chapter addresses issues of regulation and competition in the telecommunication industry, one sector which has undergone significant deregulation and opening up in India.

BASIC GOVERNANCE STRUCTURE

India has now gone through more than five decades with parliamentary executives both at the centre and in the states. One of the main concerns of the Indian constitution is to achieve social and economic democracy along with political democracy; to constitute a sovereign, socialist, secular, democratic republic of India (Austin, 1999). The multiplicity of political parties has been an important feature of the Indian political system. The dominance of a single political party gave way to coalitions and genuine political plurality, primarily in the late 1990s, which has brought the perspectives of regional parties into the decision-making process at the national level more prominently. Along with the shift in power to regional parties, one could see a drift towards disadvantaged classes (Bardhan, 2002). The adaptability of the constitution to the changing realities has been reflected in the large number of amendments (more than 80) during the last 50 years that have effectively made it an instrument of social change.

The institution of Parliament consists of Lok Sabha (Lower House) and Rajya Sabha (Upper House) in the centre and the legislative assemblies in the states. The members of the Lok Sabha are directly elected representatives of national constituencies; the state assemblies nominate the members of the Rajya Sabha. The Union represents 28 states and seven Union Territories. The ministerial character of the executive is an important feature of the Indian system that clearly stated the collective responsibility of the council of ministers to the legislature.

The constitution has laid down various measures to protect the judicial system from the influence of the executive, and also envisages an element of judicial review. The Supreme Court, the highest level of judicial institution in the country, has original jurisdiction in all disputes between the regions, and the regions and Union government. The High Courts in various states are responsible for the superintendence of all lower courts within their jurisdiction.

The constitution envisaged a cooperative federalism in centre–state relations, which ensures a harmonious interaction between the centre and the states and among the states for the common good. In addition to many commissioned studies such as the Sarkaria Commission in 1988, there are several mechanisms such as the Inter-state Council, the National Development Council and the Chief Minister's conferences that look into disputed areas between the centre and states. However, issues such as the redistribution of financial power and the sharing of water resources continue to be issues of concern between the centre and states, and among states.

DEVELOPMENT STRATEGIES AND REGULATORY LEGISLATION 1947–91

Successive Indian governments held the view that government intervention in support of large-scale investments in the public sector was necessary to achieve economic, political and social development objectives. Five-year plans have been used to organise human resources, capital and technology to achieve the targets for self-reliance and rapid industrial development. These policies were largely based on the concept of import substituting industrialisation, such as extensive import licensing and high tariffs, in the context of a mixed economy with a relatively large public sector (Arun and Nixson, 1997).

Government policies played an important role in regulating the inflow of foreign investment through restrictive legislation that affected the relative advantages of foreign investors. In the early years of independence, the activities of the public sector were restricted to a limited number of fields such as power and communications, which was extended later to non-infrastructure activities and non-core areas. Public sector enterprises were mostly the outcome of political considerations and bureaucratic rent-seeking, which constrained the choices on size, technology and location of these institutions in a competitive regime. The poor performance of these enterprises, which was manifested in low or negative returns to public investment, raised concerns about the rationale of supporting them as an engine of growth (Arun and Nixson, 2000).

Although there was marginally growing concern in the pre-reform period of the 1980s about promoting competition in the domestic market, technological upgrading and modernisation, the policy regime remained characterised by extensive intervention and the widespread use of discretionary controls. The regulation and competition issues in an open market setting took precedence over inward oriented policies during this period. Some of the prominent regulatory measures implemented during the pre-reform period are briefly discussed next.

Industries (Development and Regulation) Act, 1951

This Act was introduced to ensure that industries were not set up or not expanded without obtaining a licence. It provided the legal framework for control and regulation of important industries subject to the levels of investments, location and growth, and also allowed the government to prescribe prices, methods and the volume of production and channels of distribution. According to the government, the overall objective of industrial licensing was to allocate resources according to priorities stated in development plans. Although there were numerous amendments to the Act over the years, no significant changes were made in the basic provisions until the early 1990s.

However, over time the process of licensing acquired a very different character and became a mechanism for long-term industrial growth.

The Monopolies and Restrictive Trade Practices Act, 1969

The Monopolies and Restrictive Trade Practices Act (MRTP) was designed mainly to serve three purposes: (1) to regulate the concentration of economic power in private hands to ensure that it did not cause detriment to the public; (2) to control monopolies and prohibit monopolistic trade practices; and (3) to curb restrictive trade practices. This Act covered only private sector undertakings and did not apply to (1) any undertaking owned or controlled by government, government companies or a corporation established by or under any central, provincial or state Act; (2) any trade union or other association of workers or employees formed for their own reasonable protection; and (3) any undertaking engaged in one industry, the management of which has been taken over by any person or body of persons in pursuance of any authorisation made by the central government.

Foreign Exchange Regulation Act, 1973

The Foreign Exchange Regulation Act (FERA) was thoroughly revised and amended in 1973 to replace the old Act of 1947. The main aim of the Act was to regulate foreign exchange transactions to limit the use of foreign exchange resources which, apparently, constrained the freedom of foreign investors. This Act had given much wider powers to the government and the Reserve Bank of India (RBI) in dealing with matters pertaining to foreign exchange regulations, regulating the working of foreign companies, or companies incorporated in India in which the non-domestic interest is 40 per cent or more. The activities of Indian entrepreneurs, in the form of joint ventures, were also subjected to stricter scrutiny.

In general terms, the basic idea embodied in the industrial approval system was to make the best possible use of scarce resources. However, the considerable discretionary powers vested in regulatory agencies resulted in huge delays in the processing of applications, and the whole system developed into an institutional arrangement that promoted rent-seeking and discrimination. There was evidence of declining social profitability of industrial investment during this period (Lal, 1980). The lack of technological dynamism, the absence of competition and the protection of markets drastically restricted the development of a competitive industrial sector in India during this period (Arun and Nixson, 2001). The new economic policies introduced since 1991 marked a fundamental break with the past and drastically reduced the degree of state regulation.

REFORMS, REGULATION AND COMPETITION POLICY

Since 1991, the government of India (GOI) has introduced a series of economic reforms, including policies of liberalisation, deregulation, disinvestment and privatisation. The seriousness of macroeconomic imbalances and unanimity among political parties towards reform made this possible. The broad thrust of the new policies was a move away from the centralised allocation of resources in some key sectors by the government to allocation by market forces. Private participation in economic development has emerged as an alternative to the state-oriented development strategy in the reform period (Arun and Nixson, 1997).

The disinvestment of government shareholdings in the equity of selected public sector undertakings is an important step towards wider private sector participation in economic development. The shift in attitude was interpreted as a belated realisation by government of the poor performance of public enterprises, and the new policies were intended to bring market discipline and public accountability to the performances of public enterprises by broad-basing their management and ownership patterns (Arun and Nixson, 2000). After a decade of reforms, restraints to competition such as state monopolies and protective measures and controls are being replaced by a relatively more competitive and de-regulated open economic system. Industrial licensing was abolished irrespective of levels of investment, except for specified industries. The new policies relaxed or abolished the restrictions on private/foreign investment in key sectors of the economy such as infrastructure.

The need for regulation of economic activities is often justified as a policy instrument to minimise the effects of market failures. Several characteristics of effective regulation such as independence, accountability, transparency, clarity, simplicity, and consistency have been identified in the literature. To develop a more rational approach to economic regulation, the priority must be to establish a more coherent institutional framework (Ogus, 1994). This requires the proper allocation of functions to the regulatory institutions based on appropriate power and accountability, which is a highly contentious issue in the political economy context of India. To what extent the government is willing to surrender political control over regulatory decisions is an important issue yet to be addressed.

In India, during the period of economic reforms, private sector participation in the production and supply of utility services has increased substantially and the concept of economic regulation, particularly the issues related to prices/fees of service providers, attracts a lot of attention. The independent regulators have already been in operation in many sectors such as telecommunications and electricity. These regulatory commissions are different from commissions appointed in the past, such as the Disinvestment Commission, which were advisory in nature. In the literature, the sectoral regulators are expected to determine the entry conditions and eventually the level of competition in the industry itself. However, to what extent the issues of competition can be effectively incorporated in the regulatory structure is an important issue for most of the developing economies where adequate healthy competitive practices have not been developed.

The mutually reinforcing nature of regulation and competition policies requires active coordination between the agencies even in the early stages of liberalisation, which is important for developing countries such as India, as it is setting up sector specific regulatory bodies. The changing dimensions of market failure in the light of developments in technology and property rights give rise to more opportunities and challenges for regulatory and competition strategies. In the case of the United Kingdom, the regulators have acted as a proxy for competition in establishing the proper balance between producer and consumer interests (Pryor, 1996). However the boundaries between the roles of the sectoral regulators and the competition policy are difficult to define, and in many countries the competition authority has direct overlap with sectoral regulators (Mehta, 2002).

The nature of the national regulatory framework that has developed for privatised utilities in India is influenced to a large extent by the capacity of the system to implement regulation and by the type of markets within which enterprise functions (Cook, 1999). However, to what extent these regulatory agencies will or can be independent and accountable is the real issue in the political economy context of India (Arun and Nixson, 1997). The sequencing and timing of competition policy in developing countries depends to a great extent on domestic compulsions and needs (Basant and Morris, 2000). It is necessary for the government to take an active role in developing and maintaining a competitive environment and to redefine its role as regulator in the previous policy regime.

Regarding the scope of competition policy in a developing country, one view is that it must address issues such as (1) restraining anti-competitive behaviour by domestic privatised large firms; (2) limiting abuses of monopoly power by mega-corporations created by the international merger movement; and (3) promoting development (Singh, 2002). The competition policy should also be able to promote competition and maintain the competitive environment through the efficient allocation of resources in the economy, which should result in lower prices, adequate supplies for consumers, faster growth and more equitable distribution of income (Mehta, 2002).

Competition policy is a broad concept which covers all aspects of government actions that affect the conditions under which firms compete in a particular market and is considered as complex in its intentions and effects (Lahouel and Maskus, 1999). The governments in developing countries must establish appropriate competition policies to foster 'a liberal trade and investment regime, and that action can be taken under competition law statues to ensure that markets are contestable' (Hoekman and Holmes, 1999, p. 21). Hoekman and Holmes (1999, p. 11) further argued that

> where institutional capacity is limited, it is desirable for political structures to do all they can to make conditions as favourable as possible for pro-competitive behaviour, which includes sustaining free trade and avoiding the creation of monopolies through perverse regulation or by ill-conceived privatisation.

However, preserving and promoting the efficiency gains from trade and investment by limiting the potential problems for equity and welfare are the real challenge for a competition policy (Balasubramanyam and Elliot, 2002). All these discussions indicate the need for a broad-based approach in developing a competition policy in developing economies.

In India, the new Competition Bill (2001) aims to revoke the previous MRTP Act and the dissolution of the MRTP Commission. As a prelude to this, the government has appointed various committees such as the Raghavan Committee to examine issues relating to competition law and policy in India, which provides crucial inputs in the drafting of new legislation. The new legislation was necessary due to the incompatibility between the liberalised regime and previous policy instruments such as the MRTP. For instance the issue of predatory pricing has not been discussed anywhere in the MRTP Act (Bhattacharjea, 2000). The new legislation aims to promote and sustain competition in markets by preventing anti-competitive practices and maintaining a competitive environment. The law envisages the formation of a quasi-judicial body, the Competition Commission of India (CCI) to control the negative aspects of competition and undertake competition advocacy for creating awareness and imparting training on competition.

The CCI will consist of a chairperson, and not less than two and not more than ten other members, to be appointed by the central government on the recommendation of a selection committee consisting of Chief Justice of India, two cabinet members, the Reserve Bank Governor and the Cabinet Secretary. However, the issue of who shall be the members of the Commission has raised some discussion in India, mainly in relation to the issues of experience and age limit of members of the proposed CCI. There is a serious concern that CCI will become yet another commission which provides jobs for retired civil servants and judges. The other issue of concern is that the new commission may inherit the investigative staff of the MRTP commission who had been trained for procedural duties and have little expertise in administering a modern competitive law in its complexity (for a detailed discussion of this argument, see Bhattacharjea, 2001). In reality, the responsibilities of the commission require technically competent people with a reasonable period of experience and an understanding of the economic arguments required for the enforcement of modern competition laws.

An assessment of the new Competition Act is summarised in Table 20.1. There is an argument that the Act has provided multiple criteria and many of them are subjective. It may be the case that judgements on competition could often lead to an increase in business cost (Bhattacharjea, 2001). Regarding IPRs, the concern is that these need to be addressed adequately in the Act to check the transgressing activities of firms in a rapidly changing global knowledge-based environment (CUTS, 2001). CUTS has further argued for the incorporation of appropriate incentives and measures in the Act to encourage firms and their employees to inform the CCI of reprehensible activities, and also recommends a reconsideration of clauses 3 and 27 of the Act to deal separately with general anti-competitive agreements and hard core cartels.

Table 20.1 Competition Act of India, 2002

Highlights	Lowlights
• Anti-competitive agreements such as price-fixing, output restriction, market allocation and bid rigging prohibited per se • Regulation of mergers and acquisitions above a threshold and prior notification optional • Higher penalties for offences, up to 10 per cent of the average of the turnover for the last three preceding financial years • Unfair trade practices omitted – pending cases to be transferred to the consumer courts • Establishment of CCI and Competition Fund	• CCI is required to adhere to the policy guidelines from the central government from time to time – independence of the commission is in doubt • The bill appears soft on serious competition abuses such as hard core cartels • Competition abuses due to Intellectual Property Rights (IPRs) not addressed well • Relationship between CCI and other sectoral regulators are not very well defined • 'Exemptions' from the Bill are left to the discretion of the central government without any guidelines

Source: Adapted from CUTS (2001).

REGULATORY AND COMPETITIVE PRACTICES IN THE TELECOMMUNICATIONS SECTOR

Policy Reform and Organisation Changes in the Telecommunications Sector

The Indian telecommunications sector was wholly under government ownership until the mid-1980s, and in 1986 public sector corporations such as the Mahanagar Telephone Nigam Limited (MTNL) and the Videsh Sanchar Nigam Limited (VSNL) were created to allow greater autonomy in decision-making, and to facilitate public borrowings that would not have been possible under a government framework. However, policy formulation and regulation remained with the Department of Telecommunications (DOT). The MTNL was mainly constituted to look after the operation, maintenance, and development of telecom services in Bombay and New Delhi. The VSNL was set up to plan, operate, develop, and accelerate international telecom services in India. In 1989, the Telecom Commission was created with executive, administrative, and financial powers to formulate and regulate policy and prepare the budget for the DOT.

In line with other economic reforms, the telecommunications equipment manufacturing industry has been de-licensed and de-reserved since 1991. Automatic approval of foreign equity up to 51 per cent has been allowed for foreign investors engaged in the manufacture of all telecommunications equipment. The value added services in the telecommunications sector were opened up to private investment in July 1992 with the objective of achieving international facilities.

The National Telecom Policy (NTP) announced in 1994 specified the major objectives of the reform in the telecommunication sector in India. It required telephone services on demand, the achievement of a universal service obligation, assurance of world class service to subscribers and the universal availability of basic telephone services. This policy also paved the way for private sector participation in basic telephone services, particularly local telephones. However, there is criticism that the policy failed to provide the mechanisms to achieve the objectives such as universal access and service goals (Gupta, 2002). Although the 1994 policy was instrumental in accelerating private participation in the telecommunication sector, the poor design of auctions and the licensing conditions resulted in delays (Arun and Nixson, 1998). In 1999, a new NTP was issued which contains guidelines for contentious issues such as high licence fees, interconnections, constraints on service provisions and opening up of satellite services to foreign companies. Critics have argued that the policy failed to take a stand on the privatisation of incumbent companies and retained the capacity of the government to intervene in the competitive process (Gupta, 2002). This revised policy has incorporated an element of revenue sharing with operators rather than licence fee arrangements.

The Department of Telecom Services (DTS) was created in 1999 to separate the DOT's service role from policy and licensing, and the DTS was converted in 2001 to an independent company called Bharat Sanchar Nigam (BSNL). This raised huge opposition from labour unions and the government had to compensate the employees with a free phone installation, free local calls to a certain number, and no rental charges for a telephone until a specified time. The VSNL lost its monopoly status as the sole internet service provider (ISP) in the reform process as the GOI allowed private participation for ISPs, and thus licensing was made almost free. The government also treated VSNL and other providers indiscriminately, and provided the same rights to work with international carriers in order to have access to undersea bandwidth. Again, in typical fashion, to compensate the losses for VSNL, the government granted a nationwide licence for internet and a free licence for long-distance calls, which was cancelled later due to a belated realisation of the negative impact of this decision on the growth of the sector.

Telecom Regulatory Authority of India

In the telecommunication sector, traditional regulation was aimed at protecting the monopoly status of government-owned operators to preserve revenue and to maintain the sustainability of cross-subsidisation policies. Even in OECD countries, it was difficult for policy-makers to make the intellectual leap needed to convince opponents that competition in the telecommunications sector had benefits (Pryor, 1996). Also, the time needed to obtain policy consensus at bureaucratic and political level in order to bring about policy changes should not be understated. The public telecommunication operators have had traditionally highly unionised work forces, and given the size of employment in most economies, these unions proved to be influential in the process of reform. However, as we discussed earlier, the institutional design of a regulatory agency based on transparency and accountability enhances the confidence of both investors and consumers.

In 1997 the Telecom Regulatory Authority of India (TRAI) was set up, which was considered to be a bold initiative. The objectives of TRAI are

> to protect the interests of consumers, regulate telecommunications tariffs, settle disputes between service providers, ensure compliance of license conditions, bring about technical compatibility and inter-connections between different service providers, regulate arrangements amongst service providers in respect of sharing revenue, levy fees, facilitate competition, promote efficiency, provide a level playing field for fair competition among the public and private operators and to give further content to universal service obligation. (GOI Economic Survey, 1996–97, p. 169)

According to the composition of the TRAI, the Chair should be appointed for a period of five years and the members for a period of five years or up to the age of 62, whichever is earlier. A member of the TRAI can be removed only on the recommendations of the Supreme Court on the basis of a specific enquiry held by it into his or her misconduct. These provisions are supposed to protect the TRAI from unnecessary government interventions and provide more functional autonomy and independence. The TRAI has the power to seek information on all aspects of a service provider's activities and to investigate any matter which in its opinion constitutes public interest. The Authority has an inbuilt dispute settlement mechanism, including procedures to be followed in this regard as well as a scheme of punishment/fines in the event of non-compliance with its orders. However, the TRAI was not given responsibility to issue and revoke licences, but only to recommend them. The TRAI divests the DOT of several regulatory functions it has experienced all along on behalf of the government of India, and brings its service-providing and tariff-seeking functions under the regulatory jurisdiction of an independent agency. However, the DOT retained policy-making, licensing, and operative powers within the same organisational boundaries.

In practice, the Minister for Communications nominated members to the TRAI and most of these members were former civil servants, who throughout their life were practitioners of the 'permit-licence-quota system' and did not include anyone who could take care of consumer interest, which is one of the most important objectives of the TRAI (Chowdary, 2001). There are instances that even a serving member of the Telecom Commission of the DOT was appointed to the TRAI. The majority of the members had no communications background nor were they businessmen, economists, industrialists, consumer activists or public policy makers. This episode shows that one of the competitors became a member of the TRAI, which is primarily concerned with the resolution of disputes between the competitors, and this was mainly due to lack of transparency in the selection and appointment of the members of the regulatory body (Chowdary, 2001). The cases discussed later in the chapter suggest that the lack of support for the TRAI influenced many foreign investors to pull back from the telecom market, which has received the highest amount of foreign investment during the reform period.

In 1999, the Committee on Telecom and Information Technology Convergence looked into the emerging issues in the sector and provided inputs to amend the TRAI Act in 2000. The new Act has changed the nature, composition and powers of the regulatory commission, and the regulatory role of the TRAI has been split from dispute settlement. However, the new TRAI has powers to recommend the introduction of new service providers, technological improvements, quality standards, and the fixing of terms and conditions of licences (Gupta, 2002). The new Act also reduced the number of members to four (out of them, two are part-time members) and removed the condition that the Chairperson should have a background in the judiciary. The new Act has also constituted the Telecom Dispute Settlement and the Appellate Tribunal (TDSAT) to adjudicate disputes between a licensor and licensee, service providers, and between a service provider and a group of consumers. However, there are criticisms that the new Act has not explicitly addressed issues relating to telecom standards, intellectual property rights and competition policy (Basant, 2001). It has been further argued that the lack of clarity in the allocation of powers between the TRAI, the TDSAT and the competition authority could lead to delays in litigation (Basant, 2001).

In one of the legal battles between the DOT and the TRAI, the cellular operators had alleged that the DOT had unilaterally increased the tariffs for calls made from ordinary telephones to cellular mobile phones (Aircel Diglink India Limited and others vs. Union of India and others). The DOT appealed against the TRAI order which favoured cellular operators in the Delhi High Court and asked to curtail the scope and powers of the TRAI. The High Court's judgment was against the TRAI decision, which opened up the possibility of challenging TRAI decisions in all the High Courts in the country. However, the provision to appeal TRAI decisions in the High Courts was removed from the new Act, making this possible only in the Supreme Court.

Technological changes are transforming the structural features of the telecom industry in an unprecedented way and call into question the nature and scope of regulation itself. The issue of technological convergence raises the subject of rapidly changing definitional issues in the telecom industry and the contestable nature of the increasing number of segments of the telecom markets (Basant, 2001). In such a situation, the inconsistent regulatory policies across various delivery mechanisms could distort the growth of the industry. In India, the proposed Communications Convergence Bill 2000 suggested the formation of an independent commission consisting of specialists from various fields to establish a modern and competitive communications infrastructure, which could tackle the issues of convergence among various sectors, and provide communication services at an affordable cost.

Competition in Basic Services

As of 1994, basic service provision had been planned as a duopoly between the DOT and a selected service provider. In 1995, with the intention that the private sector would provide 1.77 million telephone lines and 0.21 million villages with public telephones, the GOI started to initiate limited competition in basic services. Several service providers, one for each of the 20 circles into which the entire country had been divided, would compete with the DOT for basic services (for a detailed discussion on this process see Arun and Nixson,

1998; Gupta, 2002). Despite an increase in the number of villages connected by phone over the years, rural connectivity remains a matter of concern. Even in those villages which have been connected, provision remains poor for services such as public telephones, long-distance facilities and other value-added services. Tele-density increased from 0.8 per cent in 1994 to 3 per cent in 2001, but this is below the government target of 7 per cent in 2005 (Gupta, 2002).

To address these issues the TRAI suggested unlimited competition for basic services along with domestic and international long-distance services, and has also recommended the use of alternative technologies such as Wireless Local Loop (WLL) (allowing limited mobility with handsets) for a rapid expansion of basic services. Cellular operators objected to this and suggested it is nothing more than a substitute for cellular services. They argue that the decision would disrupt the level playing field as cellular operators pay higher fees for entry and basic revenue share arrangements compared with basic service providers (Gupta, 2002). However, the TRAI has decided against the objections by cellular operators and treated the WLL technology as a supplementary facility for basic services. The TRAI also noted that the service provided by the cellular operators is superior to what will be provided by the basic service providers by using WLL and as a result will not adversely affect business (Gupta, 2002). The DOT has recently implemented the proposals of the TRAI despite the resistance from cellular operators. The introduction of effective competition in the domestic long-distance sector was made possible only through the intervention of the Prime Minister's Office in the policy-making process against the interest of the DOT (Bagchi, 2000). Currently, other than BSNL and VSNL, two private companies (Bharti Group and Reliance Industries) are also operating in the domestic long-distance services. However, a recent survey by TRAI during the period October 2001–June 2002 shows that operators in the basic services provision are short of meeting the standards for network reliability and availability. This poses further challenges to the TRAI and the basic service providers to make the industry more competitive and beneficial to consumers.

CONCLUSIONS

The legislative changes in regulation and competition prove beyond doubt that India has come a long way from a closed economy. The Indian situation reveals that as the economy opens to competition, regulating a market place requires a different set of resources and capabilities to address the emerging issues. The corporatisation of government departments brought more freedom and flexibility to take market-oriented decisions, and enhanced the level of accountability. In the telecommunications sector, regulatory activities in the early stages of competition were heavily involved in preventing the incumbent from using its market position. Although the TRAI has established some elements of transparency and leadership in its participatory style of functioning, it is imperative to develop more initiatives based on technological development to enhance competition and to avoid regulatory capture by the previous incumbent. The regulatory authority's decision to allow WLL in the basic services is expected to reduce the cost and enhance rural connectivity and tele-density. The new licensing regime of a one time entry fee and the rest by revenue sharing is also a change in a positive direction compared with the previous high licence regime. However, there are still some contentious issues, such as convergence and interconnection, that need to be addressed with appropriate regulatory guidelines and/or industry negotiation on agreements.

India needs to examine more closely the international experiences of regulation and competition in developing its own specific strategies. As in many developed countries, there should be a national consensus to keep the issues of regulation and competition out of the political agenda, which is still not happening in India. As India moves through the reform process, the political parties need to recognise the views of subject experts. To what extent the government is willing to surrender political control over the decisions on regulation and competition depends on whether the political parties are prepared to treat these issues on the basis of the long-term national interest, irrespective of their position in power.

REFERENCES

Arun, T.G. and F.I. Nixson (2001), 'Liberalisation and the manufacturing sector: the Indian experience during the 1990s', in O. Morrissey and M. Tribe (eds) *Economic Policy and Manufacturing Performance in Developing Countries*, Cheltenham: Edward Elgar.

Arun, T.G. and F.I. Nixson (2000), 'The disinvestments of public sector enterprises: the Indian experience', *Oxford Development Studies*, **28** (1), 19–32.

Arun, T.G. and F.I. Nixson (1998), 'The transition of a public sector monopoly: India's experience', *Journal of International Development*, **10**, 387–95.

Arun, T.G. and F.I. Nixson (1997), 'Privatisation and foreign participation – the Indian experience', *Journal of Asia Pacific Economy*, **2** (2), 201–24.

Austin, G. (1999), *The Indian Constitution*, New Delhi: Oxford University Press.

Bagchi, P. (2000), 'Telecommunications reform and the state in India: the contradiction of private control and government competition', Occasional Paper No. 13, Centre for Advanced Study of India, University of Pennsylvania.

Balasubramanyam, V.N. and C. Elliot (2002), 'Competition policy and WTO', paper presented at the WTO and Developing Countries' Conference, King's College, 13 September 2002.

Bardhan, P. (2002), 'The political economy of reform in India', in R. Moham (ed.) *Facets of the Indian Economy*, New Delhi: Oxford University Press.

Basant, R. (2001), 'Interface between sector-specific regulatory bodies and competition agencies: a case of the Indian telecommunications sector', India Infrastructure Report, 3i Network, New Delhi: Oxford University Press.

Basant, R. and S. Morris (2000), 'Competition policy in India – issues for a globalising economy', *Economic and Political Weekly*, 29 July 2000.

Bhattacharjea, A. (2000), 'Predation, Protection and the "Public Interest" ', *Economic and Political Weekly*, 02 December 2000.

Bhattacharjea, A. (2001), 'Competition policy: India and the WTO', *Economic and Political Weekly*, 22 December 2001.

Cook, P. (1999), 'Privatisation and utility regulation in developing countries: the lessons so far', *Annals of Public and Cooperative Economics*, **70** (4), 549–87.

Chowdary, T.H. (2001), 'Competition in international long distance telecom service', *Economic and Political Weekly*, 1 December 2001.

CUTS (2001), 'Competition Bill of India, 2001', Briefing Paper on Competition Bill, Consumer Unity and Trust Society (CUTS).

GOI (1994), *New Telecom Policy*, New Delhi: DOT.

GOI (1997), Economic Survey, New Delhi: Ministry of Finance.

GOI (1999), *New Telecom Policy*, New Delhi: DOT.

Gupta, R. (2002), 'Telecommunications liberalisation – critical role of legal and regulatory regime', *Economic and Political Weekly*, 27 April 2002.

Hoekman, B. and P. Holmes (1999), 'Competition policy, developing countries and the WTO', Washington, DC: World Bank (WTO 2000 capacity building project background papers).

Lahouel, M. and K.E. Maskus (1999), 'Competition policy and intellectual property rights in developing countries: interests in unilateral initiatives and a WTO agreement', paper presented at the WTO/World Bank Conference on Developing Countries in a Millennium Round, WTO Secretariat, Geneva.

Lal, D. (1980), *Prices for Planning*, London: Heinemann Educational Books.

Mehta, P.S. (2002), 'Competition policy in developing countries: an Asia-Pacific perspective', Bulletin on Asia-Pacific Perspectives, United Nations Economic and Social Commission for Asia and the Pacific.

Ogus, A. (1994), *Regulation – Legal Form and Economic Theory*, Oxford: Clarendon Press.

Pryor, A. (1996), 'Use of competition policy to facilitate market access in relation to regulatory reform', in *Regulatory Reform and International Market Openness*, OECD Proceedings, OECD.

Singh, A. (2002), 'Competition and competition policy in emerging markets: international and developmental dimensions', Working Paper No. 246, ESRC Centre for Business Research, University of Cambridge.

21. Telecommunications in Guyana: from state ownership to de-monopolization?

Claude V. Chang

INTRODUCTION

The fundamental changes in telecommunications worldwide over the last six years have not been lost on Guyana. To the incumbent People's Progressive Party/Civic (PPP/C) government of Guyana, 'a phone in every home' and bringing Internet access to every school child in Guyana were campaign promises too good to pass up in the 2001 general elections – such were the perceived expectations for telecommunication services.

Even before electioneering began in earnest the Guyanese President, Bharrat Jagdeo, registered his dissatisfaction with the slow pace of network rollout and threatened to de-monopolize the industry. In his view, information technology (IT) is central to economic development and to achieving the objectives of the Poverty Reduction Strategy Programme (PRSP) required under the Highly Indebted Poor Countries (HIPC) Initiatives and the International Monetary Fund's (IMF) Poverty Reduction Growth Facility (PRGF). It also figures prominently in the National Development Strategy (NDS) developed by a cross-section of civil society in Guyana.

For its part, the incumbent monopoly provider, Guyana Telephone & Telegraph Company Limited (GT&T), has taken the position that since privatization of the industry in 1991, it has improved both the quality of and access to telecommunications services. To support its position, the company points to the increase in investment in plant and equipment and to the increase in the number of service connections since 1990. It further claims that its progress has been hampered by adverse regulatory practices.

With the re-election of the PPP/C in 2001, the campaign promise on the issue of de-monopolization has proven to be more than just rhetoric. GT&T's parent company, Atlantic Tele-Network (ATN) of the US Virgin Islands, however, has held that a 1990 Agreement with the government is inviolable. The issue has been made more complex by a changing perception of regulation and competition, and convergence of public voice circuit-switched networks (public switched telephone networks) and the connectionless packet-switched data networks.

HISTORICAL PERSPECTIVE

As with most former British colonies, the telecommunications service in Guyana was combined with the postal service. However, in keeping with the trend to de-link telecommunications from postal services, the Guyana government created the state-owned Guyana Telecommunications Corporation (GTC) in 1967.

From 1 March 1967 to privatization in January 1991, telecommunications services were provided by a state-owned corporation, with authority to set rates residing in the Deputy Prime Minister, in the absence of a separate regulatory body. Hence, notwithstanding corporatization, GTC continued to have linkages to the political directorate. Further, its foreign exchange earnings (second only to that of the Guyana Sugar Corporation) were required to be paid directly into the government's account at the central bank and came under the control of the Ministry of Finance.

The deterioration of the Guyana economy, attendant on the exogenous shocks of the 1970s and 1980s and an external debt that had become unserviceable, negatively impacted on the operations of GTC despite its profitable status. Guyana had adopted a socialist-type economic model of development in the 1970s, with import substitution a fundamental development strategy requiring diversion of scarce resources from state-owned enterprises such as telecommunications.

At the end of 1990, the installed telecommunications base was estimated at 21 000 main lines and teledensity was only five telephones per 100 persons. International Direct Distance Dialling (DDD) was minimal, with most overseas calls being placed through an operator. Persons with access to a telephone were conservatively estimated at 52 000, and most public call boxes were either not working or vandalized (GT&T, 2000). Under the IMF's Enhanced Structural Adjustment Facility (ESAF), privatization of state-owned enterprises became a condition of loans, with telecommunications services as a first-tier enterprise to be privatized.

THE PRIVATIZATION OF GTC

Attendant on its agreement with the IMF, the government of Guyana negotiated the sale of 80 per cent of GTC for US$16.5 million to ATN on 18 June 1990. The price was based on the valuation of US$20.0 million put on GTC by Merchant Bankers, S.G. Warburg. At this valuation, GTC was sold not as a profitable going concern but on the basis of its estimated break-up value. Indeed, as a going concern, according to Anand Goolsarran, Auditor General of Guyana, a valuation of US$63.0 million would have been more appropriate (a figure arrived at by Jonathan Miller, adviser to the government on privatization, employing a price earnings ratio of seven times net income) with a minimum price of US$45.0 million.

GT&T was formed as the successor corporation and commenced operations on 28 January 1991. As part of the sale agreement (henceforth, the Agreement) GT&T assumed the outstanding debts of GTC of US$15.8 million: US$5.3 million to international carriers and US$10.5 million to Northern Telecom for switching equipment. As part of the deal ATN was given an 'Advisory Service' contract, at an annual fee of 6 per cent of gross revenues. This fee was fixed ex-post by the ATN-controlled Board of GT&T and without approval of the government. In terms of costs, this amounted to US$1.5 million in 1991[1] and provided a payment to ATN equal to approximately 7 per cent on its initial investment in the first year of operation as a privatized entity. The Agreement also provided for advisory fees and dividends to be paid free of any withholding taxes. The fees were also exclusive of the expenses that ATN routinely charged to GT&T.

For its part, ATN warranted to 'perform all of its obligations and undertakings required by this Agreement'[2] and committed GT&T to:

- increase service connections 'of at least 20,000 additional subscriber lines to the existing number of lines estimated at 21,000, within three years of the date of closing' of which 5000 were to be within the first twelve months, 7000 in the next and 8000 in year three. It also undertook to provide telephone or radio telephone services along Guyana's coast and in the interior within the same time period;
- within 24 months, to achieve the contractually guaranteed quality of service performance according to measurement of service indices recognized in the industry;
- guarantee employment for a period of 18 months;
- provide full public interest services – including a universal service obligation (USO);
- not increase subscriber rates for a period of three years from the date of closing, except: (a) in the 'event of a substantial increase' in the exchange rate over a six-month period; (b) a change in the long distance charges payable to foreign correspondents; (c) to cover the increased cost of providing services to the interior; and (d) in the event of natural disaster;
- introduce in a timely fashion current technological advances;
- allow for customer provided equipment.

FIRST ADDENDUM TO THE AGREEMENT

Prior to the passing of the Telecommunications Act 1990 and the Public Utilities Commission Act 1990 (PUC Act 1990), certain sections of the Agreement were modified by the 'First Addendum to The Agreement' between the government and ATN, dated 20 December 1990. Of significance under this Addendum:

1. foreign currency liabilities of the former state corporation transferred to GT&T were lowered to US$4.3 million;
2. GT&T was permitted to bill special users in US dollars based on the volume of their long distance calls. This limited the company's exposure to currency fluctuations;
3. GT&T was given 'the right and responsibility to determine the methodology in pursuing the objectives determined by the Public Utilities Commission (PUC) from time to time';
4. GT&T was allowed to increase rates 'to cover the full cost of any taxes, licence fees or increases in government charges or any new taxes or imposts, of any nature whatsoever' for a period of three years from the commencement of operations. This allowed the company to recover the initial licence fee of US$25 000 and the annual fee of 0.1 per cent on the gross revenues of the licensee's system business by way of increased rates.

ATN was also able to secure amendments to sections of the PUC Act 1990 which it did not favour. Of significance were amendments to Sections 29(2), requiring the imposition of a penalty 'only if failure or refusal referred to therein is without lawful excuse' and then only 'after opportunity were given for compliance'.

GT&T'S OPERATING LICENCE

On 19 December 1990 GT&T was granted a 'Licence to run Telecommunications Systems'. The licence was subject to the Telecommunications Act 1990, the Public Utilities Commission Act 1990, and the Agreement. Conditions of the licence are similar to those of British Telecom (BT). However an overarching condition of GT&T's licence is that the Agreement prevails in the event of a conflict between it and any other regulation.

By its licence, GT&T is authorized to run the telecommunications system and 'to provide or undertake the following services throughout the licensed area':

- public telephone, radio telephone, pay station telephone systems, national and international voice and data transmission;
- sale of advertising in any directory of telephone subscribers;
- switched or non-switched private line services;
- supply of terminal and customer premise equipment;
- tele-fax, telegraph and telex services; and
- cellular radio telephone services.

With respect to the first three services in this list, GT&T has been granted an exclusive licence for a period of 20 years, with the option to renew for a further 20. The period of exclusivity is limited to ten years in the case of the fourth and fifth services in the list. With respect to cellular radio telephone services, the licence is non-exclusive for a period of 20 years.

In view of the non-exclusive licence with respect to cellular radio telephone services, GT&T is obliged under Condition 13 of the licence to enter into an agreement with any licensed operator 'to connect and keep connected, to any of the Applicable Systems that Relevant Connectable System'. The implications of this condition as it applies to competition are examined later in the chapter.

Universal Service Obligation (USO)

Condition 1 of Part 2 of the licence imposes the burden of providing telecommunications services 'to every person who requests the provision of such services at any place in Guyana . . . by means of the Applicable Systems'. Condition 2 further extends the burden of universal service to rural areas. This condition forms the basis of the expansion requirements imposed on GT&T, as articulated in the Agreement, and is central to the validity of the company's operating licence from the perspective of government.

THE REGULATORY FRAMEWORK

The regulatory framework is embodied in the Telecommunications Act 1990 (Act) and the Public Utilities Commission Act 1990 (PUC Act 1990), as superseded by the Public Utilities Commission Acts of 1997 (PUC Act 1997) and 1999 (PUC Act 1999). This framework is examined in the context of the interaction of the monopoly provider with the government's Public Utilities Commission (PUC) and consumers, alongside differences in interpretation of the roles of the parties

The Telecommunications Act 1990

Modelled on the UK's Office of Telecommunications (OFTEL), the Act provides for the appointment of a Director of Telecommunications (DOT) with responsibility for regulatory issues and for advising the minister on policy matters. However, no director has yet been appointed. Section 4 of the Act requires the minister or the DOT:

- to ensure that reasonable demands for telephone and telegraph services are met, including the provision of emergency services and public call boxes;
- 'to promote the interest of the consumers, purchasers and other users in Guyana in respect of the prices charged for and the quality and variety of telecommunications services provided';
- to maintain and promote effective competition subject to 'any monopoly or exclusive right';
- 'to promote efficiency and economy'.

With respect to licensing, the minister, after consultation with the DOT, is empowered to grant a licence under Section 7. Of significance is that sub-section 7(4) provides for an exclusive licence to be granted, while sub-section 7(5) authorizes 'the connection to any telecommunication system to which the licence relates' of any other telecommunication system.

Section 8(1) of the Act specifies the licensee's conditions of operation. These are:

- to provide such telecommunication services as are specified in the licence;
- to connect to any telecommunication system to which the licence relates, or to permit the connection to any such system of such other telecommunication system;
- not to show undue preference to, or exercise undue discrimination against particular persons, with respect to any service provided;
- to publish the method that is to be adopted for determining the charges and other terms and conditions that are to be applicable to services to be provided.

By the provisions of Sections 4, 7, and 8(1), therefore, all licensed operators are required to conform to the requirements for universal service, reasonableness in rates, and competition, and to operate efficiently and economically.

The Public Utilities Commission Acts 1990, 1997, and 1999

The 1990 PUC Act informed the regulatory framework until it was superseded by the PUC Act 1997, which was in turn superseded by the PUC Act 1999. In reviewing the PUC Acts, only those aspects that have been revised are compared and contrasted to indicate the effects of the changes.

The 1990 Act was the first attempt at utility regulation in Guyana and was consequent on the privatization of GTC. As such, the 1990 Act took cognizance of the Agreement between the government and GT&T with respect to its overriding provisions. For example, Section 26(2) of the 1990 Act gives guidance to the PUC as to what is a reasonable or adequate standard or quality of service, which is based on the Agreement or, indeed, on any agreement between the government and a public utility. Such guidance has been clarified by Section 25(2) of the PUC Act 1999 to include agreements 'for the privatization or capitalization of a public utility'.

The general provisions of the 1990, 1997 and 1990 Acts are standard as to the appointment, authority and function of officials. Section 22(3) of the PUC Act 1990, as affirmed by the 1997 and 1999 Acts, established the PUC as an independent regulatory agency. However, although funding is by way of annual assessment on the utilities, the PUC is required to seek budgetary approval from the National Assembly.

Operationally, the PUC Act empowers the PUC to initiate and conduct investigations into the operations and standards of service of any utility. Section 65(1) of the 1999 Act further authorizes it to recover all expenses, including litigation expenses, arising from any investigation or proceeding under the Act. In addition, the 1999 Act requires the utility to submit for PUC approval any expansion plan, including its source of financing. Furthermore, on its own initiative, the PUC may order the public utility to construct and maintain any extension of services, which in its opinion 'provide sufficient business to justify the construction and maintenance of such extension'.[3]

In the determination of rates, Section 33 of the 1990 Act refers to the Agreement and requires that 'the Commission should give effect to such agreement'. The 1997 Act strengthens this provision by requiring the Commission to be 'bound by and shall give effect to the Agreement'. Also, 'in the event of a conflict between such agreement and an existing law' the agreement shall prevail.[4] This provision was further clarified in Section 33(b) of the 1999 Act to have either the Agreement or the licence prevail in the event of a conflict between the law and the Agreement or licence. Moreover, by Section 34(2) of the PUC Act 1999, GT&T is authorized to demand and receive different rates from different classes of consumers. However, Section 40 of the 1999 Act restricts such rates to those approved by the PUC and no utility is entitled to vary its rates, either up or down, without the approval of the PUC. Furthermore, Section 44(1) places the burden of proof with respect to reasonableness of the rates on the utility.

As to authority and enforceability, by Section 66(1) of the PUC Act 1999, an order of the PUC may be executed by the High Court as 'if it were an order made by it' on application of any party to any proceedings before the PUC. This section notwithstanding, the evidence suggests that the PUC is reluctant to act as authorized by its enabling legislation and has consistently deferred to the Courts. The Guyana Court of Appeal, in its decision on 'Civil Appeal 40 of 2001', effectively ruled that PUC orders are enforceable as issued in accordance with the Acts.[5]

It should be mentioned here that the PUC Acts do not require public comment on regulatory issues, in contrast with the accepted approaches in some other countries, such as Singapore. In Singapore the Info-communications Development Authority (IDA) routinely invites public comment as an integral part of its regulatory process.[6]

REGULATORY AND PERFORMANCE ISSUES

On the surface, Guyana's regulatory system may seem to embody the qualities of a workable framework. However, conflicts between the regulator (the PUC) and the US-based investor (ATN) have occurred frequently. In particular, the Telecommunications Act 1990 has provided an incomplete framework in the absence of the appointment of a DOT, whose duty and responsibility were to be fashioned after those of the DOT of OFTEL in the UK. Moreover, the PUC Acts of 1997 and 1999 have progressively eroded the authority of the PUC, requiring as they do the subjugation of the PUC to third-party agreements with the government or to licences granted by it. In conjunction with a weak Telecommunications Act, this is a manifestation of the ability of an investor to influence the regulatory framework of a country. The burden of regulation falls on the PUC, which looks to US regulatory tradition and concepts (albeit selectively) for guidance. Administratively, the PUC is made up of four part-time members drawn from the private sector and civil society, and a full-time chair drawn from the judiciary. The staff of the PUC includes a Secretary to the Commission, an Assistant Secretary/Legal Officer, and a Financial Analyst. However, none of the staff members has had any prior experience in utility regulation. By contrast, ATN is an experienced provider of telecommunications services in the US and possesses at-will access to substantial regulatory expertise and financial resources. More importantly, ATN brings an aggressive approach to regulation honed in the US Virgin Islands. It is against this background of a regulatory regime informed by political expediency and a process of learning-by-doing on the one hand, and a highly motivated profit-seeking investor on the other, that the effectiveness of regulation and the company's performance are now examined.

Effectiveness of the Regulatory Regime

In the absence of significant technical expertise, the PUC is vulnerable to manipulation by the company, as evidenced in the transcripts of hearings held by it over the years. Given the part-time status of commissioners, the PUC is often seen to be guided, if not chided, by company officials. Moreover, GT&T/ATN's confrontational approach to PUC proceedings, backed by extensive legal and financial resources, has arguably served to intimidate commissioners, staff, and consumer advocates.

In addition to effecting favourable changes to the Agreement and to certain provisions of the PUC Acts, GT&T/ATN has managed to stay several decisions of the PUC by court action. For example, in early 1998 there were several issues pending judicial determination, among which were appeals against PUC Orders to GT&T:

- to cease collecting a surcharge for lost revenues;[7]
- to cease paying advisory fees to ATN;
- to increase the number of telephone lines in service, as ordered in October 1997;
- to cancel promissory notes issued to ATN, which were not previously approved by the PUC.

GT&T has also challenged the legality of an investigative task force set up by the Minister of Trade and the Commissioner of the Inland Revenue Department (CIRD) to investigate the company for possible tax evasion (ATN *Annual Report*, 1997). These and other issues subjected to legal challenge have elicited the observation that, 'It would not be overstating things to say that telecommunications regulation in Guyana is subject to an unusually high degree of litigation gridlock' (Intven, 2001, p. 29). The effect of this high level of judicial intervention has been to delay regulatory proceedings and to undermine the credibility and effectiveness of the regulatory process.

In addition to litigation, GT&T/ATN was able to secure the removal of the Chairman of the PUC on the grounds that his actions showed a definite bias against the company. It also recruited the Commissioner of the Inland Revenue as its Treasurer. These actions support the observation that an investor will seek to influence the regulatory regime either by changing the rules of the game or by changing officials.

With respect to the requirement to operate efficiently and economically, in regulation there is an underlying presumption of a partnership between the utility and the regulator, in which the utility, in return for a guaranteed income stream, adopts responsibility to provide services efficiently. However, a review of the accounting records of GT&T suggests that there have been inadequate incentives to operate efficiently. Without adequately qualified staff to monitor operations effectively, the PUC is often forced to accept the costing information that GT&T submits to it. No on-site audit has been conducted by the PUC to verify the accuracy of the company's cost of service submissions and/or the relevancy of the expenditures claimed. It is therefore a curiosity that, despite the authority to investigate and recover attendant expenses from the utility being investigated, the PUC has appeared reluctant to pursue the kind and level of investigations necessary to ensure compliance with the regulatory rules.

Performance Issues

GT&T is subject to rate of return regulation. In exchange for meeting its obligations, the company is allowed a minimum rate of return on its capital, which has been set at 15 per cent. The obligations are assessed in terms of the conditions of the Agreement and the operating licence. In spite of this, by its own admission GT&T failed to meet the expansion requirement of 20 000 new connections in 36 months, as specified in the Agreement. By the end of 1993, access lines stood at 29 448, an increase of only 8448 from the 1990 figure of 21 000.

In its defence, the company has claimed that inadequate charges are the cause of its inability to finance the expected expansion programme. However, under the Agreement, ATN warrants GT&T's financial capacity to carry out the investment. Moreover, nowhere in either the Agreement or the licence were charges made a condition of the agreed expansion programme. Furthermore, the PUC has clearly stated that higher charges will be granted when the company *fulfils* its service obligations as specified in the Agreement, the licence and the PUC Act 1990.

Allied to the argument over telecoms charges, GT&T/ATN, has taken the position that 'its failure to receive timely rate increases, to which GT&T was entitled, to compensate for the devaluation in Guyana currency which occurred in 1991, provides legal justification for GT&T's delay in completing the Expansion Plan' (ATN *Annual Report*, 1997, p. 11). However, as shown in Figure 21.1, operating revenues increased significantly in the first six years of operations, with net income, advisory fees and net cash flow all trending upwards. Also, as shown in Figure 21.2, in the first six years of operations, with the exception of 1993 and 1996 in which the return on investment (ROI) and the return on equity (ROE) fell below 15 per cent, ATN earned more than the agreed 15 per cent minimum rate of return. Also, GT&T's revenues are principally derived internationally and are settled in foreign currency, which therefore serves to insulate rather than expose it to currency depreciation. Moreover, 'From February 1991 until early 1994, the Guyana dollar remained relatively stable' (ATN *Annual Report*, 1999, p. 20).

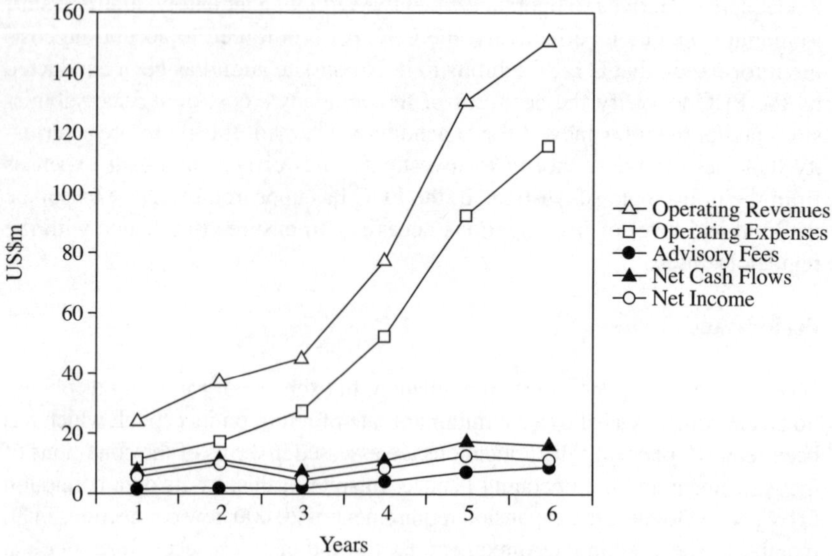

Source: Constructed from GT&T's 1998 Budget.

Figure 21.1 GT&T's gross revenues, advisory fees, cash flow and net income (US$m): 1991–96

The following issues should also be taken into account:

1. The company revalued its fixed assets in March 1993, December 1994 and December 1997, thereby employing a rate base at replacement cost in what is otherwise a historic cost accounting regime. This revaluation amounted to approximately 25 per cent of the company's fixed assets. Also, the company routinely capitalizes certain operating expenses, up to 40 per cent, without reference to actual construction activity. This approach to accounting has had the effect of increasing the rate base and distorting the achieved rate of return.
2. GT&T began in 1992 to record substantial interest expenses (reflected in operating expenses in Figure 21.1), attributed primarily to financial transactions, which, according to the former chairman of the PUC, included local borrowings by GT&T to finance 'up-stream loans from GT&T to ATN as well as one of its subsidiaries, Puerto Rico Telcom, that was at the time, on the brink of bankruptcy', and subsequently to service reverse-loans from ATN 'at an interest rate of 32%' (Tyndall, 2001).[8] Indeed, long-term debt at GT&T increased from US$11.1m (mainly to Northern

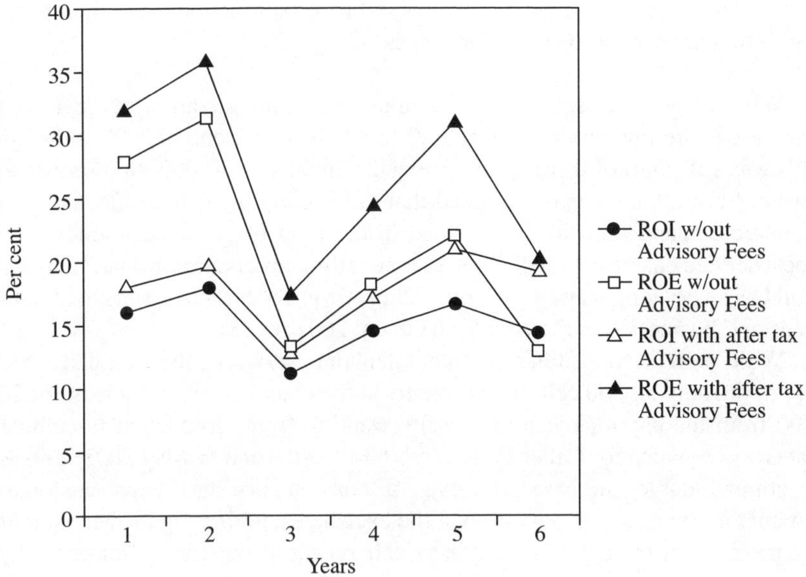

Source: Constructed from GT&T's 1998 Budget. ROI = Return on Investment; ROE = Return on Equity.

Figure 21.2 Comparative percentage returns to ATN from investment in GT&T: 1991–96

Telecom) in 1990, to US$23.0m in 1991, and to US$42.1m in 1993. Concurrently GT&T's debts, 'due to ATN' increased from US$0.9m in 1991 to US$25.9m in 1995. By the end of 1996, however, 'debt to ATN' and long-term debt were reduced to US$1.1m and US$4.1m respectively (GT&T 1998 Budget). These reductions totalled US$51.1 million (US$24.8m to ATN) and coincided with an increase in ATN's 'shareholders' equity' of US$44.6m in 1996 (ibid.).

3. A review of the finance agreement with Northern Telecom indicates an average rate of interest of 10.5 per cent payable. However, ATN claims that the 15 per cent minimum rate of return applies to the assets employed and bears no relationship to capitalization. It is an aberration of regulatory practice, however, not to premise an allowable rate of return on the cost of capital.

In response to such criticisms GT&T/ATN has stated that:

- 'contrary to what the Regulator and Government would have the public believe, GT&T *fulfilled its commitment to install 20,000 new lines during the first 3 years of existence*'.

- 'The so-called Advisory Fee was in fact established as a pre-incorporation agreement' (GT&T, January 2002, pp. 6&7).

With respect to service connections since privatization, GT&T had increased wire-line service connections to 80 000 by the end of 2001, although this was still short of meeting the demand estimated at 70 000. In response to this criticism, the company claimed that the waiting list is not reflective of a realistic demand for wire-line service in the light of the uneconomical low local service charges. Nonetheless, the prevailing observation is that, 'Guyana still has a very long way to go to providing adequate levels of access to all citizens and businesses in the country' (Intven, 2001, p. 23).

With respect to cellular mobile telephone services, the company had approximately 30 000 cellular customers at the end of 2001, an increase of 20 000 from the previous year, primarily resulting from a reduction in cellular rates and a switch to 'Caller Party Pay' (CPP) at the end of May 2001. This is a commendable increase, however a consequence has been customer complaints because of congestion at the exchanges, prompting the Minister of Tourism, Industry and Commerce to call on the company to 'immediately cease adding new subscribers to the system' (*Stabroek News*, 2002).

In response to such criticisms, GT&T/ATN has pointed to the level of investment it has achieved and especially in comparison with comparable income communities (mainly African, which are rural and widely dispersed). Nonetheless, at the end of 2001, 'poor or non-existent service to many small communities . . . severe problems in calling Guyana from other countries, and comparatively low levels of cellular telecommunications services' were observed (Intven, 2001, p. 23). Also, according to an Inter-American Development Bank (IDB) internal report,

> teledensity (number of telephone lines per 100 inhabitants) is only 7 in Guyana compared to 37 in Bahamas, 42 in Barbados and 20 in Jamaica . . . Internet usage (users per 10,000 inhabitants) is only 35 in Guyana, compared to 498 in Bahamas, 223 in Barbados, 224 in Jamaica and 233 in Trinidad and Tobago. (IDB, 2001)

However, in terms of main lines per employee, an International Telecommunication (ITU) benchmark for measuring efficiency, GT&T is now at the upper end of the international performance range, with around 125 main lines per employee.

Audio-text Service

Over the years, GT&T/ATN has been severely criticized for providing certain audio-text services through the telecommunications facility. A prevailing view is that Guyana has become a conduit for pornographic material. According to the former chairman of the PUC, Joseph Tyndall, not only is the provision of such service 'illegal', but also the possibility to switch such traffic through Guyana was not disclosed to the government during the privatization negotiations. Furthermore, the outflow of large sums of money with respect to this service has been a major concern for both the government tax authorities and the PUC under the chairmanship of Joseph Tyndall (Tyndall, 2001). In terms of volume, traffic data show that audio-text 'inpayment minutes' progressively increased from 2.3 million in 1992 to 101.8 million in 1995, before falling back to 13.0 million in 1996 (GT&T 1998 Budget). GT&T/ATN's position in 2002 was that 'irrational regulation . . . was one of the principal factors that drove the company to participate in the audio-text business' (GT&T, January 2002, p. 7).

COMPETITION AND DE-MONOPOLIZATION

The issues of competition and de-monopolization in developing countries are complex, incorporating as they do issues of natural justice, fair trade, universal service obligations, predatory pricing and the abuse of market power, on the one hand, and the legality of de-monopolization in cases where privatization agreements speak of exclusivity for the incumbent service provider, on the other. These issues are now examined in the Guyana context.

Competition in Guyana

On the issue of de-monopolization, given particularly the constraints in the agreements and licences already discussed, the regulatory regime adopted in Guyana for telecommunications appears to be an inferior disciplinary mechanism on management behaviour compared with competition in the market. This is clearly evidenced by the lengthy delays in the decision-making process at the PUC, the very high levels of litigation affecting regulatory decisions when they are eventually made, and the very high rates charged by the incumbent monopoly provider for value-added services, including international dial-up services and lease-lines. Indeed, many Internet Service Providers claim that GT&T's pricing policy for its lease-lines and 'E1s' constrains their expansion into providing Voice Over Internet Protocol (VOIP) services in Guyana.

GT&T in a letter to the Prime Minister has taken the position that VOIP violates its operating licence, and 'has become a strategy to destroy GT&T's viability'.[9] It has therefore sought intervention by the Prime Minister to restrict bypass of the company's international gateway, which it claims is being violated by the use of satellite technology – primarily by *I-Net*, a company that has been licensed to provide data transmission (packet-switching) services. In response, the Prime Minister has taken the position that there are many grey areas in the issues raised by GT&T, the determination of which is best left to the courts.

Interconnection

With respect to competition in the market for cellular mobile telephone services, GT&T's obligation to provide interconnection is clearly defined.[10] Such interconnection is by means of private negotiation between the parties, with intervention by the PUC if the parties fail to reach an agreement.

GT&T's sole competitor in this service area is Caribbean Telecommunications Limited (CTL), which has been licensed to provide cellular mobile telephone service in Guyana and which has an interconnection agreement with GT&T. However, by various means employed by GT&T, including litigation, interconnection to the Georgetown exchanges by CTL has been thwarted. For example, although the Guyana High Court on 11 May 2001 upheld CTL's contention that it had a right to interconnection in Georgetown, by the end of 2002, the company was still not interconnected to GT&T's Georgetown facilities because of further judicial proceedings. Meanwhile, GT&T increased its cellular mobile telephone customers from less than 6000 at the end of 2000 to over 50 000 at the end of April 2002.

De-monopolization

The trend towards de-monopolization of telecommunications internationally provided the Guyana government with the impetus to seek de-monopolization of GT&T, notwithstanding a legally binding agreement that speaks of a period of exclusivity. Supporting the move away from regulation of entry, exit and price is the realization that, within Guyana, imperfect competition is preferable to imperfect regulation – if only because of the high costs of regulation and the limitations monopoly imposes on service development. Indeed, regulation appears ill-equipped to deal with the issues of universal access and service, performance efficiency, and service innovation such as VOIP, especially in the light of changing technology.

ATN has taken the position that it has the legally binding Agreement that grants GT&T monopoly status. However, negotiations between the parties on de-monopolization have restarted.

CONCLUSIONS

While a country dependent on foreign direct investment must often provide incentives to foreign investors and must be seen to uphold legally binding agreements, changes in economic fundamentals and technology militate against maintaining practices and agreements over a long period of time, especially as they become no longer appropriate to the needs of the country. In the case of telecommunications in Guyana, the following observations are offered:

- Rate of return regulation as a surrogate for competition is not only cost-inefficient but also ineffective as a means of controlling the abuse of market power. Competition is necessarily a first-best choice in promoting telecommunications in terms of increasing both access and capacity.
- Public policy initiatives that seek to redress social imbalances and market failure are often undermined by inconsistencies in interpretation and application of regulations. In Guyana telecommunications regulations are imprecise and have not had the benefit of public scrutiny.
- The regulatory process becomes vulnerable to industry capture and rent-seeking in the absence of transparency and public accountability.
- The convergence of IT and telecommunications has radically changed the dynamics of the industry, rendering contracts relating to exclusivity, universal service obligations and rates of return inconsistent with technological advances and the notion of natural justice.

Finally, arguably recent de-monopolization agreements between the governments of Jamaica and the Eastern Caribbean countries and Cable and Wireless provide a workable model for future telecommunications reform in Guyana.

NOTES

1. GT&T 1998 Budget.
2. Section 3.4 *Agreement between the Government of the Co-operative Republic of Guyana and Atlantic Tele-Network*, 18 June 1990.
3. Section 27(1), *PUC Act*, 1999.
4. Section 33, *Public Utilities Commission Act*, 1990.
5. Court of Appeal, 18 December 2002.
6. Section 26(1) *Telecommunications Act*, 1999, Info-communications Authority of Singapore, Republic of Singapore, 2000.
7. In September 2002, the Guyana Court of Appeal ruled in favour of GT&T on this matter.
8. It should be noted also that such loans are proscribed by the US Federal Communications Commission.
9. Letter from Sonita Jagan to Juan Belt, Inter-American Development Bank, 10 July 2001.
10. Condition 13, GT&T Operating Licence.

REFERENCES

ATN (Atlantic Tele-Network, Inc.) *Annual Reports*, 1997 and 1999.

GT&T (Guyana Telephone & Telegraph Company Limited) (1998), *Budget, Executive Summary*, Guyana.

GT&T (Guyana Telephone & Telegraph Company Limited) (2000), *A Decade in the Development of an Industry*, Guyana.

GT&T (Guyana Telephone & Telegraph Company Limited) (2001), Letter to Prime Minister, Modernisation of Telecommunications (MIF/TC-00-2068), Guyana.

GT&T (Guyana Telephone & Telegraph Company Limited) (2002), *GT&T, an Industry in Distress*, Guyana.

Guyana, *Government of Public Utilities Commission Act*, 1990.

Guyana, *Agreement between the Government of the Co-operative Republic of Guyana and Atlantic Tele-Network*, 18 June 1990.

Guyana, *Public Utilities Commission Act*, 1997.

Guyana, *Public Utilities Commission Act*, 1999.

Guyana, *Public Utilities Commission, letter to GT&T dated 17 May 2001*.

IDB (Inter-American Development Bank) (2001), *Profile 1, Guyana: Information and Communications Technology Project (GY 0066)*, 5 July, Inter-American Development Bank.

International Telecommunications Union (1999), *Trends in Telecommunication Reform, 1999: Convergence and Regulation*, ITU: Geneva.

Intven, Hahk (2001), *Consultation Paper on Reform of the Guyana Telecommunications Sector in Guyana*, Guyana.

Stabroek News (2002), 'Nadir calls on phone company to improve cell service', 11 April: 11.

Tyndall, J. (2001), 'The GT&T dividends issue – nothing much to shout about', *Guyana Chronicle*, 20 March.

Index